The Postwar Japanese System

THE

POSTWAR
JAPANESE
SYSTEM

*Cultural Economy and
Economic Transformation*

William K. Tabb

New York   Oxford
OXFORD UNIVERSITY PRESS
1995

Oxford University Press

Oxford   New York
Athens   Auckland   Bangkok   Bombay
Calcutta   Cape Town   Dar es Salaam   Delhi
Florence   Hong Kong   Istanbul   Karachi
Kuala Lumpur   Madras   Madrid   Melbourne
Mexico City   Nairobi   Paris   Singapore
Taipei   Tokyo   Toronto

and associated companies in
Berlin   Ibadan

Published by Oxford University Press, Inc.
200 Madison Avenue, New York, New York 10016

Oxford is a registered trademark of Oxford University Press

Library of Congress Cataloging-in-Publication Data
Tabb, William K.
The postwar Japanese system :
cultural economy and economic transformation
/ William K. Tabb.
p.   cm.
Includes bibliographical references and index.
ISBN 0-19-508949-9. — ISBN 0-19-508950-2 (pbk.)
1. Japan—Economic conditions—1945–1989.
2. Japan—Economic conditions—1989–
3. Japan—Social conditions—1945–
I. Title.
HC462.9.T14   1995   330.952'04—dc20   94-20889

2 4 6 8 9 7 5 3 1

Printed in the United States of America
on acid-free paper

Preface

Everyone who writes about the Orient must locate himself vis-a-vis the Orient; translated into his text, this location includes the kind of narrative voice he adopts, the type of structure he builds, the kinds of images, themes, motifs that circulate in his text—all of which add up to the deliberate ways of addressing the reader, containing the Orient, and finally representing it or speaking in its behalf.

EDWARD SAID [1]

The world is just out there, but descriptions of the world are not.

RICHARD RORTY [2]

The Orient of which I write is a different one than that of Edward Said in this preface's epigraph; we face similar problems of social construction. There is an ensemble of relationships among the works cited, audiences addressed, and judgments as to the level of ''proof'' or argumentation and definition of place that inform any such effort.

There are also problems in writing for people with very different levels of prior knowledge. I have chosen to be inclusive, to explain what is familiar to experts and to offer a work of synthesis with interventions in a number of contested areas. The text is not jargon-free, but I have tried to make it user-friendly. The book is written for patient scholars who will put up with material that is covered more completely elsewhere, but who are interested in the broader discussion of Japan as a signifier for diverse ideological positions, broad-minded economists who are willing to stretch methodological tenets of the profession, policy makers who will take a longer view, and general readers willing to pursue a current-events topic in more taxing institutional, historical, and comparative perspective. I have tried to let parallel conversations be heard while providing a coherent framework within which they can be considered.

The present effort results from a happy confluence of factors. The first is an invitation to be a visiting researcher in Kansai University in Osaka for the fall term of the 1990 academic year. Networks being what they are, this also meant numerous invitations to lecture at conferences and in business programs and economics departments at other schools. The second was the receipt of the President's Award, originated and bestowed by the CEO of my college, Shirley Strum Kenny, to lucky faculty members of a semester off to engage in some worthy research activity, and of a Professional Staff Congress-City University of New York research grant to study the regional impact of Japanese economic development in the postwar period. The invitation and the awards enabled me to live in Japan with my family, to travel extensively, and afforded time off upon my return to write.

Living in a country in a family setting is very different than merely visiting at intervals. In the former situation one gets a feel from the ground that one can never have as a guest, no matter how well treated (as one invariably is in Japan). There is more time for chance conversation, and I had many serendipitous talks with strangers, local merchants, and the parents of my daughter's schoolmates. There are the neighbors, friends, and professional colleagues of whom only three will be mentioned—my host, Shigeru Yokota, and the senior urbanists who welcomed me and spent such "quality time" with an ignorant *gaijin*, Kenichi Miyamoto and Tokuei Shibata.

I owe enormous debt to the Japanese members of my research team, with whom I have worked for a number of years. I have learned so much from them in informal conversations as we toured steel mills and auto plants, ridden buses to garment factories, and the *shinkansen* to numerous conferences. A three-year grant from the Ministry of Education of Japan to conduct an interdisciplinary team study of Urban Problems and the Transformation of Industrial Structures underwrote our many field trips and the preparation of our interim report in May 1990 of the Monbusho International Scientific Research Program. I would also like to express my gratitude to Keiichi Yamazaki for his yeoman efforts as my research assistant during the fall of 1990. One more individual needs to be named with my great gratitude—Jackson Bailey, lover of things Japanese and teacher of that country's history extraordinaire, who I had the good fortune to encounter as a freshman at Earlham College many years ago. His energy and enthusiasms proved infectious. Thanks, Jack. I apologize to him in this assignment for omitting macrons (which are used to indicate long vowels) and for the given name, family name order of presentation for Japanese instead of the family name first of the Japanese convention.

A number of colleagues read parts of different drafts of the manuscript. I wish to thank Paul Attewell, John Bowman, Michael Edelstein, Michael Krasner, Lenny Markowitz, and Mike Wallace, all of the City University of New York, who brought their expertise as sociologists, economists, political scientists, and historians to the task of critically reviewing this work. I am fortunate to have such colleagues and to be part of an intellectual community in which cross-fertilization allows an economist to teach sociology, offer courses jointly with literary critics, lunch regularly with anthropologists, and work out curricular reforms with philosophers.

New York
September 1994   W. K. T.

Contents

The Postwar Japanese System

Introduction

To the great trading nation, to the great manufacturing nation, no progress which any portion of the human race can make in knowledge, in taste for the convenience of life, or in the wealth by which those conveniences are produced, can be a matter of indifference. It is scarcely possible to calculate the benefits which we might derive from the diffusion of European civilization among the vast population of the East.

LORD MACAULAY, 1833[1]

Passing away from the European races, we find Japan a bold claimant for leadership of the East on lines that are mainly Western. Her insular position, contiguous to a great Continent, is almost as well adapted for the development of industry and trade as that of Britain. She has learnt so much during the last thirty years, that she can hardly fail to become a teacher ere long. It seems indeed that stronger food than they now have will be required to enable her people to sustain continuous, severe strain; but the singular power of self-abnegation, which they combine with high enterprise, may enable them to attain great ends by shorter and simpler routes than those which are pursued where many superfluous comforts and luxuries have long been regarded as conventional necessities. Their quick rise to power supports the suggestion, made by the history of past times, that some touch of idealism, religious, patriotic, or artistic, can generally be detected at the root of any great outburst of practical energy.

ALFRED MARSHALL, 1919[2]

Nihon ishitsuron, "Japan is different." Its version of capitalism is a new model, one that for good and for ill other countries have emulated even as they may fear the Japanese themselves. The model they are attempting to copy, however, is no longer representative of a changing Japan. The Japan of consensus thinking is now history.

It has now been transformed by globalization forces that have led not so much to an opening up of the country, although that has to some extent happened, as to Japan's restructuring its system on an internationalized—and especially regionally—cohesive basis. The most interesting lessons to be learned from Japan have to do with its struggle to define what may be called a nationalistic model of internationalization. How does a country preserve what

3

it has achieved, promote full employment, and develop greater value added activities by continuously upgrading its labor force and corporate entrepreneurial capacities while preserving its social fabric from the disruptions that can be caused by the demands of globalization?

Dynamic developments in the world capitalist system intrude to shake our mental map as well as the actual social formation named Japan. In the latter part of the postwar period Japan came to exist within the American unconscious, Marilyn Ivy writes, "as an almost comfortable figure of danger and promise—the danger of foreign capital and the promise it offers if domesticated."[3] One form that mental domestication has taken in some American minds is a total denial of the role the developmentalist state has played in Japan's economic development. Management guru Peter Drucker, for example, writes that "there is not the slightest evidence that any government policy to stimulate the economy has an impact" and that "Japan's industrial policy of attempting to select and support 'winning' business sectors is by now a well-known failure."[4]

Richard Beason and David Weinstein offer an econometric test of the thesis that industrial policy in Japan has mattered. They find it has not. Their study highlights many of the issues that are so controversial and will claim much of our attention. They see the case study literature and historically specific institutional investigations of the sort stressed in this book to be fatally flawed. Their method reduces industrial policy to government targeting of industries. They find "many of the targeting programs that allegedly caused resources to shift into high growth sectors were actually used far more frequently in low growth sectors."[5] Targeting in their view has therefore been a big failure. But what do such studies actually measure? Important conditioning events such as the forcing out and the keeping out of U.S. auto producers or letting computer makers in only after forcing them to license critical technologies, actions that cost no money and do not show up as tariffs or quotas, have no place.[6] Beason and Weinstein's sophisticated translog production functions "test" a model that assumes any unconventional targeting (that they can't measure) is proportional to what they do measure. This is precisely what so many of the students of Japanese industrial policy question. American producers have not had access to Japanese markets except on terms molded by the Japanese. That their impacts of industrial policy are found more heavily in declining industries is explainable by what they don't measure. Their presumption that the reason declining industries receive so much assistance is simply a matter of political corruption is also open to question.

Many Japanese would be inclined to see this as a typical American attitude, one which mistakes an undeniable aspect that can and does affect government programs for the totality of industrial policy. Every Japanese decisionmaker has a personal story to capture his understanding of such American views. Tetsuya Terazawa tells visitors to his office at MITI (the Ministry of International Trade and Industry) about how at the Harvard Business School, studying a failed airline, as his class watched a video of the CEO being interviewed, the president noted with pride that through it all he had never sought government help. The class, Mr. Terazawa recalls with astonishment, broke into applause. "There is strong resistance to government intervention in America. I understand that," he said. "But I was shocked. There are many stakeholders in companies. What happened to all his employees? We have not reached a point where we can make such cold hearted decisions." Mr. Terazawa added: "It is something quite close to a religion. You cannot argue about it with most people. You believe it or you don't."[7] The purposes (plural) and methods of industrial policy (typically changing and matters of administrative guidance that are difficult to approximate using tariff and other subsidy levels) need to be explored in the fuller context of Japanese experience. In undertaking this task, I will stress that economic laws work in situations that are historically contingent and at the time they were undertaken unique to Japan.

The argument here has a number of parts. The first is that a model of corporate development emerged in the postwar period that was very different from the dominant multidivisional structure and Taylorist work relations of the American one, as different as the latter was from the Marshallian firm of the nineteenth-century England. Second, the Japanese developmentalist state and other key institutional features of this model, from its trade unions to its governmental industrial policy, and electoral politics combined to form a unique social structure of accumulation or system of regulation or societal reproduction that set it apart both from other nations as well as in important respects from Japan's own past and its future. Third, the coherence of this system has sufficiently eroded that we must now speak of the end of the accommodations that is here identified as the Japanese postwar system. The end of the postwar Japanese system has implications for other developmentalist states because Japan, while unique in major respects, is also part of a class of national economic formations of late industrializers that have operated far differently than the laissez-faire understanding of economic growth suggests a successful nation would be able to do. Finally, an internationalization of the Japanese political economy has taken place signaled by the break in 38 years of Liberal Democratic Party rule in what may be called a modernization coup. A new regime is emerging in Japan based on commitment to reforms that will make Japanese transnational corporations more competitive in the post-Cold War era and which represent a break from the nationalist development state practices that had been followed for over a hundred years. This shift, which will not be easy for Japan, involves new forms of interdependence. The way Japan navigates these is unlikely to be the same as the manner in which the United States chooses to do so nor is it likely to accord in important respects with American judgment of how Japan should change.

Method and Social Investigation

How to view a social formation at a point of time or over some extended period is a matter of some dispute among social scientists. Some use models that presume a unity, extrapolating trends backward and forward in some linear fashion. Others accept a perpetual instability of meaning. Still others use con-

structs such as social structure of accumulation or regulatory regime to privilege quasi-fixed relations valid for an extended period of historical time. This
study is closest to the third of these. I find this method useful because attention
can be focused on how a society can develop a protracted stability over decades. The characteristics of a social structure of accumulation can be identified
by characteristics that over time come to be fetters on the society's further
development.[8] Treating the Japanese system in the years of the postwar era,
the golden age of capitalist development, as an ideal type allows comparison
with what came before and after. It also allows consideration of the trajectory
of Japanese development in historical and comparative terms, giving attention
to the emergence and transformation of institutional forms and cultural attitudes supportive of economic developments.

This book balances elements of historical, comparative, and institutional
analyses that include within its political economy framework anthropological
and sociological moments along with those of politics and economics. It is
concerned with how Japanese capitalism emerged, developed to its classic
form, and continued to move toward a globally imbricated, and less-stable
social formation. It revisits the extended period of Japanese economic development and discusses the dramatically different situation that emerged with the
end of the postwar era (conveniently dated by the death of the Showa Emperor
as well as the fall of the communist system in 1989 and the end of the Cold
War). Japan has evolved under the pressures of the financial overextension
built up during its "bubble economy" in the 1980s in which speculation ran
rampant, undercutting the productionist strength of the "real" economy in
the context of global economic slowdown.

Japanese industrial triumphs, while extensive, are concentrated in two major sectors—two-thirds of all Japanese exports to North America in the early
1990s came from auto and electronics manufactures, and a large proportion of
Japan's export surplus to East Asia end up as motor vehicles and consumer
electronics products sold in the United States. While it may be argued that
low-cost Asian imports have increased the standard of living of Americans
ceteris paribus, "all other things" have not in fact been equal. In a period of
slow global growth and underemployed resources there has been to some
extent a substitution of growth in the Asian Pacific region at the expense of
stagnation in older industrial areas in Europe and the United States. While
free-trade models suggest such costs are only short run and a new full employment equilibrium will be established in which all participants will find themselves better off, the transition costs proved high and the long-term prospects
of many working people appeared bleak enough to raise serious fears and
political disquiet. Among economists low-growth rates raised the question of
what was to follow what came to be seen as the post–World War II Golden
Age of Capitalism. Excluding the former communist nations, the world's rate
of economic growth slowed from 5 percent in the 1960s, to 4 percent in the
1970s, to 3 percent in the 1980s. In the 1990s, too, as each nation tries to export
at the expense of others by holding down wages and social spending aggregate
demand remains slack, competitive pressures remain strong, and the public

policy conundrum everywhere is the same, "Where are the jobs and especially enough good jobs to come from?"

Economists have long been aware that conventional inputs explain little of the observed rate of growth of output.[9] By the late 1970s the United States appeared to be losing international competitiveness (loss of economic rents, the temporary extreme advantage resulting from the wartime losses of productive capacities among our competitors). As growth theory once again became a growth sector within the economics profession, doubt began to be raised as to whether economists had a very sound grasp of even the "facts" of the situation. Disagreements over measurement, seemingly minor technical matters, assumed significance for theory. In his presidential address to the American Economics Association Zvi Griliches suggested that "major portions of actual technical change have eluded our measurement framework entirely."[10] In the midst of a major revolution driven by microelectronic innovation and its impact on transaction costs and especially information technology, economists strove to develop an understanding of the process of disequilibrium growth.

A consideration of the economic development of Japan perforce involves a consideration of the new thinking that is affecting studies of economic development, international trade and other classic topics. It becomes in some ways difficult to build from existing understandings. To take the case of "capital," seemingly the most basic of economic constructs, reification has proceeded to such a point that it becomes difficult in the context of much textbook economics to accept the importance of transmission of ideas and their coherent appropriation as central to growth in addition to traditional measures of saving and physical investment.[11]

The allocation of given resources within an unexamined context of existing cultural patterns, values, and attitudes, and the assumption that buyers and sellers have no control over supply and demand assumed by mainstream models create a number of presumptions that are increasingly being addressed, in significant measure because of the Japanese example. Leading economic journals feature articles in which there is evidently an incentive for countries to pursue industrial policy in which "a well-informed government might increase national welfare by providing incentives to firms to adopt a new technology even when it is currently less productive than old methods."[12] Part of our effort is to partake in this movement to broaden what it is economists do and to recapture the creative complexity and holistic analysis that once characterized political economy.

A key component of this rethinking has been middle range conjunctural formulations such as regulation theory and the social structure of accumulation literature. In the case of Japan, the overaccumulation of capital in the 1980s represents a complex instance of the exhaustion of a mode of development. As growth rates slowed, high profits could not find outlet in expanded real production, yet the general abundance of the period allowed their absorption in pecuniary speculative investments (in real estate and stock markets). The statist controls and guidance of capital allocation were undermined (in contrast to earlier periods of capital shortage) and the maturing of Japan-based transnationals with increasingly globalist perspectives created tensions with the nationally imbricated state bureaucracies. The slowing of real economic growth, the internationalization process, the loss of both direction and control by the ministries, growing corruption, and the leveraging of speculative activities all validated a short-term profit-seeking mentality. The very elements of postwar success became fetters to necessary adjustment to new conditions.

The Presentation

In the first chapter Japan is situated in terms of the ways it has been "seen." It draws on the anthropological construct of culture and the sociological conceptualization of social facts, offering an understanding of the economic culture of Japan and how seemingly familiar economic institutions embedded in the Japanese context must be understood in their own terms and are not to be presumed to be the same as our own. Economists looking for "rational economic man" should be assured that nothing said suggests that Japanese as individuals do not seek their own self-interest as they understand it, only that the constraints upon them are different and so rational behavior may, until the system is understood, seem strange or different in presumably uniquely Japanese ways. The second chapter introduces the elements of difference in the corporate form, the state, and cultural economy that will be important to the study. The contingent nature of economic structures is typically underestimated, and not only with regard to the Japanese. The historical embeddedness of a social formation is also given short shrift by economists and policymakers looking for quick fixes.

Much discussion of the Japanese economy concerns the interlocking elements of the postwar Japanese system that I am suggesting is a time-bound construct that came into being under unique conditions and is now passing from the scene in important respects. There is a lag in how we see this system of governance, production, and labor relations. The roots of the Japanese system go back to the fear of foreigners in the Tokugawa Era; the emergent developmentalist state grew in the fertile soil of the Meiji Restoration of 1868. The system is the product of national resolve, elite control, and of Japan's ability to take advantage of foreign learning. Chapter 3 takes this story to World War II.

Picking up the development of the Japanese postwar system Chapter 4 pays attention to the American role in restructuring the Japanese political economy and to the rebuilding effort under Japanese control as it responded to external challenges and opportunities. The capacity to act coherently comes from the particular accommodations made to the overarching economic nationalism of the postwar Japanese system that guides the *keiretsu* (the large corporate groupings that dominate the modern Japanese economy), the industrial relations system, political governance, and bureaucratic guidance institutions.

Chapter 5 is devoted to a discussion of the automobile, the most important instance of Japan's ability to enter an industry dominated by the United States and successfully challenge its position. American overconfidence and initial attempts to apply both foreign procurement and domestic automation reflected a misunderstanding of the nature of the Japanese challenge before coming to terms with the essence of the Japanese route. The Toyota manufacturing system involves labor and production process innovation, supplier and customer relations that are contrasted to the traditional U.S. approaches. Fortunately, the key elements of the Japanese system can be learned and to a remarkable extent have been by many U.S.-based producers.

The Japanese labor relations system is discussed in great detail in Chapter 6 in which the long working day, week, and year, the intensity of effort, and other strains that are the norms of Japanese industry will be detailed. Much of the analysis of extreme exploitation and alienation is missing from the usually laudatory appreciations of the Japanese model. Work life in Japan is a far more complex matter than the usual treatment of quality circles and teamwork would lead us to believe. That Japanese homes are small, if not universally the early postwar "rabbit hutches," is better known, but there is a complexity to regional patterning that is less familiar. There is both the unicentric concentration in the Tokyo metropolitan area and the wider Tokaido region, with its social costs of overcrowding, as well as the problems of the depressed regions of the periphery. Chapter 7 tells the story of uneven growth patterns and the politics involved in urban and regional policymaking from the structured corruption of mainstream politics to the importance of citizens' movement activism in the postwar era.

The "bubble economy" of the 1980s in Japan was a time of speculative excesses that contrasts with the image of Japan as the producer nation in which the engineer dominates the price system. In Chapter 8 the story of the impact of the slowing global economy fueling speculative excess is told along with the corruption of the market-insider relations that became evident to all once the bubble began to deflate. The role of the Ministry of Finance and the *zaikai* (the movers and shakers of Japanese economic life) as well as the shadier underworld are discussed.

In Chapter 9 trade antagonisms and the debate over industrial policy that generated so much heat during the 1980s, threatened open trade wars in the 1990s, and which remains at the core of the usual U.S.–Japan economic policy discourse are considered. It distinguishes three debates within this broad area: competitiveness, the restructuring of the capitalist system of production, and globalization trends. The task is to show how these approaches focus on overlapping but distinct issues. The semiconductor industry and high-tech competition more generally are discussed in some detail. The suggestion is made that industrial policy continues to be integral to Japanese development but takes very different form in the 1990s in which internationalization of economic relations become preeminent. As the chapter should also make clear, American resurgence in many high-tech fields comes about through a unique combination of learning from Japan and evolving uniquely American responses to the new mode of accumulation revealed by the application of the very technological revolution itself.

The globalization process, especially the emergence of an Asian regional economy, the localization of production by manufacturing firms in their major market areas, and the formalizing of strategic alliances among trilateral producers suggest the need to revise many of the premises of both nationalistic and free-market policy strategies. The tenth chapter pulls together the key international tendencies that have forced significant changes on the postwar Japanese model and call for serious rethinking on the part of those who would wish, in a new era, to follow older recipes. The new understandings of competition that have been emerging are the topic of Chapter 11.

The final chapter brings together many of the themes of the book and looks at issues that will shape policymaking and competitiveness strategies in the twenty-first century. The implications of increasingly internationalized giant corporations and the embryonic beginnings of world governance structures such as the International Monetary Fund and United Nations police-keeping suggest a new institutional environment for macroeconomic policymaking. These changes raise issues for world system operational stability and of social identity. Unlike the business-oriented literature that considers such questions from the perspective of corporate strategy, my focus is on a broader, inclusive vision of society. The social underpinnings of economic transactions and the noneconomic factors that constrain political and economic choices are our concern. Throughout, comparison to the Anglo-American economic norms are made explicitly or implicitly. For many readers the reason to study Japan is to understand their own societies in comparative perspective. Part of the difficulty we have in trying to do this is that we presume too much. We see with eyes that seek out the familiar and interpret what is new to us as if it were what it would be at home. Before we can undertake the task we set for ourselves we must talk at length about ways of seeing.

In the 1990s, as some of Japan's seeming strengths, its educational system, financial institutions, and close corporate-government cooperation, appeared as disadvantages—the Japanese were said to lack the imagination for success in the burgeoning entertainment–communication field, their overprotected financial institutions unable to understand and so properly price risk, and the excessive bureaucratic regulations of the developmentalist state to stifle innovation. At such a juncture it is important to pay even closer attention to the ways institutions that respond so well in one historic context can retard necessary change in another, to consider how success can breed *hubris*, but also how a nation's cultural economy can offer resources needed when facing challenges and provide energies for overcoming them.

1

From Garbagne to the Coast of Bohemia, or, Assume a Japan

"If I want to imagine a fictive nation, I can give it an invented name, treat it declaratively as a novelistic object, create a new Garbagne, so as to compromise no real country by my fantasy . . . I can also—though in no way claiming to represent or analyze reality itself (these being the major gestures of Western discourse)—isolate somewhere in the world (far away) a certain number of features . . . , and out of these features deliberately form a system. It is this system which I shall call Japan."

ROLAND BARTHES[1]

"For the real environment is altogether too big, too complex, and too fleeting for direct acquaintance. We are not equipped to deal with so much subtlety, so much variety, so many permutations and combinations. And although we have to act in that environment, we have to construct it on a simpler model before we can manage with it. To traverse the world men must have maps of the world. Their persistent difficulty is to secure maps on which their own need, or someone else's need, has not been sketched in the coast of Bohemia."

WALTER LIPPMANN[2]

Roland Barthes's choice of Japan to make a point about the nature of the reality we create and then believe in was hardly arbitrary. Westerners have long created Japans that fit our needs, ambivalence, and confusions. The naming "Japan" is a Portuguese mishearing of a Malay corruption of the Cantonese mispronunciation of the Chinese term for the country known to its inhabitants as "Nippon" or "Nihon."[3] So much confusion and arbitrary order is suggested that the postmodernist critique of social science seems particularly apt. The Japans that confront the reader casually browsing the well-stocked special-interest shelves find Japans in profusion, each seen alongside others seeming something close to a novelistic construction of reality. To many Japanese these

11

constructions share a universal characteristic, they are "images Americans create to vent frustrations upon." This leads, Tomoharu Washio, Executive Director for Research and Planning of Japan External Trade Organization (JETRO) angrily wrote in February 1994, just before the Clinton-Hosakawa summit standoff, to a "shadow boxing" in which negotiations are based on illusion and so carry unnecessary, harmful baggage.[4]

I am more inclined to think that while the construction of reality involves subtle readings, with many possible permutations and combinations in which our own needs and those of others deceive and bias our investigation, that nonetheless useful coherences can be created and employed to guide our understanding and action. The problem begins when constructs differ so markedly that meaningful conversation is seriously impeded. This is the case with America's confused views of Japan.

The growth of any nation is a combination of the patterns of its different sectors, regions, and class fractions. At different times some formulations of the core essence of what is happening are very different than at other times. Since the parts we stress at one point in time came into being and erode, there are ample grounds to disagree on defining a subject at any particular moment in history. It is especially difficult to accept any one version of Japan. Modalities of growth and instability revolve around a process of combined and uneven development that seem to present us with an unstable subject matter.[5]

There are four levels on which the Japanese economic experience should be understood. The first of these is in terms of *competitiveness*: How are we doing in relation to "them?" Much of the discussion has stayed on this level. Japan, however, also developed a new model of production, one that through the postwar period shouldered the United States out of first place in a range of products, and led American firms to adopt Japanese techniques and modes of organizing production. Second, therefore, Japan represents on a *transformational level* a more advanced stage of capitalist development that others emulate to mutual advantage. Third, Japan's growth needs to be seen in an *internationalization perspective*. Both the United States and Japan are part of a single world economy and through the commodity chains and webs of production that have developed in the postwar era Japan is part of a larger process of internationalization within a world system. Finally, the uneven and combined nature of capitalist growth over space and time suggests that long wave cycles of expansion and stagnation affect the national economies within a *world system* framework. The slow growth of the world capitalist system from the early 1970s creates a larger constraining climate in which all decision makers and ordinary citizens live their lives and determines whether there will be a leveling up to bring about a new global balance or a leveling down. The cultural signifiers through which these deep structure economic forces make themselves felt are also part of this story and their understandings intrude on each element of its telling.

It is hard to make the turns that come with new historical eras. The postwar period ended leaving the United States as the only superpower. Our president spoke of a New World Order and there was little doubt he meant a new U.S.

hegemony. The United States came out of the postwar era with its Cold War mentality intact. However, without a Soviet bogeyman to distract us from seeing ourselves and what was happing to our own nation, we were slow to recognize the presence of a new *economic* superpower: Japan. When the alarm bells starting ringing, the concerns that were put on images called Japan seemed as arbitrary as the mishearings and the namings. Some of these involve Japan and orientals—the "others" to be distinguished with the rise of the Pacific economy in the midpostwar period.

There is still a newness to our thinking about Japan and much fashionable contradiction in our descriptions of these "others" who

> are the most innovative imitators, the hardest working hedonists, the lewdest prudes, the most courteous and cruellest and kindest of people. Rich and yet wealthless, confident but confused. . . . They are convinced of their own culture's supremacy, yet suffer from an inferiority complex that makes all others look simple. They hold tradition precious. They adapt.[6]

Are they like us down deep? Do they respond to the same incentives in the same ways we do? The answer is *yes*. Japanese *would* respond to the same incentives the same way we do *if* they saw themselves in the same situation faced with the same choices; however, they often are not. The context of decision making in Japanese society is different. The constraints within which choices are made are not the same. The institutions that constrain behavior may have the same labels—"corporation," "labor union," "democratic political system"—but these words represent different phenomena in Japan.[7]

For the nonexpert there is the dependence on academics who have their own language, and much of their internal discourse that involves efforts to impose preferred terminology as labels for social reality. Thus, for many experts of political science the issue of whether Japan is best labeled "authoritarian pluralism" or "bureaucratic-exclusionary pluralism" is of great significance. In other discourses the preferred usage, "sponsored capitalism," is considered by some a better categorization than "development state capitalism." For others, the oxymoron "laissez-faire-oriented intervention" holds great salience and avoids the objectionable use of the Ministry of International Trade and Industry, "planned markets." There are many such conversations that only occasionally intersect. Moreover, there is visceral reaction on the part of each subspecialty to avoid contact with the others, perhaps out of hubris that their own approach is superior, or perhaps simply due to fear of disclosing their lack of understanding of ideas that if taken seriously would force a rethinking of their own well-worked-out stance. In-Groupness afflicts academic specialists as well as national chauvinists.

Fear of the Other

From the British Empire's self-confident racism, expressed so well by Rudyard Kipling ("The Japanese should have no concern with business. The Jap has no business savvy."), to the pronouncements of that great standard bearer of American Empire, John Foster Dulles, the white imperial powers have under-estimated Japan. In the mid-1950s, Secretary of State Dulles, in briefing President Eisenhower, indicated that there was little future for Japanese products in the United States. In one of those routine TOP SECRET—EYES ONLY memos Dulles recorded his lengthy meeting with Premier Yoshida, who he "frankly told Japan should not expect to find a big U.S. market because the Japanese don't make the things we want."[8] This transition of perception, which frequently retains a smug superiority, is present both in Anglo-American thinking, and among other Westerners as well. Charles DeGaulle remarked after a summit gathering with Hayato Ikeda, "I had the impression I was meeting a transistor salesman rather than a prime minister." A quarter of a century later, the Gallic swagger had turned bitter, reflecting panic as well as snobbery. In 1991 the French prime minister, Edith Cresson, said of Japan, "They are in a position to destroy any industrial target they decide to de-stroy." While denying she had called the Japanese "ants," she added, "I say they work like ants," and went on, "but we don't want to live like that. I mean, in the small flats, with two hours to go to your job and—we want to keep our social security, our holidays, and we want to live as human beings in the way that we've been always used to live."[9] When President Bill Clinton sought familiarity with Russian President Boris Yeltsin in the strangeness of a post-Cold War summit, he "joked" about the Japanese whose "yes" could not be trusted.

The Japanese have not been without their own chauvinistic contempt for the barbarians. There is a duality of Japanese identity in some respects akin to the duality W. E. B. Du Bois described of being one and other with whites. Although African-Americans and Japanese may draw back at such a parallel, and indeed the cultural specificity and historically vastly different determina-tions in the two cases set them apart, the essence of being "one and other" for Japanese can be as real as it is for many African-Americans. They have been made honorary Aryans, members of the OECD and the Group of Seven, yet they are not fully accepted. They can afford to eat at the lunch counter—indeed they may well own it—but they are resented.

Part of what passes as cultural in contemporary discourse is crucially about separatism and is best considered in ethnic or racialist terms—a belief in innate differences among peoples in which identity politics has its ugly side. Sepa-rateness can be raised to belief in a degree of difference in which exorbitant claims of superiority are implicity or explicitly made. Considerations of culture are rarely innocent of fear of the other. It is an insecure world we live in and habits of the heart can be formed in antagonistic definitions of self and other. Both positively and negatively Japan has always used the West as a standard while maintaining its separateness.

For the West Japan's service as a floating signifier acts as a barrier as well. The struggle over whose definition of what kind of Japan is accepted is in large measure simultaneously a discourse of self-study. We know ourselves in our understandings of our significant others. Whether that other is benign, however (our bright student but still subhuman native or loyal, talented servant), or threatening (the evil Oriental or wily economic competitor), whether there is a stereotyping of the mysterious East or an assertion that they are really basically like us, representation in terms of our own needs and desires concerning who the other is reveal that Japan looms large in the Western psyche.

That Americans and Japanese are individuals who act according to their sense of self-interest within the constraints allowed by their social institutions tends to be understood better by Japanese than Americans. Their institutional moorings are designed to constrain and guide in the interest of the collectivities of which they are a part and to give individuals meaning in terms of their group memberships. Americans are more apt to think that external constraints by any group, including government, are bad. We seek to escape constraints to the maximum extent possible. The Japanese know the limits of such a possibility. They should, because the limits are tighter in their society. Lately, though, in the United States there has been less talk of individualism and more discussion of the collapse of our social institutions—the family, the community, and government. We find too much freedom and the lack of stabilizing structures to be less beneficial because they leave individuals less protected, with fewer resources to call upon.

What is constant over Japanese experience, at least since the Meiji Restoration of 1868, the revolution from the top that established the conditions out of which modern Japan was created, is the drive to learn, to assimilate what is thought useful, and to maintain independence through developing strength the Western imperial powers would have to respect. Their success in mastering foreign learning has brought disruptive change. DeGaulle, with visions of French grandeur, proved a delusionary prophet. The low diplomatic profile, the cautious former bureaucrat's primarily business orientation that made growth and profits the underlying rationale for state activity, led to achievement, and perhaps the overachievement over which the contemporary spokeswoman for French national interest fumed. The French were not alone.[10]

Watching the Pontiac dealers in the New York area's television ad, "It's December, and the whole family's going to see the big Christmas tree at Hirohito Center," which employs irony and plays on the perception of the public's pent up anger: "Go ahead, 'Keep buying Japanese cars' . . . " and concludes "Enough already," one does not know whether to be more shocked by the grossness of anti-Japanese sentiment vented, or the desperation of U.S. auto dealers, who apparently thought they could not compete in any other manner.

Yasuhiro Nakasone, that tall, confident nationalist advocate of a stronger Japanese military, the Japanese prime minister during the golden "Ron-Yasu" days before trade and political differences grew so overwhelming, liked to speak of Japan and the United States as *unmei kyodotai*, a community bound together by a common destiny.[11] His successors and predecessors going back at least to the time of the occupation, when Washington guided what was understood on both sides as a mentor–pupil relationship, have shared this view. As the postwar era came to an end there was the increased perception that the competence and capacities of the United States as world leader have diminished. It was not that the Japanese political leadership had not wanted to accommodate Washington. Rather, it was that there were limits to the followership they could offer. The United States had not thought very clearly about Japan's response to what seemed like a historically sudden, and not unambiguous, demand that they play a larger role in world affairs. Even Nakasone, who not even DeGaulle could mistake for a transistor salesman, told President Reagan at the 1983 Williamsburg summit, in a story he repeats to this day, "You be the pitcher, I'll be the catcher." He understood and accepted the nature of the bilateral relationship with the United States and accepted terms in a spirit incomprehensible had such sentiments been expressed by any other ally. The spokesman for a loyal Number Two, however, did go on to tell the U.S. president, "But once in a while, the pitcher must listen to the catcher's good advice." It is this unwillingness of American leaders to listen to Japan that increasingly grated.

Japanese have tried to understand the logic of America's positions and to assume a reciprocal long-term friendship. They saw the United States as taking Japan for granted, and also that the United States viewed Japan instrumentally. Japanese saw the United States as fickle and petulant, easy to anger, and shifting our stance toward them in sudden moods of distemper. From a Japanese viewpoint it seemed the United States was constantly finding petty, but symbolically important, ways to rub their noses in the dirt, reminding them that they are not considered in the same terms as our other allies. Examples abound of none-too-subtle reminders. When Fujitsu was not allowed to buy Fairchild Semiconductor Corporation on national security grounds in 1990, it was noted in Japan that there were few complaints when Fairchild was sold to Schlumberger, a French firm. To the Japanese the message was clear: "We are not really trusted to the degree America trusts the Europeans." The irony, of course, is that Japan has tried hard to play the role of staunch ally despite U.S. condescensions over the years.

At the start of the 1990s the United States and Japanese economies together accounted for 70 percent of the major industrialized nations' GNP and 40 percent of global product. One did not have to be Japanese, a lobbyist for that country, or a "Japan-symp" in language appropriate to the new Cold War, to appreciate that we needed to address rising tensions in what former U.S. Ambassador to Japan Mike Mansfield long ago labeled our most important bilateral relationship. To go on as though nothing has changed in the power relationship between the two countries would prove costly all around. There is danger that despite all the ink that has been spent on the nature of the Japanese system, the lens through which we view the world obscures the nature of the challenge the Japanese economy poses. Public discussion of Japan in the United States remains dominated by the short run in which much public thinking takes place and most politicians and business leaders live.[12] The deeper discussion should concern the trajectories of the two economies as institutional systems. It also involves confronting what type of international economic regime is desirable in the post-postwar period.

Even as we asked about better relations between the two nations there was the gnawing fear, at least among many working people, that our upper class was busy selling us to the Japanese and that elite understandings of sharing the spoils excluded ordinary people in both nations. The other is not just a culturally different group. It is instead a class society, as is our own, and we may not all be "in this together" in quite the same ways. We cannot talk about the central question, which is what kind of world we want to live in and how to get from here to there, until we first gain some clarity on the meaning of Japan inclusive of these complexities. The deeper issue is not competitiveness. Rather it is what sort of international social order can provide a context for a positive sum interaction among the world's peoples including, but surely not limited to, Japanese and Americans. These levels of analysis give us a multilayered framework for getting beyond the dichotomies that prevail in much of the extant discussion.

The Taxonomy and Imagery of Explanation

Many of the "explanations of Japan" can be fit into the classification structure of a two-by-two matrix in which the columns read: "Japan as unique" (historically, politically, culturally), or, alternatively, "Japan is not unique" (Japan's economic performance can be adequately explained by applying the various theories used by political scientists, economists, and others, there is little need to emphasize distinctive conditions and characteristics).[13] The two rows are: "Japan as demon," presented by harsh critics who condemn it as an unfair player and a collective conspiracy to undermine the West, and "Japan as benign," which reflects admiration for almost everything Japanese and sees it as a model for other societies. This simple matrix could be expanded to include important differences within each of the four boxes. For example, conservatives who see Japan as benign and a model for emulation stress the hegemony of the entrepreneurial sector, the originating role of the business sector, social harmony based on low public participation in redistributive welfare state programs, volunteerism based on strong family ties and responsibility, and in general a competitive economic structure, with a drive to do one's best and conquer markets everywhere. Liberals, on the other hand, privilege the long-term planning capacities of the Japanese state, the subordination historically of finance to production with severe limits on foreign investment, state support through subsidies, protectionism, and guidance for targeted industries picked to conquer world markets. They have their own Japan.

It would also be possible to divide analyses into those that stress initial conditions and those that do not. Country size and resource endowment are powerful influences. Some suggest the resource-rich United States, with its vast internal market and commanding technological lead at the end of World War II, could safely celebrate free markets and comparative advantage. The natural resource–poor Japanese, if they were to get rich, had to find a shortcut to becoming a technologically advanced society capable of producing exports with high-income elasticities to pay for its huge and growing demand for raw material imports. If it had to change its comparative advantage, infant industry protectionism was inevitable. Much can be explained about the two nations going back further, to before the Meiji Era and the rise to industrial prominence of the United States at the end of the nineteenth century. Initial conditions and rational choice theory might be thought capable of explaining all crucial elements. A larger matrix could be constructed to capture the diversity of dualistic sets in our thinking about Japan. The approach taken here is to try and break out of these boxes.

There are elements of unique national character. The pattern that emerges in the literatures is complex since many Westerners and Japanese experts are on the same side on key issues, facing other experts, both Western and Japanese, with very different understandings of Japanese realities. The task is to articulate these with coherence yet respect for ambiguity. To come to too easy a reconciliation is to foster false understandings and to be part of the problem. The goal is to present a coherent story, though not necessarily always a neat and unambiguous one. The problem is very often in our reading or misreading of culture. *Culture*, as I will use it here, is not that which is left over after the political, economic, and other categories of explanation have been explored. Rather, it is integral to a proper understanding of these categories. We need to pass beyond Roland Barthes imaginary Garbagne, avoiding the dangers of mislabelings on the coast of Bohemia, and establish a Japan suited to our true needs. There are so many "Japans" out there competing for the claim to represent that nation in our subjective understanding. There is also a fashionable preference for ambiguity that seeks to embrace the multiplicity of realities as equally "true" that needs to be transcended.

The issue of culture impinges on the economic sphere in two ways. The first is in what is called *popular culture*—movies, mass market fiction, and so on. There is a reflection of the fears and uncertainties that affect American policymaking and politics in popular culture that is worth brief deconstruction because it shapes public awareness and constrains policymaking. Second, culture is used as the categorization of last resort. "Culture" explains what cannot be explained any other way. When our differences with Japan are said to be a matter of culture, the speaker is in effect saying there is little else to be said on the matter—"East is East and West is West . . . ," and all that. In this usage culture is the great residual, the catch-all random error term of the statistician for what remains unexplainable in the regression. The emotional weight loaded onto this residual has been substantial.

With regard to the appearance of Japan as a global economic superpower and the new meanings of Asia, the phenomena came fast, but the disturbing "lesson" came more slowly. Asia forced itself from the periphery of American consciousness to a more central place as a result of poorly understood military involvements and then through a deepening trade relation that seemed increasingly unbalanced and a cause for alarm.

It was not acknowledged in Korea. It was learned in Vietnam and suppressed by events in other parts of the world—Grenada, Panama, Kuwait. Decades after the Vietnam War the assertiveness of a new "yellow peril" sticks in the throat. In countless novels and memoirs and in the stage musical *Miss*

Saigon, with the fulcrum still Vietnam, Americans grapple with their announced purpose "to do good" and the troubled realities to which their noble intentions contributed so perversely. It was surely in Vietnam that America's post–World War II illusions were mortally wounded, that the American Century was truncated. This backwater trouble spot of the Cold War period became the leading region in global economic development. The fear of Asian falling dominoes gave way to an awe as these nations became the Asian dynamos.[14] Given important cultural and political differences, U.S.-Asian clashes continued to have a racial caste.

From the slave ships to the Black Ships that forcibly opened Japan to U.S., trade contact between the white race and others has carried the presumption of Western superiority. There have been moments of real fear—slave revolts, the Bandung Conference and the establishment of the nonaligned movement, OPEC, and even Sputnik, since the Soviets carried the mark of the Asiatic Other and that of the swarthy moor, Red Karl himself. Such fears are alive again in the Japanese challenge. The terms on which "the other" will have to be encountered is again contested. These images of a once pliant, feminine East turning on the dominant, male West, seeing its true nature, taking advantage of that knowledge far more effectively than that other great "Other," the black slave who, after all, had rebelled but not prevailed, as the Asians now threaten to do, is a disturbing prospect for the Western mind. We hear more powerful Asian voices, more self-confident, coldly reasonable ones that insist firmly, assertively.

In the contemporary confusion over whether Japanese are our friends or enemies they are portrayed as evil and superhuman, as wise and meek, polite, and exceedingly competent. Mass culture reflects this ambivalence. In the popular *Teenage Mutant Ninja Turtles*, the Japanese gang leader is bestial and barbaric; however, the movie gets its contemporary stamp from the fact that Master Splinter, the Yodo stand-in, is also Japanese. As Gish Gen writes,

> It is as if Fu Manchu and Charlie Chan were cast into a single movie—seemingly presenting a balanced view of the Japanese as good and bad. But the fact that the "good" Japanese is a rat means that slanty eyes belong to the bad guy. And as individuals the Japanese are still portrayed as sub- or superhuman, possessing fabulous abilities and arcane knowledge.[15]

Gen suggests that perhaps it is a sign of a fitness-crazed age that the arcane knowledge centered on is the single aspect of Asian culture that is found so enthralling (as it is also in *The Karate Kid* and *Iron and Silk*). I think it more likely, however, that martial arts is a metaphor for another kind of seeming superhuman strength—economic prowess, the ability to magically turn out brilliant consumer goods, technological wizardry, and to work harder, and to be smarter at the same time in factories that use sophisticated techniques to levitate heavy components using privileged knowledge. These are certainly fabulous abilities compared with the Rust Belt familiar to movie watchers of the 1980s America, but, to a degree Marx would have appreciated, the Japanese were the messenger, not the message. Just as the United States had replaced Great Britain as the workshop of the world, Japan represented the cutting edge. Japan unsettled the Great American celebration at its seeming moment of greatest triumph.

Another cultural landmark of sorts was the publication of Michael Crichton's detective novel that was renewed again with the release of the film version of *Rising Sun*. The book's reception tells us a great deal about the mood of the country in the early 1990s and the unsettling influence of Japan. The book had the odd honor of a front page favorable review in the *New York Times Book Review*, which likens its likely impact to that of *Uncle Tom's Cabin*. On the same front page was an essay by Harvard policy analyst and soon-to-be Clinton administration secretary of labor, Robert Reich, denouncing the book as yet another example of Japan bashing. Concern over *Rising Sun* was surely understandable. As one alarmed reviewer pointed out, it was likely to be the only book many Americans would ever read about Japan and was written in a way that was calculated to inflame passions.

The *New York Times* movie reviewer Vincent Canby declared,

> Its story suggests an updated version of *Invasion of the Body Snatchers*, in which the aliens are little yellow men who dress in dark suits and, like Godzilla thrive on carcinogens. Why else would they smoke cigarettes nonstop? The message of *Rising Sun*: unless we come to our senses, we'll all wake up one morning and find ourselves turned into Japanese pod people.

A few pages after Canby's review, in the same day's paper, Ryu Murokami's film, *Tokyo Decadence*, with its bullying coke-snorting Japanese business type whose sado-masochistic relation to his dominatrix suggested an equation of sexual humiliation and lack of self-respect, was not considered to be a representation of all Japanese businessmen. Nor was Murokami's movie, or his novel upon which it was based, *Topaz*, considered too dangerous for distribution in America. Perhaps this was because Murokami, as a Japanese, was allowed to show the darker side of life in his country, and besides, few Americans were likly to see a foreign language film with subtitles. [16]

The truth is in the mirror we hold to the Japanese reality and the truths we see in that mirror are uniquely our own subjective ones. It is a subjectivist's construction. The intensity of Crichton's warning that Japanese economic warfare challenged Americans ill-prepared and naively unconcerned and ignorant of what they faced was profoundly disturbing to romantics and one-worlders of all stripes, but it struck a responsive chord in America's traumatized psyche.

Thoughtful Japanese are also worried. The Japanese way of being "does not pass muster in international society," in a world "in which we cannot make the other understand if he or she does not want to hear," Makoto Kuroda, one of the most powerful figures of the Japanese Establishment, explained. "In Japan, there is a cultural system under which people can communicate without words by reading other people's minds," writes Kuroda, managing director of Mitsubishi Corporation and former vice minister of the

Ministry of International Trade and Industry. [17] The cultural system is not un-important to our discussion and it is surely not limited to books and film.

History is crated in an open-ended manner that requires each generation to rewrite what has passed in terms of its own lived experience. Because there are different local histories, the truth as seen by different communities of identity construct different global narratives. The self-contained reality of a Japan that learns from the outside, sets goals to emulate and catch up with one foreign model after another—the Chinese and Koreans, the Dutch, the Germans, and finally the Americans—found itself a reluctant Number One candidate in a world in which rank is threatened by a wealth of uncertainties in a world system open to disruptions of profound and unpredictable sorts. To be of the larger world is to be hostage to unwilled interdependencies. Such a situation breeds pressures to build walls to protect and stimulates an under-standing that risks must be taken in negotiating accommodations before any new globalist regime emerges capable of replacing the Pax Americana. But what sort of system? How much reliance on free markets? How much media-tion by states? The Rashomon Mirror allows each to see its own truth.

The Rashomon Mirror

The Rashomon was the large gate constructed in 789 when Japan's capital was moved to Kyoto. Eight hundred years later, with the decline of west Kyoto, the gate was a crumbling edifice. In Ryunosuke Akutagawa's short story, ''Rashomon,'' which provides the ambiance and the frame for the screenplay by Shinobu Hashimoto and Akira Kurasawa of the latter's 1951 film *Rashomon*, Akutagawa describes the great devastation of Kyoto and how it became cus-tomary to bring unclaimed corpses to this gate and abandon them. After dark it was a ghostly place.

In the grove in ''In a Grove,'' Atakagawa's story upon which the movie *Rashomon* is based, the different participants told of the same events, each from their own perspective. They were all Japanese, of course; Japanese living in a time and place not our own. Their minds, their knowing and rememberings, like ours, are separated from what other participants know to have happened. Each is characterized by a consciousness unique to itself and situation-bounded.

Understanding the impact of seeing through the Rashomon Mirror is not counsel for despair. I do not accept the idea that there are no conclusions about Japan that can be considered valid. Rather, the multiplicity of viewpoints and ways of seeing must be subject to scrutiny and brought into a coherence open to inspection and comparison with others. For many readers, surely most of those who have been trained in economics and most social sciences, this is an invitation to become unscientific. Understanding of the past, present, and future, however, is revised with the unfolding of events, the passage of time. A new past is created by a more recent past. Social science is properly an evolutionary science. Social laws can only be tendencies that are historically contingent and open to human agency. I can only appeal to the specificities of this inquiry to convince such readers of the usefulness of a broader perspective. The claim of modernist social science is in part the assertion of its clear narrative, its ability to aggregate what in literary presentation and among the "soft" social sciences are only a pile of stories, incidents, and anecdotes.

Where one comes down in each instance says more about the reader than the text. There is a tendency for a coherent reading of Japanese society in most reports that, while problematic, is understandable as a function of intertextuality in that the same events appear quite different in alternate tellings and tales. One way out of the dark night of the Rashomon is to listen to the stories and weave them together.

Unlike the events in the woods described in the multiple narratives of the storyteller on a narrow and artfully crafted canvas, our themes sprawl awkwardly. The task is to impose some coherence on a confusing babble from reporters, onlookers, and participants in different roles. To provide focus I tend to restrict main attention to viewpoints that I will denote as *international* and *national*, dividing each into class perspectives, corporate and worker. Other views will intrude. They are compelled to do so because they, too, are part of the story; however, I will basically tell of the achievements and tensions of the Japanese system. The tale combines moments of regional disparities and the lack of regard for the lives of real human beings in the workplace and communities whose interests are seen through the lens of self-interested political figures and long-standing relationships of mutual accommodation with powerful corporate interests. To tell the story that makes sense of these different locations is to look beyond the Rashomon Mirror and to see beyond the darkness that seems to cloud the American fear of Japan.

At the end of the Rashomon story a dismissed servant newly turned robber looks out into "darkness . . . unknowing and unknown." Perhaps he looks out at the dark night of the soul. Perhaps he is the displaced Japanese looking incomprehensively and apprehensively at what had happened to his country and its social order. It is difficult to know. The author maintains aesthetic distance. His work has been described in terms of texture, tone of detachment, and wit underlying a perfect glaze. The literary critic Howard Hibbett tells us, "It suited his ironic taste to play the illusionist who leaves his audience staring blankly into a mirror." [18] The period of decline was followed by the rebuilding of the nation, a unity, and then the demands of the Western world that might have, but did not, lead to a new decline and a domination by stronger foreign powers. In the early 1990s, many of those dismissed from their once-secure jobs at General Motors, General Dynamics, and many of the other generals of American capitalism looked out into an encroaching darkness, unknowing and unknown. Japan came to act as the mirror we stare at to see ourselves.

Culture and Economy

I enter this terrain of culture with some trepidation. I have been trained, after all, as an economist, and the first thing we learn is to stay away from the other social sciences. To stray too far risks professional ridicule. It is for others to learn from us. There are serious concerns of status loss here. A pecking order is involved. More immediately, however, *culture* is a much embattled term among anthropologists who are able to distinguish hundreds of distinct definitions of the word. The construction of culture is related to that of a social order separate from others, marked off by the intensities of social relations and the observation of common customs. One consequence of economics abandoning its concern with how socially organized populations produce and support their polities and becoming instead a study of how demand creates markets was the invention of economic anthropology.[19] If we understand culture as the social legacy the individual acquires in a group, a storehouse of pooled learning, a set of techniques for adjusting both to the external environment and to others, among Clyde Kluckhohn's definitions, or examined Clifford Geertz's extension of Weber's semiotic proposition that "man is an animal suspended in webs of significance he himself has spun" by taking culture to be those webs and "the analysis of it to be therefore not an experimental science in search of law but an interpretive one in search of meaning," then we move to the heart of why economics as it is practiced cannot adequately explain economic development.[20]

I raise the issue of culture *not* to describe the institutional features of the Japanese economy as cultural in the sense of being rooted *causally* in values, beliefs, and so on. Rather, I suggest institutions are created in response to specific material conditions as the product of strategies carried out by groups in struggle with one another but within the context of an overarching consensus of the larger group of Japanese in a relation of resistance to the potential of domination by the outside world. It is this goal-oriented imperative behind the cultural constructs that I think is of key importance. It has informed much of the way institutions are structured and norms have evolved. That such values, once in place, may become active historical forces must also be reckoned with for they guide our understandings and perception of interest. As Edward Said has described cultures, they "are humanly made structures of both authority and participation, benevolent in what they include, incorporate, and validate, less benevolent in what they exclude and demote.[21] It is the double moment of affirmation and denial that Said includes in his definition that gives it salience for the task at hand.

In my consideration of culture I am concerned with material constraints and consciously designed institutions. Culture embraces more than the world of symbols and significations. It is rooted in the material world, in the social world, as well as the human imagination. The cultural dimension is essential; the anthropologists try to teach us that to understand a people's culture exposes their normality without reducing their particularity. Cultural materialists understand that relationships among the parts of a system evolve in a mutual relationship of part to system, and so change as they are both transmitted from generation to generation and (re)created or changed in social praxis. Culture is not immutable. As shall be seen, as the conditions of the postwar expansion came to an end, aspects many Japanese had taken for granted as part of their cultural system began to disintegrate.

Culture in this institutional context is inclusive of the expectations each firm has of its customers and suppliers, its competitors, the financial institutions, government agencies, and labor organizations with which it deals. It offers inducements and sanctions that shape a system of collective action in a context of which individual and organizational choice is constrained and tutored. Mutual adjustment involves a complex of interactions, cooperative and competitive impulses, and actions. The mix and the specific content differ across nation-state formations, over time, and within nation-states by locale, industry, and subculture. The choices that are made condition future possibilities. They close off options, lead to the development of certain capacities and not others, or form norms that become part of future givens. Agency and structure interact continuously. Contingency shapes developments. Some choices increase capacity for future change; some reduce flexibility.

A *social fact*, following Emile Durkheim, is "a category of facts with very distinctive characteristics: It consists of ways of acting, thinking, and feeling, external to the individual, and endowed with a power of coercion, by reason of which they control him." [22] People in different cultures express their thoughts and engage in actions based on a system of beliefs and practices that embody social expectations. There are conventions of custom that constrain behavior and even one's ability to think about issues. Durkheim was well aware that his use of the word *constraint* risked "shocking the zealous partisans of absolute individualism." Indeed, economists' notions of economists freely choosing out of their own free will ignore these conditioning social facts. Here, I side with the sociologists, as any sensible economist does.

One can go further, agreeing with Thomas Rohlen that American individualism "is an attempt to deny social structure itself." [23] The American presumption is to take an individualism of an unbounded freedom in an egalitarian society where anyone no matter how humble their origin can rise to the top as a starting point. Merry White suggests that

> Western public morality . . . is based on individual rights and individual self-realization. This presumes that a person will create his own social and economic relationships rather than inheriting them, that explicit contractual rules will characterize the relationships, and that an abstract legal system will enforce them. What is assumed to be permanent are the individual and the contract, not the social nexus. In Japan (and in much of the non-Western Asian world) morality is grounded in respect, duty, obligation, and responsibility within permanent reference groups that channel an individual's energies. [24]

Because respect, duty, and obligation are so far from the way most Westerners—and especially Americans—view transactions, there is a tendency to smile and think the Japanese naive and that with greater contact with our way they will "wise up." The situation is actually somewhat different. There is surely cheating, outlandish criminal behavior, and other manner of significant dishonesty in Japan, but in most situations such behavior, if undertaken as an individual in an opportunistic fashion, is counterproductive. To be known as someone of this sort is to guarantee being shunned by many one wishes to do business with and indeed with many with whom it is essential to interact. There is both security and support in groups and as well as incredible pressure to work hard in the interest of the collectivity. There is also pressure to earn the trust of network co-members because others can judge an individual's capacities and effort expended far more accurately than can be done in the loose groups in the West. The cost to group members because of the inferior performance is significantly greater. Because social ties and personal sense of worth are connected closely to group memberships and loyalty is key to acceptance, the pressure can be unbearably intense—much of the function of Japanese education and corporate indoctrination procedures is to strengthen the individual to bear it. A more intense level of average work intensity compared with average performance in the United States is the result. It must therefore be added that it is the institutionalized corruption of the system that is the result of groupness and reciprocity, as will be discussed later.

Such differences in what I think of as the cultural economy of our two countries are far from academic. In 1991 when President Bush was preparing to steam into Tokyo on his ill-fated trip to force open the restricted markets of Japan like some latter-day Admiral Perry (complete with the fire power of an entourage of corporate America's top guns), Arnold Brenner, an executive vice president in charge of Japan operations of Motorola, one of our most effectively competitive companies in that market, warned: "For an American company it is always going to be especially tough to break in. It has nothing to do with government. It has to do with a structure and a philosophy."[25] The international economist Rudiger Dornbusch explains that what the United States calls protectionism and wants removed is in fact a complicated business. It has "multiple layers, like an onion, and the innermost layers are cultural."[26] As we shall see in the next chapter it actually has had and continues to have something significant to do with government, both laws and regulations and, as Brenner says, a structure and a philosophy. It is also necessary to underline that these were developed in response to concrete situations and have worked for the Japanese. To ask them to abandon them because it suits our interests or an American sense of fair play is therefore asking a great deal.

Social facts are also reflective of the existing physical economy, the capital stock with its composite vintages of equipment with their specific technologies, and the physical infrastructure of collective and individual consumption. In historic time the physical economy has a life duration only partially determined by physical durability, the economic cost of replacing its constituent elements, and the dynamics of change in technology itself. Understandings of the world, expectations for the future and attitudinal factors that we group with the cultural economy influence when and in what manner the physical economy will be renewed. The existing physical economy limits subjective expectations and preferences concerning potential and actual renewal. The cultural economy refers to those parts of the wider culture that impinge upon and coerce individuals as economic actors. This cultural economy is manifest in institutions. These institutions are socially constructed. Understanding the ways in which economic institutions are created and change is once again an acceptable part of economics, if not quite in the mainstream of professional practices.

Culture encompasses that middle ground between universal characteristics of our species and the individual's idiosyncratic characteristics. The term encompasses the traits, behavior, and modes of thinking shared by members of a group, in this case of a nation-state, distinct and distinguishable from others. I do not mean that all Japanese share these characteristics, or that those who do so respond in the same way and to the precisely similar degree. Far from it. There are subcultures based on regional differentiation, gender, occupation, social strata, and so on. The self-awarenesses and sense of boundaries, of what is permitted and proper behavior for a group member, the shared pattern of socialization that anthropologists convey in their use of culture, is also a matter of organizational form. It calls forth patterned responses to incentives; indeed, it conditions and structures such responses.

The term *culture* is also used in yet another way: It indicates differences based on invidious comparison. That usage, too, is unfortunately relevant. The Japanese were the most alien enemy the United States ever fought in an all-out struggle. In no other war with a major foe, the anthropologist Ruth Benedict tells us, "had it been necessary to take into account such exceedingly different habits of acting and thinking."[27] From an American viewpoint the Japanese combine an incomparable traditionalism with a ready adaptability to extreme innovation. During the war American psychologists rushed to produce portraits that were contradictory in the extreme. The Japanese can be incomparably polite, loyal, and generous, but they can also be insolent and overbearing, treacherous and spiteful, and robot-like in discipline. Such seemingly conflicting characterizations are the very warp and woof of Benedict's classic study and, indeed, of much that is written about the Japanese.

On the charts that consultants and other experts in Japan like to hand out, the characteristics of the Japanese are to be homogeneous; America's are heterogeneous. There are often two columns: passive versus active, group conscious versus strong individuality, government as protector in Japan versus government as enemy of business in America. They may also contrast sumo with its extended preparation and much positioning before a quick and decisive contest followed by a polite bow to boxing in which slugging it out for ten rounds or until only one person is left standing is the norm. There is also the contrast between the Japanese "wet" pathos and emotionalism to America's "dry" logos, logical and legalistic approaches to making agreements. Finally, the Japanese speaker finds some way to point out that the U.S. position is: "Our rules are the world's rules. Come play by our rules." There is surely something to such distinctions. Many Japanese seem to think so.

This model of patient unremitting work, studious and creative effort, and respect—respect for one's company, co-workers, customers—is an incredibly powerful indoctrination. Variations on these themes pepper the pep talks that are integral to Japanese corporate life. The culture of work that the Japanese corporation tries to instill is, in the contemporary American youth culture vernacular, totally awesome. The balance of elements and the contradictions are long-standing and run deep, providing a difficult coherence and continuity. In the year 604 Prince Shotoku's Constitution of 17 Articles proclaimed the injunction, "Revere place and hold harmony as the basic principle." This first article showed the influence of Buddhism and reflected a tricky balance. Harmony is created when people know their place and act accordingly. In this ancient sense, in today's land of the rising yen, awareness of place means a new balance to preserve harmony with the United States. Because the balance of power between the two has changed, harmony requires a greater amount of take for Japan and a higher degree of give on the part of America. Americans, however, may not choose to revere place when trading places puts them in a less-advantaged role in the relationship.

The Japanese restraint, which was demonstrated through the postwar period, was embedded in a larger sense of hierarchy and proper relationships. What is appropriate behavior for a subordinate individual or groups in the face of the requests of a more powerful superordinate would be different if relative status was not such. This is why America came to meet a Japan that can say *no*. Self-confidence and achievement breeds changing places in multidimensional senses. Relative decline, by Japanese cultural norms, should induce modesty and restraint. This is not the American way. The Rashomon Mirror reflects distinctive truths to different people and groups, but the image changes over time as the construction upon which Japan is based undergoes development and the observer, person, or symbolic collectivity of nation also changes. Heroclitus' river flows on and what people will see as they look into the Rashomon mirror in some future time cannot be known. Today is a future few if any of those who looked at Japan during the American Century saw. We were unprepared to treat the Japanese with anything but condescension.

The call for collective leadership and greater cooperation among the leading economic powers takes place as always in the context of mutual recriminations and, as Lenin would no doubt add if he were around, inter-imperialist rivalries. The pecking order does not stay constant. British hegemony lasted less than thirty years, from the late 1840s to the early 1870s. U.S. hegemony 100 years later showed similar lasting power, from the 1940s to the early 1970s. Perhaps future historians will date its eclipse from the end of dollar convertibility into gold at a fixed exchange rate in 1971. Perhaps too 100 years from now historians will date a Japanese dominance from the end of the Showa Era. As we live through these changes it is more difficult to know. Before Japan's growth rate slowed in the early 1990s forecasters maintained that if present trends continue, and based on what appeared like conservative projections, the Japanese economy would surpass the American sometime in the early twenty-first century, which is not so many years from this writing—if the financial fragilities the system also manifests, which will be discussed at some length, do not take too great a toll first. It is also the case that the world has known extended periods during which no nation has been able to play a hegemonic role in which inter-imperialist rivalries and international instabilities, wars, and rivalries have augured poorly for the lives of the ordinary folk as well as sleepless nights for their leaders. The very construct of national hegemony may prove out of date in a twenty-first century of interpenetrating globalist development.

Nostalgia

While the popular cartoon family in the United States, "The Simpsons," features Bart's iconoclastic disrespect for his elders and their loser culture, a humor of the knowingly downward mobile and a socially troubled society, the long-running Japanese cartoon family's star is Chibi Mariko-chan, who lives in her three-generation family in the traditional setting that contemporary Japanese miss. She consistently gets a 30 percent or better rating. From experience I can relate what it is like to sit crosslegged on the floor around the low Japanese table under a heavy tentlike blanket that goes under the table cloth and keeps the heater's warmth from dissipating into the cold of a winter evening. The homes have no central heating and this functional arrangement makes the family meal a warm occasion. When the program is aired each Sunday at 6:00 P.M. homes all over the country resonate to the nostalgia of small city life circa 1970, in the days just before the world sat up and took notice that something new was happening in Japan. Whether the home you are in is that of a traditional merchant or a sophisticated salaryman who knows all the tricks of moving his company's merchandise, the smile on the father's face as the program creates this magical, trouble-free world is something to behold. As a tonic to the long commutes and loss of ties to parents and home prefectures the Sakura family almost has the resonance *I Love Moma* and *Molly Goldberg* did to an earlier generation of Americans. It is a warmer, wetter version of Ozzie and Harriet, a Japanese-style *Leave it to Beaver*, culturally transposed. Chibi is not a rerun. Kids today have Chibi Mariko-chan watches and groups of children will sing her theme at the drop of the first bar of the song.

The same nostalgia fuels the immense popularity of Tora-san, the likeable, romantically ill-fated traveling salesman who lives in Shitamachi, the old commercial section of Tokyo, who returns home, always on the old train, never the high-speed *shinkansen* (bullet train), to find a love interest that bittersweetly never works out. In Tora-san's Tokyo, the houses are wooden, with paper-screen doors and *gesselshaft* abounds. Bumbling, naive, buoyantly optimistic, and loving concern for others overflows because stubborn fidelity to things past is the well-understood secret of the forty-four Tora-san films (so far, they come out regularly twice a year and make the title role actor, Kiyoshi Atsumi, instantly recognizable to any Japanese). Tora-san, like Chibi Mariko-chan, reassures with the familiar—things as they were, but no longer are. Sophisticates dressed in designer clothes in trendy nightspots may dismiss such cloying iconography, but the rapidity of Japan's rural to urban transition and breathtaking one-generation rise to affluence has left a cognitive dissonance to which such cultural artifacts speak.

Nostalgia is an opiate. Anyone who has seen Yasujiro Ozu's 1953 movie *Tokyo Story*, a realistic and hard-hitting look at this period of rapid urbanization, gets a better sense of the pain involved. Nostalgia is important because new forms are partially legitimated by longing for the old village that is now remembered through rose-colored glasses. In Japan the ubiquitous *karaoke* sing-along bars, often with videos that play the words and offer visual accompaniment to the half-crocked salariman's sincere, if maudlin, rendition of an old hometown favorite memory, is an experience that reminds one of the recentness of Japan's rural–urban migration. They are the functional equivalent of the immigrant sugar candy Hollywood spun in the 1930s, like the Irish-American Hollywood memory of the Old Sod. In a relatively drug-free culture, *karaoke* and *pachinko* (a sort of slot machine game of skill and chance) parlors are the opium of the masses.

Some cultural differences appear to be indigenous and to go back in Japanese history for centuries. Others seem to have been formed and in a sense depend on attitudes toward the West, responding to external challenge with a national unity of purpose that is quite functional, rational behavior in a collective sense. The closed nature of Japanese society faced by such a challenge led to a tight code of behavior that was deeply internalized. In a national social formation such as the contemporary United States, in which individualism is privileged over community, there is a need for explicit and strictly defined rules and regulations put into legal codes that can rigorously be enforced. Harmony is less forthcoming in ways that the Japanese culture permits and encourages. In Japan, where a culture of consensus-building provides a whole host of accommodating mechanisms, self-interest leads to different behavioral choices, freely chosen by individuals within the existing constraints. The overarching social institutions and expectational norms are dissimilar and social relations, including economic ones, are played out differently.

It is often explained to visiting Americans that the Japanese people once belonged to a village unit (*furusato*), and now belong to their company instead. They are used to their lives being organized collectively and submitting their individuality in a manner Westerners would be unwilling to do. One highly placed respondent I interviewed, a man who after graduating the right school (the University of Tokyo) from the right faculty (law), working at the right ministries and embassy assignments (MITI and Washington), "retired" to a distinguished career at the top of one of Japan's most powerful corporations. He then retired again, and now advises the government in a very sensitive area of trade policy, rhapsodized over former Prime Minister Takeshita's "My Home Town" plan's 100 million yen to every city, no matter how big or small, to build community because, he said, in an industrial society we need to create a fused *furusato* in people's minds, to merge the old with the new corporate home. At the core, Japan's elite believes (perhaps not altogether cynically, although calculation is surely present) in an ideal of community.[28]

These questions of cultural coherences and perception are central to an understanding of the seemingly more hard-headed issues of economics: competitiveness among nations, the sources of growth, investment, entrepreneurial sophistication, new product development, labor productivity, and so forth. They are the historically created context within which the specific mechanisms of the Japanese system were developed. Because the cultural experience of nations are distinct, those whose historical experience has been different experience difficulties when they attempt to adapt Japanese patterns.

In my view Japanese economic success has been based on four factors: (1) a powerful national consensus implemented by a cohesive elite, (2) the institutionalization of entrepreneurship within a new type of governance system that extends to both corporate entities and the developmentalist state and is (3) embedded within supporting institutions of the cultural economy, and (4) the most effective system of work organization, labor control, human capital development, and incentive structures yet developed. Each of these elements is in itself complex and none can be expected to continue in their present form. They, like all national characteristics, are historically formed and subject to constant pressures for change. They are products of contingency and agency, as well as what used to be called, in a now unfashionable terminology, laws of capitalist development. The difficult part is combining economics with structural analysis and an appreciation of cultural specificity. In the next chapter the contours to this synthesis are presented.

There is another complex of issues that have to do with the globalization process in which Japan as well as the United States take part. Competition is also about economic transformation, the changes and development in the capitalist system itself. The next and final section of this chapter deals with *kokusaika* (internationalization), the *kee-wahdo* (key word) of contemporary Japan. It covers everything from Japanese responsibility to increase foreign aid to holding earthquake drills in English in the foreign enclaves of Tokyo's internationalized central wards. Internationalization has been a long-standing practice in Japan. Since 1871, when the Iwakura Mission spent eighteen months on a world study tour to learn all aspects of modernization from the West, absorbing foreign learning has been integral to Japanese development. In the postwar era foreign experts in all fields were brought, wined, and dined. What was felt to be of value was adopted. The Japanese listened, no matter how foolish the advice, and always expressed deep gratitude to the visitor. They still do. Today, however, while their hospitality is as wonderfully generous as ever, they grow less willing to accept one-way conversations in which Americans tell them how things should be done.

The Economics of Economic Development

Marx once noted that Americans were unable to conceive of rivalries in the world market as integral to the way capitalism works. Americans, he wrote over 100 years ago, saw conflicts "as soon as they appeared on the world market as English relations." Substitute Japan and the current solipsistic bias is captured. At the end of the postwar era, it was Japan not playing fair and that was cheating us of our natural place as Number One. Others begrudgingly admitted that they do work harder, and maybe smarter, too. Either way, our relative decline was seemingly caused by Japanese success in the postwar era. Japan's rise, however, is also about the development of a new model of capitalism, a new stage of that dynamic system that is influenced by the movement away from nation-state–centered political economy to the study of the process of global economic fusion even as scholars and others strive to measure its dimensions.

The tendency to see the world economy only in terms of our most significant rival obscures the manner in which economic competition and government policies are changing the world system while being restructured by it, and the degree to which the global changes reflect shifts in technology and the organization of production that need to be studied. A problem of serious underconsumption was widely evident at the global level by the early 1990s even as each nation-state saw the problem as one of underinvestment and supply-side difficulties and so tried to control wages and government spending so that its corporations could be more competitive. In this regard the analysis here is different from that of economists who think the United States simply has to save and invest more. If the nation in fact did so it would also lower the global growth rate. Balancing aggregate supply and demand really does have a Keynesian dimension. The difficulty is that balance is necessary at the global level and there are not the mechanisms in place to address this problem effectively.

There are three aspects of the stagnationist trend evident over these decades at the level of the world system that are of interest. The first is that industrial production dramatically slowed in all advanced nations, dropping a full percentage point in each decade from the 1960s through the 1980s. It was this industrial stagnation that set the context of the intensified international competition and the triumphs of Japan (and also Germany). Second, as industrial production slipped, direct foreign investment increased. Third, the growth of finance that accompanied this decline was both inadequate to replace productive activities as a source of growth and contributory to global economic instability.

A transformation took place over the postwar period. In manufacturing, the Japanese pioneered a new stage of capitalist development with lean production, just-in-time inventory handling, the white collarization of its blue collar production work force, and institutionalizing entrepreneurship by extending the capacities to innovate and increase efficiency in production and design as a continuous rather than a discrete process. It has achieved breakthroughs by collapsing the distance between manufacturing and information-based services. It invented what Tadahiro Sekimoto, president of NEC, calls 2.5 industries that produce goods with a high-software component, not traditional products making heavy use of electronics and microprocessors. These are knowledge intensive and so have a high "service" content.

The 1960s was Japan's most remarkable decade of economic growth as industrial production rose by 15.9 percent per year on average compared with only 4.1 percent for the 1970s and 3.9 for the 1980s, much slower but still better than its rivals. The comparable U.S. rates were 4.9 percent, 3.3–2.6 percent in the 1980s. For West Germany the respective rates were 5.2, 2.3, and 1.8 percent.[29] The speedup of direct foreign investment in the 1980s came at a time of this dramatic slowdown in domestic economic growth. Between 1983 and 1989 the outflow of direct foreign investment increased almost 29 percent per year while world exports rose by only 9 percent and world product hardly at all. Much of this foreign investment was concentrated in banking, finance, and insurance. This was true for Japan and for the United States. The amount of Japanese direct foreign investment in finance, insurance, and real estate exceeded that in manufacturing at the start of the 1990s.

The success of European and Japanese recovery from World War II created overproduction and severe adjustment problems even as their renewed competitiveness put strains on what had been the seeming invincible economic machinery of the United States. For Japan, the great leap forward in terms of industrial production came in the 1960s, as we noted earlier. While output increased at a respectable rate after that (by world standards), its performance was far less impressive. As America demanded concessions from Japan, the Japanese felt unfair pressure from a nation that was richer than they, did not work as hard, and did not appreciate that Japan had its own problems. Production and profits based on selling useful commodities gave way to finance and to speculative investments. The excesses of Japan's money culture in the decade of greed put even the Americans to shame. At the end of the 1980s, as fear of Japan reached its fevered peak, the new enemy seemed to run out of steam, the air appeared to go out of its bubble. Developments in the first half of the 1990s led to a reassessment of the Japanese model as the growth rate plummeted. In 1993 the Japanese economy grew by only one tenth of one percent adjusted for inflation, the weakest performance since oil-shocked 1974. As the recession continued (it was the longest downturn since the war years four decades earlier), efforts to increase exports ran against resistance from Europe and especially the United States. Another turning point had been reached. The postwar period had come to an end for Japan as well as the United States.

Some observers suggest that the twentieth century technology paradigm has been exhausted. A host of new terminology—post-Fordism, flexible technologies, niche production, commodity chains—is used to describe the economy that supplanted the Fordist assembly line production system of long runs of standardized items. Yet, the way these shifts have been internalized in the Japanese system are quite distinct from both our traditional ways of doing business and the new forms of flexible production based on local economic cultures. The Japanese *keiretsu* form and the production system and labor relations regime that is dominant cannot be understood simply in terms of how corporations behave or of government subsidies and protectionism. They are about how a whole society works and does not work. At the same time, what is taken as "the Japanese system" represents only a small part of total employment and a minuscule proportion of firms. Matters are complicated by the networks of subcontractors and even the significant presence of local small firms manifesting patterns quite similar to Third Italy and other flexible production regions in other parts of the world. Such complexities are elided in much that is written about Japan.[30]

I am using the term *the Japanese system* in much the same way *the American system* was used in the middle of the nineteenth century from about the time of the Crystal Palace Exhibit (1851), where it became clear for the first time that use of interchangeable parts in assembly and other organizational innovations of American mass production had created a set of new techniques in manufacturing that came to be called "the American system." European governments were soon dispatching delegations to come to America to see it first hand. Over time as they caught up the name retained meaning only for the economic historian. Similarly, as other nations adopt just-in-time techniques, collapse chains of command, restructure work relations using team concepts, put engineers on the factory floor, and so on, the term *the Japanese system* has less unique meaning. Most American firms have by now had a decade or so of experience with techniques developed in Japan. Their achievement is obvious in the stronger competitive position of many American products.

The transformational analysis of capitalist development suggests that the emergence of the Japanese system signaled a new state of capitalist development. The very aspects that defined the older American system—Taylorism, inflexible production, the single "skilling" of workers who were discouraged from playing roles as thinking, creative agents in the production process and their lack of connectedness to the rest of the total production process, fit the goal of long runs of standardized production using fixed and supposedly best-available technologies. The American manufacturing system did not differ from the Japanese in being a stratified form of organization (in Japan hierarchy is quite pronounced and commands great respect); rather, it differed in devaluing the workers as thinking active participants who could be encouraged to contribute to the company's bottom line and growth potential. The Fordist model assumes a stability in which fathers were followed by their sons into steel mills and auto plants in a promotion system with seniority-based transfer rights guaranteed by a complex contract with management. They received generous compensation by the standards to which the workers of the world were accustomed at the time.

The Japanese system's success challenged the U.S. production system and then undermined these accommodations. From being a celebrated success story, one in which the pragmatic Americans responded to any suggestion for improving their model with an "if it ain't broke don't fix it" reply, it came to be recognized that many of the breakthrough qualities of the U.S. model had become rigidities that now had to be overcome. The initial efforts to respond to the Japanese were through outsourcing, to make an end run around the high costs and now lower efficiency of home production, the shutdown of unionized and older plants where work rules generally built up over decades by management as much as by unions were now seen as an obstacle to flexible production, and a restructuring through mergers and acquisitions. The change that created mean and lean companies, resentful workers, and confused customers (as well as a debt structure that enforced a short-term mentality on managers in the U.S. institutional context. Rethinking productivity and comprehensive quality took longer and was preceded by public relations claims that change had been successfully achieved. A significant amount of learning from the Japanese has gone on. The older American system is in retreat. Embracing things Japanese with an uncritical acceptance represented an unwarranted extrapolation from a set of relationships that were themselves undergoing change and in any event had been far more complicated than celebrants had understood.

While Westerners, and indeed some Japanese, celebrate the appearance of horizontal work relations and peer consultation and groupness in decision-making as indications of the democratic nature of Japanese firms, for example, hierarchy is always present even if this is not obvious to outsiders who focus on the process of discussion and consensus formation. Similarly, Japanese typically do not mean a delegation of authority to those further down the hierarchy by *decentralization*; rather, they mean a taking up of responsibility for objectives by more active participants.[31] Despite the claims of much of the celebratory literature participation is an obligation and not, for the most part, an opportunity for employee self-actualization.

It is one thing to say that the Japanese system proved a more competitive model of capitalism, one U.S. firms have done well to emulate, but quite another to set Japan up as some ideal either for others or the Japanese themselves. Further, an economic system encompasses far more than corporate forms of production and industrial relations. The governance system of the developmentalist state has guided Japanese economic expansion and transformation. The particulars of Japan's civil society, state formation, and economy form a historically specific social formation that needs to be understood as a totality and studied in terms of their evolution and internal and external tensions. Characteristics that seem to explain success in one period may appear as problems to be overcome in the next. The tiring debate over free markets versus a greater role for the state in guiding economic development—because it typically does not take the long view, because it does not take an evolutionary approach to institutions, or seek to explain how changes in corporate and state governance and technological developments create new possibilities and obstacles—is often a two-dimensional debate between caricatures. Our task is to give historical depth to the debate and to embed what would otherwise be a theoretical and abstract discussion in its cultural matrix.

2

Competition, Culture,
and the Economy

"At times like this we naturally think about reinforcing the barricades
to hold back the invader. But purely defensive measures might well
make us even weaker. In trying to understand why this is so, we
stumble across the key element. This war—and it is a war—is being
fought not with dollars, or oil, or steel, or even with modern machines.
It is being fought with creative imagination and organizational talent."

J. J. Servan-Schreiber, *The American Challenge*[1]

"What's the ultimate secret of your success? In the beginning you were
in no position to cut costs by volume purchases. Maybe it was your
fashion sense? . . . 'I just kept on doing whatever was necessary, as
best I could, with stubborn persistence. There's no other secret,' Ma-
sako explained."

Arai Shinya, *Shoshaman: A Tale of Corporate Japan*[2]

The Japanese competitors who challenged the American corporations that
dominated the global economy for much of the postwar period had an existence within a private enterprise system that can be described as capitalist—
but "capitalist" requiring a modifier or two. Following Chalmers Johnson, it is
developmental-state capitalism or an organization-oriented as opposed to a
market-oriented system (in Ronald Dore's taxonomy). The relationships of
the enterprise form that proved so successful in the postwar era needs to be
specified.

In this chapter the nature of the Japanese firm is sketched in broad strokes.
Its specification and the system in which it is embedded can be better understood with the help of economic theory, but not by a standard textbook orthodoxy[3] or a "universalistic" institutionalism. Rather, the framing of Japan manifests cultural uniqueness, which helps to explain what it is that the Japanese
business unit does differently in terms of relational contracting within a power

matrix internal to the firm, with its suppliers and customers, and in the context of the Japanese cultural economy and state–market relations. [4]

Thinking About the Japanese Firm and Political Economy

It is the dynamic advantage of embodying organizational-specific capital, human and physical, so as to be uniquely appropriable by the firm that gives cohesiveness to the Japanese enterprise as a competitive unit in relational transacting. [5] The performance of many actual Japanese firms depart from the ideal type representation. Companies, especially those that do not compete internationally, may be backward-looking and inefficient. Particular strategies and foci of strength may likewise differ among successful corporations and between weaker ones. It is not possible to generalize about all businesses in any economy without significant loss. This needs to be borne in mind as I use the representation method that characterizes *the* Japanese enterprise in contrast to *the* American one. A second warning needs to be posted with regard to U.S. practices that have changed dramatically in the direction of emulating the Japanese model. A third qualification is in order. I believe Japanese corporate practice and the larger political economy in which it is embedded are undergoing profound transformation, indeed decomposition. Much of the model that will be detailed emerged in the postwar era, and by the end of that historical period many of its basic characteristics were under attack if not undergoing outright revision.

Since long-term profitability for an economic enterprise can be seen as related to market shares, vanquishing competitors, and reducing incentives for others to enter the markets, a growth orientation can be said to maximize profits in the long run even if it appears to ignore static criteria of profit making and comparative advantage. Many Japanese economists make the claim that there has been a bias toward growth over profit per se. This is caused by the lifetime employees of the firm's desire to see a healthy expanding company as a source of promotion and security. Their incentives in this regard are greater than in an American-style company because gains are shared more substantially with permanent employees and the firm is more committed to the worker over his (rarely her) career. Structures of belonging encourage employees to work harder. That these choices are "coerced" by the structures of incentives they face may be true enough, but there is no reason that these constraints are any less legitimate or effective in terms of long-run criteria than are the ones faced by Americans.

That the firm need not be (and best not be) a passive vehicle for the workings of the invisible hand has long been recognized by economic historians. Indeed, Alfred Chandler has demonstrated how the United States took the lead starting more than a century ago. He found that success depended on the entrepreneurial aspects of management, the building and adjusting of personnel. In Chandler's terms, while mainstream explanation is about structure, what needs looking into is strategy. "Structure has been the design for integrating the enterprise's existing resources to current demand, strategy has been the plan for allocation of resources to anticipate demand.'' Creating organizational structures that worked to achieve goals was what separated more successful firms from others. It was the visible hand that was responsible: ''Modern business enterprise took the place of market mechanisms in coordinating the activities of the economy and allocating resources.''[6]

The American corporate structure, however, as it grew more complex at the end of the nineteenth century while it internalized planning, responsiveness, and even control of the external environment to a remarkable degree, was embedded within a political economy in which the state played more of a regulatory than a developmental role. Sectional interests and the broader lack of consensus prevented subsidy to particular industries in an open manner, and mass movements, the populists and the Wobblies for example, exerted pressures on the prerogatives of capital.[7] The single-minded, organized nature of the Japanese political economy made for different possibilities. The state form in Japan, with a stable ruling coalition and a powerful bureaucracy, offers a not unrelated point of contrast.[8]

The Japanese Corporate Forms

The group nature of Japanese society and unchallenged management by the nation's elite made it possible to form first the *zaibatsu* (the giant families of enterprises under common control in the pre–World War II period), and then the *keiretsu* (interlinked enterprise groups more loosely related in the postwar era) as vehicles to promote single-minded economic growth. The family of related and interpenetrating *kaisha*, giant corporations with their *kogaisha*, or child companies and institutionalized presidents' committees are the corporate side of Japan, Incorporated, the amalgam of Big Business and Big Government; politicians and bureaucrats are among the unique control mechanisms of the system. That high-government officials retire to powerful positions in the corporate world, the phenomena in Japanese *amakudari* (literally translates as ''descent from heaven,'' which conveys the relationship of power involved) provides for a closeness and information sharing among these key institutions of the Japanese system. Information sharing extends to the shop floor.

The Japanese system replaces Taylorism and Fordism with flexible production. Frederick W. Taylor, the father of American-style factory efficiency, had assumed it was the burden of management to gather together all knowledge that was possessed by the workers and then remove them from the brainwork of the operation.[9] By replacing their judgment with management discretion over every detail of production Taylor thought far greater efficiency was possible. In his view the ''full possibilities'' of scientific management ''will not have been realized until almost all of the machines in the shop are run by men who are of smaller calibre and attainments, and who are therefore cheaper than those required under the old system.''[10] Henry Ford took the idea of the division of labor and standardized the production of car parts, put the assembly operation on a moving line and lowered the price of the product so dramatically as to introduce at one and the same time the most successfully merchandised mass market consumer durable as well as the most efficiently produced product of his day. In addition, by paying high wages he solved at one stroke the disturbing interference of large turnover and slack labor control and appealed to a Keynesian rationale (he was providing himself with his own customers—a marvelous bit of misleading self-promotion). [11]

The Japanese system goes some distance toward incorporating the worker as compared with the Fordist model that is overly bureaucratic and suffers from the nonporous separation of thought and execution, as well as hierarchically rigid information and command flow mechanisms that squander the tacit knowledge and creative capacities of those on the front lines of the production process. By structuring group participation to direct maximum pressure on the worker to exert himself or herself both physically and mentally, the Japanese system increases the productivity of the worker. Investment in human capital, learning by doing in a long-term employment setting, and a bonus-driven, team-responsible context diminishes agency problems at the level of the production work force. Over time the experience with mutual problemsolving demonstrates the advantages of cooperation and exerts a peer pressure on all to give their best. Radical organizational change is possible since the workers have more rounded training and task experience, will share productivity gains, and do not fear job loss as a result of rapid technological change. Job rotation, team effort, and security have a similar impact on white collar and managerial personnel.

In the ideal type American factory the extreme division of labor so simplified tasks and isolated workers (that was Taylor's design) that static efficiency was to be achieved at the expense of workers not knowing enough about the total production process and, equally important, not being trusted enough to be able to pursue the source of the problems at their own work station to their origins elsewhere in the production process. "Management," as Kelley and Harrison note, "cannot rely on individuals to generate solutions to problems of which they are unaware." [12] Thus, worker involvement in a Taylorized environment is of limited value. It is difficult to replace layers of inspectors, supervisors, and coordinators through production worker involvement unless the worker's role is conceptualized quite differently and the goal of static efficiency replaced by a dynamic understanding of fuller utilization of worker potential. By the 1980s this was the standard message of management "how-to" books that crowd the shelves of business school libraries. In the 1990s it was well integrated standard operating wisdom in America's leading companies. The American corporations were less successful in marrying long-term employment guarantees for primary workers to a labor relations system in which growing numbers were contingent workers.

The larger meaning of the Japanese system is captured in Harvey Leibenstein's concept of "X-efficiency." Leibenstein pointed out "the simple fact" that neither firms nor individuals search out relevant information as fully or work as hard as they could. The Japanese gains have extensively been in terms of X-efficiency. He sees the Japanese as establishing more substantial "effort conventions." These are enforced by peer group standards and, I would add, made rational for individuals by the golden chain of career length employment and the exceedingly high cost of job loss. Leibenstein's insights that firms typically operate within and not on their production possibilities frontier and that for a given output costs are generally not minimized flies in the face of conventional neoclassical economics, but it is surely right.[13] While all firms function at some degree removed from their theoretic absolute efficiency, the Japanese have developed mechanisms that create norms leading to a closer approximation of maximum efficiency.

Flexible production involves both a new regime of production and a system of labor regulation. The reorganization of the factory, learning curve forward pricing, the extreme use of leverage in the context of patient capital, and work teams that see projects through from conception to normalization of production are all elements that shall be discussed at length. I shall also talk of the less-pleasing Japanese reality of intense alienation and the most successful system of labor exploitation yet developed. Part of its economic success, and contributing in large measure to its achievements, is a system that can coerce labor and extract physical and mental effort more efficiently than any other workplace regulatory regime yet devised. The system is brilliant and cruel. It builds obligation and elicits (or, critics would say, coerces) a compliant cooperation.

In considering the different views in the Japanese system and the American one, the term *nemawashi* frequently appears. *Nemawashi* literally means a root binding. When a plant is uprooted and moved to another location, each of its delicate little roots is carefully prepared for the change so that it is not injured and the plant as a whole does not suffer a shock to the system as a result. *Nemawashi* can also mean lobbying or logrolling. The first usage implies that everyone's feelings are respected in any decision and their individual needs in a situation considered when changes are made. The second suggests more of the give and take of a group process in which all participants pursue their interests paying attention to those of others who may be in a position to forward or inhibit those interests, paying off as best they can in exchanges or whatever to get what they want in a particular situation, understanding that the same players will be involved in other negotiations and that how each is treated affects this outcome as well as future ones. *Nemawashi* can also translate as "laying the groundwork." The Japanese common practice of careful preparation for a change, rather than a "let the chips fall where they may" stance of laissez-faire free marketeers, is calculated to minimize long-term costs of decisions made. The butt heads adversarial roles risk a loss to both parties, where cooperation might yield a win–win one. The Japanese term may not be familiar, but the idea has been embraced and made part of redefinitioned corporate cultures in many American firms.

The Japanese company builds its organization paying close attention to the capacity of individuals and departments that work well together. It has less inclination to buy services from outside consultants. New projects can be undertaken by specially selected teams composed of people with wide experience in the company who will stay with the firm through all phases of the project's development.[14] Firm-specific capacities can be developed well in advance of a payoff because short-term returns are not essential compared with the same investment made in the United States. The Japanese system gets the new product to market faster and with better quality control because of this team approach, as American businesses learned. The degree of autonomy of the group and the prerogatives of its leader are not absolute matters; rather, they are negotiated and reassessed by upper management and change over time in response to performance. There is no technique or relationship that is absolute. At the same time while patterns are contingent there is a predictability to their continuance and a shared understanding of the grounds for their modification.

The team of course has a leader who does offer guidance, exercises judgment, and is responsible for the project to higher-ups. This person is in charge of the project from design through the shakedown period of actual on-line production. Because technical and organizational leadership go together, the *shusa*, or leader, has been called "the new supercraftsman" by MITI, although he can also be a hard driving boss. The many skills required to pull the team together and draw on the essential component skills position successful team leaders in the entrepreneurial role. These are not uniquely Japanese skills. They can potentially be learned by anyone. They do, however, extend the concept of entrepreneurship into a different institutional setting than does the Western notion, which often links ownership and risk taking in an ideological and narrow fashion. Control by supercraftsmen rather than by bean counters has had powerful implications for our two management systems.

The theory is not always so impressive in all particular cases, but the notion that it is everybody's job to keep well informed is part of a total package that includes some people in the firm reading everything available on world market trends and the state of evolving technologies. Foreign specialists are invited regularly. They are well paid, generously treated, and listened to—respectful Japanese do not interrupt to show off their own knowledge. The goal is not to show that you are bright, as it often is in America, but to get the most useful information. Those being groomed for the top are often sent as young trainees to the United States and elsewhere to get a feel for Western culture through immersion. Similarly, the rotation of employees among jobs makes sense. Employees receive a better overview of the firm and whatever short-run inefficiency results are amortized over a long relationship.

An inclusive stance toward firm workers has a number of dimensions. A significant portion of Japanese blue collar workers are called upon to use intellectual skills that are more akin to white collar technicians and engineers than to the "check your brains at the door" blue collar operative of the Taylorist dispensation. Because such workers need to use skills and exercise judgment in frequent nonroutine and unusual operations on the shop floor, the gap between production workers and scientific and technical personnel is much less in Japan than it is in the United States. In the Japanese system a worker's cooperation is crucial since quick adjustments based on subjective judgments are crucial to economies of scope—again as U.S. firms faced with Japanese competitors have found out. American companies have tried to imitate this aspect of the Japanese system using quality circles and other Japanese management techniques. More is involved, however, from close proximity to long-term suppliers to the *keiretsu* form of intercorporate linkages, which had been absent in the American system.

The cultural difference between a people who are used to arguing or contending in a confrontational sense as a style of coming to agreement (the marketplace of ideas in America, where the strongest statement of opposing positions is thought to bring the best decision), or the American legal system, with its sharp adversarial nature, quick to threaten lawsuits and strong on legalism over harmony, contrasts sharply with the Japanese decision-making structures, with joint effort to arrive at the best solution given. This is an important element because the relative status of the parties involved is structured to leave organizational and interpersonal relations intact and, it is hoped, strengthened. While there is a tendency to romanticize the cooperative element and to avoid looking carefully at the intense competition, frequent animosities and tensions among players presumably on the same team, office politics, and corporate and governmental struggles do play out quite differently in Japan. Also, if discussion goes on too long, if further consultation postpones needed decision making and becomes avoidance of responsibility, then Japanese corporate leaders are ready to step in to move processes forward. They will, however, tend both to wait longer and to have greater respect for process.

In the Japanese equation right is not based simply on the facts as they might be understood in the United States, where rich and poor, the powerful and the humble, are supposed to be equal before the law, but there exists instead a sort of situational justice in which the powerful are not easily challenged and the official story holds sway even where there is ample reason to believe it is a convenient fiction. As Anthony Woodiwiss has phrased the matter, "Japan is not a society in which resort to the law is a sign or source of strength."[15] Japanese judges will tell petitioners to work it out and not bother the courts with matters that can be accommodated without confrontation and loss of face in a public airing of a grievance. Central to the Japanese model of law and of litigation in particular, as Frank Upham's treatment of the subject demonstrates, is "the elite's attempt to retain some measure of control over the process of social conflict and change."[16] The powerful get their way without recourse to the courts. Others learn to pay deference to authority and status. The Japanese also tightly limited the number of lawyers, judges, and prosecutors they allow to enter practice each year as a very direct means of delimiting litigation possibilities.[17] Hierarchy is fundamental in Japan and the "cooperative" company culture and societal ethos exist within a society in which the members are always deeply aware of their place.[18]

The *Keiretsu*

Cross-shareholding increased sharply in Japan in the mid-1960s. With successful growth came fears that foreign firms would attempt to take them over.

The percentage shares held by other domestic corporations with long-term relationships to particular corporations (other *keiretsu* members, suppliers, customers, banks, and so on) typically reaches 70 percent or so, but it exceeded 40 percent for the first time only in 1965, topped 50 percent in 1969, and reached two-thirds by the end of the 1980s. The Japanese system has no place for a market in management rights. While some observers see greater management autonomy and a decline in "groupism" as a result of the growth of internal financing (more reliance on equity issues and less on loans from main banks), [19] the most complete study of the data shows that as of the late 1980s over 90 percent of total capital flows were mediated by financial institutions. The change in financing from bank loans to security issuance in the late 1980s and into the 1990s made little difference to the substance of *keiretsu* relations. As Gerlach reports, "the internalization of equity capital within the same group is now actually higher than for bank capital." [20]

Despite strains in the *keiretsu* and shifting in the degree of closeness and distance among group members that rather than being new have always been present, a sample of the 200 largest Japanese industrial firms shows that, excluding double counting of relationships, in nearly half the cases (48.9 percent) where a company is a leading shareholder there exist relationships as a top-ten lender, a leading trading partner, and/or a dispatcher of one or more directors. Moreover, corporate shareholding for large Japanese firms is about twice as concentrated as it is in the United States, four times more stable, five times more likely to involve simultaneous board positions among the same companies, and seven times as likely to be reciprocated. The proportion of transactions taking place with firms in the same group is over ten times higher than the average with firms in other groups indicating significant preferential trading. Gerlach's data suggests that we should be cautious in interpreting examples of *keiretsu* members dealing with outsiders as meaning that relational contracting is falling into disfavor in Japan. Similarly, in the hard times experienced by the Japanese economy in the long downturn that started in 1989 and continued well into the 1990s, pressure to sell off stock holdings in other companies to raise badly needed cash was discouraged by the constraints of Japan's cultural economy and its institutional checks.

Dense networks of transactions and stable patterns of exchange based on a shared perception of mutual interdependence continue to exist. Linkages offer important advantages to group members. Nissan, for example, depends on long-term relations with Hitachi Electrical for pollution-control devices and Hitachi Chemical to develop silicon ceramic materials for engine parts. Hitachi Shipbuilding provides custom body stamping presses and ships to transport their cars to America and other markets. Toyota is a Mitsui affiliate. These linkages and long-term working relations speed up technology transfers. They also allow the same large corporate groups to scan the technological horizons and to move quickly into new fields by creating their own startups, not by buying up promising companies as a U.S. conglomerate would. The chairmen of Mitsubishi companies have Friday lunches (at the Mitsubishi Club, of course) to discuss everything from politics to the direction of the group; however, the constant function is to build and reinforce relationships among the presidents of Mitsubishi Heavy Industries, Mitsubishi Electric, Mitsubishi Motors, the Mitsubishi Bank, and the other family members.

The horizontal *keiretsu* company councils keep abreast of emerging technologies and move to create new entities to enter promising markets by drawing on talents and support of any or all allied members. Thus, new firms can use financial resources and expertise, technology and marketing skills of related firms. Indeed, *keiretsu* members can be an immediate, large market for the output of such new firms. Firms with a surplus of workers can make them available; indeed this way of placing redundant workers and surplus workers may be a motivation for starting new businesses. In an expanding economy this system has substantial advantages. In time of recession the deep pockets of the group help weaker firms. Japan has yet to experience the sort of sustained downturn that would put severe strain on these accommodations, although there is indication that the linkages are becoming less binding.[21] In the early 1990s, as prolonged recession strained the Japanese system, there were well publicized instances of contractors being dropped for poor performance and of the government allowing badly managed firms to go under but despite some telling anecdotes it would take a greater crisis to fundamentally displace the system.

Markets, Firms, and Historical Specificity

Japan's experience brings to the fore the ambiguity, and perhaps more an imprecision and obfuscating sloppiness, in popular usage of such core mainstream concepts as profit and cost. The divergence between short-run profit targets of U.S. firms and long-run market-share goals of Japanese firms, which was presumed by them to be consistent with long-term profit maximization, continues to hold for manufacturing and service activities (but not in the important exception of speculation, especially in land and financial instruments in which the Japanese pattern is quite similar to the American one and flows from the same "free cash problem.")

Western free-market thinkers have generally assumed that the firm that maximizes short-run profits is the most efficient since the long run is only a series of short runs put together. Yet, maximizing based on immediate givens may result in a success that may not be quite what a firm expects, something like climbing to the top of a mountain only to look out to see the soaring peaks of higher mountains that were not visible from the base of the one climbed. The Japanese often appeared to move slower in the very short run, and even for a series of short runs in which the Americans seemed to be ahead, or so it seemed. In the somewhat longer run they turn out to have done much better. Over the postwar period the time it took particular industries to leapfrog their American competitors appeared in historical terms not to have been very long.

A number of institutional factors are at work. Some American economists blame the tendency of our large corporations, which had grown to maturity, not to pay out enough of their profits in dividends and allow the stockholders to redeploy capital through the market. One influential school of thought associated with Michael Jensen suggests that the reason mergers and buyouts in the 1980s were good for the economy is that they created a market for corporate control and forced companies to pay out earnings instead of retaining them. The problem is with undependable economic agents. In the light of the Japanese experience of companies paying out very little and using funds to continue to grow internally rather than buying new divisions or discarding old ones, this theory must be considered suspect. One might look instead at the Western bias to high profit margins and high dividend payments over reinvestment as the culprit. The Japanese took the route of lower profit margins and went for growth even in so-called mature markets, adding capacity while their fatter competitors soon lost market shares.

Enough has been said that it should come as no surprise that the individualism that is the starting point for most Anglo-American thinking on economics is in need of some reconsideration when we talk about Japan. The entrepreneurial function is not a matter of the isolated genius alone so that to claim entrepreneurship as an individual achievement as the motor force of history is to claim both too much credit for the individual person of genius and too little for the contribution of entrepreneurship as a process depending on a larger culture and political economy. It is to that larger conditioning environment and the phenomenon of societal entrepreneurship that I now turn.

In the more open world economy of the postwar era, knowledge and creativity were rapidly turned into low-cost innovative products and quickly brought to market. As Michael Porter has written "nations succeed in industries where they are particularly good at factor creation."[22] Differences in national values, culture, and the structure of their institutions—not labor costs, interest, or exchange rates—may be the more important class of variables to "get right" if a nation is to be successful. There is no magic key. It is not either/or but usually the mix that creates a climate for and a practice of economic development. It is this aspect of what is involved in entrepreneurship that is missing in the highly politicized discussion of "building an entrepreneurial culture," which played such a prominent role in Margaret Thatcher and Ronald Reagan's efforts to restructure their respective nation's cultural economy, efforts that succeeded only in privileging buying and selling over producing. Indeed, when the Japanese accepted a permissive market freedom in the 1980s, which to earlier regulators would have seemed irresponsible, the nation moved into a period of harmful speculative excesses.

The Japanese success has been based on the entrepreneurial firm, "an enterprise that is organized from top to bottom to pursue continuous improvement in methods, products, and processes. The pursuit of continuous improvement," as Michael Best has written, "is a production-based strategy that has redefined the meaning of entrepreneurial activity from its traditional individualist approach to a collectivist concept."[23] Such an entrepreneurial firm, which seeks superior product design and relies on persistence to detail and the integration of thinking and doing, which involves itself in up-to-the-minute shifting patterns of commodity and service exchange networking, is a very different creature from the stylized American corporate entity. The Japanese firm as it exported to the American market created a challenge in the new form of competition it brought.[24]

Economists have come to appreciate the importance of process innovation, making products someone else invented better and for a lower cost than those who pioneered the product's development. In the 1950s the first industrial robots were developed in the United States, as were the first transistors. The "hot sellers" of the 1980s—VCRs, CD players, and fax machines were not invented by the Japanese any more than the camera, the automobile, or the color TV (the VCR and the fax were developed in the United States; the CD player by the Dutch). Japan's expertise on production technology, however, meant that they were able to "take away" products from those who first invented them. Such agility will be crucial in the global competition of the twenty-first century.[25]

The institutional framework of a nation will shape the direction and influence the speed of the acquisition of knowledge and skills that will be decisive for the economy's long-run development. Institutions can reward restricting output and repress innovation that devalues existing capacities, or the institutions can encourage their introduction and foster technological breakthroughs. This means that societal entrepreneurial skills are crucial to the prospects of nations. Competence in adjusting to change by firms and other institutions has learning effects that mean future challenges can be handled more smoothly and at lower cost. By working together, affected actors can gain from cooperation. Predictability and compliance to jointly entered agreements means all can take consistent actions in the knowledge that others will reciprocate on expected terms.

Institutions and Their Ownership

Consider the situation of Tamotsu Aoyama, managing director of Koito Manufacturing Company in 1990. Aoyama's name is hardly familiar, even in Japan. His company is relatively small. It makes car headlights. His most unwelcome and largest single stockholder, T. Boone Pickens, Jr., the Texas oil man and well-known greenmailer, was more famous. Pickens, following the U.S. custom, demanded a seat on Koito's board of directors and a say in running the company commensurate with his large holdings. Aoyama refused. The American was not a stable stockholder. There were some questions of why he had bought the shares, who might be behind him, what their intentions were, and so on (Pickens had bought the stock from a prominent Japanese greenmailer who had failed to intimidate management). That Pickens held 25 or 26 percent of the stock, having paid $1 billion or so was not a primary concern. Pickens, on the other hand, said: "When you buy a stock in a company you're one of the owners. You don't have to work your way in with management; the management has to work its way in with you."[26]

Toyota Motors directly owned only a small part of Koito stock, but its influence on the company was dominant. It provided Koito with its president and vice president and bought its output. The financial data, to which the company (Koito) refused its largest stockholder access, had an almost mystical quality. The data is whatever Toyota said it was. If Koito's profits were thought to be too high (by Toyota), they were lowered when Toyota said they should be by changing prices paid on parts delivered to Toyota. When political figures in the United States raised the prospect of "forcing Koito to act properly" (i.e., like an American firm would), they were laughed at in Japan. Should the Americans have invested bargaining capital and actually succeeded (very doubtful on the face of it), Toyota might simply have stopped buying from this now foreign entity, and a new Koito would have been created to meet Toyota's requirements. Pickens, after some embarrassment, withdrew from the field.

The story of what it had all been about for him is less important than what the tale tells us about how business is done in Japan. It suggests that the transaction costs for large Japanese firms tends to be lower than elsewhere because both sides recognize an obligation to proper maintenance of an ongoing relationship and that neither a brash Texan with access to $1 billion nor much else is going to be allowed to get in the way. There is a deep obligation of conscientiousness and sincerity in dealings. The Japanese system is one of relational contracting and not arm's-length sequential or spot contracting, as has been traditional in the United States for similarly situated firms. In addition, an individual stockholder's rights do not amount to much, in contrast to the American situation. Now, consider the explanation of the behavior of large corporations based on American-type transaction costs thinking.

In the U.S. economics and finance literature it is assumed that there is potentially great uncertainty about the quality and reliability of delivery of purchased inputs. Such fears of interrupting the flow of production or of suffering unacceptable quality input materials can be reduced by strict contractual agreements. By bringing matters directly under the control of the firm, however, or by producing the inputs in-house, they can be reduced still further. Such an expedient also economizes on time and effort in negotiating contracts. On the other side of the cycle, there is danger of underutilizing capacity. In slack periods a major purchaser can also play one supplier against another to reduce prices, even below variable costs in the extreme case. Market purchase is thus not without advantages.

This sort of thinking, prevalent in the Anglo-American literature, does not explain parent–supplier relations very well. Japan has far too much subcontracting and rather too little in-house production compared with the American norm (although if the market test is accepted, it is the Americans who have it wrong since they are moving to the Japanese pattern). The Japanese, rather than cutting a supplier off when a less-expensive alternative appears, helps them learn to be more competitive, perhaps lending their own experts to offer technical advice, coming through with a low-cost loan for state-of-the-art equipment, or training the subcontractors' workers. Price and other conditions may be better elsewhere, but the company stays within its network of affiliates. Internal firm organization is based on a gain-sharing concept in which employees, suppliers, customers, and managers all come before juridical owners. This is said to be a modern reflection of the *ie* principle of group organization in which collective goals of continuity and expansion of hierarchical, but inclusivity, guide decision making. This stakeholder approach has been severely criticized in the financial literature of the United States.

In the American version of capitalism the owners are entitled to the surplus produced by the enterprise and need to be on guard against those other interests that are always trying to grab what rightfully belongs to the owners. Ironically, the worst offenders are no longer thought to be the greedy workers, but management that skims the kitty and refuses to disburse what the owners have coming. Michael Jensen argues that the corporation as we have known it in America is a fundamentally flawed form of organization because it separates ownership and control, distorting the incentives faced by management who, because they do not own all the stock, do not bear the full risks of the consequences of their decisions. This imposes agency costs on stockholders. These are the costs of monitoring managers to be sure that they (the stockholders) get as close to every penny they have coming as practical.

The threat of takeover, an active market for corporate control, reduces these agency costs by disciplining managers. For this reason takeovers, leveraged buyouts (LBOs), and other manifestations of contestation for control increase efficiency (as Jensen and others of this way of thinking understand efficiency). Jensen's free cash flow theory suggests that growth-oriented objectives of management and value-maximizing objectives of stockholders diverge. Since the return on new real investment is less than the relevant cost of capital, investors would be better off if cash earnings were redistributed. By replacing equity with debt companies are forced to pay out cash. This is a good thing, says Jensen, whose work relates to the U.S. case.[27]

The Japanese system works the other way around. The lead bank becomes an active participant in the management of a client firm when the company gets in trouble. Payout to owners comes last (after other stakeholders). Indeed, the very relevance of such an argument is doubtful in any blind application to Japan, where, as Michael Gerlach writes,

> Credit, in the form of bank loans, has come to resemble equity in allocating creditor flexibility in repayment by deferring interest and principal payments and reducing the "compensating balances" that corporate borrowers need to leave in banks during times of financial adversity. . . . Common stock, in contrast, seems to take on many of the characteristics Westerners associate with debt. Shareholders demand relatively fixed returns on their investment . . . but do not ask for active influence over management.[28]

Berle and Means made the same agency cost argument Jensen does in their classic *The Modern Corporation and Private Property* in 1932. Why did LBO activity and contestation for American corporate control develop only in the 1980s? A number of factors came together. Tax law changes, capital costs, and undervalued equity markets are most frequently cited. The issue is complex and a close consideration of the arguments would take us beyond our immediate purpose here, but declining rates of return since the mid-1960s and rising capital costs since the late 1970s are the neoclassical culprits. These in turn, however, reflect the exhaustion of investment opportunities as perceived by American manufacturing, which had saturated markets and faced lower cost competitors globally as the other advanced industrial nations recovered from World War II.

Speculative investments and asset rearrangement took place in the context of a downsizing of U.S. productive capacity in basic industry. Thus, while management may have milked old-line companies, this was rational behavior given the incentive structures of U.S. capitalism (as distinct from those of a developmentalist state capitalism like Japan or Germany). The leveraged buy-outs and mergers and acquisitions were a no-nonsense disinvestment and redeployment of capital that met the market test of efficiency under American rules. The problem is that American rules reflect a very limited understanding of social efficiency (which it collapses to the bottom line private calculation of owners). They are not good rules in a world system in which others play by better ones. Indeed, dramatic rule changes accepted in Reagan-era America moved U.S. corporate governance in the wrong direction. "[T]he financial 'debt' instruments developed in the acquisitions and restructurings of the 1980s violated almost every principle of prior law with respect to the distinction of debt and equity," as Bulow, Summers, and Summers have argued.[29] Laissez-faire ideological tools were used to redefine property rights away from traditional American practice and still further from the Japanese system's approach. Institutional constraints and the lack thereof are crucial. The Japanese system did better so long as the developmentalist perspective dominated. In the 1980s, as the real economy slowed down and speculation increased, producing a larger and larger share of profits, banks came to be part of the problem rather than the mechanism of securing economic development. The close working relationships that secured coherent development also lent themselves to easy abuse as familiarity led to pack thinking and group aggrandizement. Once Japan had caught up with the West its cohesive growth orientation no longer bound its key players.

Economic Theorizing and Institutions

The example of Japan has encouraged some economists to demonstrate from neoclassical premises how the existence of externalities or national level economies of scale can mean that policies to coordinate firms' incentives may be beneficial and that some sorts of coordinated or managed trade may be desirable.[30] Unlike in the usual trade models based on perfect competition, in the more realistic world in which resources are underemployed and oligopolies with a significant degree of ability to create new market outcomes prevail, subsidies to domestic industries can result in expansion of market shares at the expense of foreign rivals by creating quasi-rents, the rewards of getting there first with a unique product. Customers in both countries may benefit, but jobs and profits will be redistributed. To the extent that there is a cumulative learning process involved in being first in one round generates resources and abilities that offer advantage in further product development races.[31]

Quasi-rents, the rewards above normal profits that temporarily accrue in a competitive market, can also aggregate for a nation that has innovated institutionally. Economists have generally been confident that competition leads inferior institutions to be "driven off the market," as it were, by those institutions that better meet human needs the way successful firms drive out less competitive ones.[32] The problem with such a conclusion is that there are no pure markets for institutions in this sense. Powerful vested interests, whether military dictators, landed oligarchs, or, in the core nations, interest groups from farmers to merger and acquisition mavens can influence the legislative branch to subsidize or legitimate actions that may not be in the public interest. Some demonstrably bad institutional forms have existed for centuries without the magic of the marketplace cleaning things up. Such lags can devastate nations that find their institutional arrangements making them less competitive.

Markets are without doubt tremendously powerful as efficient allocators, but the incentive structures under which they operate are terribly important and can be (re)constructed and modified to bring about more rapid economic growth. This contention in turn reflects an understanding of static efficiency, the allocation of scarce existing resources among various and competing ends in which the attributes of resources are taken as fixed and known. In the Japanese system there is greater awareness that growth is about knowledge-based innovation, not about static replication. Such a perspective leads to a stress on entrepreneurship as a process of creation of new information and offers insight into the way "entrepreneurship" that, at least since the time of Joseph Schumpeter, has never fit easily, or really fit at all, into the neoclassical understanding of economic development.

Every social environment has its own ways of filling the entrepreneurial function. The entrepreneurial function as, Schumpeter made clear, "may be and often is filled cooperatively." With the development of the large-scale corporations, he wrote more than half a century ago, "this has evidently become of major importance: aptitudes that no single individual combines can thus be built into a corporate personality . . . "[33] Contemporary concerns in the United States over corporate cultures represent a belated awareness of this insight. Experts give advice concerning creating and merging people and companies so that entrepreneurial functioning can be made more efficient and so that constant innovation can be smoothly institutionalized. As noted earlier it is just such an understanding that informs Japanese corporate organization.

Entrepreneurship in the Japanese system, more so than elsewhere, perhaps tends to be a collective force, a complex social construction that institutionalizes the entrepreneurial role in a group process of constant product and process innovations that have helped the Japanese forge ahead. The nature of this process relies less on a once-and-for-all perfection of the particular product and more on stress on continuous process innovation. This has given Japanese companies and those who adopt their stance toward human resource management an important edge. Leadership is exercised, some individuals stand out and make the fast track. The group context is supreme, however, and some companies have even owed much to the ambition, drive, and skills of one personality or of a few leading figures.

Shigeru Sahashi, a noted former MITI vice minister, liked to quote Schumpeter to the effect that "the competition that really counts in capitalist systems is not measured by profit margins, but by the development of new commodities, new technologies, new sources of supply, and new types of organization."[34] Institutional entrepreneurship involves adaptive efficiency, reacting to situations creatively, undertaking risks to solve problems rather than avoiding them or putting off necessary change. For a firm or a society it involves providing incentives that elicit productive change. Market pressures help, but the free-competition model underestimates the extent to which subsidies and other forms of risk reduction can alter the payoff matrix individual and corporate actors face. Adaptive efficiency creates new patterns. Allocative efficiency creates economies within old patterns. Adaptive efficiency means reacting to situations creatively, undertaking necessary risk to resolve problems rather than avoiding them and putting off needed changes. It means providing incentives that elicit productive change.[35]

Entrepreneurs create a loop to obtain information to match a new situation that enables the identification of a total structure in the new context and enables this information network to replace older ways of doing things. It is possible that such a usage of entrepreneurship can be applied to continuous incremental innovation, undermining the exclusive usage of the term *entrepreneurship* that has been associated with big leap theorizings, incorporating a broader understanding of innovation and economic growth. The Japanese innovator is not Schumpeter's creative destroyer, but the one who discovers unexplored potential linkages. The network or information-centered understanding of entrepreneurship may be a better fit for the contemporary stage of capitalist development.[36]

Japan and the Norms of Capitalist Development

The large Japanese corporations for whom economies of scale were important in the postwar period, in stressing market shares above profit as the driving imperative, has functioned differently than did U.S. firms in the same years for whom overcapacity and oligopolistic accommodation were the problems and whose concern was short-term profitability. The American large corporation in the postwar era considering, perhaps, a three-year-payback period, made qualitatively different decisions than did a firm that planned over a longer time period, used forward pricing to win market shares, and then moved down a learning curve over an extended time horizon.

Given this difference in understanding competitiveness, the Japanese firm more often succeeded by the test of what increasingly became the international market in which all large firms were forced to compete. The mechanics of the Japanese firm that does not separate design and production by assigning them to different experts, uses collaborative teams, institutionalizes innovation, and so on was formed in an environment quite different than that presumed by the American corporation in the early postwar years. Fortunately, these techniques can be copied. Many American firms have done so moving beyond Taylorist work practices and Fordist production methods. Even the best U.S. corporations, however, have functioned within a context established by American laissez-faire proclivities, the U.S. legal system, and governmental practices.

It is not a simple matter of "government should . . . " or "the state should not. . . . " There are different types of governance structures of differing capacities, and one applies generalizations to particular cases at one's hazard. The Japanese success with what Robert Wade has called "governed markets" has included high levels of productive investment in key industries guided by government incentives, controls and other mechanisms to reduce risk for private actors so that they allocate resources in ways that would not have taken place without state guidance. The workings of governed markets are not to be determined by the size of government spending. Far more subtle mechanisms are at work that the economists' statistical tools can only partially explain.

The American behavior pattern was not irrational through the first half of the postwar period when the United States strode the globe as the Great Free World Colossus. By spending more we stimulated demand and provided jobs for workers at home and assisted reconstruction and development abroad. Our corporate leaders formed informal alliances to avoid messy price competition. By introducing planned obsolescence they ensured growing markets. Our government, by pursuing a tax and spend set of policies built around military Keynesianism, and our consumers, by going into debt to live better, were acting in a manner functional to the prosperity of the United States and the better economic health of the world. Without such an expansionist bias the economy would have grown more slowly and more frequently slumped into recession and even depression. If these strategies seemed to be working so well, what happened? The answer is that all else did not stay equal. There was the recovery of Japan and Western Europe, global overaccumulation, the rise of the New Industrial Economies, and greater international competitiveness in a context in which the United States provided a relatively open market ready to absorb the products of increasingly strong competitors while being slow to recognize that resting on our laurels and the institutions of our increasingly outmoded cultural economy brought with it competitive shortcomings. These became evident as the postwar period wore on.

Because the Japanese faced intense domestic competition, and, in the context of the Great Race to catch up with the West, there was a growth bias strongly built into their economy, there was not at all the same collusion to prevent new destabilizing products from reaching the market or implicit agreements to set umbrella prices over all participants so that less-efficient firms would not be driven to the wall in a system of oligopolistic interdependence (as in the United States). Instead, there was a structure very much the opposite that bred dynamic risk-taking underwritten by a state that encouraged campaigns to expand market shares at the expense of profits and fostered technological breakthroughs as the means of competitive victory.

In my view the reasons for the limited successes of the Keynesian regime and the old international order would be better understood if the following elements of revisionist thinking were accepted. It was the recovery from World War II, the overexpansion of productive capacity, and increased international competition that did in the limited, or in Joan Robinson's phrase, the Bastard-ized Keynesianism prevalent in the United States and elsewhere. It is not unreasonable to see the Keynesianism that was widely practiced as a limited compromise in the extension of state influence over the private economy. The state created opportunities for entrepreneurs by expanding effective demand, but in an increasingly globalized economy did not pay sufficient attention to the need for structural adjustments and the formation of an international re-gime that would provide for articulated expansion. It did not "coerce" through administrative guidance or set balances between public consumption needs and private accumulation.

Whatever long-term planning existed remained the prerogatives of private enterprises and investors who retained control over much of society's surplus. Despite rhetorical endorsement of antitrust, the United States in the heyday of 1960s liberalism had a market structure of oligopolistic interdependence in which large, powerful, and seemingly eternal firms shared umbrella pricing, which provided a quiet life for the well-fed. Competition took place around the edges in design changes whose importance was magnified through advertis-ing's extravagant claims.

The American system, which was said to be the envy of the world, was taken to be a result of innately superior American talents but, in fact, rested on a huge internal market, abundant resources, and the lack of meaningful for-eign competition. As our resources base became exhausted and in any event played a less-important role in a more service-oriented economy and recovery from the war showed that the American Century was highly contingent things changed.[37] By the end of the postwar era Americans had lost much of their historic confidence. The quiet life of corporate America was shattered. It took a long time, however, for the comfortable occupants of the executive suites in Pittsburgh, Detroit, and elsewhere to meaningfully internalize what was occurring. It was not stupidity. These were intelligent people. It was force of habit, bad habits as it turned out, for the new international order into which they were thrust. With hindsight the differences are clear enough, but making basic changes is nowhere easy. Indeed, having been so far ahead of everyone else may have been part of the cause of the slowdown of the world leader. The earlier success of the United States (and of Germany) in the late nineteenth century have been understood to have retarded British growth in the key years 1870 to 1913 when it lost its hegemony.[38]

It is easy to forget that in the 1950s all those men in grey flannel suits, loyal and disciplined, who as a group produced technological miracles, were American. Conformity and tractability are now seen as Japanese characteris-tics. The Americans have become less dependable. In the 1950s and 1960s, years of oligopolistic interdependence, overproduction was the problem. Tacit collusion and covert price fixing were widely practiced. In a world of American corporate giants the sort of behavior Adam Smith had in mind was neither possible nor thought desirable. Following price leadership and planned obsolescence were criticized by some liberals, but, as John Kenneth Galbraith also wryly noted, these "uncompetitive firms" that the Justice Department might see as possible lawbreakers were the very ones visited by foreign executives wanting to learn how to do as well. The Americans seemed unstoppable. Writing of *The American Challenge,* Jean-Jacques Servan-Schreiber noted that "the successful takeover of Europe came from America's highly organized economic system based on large units, financed and guided by national government." "Most striking of all is the strategic character of American industrial penetration. One by one, U.S. corporations capture those sectors of the economy . . . with the highest growth rates."[39] It was not long before books were being written on "the Japanese challenge" in which the preceding passage was recycled in different forms with only the slight modification of some name changes.

Entering the Post-Postwar Era

Technological change involving computerized handling of information and communications, which some have called the Third Industrial Revolution, occurred simultaneously with Japan's long drive to catch up with the West. The end of the Cold War was at the same time. The extent to which these major developments are interlinked causally will be debated by historians. However, the Soviet system's inability to innovate, to satisfy consumer demands, and to deal with bureaucratic inefficiency, along with Japan's market-conforming and market-creating institutionalizing of the entrepreneurial function in a corporate–state alliance, and the United States' willful insistence on maintaining outmoded practices (indeed, attempting to force them on others) are surely all factors in this restructuring. That Asian newly industrializing economies were able to put Japanese lessons to good practice and U.S. firms found they could adopt many of the same techniques suggested a more generalizable progress, but one that required a different set of governing perspectives to be adopted from those the U.S. had come to regard as basic in the postwar era.

The central conditioning context in which Japan was constructed in the mind of America was the Cold War, especially the leadership role the United States had assumed of the "Free World." That we had chosen ourselves for unilateral leadership was less important than the fact that no one had effectively objected. In Japan the guiding consensus had been the goal of catching up with the West economically. In the United States economic questions were less important because U.S. preeminence into the indefinite future was presumed. The country was Number One and there was no Number Two in the immediate aftermath of the war. The Keynesian welfare state at home and the projection of military might abroad supported an open trading system in which free markets extended to free trade and were unquestioned as public goods.

There was little doubt in the minds of the nation's leaders that the United States would benefit from such policies and so, it was said, would the rest of the world. Globalization, then, was a process of extending the benefits of such economic freedoms to consumers everywhere.

With the winding down of the Cold War, and even before the crumbling of the Evil Empire was dramatically evident, Americans were telling survey researchers that "our economic competitors like Japan pose more of a threat to our national security than our traditional military adversaries like the Soviets," and that Japan and Western Europe's increasingly strong economies hurt national security because they threatened our own economy. [40] Indeed, for some time Americans had seen the United States using Japanese trade practices as a scapegoat. [41] They did not need a Massachusetts Institute of Technology report to see our real economic problems as being "Made in America." By better than two-to-one margins the American public, at the end of the 1980s, thought improving efficiency and productivity of U.S. industry rather than forcing other countries to adopt fairer trade practices was the better way to reduce the trade deficit. At the same time these polls suggested that the average American was thinking worse thoughts about Japan than they had previously. [42] Negative opinion grew in direct proportion to pessimism concerning America's economic future. [43] Unfortunately, the terms in which change was conceived in the United States and also in no-longer-so-Great Britain were backward looking and called for the recreation of a supposed golden age of competitive capitalism. Such ideological presumptions set these nations apart from Japan in fundamental respects. It is useful to spell out the differences in some detail as an exercise in comparison and contrast.

Flexibility and Enterprise Culture

There are those political figures working within a neoclassical economic context in both Great Britain and the United States who have attempted to construct lessons of Japan as an endorsement of flexibility and an enterprise culture that they wish to impose on their own political economies. Ronald Reagan, Margaret Thatcher, and their immediate successors appropriated a use of these terms—*flexibility* and *enterprise*—which they contrasted to liberal welfare-state–oriented economic organizing principles, claiming Japan as a case of a successful market economy. Yet, the usage of flexibility and enterprise culture are quite contextually specific. There are ways in which the laissez-faire protagonists in the West act in a manner consistent with the Japanese pattern, but they miss what has been the core pattern. Those in the Thatcher and Reagan camp on the issue seek to build an enterprise nation by getting government off the backs of business. Enterprise culture, flexibility, privatization, and deregulation—the buzzwords of the 1980s—were all descriptive of aspects sweeping away an older regulatory regime. They are the negative moment in dislodging the Keynesian state. That Japan followed the Anglo-American pattern, deregulating and privatizing such former state enterprises as the phone company and the railroads would lend support to the view that this worldwide trend was consistent with the Japanese model. From such an appraisal of the historically progressive nature of the Anglo-American thrust, enterprise culture can be seen as being about the attitudes and values, embodied in self-understanding and institutional activities, that represent a project of reconstruction of the cultural economy.

The Reagan–Thatcher enterprise culture, however, was and, to the extent it is a continuing force, remains an effort to create individuals who are self-reliant and not dependent. The two are assumed to go together. This is in contradistinction to the Japanese pattern. The properly socialized enterprise individual in Japan is enmeshed in a collective ethos and business community set of relations that assumes dependence on others as a positive thing and the extension of oneself for the good of the group as a necessary part of individual success. At base there is a fundamental disjuncture as to the conduct best calculated for achieving success in the marketplace and the role of the individual in the enterprise—and so the definition of a desirable enterprise culture—between the conventional Japanese understanding and the Anglo-American view that is at its most extreme in the Thatcher–Reagan formulations prominent in the 1980s. Sink or swim is hardly the advice a Japanese manager gives to an employee expected to hustle for the good of the company. Individuals are given all the support possible, but they themselves must work to the utmost of their potential in this supportive atmosphere. The environment for the Anglo-American in the enterprise culture is that he, or perhaps she, can count on only themselves.

As critics of Reaganism and Thatcherism (to stay with the namesakes of the most influential exponents of the approach that has outlasted their tenure) suggest, such extreme volunteerism as the basis of human community denies the relevance of social constraints and imposes moral judgments as external goad and punishment. Both in other Western traditions of social solidarity (corporatist, universalistic, and other forms of solidaristic models) and in somewhat different ways in the Japanese setting, we find conceptions of responsibility that see it instead as "a human potential whose realization depends upon a number of specific social conditions and learning experiences, themselves often of a non-individualistic nature, and requiring various collectively provided resources and opportunities."[44]

The 1989 Organization for Cooperation and Development (OECD) *Labour Market Flexibility* report finds that *flexibility* in both France and the United Kingdom means "the ability to lay off workers" or impose "flexible working hours." In Germany and Sweden, on the other hand, it meant "multiskilling and broad qualification" and "training all employees." After reviewing contrasts in usage Anna Pollert writes, "those believing they are sharing the same debate on flexibility at an international level may be describing quite different processes within incommensurate economic, legal and institutional contexts."[45] We would also want to time date our generalizations because they are historically contingent, culturally embedded, and subject to the influences of changes impinging from the larger world system over time.

The flexible long-term employee in Japan is an especially privileged worker compared with those who complement his work elsewhere in the production system. Indeed, the primary worker in a large corporation is not flexible in the most fundamental sense in which the term is used in the Thatcherite discourse. His job is protected. There is relative inflexibility in terms of a lifetime commitment by the firm to provide him a job. The flexibility is in secondary labor markets where workers enjoy no such protection. It is the insecurity of the temporary workers that is the price paid for the security that permanent workers in Japan enjoy.[46] The stability of core employees sits atop the flexibility (or instability) of the larger number of secondary workers. Providing such disadvantaged workers with stability would be to introduce inflexibility into the system. Thus, the easy identification of flexibility as good and rigidity as bad is misleading. The primary workers' lifetime employment is a rigidity that permits, empowers, and encourages them to behave flexibly. Adaptive capacity in one part of the system rests on rigidities in another part. Redistributing risk within the total system involves both equity and efficiency issues that are typically skated over in the management literature and too often in public policy discussions.

It is not clear in this regard that the "flexibility" top management has in the United States to compensate itself vastly more generously than executives elsewhere is not a source of inflexibility on the part of resentful workers in their employ who are quickly fired to achieve short-term cost savings. For the British case, despite much talk about cooperation, it has been argued that flexibility has been "a tactical survival plan related to recession, not a strategy" for participatory transformation of the stagnant economy.[47] Moreover, it is not all clear that even if the Thatcher–Reagan strategy were to succeed their countries would be better off. Makoto Itoh speaks for many other Japanese economists in asserting that "at the root of the 'British disease' and of American difficulties in industrial restructuring is their failure to secure strong motivation of general workers in workplaces, despite the presence of a typically capitalist market economy."[48] While the ultimate wisdom of Thatcher–Reagan economic thinking takes us beyond our immediate subject there are surely grounds for skepticism. Part of the inadequacy of the theoretical underpinnings of such ideologically driven economics is the insistence on a sharp dichotomous definition of planning by firms and government versus market allocation. Exchange in the Japanese case combines use of markets with aspects of tradition, relational networking, and social harmony enforced and guided by state activity in which long-time horizons, individual memory in committed group institutional settings, and nonmarket reciprocity are key.

The fascination with corporate culture comes from the belief that you cannot fundamentally change a firm's behavior (response to new situations) without changing the culture (the way employees organize their thinking about a situation, the starting assumptions brought to ways of seeing and understanding). This is as true of a nation as it is for a corporation (and is why the Reagan–Thatcher stress of "the magic of the marketplace" and revitalizing "enterprise culture" was more than politically motivated rhetoric). Corporations do exist within a larger cultural economy of their society, but this is an insight that cuts against much of what Thatcher and Reagan attempted to do. If in the larger society individualism devolves into greed and the celebration of selfishness, then attempts at developing a team effort within a particular corporation are made more difficult. A history of antagonistic relations with suppliers and production workers is not easily overcome.

Finally, rather than taking the mainstream understanding of the commercial enterprise as the paradigm for all other institutions (e.g., so that health care or education are run on "business principles"), denotes both an "extremely wide-ranging process of 'de-differentiation' of previously distinct modes of organization, self-understanding and conceptual representation,"[49] and a representation of a narrow understanding of the cultural range of successful enterprise. The neoutilitarian teleology of the neoclassical approach implies that one knows the best arrangement and that it should always win out in a Social Darwinist marketplace if only it were not for government intervention by bureaucrats and others who think they know best. Such a method, however, would be problematic even if market outcomes were always most desirable because it evades the question which kind of market.

Markets need to be structured. To show that some social creation is useful is not to explain its origin or why it is the way it is. Functionalism can characterize usefulness, but it does not confer specific nature on social phenomena. One does not just whistle into being an enterprise culture just because one thinks one knows what it is and what it can do. As Dirkheim writes: "The idea we have of their utility may indeed motivate us to put these forces to work and to elicit their characteristic effect, but it will not enable us to produce their effect out of nothing."[50] Toward the end of the book there is discussion of how the positive aspects of the Japanese system can in fact be more strongly incorporated into Anglo-American cultural economies by strengthening some of the very institutions the Reagan–Thatcher efforts were bent on destroying.

The Japanese System in Comparative Perspective

The Japanese industrial relations system will be described in detail in Chapter 6, but I will consider here, in the context of enterprise culture, what team effort means in the Japanese case and how efforts to enlist worker cooperation have been viewed in the ideal American case or, even more extreme, in the English case. Team effort means if one worker does not perform a task, then other members of the team must. Therefore, if one does not do what the company expects, then other workers must do more than they had expected to do and the errant worker is blamed by teammates. The peer pressure can be intense. It is in the context of such an industrial relations system that workers who do not take earned vacation time can be understood. Overworking oneself is an act of responsibility to one's fellow workers. As we shall see such attitudes were coerced—not freely extended—but they are nonetheless a reality in the Japanese system.

In the traditional Anglo-American system such an attitude would bring ostracism. Anyone who purposely sought such work intensity would be a ratebreaker and face retaliation from fellow workers. Peer pressure leads to-ward relaxing norms and a constant "them versus us" outlook in shop floor struggle. In the United States a go-getter would traditionally be told to slow down because otherwise everybody will be pushed to adjust to a faster pace. No one takes less than their time off unless generously compensated by the company. In Japan peer pressure is used to undermine working class solidar-ity. This is one reason American managers adopt Japanese-style practices, as the British once looked to American ways of managing.

Attitudes are significantly influenced by the incentive structures and insti-tutional workings under which people find themselves. The clichéd "I'm all right Jack" attitude of British working class culture was formed in the period of decline in which British capital milked their industrial plants and failed to reinvest. Workers gained little through collaboration. Only a resistant mili-tancy and upping the ante seemed to secure gains. Over time the class struggle became a negative sum game and the United Kingdom experienced economic stagnation. Capital, however, always had the upper hand and came out with its assets in diversified investments around the world. The localist workers' movement could resist, but it could not win without gaining control over the mobility of capital.

The context of British manufacturing inefficiency is historically twofold. First was the tenacity of the Marshallian firm whose owners were unable to adjust to modernized forms of organizing the large-scale capitalism that was pioneered by Chandlerian multidivisional corporations in the United States. On the labor process side, the British firms in which the founder had the command of craft technology necessary to lead a workshop degenerated under the Oxbridge-educated heirs distanciation from the shop floor. Worker control on the craft union model became dominant. The second level of failing was the inability to develop a coalition within England that could control the trajectory of British development by gaining coherent leverage over the resources com-manded by residents of the national economy, but whose efforts to maximize their own well-being precluded domestic adjustments and capital constraints oriented toward developmentalist goals. The political will did not exist among British elites to adjust to new circumstances in a manner capable of revitalizing the nation's competitiveness.

To consider the paradigmatic automobile case, manufacturers in the En-glish industry from the early twentieth century tended to rely on craft workers to plan and coordinate the flow of work on the shop floor. As Austin and Morris became mass producers, and well into the 1960s, there were scores of separate craft agreements in any one auto plant. Low fixed costs, possible because of the craft knowledge of the workers, did not make up for the lack of technological dynamism that came from a stronger corporate engineering capacity that integrated planning, design, execution, and follow-up with con-stant improvement of the Japanese system, or even the mass production stan-dardization of the interim Fordist model of Detroit's heyday. The resulting lower profits and wages of the U.K. auto industry was not uncharacteristic of British industry more generally. The nonexpansionary strategy of family owners unwilling to lose control or to rely on middle management along American lines left the British firm increasingly behind.

The English elite sitting atop the corporate pyramid and staffing much of upper management was classically educated (and lacked the engineering school background of American staff and line management). There were British managers who came up from the ranks, but they did not easily communicate with the elitist ownership class. The gap between the cultures was never easily breached. Class division in England was extreme and binding. The American system allowed both for more mobility and more communication across class lines. Its structure was also different, allowing an expanded management core to go further down the corporate hierarchy, where in Great Britain the structural disjuncture between top and the shop floor was far sharper. Middle class education in an enlarged management cadre meant communication was easier further down the pyramid. The American difficultly was that the distance from top to bottom grew too large. One achievement of the Japanese system was to flatten the pyramid. This could be achieved because the workers were incorporated to a far greater extent as cooperative agents in the production process, unlike in the American Taylorist system in which the most extreme separation of conceptualization and carrying out tasks was the model.[51] The Japanese system never accepted either the class rigidities of the British nor the stockholder dominance of the American systems. The larger society constrained each of the three systems of nation-state–based capitalism. There were clearly serious "attitude" problems, but these developed in reaction to what was happening to workers within an institutional framework over which they had only the most limited influence. American capital under challenge eventually proved more flexible.

Thinking About Economic Institutions and Competitiveness

Most American economists in the 1970s and 1980s denied the characterization of Japan as a developmentalist state. Whether the Japanese system was more like ours and so just another brand of a wider capitalist phenomenon or something more unique and so requiring definition in terms of difference more than of similarity, remains contentious. The issue increasingly becomes one of convergence. The West, it was alleged, has made the historic move away from an earlier Keynesian dispensation. Japan, leaving aside its degree of state intervention in the past, will now become a mature economy and follow the same free market rules we do. The opposing view, and the one I find more convincing, is that some Global Keynesianism and transnational regulation will emerge after a painful period of the excesses brought upon us by extending the rule of unregulated markets and that the Japanese model will prove more influential in shaping this integrated global economy.

If institutions existed in a zero transaction cost framework, then history would not matter. Relative price or preference shifts would immediately produce new equilibrium positions, as they do in so many of the mainstream economist's models. Institutions, however, do not adjust instantaneously. Restructuring in the real world takes time and is costly. These "adjustment costs" should not be glossed over. Indeed, they are the very matter of human social experience. A lack of awareness concerning the importance of institutions makes America unable to see what needs to be done as a matter of conscious national policy to restore a healthier U.S. society. It also blinds us to new global realities that call for joint decision making with Japan on matters of mutual concern and with the larger world community, which is badly in need of a new institutional framework to set rules of trade, aid, investment, and finance. Such matters cannot be left to the market. It is the need to offer constructive incentive structures to individual decision agents that must be faced.

The United States is having trouble accepting a new global framework that it does not dominate. The Japanese are more willing to negotiate new rules because they are not trying to freeze in time an order whose time has past. Americans are reluctant in part because of our predilections for a "market," not Big Government(s)' solution, but also perhaps because the United States does not want to accept less authority or a set of procedures under which a loss of hegemony is feared. The realities of international financial fragility, however, and the costs to the United States of continued marking time are substantial. The Japanese, too, are part of the world system. They cannot avoid the pressures of the world system, although they alone with all other nations work to minimize them. The institutional innovations of the Japanese system presume an expanding economic context. Without it they, too, are in serious trouble. This is why comparing the two systems in static terms is not sufficient. The historical embeddedness of institutional arrangements must ultimately be grasped within the larger framework of an evolving global capitalist system.

The present situation arises out of a centuries-long evolution of the world system in which nation-states were formed and played an important role in shaping economic decisions and individual consciousness concerning available options. A long look at Japan's history tells us a great deal about the attitude and assumptions Japan brings to contemporary negotiation and the institutional forms it has found natural to adopt domestically that influence its views on the best norms for a new world order. The next two chapters discuss relevant aspects of Japan's economic development.

For well over a century Japan's national purpose was to become an equal to the Western powers. The mechanisms that were the vehicles for its remarkable success—the unity of its elite, the use of state power to speed structural adjustment through administrative guidance, protection and subsidy, one party rule, patient group consensus formation, and suppression of individualism—became rigidified and obstacles to a necessary restructuring. To understand this new turning point, it is necessary to review the long history of how Japan came to successfully challenge the West, to see first how the postwar system was formed, and then, to see how Japan became less able to accommodate needed change by the early 1990s.

3

The Modernization Process

"Barbarians are, after all, barbarians. It is only natural that they adhere to a barbarian Way, and normally we could let things go at that. But today they have their hearts set on transforming our Middle Kingdom Civilization to barbarism. They will not rest until they desecrate the gods, and destroy the Way of Virtue . . . Either we transform them or they will transform us—we are on a collision course."

SEISHISAI AIZAWA, eighteenth-century scholar

"I am therefore convinced that our policy should be to stake everything on the present opportunity, to conclude friendly alliances, to send ships to foreign countries everywhere and conduct trade, to copy the foreigners where they are at their best, and so repair our shortcomings, to foster our national strength and complete our armaments, and so gradually subject the foreigners to our influence until in the end all the countries of the world know the blessings of perfect tranquillity and our hegemony is acknowledged throughout the globe."

MASAYOSHI HOTTA, nineteenth-century official

To take a snapshot of a society is not the same as to trace its trajectory through time. To construct an ideal type is a different project than to examine the complexities of an existing evolving social formation, and to claim to understand something of the present is hardly sufficient to forecast the future. The cacophony of expert advice attests to all of this as levels of analysis, and modes of discourse create a welter. In the last chapter I made the case for the importance of a careful examination of institutions and understanding cultural context in comparative economic analysis. In this chapter I will first address issues of economic development in Japan. The focal point through which we look at Japan is the Meiji Restoration. Through it we shall see the Japan that existed before it and the Japan that was created by it. In the next chapter I will return to the postwar period of Japanese economic growth in the historical perspective needed to understand sectoral investigations and the policy issues that are to follow. The last section of this chapter forms a bridge. It gives attention to the key period of class struggle and political turmoil at the end of World War II that set the tone for the emergent Japanese system.

The long trajectory of Japanese capitalism is one of an adamant disarticulation. The Tokugawa Regime, as it is called in the West, closed Japan off from the world for over 200 years during the age of exploration as effectively as it could, wishing neither to be explored nor to have foreign ideas and ways undermine their reign.[1] Within its isolation a strong national economy and governance structure was developed. When Japan felt interaction with the world system could no longer be put off it sought relations first at arms length and then by becoming an imperial power itself. After defeat at the end of the Pacific War at the hands of the United States and protracted rebuilding under U.S. tutelage, Japan was ready for a more extensive but still controlled insertion into the world system.

Japan in History

Japan is the only nation in the world to avoid being dominated by Western imperialism. There are a few other nations that escaped formal annexation (two, perhaps three), but, as we know from *Anna and the King of Siam*, these weak states accommodated in large measure on the terms of the Western powers. Japan is unique both in its avoidance of domination (until its defeat by the Americans) and in its success in catching up with the West economically. The achievements and the social costs of the Japanese model that prevailed between the mid-1950s and mid-1970s, and its erosion under the impact of the loss of national consensus following this success added an important dimension to world history in the late twentieth century.

Bismarck bragged about Germany that it was the country in which the kings made the revolutions. So, too, in Japan it was the ruling elite that created the new nation using state power to modernize under the tight control of a professional bureaucracy that administered and regulated economic life. Under the Meiji oligarchs Japan developed public administration, maintained a top-down paternalism with strong remnants of a feudalistic sense of obligation, devotion to duty, and hard work, patriotism, nationalism, mercantile regulation, and subsidy to promote industrial growth. Like the Germans in the 1870s and 1880s, the Japanese questioned the relevance of British classic economic doctrine to their situation and as a useful guide to their undertaking.

It should not be surprising, then, that the school of economic thought that developed during these years in Germany—the Historical School—should not also offer an approach and insight into the process of development in Japan. The emphasis on the positive role of the state, a relativistic approach to change of studying the economy as part of an integrated social whole and of not separating the economic from the political. There is little of the abstract, deductive, static quality of orthodox Western economics in either the German Historical School's thinking or in the Japanese practice. In both there is an advocacy of conservative active reform, using *conservative* to mean maintaining a concentration of wealth and power in the hands of ruling elites, but ensuring that the social surplus is channeled to economic growth. In both nations as well there was agreement that unrestricted free enterprise does not produce the best results and that nation-building, and not the allocation of existing resources to meet consumer preferences, was to be the objective of policymakers. While the historical experience of Japan is unique, therefore, much of the thinking concerning the best path forward for late industrializers is shared by similarly situated countries able to forge a nationalistic coherent drive to maintain independence and change their relative standing in the world economy.

The national consensus, forged around the Meiji Restoration in the last decades of the nineteenth century, has both a negative and a positive moment that is still much in evidence in contemporary Japan. The negative was fear of the power of the West, initially of being colonized, as China, the great Middle Kingdom, had been by the barbarians, and of being humbled and subjugated. Economic development was to be achieved through learning from the West while applying Japanese "spirit" to the collective discipline of the task.[2] This second element, pride in Japanese identity, unity, and purity, symbolized by the divine emperor (descended from the sun goddess herself), combined with the first to produce the inferiority–superiority complex that Japanese culture still manifests. Both victims of white racism, and racialists themselves, the drive engendered by these fears and chauvinistic hubris have produced great achievement and tragedy. The polarities may be combined to create new dreams and dangerous antagonisms in the future, especially as they conflict with the now less secure psyche of the United States. In a sense Japanese development has been continuous over more than a century despite serious interruptions in its upward trajectory. The clashes have come when its expansion intersected powerful rivals.

The Tao of Japanese Modernization

Japan was not accepted by the West as any but the most junior member of the club until well after World War II, and the Japanese have a long history of feeling inferior to the West. Looking over 200 years of intercourse between Japan and the West, John Whitney Hall remarked, "Each generation of Japanese has had its particular sensitivities as to where Japan fell short of the Western ideal."[3] This remained true even after Japan had caught up to and surpassed the West by many measures.

Japan must be regarded as not simply a modern society, but the most modern of societies by the measures of modernization: widespread literacy, comparatively high per capita income, extensive geographical and social mobility, a relatively high degree of commercialization and industrialization, an extensive and penetrative network of mass communications, widespread participation and involvement by members of society in modern social and eco-

nomic processes, a relatively highly organized bureaucratic form of governance, and an increasingly rational and secular orientation of the individual to
"his" environment based on the growth of scientific knowledge—these being
the criteria of the classic developmentalist texts of modernization theory.[4]

The modernization of Japan is often dated from the Charter Oath of April
1868 in which the reformers of the Meiji Restoration, that revolution from
above masked in the rhetoric of renewal, announced their determination to
abandon "absurd customs"[5] of the past and to seek knowledge throughout
the world. In fact, this was to be done in a way, as Sir George Sansom reminds
us, that has come to be seen as thoroughly Japanese. They "borrowed and
discarded as seemed fit to them, performing eclectic feats which bear witness
to the toughness of their native tradition."[6] Knowledge of events elsewhere in
Asia imparted an urgency to the task of organizing a response to Admiral
Perry's demands and the possible future for Japan that those who made them
were understood to have in mind. *Gaikan* (foreign threat) has remained a
potent force for change ever since. Foreign Minister Kaoru Inoue told his
compatriots it would be necessary to make Japan "a newly Westernized country among the nations of Asia" in order to achieve repeal of the unequal
treaties their country had inherited from Tokugawa days. To "escape Asia"
and "enter Europe" became the overriding goals of the Meiji reformers. When
Japan again turned toward greater involvement in Asia starting in the early
twentieth century, it was as an imperialist and would-be "Western" power
approximating in attitude the United States in a parallel claim to its civilizing
mission and manifest destiny.

The economists' story of the Japanese miracle is usually at most an account
of the last half century. For our purposes the 1868 Meiji Restoration is a key
event, the focal point for understanding Japanese history. It is the period in
which the old order is transformed and it fits nicely into a Rostovian take-off[7]
(few countries do as well) because of the remarkable emergence of a modernizing industrial state after the centuries of the tradition-bound Tokugawa Period,
in which the preconditions for modern growth were laid.[8] In undertaking this
historical review we will be "concerned with the pastness that lingers in the
present and has entered formatively into its character," to borrow a lovely
formulation from Anthony Giddens.[9] It is this element of historical sociology
or institutionalist economics that, in tracing the antecedents and the logic of
development of Durkheim's social facts, acts to place the present moment in
the context of the Japanese cultural economy. These social facts are part of the
self-definition of individuals in society who make choices under constraints,
even if economists do not generally recognize their existence or importance.
"Air," however, as Durkheim reminds us "is no less heavy because we do not
detect its weight."[10] Japan's successful modernization was built on a very
different base than was the single trajectory modernization theorists assumed
in their one-size-fits-all model. To appreciate the changes wrought by the Meiji
Restoration and its continuing unique legacy we must go back to its antecedents to examine the complexities of continuity and disjuncture in Japanese
economic development.

Tokugawa Japan

In 1640 all foreign contact was ended except for a small and closely regulated Dutch trading post at Nagasaki. The death penalty applied to any Japanese attempting to leave or return to the country and the construction of oceangoing vessels was prohibited. As late as the early nineteenth century Japan was at a stage of development comparable to that of Western Europe in the late Middle Ages. Its rulers' attempt to freeze society in a rigid hierarchical mold was not altogether successful because, while repression was effective, population growth, the demands of a parasitic ruling caste, and the mismanagement of public finance produced a disordered economy, and peasant insurrections reminiscent of fourteenth-century Europe were tearing the social order apart from within.

In feudal Japan millions of peasants lived in self-sufficient villages, artisans produced traditional crafts, and most people were farmers cultivating rice, the overwhelming majority of whom were unfree and poverty-stricken peasants who lived and died in the villages in which they were born. When historians write that Japan was an old and highly sophisticated civilization that had developed in a splendid isolation that is the fortune of few nations on our troubled planet, their attention is focused on the lives of the nobility. Tokugawa Japan may have been a culturally sophisticated society at the top, but it was also a feudal version of the modern police state.[11] There were strict class lines. Dress and rights to carry weapons were circumscribed and traditional authoritarian rule was the order of the day. Limited trade existed, and it was mostly in luxury goods. In the cities workshop production was subject to guild regulation. In many respects Tokugawa Japan brings to mind that other great nation of islands, Great Britain.[12] Upper class life had the same qualities of colorful gaiety as Restoration England even if the police state atmosphere of Tokugawa Japan was more oppressive and economically restricting. A large feudal class was maintained by an illiterate, hard-working peasantry, who were forced to contribute 40 percent or more of their rice crop as feudal obligation in addition to rents to the landlords. The burden on the peasantry of supporting a large and nonproductive samurai or warrior class was great. The merchants, though they could grow rich and even marry into higher classes, were themselves social outcasts and subject to arbitrary financial levies. Commerce was inhibited by regulation of occupational choice, travel, and trade with the outside world.[13]

Contemporary scholars looking back on the period are wont to stress two aspects of the social order that seem especially relevant for the modern period. The first is that in the Tokugawa Era the family business, or house, was an entity with a life beyond that of its individual members. All family members shared a responsibility to build the business, and they shared in its success. How unique these Japanese merchant houses are in comparative perspective is another matter (Venetian, Dutch, and British experiences come readily to mind). The closed nature of Japanese society is perhaps the more historically unique aspect of the system. The more open economies undermined incentive for continued loyalty of employees and intense "groupness" to a degree absent in the Japanese case. The second feature is the role of education. Writing of this period Thomas Rohlen asserts that:

> Most fundamental was the fact that Japanese civilization was highly evolved as far as the place of learning was concerned. Literacy was a requirement for holding power, the basis of administration, and central to almost all aspects of culture creation. The merchant class participated in this pursuit of learning, and among well-to-do farmers and artisans, there were some who acquired fame or power on the basis of their scholarly achievements. Many kinds of skills and arts were organized on the basis of intensive apprenticeships or formalized learning schemes (*michi*) that wedded status, ambition, and personal development to the acquisition of practical skills. In essence, study was an important prerequisite of getting ahead throughout Tokugawa society. [14]

As a governance structure the Tokugawa regime was also responsible for a debasement of the currency and heavy taxes. There was extensive borrowing by the shogun (who ruled supposedly in the emperor's name and who held the real power), and by the regional feudal lords, the *daimyo*, who were strapped for funds to support their luxurious living, the necessity to maintain two establishments (one in the capital where their families remained as veritable hostages when the lords went home to their estates), limited rental income, and inflationary pressures. The merchants, although hemmed in by tradition and restrictions of all sorts, grew rich while chafing under their enforced lower status. By the end of the era many lower samurai were finding themselves unemployed as their masters could no longer afford to retain them.

The pressure of Westerners imposing unequal treaties on Japan's neighbors, including the ancestral home of their cultural roots, China, catalyzed them. Pressures resulting from population growth and the crude, cruel, and unbearable exploitation and mismanagement by the shogunate all contributed to its overthrow by an alliance of the outer clans or *han* (those powerful *daimyo* furthest from the shogun's direct power), lower samurai, and the merchants, both, although in different ways, suffering status deprivation.

When the *kurobune*, the American navy's Black Ships, appeared in 1853 under Commodore Matthew Perry and forced entry and imposed unequal treaties on Japan, the rotting structures of Tokugawa Japan crumbled. Japan, which had basically been isolated for 250 years and had not been successfully invaded for 1,200 years, was breached by foreign military power. The treaties that forced Japan to open her economy to foreign trade (and forbade her to impose tariffs of more than 5 percent) were deeply resented by the Japanese. The dislocations to domestic production, from cotton spinning and weaving to sugar growing, were disastrous. The deindustrialization of the craft-based economy was painful and disorienting. [15]

The Japanese became determined to regain their independence by catching up to the West, and this was evident from the first contacts the Americans made. Perry reported that: "Those who were admitted on board the ships were equally inquisitive, peering into every nook and corner accessible to them, measuring this and that, and taking sketches after their manner of whatever they could lay their eyes on." Our first ambassador, Townsend Harris, took four years to negotiate what America thought Japan had promised Perry, and this "rapid progress" can perhaps be attributed to Harris' having convinced the shogunate officials that the United States, unlike the Europeans, had no territorial designs on Japan and so it was better to deal with us. The Japanese were aware that an Anglo-French fleet had burned the port of Guangzhou in 1857. The emperor's court, however, rejected the shogun's treaty with the Americans, an indication that a new wind was blowing.

In the four key *han* that rose up to overthrow the Tokugawa regime a bureaucracy had developed that was part of the reform movement. Well before the event called the Restoration, the bureaucracies in the leading southwestern *han* were well poised to take over central power.[16] After 1868 the elder statesmen used this bureaucracy to guard against the encroachments of parliamentary politics; this bureaucracy succeeded remarkably well as the bulwark against democratic government from those days to this. The Meiji Restoration was a controlled revolution by a coherent elite. It was not a popular uprising that required concessions to the masses as the democratic revolutions against the old order tended to be in Europe. The transition is described by John Dower as a subtle one:

> The feudal regime was never overthrown, but selectively and in piecemeal fashion eased out from above, in a manner which brought about changes in the relations of production but not in the essential locus of power. What the early Meiji leaders accomplished was undeniably brilliant in its own terms. It was also a "grafting operation," which implanted critical and enduring distortions in the structure of the modern state, as seen most notably in the nature of the 1873 agrarian settlement, where property remained unliberated, despite institutionalization of private property, and this surplus was expropriated for the state and new industrial sector. Moreover, the political consolidation affected by the early oligarchs *institutionalized* repression, authoritarianism, and class rule.[17]

This, however, was hardly the whole story. There is also the idealistic moment of nationalism and the burning desire for independence and greatness as well as for real development that would spread its benefits more widely than simply a scheme to enrich a new ruling class. There was, in the words of the Confucian scholar and government advisor in the late Tokugawa era, Nobuhiro Sato, a sense of proper economic relationship and developmentalist mission:

> *Keizai* [economy] means managing the nation, developing its products, enriching the country and rescuing all its people from suffering. Thus, the person who rules the country must be able to carry out his important task without relaxing his vigilance even for a single day. If this administration of *keizai* is neglected, the country will inevitably become weakened, and both rulers and people will lack the necessities of life.[18]

Sato's model for a state-controlled economy required a strong state capable of insuring proper attitudes, active in training and socializing its work force and in introducing new technology from abroad. His study of Europe convinced him that trade could enhance a nation's wealth and power. He likened Japan to England in its geography and its potential in much the same way Alfred Marshall did (see our opening epigraph). Sato's sense of Japan's mission, while perhaps more idealist than others, was not unusual among the builders of the modern Japanese state.

Learning from Abroad

Fortunately for Japan the Westerners were occupied elsewhere in the second half of the nineteenth century, giving Japan needed breathing space to prepare to enter the world of contending military powers. Japan was quite peripheral to the main action and was seen mainly as a refueling point. China was the prize. The Opium Wars in the 1840s and the great revolt in India in the late 1850s kept Great Britain busy. The Crimean War, which started in 1854, the year of the first foreign treaty with Japan, also kept Great Britain and Russia occupied. France was in Mexico supporting its emperor, Maximillian, and getting ready to take on Prussia in Europe. Even the United States could not follow up Perry's threats because of the Civil War. While the world more or less left Japan alone, Japan went out to seek foreign learning to better prepare for what were seen as inevitable conflicts. In an age of imperialism Japan was either going to learn to become a successful belligerent or be swallowed.

Almost immediately after assuming power the key leaders of the new government (having received their colleagues' pledge not to institute major changes in their absence) set out to learn by visiting the major nations of the world. These men, led by Prince Tomomi Iwakura, were all products of the feudal era who set out to seek knowledge "so as to strengthen the foundations of Imperial rule."[19] No matter what valiance one puts on the value system and consciousness out of which such chutzpah comes, this was one of world history's most unique undertakings both in terms of the importance placed on learning from abroad and the confidence in collective commitment that allowed such trust.[20]

When the more than 100 members of the Iwakura Mission returned after nearly a year and nine months in the United States and Europe following discussions (unsuccessful) on revising the unequal treaties, they had enough knowledge about their enemy and role model to realize that drastic and totalizing reforms along Western lines, along with technological innovation and knowledge of international political culture, were necessary before Japan could hope to negotiate on an equal footing with the West. The five volumes published under the title, *Journal of the Envoy Extraordinary Ambassador Plenipotentiary's Travels through America and Europe*, contains minute records of impressions and reactions. It is a thorough and systematic assessment of the West. It set a precedent for the kind of reports from embassies, trade offices, and the like that continue to keep Japan better informed about the West.[21]

Two years after Admiral Perry's arrival the government opened a translators' school in Edo. It later broadened its curriculum to include military science, metallurgy, and cartography, as well as history, physics, and other subjects whose mastery are required of a great nation. In 1877 the school was brought together with several other educational institutions to form what became Tokyo University, in the Meiji Era Tokyo Imperial University. It was, and is, there that Japan's elite administrators were, and are, trained. Among its early teachers, an American economist, Ernest Fenelossa, taught neoclassical economics. A student diary of the day recalls of this approach that it tries "to find out some universal which explains everything. He speaks of exchangeable quantities. . . . Law of Demand and Supply. Law of Cost of Production. Law of Utility. Law of Labor. There are many such assertions. But they are valueless and the real use of Pol. Econo. is to find out certain forces which are acting actually."[22] This penchant for stressing how things actually work and could work in specific situations over bland principles universally deemed applicable has been an essential feature of Japanese economics.

Liberal and utilitarian philosophy was not (after initial investigation) terribly influential in Meiji-Era Japan, which lacked a modern developed entrepreneurial class. Japan's leading economic figures were more than willing to take assistance and advice from state bureaucrats with whom they shared class background, personal friendships, and family links. They had every reason to see an activist state as a good thing. With the translation of Frederick List's *National System of Political Economy* and growing acquaintance with the German historical school, English neoclassical thought fell into disfavor. As List's translator, Sadamasu Oshima, noted, one should not simply read the English texts and apply them to a country in different circumstances. Such men were well aware that as a late modernizer Japan had more in common with Bismarckian Germany. The capitalism that was introduced was a state-dominated version.

Under the new regime feudal property rights decreased, restrictions were abolished on freedom of movement and on internal trade, and new freedoms were established—property rights in land and to enter new occupations. A new leadership class coalesced of young samurai-*chonin* (merchants) with long-time horizons and leadership from *daimyo* with a breath of vision. There was a stress on ancient greatness and nationhood, and yet there was also an openness to new ideas, "foreign learning." Guilds were abolished and a new curriculum, modeled on Western schools, was made compulsory. The Buddhist Church was disestablished, and Western dress was encouraged. Even today in the heart of Tokyo stands a beautiful park modeled on those in Europe, quite distinct from the traditional parks found elsewhere in Japan. It was built to impress the Westerners who came over 100 years ago in the same spirit that those interacting with foreigners were ordered to adopt Western dress.

It is not that the Japanese were ignorant of science and mechanics before the coming of the West. When visiting a regional museum in Okayama, I came upon an exhibit featuring a local notable, Benkitchi Ono, an inventor. In the display was a self-propelled robot in human form that he had built in the early

1830s. Its major function seems to have been to bring visitors tea. The exhibit is one reminder that Japanese had an interest in machinery, in the potential uses of innovative technologies, but it was not until the Meiji era that there was incentive for such knowledge to be called upon for practical application. By the turn of the century an American, Robert Porter, in a report to the National Association of Manufacturers wrote:

> There never was a people so completely absorbed in industrial and commercial questions as the Japanese at this period in their history. Emperor and prime minister, the cabinet, members of the Imperial Diet, and minor officials are all imbued with the progress and future greatness of Japanese manufacturers, in commerce, and as the dominating nation in this part of the world. At public dinners, on official occasions of all sorts, the drift of remarks is, what can be done to help the material progress of Japan. The vernacular papers have taken this up, and enterprises of all sorts are exploited with the vim and vigor displayed in the building of the country.[23]

The Japanese walked a fine line. They prevented foreign control while seemingly acceding to the requests of the great powers. The Japanese assimilated the Western ways that they found useful, but they avoided foreign domination. The total cost of foreign technicians and study abroad came to 6 percent of the central government's budget between 1868 and 1872. The government was the dynamic factor in development. It incurred development expenditures and collected taxes on a truly impressive scale. These high taxes were paid by the peasantry, which, in effect, financed modernization.

The government itself built railways, set up banks and insurance companies, shipyards, cement plants, cotton mills, and a glass factory. These early businesses almost always lost money initially, but they showed the way, blazed the trails into the desired future. The state acted as the entrepreneur, nation builder, and economy developer. After the enterprise was made to work it was sold off, typically at a low price, and usually to well-connected families. This was the source of many of the *zaibatsu* empires that were to dominate the Japanese economy fifty years later. For example, Hachiroemon Mitsui bought silk mills from the government. The founder of the Mitsubishi empire obtained government shipyards, and Mitsubishi shipping received large subsidies so that it, and not foreign interests, could control Japan's international trade. It became the world's largest shipping company. As Allen reports, "It can be said with truth that there was scarcely any important Japanese industry of the Western type during the latter decades of the nineteenth century which did not owe its establishment to State initiative."[24] At the same time it was the great *zaibatsu* entrepreneurs who shaped, indeed invented these great corporate entities. Hikojiro Nakamigawa built Mitsui around a mining base. Heigoro Shoda expanded Mitsubishi from its start in shipbuilding into machine making industries. Such entrepreneurs did not follow the market. They were its architects.

Iwasaki, the samurai who built Mitsubishi, offered a set of remarkably contemporary house rules: Organize all enterprise with the national interest in mind; never forget the pure spirit of public service; be hardworking, frugal, and always thoughtful concerning others; treat your employees well and utilize personal property; and be bold in starting an enterprise, but meticulous in its prosecution. Other aspects of modern Japanese practice were evident in these beginnings. Collaborative work relations, rationality, familylike obligations, concern for reputation, fear of bringing shame to the firm as family, and state sponsorship are long-standing Japanese conventions.[25]

Building national champions through incentives, directives, and subsidies has been the long-standing policy, and it was and is combined with encouraging intense domestic competition among these privileged firms. This competition was and is directed at maximum efficiency and growth, providing firms with the resources necessary for successful constant innovation. Its goal is not lower prices to benefit consumers. The process was development-driven and focused on production and investment, not on consumption and increased mass living standards. Western economics understood the development process in terms of consumer sovereignty and seeing that there were many small competitive firms in the marketplace none of whom could exercise power over price. This has never been the Japanese way. Nor was democracy a very large part of this modernization process despite waves of popular struggles into the 1880s and again in the 1920s.

In the 1870s and 1880s a people's right movement was actively learning from foreign examples. In reaction the government cracked down to control school textbooks to foster reverence for the emperor in place of discussion of the American Declaration of Independence. Humanism, secular or otherwise, was not a nation builder to an authoritarian regime. The 1880 equivalent of the minister of education expressed the view that "teachers were not independent scholar-educators, but rather public officials, official guardians of morality, responsible to the state." As part of this drive when the University of Tokyo was reorganized as a school for government bureaucrats, law school graduates were granted special exemptions in the higher civil service examinations even though the board of examiners, then as now, was dominated by University of Tokyo professors. The controlled nature of education was obvious from top to bottom where for the masses obedience, loyalty, and subservience to a remote and unquestioned imperial rule was the message of educational reform. The Constitution of 1889 was prepared by the Imperial Household to be presented by the emperor as a gift to his people. There was little discussion of this document, which owed much to German theories of bureaucratic constitutionalism gleaned by Japanese sent to Vienna and Berlin to attend lectures. Indeed, Carl Frederich Hermann Roesler was brought to Japan to help write the Constitution. The legacy is a significant burden to the prospects of democracy in Japan even today, as will be discussed in Chapter 12.

As Gavan McCormack and Yoshio Sugimoto have written, "Through the course of Japan's modernization and industrialization from the Meiji Restoration onwards the common people were dragooned, manipulated, mobilized, and exploited in the relentless pursuit of the elusive goal of equality with the

West.''[26] Conservative rule has been unbroken since the Meiji Era. Japan remains a controlled society. This, too, is part of the story.[27] As in Bismarckian Germany of the same period, where the prime minister ruled in the name of the king and was not responsible to parliament, the army remained under the king's control, and a system was created in which the imperial bureaucracy wielded great power. This was true in Meiji Japan. The leaders created a weak parliament and ruled through the bureaucrats they appointed and who spoke for the national interest.[28] The selection of bureaucrats by open and competitive examination gave them some claim to be above vulgar politics and the party-elected representatives of local or particularistic interest groups. In pre–World War II Japan they ruled as officials of a divine emperor and carried the respect earned by their competitive examination success and presumed sacrifice for the public good. These officials retained a special caste status even after they no longer came from samurai backgrounds.

The contours of the bureaucratic role were established early in the Meiji period. Thus, it is possible to locate the basis for industrial policy in long-standing features of the cultural economy. A more detailed treatment could include the experimental boldness of particular individuals in this elite class of bureaucrats in a subculture that invented the forms of Japanese state-led development through trial and error. One may mention as a model early state builder Hirobumi Ito, who played a high-profile political role; "pragmatism, flexibility, moderation, and preference for compromise and workable realistic solutions" characterized his work and that of his peers.[29]

Since only a handful of Japanese knew anything about foreign trade and few spoke foreign languages, the government was concerned that the foreign trading houses that were then functioning in Kobe and Yokohama might dominate Japan's external trade and the shipping companies of the European nations would control transport. The state therefore created domestic trading monopolies by protecting and extending privileged treatment to the well-connected houses: Mitsui, Mitsubishi, Marubeni, and C. Itoh (the latter were Osaka-based textile merchants). In 1875, Mitsubishi was given a government loan to buy out the American Pacific Steamship Company's Tokyo–Shanghai route. In 1880 the British- and French-owned postal services were nationalized to reduce foreign influence.[30] It is also from this period that the postal system (established in 1875) became a major source of capital. It regularly received greater amounts than did the private banks and reached into the smallest towns. No wide public market for securities was allowed to develop; therefore, the state and the large *zaibatsu* banks had a monopoly on credit allocation.

At the same time the government moved to control imports. Unlike other less-developed nations, where imports consisted of luxury goods for the local ruling elite and cheap goods for mass consumption, the Japanese state as doorkeeper allowed in those intermediate inputs, necessary raw materials, and capital goods to support the industrialization process. This trade was carried on by what became the *sogo shosha* (the great trading companies), and was financed by banks set up for this purpose. Japan was one of the only nations of the underdeveloped world where foreign merchants and bankers did not dominate export and import trade. By keeping foreign capital at arm's length and preserving its indigenous consumption patterns, it avoided the demonstration effect that doomed most colonized peoples to dependency on foreign-produced "necessities."

Foreign control over Japan's international trade fell from about 90 percent in 1890 to about half in 1920, first as Japan's own coastal shipping, which in 1880 had been in the hands of foreigners was taken back and policies of promoting domestic shipping, buying foreign-made ships and virtually giving them away to Mitsubishi and others, in some cases even guaranteeing dividends to investors and, when Japanese firms were strong enough, banning foreign ships from certain ports starting in 1894, finally banning them all together (in 1911). The government had many instruments of industrial policy from generous postal contracts to navigation bounties. Such subsidies between 1900 and 1914 accounted for more than three fourths of the total net earnings of Japanese shipping companies, with authorized capital of more than 300,000 yen. By 1913 half of Japanese rapidly expanding overseas trade was carried on Japanese ships, compared to less than 10 percent before the war with China.

Close to half of the Ministry of Industry's budget at the end of the nineteenth Century went to pay the salaries of foreign technicians who brought knowledge with them and transmitted what was needed for Japanese industrialization. Japan also imported machinery that could not be made at home. In 1910, to take one revealing example, Japan was still not making textile machinery, although it was a major textile exporter and even though it had completed the largest battleship in the world, the *Satsuma*. The industrialization process was focused on building the military.

At the turn of the century only 1 percent of the population worked in factories. The majority were women, predominantly in the textile industry, who were brutally exploited and totally disenfranchised politically and socially, having been sold into factories by male family members. One in four was under the age of sixteen. This practice of using "half-paid" young women in the most labor-intensive industries, especially textiles, remained a mainstay of the Japanese industrial system well into the 1950s. Steven argues that young women formed the core of the industrial proletariat from the Meiji industrialization onward: "Their appalling wages and conditions remain the central feature of factory work to this day. All the extraeconomic pressures the society could muster, from its feudal hierarchies and ritualized authoritarianism to the overbearing patriarchal practices of the samurai class, were brought to bear on these women."[31] The pattern of rapid growth relied on a grossly unequal distribution of income, wealth, and power, an absence of political democracy and human rights. Writing of the years well into the modern period, Lockwood says, "For Japanese capitalism displayed an all-too-callous disregard for the immediate well-being of the worker in the factory and the field. It perpetuated evils like child labor and tenant oppression long after the remedies were at hand."[32]

The beginnings of the contemporary industrial relations regime can be traced from these years. Before World War I, as labor shortages developed, employers agreed not to take on the former employees of other companies immediately after the worker had left another company. They also adopted a pay arrangement known as the *nenko* system of ranking by years of experience. This meant a worker would have to start again at a second company. This encouraged workers to stay put whether they were happy at their job or not since the cost of starting at the bottom was substantial. Putting in time, however, often did not bring security or, if it did, not for many years. Studies of the steel industry in the 1920s show that this system did not allow the average worker to reach the status of permanent employee until they were about forty years old: "Until then, on the basis of his lack of loyalty or his failure to obtain the requisite skill level, he could be forced to leave the firm."[33] The institutionalization of temporary workers, most of whom worked long term, also date from these years. Such workers received lower pay, and were given no job security or fringe benefits. In the early 1930s, 21,000 workers of the Yawata Iron and Steel Works (70 percent) were under temporary status. In steel, in mining, and in other sectors strikes and violent repression of efforts to organize mark the history of Japanese industrialization.

In Japan there were no foreign concessions and trading activity was severely restricted from the beginning of Western involvement; when foreign investment did begin in a significant way in the late 1920s, however, when some American firms established branch plants and acquired minority interest in Japanese companies, they did so through offers of patent rights, advanced equipment, and engineering skills. Quantitatively, such investment was negligible. Foreign entrepreneurs made less of a contribution to Japanese industrial growth than they did in any other developing country in the world. Equipment was purchased and reverse engineered. German doctors staffed medical schools. French jurists shaped the criminal code revisions. American agricultural extension workers served frontier settlements in Hokkaido—and Japan prospered. Indeed, it can be suggested that the Industrial Revolution came full circle in 1929 when rights to manufacture the Toyoda automatic loom was acquired by Platt Brothers of Oldham, England. The Toyoda family impact was to mark another milestone when the automotive company that was then not born a half century or so later entered an agreement with General Motors—the world's largest corporation—to teach GM, in a joint venture at the latter's Fremont, California, plant, how to make cars. We will pick up this story in Chapter 5.

Japan did not recover its tariff autonomy until 1911 when its military strength had won it begrudging respect of the Western imperial powers. It was only after this that it could break the pattern in which it exported unprocessed silk, tea, and other raw materials and bought manufactured goods from America and Europe. At the same time, unable to protect the development of domestic industry by tariff Japan was encouraged to pursue other forms of state intervention, to focus its subsidies, to foster certain key industries, and to encourage trends toward monopoly. The government gave businessmen low tax burdens and used banks to channel funds to industry. Because the government discouraged foreign investment, even after liberalization in the 1920s, as of 1930 about three quarters of the foreign capital in Japan was in the form of loans to the Japanese government. The policies of discouraging foreign investment and, as we have seen, of buying back foreign-owned, domestically located productive assets was long standing. Indeed, these policies had been urged on the Iwakura Mission by Bismarck himself. While the government had initially pioneered through direct state ownership, investing in railroads, factories, and mines, the cost in corruption was simply too high, and policy wisely moved to indirect sponsorship, thereby granting favored large merchant houses exclusive licensing and other privileges that set the basis for the expansion of the *zaibatsu*. After 1880 state spending for armaments, transportation, and other strategic sectors accelerated growth. Spending was concentrated in metals, machinery, and shipbuilding with the government underwriting industrial development and insuring profitable accumulation by providing guaranteed markets and generous payments. Intervention grew more extensive again in the 1920s and especially 1930s as the military sought to expand Japan's industrial capacities. Between 1931 and 1936 the Ministry of Commerce and Industry, MITI's predecessor, pursued policies known as the Oshino-Kishi line, under which special attention was given to government promotion of heavy and chemical industrialization.

The high visibility of the *zaibatsu* should not be allowed to obscure the wide variety of enterprises that ran from handicraft production operating essentially on a precapitalist basis to suppliers subcontracting to larger firms. The Japanese retain a penchant for allowing the mutual survival of firms of different sizes and patterns of development to coexist, which both minimized dislocations and allowed symbiotic linkages. Economic historians report the "almost bewildering array" of business patterns and "an equal diversity in the play of forces determining prices, output, and technology." Social tradition and political manipulations imposed a framework in which what we call private enterprise operated. [35] The modern Japanese economy shows the effects and continuity of these patterns of organization and resource allocation. [36]

The importance of small business people, especially the owners of tiny factories in Japan in these years were, as they continue to be today, exceedingly important, even as their status and incomes is no better than a factory worker's in the primary sector. Many of these are not independent entrepreneurs in the sense that they often secure their raw materials, credit, and markets from a larger industrialist. This pattern developed in the nineteenth century as the great trading companies, Mitsui Bussan (backed by Mitsui Bank and offices around the world), could plug small manufacturers and merchants into their global network. The large enterprises, Sumitomo or Mitsubishi, had and continue to have the power position. They squeeze those all the way down the pyramid. The adaptability of the small business people to new opportunities and the way the large and the small, the state and the private, were melded in complex interaction brought impressive external economies in national development growth. Writing of this system at the end of the nineteenth century Lockwood explains, "If the dynamics of economic expansion owed much to the Meiji bureaucrat and the Mitsui executive, its substance came in no small measure from the responses and capabilities of the small peasant, trader, and industrialist."[37]

Foreign wars played major roles in Japanese development. The first with China (1894–1895), brought on by bureaucratic designs on Korea, increased the power and prestige of the oligarchs, undermined the movement toward democracy, and set the stage for an imperial future. The war boom stimulated the economy. It also gave Japan the clout to terminate the humiliating 1858 unequal treaties with Western powers that had provided for extraterritoriality and delayed the most obvious form of infant industry protection. The war with Russia (1904–1905) won Southern Manchuria from the czar and further developed Japan's industrial, financial, and military capacities. Like the war with China it was short and not very costly (to the Japanese elite). In the West these wars showed Japan's violent and aggressive nature. To Japan they were necessary as part of gaining the strength to resist the imperial powers. The West condemned them for acting in the same fashion Great Britain, France, and the others had long practiced. While Japan was of course defeated in World War II, it had added occupied China and Korea to Japan's conquests. In the five months after Pearl Harbor, Japan controlled territories containing one quarter of the world's population.

Japanese imperialism was neither the Schumpeterian version, "the object-less disposition on the part of a state to unlimited forcible expansion," nor Lenin's "inevitable product of capitalism in its monopoly stage." Rather, it was a matter of opportunistic raids to increase primitive capital accumulation by a small resource-poor island nation whose leaders sought equality with the great powers of Europe. It was an effort led by military bureaucrats to see that Japan survived as an independent people by internationally "becoming one of the boys." The weak Japanese capitalist class had hardly emerged as the domi-nant force and was more client than master of state power. Japanese imperial-ism was as harsh as any other, yet in terms of developmentalist potential, while much is made of the legacy of British rule in India, for instance, Beasley reminds us that "it is no coincidence that Taiwan and South Korea are two of Asia's most successful recent examples of industrialization, that the Man-churian provinces have remained a centre of Chinese heavy industry . . . "[38] In the postwar period many key government officials in Taiwan and South Korea had long-standing relations and often personal ties to Japanese business and political leaders that could be drawn upon in the postwar period.

The flooding of Japanese goods into foreign markets in the depression decade added to the anti-Japanese hysteria, although the Japanese trade "menace" at its peak was not very great—less than 4 percent of world exports. The panic in Western business circles resulted from awareness that Japan's increased technical prowess, business organization, and its success in particu-lar product lines and markets (preeminently textiles in Asia) augured poorly for the future. The Japanese shook up higher-priced cartel-like producers, who did not want to admit their competition.

The contemporary debate is in many ways a replay of the early 1930s, when much was made of the Japanese government's subsidizing of exports.

Actually, direct subsidies were far smaller than they were in the United States at the time. The broad economic policies, taxation, and credit extension by the developmentalist state bureaucracy and affiliated banks were more important. An issue that remains from this period may turn out to be of substantial importance. It is the way Japan and the other combatants of the Pacific War think about the causes of that extended conflict and its contemporary relevance.

There are two schools of thought on Japanese expansionism in the 1930s.[39] The first, which is in accord with much postwar modernization thinking, is that Japan had the most to gain of any nation from an open world trading system and that it was only the selfish and short-sighted policies of the imperialist powers that forced her on the path of colonial empire building that led to disaster in World War II. There are those who would argue that had Japan pursued a statesmanlike settlement in China, war could have been averted even as late as 1936 and that a liberal world trading order was possible. Writing of the nation's counterproductive imperialist military expansionism in the interwar years Lockwood, for example, declares: "Certainly Japan's major trading stake lay in multilateral world trade. Her *economic* interest argued for combatting the rise of economic nationalism, not contributing to its spread."[40] Such interpretations stress the cost of military budgets in foregone opportunities for education, farm relief, and other social investment and welfare related spending. Those who stress the drain of empire on the building of modern industry ignore a number of its positive aspects. Militarism preserved Japan's independence from the West, no small feat, and increased bargaining power in a dog-eat-dog world of interimperialist rivalry. Even as Japan entered into war with the United States it was widely understood to be a "mistake" at one level, but unavoidable.

The second perspective and the one with which I have greater sympathy suggests that accommodation was never really possible. The Western imperialists would have only allowed Japan a second class role in world affairs and had maneuvered to keep her down. In this light it is less the recklessness of Japan's military extremists than the no-win box to which the West consigned it that forced war on Japan. Racism is an important component of Japan's being refused membership in the imperialist's club. Japan, for example, won a majority vote for a formal declaration of racial equality to be written into the Versailles Treaty. Woodrow Wilson, as chairman, ruled it out of order on the grounds that the vote was not unanimous. The Four Freedoms notwithstanding, colonial empire was at stake and the darker races were already getting restive.

To summarize, in Japan the state has been in a close collaborative role with its dominant corporations since the Meiji Restoration. Indeed, it created them to a significant extent and sponsored industrial growth through continuous guidance, subsidy, and protection. For Western economists the experience of Japan changes some of the assumptions about the nature of the capitalist system and the individualistic model of economic growth. In a sense the state in Japan since the Meiji Restoration has acted as the collective entrepreneur within the larger mandate to catch up with the West, preserve Japan's independence, and assert the strength of the national character. Economic nationalism is not unique to Japan, but its success has been so outstanding that, as I have noted, it forces a reconsideration of much of the conventional wisdom on the subject of the nature and causes of the wealth of nations,[41] for "what Japan managed to do was to split up three factors which imperialism often tries to pretend are inseparable: technical 'know-how,' actual imports of the product of advanced technology, and foreign capital."[42]

Japan's developmentalist state with a century or more of unquestioned power and bureaucratic authority attracts the best and the brightest to public service. The version of nationalism that provides its rationale is a rounded concept that includes the requirement of informed economic strategy and which puts short-term behavior in a longer-run context. Once in place a path-dependent process is self-reinforcing, yet flexibility is privileged to a high degree. For our purposes we need only underline that pragmatism, not dogmatism, is the guiding star. Responsiveness to conjunctural factors, not ahistoric theorizing, is uppermost.

The need to catch up as an outsider, and the perceived cost of failing to do so, created a national consensus and intense willingness to learn from others which was absent in other places. Similarly, thinking in terms of polarities and exclusive opposites, so favored in the ideologically imbricated development discourse of Anglo-American thinking, was scorned by the Japanese economic planners as well as business leaders. In the aftermath of World War II these same understandings guided a Japan liberated in defeat from the militarist form its society had assumed in the high period of imperialism. The postwar order the United States created offered an umbrella under which the Japanese, despite widespread criticism of America's continued imperial presumptions, could rebuild and become a global economic superpower. The next chapter brings this historical account from the end of World War II to the contemporary period. One task, however, remains for the final section of this chapter. It is to describe the important developments in capital–labor relations that occurred at the end of the war and had important ramifications for the development of both the Japanese economic and political systems.

The Emergence of the Industrial Relations System

The class struggle (very much in the Marxian usage of the term) aspect of the postwar period requires detailed attention because it is during these key years that labor relations developed a unique ability to induce worker involvement that characterizes Japanese capital–labor collaboration. In the aftermath of Japan's surrender there were widespread militant takeovers by workers. The first of these was at the *Yomiuri* newspaper, where the publisher had been a leading sponsor of the Imperial Rule Assistance Association, a staunch militarist, and a major reactionary figure. The workers took over the newspaper and ran it themselves along radically democratic lines. At Mitsui's Bibai mine in Hokkaido, a place that had given searing dimension to the term *wage slavery*, the workers took over and cut the working day from twelve to eight hours while increasing production under worker control from 250 to over 650 tons. The people's court set up to try top management sent shockwaves through the upper reaches of Japan's ruling strata. Labor's power temporarily and to an impressive if finally limited extent overwhelmed capital. It had been argued for decades by the Japanese elite that their workers, unlike those in the West, did not need unions since the master is loving toward those below and takes tender care of them. Like slave owners in the American South before the Civil War smugly criticizing the inhumanity of labor's treatment under free labor markets in the North, the Japanese paternalistically contrasted their treatment of workers to that by American and European factory owners.

Largely because of SCAP's (Supreme Commander for the Allies in the Pacific) New Deal stance toward labor unions, membership rose from 7 to 50 percent of the labor force between 1946 and 1948. Under General MacArthur SCAP ruled Japan until 1952 when control reverted to the Japanese. This was the first (and only) time in Japanese history that free industrial unionism as we know it was encouraged. The status of the former ruling *zaibatsu* that had been the core of the imperial war effort was shaken by the jailing and purging of its leaders. The left, socialists and communists, who had opposed the militaristic system, had won the respect of most workers, and the whiff of class warfare was in the air. In the first six months of 1946 over 150,000 workers were involved in the seizure of over 250 factories. They expelled the managers and ran the factories themselves. These radical workers challenged both the authoritarian order and the fundamental notion of private property. In the early Cold War years harsh legislation was introduced to diminish the influence of communists and other militants. Some 120,000 workers considered Communist Party sympathizers lost their jobs, along with hundreds of thousands of others in the 1950 Red Purges that were held in factories, public enterprises, and the media. The change in U.S. policy was dramatic. From support of independent unionism to orchestrating the McCarthy era in Japan, the Americans shaped Japan's postwar destiny to a remarkable degree.

In 1948, General MacArthur deprived civil servants of the right to strike; therefore, when postal and railway workers struck in defiance, dismissals of presumed communist troublemakers could be justified. Selective dismissals and the creation of enterprise unions under company control created a pattern of corporatism without labor.[43] The market power of workers was reduced by limiting property rights in a particular job or skill. The practice of job rotation makes workers generalists. Their skills and experience are specific to particular firms and thereby less transferable.[44] The multiskilled worker needs to do a series of job-specific tasks. There is not a great deal of creativity in this. Instructions need to be followed precisely and slack time is dramatically reduced. All of the worker's physical stamina and dexterity is called upon, as well as his or her ability to think out how to design the job to be more productive. The Japanese, in a context of control of the worker by the company, designed a system that makes the workers share their knowledge.

Between 1949 and the end of 1950 about 700,000 workers lost their jobs as the Dodge Plan austerity took hold. Militants were fired first, and industrial reorganization was then used to weaken the leftist unions. The purges were extended to universities and a McCarthyite period weakened labor and the left quite substantially. As jobs became scarce enterprise unions gained strength over workers. It is in this period that the great wage differentials between large and small companies became institutionalized and the structure of postwar industrial relations was established. Low wages and weak unions resulted in the largest capital-to-labor advantage in the distribution of income of any industrialized nation in the world (except for South Africa), which constrained living standards and promoted accumulation.

By the 1950s the Cold War had changed American priorities, and the former war criminals were allowed, indeed encouraged, to reassert their control, and the leftist unions were mostly smashed. The establishment of a rival representation system, an ultraconservative companyist version of the business unionism, was established. Union membership peaked in 1949 at 59 percent of the labor force, but it was down to 26 percent by 1989. In Japan the victory was not simply one of collaborationist unionism over a Marxist one; rather, it was one of the extreme dominance of capital over labor. It was symbolized in the auto industry by the "Everlasting Peace Treaty" that was signed in 1962, which established a principled agreement that labor–management relations "are not to be considered to be relations of class antagonism, but to be relations between human beings" and that problems are to be resolved by consultation based on trust. In translating, Professor Masaki Saruta has suggested the phrase "oneness of labor and management" rather than "cooperation of labor and management" to convey the reality of labor's absolute subordination to management signaled by the treaty, a treaty of the surrender of the hotly contested battle over class militancy versus paternalistic control.[45] As the Cold War heated up, a coalition of government and employers allied with anticommunist and collaborationist-oriented workers to attack class conscious trade unionism root and branch. The trade union laws were amended to isolate those labeled militants. Alternative unions were sponsored to woo workers away from those dominated by the Left.

Enterprise unionism under conditions of postwar dislocation and the overwhelming power of the government, corporate, and SCAP attacks on class-conscious militancy seemed essential to many workers. The *Densan* system (named after the union federation involved in the first systemization of a seniority wage system) guaranteed a minimum wage by age group and length of service along with a complex system of payment that tied "a living wage" to a formula involving family size as well as the ability of the worker. The system also allowed the company to claim the surplus above this "living wage," which was typically reinvested in a rapid growth program. The worker received less pay but more job security. The enterprise union had no interest in working conditions or pay in subcontractor plants. United industrial action was thus discouraged. The communist unions resisted this direction, but they were met with the united force of capital and the state. Capital sponsored company unions, the police broke up demonstrations, and MacArthur banned strikes that threatened to cripple the economy.

"The consequences of these developments," Taishiro Shirai writes, "should be clear, the workers were firmly under management's control as company-men, whereas union activities at that level progressively lost their effectiveness. The result was a situation in which unions could hardly resist or regulate the effect of management's introduction of new technology, or drive to increase production." [46] The emasculation of trade unions was one of the preconditions for the extremely rapid increases in productivity and labor intensity in Japanese industry that began in the late 1950s. In particular since the late 1960s this emasculation has facilitated the efforts of the Japanese Federation of Employers' Association to implement and expand management systems designed to produce the utmost efficiency of labor.

This system was created in the 1950s, although some elements do go back to the 1920s, as noted earlier, and the paternalism is, as analysts have pointed out, consistent with feudal relations. It is *not* however a centuries-old set of practices; rather, it is a conscious construction of these postwar years. Rather than being an old traditional culture–bound set of arrangements, the defeat of class-conscious unionism by the united efforts of management, government, and SCAP was the product of protracted class warfare in the postwar period. [47]

Social control in Japan in these years is reminiscent of the experience of workers in early industrial America. Young women off the farm sent to Sony had much in common with the famous factory girls in the Lowell textile mills a century and a half earlier. At Sony a company union was created in 1961. Shigeru Kobayashi, a key unionbuster for the company, describes in his book, *Sony Makes Humanity*, how he helped to give workers "a sense of purpose" and "of meaning in their lives." Those not responding to his generosity were fired or given punitive transfers or disciplinary wage cuts as an incentive to improve their receptiveness. He also set up "worker's schools" where the worker-student rose at 4:45 A.M. and started work at 5:30. After working for an hour and three-quarters they had twenty-five minutes for breakfast, resumed work until 1:15, and went to school after lunch and studied until 5:30. These were high school students. They were organized into "cells" of five to eight under the supervision of leaders, called "sisters," who had been with the company for a longer time. They slept on double bunks four or six to a small room. No visitors, including parents, were permitted ("It wouldn't be fair if your parents came but other girls couldn't, would it?"). Love affairs had to be confessed to the leader, who also humiliated the young women in front of their group if their work or self-criticism was inadequate. Village girls removed to such an environment were very productive on Sony's behalf. They had little alternative but to return home in disgrace. [48] Three decades later Sony President Akio Morita was calling for Japanese to work less hard and enjoy life more, while criticizing Japan's workaholic culture. The objective conditions, and so the strategic designs of this company's leisure-time marketing, and of

Japanese capitalism as a whole, had shifted dramatically over the intervening decades.

Once they took the initiative away from labor, capital was aided by their ability to discipline new arrivals who poured into the factories in the postwar period. Within thirty years, the size of the self-employed agricultural work force had decreased to one third of its initial level. The size of the working class had almost trebled. No Western industrialized country has experienced such a dramatic transformation. Through the postwar era a large part of the industrial labor force from the farm tended to be self-restrained. The typical response when the company makes new demands was, "Oh well, we can't have everything our way". The naivete and powerlessness of the new arrivals meant that "even though the feudal elements of the prewar labor relations system have disappeared, it is still only **after** the signing of the employment contract that workers become aware of the precise form of work they are to perform, and only **after** they are employed that their precise occupation within the company is decided."[49] Competition for promotion and transfer to better work was and remains so intense that workers put in unpaid overtime and all the rest of the cooperative gestures for which the Japanese worker is famous. Such circumstances, which include company-specific pensions and seniority wages, encouraged the Japanese to identify their own welfare with that of their companies. The most prestigious companies offered housing, company vacation resorts, and outings (i.e., the generous bonuses)—the system seems to combine the best promises of early Soviet communism and the successful perks of consumer capitalism. The idea is that the quality and harmony of the work force comes first and output flows naturally from a close-knit production system that combines central direction with maximal decentralized contribution to the constant recreation of product and production process as part of this Japanese-style capital–labor accord.

It is important to note that small enterprises (those with under 100 workers) employ two thirds of the labor force and produce half of total output. Nearly half the jobs in manufacturing are in establishments with fewer than fifty people (compared to 15 percent in the United States, although the average size of American enterprises has been dropping fast). Self-employment and workers in small family enterprises are over one quarter of the Japanese labor force. Very few industrial relations studies are made of these workers, except by anthropologists who might study, for example, the briefcase manufacturers, located primarily in two Tokyo wards, who employ an average of twelve workers each, and the other cluster industries in which piecework is the norm and work at home is part of a complex subcontracting system that includes minuscule family businesses employing women and children.

Japan is at least twice as dependent upon such small shops as other advanced industrial nations. These are a key, but typically ignored, part of the story. This is because the giants of Japanese industry are the firms the West competes with, and while they also depend to some extent on such tiny businesses as lower-tier suppliers, the focus is on the advanced technology and labor practices of the largest, most visible, and internationally important plants.

Much of what I have to say about attitude toward work is at least as visible in small enterprises where the motivation for family members and individual small entrepreneurs is great indeed. The work culture is evident in most areas of the economy. For example, a good sushi chef, a master *itamae*, may serve a ten-year apprenticeship that starts with scrubbing floors and washing dishes, preparing sushi rice, and getting knocked around by senior chefs in thirteen-hour days, six days a week that are devoted to sushi.

It is also important to remember that "lifetime" employment is not a given in perpetuity in the Japanese system. It is an artifact of an expanding economy. When an industry collapses thousands of workers are "retired." In the wake of the OPEC price increase, in the 1974 recession firms entered "Operation Scale-down" (*genryo keiei*) and labor costs were cut back, interest burdens were reduced, and rationalization was undertaken. The Employment Insurance Law was modified to underwrite the cost of firms retaining workers. Still, unlike in America, wide-scale unemployment did not accompany the deep recession. Some reports suggest that

> Designating specific workers for dismissal is particularly taboo, and was virtually not done. Every imaginable device to reduce employment within the constraints of these values was used, from leaving the positions of retiring employees vacant to personnel reshuffles, temporary transfers to other companies, and calls for voluntary resignations.[50]

Of course, from labor's perspective some of these voluntary resignations were close to summary firings brought on by intense speedups. The company unions did their part, not defending the workers thus abused and in asking only token wage increases, accepting declines in real wages, and making the rationalization possible and relatively less painful for their corporations. For some observers the dramatic decline in wage increases was "a signal achievement for efforts at reducing labor costs" in the latter half of the 1970s. As Nakamura also writes, however, "The most important consequence of Operation Scale-Down has been the deterioration in employment conditions that it produced."[51]

While Operation Scale-Down seemed at the time to signal the end of rapid growth, the decline was not even in its impact, productivity gains improved dramatically through this period, and a new production regime was created that was dubbed "lean production." It involves far fewer workers than Fordist mass production and has some things in common with the much-touted flexible accumulation of the Third Italy, but is essentially quite different in its revolutionary potential.[52] The gender aspect of this general phenomenon should be noted. At the end of the period of high growth women accounted for about a third of all employed workers, but were close to 60 percent of all factory workers and a little under half of office workers. On average women received less than half the wages received by male workers. Their exclusion from the protected jobs and their being forced out during child rearing and then being allowed back at lower wages are a key contribution to rapid capital accumulation during the period.

Since the mid-1970s, female workers have been added at twice the rate of increase in the male work force. Hiring was done by small firms as the large ones subcontracted more to undercut the status of higher-cost male workers in primary firms. Older people, past the compulsory retirement age of fifty-five, later sixty, and without adequate pensions, were brought back to the labor force as low-cost labor as well. Also, to meet labor demand, temporary employment agencies are a fast-growing sector. Most of the largest manufacturers themselves operate at least one subsidiary in this business. Permanent workers are also laid off in hard times and more temps are hired. The figures on workers fired are highly problematic and make generalizations difficult to make. The pressure to retire voluntarily is exceedingly strong. Failure to volunteer when asked to leave means becoming designated for dismissal in any case, but with fewer postretirement benefits. Employees can also be transferred to subcontractors, who may then fire them. They may be counted as temporarily not at work and encouraged to find employment elsewhere since their chances of being recalled approximate zero. They would still not be counted as having been fired.

"It is astonishing," Chalmers Johnson has written, "how easily admirers of the tranquility of Japanese society during the 1970s forgot the strikes, riots, demonstrations, and sabotage that marked the period 1949–1961."[53] Much is at stake in this forgetfulness. The political exclusion of labor has been an important component of the Japanese "miracle." It allows the single-minded pursuit of capital accumulation in the context of a higher capital-to-labor ratio of national product than elsewhere in the industrialized world. Through the years of high-speed growth between 1953 and 1972 capital's share tripled as labor productivity grew far more rapidly than real wages. In 1965 labor's share of gross value added was under 40 percent. For the United States it was over 50 percent, and while there are problems with such simple comparisons, they indicate one measure of capital's dominance.[54] T. J. Pempel, summarizing the era, writes:

> Virtually all key aspects of Japanese or Japanese foreign economic policy would have been impossible in other industrial societies where organized labor plays a regular, or at least a periodic, role in the formal governmental and policy-making progress.[55]

These years of the immediate postwar period were a turning point in terms of larger politics as well. In the 1946–1947 elections the socialists emerged as the largest single party, although the conservative liberals and democrats (who were to merge in 1955 to form the party that has dominated Japanese politics) held a comfortable majority. The socialists formally headed the government, but had neither the votes in parliament nor, as importantly, the capacity to take on the conservative bureaucracy that ran the state. Indeed, agreeing to exclude their own left wing from cabinet posts and accepting a low real wage policy to fight inflation, they disappointed their electoral base. Taxes rose, scarcity intensified, and unemployment spread. As the socialists were hammered from the right and attacked by the communists who objected to such a "sell-out stance," the government fell in early 1948. The left was not to chal-lenge the conservatives effectively for the next forty years at the national level (although it did at the local government level with great effect in the 1960s, as we will see in Chapter 7).

The Japanese workers act as international ratebusters because the condi-tions they accept spread to the workers of the world whose firms must com-pete with theirs. Therefore, even though most of the literature on the Japanese miracle has little of a critical nature to say about the industrial relations system, this history and the present situation, which will be described in Chapter 6, are important pieces of the story.

There are surely those who would draw the conclusion that smashing inde-pendent and leftist trade unions makes good economic sense, but surely this is neither a necessary nor sufficient condition for economic recovery after military defeat. The German postwar system with its powerful works councils' shop floor control and union representation strength (50 percent of management boards), social democratic party, and the centrality of worker education and training, apprenticeships, and high income for labor offers another model of economic miracle.

In countries such as the United States where organized labor is weak this pressure has been intense since the cost of adjustment has been borne dispro-portionately by the working class. Income disparities between the upper 20 percent of Americans and the "bottom" 80 percent widened in the 1980s more than in any other single decade for which there are statistics to make a comparison. In 1990 the average American worked 164 hours more than twenty years earlier, the equivalent of an extra month's labor time per year. Juliet Schor, who has studied the impact of modems, fax machines, and voice mail in extending the work day to after hours work at home for white collar workers in the context of intense competition for jobs, has suggested that without some change in the trends things will continue to worsen.[56] Perhaps we are turning Japanese.

4

The Japanese System in the Golden Age

"Whenever an economy or a sector of an economy adapts itself to a change in its data in the way which traditional theory describes, whenever, that is, an economy reacts to an increase in population by simply adding the new brains and hands to the working force in the existing employments, or an industry reacts to a protective duty by expansion within its existing practice or to a fall in its demand by a contraction within its existing practice, we shall speak of *adaptive response*. And whenever the economy or an industry or some firm in an industry do something else, something, namely, that is outside of the range of existing practice, we shall speak of *creative response*."

JOSEPH A. SCHUMPETER[1]

"We do not make something because the demand, the market, is there. With our technology we can create the demand, we can create the market."

SOICHIRO HONDA[2]

As we saw in the last chapter, Japan was gaining on the United States in the pre–World War II decades. Losing the Pacific war had devastating consequences. It was not until the mid-1960s that Japan again reached its prewar per capita income relation with the developed Western nations. The climb was not easy.

At the end of 1945 13 million were unemployed, and 32 million employed in the Japanese work force. Under the priority production system subsidies were extended to basic industry and wages were kept down. Wages were fixed by the government for public employees sufficient for basic food consumption of 1,550 calories a day. Many workers in private industry received less. The proportion of subsidies to unit costs of products in many industries was exceedingly high. For example, in fiscal year 1948 the level of subsidies was 70

86

percent in the iron industry, 40–45 percent in rolled steel production, and 40 percent in ammonium sulfate production. The proportion of public spending devoted to various production subsidies rose from 10 percent in 1946 to between 20 and 30 percent in 1947–1949. As noted in the last chapter MITI inherited regulatory powers from procedures developed under particular legislation passed in the climate of the war emergency.[3]

Before World War II, close to half of the cultivated land in the country was leased to tenants whose rights were precarious—their bargaining power was nil due to rural overpopulation and semifeudal social relations were dominated by the landlord class. In the world system, Japan's role was to import antiquated machinery from the United States and the United Kingdom. Use of a lower-wage labor force produced the typical less-developed-nation exports. In 1926, for instance, over half of Japan's industrial workers produced textiles (bound mostly for India and China). The U.S. advice in the immediate post–World War II period—that Japan should continue to pursue labor-intensive industrial growth in accord with its obvious comparative advantage—was rejected by the Japanese bureaucrats. They saw that following such advice would delay, perhaps preclude, long-term self-reliance and the prospect of economic maturity. Western theory assumed specialization based on existing factor endowment. The Japanese, with their eye still on modernization and catching up with the West, had other ideas.

In 1951 the Japan Development Bank first offered special loans for commercialization of new technologies. Since 1952 the Japanese government has offered special depreciation schedules for testing and research equipment and since 1958 for the commercialization of new technologies. In 1967 the government provided subsidies for the development of cargo planes for the private sector. While directed recovery is seen by some observers as approaching almost a central planning system it is more useful to see the Japanese government at each phase of its development adopting whatever approaches and techniques thought to be needed. This was never a matter of ideological commitment to specific policies. When the worst of the recovery years were past, assistance continued in proportion to perceived need. The industries assisted and the means chosen continued to change.

The American occupation did not encourage such subsidies. Rather, it demanded balanced budgets. SCAP, however, did endorse land reform, which was important to breaking the back of the old landlord class and bringing modern democracy to Japan. Postwar reform in Japan is called *sengo kaikaku*, which conveys a postwar adjustment of the prewar regime, not a democratization. The key political figure of the era was Nobusuke Kishi, who had been among those most prominently charged as a war criminal. He had been minister of munitions and worked closely with Tojo in Manchuria, where he was part of a group of extreme right-wing nationalists and gangsters active in China before and during World War II. Many of these came to hold prominent positions with U.S. encouragement during the Cold War years. Charges against Kishi and others were dropped by the Americans and he came to lead the government in 1957. The 1992 gangster–politician connections revealed in the *Sagawa Kyubin* affair, which brought down Shin Kanemaru, Japan's fore-most political power broker is in direct lineage from the gangster–politician relations established in these years. This will be discussed in a later chapter.

The centerpiece of most Western accounts—land reform—was carried out under conservative auspices. Along with a system of rice subsidies and protectionism this tightly bound the rural population to what became the Liberal Democratic Party (LDP) after the merger of the two conservative parties in 1955. The powerful farmers organizations and a districting system for elections dependent on 1947 population distribution, which the LDP refused to comprehensively revise, gave the farmers three times the influence of urban voters in parliamentary elections through the postwar period.

The industrial economy of pre–World War II Japan was organized on the basis of private property, but with a degree of monopoly control and a dominance by the giant *zaibatsu*, which, while they rarely held a monopoly on a particular product, together dominated the economy. After World War II use of the old names and insignia of the *zaibatsu* corporations, the corporate elites controlled by Japan's leading families—Mitsubishi, Mitsui, and so on—were forbidden. Rather than holding back centralized development of the Japanese economy, "The breakup of the *zaibatsu* prepared the way for the demise of the era dominated by finance capital and the arrival of the new industrialism."[4] It was the new corporate groupings, some produced out of transformed *zaibatsu* groups, but others built up by new players and forms, upon which postwar growth was based. While smaller firms played an important role in the accumulation process modernization of technologies, the achievement of economies of scale in heavy industry and the plowing back of monopolistic profits drove the engine of rapid growth.

Yutaka Kosai wrote that looking at "the kind of gluelike sticking together done by politicians, bureaucrats, and businessmen during the postwar reconstruction, although quite open, may be quite worthy of being called state monopoly capitalism."[5] The society was profoundly undemocratic, "perpetuating inequalities of income and opportunity in modern Japan almost as wide as those of feudal times." Writing in the early postwar period Lockwood went on to describe how these relations were carried over "into modern industry the traditions of hierarchical status and authoritarian control which was so inimical to political and social democracy."[6] State power was used to bring about economic development under near authoritarian auspices.

In fiscal 1946 almost 20 percent of the national budget was allocated to industry-related purposes and state guidance was important to the direction and character of economic and regional development. In 1947 Priorities Production Policy guided and underwrote reconstruction of designated industries (coal, electric power, iron, and steel). Subsidies to such industries amounted to 30–40 percent of their total cost and took almost a quarter of the fiscal 1947 budget. The Reconstruction Finance Bank (established in 1947) channeled capital to priority industries as well. Administrative guidance was used to intervene within particular sectors as well as to allocate across them.

In 1952 MITI's special depreciation schedules, designed to encourage the pattern of investments it wanted, allowed the writing-off of as much as 50 percent of expenditures for plant and equipment, which contributed to the reconstruction of Japan. MITI used its power to license and approve investments and imports to control industrial activity. Capital goods and needed raw materials were let into the country on favorable terms. Consumer goods were not. Direct foreign investment (DFI) was discouraged except in cases clearly linked to domestic producer needs and portfolio investment by Japanese nationals abroad was prevented. From the 1950s the Japanese government actively participated in DFI activity projects from Alaskan pulp mills to Sumatran oil development. The government planners saw to it that Japanese companies were guaranteed ample supplies of low-cost copper, zinc, bauxite, iron ore, and so on, often in joint ventures with foreign governments.

Those with money for hire had to accept whatever return they could get in the controlled domestic financial markets. The funds were then made available on favorable terms, mostly to the largest Japanese corporations. This does not mean, however, that other companies did not play a crucial role in postwar economic development. Some economists have even stressed that it was the small and medium-size companies that assumed "large if not dominant roles in Japanese industry."[7] Their role remains important. Capital spending by small and medium-sized enterprises was more than 40 percent of total corporate capital outlays in the 1980s. Furthermore, many of these firms over this period used sophisticated technologies.[8] For all sectors, from the end of World War II to the mid-1960s, royalties to foreigners equaled about 20 percent of expenditures on technology in the private sector. Technology agreements were scrutinized on a case by case basis until 1968. MITI entered into the details of negotiations to get a better deal for their clients. "It also sought to insure that technology licensing would quickly lead to Japanese absorption of the new information and would allow the Japanese partner to take over complete production at the earliest possible date."[9]

Many of the institutional innovations of the period were not unique to Japan, although Japan seemed able to take ideas that they borrowed from abroad and make more of them. For example, other nations had postal savings systems, but they became secondary to private banks everywhere else in the capitalist world. The Postal Savings System, part of the Ministry of Post and Communication (which still buys about half the bonds issued by the Japanese government), was key to aggregating the savings of millions of the nation's small savers in the early postwar recovery period.[10] These funds financed the expenditures of the Fiscal Investment and Loan Program (FILP). The Postal Savings System had more branches nationwide than there were branches of private banks. They still do, and while the system today holds only 30 percent of all personal savings, this is still a market share the analogous facility in the U.S. postal system even in its heyday could not have dreamed of attaining. This is because the developmentalist state built this instrument into a powerful vehicle to encourage a high savings rate by making these accounts more attractive than those they allowed private banks to pay with tax-free interest.[11] The Finance Bureau of the powerful Ministry of Finance (MOF) controls the FILP and supports expanding postal savings.[12]

Like many other nations after the war the Japanese controlled capital flows. Unlike those who saw such a measure as a temporary evil, however, the Japanese used capital controls as an integral part of industrial policy. The Foreign Exchange and Foreign Trade Law (1949) prohibited external transactions in principle, with exceptions granted on a case by case basis only in instances in which they met very specific notions of the national interest. It was not until December 1980 that a new law came into effect that provided for freedom in principle, with prohibitions of transactions as the exception. The new Foreign Exchange Law referred to "freedom of exchange, foreign trade, and other external transactions, with necessary but minimum controls." In addition to not containing the phrase "freedom in principle" it authorized delays and prohibitions of transactions that in the government's judgment "might" lead to certain undesirable results. Article 21 of the law provided for the licensing of any capital transaction that "might" result in drastic currency fluctuations in exchange rates or adversely affect Japan's capital markets. Through the postwar years the government exerted administrative control on foreign borrowing and the uses of foreign exchange received by exporters.

Another important import was the concept of *quality control* (QC). It was the Americans at GHQ who recruited W. Edwards Deming to teach QC methods in Japan after the war. Deming had his basic text on QC methods translated into Japanese (and donated the royalties, which were considerable, to establish a QC award that the Japanese named the Deming Prize, which they started awarding in 1951). Deming's status is godlike in Japan. His portrait today hangs in the main lobby of Toyota's headquarters (along with two others of Toyota's founder and its chairman—both of which are smaller than the one of Deming). He was ignored in America until Ford finally brought him to Detroit in 1981, *and General Motors three years after that*. Another important influence from America was A. V. Feigenberg, head of General Electric's QC department, who promoted the concept of total quality control, extending QC to market research, product development, design, and procurement. While Feigenberg had published his ideas in the *Harvard Business Review* in 1956, it was the Japanese, not the Americans, who paid attention to his thinking.

Japan, at U.S. insistence, imported antitrust laws, but adapted them to their long-standing preference for encouraging large, powerful companies to dominate their economy by proceeding to ignore the American-style legislation. While efforts were made with some success to break up the *zaibatsu* in the postwar period, the *sogo shosha*,[13] the giant trading companies that had been the heart of the *zaibatsu*, were allowed to regroup and were favored with scarce foreign exchange with which they dominated import businesses. The capital-poor manufacturers depended on them to market their products and raise investment funds to keep them going. Even as these manufacturers grew, the superior information and other services provided by the *sogo shosha* with their globe-scanning antennae spotted new markets for Japanese products and made the connections quickly and efficiently. They accepted hair-thin profit margins, but on huge volume. With the shift in manufacturing away from standard commodities and the growing importance of consumer relations and service, many Japanese firms developed their own distribution channels over the postwar period, and the winter of the *sogo shosha* descended, pushing them into new areas ranging from information processing to satellite broadcasting and project development packaging for developing nations. In the immediate postwar years, however, they were crucial to Japan's recovery and growth.

The role of the United States in the restructuring of the Japanese political economy in the years of the occupation (beyond bringing Deming to their attention, no small contribution), while an intriguing story, is only tangentially important to the developments most relevant to the present undertaking. There are interesting comparisons to be made, for instance, of the U.S. role in Japan and Germany.[14] There are issues of the personalties involved from Douglas MacArthur on down. The diverse group of Americans who were assembled to administer the occupation of Japan as a group not only had divergent views of their mission, but they knew relatively little about the country and in the mood of postwar victory felt little compunction to learn a great deal about it even as they went about the business of remaking the nation.[15] Most important to America's role, however, was the limited democratization it brought to Japan and its role in finally allowing a modified authoritarian regime to retain power through the postwar years in which there was a substantial leftist challenge. U.S. assistance was also critical somewhat later to Japan's getting World Bank loans and admittance to multinational economic organizations over the opposition of European and Asian governments. Japan's early acceptance into the community of nations after World War II was under U.S. sponsorship and through American insistence. U.S. wars, hot and cold, were also important.

Through the global postwar recession of 1949–1950, the United States insisted that Japan follow the orthodox deflationary program of the Dodge Line (named after the conservative banker, Joseph Dodge, who advised Japan's economic decision makers on behalf of the American government). Japan pleaded for relief from this killing austerity. Then, as Robert Angel describes events, salvation came from an unexpected source:

> Just two months after . . . the Korean tinderbox burst into flames. . . . As the only nearby industrialized nation with adequate manufacturing capacity, Japan's underemployed factories and work force benefitted enormously from Korea's misfortune between 1950 and 1955, first as suppliers of war materials and services for United Nations forces and, after the July 1953 armistice, as suppliers of materials needed for the reconstruction of South Korea. Former economic planning official Tatsuro Uchino estimates that special procurement, broadly defined, during the period pumped between $2.4 and $3.6 billion into the capital-starved Japanese economy and accounted for an amazing 60 to 70 percent of all of Japan's exports. Also significant for Japan's postwar economic development, this unanticipated expansion of demand was strongest in industries such as textiles,

steel products, and automotive equipment, the very sectors that would lead Japan's export drive during the 1950s and 1960s. [16]

After the start of the Cold War the American command reversed its course. These restrictions were lifted under the impact of the Korean war. The war was also an economic turning point. By June 1951, one year after the outbreak of the war, the index of manufacturing production (in real terms) was 50 percent higher than it had been in June 1950. [17] Special U.S. procurement from 1950 to 1957 was over $1.5 billion. Normal exports (in 1949) had been $0.5 billion. The boom also helped other exports as the world economy expanded as part of the Korean war boom. In this period Japan had surplus unemployed labor and a huge rural reserve of potential factory workers. Wage growth was minimal, and after the historic defeat of class conscious unionism in the early 1950s (a topic that claims attention in Chapter 6), labor's share of national income was reduced.

Through the 1950s the United States, as a matter of national policy, facilitated the entry of Japanese goods into this country. A 1953 National Security Council document, for example, declared that increasing access to markets in the United States was necessary to eliminate economic deterioration that "creates fertile ground for communist subversion." John Foster Dulles, pessimistic about Japan's economic capabilities, as we have seen, pursued international trade agreements favorable to Japan, and the administration ignored complaints from American firms concerning Japan's unfair trade practices. President Eisenhower personally worried about Japan's chances of recovery and the communist challenge, urged American industrialists to buy Japanese products even if they did not meet U.S. quality standards. Foreign aid to the tune of hundreds of millions of dollars was added to Defense Department procurement contracts.

The Okano Plan of the early 1950s (named for MITI Minister Kiyohide Okano), was premised on the need for heavy and chemical industrial development in order to build up capacity for export of products with a much higher income elasticity than Japan's traditional light manufacturing. The plans for rapid growth to the end of the 1950s were opposed by the MOF, which would not even provide basic financial data the Economic Planning Agency needed. The accession of Hayato Ikeda to the prime ministership broke this resistance. Ikeda had been the highest ranking career MOF bureaucrat before his *amakudari*. [18] As prime minister he had great leverage over the retirement prospects of his former subordinates, who came to see things his way as he maneuvered the MOF into supporting his Income Doubling Plan. In exchange for the ministry's cooperation it was also given greater power in intrabureacratic rivalries. [19] While I will have more to say about politics, both electoral and popular movements, in Chapter 8, it is of interest here to mention that a 1963 Public Security Agency Report, following the Ikeda plan's success, declared that "the general expectations of rising living standards are now overwhelming and diffusing the progressive political movements." [20] "GNPism" was well established as the consensus politics of the Japanese system from this time forward, although, as we will see, it was costly in terms of health degradation and environmental depredations. The basic living standard lagged seriously behind the expansion in per capita GNP.

When pressured to remove subsidies to the shipbuilding industry during the recession of 1953–1954, administrative measures were taken to allocate sugar-import permits to exporting shipbuilders based on their individual need. These not so hidden subsidies (sugar was in short supply and sold at very high prices domestically) allowed the export price of Japanese ships to be cut by 20–30 percent. Such an example confirms Chalmers Johnson's definition of industrial policy that "may be positive or negative, implicit or explicit. Put negatively, industrial policy refers to the distortions, disincentives, and inequalities that result from uncoordinated public actions that benefit or restrain one segment of the economy at the expense of another." As this example with shipbuilders and sugar quotas suggests, however, to see only the distortion is to miss the positive moment, government activity that "leverage upward the productivity and competitiveness of the whole economy and of particular industries in it."[21]

While it is appropriate to emphasize the differences between Japanese economic practice and that derived from Anglo-American economic thinking, Japanese economists were influenced substantially by the main currents of modern Western economic thought from Keynesianism to monetarism. The applications in the Japanese context, however, have often been quite different. Osamu Shimomura, who has been called "the first and most enthusiastic prophet" of Japanese high growth, derived much of his underlying methodology from English-language Keynesian models such as those formulated by J. R. Hicks. The "Shimomura Thesis," which he put forward in the late 1950s and which offered intellectual moorings for Ikeda's National Income Doubling Plan, was the simple assertion that "in the final analysis, the growth rate will more or less parallel the size of private fixed investment as a percentage of GNP."[22] Japan's high savings rate allowed a particularly high rate of private fixed investment, hence Shimomura's optimistic forecast. Such high growth would not be inflationary, as many had feared, because, Shimomura explained, the rapid capital investment would embody new technologies and thus increase productivity sufficiently to offset its contribution to increased demand. Further, there would be no foreign exchange constraint because the application of up-to-date technology would increase Japan's competitiveness. A bold expansionary policy would be a gamble that would pay off. He was right. As Shimomura wrote in 1962, "Future possibilities will be opened up and realized, not by a conservative, negative policy of 'safety first,' but by resolute and creative vigor."[23] Ikeda's policies were not unlike President Kennedy's Keynesian experiment. They were, however, on a bolder scale. The institutional environment of Japanese capitalism of the early 1960s supported such boldness. In the United States anything so ambitious would have been powerfully inflationary. We lacked the industrial policy concomitants for successful significant expansion.

Miyohei Shinohara and other economists stress wage restraint as they measured the impact on growth rates of using new imported technology while wage increases were kept well below the rate of the productivity increases fueling accumulation. He and others also demonstrated the importance of the undervalued yen in stimulating exports. Hiromi Arisawa coined the term *niju kozo* as the Japanese equivalent of dualism and sparked a debate over the nature, origin, and implications of the Japanese model of stratification in labor markets and their central role in the production regime.[24] The rise in the ratio of capital to labor resulted in lower production costs for export industries. Under the existing fixed-exchange rate system that undervalued the yen, which the United States had established, exports expanded. From the Shinohara perspective the growth in exports was basically due to changes in the terms of trade (measured as the ratio of export to import prices). This price effect made Japanese products internationally competitive. Other economists, among whom Kojima may be the most important, stressed the expansion of foreign incomes as the key factor in Japan's export success. For the 1950–1970 period rising foreign incomes is estimated to have accounted for 90 percent or more of Japan's export growth although price effects played an increasing role in the 1970s. It was in these years that exports became a major factor in the pace of Japan's growth.[25]

In 1965 Japan's balance of payments moved into surplus for the first time in the postwar period and stayed there, in part by restricting imports. The previous year, 1964, Japan became an Article 8 member of the International Monetary Fund (IMF) and a member of the Organization of Economic Cooperation and Development (OECD) and so could no longer officially limit capital movements, but it left in place hundreds of restrictions on import items in violation of the General Agreement on Trade and Tariffs (GATT) rules, for which it was censured at GATT's 1968 meetings. Until 1967, all overseas investors had to receive special permits from the Foreign Investment Council. After that date licensing was gradually lifted, although informal controls remained. Also in 1967, taking a page from Uncle Sam-sensei's notebook, Japan initiated and financed the Asian Development Bank (ADB) and upped its foreign aid (tied to the purchase of Japanese goods). By custom the head of the ADB remains, as they say, Japanese.

In the early 1960s MITI had sent a team of experts to Europe. While their report, *The Infiltration of U.S. Capital in Europe*, was never made public, it was widely read and discussed by Japanese decision makers, who concluded "the American challenge" was best met by preventing direct investment (or infiltration) by U.S. firms into ownership positions in Japanese firms.

In 1969, Japan passed West Germany to become the second largest capitalist economy in the world. "The Japanese economy for the 1960s can be summarized in short," wrote Kenichi Miyamoto, "as a period of a high degree of capital accumulation, and during this decade Japan literally became an enterprise state."[26] Exports did *not* explain Japan's performance during its high growth period of the early 1950s through the early 1970s. Westerners tend to be preoccupied with the role of foreign trade in Japanese economic growth because it is in this area that Japan impinges upon the rest of the world, yet its exports over those years averaged 11 percent of GNP, which was less than France, Germany, Italy, Great Britain, or even OECD Europe as a whole. The Japanese development followed an organic process in which the major determinants were thought of first in terms of capital spending priorities, market extension and diversification, increasing productivity, and expanding their domestic economy. The drive to export came first out of the need to import and only later as a means of maintaining profit rates and using capacity generated. In this pattern they followed the path of Great Britain and the United States.

Once Japan had recovered from its wartime devastation and had laid the basis for secure growth its exports to the United States began in earnest. They were concentrated in a narrow range of consumer products that came in waves: radios and motorcycles, then color TVs and automobiles, and later sophisticated electronics products. The impact of the undervalued yen became increasingly evident, but it was not until 1971, as part of a general response to its deteriorating trade position, that the United States took any serious action. During the Vietnam War Japan and most of the allies helped to finance U.S. intervention by supporting the dollar by building up their own dollar reserves far beyond all reasonable bounds. Both Germany and Japan depended on U.S. military protection. In the case of Germany this was because of the special position of the Federal Republic with regard to the East. Therefore, they accepted U.S. leadership and requests for burden-sharing through financial support. In 1971 President Richard Nixon chose to claim a redistribution of resources by devaluing the vast dollar holdings of our allies.

At the time of the Nixon *shokku* (1971), Japan had a $3.2 billion trade imbalance with the United States. The U.S. responded to its increased inability to meet its international obligations while maintaining its living standard beyond its means by devaluing the dollar without consulting the Japanese about ending the 360 yen to the dollar rate that had prevailed since 1949. Prices of Japanese goods in American markets jumped upward in dollar terms. The United States also introduced restrictions on the number of Japanese products that could be imported. In response, in 1972 Sony opened the first Japanese manufacturing plant in the United States and exporters scrambled to diversify their markets away from their extreme dependence on American consumers.

The oil shock that soon followed led to a recession in Japan. The growth rate that had been almost 10 percent in 1973 fell to −1 percent for 1974. In the contraction corporate investment rates plummeted, and so they were able to finance their limited investment needs out of even their reduced earnings. The large borrower of this post-OPEC period was the Japanese government (to support huge amounts of deficit spending). This had an exceedingly important implication, which will be taken up again in Chapter 8. The banks no longer depended on the government for overloans, as they had in the first half of the postwar era, but were creditors to the state instead. They also became less vulnerable to bureaucratic controls. The banks demanded and got new interest rate freedoms. Corporations—Matsushita was the first in 1975 soon followed by others—issued dollar-denominated convertible debentures. In 1977 Euroyen bonds were allowed on a restricted basis. By the 1980s, to get ahead of our story for a moment, Japan's current account surpluses had not only recovered, but they had risen to new heights, which meant still less ability by the MOF to regulate financial markets. The wall between Japanese and world capital markets had been breached. Interest swaps and other new financial instruments, which had been developed in the United States, grew in popularity. Regulators, pushed by their bank clients and the pressures of foreign bankers, governments, and the new international competition in finance, were forced to loosen up. As we shall see this has had significant ramifications on the Japanese system.

In the 1970s Japanese corporations and MITI responded to higher energy costs by moving rapidly away from the "heavy, thick, long, big" industries (ju-ko-cho-dai) such as steel, shipbuilding, and chemicals. These were replaced by light, thin, short, and small (kei-haku-tan-sho) services and high-technology products. Japan's success in hai-teku (high tech) was at first attributed to a quickness in copying American technologies. The lack of creativity widely attributed to Japan by Americans and others in these years is reminiscent of the same sort of hubris shown by the British toward Americans a century earlier.[27] Japan quite consciously moved toward the creation of an information society in the post-OPEC years.[28] The importance of "soft" inputs in such an economy also had implications for the trajectory of the Japanese system. From the late 1970s a number of high-level policy advisory committees recommended shifting from Japan's traditional economic priorities based on the "hard" economy (centralized production by heavy industry) to a "soft" economy of services and especially information-oriented production. A blue ribbon MOF-sponsored Research Committee on Policy and Structural Change in the Economy a decade after the first OPEC shock popularized a new term, softoku (from the English "soft" and the Japanese suffix ka meaning change or transition to). In their report they stressed that this shift to intellectual products that used and handled information required a shift to smaller decentralized systems.

After the first OPEC shock and the still more dramatic restructuring of the Japanese economy Japan moved increasingly to export specialization in sectors with high-income elasticities. This, of course, was not a new orientation. The Report of the Industrial Structure Advisory Commission a decade earlier (November 1963) had noted that "if we specialize in income elastic products then to that extent we can also anticipate a rapid growth of exports." The continued success of such a strategy is demonstrated in Economic Planning Agency calculations. Over the period 1975–1987 the income elasticity of Japanese exports was 1.43. According to their estimates close to half of the growth of exports in the first half of the 1980s was due to increased income abroad (the other half to depreciation of the yen).[29] While the high yen value after 1985, however, reduced Japanese exports to the United States, it was by far less than many experts had expected. This was because of American preferences for Japanese-made consumer products, especially automobiles.

Wakasugi, looking at the growth rate for total factor productivity in the United States and Japan over the years 1979–1984, concluded that even if we assume that production factor costs rose equally in the two nations it would take close to a two percentage point drop in the value of the yen *annually* to keep the balance of trade from getting worse, given the U.S. lower growth in productivity. A 2 percent drop annually may not seem like much, but over time it would represent a sharp diminution in the return to America's most immobile factor of production—labor. Unless something happened living standards would fall by half within a thirty-five-year generation in the United States. As Rob Steven explains the 1985 yen revaluation did not help Japanese consumers as much as might have been expected either.

> In spite of the fall in import prices and the additional dive in oil prices Japanese workers were too weakly organized to win any other gains from the higher yen for themselves. It was a constantly remarked on phenomenon by the press that the consumer price index failed to follow the plunge in the wholesale prices brought on by the revaluation. Capital was able to appropriate almost the entire benefit of cheaper imports, which it used to compensate for the pressure on profits due to the surge in export prices. Whereas before September 1985, the lower living standards of Japanese workers in relation to their U.S. counterparts to some extent corresponded with their lower money wages, afterwards the situation was almost incomprehensible. Japanese money wages rose above U.S. money wages, but its real wages were still only a bit more than 60 percent of American real wages. [30]

While Steven's figure of 60 percent of American real wages in the years immediately following the yen revaluation may be questioned (other analyses place it at 80 percent), the point he makes seems irrefutable: The average Japanese did not benefit significantly from the stronger yen. This was especially true because housing costs skyrocketed with the lower interest rate policies the government used to stimulate the domestic economy in the face of expected loss of exports. The move stimulated speculation, among other areas, in land prices.

The Success of the Japanese System

Japanese companies responded to the higher yen with $2.5 trillion worth of investment in new plant and equipment from 1987 to 1991, dramatically outspending their American rivals by so much as to lay the basis for a new round of new technologically advanced products from long-term batteries to liquid crystal display televisions. In some key sectors (e.g., electrical manufacturing) there is evidence that productivity growth was so high that Japan was able to maintain competitive pricing in many areas despite the sizable appreciation of the yen, although it did create pressure for increased offshore production and a new internationalized production strategy. This will be discussed at length in Chapter 10. [31]

The outstanding success of the Japanese system by the 1970s created questions concerning cherished Western assumptions about markets and the most efficient means of organizing production. The developmentalist state generated uncertainty about the best role of government in the capitalist economy, making obsolete much of the conventional wisdom on the proper scope of the regulatory state, a debate that has been heating up for some time.[32] Interestingly, both Deming and Joseph Schumpeter had argued far earlier that major breakthrough innovations do not come from small competitive firms; rather, they come from large monopolistic ones. Their view remains unpopular in America, but it is conventional wisdom in Japan.

The Japanese corporation, the regulatory institutions of the state, and the culture of civil society in which they are embedded are as different from the corporate form, and the ideology and social support structures that emerged in the United States were from the culture of craft production. In this I am in agreement with Hikari Nohara's affirmative answer to the question, "Is the Japanese System a breakthrough?"[33] I, too, see "a very big change" in capitalist development. It is akin to the great depression era at the end of the nineteenth century out of which the American corporate form emerged.

The phenomena that had been characterized in the title of one popular book as *Trading Places*[34] resulted from the innovation in strategy and structure to be found in Japanese economic institutions. Economists studying these same issues from a neoclassical perspective interpret the difference in growth rates using conventional quantifiable economic variables. Investment rates in Japan in the late 1980s averaged 24 percent compared with 16 percent in the United States. Domestic savings rates that equaled 28 percent of GNP compared with 13 percent, supply-side investments in education and on-the-job training contributed to human capital formation, and so on. The strong dollar in the first half of the 1980s, also important for half of Japan's GNP growth, can be attributed to net exports.[35] Such factors are able to "explain" these developments statistically.

In fact, it can be argued that America's problems were created by its own government's misguided policies. It has been suggested that rather than Japan doing anything to create a balance of payments surplus of any unreasonable magnitude, it was the United States that followed "state-led" policies that caused its own problems. From such a perspective it can be pointed out that for twenty-two years, from 1961 through 1982, Japan's balance of payments remained fairly steady, fluctuating only slightly between surpluses and deficits (the aggregate surplus over the twenty-two years was only $35 billion). The surplus jumped to $21 billion in 1983, to $35 billion in 1984, and it kept growing into the late 1980s. Some Japanese economists argue that since Japan took no special steps to promote exports at that time, the explosive growth in exports that began around 1983 must be due "to outside factors," and the one they seem to have in mind was the rapid growth of the debtor status of the United States. The villain from this perspective is Reaganomics, the gamble that a tax cut would promote growth and the government would attain increased tax revenues at lower tax rates—the Laffer Illusion. There is certainly truth in this analysis, but is it the case that "this and this alone is the source of the economic problems now plaguing Japan–U.S. relations?"[36] Such a view is short sighted. It does not consider the context out of which Reaganomics on the one hand arose, and the singular achievements of the Japanese developmentalist state and its evolution in the postwar period on the other. These are the matters that need to be explained.[37]

To summarize the argument to this point, Japan in the 1960s and 1970s was able to import production technology and improve upon it. In the 1980s it was able to forge ahead in a manner that cannot be reduced to a high rate of investment or satisfactorily explained by other neoclassical growth model variables. It was the Japanese production system itself that must be examined as an innovative breakthrough akin to the multidivisional firm and related developments that set the American corporation apart from the British ideal type, the proprietary firm. The Japanese innovations were the institutionalization of constant improvement in place of the intermittent new design and long runs of standard products of the Fordist era (i.e., the flexible manufacturing system with its tight process controls and inventory management). The keys were the reinvention of automobile manufacture, especially but not exclusively the *kanban* or just-in-time order entry system and precision control of parts and process scheduling, the white collarizing of blue collar industrial workers more broadly so that knowledge-based learning-by-doing could be dramatically accelerated on the shop floor, and the spurt ahead in consumer electronics and other sectors in which large amounts of patient capital was available.

The role of MITI's historic task of nurturing Japanese industries until they could compete in any market in the world is well known. The centrality and success of industrial policy is also a matter of some dispute, partly as I have suggested because it was undergoing change constantly and was never transparent, and partly because it was quite different in major industrial sectors, less important in auto, and more crucial in semiconductors, for example. The industrial policy strategies adopted by MITI, as Shinohara points out, that "tried to take into account potential intertemporal dynamic developments rather than automatically applying the ready-made static theory of international economics, proved to be a wise choice."[38] In terms of production the Japanese strategy was to reduce costs through pushing the learning curve not simply through economies of scale and by institutionalizing constant improvement and innovations.

There has been no change in Japan's industrial policy objectives over the years covered in this chapter; rather, there has been a continuity in the basic approach of targeting industries, activities, and even firms for promotion. The forms of assistance have changed over time. The sectors encouraged have shifted. There have been changes in the mix of tools employed. The policy has remained. It would be odd indeed if the degree, kind, and targets of government intervention had not changed. To jump to the end of the time period covered for a moment, in the 1980s and 1990s precompetitive technology development was seen as crucial and cooperative research and development consortia were organized and funded by MITI's Agency for Industrial Science and Technology (AIST). AIST national technology projects in these years included development of hydraulic mining systems for harvesting manganese nodules from the ocean floor, automated sewing machines for the textile industry, and "high-power" chemical products such as dyes and insulating materials using marine life resources. More familiar projects included advanced robot technology, interoperative data base development, and lasers (for laser-beam printing, videodiscs, and fax machines). [39]

At the level of the social formation the developmentalist state, administered by elite bureaucrats, a national consensus to overtake the West, and a powerful set of complex policy instruments reflected at one and the same time a rejection of laissez-faire thinking and a deep understanding of how markets could be commanded. Japan as the paradigmatic strong state erected barriers to prevent external control, and created, under state direction, a concentration of power within a cohesive indigenous capitalist class. It regulated the flow of capital and profit, channeling savings and forced savings, limiting to the extent of forbidding capital exports until development was most firmly and unshakably established. The state guided and subsidized diversification of production and used elaborate rules, formal and informal, to manipulate and significantly indirectly administer the economy. The departure from the economist's conventional wisdom cannot be overstated. [40]

These characteristics of a strong developmentalist state should not be seen in opposition to capital, as it sometimes is in the Western laissez-faire–influenced literature, but as a variant of capitalist development in which the state secures privileged access to resources, technology, and markets for "its" capitalists. While occasional tensions between state technocrats and corporate elites may of course be manifest, they are over judgments of the distribution of particular short-run costs and benefits, and only infrequently over long-run strategic orientation or national goals. When they are of the latter nature it is the bureaucrats who a priori are usually judged to have the interests of the Japanese people at heart, not the corporations.

The remainder of this chapter takes up these issues in the following manner. The next section traces the historical development of the Japanese and the American postwar-era structures of accumulation and compares their essential features in the light of received mainstream economic doctrine. The section that follows examines the regulatory framework of the postwar period, more closely detailing the unique characteristics of the transnational Japanese corporation and the social institutions in which they were embedded. Special attention is paid to the financial sector.

The Postwar National Regimes of the United States and Japan

In the immediate post–World War II period, the U.S. advice that Japan should pursue labor-intensive industrial growth in accord with its obvious comparative advantage was rejected by Japanese bureaucrats. They thought that to follow such advice would delay, and perhaps preclude, long-term self-reliance and economic maturation. Comparative advantage theory in the static version assumed self-reliance was the inferior strategy compared with specialization based on existing factor endowment. Nonetheless, heavy industry, not toys, were targeted as the priority because, unlike the conventional mainstream economists, Japanese planners did not think all economic activity, any industrial mix of equal value to any other. Linkage effects were of strategic importance. Steel, for example, was the rice of the industrial economy of the 1950s, integrated chips, the rice of the 1980s. Planners saw the sectorial priorities chosen today as setting the prospects and possibilities of tomorrow.

The nature of late industrializers encourages a developmentalist-state consensus to privilege growth and the formation of a modernizing elite to carry out this collective purpose (in preference to letting the invisible hand, so helpful to those who got there first, do the job). The pattern is evident: Germany as compared with England, Japan vis-a-vis the United States. The drive to overcome backwardness acts as a goad in good Toynbeesque fashion. It is for the late industrializers that the better case can be made for the existence of Galbraithian technostructures. With fitting irony, it was in the public sphere that an elite, highly trained self-confident bureaucracy shaped developments, restraining and guiding application of the price system. Veblen's engineer, it seems, was also more likely to speak Japanese. The logic of the professional managerial class was given scope, because a late industrializer favors adoptive and pragmatically effective developmentalist strategies, not because of any ideological commitment to collectivism, as laissez-faire theorists might have feared. Nationalism among late industrializers encourages an active state role. Despite significant deregulation and greater openness to foreign investors, Japan remains nationalist in its basic thinking even in the post-postwar period as it copes with the need to transform its basic economic institutions to better harmonize with the rest of the national economies of the world system.

Changing existing comparative advantage, achieved by thinking in transformational terms, suggested a host of strategies to Japanese planners. These included purchasing technology to prevent foreign control, creating a pattern of interlinked ownerships by spreading stock among suppliers, customers, and other family member corporations to deny their availability to those who wished to take over a firm. This forced foreign companies seeking access to Japanese markets to pay with trade secrets and advanced technology that the Japanese firm could appropriate and, they hoped, improve upon—a reflection of the strategic orientation to building comparative advantage that separated Japanese practice from economic orthodoxy. By choosing products with high-income elasticities (most notably electric and electronic consumer durables), Japan put emphasis in areas with strong future prospects. They chose winners and strove to dominate their markets. Most of the innovative forms of statist policy, the "promotional interventions"[41] that came to characterize the Japanese developmentalist state model, were deliberately created and rationally shaped after World War II.[42] They were not, however, made up out of new cloth. Our historical discussion shows precedents that allow claims to a seamless continuity. Such claims, however, are exaggerated to the point of distorting the postwar creative institutional achievement.

An indicator of the scope of Japanese success was the speed with which it got out of declining industries even if they were at the time successful but destined to decline. In 1955 Toyobo, the cotton textile manufacturer was the number one exporter. A decade later it was Mitsubishi Heavy Industries, with a stress on shipbuilding. In 1975 it was Nippon Steel. A decade after that Toyota was the number one exporter. The administrative guidance and close working relations with the *keiretsu* will be discussed in subsequent chapters in greater detail. Here, let us simply note that rapid and flexible adaptation to changing technologies and market conditions has been the signiture of Japan's success.

Because in the mainstream model, as one Reagan economics adviser explained, it is of no consequence what a nation produces—"potato chips or micro chips." As long as exports and imports balance, then the mix from such a perspective is theoretically unimportant (except for national defense considerations). A Japan exporting and dominating cutting-edge, technologically driven products and importing an equal value of raw materials from the United States would not be a problem since there would be no balance of payments deficit involved. Yet, if learning by doing, economies of scope, and learning curves are important, then such a view is surely outdated. Generalizations concerning state-led development are plentiful and the scholarly literature of the leading success stories—Taiwan and Korea are most notably a Rorschach test for the ideological inclinations of readers as well as for the analysts themselves. The patterning of powerful state agencies that link analysis, decision making, and operational authority to broker, if not control, private investment and production as they modify the cost structure and risks faced by other decision makers to sequentially guide choice and the changing tactics and strategies of developmentalist states, are by now well documented. [43]

U.S.-style economic analysis does not place importance in historical time, but privileges ideological positions on a moralistic basis. U.S. trade negotiators are often fighting the last battle after it is over by asking that unfair trade barriers be dismantled and discussing the matter until long after the U.S. comparative advantage in the particular product area is gone. In reversible timeless models such losses are easily turned around. In historic time things are more problematic. American producers have been driven out of field after field from VCRs and televisions to, perhaps, in the not so distant future, computers and commercial aircraft, where they now hold a significant lead. In deciding what should be done U.S. negotiators are only beginning to understand the embeddedness of Japanese practice and their long-standing development. To change them requires a social engineering that is more complex than making demands that "markets be opened now."

Financial Markets

The capital cost advantage Japanese firms enjoyed through the postwar period were based on institutional innovation. It is not simply that Japanese save more than Americans. Guided savings aggregation and selective investment were born of necessity. Even after the worst of the Pacific conflict's aftermath had passed, total financial assets held by the Japanese nonfinancial sector in 1953 were 3 percent of the corresponding figure for the United States. By 1959 the ratio had risen to half. Because there were no large pools of capital corporations could draw on after the redistribution of wealth sponsored by the occupation, special institutions had to be created. The existing commercial banks were too weak to extend the long-term credit Japanese industry needed. Government funds were required to underwrite investment. These funds were gathered in postal savings deposits, postal life insurance, and postal annuities. They were allocated to priority industries, mostly in the form of long-term credits, by the private banks, who depended on Bank of Japan overlending.

If such government loans had not been continually forthcoming, then the banks would have been in immediate trouble and the Japanese miracle could not have been financed. Thus, the Bank of Japan had strong leverage over private financial institutions, power bureaucrats used to guide investment. Banks had to enter industries in support of MITI priorities even if their natural caution would have led them to hold back or risk being frozen out in riskless lending elsewhere. The authorities kept interest rates paid to depositors low and subsidized loans to favored industries. Firms that were able to develop long-term relationships with banks were more secure. In times of tight credit they would not be cut off. Since strong corporations insured the safety of the bank's money, a mutuality of interest developed, not unlike in the German case.

Studies show U.S. firms paying up to 8 percent more than Japanese ones for capital at the start of the 1980s. The gap was cut in half by mid-decade, and it disappeared, according to some measures, by the start of the 1990s. Such calculations are inherently tricky because capital cost differences should be measured standardizing for risk and total return. Japanese companies have generally been less risky than comparable American firms because the former enjoys having their stock significantly held by affiliate companies and banks who also benefit as equity holders from the profitable investments to which their loan capital is put. If one is interested in the difference in the cost of capital between nations, then attention needs to be paid to the institutional setting that powerfully affects investor risk. Smooth passage of information between lenders and borrowers in Japan reduces uncertainty. Creditors are more likely to help a troubled company than to let it go into bankruptcy. Investors with good relations to their bankers are cushioned against the risk of loss. Without the same conflict of interest between insiders and outsiders capital structures are very different in Japan and the United States.[44] The emergence of a single money market in which capital is free to seek the highest possible return consistent with the risk propensities of investors does not therefore mean that U.S. firms face the same cost of borrowing as do Japanese firms, which enjoy *keiretsu* and state support against failure.[45] How important lower capital costs has been in understanding the ascendancy of Japan is itself a growth industry among economists.

The conceptual issues are complex. Measuring capital cost in one area soon leads to interrelated ones. Different measures of rate of return on invested capital have their own complex conceptual and measurement problems. I would like to discuss the issue of capital cost further for two reasons. The first is its intrinsic importance. The second is because it is one instance of many in which the neoclassically oriented economists use methods that seek precise determination where the conceptual context remains murky and so seemingly exact findings remain suspect. In short, the debate over capital costs is a case in which most economists discuss Japan within a framework that, while technically sophisticated in technique and not readily accessible to those lacking specialist training, takes as given the very issues problematized in this study.

For non-economists the issues involved in adjusting book-value earnings, inventories for inflation (harder than one might expect since different accounting methods are used in the two nations), and so on may be one big bore. Yet, it is useful to pursue the matter briefly to see how governing institutional practices differ.

There is a set of interdependent questions that neoclassical economists have done impressively in investigating empirically. For example, while it is widely held that large Japanese corporations through the postwar period accepted lower profit rates than did their American counterparts, Ando and Auerbach examined earnings–price ratios and total returns to debt plus equity for a sample of firms. For the period they studied (1966–1981) they found that there was no evidence that Japanese firms had a lower rate of return on capital. [46] Depreciation schedules for American investment are uniformly more generous than are those for Japanese investment. It is on just such issues that such findings— that it is Japanese firms, not U.S. ones, that are taxed more heavily on their real equity income at the corporate level— are made.

Neoclassical growth models assume that higher savings leads to higher investment. What do we make of the fact that U.S. tax policy is strongly proinvestment and Japanese policy is strongly prosavings? There is also the matter of lower capital costs to the Japanese firm in yen compared with the dollar cost to American companies that results from a premium due to the expected long-term appreciation of the yen. Do we want to consider the fact that comparative capital cost analyses are also complicated by differences in accounting conventions, the treatment of pension liabilities, tax treatment, and all sorts of other factors that are taken into account by those paying careful attention to institutional context. As one leading expert told a research conference on the issue, "it is increasingly understood today, not only in finance but also in other aspects of industrial policy, that a subtle set of dependencies, power relationships, and informal understandings was in operation . . . " in the way Japan constructed its financial system and allowed for guided capital rationing. [47] The American finance literature, which is heavily of the opinion that efficient capital markets are necessary to discipline managerial behavior [48] and which advocates perfectly decentralized financial markets, may not have considered the advantages through the postwar period of the Japanese development state's intervention, tight regulation, credit rationing, and guidance of corporate finance.

In fact, there is a see-sawing of many generalizations that are part of what informed opinion "knows" about Japan in relation to the U.S. economy. The welter of calculations that have to be made before one can say anything on any of these issues is immense. Other forms of subsidy must be considered. So, too, must other forms of taxation (on personal income, wealth taxes) and outcomes will vary by types of investment. Shoven and Tachibanaki calculate marginal rates for eighty-one classes of investment. This is really only the beginning since their classes include only three industries, three assets, three types of investors, and three types of financing. Is the United States, then, the norm? What of Germany, the United Kingdom, Korea, or Taiwan?

Some economists attempting to clarify just what it is that the Japanese developmentalist state does differently speak of the subequilibrium interest rate disequilibrium policy. I think, however, that it is perhaps more useful simply to grant that "it is increasingly understood today, not only in finance but also in other aspects of industrial policy, that a subtle set of dependencies, power relationships, and informal understandings was in operation rather than a system of reliant on simple directives,"[49] and that institutional texture may be more informative than translation into mainstream terms. The economic principle involved is simple enough. Such regulation in the earlier period is best seen as "taxing" depositors (who received lower interest rates) and redistributing from small depositors to productive investment. The savers were not given alternative financial instruments and so had no choice. Their interests came last. To give them incentive to save, however, small savers were exempt from taxation, and that partly made up for the lower rates. Today, tax avoidance through the holding of multiple postal savings accounts to avoid ceiling limitations is a major revenue cost to the government, yet these accounts still, along with surpluses in welfare pension funds, provide huge amounts to Japan's unique "second budget," the Fiscal Investment and Loan Program (FILP). FILP is nearly half the size of the general account budget and is used for government investments. It is run by the Finance Ministry's Trust Fund Bureau. The safety feature of controlled markets in Japan reduces risk even in today's more open global capital markets.

This second budget is the source of low interest loans, highway construction, and financing loans to developing countries. Historically, it has been the source of the dominant share of Japan's capital accumulation and subsidized loans to industry and for infrastructure. By the mid-1970s the corporate sector had sharply reduced its net borrowing as their successful growth made internal financing possible to such an extent that many had surplus capital. As Japanese firms went multinational, they have also had access to world money markets and so could escape, to some extent, the influence of Japanese capital allocation constraints. In the 1980s, it became increasingly difficult for the MOF to control the banks themselves as new financial instruments adopted from the West begrudgingly had to be accepted by regulators. Yet, when the stock market headed south, and the banks watched their capital base shrink and bankruptcy prospects loom, the MOF in 1993 was able to engineer a stock market recovery through an impressive demonstration of administrative guidance.

This is perhaps an appropriate point to say something about the way leverage was used to induce growth in postwar Japan as compared to the United States. The institutional context is again the relevant factor. Early in the recovery the Japanese industrial system took on one of its most distinctive characteristics. As Chalmers Johnson has written:

> The pattern of dependencies in which a group of enterprises borrows from a bank well beyond their net worth, and the bank in turn overborrows from the Bank of Japan (BOJ). Since the central bank is the ultimate guarantor of the system, it gains complete and detailed control over the policies and lending decisions of its dependent "private" bank. [50]

The enterprise borrows 70–80 percent of its capital from the banks, who borrow from the BOJ. MITI policies guide lending policies. There is no pressure from impatient stockholders, who want the highest payout possible. In the American case high leverage makes a firm more vulnerable in an economic slowdown to possible bankruptcy and forced sale of assets. It is starved for investment funds and dares not invest unless the payoff is immediate. A fall in stock valuation makes it subject to possible hostile takeover. Comparing the meaning of leverage in the two systems, it is difficult to be persuaded by arguments for the superiority of our market-driven system over Japanese "planned markets" in the abstract. In practice, as we'll see, the close relationship in the Japanese system in the 1980s opened it up to a structured corruption when regulators accepted, and perhaps personally profited from, less than vigilant oversight.

Another Japanese institution, the large trading company, supplied financing through trade credits that are especially important to smaller businesses with less access to bank loans. Nine large trading companies, the *sogo shosha* mentioned earlier, account for more than 70 percent of the value of Japan's custom cleared imports. MITI allocated market shares and sponsored cartels to make governance easier and actually assigned an enterprise in which it had an interest to a trading company if it did not already have an affiliation. America had no need to develop such specialized tools given its overwhelming economic superiority in the immediate postwar period. Free trade and unlimited foreign investment as mandated by laissez-faire norms were rejected firmly in the Japanese model. Up to the mid-1970s, MITI prohibited such activity under the Foreign Exchange Law, and later through a mixture of formal and most effectively informal mechanisms. In extreme cases foreign entry remained blocked for decades after the war's end. It was not, for example, until the fall of 1991 that MITI announced that it would end restrictions on entry into the Japanese silk and woolen textile industry. Japanese firms were limited in countless ways in their business dealings and saw it in their own interest to cooperate if they were to earn governmental favor. Consider, from this perspective, Murakami's opinion:

> MITI's investment guidance and MITI-guided recession cartels were effective in avoiding or alleviating the adverse effects of excessive competition

or market instability. During times of prosperity, the investment race could easily have gotten out of control if no coordination had been attempted. During times of (relative) recession, overcapacity would have caused cutthroat competition, particularly in the export market, unless some kind of recession cartel had been introduced . . . coordination was necessary to control the self-destructive forces of market instability.[51]

Such intervention must be inefficient according to free market ideology. For Western economists there is something totally out of joint in the views, the tone, and the assumptions concerning economic theory in such an institutional framework. Yet, the practice of the Japanese developmentalist state increased efficiency of resource allocation in any number of important sectors.

Consider the important case of policy response in Japan and the United States to the oil crisis. The United States relied on the market to efficiently adjust demand and supply. Japanese energy policies were two sided—the economy was as quickly as possible moved from basic industries that were energy intensive to high value-added, less resource-processing goods and services. The state accelerated momentum with generous transitional assistance—the law involved was limited to only five years so that its transitional nature would be clear. Under the Structurally Depressed Industries Act, fourteen industries were specifically targeted. Excess capacity in shipbuilding, aluminum smelting, chemical fertilizers, and other sectors that were the heavy energy users were selected. Second, energy conservation became a religion in all industries.

Under MITI guidance, up to ten energy conservation engineers monitor fuel efficiency at the shop floor level in Japan's targeted industrial plants. To qualify for the job they must pass a tough examination (eight out of ten who take it fail, and engineers study a year or more to prepare for it). These energy conservationists are expected to know their stuff. This effort is hardly ceremonial. Between 1973 and 1987, Japan's economic output more than doubled, yet oil imports fell by 25 percent. Over the same years, a slower growing U.S. economy increased its reliance on imported oil. The United States moved to keep the price of oil cheap and used more of it, invading the Middle East when necessary. The Japanese relied on conservation. Energy prices, unlike those in the United States, were allowed to rise. Energy users were expected to recycle profits to energy research, and incentives provided for greater conservation. MITI forced utilities to spend billions of yen on energy-saving–oriented research. As a result Japan now has the world's best technology for solar cells, generators producing electricity from sea water, and gasified coal. High-risk research is undertaken because the firms have been provided with the money and ordered to do it. Japan favors coal and natural gas over oil because both are obtainable in politically more stable nations. Under such encouragement, Nippon Steel's Kimitsu plant (which alone consumed 1 percent of Japan's energy) converted its blast furnaces to coal in the early 1980s, cutting its oil usage from 20 percent of its total energy consumption to near zero. It also recycles its hot gases.

The results of the different policy emphases have been evident. Despite

Japan's far greater dependence on imported oil it was the United States that in hindsight has suffered most from the sudden increase in the cost of oil. In 1990 Japan imported 99.7 percent of its oil needs (the United States produced about half of the oil used domestically that year). Japan, however, had reduced its oil dependence from 77 percent of its total energy consumed in 1973 to 59 percent in 1990. Early in the twenty-first century, MITI officials expect, Japan's reliance on oil as an energy source will be below 50 percent. By then, America's dependence on imported oil is expected to become greater than Japan's. The Japanese have also been exploring for oil far from the turbulent Middle East (in sites from Southeast Asia to Africa). The Japanese government supports joint ventures with low-interest loans. As a result, in 1990 11 percent of Japan's total crude oil came from wells developed by such joint ventures between foreign countries and Japanese firms, thanks in part to Japanese governmental support.

In the Japanese case guidance has been defined in terms of promotional intervention (subsidies for desired behavior, research and development grants, government contracts, tax concessions for results). Such guidance has been market conforming, assisting developments that are efficient for the society, greasing the wheels and reducing the pain of desirable adjustments. In the last chapter note was taken of the ability of the Japanese to borrow from the rest of the world, to import machines and reverse engineer them, to invite foreign experts to teach them how to deal with problems, and to adopt foreign methods. The Japanese could draw on what suited their own needs because they had maintained their national autonomy and had not been integrated into the world system on terms established by the imperial powers. They chose to interact on a limited basis, limited by their own understanding of what would best serve their national interests.

At the end of World War II, the U.S. Strategic Bombing Survey recalled the importance of foreign machine tools and experts trained in American engineering schools who had interned in U.S. plants and then returned to Japan to build zeros at Mitsubishi. Their 1947 report has a more general applicability to Japanese procedures in the postwar period.

> For assistance other than the financial, the Japanese aircraft industry owed more to the United States than it did to its own government. It is sad, but true, that United States fighter and bomber pilots fought against aircraft whose origins could be traced back to United States drafting boards. Many Jap [sic] engines and propellers came from American designs which had been sold under license in prewar years. Many top Jap aeronautical engineers could claim degrees from Massachusetts Institute of Technology, Stanford and California Tech. Their best production men had served apprenticeships with Curtis, Douglas, Boeing, or Lockheed . . . [I]t can fairly be stated that the Jap [double sic] fought the war with aircraft on which the strongest influences in design were American.[52]

An assessment of Japanese technical achievements a half century later would convey a similar message. Americans made available at low or no cost the weapons that defeated them in economic competition across a range of con-sumer products and capital goods. If trade is seen as war, then the Americans continued policies that were self-destructive. If the spread of technology even-tually helps everyone—Americans, Japanese, and others—then these peaceful achievements of the Japanese should be seen in a more positive light. These larger issues will be addressed in subsequent chapters, but here we may note that American policy in the postwar period did act to create an open world economy in which goods and knowledge could freely travel and in so doing reversed the zero-sum nationalism that had afflicted the world in the interwar years and, in the minds of many, had prolonged the depression.

When Lockwood wrote in the early 1950s that "this laissez-faire philosophy seems anachronistic today, as the forces set loose in the world, so stimulated by Japanese militarism itself, have returned us to the bitter divisions, alliances, and mercantilist practices of the seventeenth century,"[53] he was perhaps at-tributing too great a responsibility to the Japanese. It was the European former colonial powers that tried to hold on to their system of imperial preferences. He was also, however, calling attention to the dominant reality of the early postwar period against which the U.S. efforts to promote free trade and an open system of trade backed by a stabilizing structure of finance and interna-tional payments was aimed. Nonetheless, it was the Japanese who continued to be the most successful in practicing mercantilism policies in the postwar period, and with American blessings. In a world we shaped in the political construction of fear of the Evil Empire, a strong Japan as an American outpost in Asia was worth the price of allowing it to flout the rules of an open system. It was not until the early 1970s that the United States officially found Japan's developmentalist state policies objectionable; however, one-way technological transfers and trade restrictions and export subsidies continued.

At the same time in an open world trading system (even one constrained in various ways) two factors impact on the Japanese domestic economy that have brought pressure on its continued corporate growth. The changes in the share of total manufacturing exports attributable to exchange rate shifts is much larger than for the United States multinationals who function on a worldwide scale of production. This makes interpretation of the data more difficult in terms of what it says about the competitiveness of the domestic economy. It is true that from 1982 to 1985 the U.S.-based multinationals' share of world trade increased while that for the United States declined. However, from 1977 to 1982, when the exchange value of the dollar fell to low levels, the U.S. share of world exports went up much more than did the share of U.S. multinationals. This occurred again after 1985 as the dollar's value fell. U.S. manufacturing exports expanded nicely. Indeed, America's export volume in manufactures increased much faster in the second half of the 1980s than did either Japan's or Germany's, as did its rate of increase in manufacturing output per worker hour over the entire decade, 1979–1989. It was in the category of business-fixed investment as a percentage of GNP that Japan left the United States in the dust.

Such a picture suggests that as long as the United States is willing to depreciate its currency it can remain competitive. This, however, is no more than an accounting outcome. Such competitiveness is achieved at the price of declining living standards for working people if not for the symbolic analysts, those people who manipulate money, technologies, legal arguments, and people through advertising and other image creations[54] who live here but sell their services on world markets.

The Japanese, who were the big winners in the postwar period, could not keep growing through a combination of exporting and domestic financial self-levitation forever. At the end of the bubble economy Japanese growth stagnated, although because of the nature of the Japanese industrial relations system this did not bring high unemployment levels. It did end the *urite shijo*, the seller's market, that had allowed bright graduates to pick and choose from among job prospects and allowed American firms in Tokyo to actually have a crack at some of the more desirable prospects for the first time. Overtime work was cut back and company directors were told to take the train to work instead of company limousines. Luxury product sales fell disastrously, but living standards of working people did not fall as they did in the United States. The question was how long the slump would last and at what point it would put serious pressure on established social contract accommodations.

The post–bubble economy raised questions for analysts used to thinking of Japan as a perpetual growth machine. An educational TV special, *Slumping Japan*, caught the mood. Its anchor, Sadatomo Matsuhaira, captured a pervasive feeling when he said, "A lot of people are thinking, something is different."[55] There were many indications that the period of Japanese exceptionalism might be coming to an end. Japanese corporations, for example, began to behave in ways far more similar to those in other advanced capitalist nations. This was because the external constraints they faced in a more deregulated world economy were not all that different any more to those others encountered. During the bubble economy they had sold hundreds of billions of dollars in equity-linked bonds. These paid only 1 or 2 percent interest but gave their holders special opportunities for profiting if the firm's stock price rose, which in these years they did. As the low-cost bonds matured, however, things had changed. Falling stock prices meant they had to be replaced at market rates of 6 or 7 percent, the same interest Western firms were paying. As Japanese capital markets came to resemble more closely those elsewhere, companies found themselves constrained by high-debt servicing charges, forced to maximize shorter-term profits and to abandon their emphasis on long-term market shares. The impact was slower development of new products, fewer models in less-extensive product lines, and more strategic alliances in expensive and uncertain product development areas. Even the rise of dividend payments was closer to Western norms to placate stockholders in a falling market. Yet, Japan is not the United States. The developmentalist state and the *keiretsu* needed to reinvent themselves. They did not simply turn into a version of their American counterparts.

Sorting out what remains unique in Japan as compared with the United States in areas of finance, government–corporate cooperation, and trade policies are the task of much of the rest of the book. It is important to remember that what is being compared and contrasted are two social formations that are evolving as they meet new contingencies and draw on past traditions to develop new practices. The next chapter examines the automobile industry in detail. It reflects many of the issues that have been examined in the rise of the postwar production system. Its rapid growth demonstrated the ingenuity of the Japanese; its slow growth by the 1990s, the impact of global stagnationist tendencies and the comeback of American auto producers, the reality that no competitive victory or defeat need be permanent.

5

The Case of the Automobile Industry

"General Motors is like the Stars and Stripes to the United States. I can imagine how shocking it must be when that company is beaten by Japanese cars."

JAPANESE PRIME MINISTER KIICHI MIYAZAWA, *reacting to the news that GM had decided to lay off an additional 74,000 workers* [1]

"Americans simply don't want to recognize that Japan has won the economic war against the West."

KAZUO OGURA
DIRECTOR OF CULTURAL AFFAIRS
FOREIGN MINISTRY [2]

In the 1920s U.S. automobiles dominated world trade, and motor vehicles dominated American manufacturing exports. It is central to our story that a half century later the Toyota system duplicated Henry Ford's great achievement in revolutionizing the industry and transforming its nation's producers into world leaders. The automobile is the machine that remade the world[3]; it is also the core of the Japanese drive to export preeminence in the postwar period. While automobiles were only 2.4 percent of Japan's total exports in 1960, they accounted for nearly 10 percent a decade later, over 20 percent of the total in 1980 (the year Japan became the number one auto exporter), and more than a quarter of all exports by 1986. After that, Japanese strategy was to service foreign markets from localized production facilities, although exports from Japan continued to be a serious bone of contention because they made up most of the U.S. trade deficit. Forty-five percent of Japanese automotive production is exported. The leader of the charge was Toyota, which in the mid-1980s held 30 percent of exports and an even more impressive 43 percent of the market domestically (which was divided among ten Japanese producers and a few European luxury cars). In 1991, as President Bush visited Tokyo with an entourage of American automobile company executives, two thirds of the United States' rather sizable balance of payments deficit was with Japan,

112

and three quarters of that was caused by car and auto parts. The auto industry by itself, therefore, is a significant part of the Japanese success story and the cause of much American concerns. It is also indicative of two future developments.

By the early 1990s the gap between the Japanese and the U.S. producers was closing fast as costs rose in Japan and the Americans learned how to compete more effectively. Japan had lost its price advantage during 1986 with the appreciation of the yen, and quality improvements on Detroit's products led to their gaining market shares after 1991. In 1994, Detroit's cars were costing $1700 less than Japan's (on a sales weighted average), although because resale value of Japanese cars was significantly higher, leasing erased the price advantage of the U.S. Big Three. There need be no permanent winner producer nation. Second, while Japanese auto producers in the early 1970s made 8 percent of cars for the Japanese market abroad, it was estimated (in 1993) that by the year 2000, based on yen trends and shifting costs, 42 percent of the domestic market would be serviced from abroad. There would then be 20 percent less auto production in Japan itself than at the 1990 peak. A third development which became evident by the mid-1990s, was that in the post-postwar era internationalization of production would assume a regionally integrated character. For example, as Asian markets shaped up as the next battleground for the auto industry, Toyota moved to make a sports-utility vehicle put together from parts suppliers across Asia—electrical components from Malaysia, transmissions from the Philippines, engines from Indonesia. Nissan introduced a stationwagon designed in Thailand. The prospect for the auto industry, as for many others, is for a globalization process in which complex strategic alliance patterns reflect the growing importance of particular markets and national productive capacities. Japan's role as a dominant force in the industry's future is not to be doubted.

The Japanese achievement is immense. In 1929 the Ministry of Commerce and Industry (MITI's predecessor) published a study "Policy for Establishing the Motor Vehicle Industry," and in the early 1930s the bureaucrats urged the three largest *zaibatsu* to enter the industry. Yet until 1934 when the military forced the Americans out, Ford and GM controlled more than 90 percent of the Japanese auto market.

In 1950 the entire auto industry output was 30,000 vehicles, about 1.5 day's production in the American automobile industry at that time. By 1974 Japan replaced West Germany as the world's largest exporter of cars. By 1980 Japan led the world in the number of automobiles produced. The industry exhibits a number of characteristic features shared with other leading sectors of the Japanese economy. These range from brilliance in technological adaptation and innovation, dazzling capacity to shatter conventional wisdom concerning product and manufacturing process, and prevalence of collaborative company unions.

The automobile industry offers an important case study of the manner in which Japanese technological development has been built on a unique production system and labor-relations regime. It offers a useful case study of the manner in which the sociology of economic development is captured by relating the social structures in which it takes place to the manner in which historically specific pressures are resolved. The automobile industry is a successful example of institutional entrepreneurship and of the sort of creative response for which Japanese firms have become famous, and to which Schumpeter refers in the epigraph to Chapter 4. The dual labor market of the industry also demonstrates the different principles at work in the better-paid permanent workers of its primary sector and the low-wage temporary workers who produce much of the industry's value added, which is broadly characteristic of Japanese industrial relations. Finally, the way the Japanese transplants in America are evaluated has great importance for the broader evaluation of Japanese foreign investment strategies, their meaning for host nations, and, given the history of leadership of the United Auto Workers, the future of trade unionism.

Into the Passing Lane

Japanese auto producers give new meaning to the advantages of backwardness by creatively turning traditional logic around. The Japanese pioneered a model of focused production in their effort to enter markets dominated by foreign giants. They sought to enter where the latter were weakest with specialized products to meet specific customer needs. They later found that a wide range of small-lot products could be economically produced with the maturing of flexible production techniques. They then proceeded to do this at the cutting edge of technological innovation and product quality in mass producer markets at a number of segmented positions. The increased flexibility and quick response time that had initially been a requirement forced by a disadvantaged position increased their competitiveness. Dependence on suppliers gave them the incentive to help these allied companies become more efficient producers. This was initially a matter of limited capital and a desire to obtain lower cost parts than could be produced in-house. Over time their supplier network proved a dynamic source of comparative advantage. The choices companies and industries make have iterative consequences. Advantage at one point in time, however, need not be irreversible as the Japanese were to find in the early 1990s.

Ironically, some of these advantages of backwardness combined with a technically sophisticated cultural economy were present in the United States a century earlier as this country took the automobile, a European invention, and created a new-style industrial complex for producing a more competitive product. The most famous innovation, of course, was Henry Ford's assembly line and standardized car. Before that, however, the sophisticated supplier network the Americans could draw on was an important factor in the industry's takeoff.

> Even as early as 1885 a shrewd visitor to the United States remarked that
> "the tools and processes we are inclined to consider unusual are the

commonplace of the American shop''. . . . The automotive producer in
the United States was also served by suppliers. He could turn to dozens
of shops or plants (all like himself employing machine tools) that made
tires, wheels, engines, forgings, transmissions, and other parts, and stood
ready to supply them in quantity at a low rate. The European carmaker
could call on few if any such firms. [4]

Other American modes of organization, including the great Ford River Rouge
plant, have their counterpart in the type of innovation the Japanese have
mastered in catching up with and surpassing American producers. Also, like
the Americans, who in the nineteenth century were accused of simply copying, Japanese growth was based on adaptation.

Ford and General Motors built assembly plants in Japan in the 1920s.
''Partly as a result of this,'' a Mazda-sponsored history tells us, ''Japan's own
production continued to lag far behind.''[5] From such a perspective, it can be
said that the Japanese auto industry dates from 1931, when the government
designed a standard car with a six-cylinder, 45 horsepower engine that could
do 40 kilometers per hour. It manufactured the car in a government facility. In
1936, when Ford and General Motors accounted for about three fourths of the
motor vehicle output of Japan, the first Automobile Production Enterprise Law
offered large-scale government financial support to private companies that
would build automobiles. In a continuation of the developmentalist state strategy dating from early in the Meiji Restoration, state planners chose to create a
national industry. A half century later it dominated world markets and carried
production activities to the home turf of Ford and General Motors. Protection
from American competitors and high levels of sophisticated government support were key to the industry's success.

If Japan had followed American advice it is unlikely that all of this would
have happened.[6] The American occupation authorities had restricted car production, which they did not consider essential, in the recovery period after the
war. MITI took the opposite position. It saw the stimulating effect such a
leading sector as automobiles would have on everything from machine tools to
basic steel. MITI policies combined low-cost loans, tax privileges, and protection. It allowed firms to deduct from income any revenues obtained from
export sales and exempted machinery and tools the industry needed to import
from restrictions and taxation. When GATT forbade some of these practices in
the mid-1960s MITI invented new ones. It allowed the auto companies to
establish tax-free reserves for expenditures related to overseas marketing and
adopted depreciation schedules linked to export performance. With MITI's
determination to build the industry, car firms had no trouble raising low-cost
bank loans.

In the 1980s, Japanese automakers opened seven plants in the United
States. Over the same decade, domestic producers closed the same number of
plants in this country. By the early 1990s Detroit's no-longer-so-Big Three were
all losing money, and one out of three of that city's citizens was on welfare.
American companies' automobile output had shrunk to a thirty-three year

low. The Japanese were still adding U.S. production capacity in what was overall a sluggish market.

The stories of General Motors' misspending of $80 billion on capital-intensive technology in their effort to leap-frog the Japanese with technological fixes in the 1980s are legend—the robots that dismembered each other, smashing cars, and spray painting all over, installing wrong parts, and other nightmares come readily to the mind of industry people. The mightiest general in the United States industrial armed forces has stumbled badly. When officials from GM's Framingham plant returned from touring NUMMI, the GM–Toyota plant in California (which will be discussed more extensively shortly) seen as a model for the industry, one manager claimed that there must be secret repair areas and secret stock because NUMMI did not have enough areas or stock to be a "real" car plant. Others publicly wondered what all the fuss was about. The Framingham plant was shut a short time later. It had taken 50 percent more personhours to produce inferior cars there than at NUMMI.[7]

Summing up GM's decade-long misadventures with modernization the *Economist* concluded: "It was an expensive lesson, but GM eventually learned that it was not robots, but its own workforce, that was its biggest and most valuable asset."[8] Indeed, among the new industry lore is how workers improve things themselves, visit suppliers, develop methods to improve quality, and convince the company to get rid of faulty or "overautomated" equipment and return more control to workers. (The Japanese auto industry had not in fact automated until they had worked out basic production; i.e., gotten the kinks out. Introducing new products, processes, *and* automation at once was considered too risky.) GM's effort to leap-frog landed it in the mud. While in worse shape, Chrysler bought a major part of the autos it sold from Mitsubishi, and especially Ford, which owned a large part of Mazda and learned a lot from it, did somewhat better. Improved profits when they did come in the mid-1990s resulted in part from quality improvement in Detroit, but more importantly from the dramatically higher yen— but this is getting ahead of our story.

The saga of the decline of the U.S. auto industry in the second half of the postwar era was complemented by the impact of Detroit's own sourcing from Japan and from plants in developing nations (Chrysler was the leader, as noted, but the other two major automakers followed the same route). Under competitive pressure in the mid-1980s U.S. companies increased their "captive imports," foreign models sold under U.S. brand names, from 6 percent of total auto imports in 1984 to 20 percent in 1988. At the same time they were demanding protection from imports that were directly sold as foreign cars.[9] In the early 1990s many of their own best-known models were foreign made.[10]

Not only were U.S. labels being slapped on foreign products, but foreign firms were often owned in significant part by the American producers who seemed to be demanding protection from them. The complex and ever-changing pattern included Chrysler's holding of over one third of Mitsubishi's stock and Japan's Mitsubishi's ownership of 15 percent of Korea's Hyundai. Ford, with a quarter of Mazda, was also holding a share of Kia Motors of

Korea. General Motors, which continued to express a belief in free trade, was part owner of Suzuki and Isuzu in Japan and owned half of Daewoo in Korea (the Daewoo nameplate was not on the models they made, which were sold in the United States as GM products). Efforts of elected officials to "protect" American producers seemed touchingly naïve. The protectionist pressures, however, did encourage the Japanese to continue building plants in the United States.

In the early 1980s Japan imposed a 2.3 million unit limit on auto exports to the U.S. ("upon themselves," as the make-believe world of free trade has it, the VER fiction, of voluntary export restraints). After a decade of propping up American producers—VERs were first imposed in 1981—the most noticeable change in American auto production was that the industry had scaled back and Japanese producers had built their plants and established their supplier networks to serve the American market from within the country. Japanese exports from Japan to the United States of completed cars stayed below 2 million units. By 1987, the voluntary restraints on exports of automobiles to the United States had little impact, as Japanese companies North American production matured. In 1994 the VERs were dropped by a Japan faced with Clinton administration demands for an expansion of quantitative trade commitments from Japan.

The transplants' success taught a hard lesson. First of all there was nothing wrong with the U.S. worker that quality management could not set right. Nor was the problem tough environmental standards—the other scapegoat of the years in which Japanese cars roared onto U.S. freeways. Japanese standards were and are a lot tougher and their cars meet our standards better than do ours. In the early 1970s when U.S. automakers had blamed proposed fuel efficiency and antipollution standards for their troubles, claiming Big Government was harassing them with expensive and "unobtainable" standards, Honda shipped an Impala to its factory in Japan and modified that Chevy's V-8 engine using its own technology so that the American car met both of these standards.[11] One indication of the speed of the transformation of the automobile industry is that Honda was producing its cars in a Marysville, Ohio, plant in 1982.

American experts discovered a new level of capitalist industrialization when they took a close look at the "lean production" system of the Japanese auto industry, which at the start of the 1990s used half the work time and half the engineer hours, even half the investment in tools. They paid attention to detail, educated their workers, and had zero defects—it was all rather astounding.[12] Whether the Japanese produced cars in their own country or in ours, they seemed to do a better job.

The teacher had become the pupil and many Americans did not like it one bit. Vincent Chin (a Chinese-American, as it turned out) was killed in Michigan at the height of the random anger of autoworkers in 1982, a victim of rage at Japanese success and the lack of alternate comparably compensated employment in America. Anger and frustration were also illustrated by a local congressman, who had taken a sledge hammer to a Toyota in front of TV cameras. A film clip of the episode was shown repeatedly on Japanese television.

A less-chauvinistic response on the part of American labor would have been to look more closely at the actual experiences of Japanese workers and their assumed willingness to do seemingly superhuman amounts of work under tight company control, foregoing wage increases and hour reductions that might have been obtained as their reward for what they had done to make the Japanese companies so efficient, and the need for international solidarity and joint bargaining.

Astute students of that industry attribute the Japanese success to the company union structure and the particular style of Japanese unionism that replaced the nascent industrial unionism of the early postwar period. The fundamental shift in Japanese industrial relations "was not a cultural accident; it was planned and well orchestrated."[13] By including white collar and blue collar workers in the same union the company with the active leadership of its white collar management workers who were both members and leaders of the company union were able to control production workers in a more dramatically effective way than under any other labor relations system known. The companies built second unions with the active participation of white collar workers who saw their future in management, not in solidarity with production-line blue collar workers.

This alliance enabled "mutual trust" and "love of the company" to "extinguish the red flag" from Nissan in 1953, which was the decisive battle in the war to defeat industrial unionism in postwar Japan. Taiichi Ono, the engineering genius most responsible for the development of the Toyota production system that will be discussed shortly, said long after the events of the early 1950s that he "still considered his success in controlling the union to have been the most important advantage Toyota gained over its domestic and foreign competitors."[14] Toyota had the added advantage of having chosen to locate outside of the main population centers in Aichi prefecture, where there were few alternative employment opportunities to the young men coming off the farms. Area residents tended to be grateful to the Toyoda family. When unrest threatened in the early 1950s the company could simply send conduct reports home to families of workers. As Cusmano reports: "In Japan, especially in a rural area where people were highly sensitive to public criticism, managers found that involving the family made employees conform more readily to company policy."[15]

Toyota's influence still pervades the company town atmosphere and extends from its barbed-wire-fenced dorms for single workers with their single entrance and checkpoint to the schools that socialize the youth in the company's collectivist thinking. Most of Toyota's workers came from the countryside in the 1960s and 1970s and have been separated from their own social networks to become total Toyota people. They have little life outside of the company-organized life provided for them of company-organized and company-sanctioned leisure. When a sample of Toyota workers were asked, "Who do you consult when you get in trouble concerning your work?", only one half of 1 percent said that they consulted a union representative.[16] The decision to locate in what was then a rural backwater has served Toyota well. It was able to get work discipline and a "flexibility" from its more docile farm-bred labor force than its major competitor Nissan was unable to achieve in its more centrally located factories from a more sophisticated urbanized labor force.

After the defeat of militant independent trade unions in the auto industry the companies could enforce open-ballot elections of unopposed candidates who were chosen from a small group of labor officials using union posts as stepping stones in a career in company management. Union leaders were thus often more sensitive to the preferences of the company than to the desire of the workers. The union did traditionally get 100 percent of what it asked for in bargaining with the company, but this may have been because they met with company officials extensively before presenting their demands officially. Indeed, the distinction between the union's labor affairs departments and the companies' personnel departments were not always easy for an outsider to see.

Japan's early catching up was attributed to simply copying the U.S. industry. This was a misunderstanding of what evolved into a new and better way of making cars. U.S. efforts to catch up with the Japanese, however, were often copycat moves that failed to read important subtleties or to forge ahead of next-wave Japanese innovations.[17] As the U.S. auto industry strove to emulate the cars Japan built, the Japanese pushed to design new cars at a quarter of standard development and design costs. In the same way just-in-time organization devastated Detroit, innovation in the design process brought a second round of comparative loss.

After a decade of quota protection to give them a breathing spell to catch up with the Japanese, General Motors announced in 1992 that it was laying off 74,000 people, a quarter of its workers, closing six assembly plants, four engine plants, and eleven parts plants over a four-year period. It was the most dramatic in a series of cutback moves downscaling the once largest company in the world. As profitability of the Big Three U.S. auto producers fell, they raised money by selling their shares in Japanese firms. In 1989 General Motors sold 20 million shares of Isuzu for 20 billion yen, and Chrysler sold part of its stake in Mitsubishi Motors. If such trends had continued, it was easy to foresee the Japanese buying into the U.S. auto producers to save the once mighty from a great fall. There was nothing inevitable in such a trajectory. In 1992 the Ford Taurus edged out the Honda Accord to become America's best-selling car, and crisis in the Japanese economy slowed down the apparent juggernaut, revealing important weaknesses. American industry's ability to learn increased substantially over the 1980s.

The Just-In-Time System

Toyota changed from an American understanding of efficiency in the late 1940s. Before then, their workers, like ours, were encouraged to make as much as possible. After that period they were taught to make only what was needed according to plan. More than that was wasteful since it created unneeded inventory. Socially necessary labor time is reduced in the Japanese system in a continual process of institutionalized innovation. As a triumph of engineering and management, it represents a remarkable advance over traditional Fordist thinking. It is useful to examine the ways in which this is the case and to separate them from efficiencies arising from the more intense system of labor exploitation that is also part of the Japanese system.

It can be argued that Ford's River Rouge complex, in which raw materials came in at one end and finished cars went out at the other, was "the grandfather of just-in-time production."[18] It concentrated all aspects of Ford production in one area where everything from steel making to final assembly was carried out. The Rouge was also the home of the most militant unionists in the auto industry (the fabled Local 600 of the United Auto Workers). Unable to tame the militants, the auto industry moved to deconcentrate production to reduce its vulnerability to its workers. No new Rouge-like plants were built and the industry moved toward multisourcing and backup production facilities rather than putting all their eggs in one just-in-time–like basket. Of course, Ford's technology was primitive, but had labor been docile a similar system might have evolved. The Toyota system was made possible by the smashing of class conscious, indeed revolutionary, trade unionism in the immediate postwar years and the establishment of an enterprise version in which company loyalty was a central tenet. Toyota fired a large number of workers and then offered "lifetime" employment to a select group in return for their cooperation.

In Japan the average autoworker put in 2,210 hours in 1989, including 291 in overtime, which is higher than the average for all Japanese industries, which, of course, were much higher than elsewhere in the advanced capitalist world. As Toyota's president told a press conference that year: "These are busy times with more overtime work being done. There is no disputing the fact that working hours have increased, but in a sense this is a good thing." He went on to criticize the shortening of the work week for German auto workers negotiated by their strong sectorwide union after a militant struggle. "It seems that in West Germany, some people want to work more. When work hours are shortened too much, then we give up the right to work." In contrast, the Japanese autoworkers have given up the right *not* to work.

Both academic and industry experts and much of the informed public in the United States are familiar with the main elements of the Japanese production system: the Japanese word *kanban*, the cards that are attached to inventory and identify every part and its place in the production process and the just-in-time method of parts assembly, which "pull" inventory to the assembly line as needed can therefore be quickly summarized. *Kanban* is a kind of individualized custom production system under the control of central planning with decentralized initiative at the level of individual task responsibilities. As an organizational innovation it appears as the best way yet developed to deal with fluctuations in demand quickly and with minimal miscalculation while achieving economies of scale as well as those of scope. The computer-printed posterlike guide that is attached to the front of each vehicle that itemizes the detailed requirements for a particular item can be read by people and robot scanners. Every part has a number and each is delivered just-in-time for its intended use.

As has been noted the Japanese auto industry's just-in-time system was developed out of the necessities of a scarcity economy. The size of the postwar auto market was much smaller than was that in the United States, and it called for a different approach. Toyota's 1960 production was 155,000, of which half were *not* passenger cars. The domestic market was nonetheless intensely competitive. Success could not accommodate long runs of standardized products. Flexibility was forced by the limited size of the market and quick response was valued. The *kanban* method was particularly well suited to low-volume production consonant with low-unit cost by economizing on inventory.[19] (Toyota had borrowed the idea of replenishing stock as it was used up from the American supermarket system and adapted it to new purposes in the *kanban* system.) By the end of the postwar era Toyota was a world leader with 47,000 supplier companies.

This pull system (in which final demand calls forth specified inputs from component subcontractors) should be seen as an epoch-making change in the ways of thinking, of communicating, and of offering feedback between engineers and workers. The closely articulated production system is like a meticulously choreographed ballet. It requires training and proper worker attitude, hence the close relation between the production system and the industrial relations regime of regulating workers. The visitor watching an autoworker in a modern plant's choreographed movements is impressed by an efficiency some liken to that of a trained animal conditioned by the need to eat into an ultra-intensity of activity. Whether one is favorably impressed by the beauty of the movements or sympathetic with the plight of workers who perform these motions over and over, however, the length of the work year in Japanese plants must be an additional source of wonder. The knowledge of production workers is incorporated, and employment growth itself comes increasingly in engineering and from design jobs: such procedures institutionalize constant innovation. Until 1966 the number of units Toyota produced and the number of production workers grew proportionately. While output has risen dramatically since then the same number of production workers are employed in the early 1990s as in the mid-1960s. Nonproduction employees, who equalled the number of production workers in the late 1960s, were twice as numerous by the late 1980s.

The result of investment in engineering means constant improvement and innovation over all aspects of production, from Toyota-developed centrifugal-type paint atomizers to automatic guided vehicles (developed by the company to move materials around the plant). All of Toyota's automated equipment has the capacity to stop itself in the event of any problem. Toyota's large warehouse requires no human labor. They are computer controlled and retrieve parts automatically on computer-inputted request. Robots make turbo charger parts using precision casting equipment. Other robots use image recognition to identify parts stacked at random and retrieve the one needed as identified by the *kanban* number.

The Supplier System

Unlike the U.S. firms in the 1980s that produced 60–70 percent of their own parts, the major Japanese producers made only 30 percent and contracted out the rest through their system of affiliates. It is precisely this extensive but tightly controlled structure that has given the Japanese automakers such a competitive edge in world markets. While the Americans had moved away from dependence on independent suppliers and were adamantly antagonistic in their relation to those they kept on a short leash, the Japanese developed a different understanding of how to get the most from their suppliers.

The parts companies must race ahead to keep up with the latest technologies, which can require extensive investment on their part.[20] They can also be squeezed by the parent company. Ikko Shimizu's *The Keiretsu* is the story of "Tokyo Motors." It is based on events discussed in the press involving a Nissan supplier and is the tale of an absolute master–slave relationship. The library shelves are filled with other titles concerning the harsh treatment of suppliers and employees—*The Factory of Despair* and *Gloomy Darkness in the Auto Kingdom* capture the tone. In any event over half of the 53 percent manufacturing cost reduction in Japanese four-wheel vehicles between 1958 and 1965 was attributable to cheaper purchased parts.[21]

The system traditionally relies on subcontractors to subcontractors through five or six levels to the *nayakoujo*, or shed factories, in surrounding rural areas, where farm families work in a household form of production approximating the putting out system of the early Industrial Revolution. Of course, there has been a lessened dependence on the *nayakoujo* over time, but there are still many very tiny subcontractors who lead a precarious existence.

Many subcontractors have grown successfully right along with their parent. The Araco Corporation, for example, began life in 1947 as Arakawa Industrial Sheet Metal, Ltd., sponsored to produce parts and raw material for Toyota car bodies. It soon moved on to interior finishings and seats, then to car bodies and microbuses. By 1980 it had produced 1 million car bodies and started on Land Cruiser production sold under the Toyota label. Today, its five plants produce a variety of vehicles from buses to ambulances and vending vehicles (the kind that sell hotdogs and such from the side of the truck with kitchen facilities inside). In other plants it still makes seat frames, door trim, and other parts for Toyota. Very sophisticated technology is traded back and forth with Toyota, including transfer presses, robot welding, and computer-controlled cutting (some remotely directed from other facilities). Such first-tier contractors are impressive operations. They are closely integrated into parent-firm operations. (Our research group's visit to Araco, for example, was part of an overall tour of the company's operations designed by Toyota.)

A Japanese parent company has all subcontractor data and knows their operations well. There are few, if any, secrets. The parent firm assumes that costs will come down as the subcontractor gains production experience with a new part and prices it accordingly. The subcontractor must accept and plots to stay ahead of the curve.[22] In America there are certainly large and impressive parts suppliers as well, but they have traditionally existed in an antagonistic relation to the auto companies, who held back on technology and design, and negotiated hard for every nickel of advantage they could get. The Japanese supplier is a member of the family and takes pride in its own achievements and its affiliated partnership. It does not aspire to true independence. This combination of unity in production with close coordination and a corporate-designed system of internalized direction of tasks, constant striving for improvements in operation, and product design gave the Japanese an edge.

The just-in-time system requirement of close coordination of all aspects of production requires that labor processes of all departments are integrated, in Eishi Fujita's phrase, "as one body by perfecting high synchronization." The just-in-time system was completed in all Toyota factories in 1962, and was later taught to subcontractors. Workers are reassigned on short notice. In any case, duties are not set apart as in the rigid traditional American classification system; they overlap. In the 1960s Toyota insisted that a worker with free time was obliged to help fellow workers as necessary. This process of "observation of mutual help" was systematized further in the 1970s into a flexible manning system responsive to process changes in fluctuating production. The closely synchronized and integrated production process created a flexibility without which the new electronics-based automation technologies, such as robotics, would not have been introduced as easily and effectively.

Doing it right the first time means that in lean Japanese-style auto plants there are practically no rework areas because there is little reworking to perform. "By contrast," the 1990 Massachusetts Institute of Technology Motor Vehicle Program report tells us, "a number of current-day mass-production plants devote 20 percent of plant area and 25 percent of their total hours of effort to fixing mistakes."[23] The same sort of savings are attained by reducing inventory to an absolute minimum. When the MIT researchers originally designed their survey they had asked how many days inventory were in a plant. A Toyota manager had politely asked whether there was some error in translation: "surely, we meant *minutes* of inventory."[24] Time, of course, is money, and the Harbour study cited earlier found that the U.S. Big Three had costs per car of $600–700 for a sufficient inventory of parts. The Japanese just-in-time part delivery system meant a comparable cost of a mere $40 per car. The difference exceeded the labor cost disadvantage the U.S. producers had.

Worker Loyalty, Company Leadership

The degree of built-in quality in the work process requires that "each employee puts his entire mind on his work and assumes the responsibility of his specific job." When Toyota claims that the most important factor in the success of their production system has been mutual trust between management and labor, it is clear that without such industrial relations Toyota's production system would have been impossible. Toyota's employee suggestions—each employee makes an average of thirty-five per year, of which 97 percent (management says) are adopted, and the 6,800 QC Circles (in 1990)— are the concrete embodiment of the company slogan, "Good Thinking, Good Products." These instrumentalities provide both ideas to the company and a strict socialization to the worker whose mind becomes occupied with better serving the company. Workers are encouraged to see the work process as if they were managers themselves. Opinion differs as to the extent to which such participation empowers workers or, as critics say, conveys a false sense of partnership. Further questions arise as to worker motivation and whether outward cooperation is instrumentally a survival technique in a structured environment of coercion and class dominance. Worker suggestions are almost always for simplification of the group process and result in decreased labor time being required in production. The "lifetime" employment takes the edge off such suggestions, and the costs of not complying can be severe.

Such developments were also helped along because the company is never contested on the shop floor by a union acting independently of the company's will. At Toyota, the equivalent of foremen and straw bosses are union members. It is these people who are then typically elected union representatives. Since the red purges of 1950–1951, the election laws were tightened to prevent the nomination of insurgents. Only pro-company candidates are encouraged to run for union office.

Many production workers cannot endure the pressure of speedups, forced overtime, and shift changes. For some health is destroyed and they are forced to "retire" early despite the company's promise of permanent employment. The Toyota Labor Union cooperates in easing such workers out. The union does nothing for temporary and seasonal workers, part timers, and subcontracted workers. At major suppliers, such as Nippon Denso, no one can run for union office without the recommendation of the company union's executive committee. In other suppliers, rank and file nominees are harassed, as are those who sign their petitions. If all else fails, the Establishment counts the ballots. Counting is closed to members. At the Toyota Automatic Loom plant, and it is surely not the only such case, researchers find those who vote against the officially sanctioned slate to face punishment.

The legends of the great founders are an important element in the company mystique that serves to bind a corporation's community, to form its culture of citizenship in much the same manner as stories of George Washington and the cherry tree did to now long-dead generations of Americans. Japan is still in touch with the living memory of such men. Sakichi Toyoda, founder of the family empire, is quoted on one Toyota booklet as telling his son, "Kiichiro, I have worked hard for many years with my looms. Now it's your turn. Go do the same with the automobile." One pictures a diminutive Charleton Heston listening to a bearded patriarchal figure with a divine countenance to match the swelling music. It is remarkable the extent to which executives consume the inspirational pamphlets and books to capture the indomitable spirit of the founder, their unshakable determination to conquer mountains, and to let nothing stand in their way. Will and earnest resolve to conquer that once proud kamikaze pilots all had (at least in the movies) is now turned to corporate dominance and team success in world markets. (The money Sakichi Toyoda turned over to his son telling him to found the new venture manufacturing automobiles was the £100,000 of royalty income for his patents on the automatic loom from Pratt Brothers.)

An important determinant of product quality is the production workers' state of mind, which in Japan involves what is generally desirable from a long-term corporate perspective being maintained uppermost in the consciousness of the laborer. In the United States consciousness is not coopted so easily. The presumption is that as long as an acceptable performance by the worker is forthcoming, the company has no further purchase on the soul of the worker. The American system details aspects of his or her job and mandates a strict adherence to fixed rules. In practice workers often know better how to do the job than the writers of the manuals do, and "working to rules" is a powerful tool in a slowdown situation in which workers painfully do only as they are told and no more. In fact, everything cannot be prespecified by management.

The Japanese system combines careful training on all details and guidance with general instructions in the context of overpowering socialization, counting on the worker to know how to do the job better and improve constantly on performance. As the Toyota manual states, the company maintains a philosophy of valuing practical experience over theoretical knowledge. This signifies, according to the company, that "workers should actually improve the things they are handling and ascertain the effects of such modifications for themselves." This puts extreme pressure on workers who are expected to solve problems that are the responsibility of management in the American system. This philosophy pervades every aspect of production and is built into a number of effective mechanisms. For example, the reason the line is stopped if a defect is found in the way the production process is designed, no matter how small, is the need to improve the line's operation in the future by reengineering the glitch. By tracing the cause, which the workers can usually do, it can be prevented from occurring again. In Japan, if one pulls the cord (to stop the assembly line because some problem has been encountered), and does this "too often," it is a reflection on the inadequacies of the worker. Such behavior will affect one's future pay, bonuses, and promotion prospects negatively. In America, in Japanese-run plants, the opportunity to pull the cord has been a big plus. The question, after a transitional period, is whether the Japanese norm be implemented in American transplants. Can the full Japanese labor relations regime so dominate in American plants that the more totalizing Japanese production system can be applied?

The egalitarianism of the Japanese system is relative and constrained by a powerful incentive system of pay and status differentials, with significant material benefits going to those who cooperate most effectively in carrying out company goals. Considerable disparities in wages occur between workers of the same age and seniority. They are paid according to their supervisor's and personnel department's merit rating and, according to the grade of work to which they are assigned. This assignment reflects evaluation of the commitment of the workers, their "attitude," and their performance.[25]

The importance of technical people being able to observe things closely in day to day factory operation, to see a project through from concept to the end of the first year or so of production, contrast with the strict division between design and production in Detroit before the coming of the Japanese. Halberstam's classic description in *The Reckoning* of the way engineers designed a new model car and threw it over the wall to the production people, who had to actually make the thing work, reflected a culture in the American auto industry that was vastly inferior to the Japanese system.

Engineering is a task carried out at all levels of the company. Workers in Japanese factories, because they know more about more tasks and how they can be combined and modified even to minute degrees, can save a second or two here and there. They are able to make suggestions that save management millions. The results can be impressive. A famous MIT study drawing on the Japanese terminology reports: "We call their system 'lean' production [actually, the Japanese call it this as well] because it uses less of everything than a comparable mass-production—half the human effort in the factory, half the manufacturing space, half the investment in tools, half the engineering hours to develop a new product."[26]

David Friedman, writing on the U.S. auto industry's efforts to produce a world car and other product standardization efforts, wrote prophetically in the early 1980s:

> Market *uncertainty* seems likely to increase in the future, if this is so, flexibly organized firms will be in a much stronger market position than more standardized companies. Indeed, American companies may well create a chronic readjustment problem by trying to find a new standard design where none can survive.[27]

The Japanese industry did not adopt the global car strategy of sourcing various parts from lowest cost producers worldwide, as did the Americans. In the second half of the 1980s, as they moved to produce abroad under pressure of the stronger yen and foreign pressures, they localized production complexes (including supplier firms and even design studios) in key markets and, in the 1990s, to a different conception of the global car strategy that used multisourcing as a counter to market uncertainty. Major Japanese producers developed a capacity to produce cars in the three market areas (Japan, Europe, and the United States) that could be shipped to the other markets. By increasing or decreasing production in as many plants as needed to smooth out production globally and shifting the pattern of exports and imports to meet cost considerations (and no doubt political pressures) the sum of disruptions would be minimized.

Because of labor shortages Toyota built plants far from its home base in Hokkaido, the northernmost island, and Kyushu the southernmost one. Japanese automakers learned from their experience with U.S. transplants that longer supply lines and significant departures from localized just-in-time production could be managed. In fact, there are costs to the system in heavy pressures brought about by the immediate delivery system from lines of trucks parked on nearby roadways waiting for their designated arrival time to the constant fraying of nerves that such taut production brings in its wake. Indeed, relocation was necessary as older plants could not be easily refit or expanded in urban areas and congestion limited deliveries and forced building inventory.

By 1992, for the auto industry as a whole, labor costs were higher in Japan than they were in the United States.[28] The system itself could not be reproduced given rising costs and a surprising diminution of competitive advantage. The American auto industry was also gearing up to export right-hand drive cars to Japan, something almost unimaginable a few years earlier. The lesson that to compete globally a producer must be able to carry the battle to the opponent's home grounds had been learned.

The Transplants

When Japanese auto companies first opened plants in the United States American managers had smiled at the Japanese penchant for overanalyzing everything, investigating in great detail what went wrong in any foul up, and insisting on the ultimate goal of *baka yoke* (foolproof) production methods. When Japanese transplants screened tens of thousands of workers, giving the best prospects days of tests (everything from reading comprehension to ability to assemble small parts and getting along with others), many in Detroit said "an autoworker is an autoworker is an autoworker. You push 'em and they still won't work, but playing nice with them sure won't do anything but cue them to take advantage of you."

That attitude changed as the care the Japanese took in interviewing at length, and hours-long testing in reading, writing, and math skills, being observed in discussion groups and simulated team assignments, paid off in higher productivity and quality products. The Americans, less sure of themselves as automakers, were soon mimicking Japanese concern for quality, which became "Job One." GM, as we saw, bet on a technology fix and invested a king's ransom, but did not have the production system to use it effectively, nor the industrial relations regime to make it work as the Japanese would have. They were also pushed by competition at both ends with Korean producers who began to squeeze them at the bottom end even as the Japanese moved to take over the luxury market.

An International Metalworkers Federation report noted that Korean workers who build a Ford Festiva work 80 percent more hours per year than a U.S. Ford worker—ten hours per day, six days per week, with only one week's vacation per year, all for $1.60 an hour.[29] The U.S. producers were caught between the Japanese, whose greater efficiency was based on a combination of better management and the industrial relations regime that produced more intense and high-quality labor response and the low-wage industrializing countries with their extensive exploitation. The Japanese showed the way out of the dilemma. The question was could the American companies reverse long-standing habits. The NUMMI collaboration was part of GM's effort to do just this.

As numerous visitors have noted, "The NUMMI plant has nothing noteworthy in the way of high technology, with the exception of its modern Japanese stamping plant. . . . What distinguishes it is the Toyota production system, which means its management. It is in essence a Japanese plant with American workers."[30] Most noteworthy, NUMMI had tried carrot solutions in place of American management's stick methods. For example, NUMMI cut down on the number of workers who go out and get drunk by offering lunchtime pay for those who stayed in the plant. The Framingham officials never got it. By now those plant managers who are still employed have learned the theory, even if they still sometimes have trouble with the practice.

At NUMMI traditional U.S. labor–management relations and Big Three production practices were replaced by Japanese-style organization. The American industry standard of nearly 200 job classifications was reduced to four. The old GM plant described by a company official as "one of the worst plants in the industry" was reopened with 85 percent of the initial work force composed of former GM workers. NUMMI ran the line much faster than conventional American auto plants and the union proved cooperative to the speedups because it was anxious that "co-management" be seen to work.

A large part of what was going on in this most studied of the transplants, the NUMMI joint venture run by Toyota and co-owned by General Motors, was summed up by the local United Automobile Workers union leader, Tony DeJesus, who explained that the workers "are doing what they have wanted to do for years. There is a big break from all those grievances now that everybody is working together, well maybe not everybody, but unlike the past when "we were always defending people who didn't give a damn," now, he says, "we make it clear we won't be babysitting you any more. You're responsible for your actions."[31] The new work relations had the double edge of the Japanese system: incentive to cooperate with union help, and little mercy for those who did not perform as demanded.

Interpretation of aspects of the plant's performance are highly contested. Some workers complain, for example, that the lower absenteeism that management sees as a plus results from fear of suspension rather than higher job satisfaction, and NUMMI turnover has been high. Others do report greater job satisfaction and appreciate the job security the long arrangement promises. Different researchers have valianced such findings in conflicting ways.[32]

While Toyota claimed (in my interviews in the fall of 1990 at their Japanese headquarters) that they saw no difference in productivity between unionized workers in the United States and nonunionized employees, Nissan has seen American-style unionism as a major impediment. The U.S. president of Nissan maintained that "[we] have to be union-free in order to have the type of communication with our employees that we must have in order for us to build quality products."[35] On a tour of a Mazda plant in Japan, my guide, Keiji Motoyama (vice director of the second production department and a man responsible for production for some years in their Flat Rock plant), offered the familiar joke, when I expressed approval of a particularly innovative robotics application, that they (the robots) did not join unions and worked hard. Unions, of course, meant U.S.-style independent unions. A house version exists at the plant we were touring, but is viewed as a tool of management. It is possible that Toyota has done a better job of winning the hearts and minds of their workers, or at least a more willing cooperation, or that the front office might have given me a different impression at Mazda.[36]

There have been similar differences in interpreting GM's own venture, the new Saturn company, a company within a company that GM promised its workers (when a memorandum of agreement concerning the enterprise was signed with the UAW in 1985) would be "a different kind of company" and for its customers "a different kind of car." It was a struggle. When the first Saturn rolled off the line in October 1990 neither the buying public nor the workers were not initially all that happy. When the car did not do as well as expected (since 20 percent of workers' pay was tied to profits, they were unhappy), the workers complained that since they did not design the car why should they pay for its problems. In the fall of 1991 when GM Chairman Robert Sempel visited the Saturn plant in Spring Hill, Tennessee, he was met by United Auto Worker demonstrators complaining that management was trying to increase output at the expense of quality. Ironically, the pressure to "move the metal" came from positive buyer acceptance of the Saturn. According to independent surveys Saturn owners recommended their cars to more people than the owners of any other brand, including luxury lines. GM had tried to take advantage of the uptick in sales, but, as they did so, the defect rate shot up. The workers objected since their pay over the long run depended on the reputation and so the continued sales performance of the car. They were the long-term patient investors. The company gave in, but such problems of inter-mittent short-term time horizons on the part of GM persist.[37] Worker effort was widely understood to have made a tremendous difference in car quality. Sales took off and GM had trouble keeping up with demand. This led to cutting corners in the training of new Saturn workers who were not socialized in the cooperative team consciousness or driven to regularly work fifty hour weeks. Morale problems also rose.

These skirmishes were not new to company–labor relations in the American industry. The UAW had raised the quality issue early in the postwar period and had been told by top management to mind its own business. In 1973 Irving Bluestone, who was a UAW vice president, sent a memo to the company as well as to all of the union's locals at GM entitled, "Quality is our concern too." He warned that GM was spending half a billion dollars in warranty costs and that declining quality "may well be followed by declining sales." Dissatisfied customers, he also wrote, "often turn to foreign imports." When enthusiastic unionists posted the memos on union bulletin boards at the auto plants GM demanded that they come down because, as a company vice president told Bluestone, "quality is management's job—not the union's." This answer may explain in part why it took Detroit so long to pay attention to Deming, who stressed that the company needed to "restore the dignity of the hourly worker.'' Deming's statistical quality control method is based on the premise that defects are caused by poor systems, not by workers. The problem is always management. By tracing a problem back to its ultimate cause the Japanese modified the system so that it would not happen again. American managers preferred to blame the dumb workers. It took two crucial decades before the American auto companies learned some of the lesson. They still do not totally accept that workers want to do a good job and that it is the company that usually stands in their way, as Deming said.[38]

It has been said that the U.S. operations of Japanese automakers represent branch assembly plants and that the learning involved in innovative design and production *kaizen*ing, constant improvement, for the most part, takes place in Japan. It is there that the ''debugging'' of the assembly line takes place in the new model shakedown period before the smoothly running operation is transferred as an assembly line operation to the United States. Some learning certainly takes place for U.S., or Mexican, or European workers in local operations, but the meaningful gains go to Japan. As Candace Howes asserts:

> Since the assembly process is among the most mechanized and hence immutable parts of the production process, there is less room for worker input into the production process than in the case of the design process or batch production. If the Japanese assembly workers make necessary changes during the start-up process in the sister plant in Japan, then the work of American production workers can be reduced to that of machine tenders.[39]

From this perspective the advantages of team performance is more apt to be found in its mutual monitoring and elimination of the need for most of the expensive supervision in the U.S. system rather than involving discretionary roles in evolving new production processes, as in the Japanese case.

I hesitate to read too much into such differences, either among the Japanese and the American producers or between the two since there has been a continual learning process in which American producers have caught up in many regards only to fall behind and then perhaps to pull ahead in market share, quality, consumer satisfaction ratings, and so on. The point is not that the Japanese are uniquely suited to build better cars, but that the techniques they have introduced have set new standards for the global automobile industry and that Japanese managers can implement their system poorly and Americans can adapt it well. The shrinking quality differences among newer Japanese and American plants by the early 1990s showed a transfer of know-how to the Americans.

Competitiveness and Presidential Politics

One way to stay ahead is to localize Japanese industries in markets around the world, give them independence to buy and design locally, and adapt to local preferences, politics, and peculiarities. Thus, flexibility in approach is a large part of successful competitive strategy. Again, there is much about making a virtue of necessity in this strategy. In 1990 the Japanese auto industry engaged in production in some forty countries. They had been drawn to most of these arrangements by host-government imposition of some form of domestic content regulation, not by free trade considerations of their own economic interests in a market sense.

In the early 1980s the United Auto Workers pushed domestic content legislation as a way of saving its members' jobs. The plan, which was based on legislation already in effect in twenty nations, was dismissed in the Congress as interfering with free trade. In the 1970s Toyota, for example, had built parts-manufacturing facilities in Indonesia, Thailand, Australia, and Brazil in response to nationalist requirements. Toyota's suppliers also followed their assembly plants abroad over a decade before either located facilities in North America. Yuasa Battery, a Toyota supplier, established an Indonesian joint venture in 1975 in response to a threatened ban on imported batteries.[40] Had the United States in fact legislated a domestic content law it would have forced the *American*-owned auto companies, which had responded to their crisis by outsourcing more models and parts from abroad, to modernize their domestic facilities and to adopt Japanese techniques much earlier.

The first Japanese assembly plant in the United States, as noted earlier, was opened by Honda in 1982. By the late 1980s, 80 percent of Honda Accords and Civics sold in the United States were being produced in its Marysville, Ohio plant. Honda spent hundreds of millions of dollars on U.S. parts plants producing engines, transmissions, brakes, and other components. Honda's integrated production facility included engineering and design components. Honda moved hundreds of design and manufacturing engineers to the United States and hired hundreds of American engineers and designers as well to conceptualize and then build a new car in the United States for the American market.

When Honda Accord production had to be cut back at the Marysville, Ohio plant in 1993, Honda used the time for intensive training instead of laying off hundreds of workers until business picked up. This was, the company said, because it chose to teach workers new skills as an investment in future productivity, not because the company had made any guarantees to employees against layoffs. The tactic certainly played well in Bill Clinton's Washington with the administration's emphasis on education and training as the route to revitalizing manufacturing in America. Among the 600 courses offered by Honda were pneumatics, hydraulics, and electronics, as well as export marketing, Japanese, and quality surveying. The Big Three American producers continued to pay their employees to go home during such slack periods.[41] When the company designed its 1994 Accord it paid $0.5 million for each of sixty U.S. engine and production specialists to move with their families to Japan for two or three years to take part in the process—money well spent based on the contributions the Americans made. It is interesting that when divisions of opinion arose they were between design engineers and production engineers, not between Japanese and Americans.[42]

"Our dream is to increase our engineering and product development resources in the United States to establish a self-reliant auto company in America as part of an international organization," Honda's president told the American press. "There used to be one major player in Honda—that was Japan. Now, we will have two, Japan and the United States, with both supplying cars worldwide." This seemed a creditable prospect. Half the company's world-wide sales (and most of its profits) originate with its U.S. subsidiary. Even for Honda of America, however, the most indigenized of the transplants, its localization was not an uncontested, transparent process. By the early 1990s Honda was claiming 75 percent domestic content for the two-thirds of its cars sold in North America. Commerce Department spokespeople called such a claim by Honda and similar ones by Toyota and Nissan for their cars assembled in the United States "a sham."[43] The U.S. Customs Department (a division of the Treasury Department) found Honda to have less than 50 percent local content and claimed that Honda owed $20 million in back tariffs for 1990. The issue became murkier when the Bush administration trade representative, Carla Hill, at the same time insisted to the Europeans that "this is an American car" to gain it favorable access to European markets as a non-Japanese prod-uct. As customs investigators examined Honda's alleged domestic content at their Anna, Ohio, engine plant the officials came up with more than $700 million in parts coming from suppliers in Japan or transplant parts makers wholly or partially owned by Honda, and only $52 million worth of U.S. parts. By Honda's own accounting, the biggest item of local content added at the Anna engine plant was depreciation of the factory's equipment (machinery mostly imported from Japan). Issues of transfer pricing were also raised. Were parts coming from Japan underpriced for customs purposes to lower the value of Japanese content in the cars?

In a declining auto market nationalism was on the rise. The United States Motor Vehicle Manufacturers Association expelled Honda, its only Japanese member, in 1992. Despite announcements by the Treasury Department that they intended immediate action to stop Honda from importing cars from Can-ada duty free and of actions to collect tens of millions of dollars in duties, no action was taken. Honda's law firm's man in Washington, the Treasury Department's former general counsel, had asked for and immediately received a meeting with his former associates—and without any Customs Service offi-cials being invited. Following the meeting Treasury officials assured Honda by letter that the audit was not complete. Political pressures and counterpressures were intense. The $100 billion auto parts industry in the United States with its 600,000 workers was the largest single sector of the U.S. economy. The Canadi-ans saw the customs move as an attempt to intimidate the Japanese from investing in Canada. A former president of the Canadian Automotive Parts Manufacturers Association called the customs action "terrorism." There was little agreement within the Bush administration concerning what to do or even how to think about what was at stake. Three years after the U.S.–Canadian Free Trade Agreement the Customs Department has not issued regulations. This left the Japanese automakers free to use their own preferred methods. Toyota, asked about their questionable ways of counting domestic content for their U.S.-assembled cars, responded that they "want to accent the positive." So did the Bush administration, only it was more confused as to what that might mean. They were ideologically divided and could not agree among themselves. Their trade negotiators could hardly be blamed for inconsistency and temporizing.

The issue is of no small importance. The *main* advantage for Japanese transplants is that they buy standardized parts from nonunion transplant suppliers who pay on the average 40 percent lower hourly compensation than the U.S. car parts suppliers sector as a whole. The disadvantage for GM was particularly severe. In the late 1980s 50 percent of its parts were produced in-house using union labor (compared with 40 percent for Ford and 30 percent for Chrysler but substantially less for the Japanese transplants). Even if the transplants had paid similar base wages, benefit costs—especially medical and retirement—gave them a tremendous advantage ($2.50 to $5.50 an hour per worker).[44] Howes estimates that by the mid-1990s (from a base of 1982) Japanese auto producers would have cost the U.S. 200,000 auto jobs and American workers some $6 billion per year in annual income lost as a function of their policies of sourcing parts from abroad and replacing Big Three production with those assembled by lower-cost transplants. Still, by the 1994 model year, by the stricter U.S. government standards then in force, 73 percent of the new Accords were local content. (Honda claimed 82 percent domestic content.) Honda's fifth generation Accord for the American market, the 1994 model, was the responsibility of a U.S. design team and many of its 320 U.S.-based suppliers had worked with the team. Political pressures, the soaring yen, and Honda's commitment to an American-based car had done their work.

Things were bound to continue changing and to become worse for unionized North American workers with the entry of Mexico into a North American trade zone that offered both the Japanese and the American auto producers a low-cost venue. Mexican wages, which had been 30 percent of those in the rest of North America in 1981, were only 11 percent of those in the United States and Canada by 1989. The Latin Americans' "lost decade" had made the Mexican leaders more willing to accept loss of economic sovereignty in exchange for foreign investment and job creation. The quality of production in Mexican auto plants was high. GM's Arizpe assembly plant was the best in North America at the beginning of the 1990s. Ford's Hermosillo plant had the third lowest defect rate of any plant in the world according to the J. D. Power survey. Mexicans had accepted Japanese labor relations after some initial resistance, which the company experts chalked up to their "immaturity." It seemed they resisted *kaizen*ing which might create unemployment. As an American researcher was told: "The engineers are the ones who do the time studies because the people are not mature enough yet in this matter. Taking out a working buddy to give more work to others, well, the people are not mature enough to do that. We are trying to help them mature . . . "[45] The particular plant was a U.S.-owned one that was a direct copy of an affiliate's factory in Japan, which raises the question of what cut of auto profits American firms will get from the Japanese. The examples of world-class productivity at

North American plants also allows us to distinguish between efficient factories, many of which are found on this continent, and inefficient ones, which also exist in Japan.

Admiral Bush Steams Into Tokyo and Gives Up His Dinner

George Bush went to Tokyo in 1991 in the context of the imminent U.S. election. The purpose of the trip, the president said, was "jobs, jobs, jobs." Mr. Bush's visit, the first by a U.S. president in eight years, came at a time when the Japanese were anxious to discuss foreign affairs, especially Asia. The specter of dramatic changes in China, possible unification of Korea, and other developments affected them, and they looked to American leadership. The Japanese prime minister himself in trouble at home wanted to appear states-manlike. Mr. Miyazawa was able to get the U.S. side to sign on to some boiler-plate sentiments concerning "our global partnership," in what was dubbed rather pretentiously the Tokyo Declaration. Mr. Bush, however, ar-rived as a heavy-handed auto salesman in an exercise, as Japanese editorial writers said, to mix images, of "gunboat diplomacy." It was an odd and counterproductive meeting. On the one hand it had the trappings of the first meeting between rival superpowers of the post–Cold War era, but on the other it was a huckstering extension of domestic politics—another photo op.

Mr. Bush's crusade to open Japan's auto market resulted in an agreement by the Japanese auto companies to make efforts to sell as many as 20,000 American cars per year (in addition to the 16,000 or so then being sold through American franchise dealers). The agreement seemed to be accepting a selling quota and an instance of government-managed trade. Commerce Department officials explained that "we could not appear to be agreeing to specific num-bers," which would be quotas, and managed trade, which they were in princi-ple against. Yet, the problem with vague promises was that the United States had received them in the past and they had not been honored. Only hard numbers were likely to work, and so numerical goals were necessary if prog-ress was to be made. (Civil Rights leaders might take note here.) In any case, said the U.S. officials, the agreement had been announced by the auto executives, not by the governments. The agreement was between private par-ties, totally voluntary; indeed, they were based on "unilateral" proposals from the Japanese companies themselves and so could in no way be considered managed trade. "In no way does it constitute an agreement," a senior admin-istration official briefed reporters a few hours after President Bush had referred to "the agreement." Mr. Bush later claimed credit for the auto industry "ac-tion plan."[46] Actually, the origin of the plan, down to the specific numbers, was in a MITI proposal that the Japanese auto producers accepted as *gyosei shido* (administrative guidance), the very thing to which polite Bush Adminis-tration trade officials did not like to call attention. When the Clinton team came in there was far less ambivalence in demanding quantitative measures of progress from the Japanese. Partly this was a result of the frustrations of the Bush team.

While the president hailed the 1991 agreement with the Japanese automakers, the chairman of Ford said, "There is no agreement." It was another promise to try to do more. The Japanese negotiators agreed to targets. The American politicians chose to hear commitment rather than goal. Even if there was 100 percent success in this endeavor, however, the total cars sold would equal seven tenths of 1 percent of the over 5 million cars sold annually in Japan at a time when the Japanese were selling 30 percent of the cars sold in the United States. Further, it was likely that any increase in U.S.-made cars would be produced in U.S. factories owned by the Japanese. Under Clinton Administration prodding there were plans to buy more U.S.-made parts. (It was estimated that perhaps 80 percent of these would come from Japanese suppliers here.) The ramifications of the agreement, however, were quite important. The United States, which had advocated free markets and opposed negotiated trade, seemed to be lending its support to a changing of the rules or maybe even suggesting the Japanese accept a new game. Jean-Pierre Leng, the European Community's ambassador to Japan commented: "If the game we are playing changes from bridge to hockey, then we will want to have a hockey team."[47]

Clinton's new "hardball" (or hockey) approach came at a difficult time for Japan. Certain trends had become clear. The background of Mr. Bush's trip had been more than simply a troubled economy; it was a global crisis. The United Nation's World Economic Survey data show a zero global economic growth for 1991, down from a mere 1 percent in 1990, 3 percent in 1989, and over 4 percent for 1988. At the time of Mr. Bush's visit Japan was experiencing its worst year in over a decade. The Japanese domestic market was saturated and car sales had been stagnant for some time. As Mr. Bush was visiting Tokyo the Japanese Automobile Manufacturers Association was reporting the sixth consecutive year-on-year decline in cars, trucks, and buses exported. Things worsened for the first half of the 1990s even as Mr. Clinton's demands escalated.

In early 1993 Nissan announced it would shut its Zama plant in a move that shocked the industry. For thirty years the Zama factory had been a symbol of Japan's economic miracle. The announcement of its planned closing was denounced by militant unionists who saw it as part of a global rationalizing of production that would cost Japanese autoworkers jobs. Mazda canceled its planned Amati luxury sedan that was to be marketed in the U.S. in 1993 as a result of its first pretax loss in forty-five years. Yet, in the crisis they faced, the Japanese automakers did not follow the slash and burn plant closings of the Americans (especially General Motors); rather, they made plans, as in the case of Zama, to transfer some workers and offer early retirement to others while avoiding firing outright any of the core work force. The automakers also cut the number of options and models offered and pinched pennies in 1,000 places: Taillights were hooked up with one connector instead of two, a smaller plastic clip was used to anchor the body's weather stripping, and so on.

Flexibility in an era of slow growth and rising trade tensions placed the auto industry and the Japanese economic system more broadly under new types of pressure. As in the past the developmentalist state was there to help the companies make adjustments. Following Mr. Bush's trip to Tokyo MITI pressed Japanese carmakers to raise prices of cars sold in the United States. Norihiro Kono, deputy director of MITI's auto division, said: "We're encouraging them not to pursue market shares so aggressively. We can't tell them what to do, but we are suggesting that they raise prices, lengthen model cycles, and decrease their working hours."[48] MITI did make suggestions. It also exercised its authority and made clear that noncooperation would carry penalties. When MITI lowered the number of cars Japanese automakers would be allowed to export to the United States by 28 percent, Toyota's managing director overseeing North American operations said, "That's more than pressure. It's an order. If we violate the regulation, we will be punished."[49] The Japanese automakers were forced to speed up their timetables to produce more cars in the United States, even though their costs in doing so, given existing capacity, were higher per car delivered to the American market than they were if they came from Japan.

The politics of protectionism in the case of autos demonstrates the complexity of the matter and the cross-cutting interests involved. Toward the end of President Bush's term House Democrats offered a plan to limit Japanese sales that would have included cars produced by Japanese-owned factories in the United States. It was withdrawn after objection from Democratic representatives from districts with transplants and joint ventures. The plan was not aimed at saving jobs of U.S. autoworkers, but at protecting profits for U.S.-owned companies and the jobs of their unionized workers. (Only 3 percent of the UAW's 900,000 members were at the transplants despite a decade-long organizing effort.)

The Future

It is not clear that either the Japanese or the American companies will do all that much for employment in the U.S. auto industry. This is true for two reasons. First, because the new plants require far fewer workers so that whether U.S. autoworkers are employed by the Japanese or American car producers they face shrinking job prospects. U.S. producers, with the aid of the falling dollar, became more competitive in the early 1990s. A major MIT study found the best U.S.-owned plants in North America were nearly as productive as the average Japanese plant and very nearly equal in quality by the end of the 1980s. Other studies showed two of the three Detroit firms producing small cars more cheaply than Toyota, the Japanese low-cost producer. Second, as noted earlier, auto production within the North American market need not take place in the United States. The MIT group found Ford's Hermosillo assembly plant in Mexico to be the best in quality, both above the Japanese transplants in North America, and above the best Japanese plants. In the early 1990s Mexico began to be recognized as "Detroit South" since more American cars were being produced there: Ford Escorts, Dodge Ram Chargers, and Buick Centuries, among the over 1 million cars being made there for U.S.

and other markets. There were plans to double or triple the number within the decade. As the North American Free Trade Agreement reduced the significance of the border still further, more "American" cars will flow north, as will more Volkswagens from VW's plant in Puebla and Nissan factories in Cuernavaca and Aquacalientes. Mexico's *maquiladoras* have long provided low-cost parts to Detroit. Now, they form part of a more regionally articulated economy—Detroit South.

In the early 1990s the American producers gained market shares. The fall in the U.S. dollar had been the biggest reason for the cost advantage. But design time and quality of U.S. cars had also been exceedingly impressive. In terms of labor hours per car and total labor costs the Japanese has lost their advantage.[50] A strong yen had given the auto industry breathing space before. In the late 1980s it had used its exchange rate advantage to raise car prices, repurchase company stock, and increase compensation to industry executives—top management received five to six times their counterparts in Japan, a gap that increased in the early 1990s when salaries of top executives were cut from 20 to 50 percent in response to slumping profits.

Learning has gone on under duress in Detroit. Hard-headed "move the metal" executives had a hard time with the advice they were given about trust and "intimacy" in relations with their workers. Company cultures in America did not easily accept the need for cooperation, and signals were often mixed as companies ordered layoffs with one side of their mouths and asked for cooperation from their employees out of the other. In the absence of state-enforced protections for workers, institution of flexible relations depends on the balance of power between workers and company.

If the union surrenders shop floor control to quality circles and cooperative informal arrangements replace contract rules, the future of the workers will come to depend on the benevolence or farsightedness of the company in an economic culture that favors short-term thinking. As power relations shift, a British view of flexibility can become dominant. Ironically, the company may win by forcing cooperation on workers, but this does not mean it can expect the sort of teamwork the Japanese achieve in their home plants. There have simply been too many cases where concessions have been made, jobs surrendered to make plants viable, and the plants end up being closed. Opposition to concessions led to rebellion in the ranks. In Canada militants won election to national union leadership and broke ties to the Detroit-based UAW. In the United States it also became harder for the union to sell cooperation with management. On the other hand as the union loses power it becomes easier for the auto companies to restructure their industrial relations system along Japanese lines and to create modifications in their corporate culture.

A final important element in the Japanese production system is how management forms an obedient work organization. In the auto industry, as in other sectors, it is the "extraordinary hard work which more directly contributes to the profitability of Japanese manufacturers than the flexible job assignment system."[51] A key question is whether the Japanese managers can continue to get more work effort out of their labor force. There is an important difference between pioneering design concepts, the production system, and the industrial relations regime, although as we have seen they are intimately related, even if they can be separated conceptually. One way to think about the difference is to follow Toshio Kamo in making the distinction between efficiency-oriented reform and workers' consciousness control. The first includes job rotation, quality circles, just-in-time inventory, and so on, procedures that are accepted by American as well as Japanese autoworkers. The latter category includes personnel evaluation by immediate supervisors, company unions, shift rotation, and seniority wage regardless of task assignment. These have generally been rejected by American workers.

Same work, same pay, independent unions, and seniority rights in job choice and shift assignment—to say nothing of the right not to wear company propaganda, not to "voluntarily" attend company social functions and other sponsored events and, in general, to resist being socialized as good, well-behaved members of the family responding to gentle control by the wise parent (the company)—characterize U.S. norms of worker consciousness, especially in unionized plants. In the transplants, American workers successfully refused to have their wages based on the extent of the cooperation they demonstrated in these regards. Cooperation in the Japanese style and loyalty in these collaborative ways were for the most part not as forthcoming as the Japanese managers would have liked.

But I Don't Like Subtitles

Two movies that were playing in local theaters during President Bush's 1991 visit defined the two poles of Japanese popular awareness. The first was the latest Godzilla movie in which the legendary sea monster defends Japan against the predations of an alien power that is attempting to force Japan to adopt a foreign computer standard as a means of subjugation. The second was Mitsuo Kurotschi's *Traffic Jam*, which uses one family's attempt to make the 300-mile trip to the father's parents' home over the traditional New Year's return home holiday, which becomes travail on the level of Ulysses' journey, only a lot funnier than *The Odyssey*. The protagonist, greeted a few minutes out with a freeway sign offering the electronic message, "Stop and Go Traffic—Next 100 Kilometers," mutters, "They call this country 'rich Japan,' but who is rich? We're not rich if we can't even get home!" Both films are fun in their own way and Mr. Bush might have profitably skipped a banquet one night and gone to see a double feature. He would have gotten the message: "Japan is once more under attack by selfish and unscrupulous foreigners. We have our own problems which are quite serious and need to be addressed before helping rich foreigners who don't work as hard as we do and yet are trying to strong arm us so that they can continue to live beyond their means." President Clinton seemed even less inclined to see things from a Japanese viewpoint or to seek mutual accommodation.

The press coverage and the politicians' discussion, of course, play to the domestic audience. There is little effort to understand or communicate the view from the other side, or sides. Most important, the key question, which is how could our systems be modified so that workers and consumers in both countries could be considered within a single decision-making framework, was not asked. The discussion continued to be set in a competitiveness framework. The transformational perspective, while not absent, focused on technology and efficiency questions in which the impact of the labor process on workers was either ignored or examined through rose-colored glasses. Working in an auto plant remains a tough job. Indeed, the larger questions of hours worked, intensity of effort demanded, the way stress is managed, and how family and community life are influenced by job conditions and social relations was not really a part of the discussion. Because the Japanese advantage flowed in large part from its innovative system of labor relations, and that system has both extremely good and very bad aspects, I want to discuss it in greater detail. This is the project of the next chapter.

6

The Industrial Relations Regime

"Practically no one gets fired. And labor–management relations are, by our standards, astonishingly cooperative. In the U.S. and Europe, the 'us vs. them' attitude often impairs industrial productivity. In Japan, it is just 'us.'"

ALAN S. BLINDER, Gordon S. Rentchler Memorial Professor of Economics, Princeton University[1]

"Certainly, the strongest myth of Japanese industrial relations is permanent employment."

KAZUO KOIKE, Institute of Economics, Kyoto University[2]

"Let's think about slavery, then and now.

In the past, slaves were loaded onto slave ships and carried off to the new world. But in some way, aren't our daily commuter trains packed to overflowing even more inhumane today?

And can't it be said that today's armies of corporate workers are in fact slaves in almost every sense of the word?

They are bought for money.

Their worth is measured in working hours.

They are powerless to defy their superiors.

They have little to say in the way their wages are decided.

And these corporate slaves of today don't even share the simplest pleasures that forced laborers of ages past enjoyed; the right to sit down at the dinner table with their families."

TOSHITSUGU YOGI, who died February 1987
at the age of 47 from *karoshi*[3]

The literature on Japan stresses the greater efficiency of technology and the organization of production with a bow to the high savings rate, good work habits, and education system. Debate over the role of the state and alleged mercantilist policies typically rounds out the discussion. Just as we have seen that the Japanese developmentalist state needs to be understood historically in

140

the context of the complexities of Japan's unique development, so, too, is the idea that Japanese work hard needs to be interrogated with some care. The emphasis in this chapter is on ways in which the social relations structure production and the uniqueness of the Japanese industrial relations regime about which there are some disagreements, as this chapter's epigraphs convey.

The successful firms in each era of national preeminence do not simply adapt to market signals; they produce a new set of relative prices through boldly restructuring relations of production. This involves technological innovation, organizational transformation, and new labor relations. These three elements are woven into a new stage of accumulation. Changes in these "givens" are the dynamic propellants. Higher savings and investment rates and other neoclassical incremental changes accompany these initiating breakthrough developments.

The mainstream comparisons between the U.S. and Japanese economies, which do stress organization and technology within a competitiveness paradigm, do not typically give central importance to labor conditions and so ignore the extent to which the Japanese system is successful because it intensifies work effort and can exploit labor more efficiently. Higher productivity, intense work relations of participation, and institutionalized learning come at a price. The Japanese dual labor markets with their extreme institutionalized sexism produce a hierarchical stratification that keeps everyone in line by doling out relative privilege and enforcing obligation in ways that coerce all levels far more than the paler analogous labor market mechanisms elsewhere through the differential use of carrot and stick. For example, the prevalence of "voluntary" overtime, or the far better use of workers' mental capabilities to improve the organization of production (i.e., the fact that noncooperation is punished far more severely and is less likely in the Japanese system) are ways in which the Japanese industrial relations system is more conducive to higher productivity. As Americans are encouraged to "compete like the Japanese," the nature of work relations and the costs of job intensity need to be examined critically.

This Japanese system of intense exertion and mental control results in both the workers' greater physical exhaustion and what has been described as their "cultural and spiritual regression." Japanese workers are expected to put their companies first, before family, friends, community—everything—in a single-minded drive for greater efficiency. This is the Organization Man mentality with a vengeance. All other aspects of society become colonized by this narrow imperative. Human autonomy is reduced and the cultural space of civil society is limited. While the Japanese system of social relations of production is not unique, it carries the commodification of labor to new heights. With prosperity and greater awareness of norms in the other advanced nations there is increased resistance to such demands, and, as we will see in our penultimate chapter, raises questions about the future of the system in the post-postwar era.

The matter has been confused in public discussion. Japanese Prime Minister Kiichi Miyazawa's comment in 1992 that Americans lack a work ethic and had forgotten how "to live by the sweat of their brow"[4] was in part a rebuttal to charges that Japanese producers compete unfairly and that it was Japan's obligation to see that American companies do better. It was also, however, a defense of the Japanese industrial relations regime. The political discourse was highly emotional since it attributed blame for a system controlled by American management that did not use workers as efficiently as did the Japanese to the "lazy" American workers. It also avoided the question of whether Japanese workers should work as hard and as long as they did.

While Western critics, most centrally Karl Marx, have always accepted a cultural element in the cost of reproducing labor power, they have not always been sensitive to the extent to which it is possible. The Japanese case is most suggestive in this regard. Labor time has a cultural dimension that goes beyond relative bargaining power, labor market demand and supply conditions, and education. The historically accepted element needs to be inspected and analyzed. The coercive element embodied in the code of industrial discipline that employers impose is embedded in a larger cultural matrix that limits and augments its authority and possibilities. "Exploitation" is a more complex process than merely driving workers hard. Neoclassical economists and their models have been insensitive to the intensity of work and the organization of consent.

The rampant consumerism, with its stress on status symbols that can seem extreme to outsiders, may be related to the work intensity of the Japanese system. *Karoshi* (death through overwork) is facilitated by a regimentation that is part of the Japanese order. Mr. Yogi, whose poem introduces this chapter, is a well-known *karoshi* victim because a TV director, after reading an article Mr. Yogi's wife wrote for a newspaper, did a program called, "Why did father die?" Caught between his complaining staff and the refusal of his company, he suffered intense anxiety and mental stress. Though his job title was impressive he had little real freedom, and like many Japanese he felt he had no alternative but to meet the demands his company placed upon him.

Gavin McCormack writes,

> The *karoshi* may be the contemporary avatar of the wartime *kamikaze*—a statistically insignificant minority in the 1990s as in the 1940s—but what is striking is the prevalence through the intervening fifty years of an (officially promoted) ideology of subordination of the individual in the interests of needs of state and corporation.[5]

The widespread fascination with *karoshi* may at first seem too much ado about the phenomenon that while tragic would in the greater scheme of things appear to affect relatively few Japanese. A closer look at *karoshi* is called for, however, because the numbers involved are in fact surprisingly large and potential victims are part of a continuum that extends exploitative work relations quite widely and creates the expectational norms drilled into most Japanese.

Each year one in thirty Japanese office workers needs clinical treatment for depression, schizophrenia, or alcoholism. Such figures, however, are not as reliable as one would want. People with mental problems have historically been ostracized in Japan as elsewhere. The semi-public and private counseling programs that provide help-line advice report that company workers are regular callers. They call in part because of reluctance to go to clinics where their visits might be a matter of record for their companies. Mental health counseling in the Western sense is relatively new in Japan and most professionals stress medication and other medical approaches. The problems, however, are often caused by objective conditions on the job that need to be addressed by a transformation of work relations. As one long-term observer summarizes the situation: "The typical corporation claims almost all the waking hours of middle-class males. It totally exhausts their mental energies, and together with the informal hierarchy of schools is a major instrument for social regimentation."[6]

In most cases the victims go unknown to the broader public, although the formation of the National Defense Council for Victims of *Karoshi* is building awareness. Efforts to combat people being worked to death has become a social movement in Japan. A group of doctors and lawyers operate a hotline, *Karoshi* Emergency Call. There is also a Tokyo Association of Families Against *Karoshi* and other mutual support groups for the victims and families. The Japan *Karoshi* Foundation has even run ads in American newspapers to announce their protests declaring: "If you believe the Japanese work ethic is harming the American economy, you should see what it's doing to the Japanese," and describes some of the grisly details and the government's refusal to change a system that "has resulted in such massive corporate profits. They want things to stay the way they are."[7] The leading daily, the *Asahi Shimbun*, suggests that roughly 10,000 workers die a sudden death from too much stress and exhaustion. Yet, the government continues to stonewall. The Labor Ministry claims the relationship between circulatory diseases and fatigue has not been proved conclusively and overwhelmingly rules against workers in accident compensation cases.

Dr. Tetsunojyo Uehata of the National Institute of Public Health defines *karoshi* as

> [A] condition in which psychologically unsound work processes are allowed to continue in a way that disrupts the worker's normal work and life rhythms, leading to a build-up of fatigue in the body and a chronic condition of overwork accompanied by a worsening of preexistent high blood pressure and hardening of the arteries and finally resulting in a fatal breakdown.

The Ministry of Labor has defined overwork as a possible cause of death only in cases where the victim "worked continuously for twenty-four hours preceding death" or "worked at least sixteen hours a day for seven consecutive days leading up to death." Its rulings have declared that three or four hours of overtime every day cannot be classified as overwork. At the same time the government is loudly proclaiming the "goal" of 1,800 hours work per person per year, a goal that was set in the late 1970s in a period when work intensity was dramatically increasing and which was to have been met in 1992. That year the officially calculated work year was still well over 2,000 hours.

The real number of hours an average Japanese worker actually works is highly contested and is a subject to which we will give attention shortly.

The Ministry of Labor still uses a once highly confidential manual distributed in January 1988 to officials dealing with compensation claims that contains some revealing hypothetical cases. For compensation to be awarded for work-related death the alleged victim must have worked more than *twice* the regular hours during the *week* prior to collapse. One day off during the week prior to death disqualifies the victim for compensation *even if he or she had worked twice* the regular number of hours on the remaining six days of the week.[8]

As one Japanese study of *karoshi* observes: "What must be considered first when looking at the reasons for the enormous amount of overtime in Japan is the fact that industry relies on it."[9] Indeed, the Economic Planning Agency and the Ministry of Labor have noted that it is difficult to shorten hours because overtime acts as a buffer under the lifetime employment practice. A 1986 White Paper on Labor presented calculations by the Ministry of Labor that it would have taken a 63 percent overtime premium to equal the cost of hiring new staff. Companies faced with a legal premium of only 25 percent for overtime systematically understaff and rely on regular overtime work. The Labor Standards Law's Article 36 forces workers to accept such overtime as long as it is accepted by the worker's union in agreement signed with the company. Thus, the government's own directives limiting overtime are close to meaningless.

The RENGO-affiliated (RENGO is the counterpart to our AFL-CIO) All Japan Federation of Electric Machine Workers Unions, *Denki-Roren*, whose members work for Hitachi, NEC, and such, conducted a survey of workers in seventeen major electric and electronic goods-producing firms. They found that the average working hours in 1990 were 2,177, including about 343 hours of overtime, a forty-four hour work week based on a fifty-week year. Among workers with the same qualifications the survey showed a significant wage differential for continued service to the company. For example, at Hitachi among the hundreds of thirty-five-year-old men with undergraduate degrees, those in the highest pay rank earned 316,500 yen per month. Those in the lowest were paid 195,170 yen or close to forty percent less. This gap is almost exclusively the result of the "merit" ratings conducted over ten years by the worker's immediate superior. The system of subjective evaluation by direct supervisors to determine pay raises and promotion leads to the phenomenon of "hanging around" since being there is one important indication of loyalty.

It appears that the average Japanese works 500 more hours per year, or an average of ten more hours per week than their counterparts in France and Germany, the equivalent of three extra months per year. Even this figure may be an understatement because of so-called service work, hours donated to the company and not recorded on time cards, as well as the prevalence of work employees take home, which is greater than in other countries. Japan's banks are probably the worst offenders, with average hours worked per year still approaching 3,000 (compared with the official average in 1991 given by the government as 2,016 with 175 hours of overtime). In the banks there are hundreds of hours of overtime performed without pay. Some indication of the extent of such "service time," referred to as *sabisu zangyo*, is offered in data from a Labor Inspector raid on eighty branches of a dozen big financial institutions in 1992, when it was found that a third of the employees were improperly (according to the government's own lax standards) required by their companies to put in a large amount of unpaid overtime. The financial institutions were reprimanded, but not otherwise punished, nor were the workers paid the compensation the government judged they had coming.

Joint struggle to end such abuses is a difficult choice to make given the system. Section chiefs are given limited budgets for overtime and at the same time work schedules that are impossible to fulfill in the worker hours at their command. They personally have to sign overtime sheets that workers must personally bring to them. Thus, workers are under pressure not to ask for payment for as much overtime as they actually work and section chiefs to unlawfully not recognize overtime work that requires payment; therefore, companies can officially shorten the work week without loss of work time. Employees who complain suffer inferior work assignments and petty harassments. If they persist, they can be fired. Some, very few, have been reinstated under court order in a process that is grueling and time-consuming. A group of IBM-Japan workers succeeded after a fourteen-year struggle. Their case is far from atypical (except that they won).

Overtime, when paid, is compensated at 125 percent of hourly wages and is not included in the twice yearly bonuses, which run to about 30 percent on average of annual wages. Given the higher cost of adding new workers and this low cost of paid overtime, overwork is built in. Given all of this it is not surprising that the official calculation of the number of hours worked by the average Japanese employee is a highly contested matter. The Labor Ministry's figure for employees of companies with five or more employees in 1990 is 2,064 hours of work a year. Figures for hours worked come from the Monthly Labor Survey of establishments with thirty or more employees. Most workers in Japan (employed in smaller establishments) are therefore not included. They typically work longer hours than do the workers in larger enterprises. A special survey by the Ministry of Labor in 1986 found that workers in companies employing over 300 workers worked officially less than forty hours per week, but in companies employing under thirty over forty-five hours. Part-time workers in the large establishments are counted in calculating the average hours worked. Westerners usually base their average work figures on this series.

The Monthly Labor Survey relies on a company to provide the data. In contrast, the Labor Force Survey conducted by the Statistical Bureau of the Management and Coordinating Agency collects statistics from individual workers. Its survey finds an average of 250 more hours per week worked in a typical year than in the statistics provided by the Ministry of Labor for purposes of international comparisons. Time in work-related study groups such as quality control circles or socializing with co-workers or clients after work, rituals required of many workers, are not included in either government statistical series.

Estimates of actual unemployment in Japan involve so many measurement questions and value judgments that we must be suspicious of international comparisons. MITI itself suggests that by American measurement standards the official Japanese unemployment rate would have to be doubled. One attempt to reconcile the unemployment data suggests that if one combines the different ways of measuring real unemployment to form composite indices, the result is actually higher unemployment in Japan than in the United States over the 1977–1986 period. [10] The same source estimates that half of the active working class in Japan is part of the floating reserve army of low-paid and insecure workers who move from job to job (over two-thirds of this group is female), an estimate derived from an intimate knowledge of Japanese labor markets in firms with fewer than ten workers that employ most workers and for which data is not officially collected nor calculated in most studies by foreign labor economists. [11]

Patriarchy plays a significant role, further complicating matters. Cyclical downturns force women out of the labor force. Anne Hill writes: ''The historically low Japanese unemployment rate is in significant measure due to the large number of women employed in 'temporary' positions who appear to leave the labor force altogether during business slowdowns.'' [12] Nearly 30 percent of all working women in Japan remained self-employed or family workers (and so are not included in the average wage figures), [13] leading those making international comparisons of the role of women in the work force of different countries to conclude that the Japanese labor force continues to retain features characteristic of a developing nation. Because Westerners look at the large firms for Japan's secret of success, ''four-fifths of researcher energy has been put into investigating the careers of one-fifth of the labour force.'' [14] Thus, the high accident rate of small firms, the horrid working conditions of the majority of workers, and the far lower real pay per hour of the majority of Japanese workers are not studied. Data are not available and isolated case studies are considered insufficient basis on which to generalize.

Moreover, when we speak of dual labor markets and secondary workers we are talking primarily about sexual discrimination. Women account for 79 percent of temporary workers and 75 percent of day laborers in manufacturing. Their role as a buffer in the Japanese economy is a key aspect of the system. [15]

It is extremely difficult to reconcile the conflicting data and estimates, interpretations, and unofficial practices with officially proclaimed ones. To take another example, in early 1991 the ratio of job offers to job seekers was officially 1.4 : 1. Official unemployment was 2 percent and many employers were easing up on the rigid conformity, tying rewards more closely to individual performance because loyalty and devotion to work were allegedly being undermined by such a protracted period of full employment. Still, Japanese absenteeism was half the U.S. rate and workers on average were only taking half their allotted vacation time. Despite seemingly tight labor markets, as of the late 1980s only 6 percent of Japanese workers regularly enjoyed a five-day work week. Manufacturing production workers face compulsory overtime equivalent, on average, to 10 percent of their total working hours, but, again, such data omit most workers from consideration. Among contingent workers turnover is high, and unemployment is disguised and dramatically underreported in government unemployment statistics. Into the 1990s as disguised unemployment increased, firms kept millions of workers who were not strictly needed on the payroll; college graduates found it difficult to find work; hours on the job hardly fell as even the professional salarimen feared for their future prospects and sought to show no sign of slacking.

The average statistical worker is sexless. In fact, men work about fifty hours per week on average, women work forty. Men, therefore, work 400 hours more per year (using the Ministry's figures). When the statistics are fleshed out it becomes clearer that most Japanese men spend nearly all of their waking hours commuting and working for their companies. They have little time to be fathers, or to think of doing much housework. Japan was built on the six-day week and the longest work year in the industrialized world. The language of *geshukunin papa* (boarding house lodger fathers) and *tanshin funin* (bachelor husbands temporarily posted to some other city while their families remain behind) suggest something of the reality.[16] This image of workaholic fathers and overburdened mothers, who increasingly work outside the home at considerably lower pay than the men has created a machinelike quality to Japanese lives that is widely resented. It is also resisted by social movements for reduced hours so that a better home life is possible and to reduce sexual discrimination in the workplace and the home. On average Japanese workers take fewer than half the vacation days coming to them. This may represent an incredible loyalty to the company, as much of the literature would have us believe, or, as is more likely, results from a tremendous fear of the consequences of taking what they are entitled to and badly need.

Women workers are oppressed in special ways.[17] Few attain high rank within the organizations they work for because they are pressured to retire when they get married and have children. In 1990 only eight percent of all managerial posts were held by women and fewer than 1 percent of all women worked as managers. Almost all of the few women who do make it to section chief or higher are unmarried. The Labor Ministry interviews report company presidents as explaining that they do not know how to manage women ("They become emotional." They are also described as "shortsighted" and, of course, "don't fit in.") Only 3 percent of all professional positions at Japan's blue chip companies go to women. Japanese business continues to use a two-track system, shunting women into noncareer placements. Because the *sogoshoku*, or comprehensive employee, is expected to transfer locations when asked, work whatever hours are demanded, make complex decisions on behalf of the company, and supervise others, women are not considered suitable for such positions. They are tracked to the *ippanshoku* (general employee) category and limited to lower-level positions almost exclusively, the "mommy track" with a vengeance. It is actually easier for female junior college graduates to find employment than female university graduates. The return to female university graduates of more education is often zero as they are still typically paid the same rates as those with junior college degrees. [18] Japan's 1986 Labor Standards Law "urged" firms to "try to" equalize opportunity with regard to recruitment, hiring, job assignment, and promotion, but Japan ranks at the bottom for advanced nations in the labor market gender gap. [19] Measurement of this gap underestimates the difference between male and female earnings because of the importance of bonuses that go overwhelmingly to men. Women receive half the bonus on average, and, because they are disproportionately employed in smaller firms, they are substantially penalized in allowance for housing, family, shift work, and so on.

The systematic gender discrimination is rationalized within a larger understanding of alleged societal benefits of functionalist patriarchy. Women bear responsibility for reproducing the next generation. The life prospects of their children and the contribution their offsprings make depend on the investment their mothers make. Their husbands' capacity to do well on the job is also conditioned by a supportive home life. The mother and wife is responsible for quality social reproduction. More positively it is possible to say that most Japanese regard the family as the fundamental unit of society upon which the very future of Japan relies. Since the family is seen as ultimately depending upon the wife's investment of her own life energies in her husband and children, it is difficult to see things changing very dramatically in the work place until there is greater gender equality at home. [20] A comparison shows greater gender equality in some respects in the United States, yet women here pursue careers with knowledge of the cost to their families and especially their children. Men's unwillingness to be equal partners in parenting is obvious in both societies. Commitment to children's education and socialization is greater in Japan and women bear a different patriarchal package as a result.

The heavy responsibility of child rearing requires a single-minded focus that in such a model should preclude paid work outside the home in the years children are young. This is reflected in the "sloping M"-shaped age distribution of female labor force participation. There is a peak in the twenty to twenty-four age group (within which two-thirds of all women are employed) that declines in the thirty to thirty-four group (to a participation rate of a little over a third), and rises thereafter to a second but lower peak among forty to forty-four year olds, then follows a less severe decline from this lower second peak. The clusters do not represent women returning to their earlier jobs. Reentrants are largely contingent workers, temporary and of peripheral status. They may work full time, but they receive few company benefits. There is a clustering in smaller enterprises and low-paying jobs.

The role women play in massaging male egos is seen in the labor force activity of most young women who stereotypically work in ornamental and servant-like positions:

> Lacking any prospect of promotion, the OL [office lady, as these young women are widely called] symbolizes the auxiliary, insignificant nature of

work—simple, tedious, clerical—without authority or much responsibility, performed only to assist male bosses. Internationally notorious is her housewifely or servile role as an office waitress serving tea and cleaning ashtrays. [21]

It can be noted that the passage of the Child Care Leave Bill in Japan in 1991 (when comparable legislation could not be passed in the United States) indicates that under pressure of actual and expected labor shortages, a long-term commitment to attracting women to the labor force was receiving serious policy attention. Whether participation was seen in the context of breaking down gender segregation, however, is another matter. It is widely understood that Japan's passage of an equal employment opportunity law was not based on domestic consensus, but rather on a desire to be able to ratify the United Nations Convention on the Elimination of All Forms of Discrimination Against Women and so to avoid embarrassment before the international community. Although corporations cannot legally require women to resign upon marriage since a 1966 court decision, many continue to do so. Others illegally require retirement upon pregnancy, child birth, or reaching some fixed age up to forty.

Discrimination remains severe in both old-fashioned firms as well as in the new cutting-edge ones. Kuniko Fujita calls our attention to both the growth of part-time women workers in Tokyo to one in three compared with one in five such workers nationwide and to the decreasing earnings of women part-time workers compared with women full-time workers. The former earned 80 percent of the latter in 1977 but only 65 percent in 1987, according to Labor of Ministry figures. The wages of regular women workers is only half that of their male counterparts and, because part-time jobs increased 70 percent in Japan between 1982 and 1987 while regular full-time jobs increased by under 5 percent, there is a labor force restructuring of some significance going on in Japan that is not at all confined to small and medium-size companies, but which affects core employees as well. Contracting out, increased use of part timers, and heavier use of underpaid women characterizes Tokyo, as it does other global cities. [22]

It would be remiss to leave the topic of women in the labor force without noting the important developments challenging dominant patriarchal patterns. In 1991 a former employee at a small publishing firm in Fukuoka, 700 miles southwest of Tokyo, became the first person to win a sexual harassment case in Japan. Her boss had spread rumors about her alleged promiscuity and she had been forced to quit when she complained. [23] As I write Hitachi faces a suit brought by nine women charging that men with similar work histories are paid from 10 to 74 percent more. At Sumitomo Life Insurance Company dozens of women have joined in a suit charging the company with delaying the promotion of married women. The companies continue to deny there are any problems. Women are still forced out and have a hard time reentering the labor force at regular employment when their children are older. Despite Japan's presumed labor shortage, firms still tend to hire them only as temporary workers at reduced pay and benefit levels. Even when the company they formerly worked for takes them back their experience is ignored and they are paid considerably less than they were formerly. Such women often end up training younger women and overseeing their work.

Patriarchy, while being challenged by an emergent feminist movement, is still exceedingly dominant. It affects men as well as women for it is a system of hierarchal control both of women by men and of younger and subordinate males by patriarchs. The paternalism of Japanese corporations affects all of those who are expected to take orders and accommodate to the demands of hierarchal authority.

Yukihide Tanaka is a man who was fired for refusing an order to work overtime in 1967 by his employer, the multinational electronics and appliance giant, Hitachi. The company had also used violence to prevent Tanaka from distributing leaflets condemning forced overtime. In May 1978, eleven years after he was fired, the Tokyo District Court ruled in his favor. Eight years after that, the Tokyo High Court held that a worker cannot refuse an order of overtime work and his dismissal was upheld, the company action declared valid and lawful.[24] In 1991 the Supreme Court ruled against him on final appeal. This result was not unexpected. The Supreme Court, before the ruling in the Tanaka Case, had prejudged the matter by using his case before they ruled on it (the case was already famous) as an example of what it said in a meeting with lower-court judges was an example of an important principle:

> In view of the business operation of Japanese companies and the consciousness of workers, an agreement from each worker for each overtime work is not necessary. A comprehensive preliminary agreement is sufficient. . . . If the worker, at the time of joining the company, did not express dissent to a comprehensive agreement, it can be judged that he or she has given tacit consent.

Japan's workers are not nine-to-fivers. They have more accurately been described by *Asahi Shimbun* as "seven-elevens," in early, out late, working on weekends, holidays, and most of their vacations. The paper editorially saw the Tanaka decision as a ruling "that Japan, Inc., should remain a land of the 'seven-elevens.'"[25] Sadahiko Inoue, a researcher at RENGO, speaks for others when he says, "The Japanese have forgotten the purpose of economic advancement as they went along."[26] It seems accurate to say that the Japanese still work the hours Europeans put in during the early 1950s, the worst years of postwar recovery.

Statistically, by the end of the 1980s, Japan had achieved the highest standard of living in the world, although the seemingly simple question of who is richer is not in fact so easy to answer. Per capita income comparisons depend very heavily on exchange rates. When the yen doubled in purchasing power over a few years in the late 1980s, ordinary Japanese did not suddenly become twice as well off. Their homes did not double in size, and even the imported goods they bought, a small part of their market basket, did not decline in cost very much because of the control distributors had over foreign commodities once they entered the country.

Using the OECD's per person Gross Domestic Product figures for 1990 based on purchasing power parity exchange rates (what money could purchase in each nation in terms of comparable goods and services), the United States was Number One at $21,449 to Japan's Number Six with $17,634. However, the World Bank's per person Gross National Product figures, which used market exchange rates, had Japan third at $25,430 and the United States seventh at $21,790 for that same year (Switzerland was Number One, according to their calculations, at $32,680). There are a host of studies that seem to offer substantially different rankings, and I shall not review the technical literature on the subject. I think the qualitative differences in the social content and material mix of amenities present an interesting contrast of a rich country oriented to accumulation moderated in the 1980s by a growth in some segments of ostentatious conspicuous consumption, but a nation still consuming well below its potential compared with other nations.

By other measures of well being, such as adult literacy or life expectancy, the United States did not make it to the top ten. The 1990 Human Development Report of the United Nations placed Japan as Number One based on its Human Development Index. The United States was seventeenth. Kanemichi Kumagai, the secretary general of the leftist labor federation, *Zenroren*, claims that there is inclusion of smaller establishments (typically those with as few as ten employees) in the European wage data, but that because only larger employers are included in the data for Japan from which the international comparisons are made and because of other discrepancies, that based on U.S. Labor Department and Swedish employers' association figures "Japan's wages would rank lowest among the OECD countries."[27] For such labor leaders it is "small houses with high rents, located far from workplace" that force Japanese employees to go to their jobs before their kids get up and come home after they have gone to bed, and which make the official wage comparisons such a sick joke. Such international income comparisons are problematic in their large subjective elements, but the general order of the comparisons seem on target.

In the Western discussion of the Japanese industrial system, the greater involvement and responsibility of workers is seen as a plus, an unambiguously good thing contributing both to higher productivity and presumably worker satisfaction. The intensity of work and the heavy responsibility of the system, however, can create incredible pressure on workers even during their time off the job. A remarkably large number of Japanese workers reply to surveys in this area by saying that their job always stays on their mind. Being responsible for performance of the enterprise also leads to long hours of overtime, many unpaid, and missing meals with their families. Significant numbers of married men report hardly ever taking supper with their families and approximately half are at work at least two or three nights per week beyond their official hours. These intense pressures are not abating despite greater official attention and some high-profile announcements about efforts to reduce work time. In the past merit and seniority increases have been about of equal importance in establishing compensation, but in the early 1990s merit pay was more like 60 percent and rising. Seniority per se is becoming still less important for Japanese workers, thereby intensifying pressures to work longer hours as a sign of loyalty. The "hanging around syndrome," not leaving before one's colleagues and before one's boss, means that most nights executives, middle managers, and foremen, as well as many workers, do not get to go home until very late. With an average vacation of 6.1 days (in 1989), according to the Labor Ministry's figures, and the longest working day, week, and year among the advanced industrialized nations, the impact of such treatment of workers is the topic of a whole subgenre of literature in Japan.[28]

There is a failure to connect greater worker involvement (the secret of Japanese productivity improvement according to a long line of business school experts)[29] in which they learn the capacity to respond well in various environments and so can be switched around and given more tasks to do with the results of the greater pressures this system, accompanied by speedups and the company desire to meet and beat competitors' prices, upon the workers involved. Workers themselves may express conflicting responses. Along with dissatisfaction there is also a tendency that has been described in terms of symptoms of hostage syndrome (identifying with and developing sympathy for their captors). In hostage cases the captor has complete power and the captive's viewpoint becomes subordinate to, indeed reflective of, the captor's viewpoint. Captives may come to seek approval from captors and modify their behavior toward this goal given their dependence on them.

There is certainly a wide breath of work experiences, and the extent to which the captive syndrome is more representative or a genuine mutualism is at work, there is an extensive socialization process at work that does impose heavy opportunity costs on family life and community participation. There is also a debate over whether these relations are a postmodernist development that will be generalized across the global economy or remnants of a quasi-feudal ideology refurbished to play an important role in preserving a sense of reciprocity within a hierarchically ordered paternalistic order. The "remnants" of a feudal past provide low-cost production and close working relations. This view ignores the postwar construction of present arrangements in intense class struggle. The efficiency of this form of labor control and industrial organization links an advanced production system with a web of high-content intermediating communication capacity that can reduce transaction cost dramatically. Supervision costs are low and the colonization of the minds of workers by the company elicit cooperation that most traditionally managed American firms can only envy. Speedups and labor cost reduction, reassignment of workers, and a constant upgrading of skills in the service of better and faster production allows a more rapid introduction of new technologies and work arrangements.

Cultural Legacies and Contemporary Industrial Relations

The conventional wisdom does see contemporary labor–management relations as deeply embedded in Japanese history, geography, climate, and religion.

Thus, a Toyota publication, for example, presents the not uncommon view that the diligence of the Japanese worker reflects traditions created during centuries in which the Japanese economy was dependent on wet-rice agriculture, which requires more labor and closer care from planting to harvesting to controlling irrigation throughout the year, in which an intense cooperative effort was required. Confronted with frequent typhoons the Japanese farmers had little choice but to learn to work together collaboratively. The absent center of such a tale is of course the powerful landholding class that sat astride the cooperative process. Frequent rebellions punctuated the history of such outward harmony, suggesting that the system as it existed to sweat the peasants was structured for more than teaching cooperative work relations. Indeed, this dual reality, a sophisticated interdependence and efficient exploitation, have characterized Japan for a long time. It has never been one or the other, as apologists and critics from opposing viewpoints have maintained, but both in intimate relation to each other. If the "reds" had won the class struggle of the 1950s we would no doubt be hearing more about peasant rebellions and worker revolts as the constant theme of Japanese history.

The Buddhism and Confucianism that entered Japan in the mid-sixth century, the former teaching thoughtfulness, the latter harmony in dealing with others, underwent a transformation as it entered the country. Commentators who see these religious traditions as setting unwritten rules for thinking and behavior that place the good of the group above that of the individual, provide a sharp sense that work is a virtue, and so on, omit from their consideration the extent to which religion was molded by the ruling elite to create a stable orderly society amenable to more efficient control from above. Internalizing norms of subordination and social position meant that the Japanese elite could seriously claim "the class system disintegrated after the collapse of the shogunate government in 1867, and Japanese afterward came to enjoy full equality with each other." That is the way it happened according to the Toyota Motor Company and is taught by them to their workers and anyone else who will listen. [30]

There are similar suggestions that the samurai practice of never serving two lords takes the form today of a widespread dislike of changing jobs. Such an understanding obscures the extent to which it is material incentives and top-down systemic coercion that discourages job mobility. Social values held by the samurai become the bases of the "traditional values" of the Japanese people, initially because the samurai could pull his sword and kill commoners for any breach in etiquette no matter how slight or even imagined. Today, authority is far more subtle. That it is less noticed by foreign observers, and goes uncommented upon by most Japanese, is a tribute to its effectiveness, not to its absence. In any event, as we have seen the system, which operates despite echoes of feudal relations, dates perhaps from the 1950s or early 1960s.

The effort to paint the system as ingrained in an unchanging "Japaneseness" both obscures the recent vintage of many of its features and distracts attention from the prospect that under different situations the companies may no longer perpetuate its features. Self-interest, after all, has guided their adoption and it is inducing changes. There are important cultural influences of the West and the Harvard Business School. Management practices are changing: more job classifications are being introduced, the value of the all-around worker over the trained specialist is being questioned, incentives are becoming more individual, and many key companies have begun to move toward "merit"-based pay and promotion more explicitly. For example, in 1989, Isuzu introduced a new system in which employee's pay is 60 percent based on "merit," and the seniority part of pay peaks at fifty even though retirement age is sixty. An article from the business beat of one of Japan's largest circulation newspapers in 1990 made the point that "despite praise for the Japanese personnel development system by some Western experts, there is growing awareness in the business community that it also tends to stifle development of capable workers and skilled professionals."[31] The industrial relations system, like other parts of the institutional framework of the system, changes in response to external pressures.

The industrial relations patterning of the Japanese system is not the product of strong trade union bargaining, but of accommodating to the company and the product of an incentive system that is most profitable for the firm. Because an individual's lack of work effort will have a perceptible impact on the group bonus as well as individual compensation, peer pressure can be intense. Thus, not doing one's best is resented by fellow workers. "Attitude" and loyalty remain major considerations and mold a lifetime relationship with the company. Foremen "elder" new workers and help form them. Management also has many ways to humiliate workers, and in a shame culture many "voluntarily" quit. This is often the final step for noncooperative or otherwise unacceptable workers. The company union cooperates with this process and will not defend wayward workers who do not respond to paternal efforts to help them "straighten up." Only by internalizing company norms and giving the company 100 percent of potential does a worker really succeed. The potential gap between labor and labor power is reduced to a minimum. The worker sacrifices for the company, like the child for the beloved parent, although in practice both of these sentiments can be honored or flaunted in particular cases. They are accepted norms, but many employees find ways to circumvent expectations. Perhaps fewer do, however, than in other industrial relations regimes. The other extreme is more likely. More than 100 percent may be wrung from the worker who is used up in the process, drained, and then as a required norm cast aside earlier than in any other advanced industrialized nation.

Again the practices of "lifetime" employment, seniority promotion (with slack to reward differential merit), group bonuses, and so forth, did not become common until the 1950s and represent the triumph of corporate power over what was in the early postwar period a powerful, militant, heavily communist trade union movement organized in U.S. fashion (not enterprise unionism). Part of the success of company unionism has been to gain acceptance for the idea that it is traditional. In the interwar period turnover of skilled labor had been more than 50 percent per year. After the war Japan's shoddy products were said to result from the lack of worker motivation and commitment. The construction of the Japanese industrial relations regime was a competitiveness strategy and work intensity has increased in response to international developments.

In historical perspective 1973 represents an important marker on the path of continued high-work intensity in Japan. The impact of the OPEC oil price increase was the triggering event. It produced a global recession of some seriousness and the need for economies everywhere to retool to bring productive capacities into better accord with new energy costs. In Japan, which is almost totally dependent on imported sources of energy, an almost superhuman effort was unleashed. If the Japanese were "economic animals" before, then the pressures of the price jumps in 1973 and 1979 intensified the siege mentality, and work intensity increased in a context of global overcapacity. Growth rates of the expansionary phase of the postwar-long wave could not be maintained in Japan or the other OECD nations. Global growth slowed. Success had bred overaccumulation. Capital that could not be invested in productive activity was channeled into a speculative bidding up of assets, predominantly stocks and real estate, creating the bubble economy of the 1980s, which was followed by scandals exposed in the adjustment processes that followed and which are the subject of later examination. [32] At the same time as Japan followed America's example in moving from a focus on production to speculation, there was also continued pressure on labor to work harder to restore profit rates. While the pressures on Japanese workers increased throughout the economy it was often most intense in the sectors that were expanding most rapidly.

Teruyaki Murakami, a leader of the dissident Nomura Securities Workers Union, complains of the structural pressure in his company that produced an atmosphere in which any practice, no matter how unethical and illegal, was justified if done for the sake of the company. The overly militarist caste prevalent in most Japanese businesses enforces the need to do or die for his company as the corporate warrior. While it is a general pattern, Murakami argues that the securities scandals that rocked Japan at the end of the 1980s and the beginning of the 1990s were integrally related to the pressure on workers to produce. "In pointing out the causes of these scandals," Murakami told an international labor symposium,

> first we must take up the profit-first management of the big banks and securities companies. In pursuit of the purpose of the company (i.e., the maximization of profits), the company management introduces what is called a target system (quota system) in every division and stage of the process of labor, having workers compete with each other at all levels. Further, in order to secure the expected profits, the working relations between the company heads, managerial workers, and other workers are reorganized into a command system as seen in the military. Each worker is treated in a nonhuman way, as a mere component of the whole business operation, as if dictated by computer manuals. [33]

Less-militant workers are likely to privately grumble to bar hostesses after work about all this than to join what they see as a foolhardy effort to change the system. Moreover, if one company, say Toshiba, actually did work shorter hours, but another, perhaps its rival NEC, did not, then Toshiba would be at a disadvantage. "Companyism" that ties the worker's fate to a lifetime employer's profitability, keeps the worker from struggling for a shorter work week. Intercompany competition remains intense and industrywide bargaining is both uncommon and almost always secondary to company bargaining because of their "companyism." The union that sees the fate of its members tied to the prosperity of the company rarely objects. They accept lower wages and speed-ups as well when competition is intense and economic conditions are bad or when the company makes the case that certain measures are necessary to better "prepare for the future," a frequent rationale when favorable economic conditions prevail and the company wants union concessions.

I had the privilege of dining one night with Teruhito Tokumoto, the president of the Confederation of Japan Automobile Workers' Unions (JAW, the counterpart of our UAW), who was head of the Toyota group union before assuming his present post. He told me that to him a shorter work week and more time off was an absolute bargaining priority, but that he was not always supported on this issue by the member unions who tended to see things too much from the viewpoint only of their company. Unlike the head of the United Auto Workers in America, his views carry much less authority with the company union presidents, who do not report to him and are not subject to discipline from him, but are heads of autonomous company unions. Acceptance of the common fate of worker and company inhibits industrywide bargaining to achieve goals that are difficult, if not impossible, to win at the level of company bargaining.[34]

It seems natural to Japanese labor leaders that they should be on good terms with company officials and that the latter should pick up the check after expensive dinners. It is also thought logical that they should cooperate with corporations and the government in helping to organize labor unions in other Asian countries on a basis compatible with their system of "communal relations with a common fate," and that companies should train labor leaders at home. One significant venue is the Fuji Political College, run by the virulently anticommunist Democratic Socialist Party, which is closely tied to right-wing unions. Angry division between right and left unions is a long-standing feature of the Japanese labor landscape. It is not unrelated to division of opinion on the desirability of U.S.-style industrial unionism. The mainstream Japanese labor groups also funnel government money into training Asian labor unions in collaborationist unionism and to underwrite fighting "communism" in much the same fashion as the AFL-CIO continues to do in this country.

The theory of industrial unionism is to take wages and working conditions out of competition, to impose uniform requirements on all employers, and relatively homogeneous benefits to similarly situated workers no matter who their employer. Thus, while firms continue to compete based on product and process innovation, they do not gain advantage by decreasing wages or working condition norms below union contracted levels. The enterprise union accepts the commonality of interest between workers and their particular employer. This identification is more powerful than any solidarity with workers in other firms. An understanding is reached between workers and company that they are "in this together" and that it is the worker's job to help his or her company beat the competition. Group process in the Japanese collaborative teamwork approach does not replace individual initiative, but complements it. Each team member contributes beyond any narrow definition of task to the overall success of the enterprise and is rewarded in relation to such efforts. Because one's colleague is also one's rival and because, to some extent, their own interests are linked to the success of the group, they are unlikely to defend people who are seen as having made a mistake by management.

The consensus formed in this context is within a structure of compliance to company goals and established norms leading critics to see the Japanese enterprise unionism and collaborative work relations as authoritarian. Stanford Business School professor William Ouchi, who strongly supports the Japanese system as a better form of labor relations, puts the matter more positively when he observes that within teamwork is a strong element of company control:

> The basic mechanisms of management control in a Japanese company are so subtle, implicit, and internal that they often appear to an outsider not to exist. That conclusion is a mistake. The mechanisms are thorough, highly disciplined, and demanding, yet very flexible. Their essence could not be more different from methods of managerial control in Western organizations. [35]

In the Japanese system we find a pattern in which labor is explicitly rewarded in relation to its marginal product in a social setting designed for maximal efficiency, or if one prefers, the exploitation of labor. In this Japan is no different than other countries, but they are better at it, especially in comparison with other advanced nations. The managerial approach to succeeding enterprise models and their corresponding social structures of accumulation ignore the social costs of efforts to extract the maximum work effort from an increasingly disciplined workforce that is made more and more responsible for thinking out how to best increase company profits. As Nohara writes:

> The main characteristics of the Japanese social background include the overwhelming power of management on the shopfloor and no union other than company unions; little existence of community except within companies; the lack of extracurricular activity; and a strong conformism, very much the opposite of individualism. Without the support of these social backgrounds it is very problematic whether a Japanese model could be effectively transplanted or not. [36]

Equality thus has a very different meaning in Japanese culture, where it conveys being the same. It does not mean the right to equal treatment if you choose to be different. Equality in the Japanese context "is transformed into something having a conformist-oriented function." [37] The power of capital also extends to workers who are not direct employees, and not only to subcontractors.

It is the labor-relations system that goes with and makes possible the highly successful Japanese production system that is the key to Japanese productivity gains. Japanese managers can allocate workers at any time to any place necessary, something that is not possible in the traditional American industrial relations system in which seniority and strict job classifications are central. If an American union were unable to protect these two central aspects of the system it would not be much of a union. The balance of power in Japan is such that independent unionism for the most part does not exist in a form that would be recognized as such by U.S. trade unionists. We are talking here about ideal types. In practice the differences between the U.S. and Japanese industrial relations regimes was diminishing over these years as Japanese practices were widely adopted in the United States. Also, organized labor was getting weaker in both countries. In 1990 26 percent of the Japanese labor force was unionized, down from 35 percent in 1970 as service jobs, which in Japan as in the United States tend not to be unionized, grew. Labor's failure to organize the nonunionized takes place in a climate in which the seniority wage system is being further eroded and long-term employment is becoming less prevalent. Involuntary transfers, retirements, and outright personnel cutbacks are more common. The level of work anxiety has increased as well. While there is evidence of greater worker discontent with companyism the competitive economic climate means that workers continue to buy stimulants and "health" tonics and to do as they are told.

The Yin and Yang of the Japanese Industrial Relations Regime

The negative and the positive moments of the system coexist and together define its totality. What the management literature celebrates as zero waiting time, labor recognizes as the ultimate in speed-up and dehumanization, the reduction of the person to the more perfect machine. The multitasking that makes the work more interesting is also a tool to take advantage of the workers' skills and interest in recombining tasks that can lead to higher levels of output per worker and intensification of effort. The just-in-time delivery system, while reducing the need to stockpile at the factory, merely shifts this burden of maintaining needed inventories to the subcontractors. The need to send so many small shipments increases their transportation costs and adds to pollution, congestion, and road maintenance. The sight of trucks idling in plant driveways waiting to deliver just-in-time brings to mind a mobile polluting warehouse.

That only 15–20 percent of the work force is in these lifetime employment pools at large corporations is an important aspect of the system, dividing the working class, and weakening its potential unity because the more privileged workers have little incentive to show solidarity to the workers who have even less bargaining power than they do. The dual labor market undercuts solidarity because workers identify with their company and not with lower-paid secondary workers. While this may be viewed as betrayal from the perspective of

Marxian class consciousness, it is rational for such workers. A better year for the company is a bigger bonus for the worker. Job security makes for cooperative attitudes toward new technology and work reassignments. Lifetime employees are trained to both do things the company way and to be innovative within the narrow bounds assigned to them.

While many observers see this as a better alternative to the emphases of the traditional American system for both company and worker, the pressure on employees is intense. To fall or be pushed from a job in the primary sector carries severe consequences. Further, "lifetime employment," even in the primary sector, is not a given. If the demand for their products falls dramatically and permanently they may be fired. Employment guarantees are maintained to the extent that they contribute to the long-term profitability of the corporation in which employee loyalty is valued. When an industry collapses, as shipbuilding did in the late 1970s and into the 1980s, thousands of workers were "retired." As Tatsuo Hayashi, managing director of the Japan Shipbuilders Association, said in 1986, "The shipbuilding companies are going all out to fire workers."[38]

In the normal course of Japanese industrial development in the postwar period workers have been better treated, as we have noted, but as the harsh dismissals of coal miners and shipyard workers among others indicate, alternative employment is not always provided. Further, such a system can continue only so long as the macro economic conditions allow. As the Japanese corporation internationalizes production, if long-term unemployment becomes significant in an era of slow growth there will surely be a serious rethinking of these practices. The special treatment of Japanese workers by paternalistic employers, which is so commented upon in the West, is a complex and varied phenomenon. The glowing generalizations are not acceptable as summary statements. A quid pro quo is always involved for the bargain to be acceptable to employers and the price workers pay is high.

Japanese corporate industrial relations departments define cooperation as meaning that every worker appreciates the position of every other worker so that the entire company is bound together by ties of mutual understanding and respect. This is a positive virtue from their perspective because it implies the highest regard for human respect to the work place. An American trade unionist looking at such a proposition is likely to be more ambivalent and perhaps skeptical. On the one hand, the promise of lifetime employment and more creative participation on the job are appealing, but when the worker is told he or she must take responsibility for the constant improvement of the production process and participate voluntarily in interpersonal relations aimed at mutual self-policing to maximize efficiency and output, the bargain is often less appetizing. The Japanese managers have found a philosophy of involvement that is either quite clever or devilishly insidious, depending on your point of view.

Nohara suggests that Japanese managers learned a lot from what happened in the United States and Europe in the late 1960s; events such as Lordstown, the workers' plant seizures, most dramatically in France and Italy. The way

Japanese management dealt with the threat of such problems was unique because they sought to solve them "not by abolishing simplified and meaningless work, or by removing the division of labor, but by adding extra work."[39] That is, workers' participation in improving the product and the production process were added to the workers' original simplified work. This meant overtime for workers that, for the most part, was not directly compensated. In fact, not participating meant workers would not receive the same wage increases or rate of promotion. Noncooperators would be stuck at the bottom of the job hierarchy, where work intensity was greatest and became increasingly unbearable with age and the lack of prospect of moving on to better job assignments. Those wanting out from the lower rungs cooperated with as much creativity and enthusiasm as they could muster. Their reward was a less-brutal work environment and better pay.

Mitsubishi Electrical Company's New Qualification System uses very individualistic evaluations to maintain pressure by small groups for zero defects. NEC (Nippon Electrical Company) has the company slogan "autonomy through consensus," which seems to translate as the group has to figure out new and more ingenious ways to carry out objectives established for them by supervisors and section chiefs. When workers do not cooperate sufficiently tasks get contracted out to suppliers, groups are broken up through severance or reassignment, and longer hours and speedups are ordered by management to get the same productivity increases. Then, too, the labor aristocracy, if it wants to keep its position, has to hustle because there are more temps who want to work.

As a result of this control, as we noted in the last chapter, firms like Toyota are able to establish their own calendar, which ignores national holidays and has employees work Saturdays and Sundays regardless of any preference on their part, religious or otherwise. At Toyota, given compulsory overtime and commuting, a typical worker is away from home eleven to twelve hours per day. Forty percent of the company's manufacturing employees work more than one of their days off each month. Thirty percent work more than five extra days each month. Most join in recreational activities organized by the company on at least one holiday per month, and a third join in company-sponsored activities two days per month. In most cases, then, workers put in a long work year and do not plan their own limited free time. Western-style notions of a private independent life outside of the social relations established by the employer are discouraged by the professional and financial advantages of cooperating with company familyism.[40]

Company housing, vacation resorts and outings, serious bonuses that can double your income—these seem like a cross between the best promises of early Soviet Communism and the successful quality perks enjoyed by the upper class of consumer capitalism trickling down to the workers. Some experts attribute the seeming loyalty of the Japanese workers to this system of relations. The conventional wisdom concludes that Japan has a more successful form of capitalism because workers and managers work well together and share gains. They point out that in Japan, a chief executive's salary is only six or seven times that of a newly hired college graduate. In the United States a ratio of 50 : 1 is not uncommon.

When Sony decided to move in to the U.S. market the company allowed ten years to start making money off of its U.S. operations. They first made detailed studies of U.S. tastes and established their own sales operation from the ground up carefully and for the long run. "A foreign market cannot be built up overnight," Sony's president, Akio Morita, is fond of telling Americans who wish to do business in Japan. In his book, *Made in Japan*, pitched to America, he warns that our managers have lost sight of their basic responsibility to employees and customers. Instead of investing to sustain long-term growth, the main goal here is the fast buck and satisfying stockholders (along with fat salaries and outsized bonuses for themselves). "The remarkable thing about management is that a manager can go for years making mistakes that nobody is aware of, which means that management can be a kind of con-job," says Morita. His message calculated to contrast with the leveraged buyout-demands for concessions and widespread layoffs in the United States in the 1980s was:

> Once we have hired people, we try to make them understand our concept of a fate-sharing body and how, if a recession comes, the company is willing to sacrifice profit to keep them in the company. . . . They know that management does not lavish bonuses on itself . . . "golden parachutes" for management except a simple lifetime parachute of guaranteed employment and a lifetime of constructive work. [41]

With few or no job classifications, responsibility is widely shared. This brings into play knowledge and talent, which remain latent among workers in traditional U.S.-style firms. Continuous job rotation and teamwork is a constant teacher. By stressing problemsolving at the lowest possible level, "management" is economized. Self-management puts responsibility on the worker who, in long-term relationship with the company and the work team, gains skill and contributes more than if workers were simply pushed harder by foreman, following directions from engineers who are not themselves involved in production. Details are considered by those close to them in daily practice, who develop intimate knowledge in a learning-by-doing situation, and, most importantly, have incentives to use their insight to make production more efficient.

Most suggestions and plans that arise from Japanese QC circles are highly technical. Without a background in technology, Koike tells us, QC circle activities cannot be maintained. "Workers with white collarized skills have knowledge of the mechanisms of production and of principles or theories in their own field, though not as much as engineers. With this background, workers can devise better methods of work and production." [42] Such workers can handle new machinery more confidently and soon move beyond the manual, devising better ways to do the job in a learning-by-doing fashion. Selecting qualified workers with proper attitudes is crucial to making the system work.

Such socialization of workers, carefully screened to select those with good grades and proper work attitudes, allows engineering tasks to be carried out at all levels of the company. Workers in Japanese factories, because they know more about tasks and how they can be combined and modified even to minute degrees that may cut a second or two here and there, are able to make suggestions that save management millions. Multiskilling is a relative thing. The tasks are easily learned, but the system does assist morale and contributes to profitability. The system of individual subjective evaluation of workers by supervisors as the basis of pay and promotion enforces a collaborative stance.

Group work involves each participant contributing in a manner most effective to the total effort. Each knows the other's strengths and weaknesses. Cohorts are hired together out of similar, almost identical, backgrounds, and go up the corporate ladder together. By the age of thirty it is clear who among the cohorts will be groomed over the next twenty years for the higher positions. This is true in government as well, where things are even more competitive, especially in the most prestigious ministries. In the Japanese civil service, when the administrative vice minister, the man who runs the agency, presumably under an elected member of the Diet, chooses his successor, all remaining peers resign. The man at the top then has no peers, but consults broadly with all actors in making what are in effect consensus decisions. Some of those he consults with are former colleagues, including former superiors who have gone on to top positions in the corporate world among the firms the ministry offers guidance.

The key to understanding Japanese industrial relations in large firms is that the worker and the company each get something out of this system. The company provides job security and incentive pay to the worker. The worker knows that skill growth and its deployment will be rewarded (and slacking punished). The firm and worker share the cost of investing in human capital. Workers know they can amortize the investment over many years of seniority-related benefits. The cost of not investing and being more productive is fewer promotions and lower pay over one's work life. The cost of moving to another firm is high, even prohibitive. Thus, workers have every incentive to think about how to make the best out of their attachment to the particular firm for which they work.

After twenty years of continuous service a worker in Japan experiences, on the average, a 180 percent growth in wages (150 percent in small firms), compared with a 30 percent growth in the United States (52 percent in small firms where fewer workers stay on that long, but where those most valuable to the firm are given greater incentive to remain). The steeper earnings profile in the historical data starts from a smaller base in Japan.[43] Wages continue to rise with years of service in the United States; but they peak and then decline dramatically in Japan, after twenty-five years in smaller Japanese firms, thirty years in the larger ones. The older worker who has presumably slowed down has less incentive to stay on. Indeed, the Japanese traditional retirement age has been fifty-five (now being raised to sixty as workers stay healthier and productive longer). Older workers are encouraged or forced to retire, transferred to supplier firms (and lower paid jobs), or are under severe pressure to leave in a downturn to lower the company's quasi-fixed costs.

An employee who is forced to retire early, unless the firm gives special inducements, takes a severe loss. Retirement benefits are also backed by the company's stock. Should the firm go under, to take the extreme case, the cost of such an undiversified retirement portfolio becomes onerous indeed. There is thus both incentive to stay with the firm and to see that it is healthy. Because other members of the enterprise group hold a company's stock, they, too, have strong incentive to bail it out when it gets in trouble and watch to be sure management is doing the best possible job. When Mazda got into serious trouble at the end of the 1970s, the entire Sumitomo group increased their auto purchases to help out, and financing was made available through the Sumitomo banks. A comparison to similarly situated firms in the United States is instructive. The American firm is on its own. If it is big enough, then perhaps a federal bailout would be possible, but it is hardly routine. It would be offered under conditions that would discourage others from applying for help. Creditors might carry the firm, but each would have a strong incentive to pull out.

It is the mutually beneficial nature of the relationship that leads workers to see firm success as good for them. They therefore favor new technologies and master them quickly because they gain in higher compensation (based on supervisor assessment of their positive attitude and contribution) and the greater capacity of the more profitable firm that results to pay more generous bonuses. Growth means a chance to advance within a firm with more opportunities for its employees. This motivates middle-managers as well. The faster the growth, the faster promotions come. Thus, growth is a rational strategy for employees and employers.

To summarize, the multifaceted ways Japanese companies instill and mobilize habits of deference and internalize work discipline are a major factor in higher Japanese productivity. Authoritarian demands and a norm of obedience is less a matter of Japanese character than the brilliantly constructed labor control system. The use of ritual and seemingly consensual processes are designed to force every possible ounce of work effort and rest on a system of rewards and punishment carefully calibrated to play workers off against each other, even as it encourages them to cooperate with each other in the context of individual loyalty to the company. Critics of the system have called it "management by stress."[44]

Before concluding the chapter I want to consider one more example—the steel industry—which was hard hit in the postwar period. It is interesting to see how the industrial relations regime gets played out in a sector that is not a high flier. One sees both the resolve of Japanese industrialists and the cost labor pays for the industry's survival.

Steel, The Case of a Declining Industry

Through the years, when the United States steel industry was claiming that the high cost of compliance with "unreasonable" environmental regulations

was making them uncompetitive internationally, the Japanese were outspending the Americans, investing larger sums on environmental controls, and
cleaning up their act. In 1974, the Japanese Environmental Agency adopted
the original emissions standards of the U.S. Clean Air Act of 1970 (without
subsequently relaxing them, as the United States did). Further, such complaints in the United States proved occasion for disinvestment by leading steel
companies. The former national flagship of corporate might, U.S. Steel, even
changed its name to USX, altering its identity so totally as to disassociate with
its base industry as a new-wave omnivorous conglomerate that, as its president said, "made money not steel." Workers, of course, were laid off and
plants closed as the industry was gutted. Many other companies also refused
to seriously reinvest in the low-profit steel business.[45]

In Japan, Yoshi Tsurumi tell us,

> When it has been necessary to permanently discharge workers, as
> Nippon Steel . . . and other heavy industrial firms have done, these firms
> have assumed primary responsibility for retraining and relocating their
> workers elsewhere. When that has not been possible, government and
> corporations have worked together to distribute the social and economics
> costs fairly among management, discharged workers, local communities,
> and the banks and suppliers of the affected companies.[46]

Japanese firms voluntarily keep hundreds of thousands of workers on their
payroll, deploying them wherever possible, and setting up new businesses to
create employment for workers whose wages are seen as a quasi-fixed cost.
Some are retained in anticipation of renewed business activity in a long-term
version of labor hoarding since so much has been invested in their training.
Consider the following statement by Yasuo Shingu, who heads Sumitomo
Metals. What most impresses an American reader in this passage is perhaps
the *of course*, which I have italicized.

> We have also resolutely halved the number of personnel in the iron
> and steel section as compared to that at peak. *Of course*, we have avoided
> layoffs, relocating employees to new sections of affiliated companies, or
> temporarily transferring them to other corporations.

President Shingu then went on to make two further comments: "We are
deeply indebted to the labor unions for their cooperation in this and are justly
proud of our labor–management relationship in which top and bottom are
bound by a mutual sense of trust."[47] He also pointed out that even in a severe
recession Japan has never cut back on resources for research and development.
Indeed, in the visits of our research team to Japanese steel companies we were
most impressed by the extent of research being done. Shingu's stump speech
ended with the stirring "victory is certain." Such attitudes are common among
old-time steel men. They are not financial experts chosen to sell off the company, close plants and redeploy assets into industries in which the firm has no
historical connection as is common in the United States.

Such beneficence came at a severe price from the worker perspective. Nippon Steel in the late 1970s adopted a new *jishu kanri*, or "worker's self-management system," in which production workers put in overtime for the company, gathered data, wrote reports, and figured out how to reduce the labor necessary to produce steel.

> When we proposed reducing two men to one, complaints were heard that cutting personnel in half would be too much and that it would result in intensification of work. People also asked us where the surplus men would be transferred.
>
> But we persuaded these dissidents, saying by studying industrial engineering methods we would find ways to hold down our work load even if our personnel were cut by 50 percent. [48]

Since those with the highest evaluations by their supervisors received twice the wage increase as the average worker at Nippon there was an incentive to think productivity gains and not job retention. New workers were asked, "What do you think about strikes? What do you think about unions?" In addition, regular workers were of course paid more than the lower status outside workers, whose relative numbers were increasing and whom the more privileged were allowed to boss around, reproducing the relationship they themselves had with their own supervisors. When workers for a subcontractor tried to form a union the subcontractor was kicked out of the plant. Labor stratification was carefully calibrated to exact the greatest total work effort.

This is not to say that the firm did not do its best to create new jobs for its existing employees. In Kamaishi, its company town (or "castle town," in Japanese usage, since such places bear a striking resemblance to the feudal domain of the lord of the castle who were such town's single employer of old), Nippon Steel set up subsidiaries to grow mushrooms and make soy based meat substitutes. It set up joint ventures in its former warehouses to produce office furniture, and one of its piers is now a grain center for imported animal feed, using the cranes and conveyor belts that once loaded steel.

Japan's share of worldwide steel output peaked in 1973 (at 17 percent) and fell as lower-cost, state-of-the-arts facilities were opened in many developing nations. My own visits to Korea's POSCO works, which run twenty-four hours per day and uses little labor (but employs in-house subcontractors a la the Japanese system), revealed a showplace facility with a teaching staff and thousands of oxygen generators (trees artfully landscaping the plant), worker housing, and tennis courts. The company, then government-owned and run by a retired general, has since been privatized. Koreans had studied the Japanese well, and their lower labor costs, serious state subsidies, and protectionism had created the world's third largest steel company. They also had essential technical assistance that the Japanese were soon sorry they had extended. The Koreans followed the Japanese example of adapting cutting-edge capital-intensive technology, considered steel the rice of industry, as had the Japanese, and followed state-led development strategies that Western experts considered inefficient. Korea enjoyed one of the very highest growth rates in the world over decades. Its steel industry turned the heat up under Japanese producers.

Rationalization in Japan, however, did not mean wholesale abandonment of a basic industry. Some production was moved abroad, but key segments of the steel industry were brought back to global leadership. Intense efforts and immense resources were poured in. Most important, the attitude of Japanese steel men was one of total determination. "We built these steel plants with the sweat of the Japanese people," says Yoshihiro Inayama, former chairman of the Nippon Steel Corporation, and chairman of *Keidanren*. "To say it is better to get rid of them because foreign products are a little cheaper is ridiculous."[49] If even more sweat was required, then so be it. It was this combination of brilliant superexploitation and ferocious technological drive that characterizes the most successful Japanese cases.

In 1987, 80 percent of Nippon Steel's sales were derived from steel. Plans called for the figure to be below 50 percent by 1995. The electronics division, information/communications systems division, engineering, and urban development and infrastructure projects were all slated to expand significantly. These areas, as company officials explained, were extensions of what the company was already doing well. For example, the information/communications systems the company had developed for its own internal use were so sophisticated that it was being marketed. In America such systems would have been purchased from outside contractors. Even its research and development of biotechnology came from an expansion of existing work. (I heard similar things from other well-managed Japanese companies. Suntory, the alcoholic-beverage producer, is building on its unique knowledge of fermentation processes, gained over 100 years, to explore biotechnology fields.)

The Japanese Industrial Relations Regime

There is thus a labor relations system that goes with making the production system possible. Traditional American-style unionism would prevent management discretion in moving employees around between job classifications and disregard strict seniority. The union would also take the worker's side in many instances where in Japan the union would in effect support the company against the worker's complaint.

Explaining the system, one of the most successful Japanese industrialists, the founding Matsushita, whose iconic status we noted earlier, has said, in one of his most oft-quoted pronouncements:

> We are going to win and they [the West] are going to lose. We see beyond the Taylorist model . . . [T]he survival of firms . . . depends on the day to day mobilization of every ounce of intelligence. For us the core of management is precisely this art of mobilizing and pulling together the intellectual resources of all employees in the service of the firm . . . The intelligence of a handful of technocrats is not enough to take up the technological and economic challenges with any real chance of success.

As two industrial relations experts comment on the archetypal formulation of Japanese management theory,

> The Matsushita philosophy is two-edged. At its best it can lead to much greater work satisfaction and cooperative endeavor. At its worst it can lead to intense pressure to conform to the pressures of top management for speed-up and to the destruction of independent organizations to represent the views and needs of the work force.[51]

While many analysts stress either the positive *or* the negative aspects of the Japanese industrial relations regime, both are reflective of its reality. Because employees will presumably work for the same employer over most of their work life, a collegiality develops that has a number of positive aspects. One's fortune becomes intimately tied to the success of one's employer, and while it is possible to just go through the motions, and many do, there is also an effective pressure in most situations to do far more. Employees are not necessarily happy in this system. They have little real choice but to make the best of their lifetime commitment. Indeed, a 1991 survey of major companies found that over 70 percent of even senior employees said that they would *not* work for the same company again if they had it to do over.[52]

That the Japanese themselves are far from happy with a system that treats them instrumentally and shares out only part of the benefits of economic growth to those who produce it creates pressures for changes. In the West, the Japanese system raises different sorts of questions, especially for the trade union movement and political formations that have traditionally been responsive to labor's interests. The dilemma for such organizations is that in many respects they are locked into defending the relative privilege of older arrangements. Preserving employment classifications and jobs even when work is inefficiently organized and not economically viable is part of what unions do, as is resisting new technologies that displace workers. Rationalization is seen, not without justice, as a union-busting tactic. American workers are right to be skeptical of Japanese company unionism and collaboration. The flexibility of the Japanese system, however, creates conditions that undermine the outmoded production system in the United States.

The Japanese industrial system encourages one to think about Marx's distinction between labor and labor power, with the latter the capacity to work that is purchased by an employer and the former the actual work done in the concrete instance by the worker. Labor as a source of value is not the factor of production or commodity purchased. It is the outcome of the specific social relation between capital and labor in the historically specific setting. The Japanese production system draws on an industrial relations regime that increases the surplus, the difference between what companies pay for labor power and the productiveness of workers' labor. It is in this classically Marxist sense that the Japanese system is a superbly efficient version of capitalism. It is also a brilliantly innovative system in terms of technology. Again, to remind the reader, both of these factors, neither one nor the other alone, is responsible for

Japan's rapid growth. The orthodox Marxists do half the story right; the boost-erist management consultants the other half.

Finally, the system is not permanent. Amid the celebration of Japanese industrial practice by the early 1990s it became harder to avoid noticing that managers were reducing the proportion of their core permanent employees, contracting out more, relying on a greater number of contingent workers, and moving production offshore. These dramatic trends will be considered in some detail in later chapters. The segmentation that this chapter has described as characterizing the labor market has a counterpart in a spatial unevenness in the geographic patterning of Japanese economic development. It is to that topic that our attention is now turned.

7

Capital Versus the Regions

"'You wouldn't understand,' says a man who offers her a lift, 'your country's rich, but we Japanese, we're poor.'"

"I wondered whether to argue with him. But how could I tell him the rest of the world sees Japan as rich, when you had only to look out the window to see how poor it was?"

LESLEY DOWNER, *On the Narrow Road*

"There is no doubt that through centuries of such agrarian experience, extending up until as recently as a generation ago, the Japanese have developed customs of cooperation, risk-sharing, and ad hoc and flexible adoption to continual and incremental changes through collective efforts and diligent work habits, and have endured the penetration of communal life into their private lives."

MASAHIKO AOKI [1]

In the panegyrics celebrating Japanese postwar economic development in the West little attention was given to social cost, to the impacts of rapid growth on the environment in which Japanese live. There is also a tendency to see patterns of cooperation as going back centuries, providing a picture that elides the existence of contradictions and conflict. Examining the regional dimensions of postwar economic development gives pause to the easy characterizations of Japan's role in the world economy and offers comparisons and contrasts with other national experiences of regional policy. This chapter tells the story of this relationship between industrial and regional development stressing the manner in which sacrifice and rewards have been distributed in spatial and class-distinct ways. The policymaking actors—politicians and bureaucrats, local residents and construction companies—are engaged in an elaborate, many-sided process that decides the spatial distribution of costs and benefits and the pattern of spatial growth to be encouraged. The range of discourse is from the scandal-ridden world of national politics to the statesmanlike realm of national urban and regional policy.

169

For the most part, "Efficient Japan" is confined to those sectors that compete internationally or service such activities. Domestically oriented areas—farming, retailing, construction, and others—have tended to be exceedingly inefficient and often imbricated in politically motivated state redistribution and even in criminally corrupt practices. The extent of payoffs, the degree of taxpayer subsidy, and successful rent seeking are grounded in the political system that developed in the postwar years under the control of the self-seeking leaders of the LDP, a party that is neither liberal nor democratic and in a real sense is more a disparate coalition for self-aggrandizement than a political party in any real ideological sense. When, in 1993, it lost control of government as a result of years of cascading scandal and refusal to entertain even mild electoral reform it was replaced by a disparate coalition composed of all opposition parties (except the communists). The difficulty Japan had in the 1990s as it tried to modernize its politics was not unlike that faced by Italy or Mexico, countries where decades of one-party dominance had also created a culture of structured corruption which, while once conducive to stability, had increasingly extracted a high price on civil society.

From its inception the LDP was beholden to core constituencies for funding and electoral dominance. They have delivered favors in a systematic fashion to maintain high levels of such support. The Large-Scale Retail Store Law to protect the legion of small business people, generous rice subsidies that cost taxpayers huge amounts and then consumers six times world prices, and vast construction projects to reciprocally generous construction companies for undertakings in key electoral districts, have all been part of this system. Central control over local financing has at the same time starved the local state for funding for social welfare purposes. Indeed, local politicians tend to be judged on their skill in obtaining aid from prefecture and central governments and their contacts among higher-level decision makers. By obtaining the designation, "Scarcely Populated Area," for example, special education, social service, and redevelopment grants are available. The practices to be described are legitimized by broad understandings of social justice on the one hand and characterized by abuse of power by special interests on the other.

The Japanese system uses a crude pork barrel mechanism to address structured inequalities that are created and perpetuated by the normal workings of the economy. It is this system that was under attack by the end of the postwar period as Japan was forced to adjust its domestic institutional accommodations under foreign pressure. Indeed, a conflict, a deep fissure in the LDP's base, was evident between localist interests that had long supported, and in turn had been supported by the LDP, and the internationalists, who stood ready to sell out the farmers, small retailers, and others to a globalist liberalization of markets. In 1993 rebellious LDP leaders broke with the party over issues of electoral reform and corruption to break the party's thirty-eight years of parliamentary dominance and initiated modernizing reforms along these lines. (These reforms within continuity will be discussed subsequently.)

The evaluation of the historic rationales for Japan's redistributive politics differ. Ronald Dore has written, in the stylized vernacular of ceremonial politics, that

> One somewhat romantic way of putting it would be to say that all this expenditure is an expression at the national level of the old ethic of filial piety—the tribute that the youthful productive industrial sectors of the economy pay to the aging populations left in the villages, or, more abstractly, to the ancestral rural homeland, the original source from which the capital to build Japan's industry was accumulated.[2]

It is also the case that down and dirty politics shape the distribution of public works funds to a very substantial degree. The Japanese are not alone in distributing quality-of-life projects on politicized criteria and to pay off favored interests, but they have carried it to a high form of art. This *pattern of administration* is one of the secrets of the rapid growth of Japanese capitalism. That success has in turn been a hindrance to the development of oppositional politics in Japan, and to the development of local government autonomy.

The system has been protected by a larger web of bureaucratic self-interest, which has led to bizarre but perfectly understandable results. The Ministry of Agriculture, Forestry, and Fisheries spent decades paving over the nation's beaches to build fishing ports and spreading lucrative contracts to construction firms that provide post-retirement sinecures to ministry leaders. As it became harder to rationalize such activity, given the oversupply of ports for a dwindling fishing industry, the ministry developed a totally new strategy. It now builds swimming beaches. These come complete with extensive and expensive offshore breakwater retainers, access roads, and other accoutrements. The same firms get the contracts, and the game goes on. When Japan's Fair Trade Commission attempts to stop rigged bids on public works projects, the powerful Construction Ministry is able to squelch its attempts. Routine fraud is structural and very important to the bureaucrats, politicians, and contractors. When incriminating documents disclosing hundreds of millions of dollars of construction work surface, as in the case of high dams and industrial parks, the Construction Ministry is able to shed crocodile tears in mock outrage, impose token fines, and business as usual proceeds.[3]

Money, Politics, and Money-Politics

The poor prefecture of Shimane in western Honshu is number one in new public works spending for the decade of the 1980s. Of its five representatives three are among the most powerful LDP Diet leaders. Niigata's isolation on the Japanese fringe was greatly diminished by the costly Shioya Tunnel (to serve sixty households). It was only one boon among a great many others going to the home district of former prime minister and one of Japan's most powerful postwar fixers, Kakuei Tanaka.[4]

The pork barrel nature of infrastructure spending is one of the great constants in Japanese politics. The maglev (for magnetic levitation) experimental high-speed train that it is hoped will take passengers from Tokyo to Osaka at 335 miles per hour in the early twenty-first century in an hour (compared with four hours or so that the *shinkansen*, or "bullet train," now takes) is being tested in Yamanashi prefecture, home district of Shin Kanemaru, who headed the construction *zoku*, or "tribe," in the Diet, which oversees public construction spending. Until his downfall in a corruption scandal in 1992 he was the kingmaker,[5] the godfather of its largest faction (which was Tanaka's and then led by Takeshita, of whom more will be said in Chapter 8). Real estate developers fortunate enough to be on the inside bought up and resold parcels along the Yamanashi line's right of way sending land prices soaring. Speculative gains were in the tens of billions of yen in the prefecture. Cost overruns and concern about the environmental impact in terms of noise and magnetic radiation were successfully ignored by the powerful Kanemaru forces. The endemic corruption of Japanese politics is part of the "groupness" of the society and would be difficult to reform away.

Who you know counts in all societies, but nowhere more than in Japan, where access and mutual aggrandizement institutionalizes corruption as a core element in economic and political processes. Kanemaru, whose heavy-lidded eyes and worn skin gave his face the look of a wily old crocodile, the ultra-*kuromaku*, the figure behind the curtain, was capable of telling foreign interviewers with a more or less straight face, "You know, politics needs money. And politics is expensive. That will not change. So Japanese politicians are sometimes forced to do immoral things. That is the worst thing about Japanese politics. That is something we have to reform."[6] The interview was granted only months before he was indicted in one of Japan's bigger political scandals and some $40–50 million worth of loose yen was found in his home and office by investigators along with millions more in gold bars.

There is a tendency to underestimate the impact of the Japanese government's 25–30 percent share of fixed-capital formation on the politics and economy of the country. This is partly because the construction *zoku* and pork barrel politics seem removed from economic development policymaking. Yet, these expenditures are surely indirectly productive and complement private capital investment. The size of the sums involved both greases the political wheels and has important macroeconomic implications. If public corporations are included the Japanese government spends 7 percent of GDP (in 1985) for fixed capital formation. The United States spent only 2 percent of its GDP this way that year.

The Japanese construction industry has accounted for 16 percent of investment in the national accounts (compared to 10 percent on average in the United States and Europe), and the Big Five, now the Big Nine, construction firms have dominated the industry through the postwar period. Beside contributing to leading politicians who throw business their way the companies hire senior officials from the central government and from larger subnational jurisdictions and public corporations that are responsible for serious amounts of construction orders. This *amakudari*, common as we have seen throughout

Japanese corporate life, ensures access and preferential treatment. The largest construction companies also have interlocks with the major *keiretsu* that provide business on a mutually accommodating basis.

Gangsters also appear to be integral to the operation of the construction industry as suppliers of such services as procuring illegal immigrant labor, providing muscle for eviction services, and as partners with politicians and other land speculators. The line between formal criminals and informal criminal behavior by those whose business is supposedly governance or real estate is not easy to draw. Bribery, extortion, and mutuality among different kinds of criminals is not, of course, an exclusively Japanese trait, and the construction industry everywhere seems to have more than its share of such practices. In Japan, however, where everything is organized it is easier to see the relationships and structures of collusion. The system is one of structured corruption. The developers and builders support the LDP politicians and reward the bureaucrats for their cooperation. The speculators get their money directly or indirectly from the major banks. Everyone avoids taxes and all make out like bandits. It is a very comfortable system. Therefore, when Americans wanted open bidding on government projects, such as a new international airport in Osaka, they were confronting a core pillar of the Japanese political and economic system—prebidding collusion (*dango*) and the planned price system. Markets are organized and foreigners are excluded by project organizers as a matter of course.

The generic term *gumi*, by which the construction companies are known, is also the term for gangster syndicates. Japan is a construction state, in contrast to being a military–industrial state or a welfare state. The circular flow is from taxpayers to construction companies for massive development projects, bridges and tunnels, highways, and airports. The money goes to favored construction companies, who provide kickbacks from these regional development projects, to the LDP politicians who keep the money flowing. Japan, of course, can use the infrastructure spending. Its highways are crowded, deadly, and very expensive. On holiday weekends drivers are bound to wonder whether they have accidentally turned into a parking lot, and while the *shinkansen* may be a model beyond the hopes of American mass transit enthusiasts, it is three decades old and, by Japanese standards, ready for a radically improved replacement in the proposed magnetic levitation train. The politics through which such changes will come about, however, is a different matter.

Land prices are powerfully influenced by access that government infrastructure spending can do much to enhance. Throughout the postwar period land has been the major form of collateral for the massive highly leveraged loans Japanese industry and many individuals have contracted. Indeed, "incentives to manipulate land prices through public works expenditures, and hence to expand the range of public works projects in remote areas, are especially strong in Japan."[7] Regional policy spending and political rebates are closely intertwined in ways that make the telling of the story only the outer shell of many of the events described.

Historical Background of Regional Policy

The country's regional policy planning began prior to its industrial revolution when the agricultural settlement policy for the Hokkaido frontier and local planning of Tokyo were enacted at the beginning of the Meiji Era. If we skip over Depression Decade–efforts at public works in agricultural areas aimed at the solution to regional problems, the beginning of a substantial regional policy, one covering the entire nation, is the Comprehensive National Development Plan Act in 1950, which combined policies for land, water, and other natural resources, the prevention of flood and wind disasters (to which Japan is prone) with measures relating to the proper establishment of industries, and the scale and disposition of cities and farming villages. Finally, the measure dealt with the preservation of culture, natural beauty, and the enhancement of public welfare. This mix of goals continued in legislation through the postwar era.

Before World War II, Japan was an agricultural country. The cities and industrial districts that existed were like islands floating in a rural sea. Poverty in the agricultural districts was desperate. The gap in well being (generalizing to average class experiences in both areas) between these areas and Osaka and Tokyo was vast. Even at the end of World War II most people were still farmers.

In rural areas and in cities there was great hardship in the aftermath of defeat. Making allowance for those who returned to the land there were 10 million unemployed. The shortages of food and energy were mind-boggling. Coal output dropped from 4 million tons before the defeat to barely 1 million because the Koreans and Chinese, who had been forced to mine for the Japanese, no longer did so. The rice crop in 1945 was a disaster, inflation was rampant, and hunger a reality. Postwar industrialization was enhanced by land reform under the SCAP Command, which both freed tenants to come to the cities and stimulated productivity increases that provided food for them when they got there.[8]

In 1950 half the population was classified as peasants or fishermen. Thirty years later they were less than 10 percent, and this has continued to decrease. From 1955 to 1965 rural to urban migration was so extensive that over half of Japan's prefectures experienced absolute decline in population, and another quarter of them experienced growth rates of less than 1 percent per annum. The growth of the industrial workforce peaked in 1970. Thus, the period under consideration here encompasses a number of monumental shifts. One of the most—perhaps *the* most—dramatic shifts is the rural–urban migration in such a concentrated time period in the history of the industrialized world. There is also the equally momentous rapid shift into heavy industry and then out again into postindustrial occupations. In two generations Japan went from the farm to the high-tech economy in the most rapid economic ascent the world has known.

Japan's postwar economic history is conventionally divided into three periods: recovery, 1945–1955; the rapid growth era, 1955–1973; and what is sometimes called slow growth era since, but which was in fact prelude to a new crisis period for the Japanese system. [9] I would suggest that a clear fourth stage began in 1985, the strong yen era. These are the four periods that serve in the present discussion. To avoid confusion it should be pointed out that there have also been four Comprehensive National Development Plans. As they will be discussed, it should be clear that the shifts dividing the four growth periods influence, but do not coincide with, the four plans. The revisions and departures of the planners, however, are responsive to these changes in the larger political economy.

In fiscal 1946 almost 20 percent of the national budget was allocated to industry related purposes. State guidance was important to the direction and character of economic and regional development. The 1947 Priorities Production Policy guided and underwrote reconstruction of designated strategic industries (coal, electric power, iron, and steel). Subsidies to these industries amounted to 30–40 percent of total costs and almost a quarter of the total fiscal 1947 budget. Forced savings under conditions of hyperinflation (80 percent in 1949) and mass hunger provided the resources for economic recovery. The austerity forced by the balanced budgeting imperatives of the Dodge Line prevented a crowding out of private investment. The Reconstruction Finance Bank (established in 1947) and other governmental agencies channeled capital to priority industries. [10]

Poverty, discouragement, and isolation, which characterized the lives of many people in rural Japan in the 1950s and early 1960s, was a strong push factor. Populations declined in these areas, villages had trouble financing local needs, and an aging population created other problems. *Dekasegi*, seasonal employment for males outside the home village, was very common and further undermined community and family life. Elder sons had to remain at home orphaned between children and old folks. There were problems of finding brides for these eldest sons, as even families with older sons at home themselves did not want their daughters to marry into farm families. A *"hekichi* mentality"* [11] developed as many such isolated villages seemed places without a future. For many months *dekasegi* was really a permanent limbo for the men often doing construction in big cities. The problem has been likened to drug addiction. Withdrawal is too painful and the urge to continue great, yet there is also an aching desire for normal life to return. [12] The need to bring jobs to the villages has been a constant theme in Japanese regional policymaking. The sense of belonging to the village remains strong and explains the nostalgia I had occasion to comment on earlier, but there have been few effective strategies to address the continuing rural crisis. [13]

The single-minded pursuit of economic growth also led to a centralization of decision making and control of resources in Tokyo that undermined local autonomy and dramatically restricted democracy (defined in terms of people's participation in decision making concerning collective aspects of their own well-being). The elitist, technocratic, and centralist biases of the Japanese polity so integral to Japan's economic strategy have remained central to Japanese regional policies over time, although the mix has varied between accumulation and efforts to privilege quality of life issues. A subtext also omnipresent is the balance struck between the interests dominant in Tokyo and those locked in their orbit. Thus, we can speak of the dialectic of capital against the regions in this double sense of class and place.

The specifically spatial land policy was established by the Mining and Industrial Zone Arrangement Plan of 1956, which compiled a comprehensive industrial basis arrangement plan in order to break bottlenecks and give priority to industrial land, water, and road development in the four biggest industrial zones in the nation. This decision to give strength to strength and to focus on areas with a record of industrial achievement and an existing stock of social capital from the prewar era was to continue in the 1960 agreement to the National Income Doubling Plan of that year.

With such measures, the national land policy for industrial location established during the late 1950s and early 1960s did not seek to correct the extremely centralized regional structure of prewar Japanese capitalism through public policies; rather, it continued and expanded concentration in the preexisting Pacific Coast industrial zones. This single-minded accumulation-based strategic orientation ignored the social questions involved and created new regional problems. Indeed, the problematic aspects of the national land policy as an industrial location strategy were already evident in these years. There were problems of severe smog as a result of air pollution and of ground subsidence because of pumping up excess underground water. The coastal fishing industry was devastated, population growth dramatically outstripped provision of basic urban amenities, and land prices in and around large cities soared, pricing working class families out of accessible housing.

In response to these problems, the First Comprehensive National Development Plan (CNDP) was adopted in 1962 with goals to "prevent the cities from becoming too big and to reduce regional discrepancies," but economic priorities precluded such an outcome. The same failure has characterized the experience of subsequent CNDPs. While each has spoken to the changed position of Japan in the international division of labor and to the country's internal industrial and regional structures, each has called for a policy of dispersing industries and population. Unfortunately, they have not carried a real national commitment of resources and will power capable of achieving these exemplary goals.

The First Systematic Plans

In the first CNDP a bias toward agricultural areas can be detected that is at first surprising given the emphasis of the period on heavy industry. The plan called for building multipurpose dams on the Tennessee Valley Authority model, but there were important differences in motivation involved. The prime movers in the Japanese case were the large private companies that were obliged to work on developing domestic resource capacities they had lost with their overseas colonial holdings after the war. The flood control and especially enhanced food and electrical generation were also essential to the industrialization effort. The benefits that could be transferred directly from the countryside, such as water resources, were monopolized by the power plants. The electric power was transmitted directly to the major cities and their factories, which used the power at greatly subsidized rates. The other announced goals—land preservation, river improvements, and many quality-of-life improvements for the countryside, important targets announced by the plan—were not implemented. Indeed, government outlays for social services per capita through this period were about the same as in Tunisia or Sri Lanka and one third of those in France or Germany at the time. The purpose of regional policy was to intensify the accumulation effort and what Japanese call "growthism," not to directly increase the well being of the Japanese people.

The pressure for Japan to industrialize came as it had for hundreds of years, from the outside. After the peace pact in 1951, Japan was made to join the international system of division of labor under the leadership of the United States. It was told to meet International Monetary Fund rules. At the same time it remained heavily dependent on overseas suppliers of essential raw materials and so suffered a structured balance of payments problem. There is no need here to rehearse Japan's remarkable development of an industrial policy that contradicts the advice of English-speaking advisers with their static comparative advantage doctrines (to be discussed in Chapter 9). Key regional aspects of this policy approach were evident in the 1952 Act to Promote Enterprise Rationalization and Underwrite Heavy Industry, which concentrated development in the east coast industrial belt.

In Japan, as elsewhere, localities bid against each other to attract industry and lobby the central government for infrastructure projects. The consequences of losing are unpleasant, especially when the local governments undergo great expense and fail so that they are strapped with enormous debt and near worthless holdings of unsold prepared land. Even winners, however, have found that profits from factories that do locate flow back to the cities where the company is headquartered, and local linkage generation is slight since everything from inputs to the plant and equipment are supplied and brought from outside the region. Industrial waste, air pollution, and water pollution produce health hazards and reduce an area's attraction to residents and those dissuaded from locating there except to further despoil the environment. In effect, the region can be used up and require such a large renewal effort as to demonstrate a lack of wisdom in the original industrialization strategy from a local standpoint.

After around 1960 the nature of industry shifted from light manufacturing to heavy goods and petrochemicals. Large industrial complexes called *Kombinat* were built adjacent to the major cities, often on reclaimed land. Each contained port facilities, oil terminals, refineries, power plants, and steel and chemical plants. The major *kombinats* are on land reclaimed from Tokyo, Osaka, and Ise (Nagoya) bays. Two thirds of the nation's industrial activities were concentrated in these three areas. Nationwide reclamation planning was a complex undertaking. It began with projections of real GNP growth and estimates of land productivity in manufacturing to calculate the demand for factory sites.

Reclaimed land was projected to produce 45 percent of total land area needed in 1966. While costly, land reclamation costs were in most places less than half the price of farm land in the vicinity.

The 1962 Nationwide Integrated Development Plan financed 15 new industrial sites and seven special industrial areas throughout the country at a cost to the taxpayer of 6 trillion yen. Local governments provided infrastructure, ports, land, and other incentives, taking on debt they assumed they could repay from taxes generated by the new economic activities. The twenty-one areas chosen covered 9 percent of the total area of the nation and 15 percent of its population in over 100 cities, towns, and villages. These were not underdeveloped regions.

The timing, purpose, and relation of two pieces of legislation—the 1962 New Industrial Cities Promotion Law and the 1964 Special Industrial Consolidation Areas Act—are interesting. The latter was initiated under strong pressure from large capital to concentrate industrial development in the traditional Pacific belt despite obvious social costs and the needs for jobs in the peripheries, which had been influential considerations in the formulation of the 1962 program. Kenichi Miyamoto, summarizing the social cost of this policy initiative, writes:

> The consequences of regional development with the sole object of promoting the economy are (a) the emergence of public hazards [here he had in mind environmental costs which in his work he has pioneered efforts to detail], (b) the decline in local industries, (c) financial risk and (d) the decline in local self-government. [14]

The hold of the Pacific industrial belt increased in large measure because supplier firms were already located there and agglomeration economies for just-in-time production are important.

1960s Politics in Japan

The Japanese political system rewards the largest party over a fragmented opposition and gives rural conservative voters far more representational weight than those in the faster growing urban areas. (This is still true, but to a lesser degree after the 1994 reforms.) Local candidates affiliated with the LDP could also claim access to national government resources. The disruption of traditional ways of life and the despoiling of the environment, however, meant progressives could draw on local self-interest, pride, and antipathy to the harmful effects of growth, while the LDP party hacks often appeared less responsive to local interests beyond those of narrow business groups and patronage politics. [15]

The failure of Japanese economic growth policies at the regional level carried with it a widespread disillusionment with far-reaching consequences and a new politics, not altogether unlike those of the 1960s in the United States and Western Europe. Issues of the war in Vietnam, renewal of the security treaty with the United States, military spending and the peace constitution (Article

9), and other issues were part of a package in the leftist consciousness of the period along with the impact of quality-of-life and environmental issues that stimulated a mass movement at the grassroots level for political change.

The 1960s was a decade of incredible urbanization in Japan. The populations of the Tokyo, Nagoya, and Osaka regions expanded by 15 million between 1965 and 1975 to become 45 percent of the total population of the country. The heavy industry complexes, concentrated in the large metropolitan areas, sucked emigrants from the countryside into hastily built "bed towns." Public transit was overburdened and minimal urban and cultural facilities had been put in place.[16]

The massive spatial dislocations had a structuring impact on political organization in both new industrial development areas in the peripheries and in the rapidly growing metropolitan agglomerations of the core. Bureaucratic control was strengthened and democracy based on local participation eroded as national technocrats assumed more responsibility for development. Out of the experience of rapid growth and social impoverishment came a political critique of big enterprise domination, narrow materialism, and the fundamental pattern of economic development. The cutting edge of the urban and regional social movements was concern over pollution and the living environment more broadly.

In 1964 a people's movement against the invitation of a petroleum complex in Mishima and Numazu, and in Tokyo the election of the progressive Ryokichi Minobe as governor in 1967, signaled a dramatic shift in public consciousness and activism. Across Japan, farmers, fisherfolk, small factory owners, and shopkeepers came together with elements of the traditional left to form a broad social coalition challenging the single-minded pursuit of growth. These successes—the rejection of the Mishima-Numazu heavy chemical complex, which was the impetus for a nationwide antipollution struggle, and the adoption of a strong control program at the national level in 1967 (the Basic Law for Environmental Pollution Control), as well as the election of progressive local and regional officials—reinforced one another. Yet, the environmental law was criticized because it made environmental protection contingent on "harmony with sound economic development." The 1969 Tokyo Metropolitan Government's Pollution Prevention Act moved beyond such an understanding declaring environmental protection a basic right of citizens in Tokyo, rejecting the harmony theory of the central government and creating pressure for reconsideration of the national government's formulation. It was in this period that the popular movements insisted on smaller, fuel-efficient cars to protect the environment. In Tokyo the progressive administration insisted it would only buy cars that met strict standards. After claiming they could not be met the auto industry complied. This positioned them to take advantage of the OPEC-induced gasoline price jump and the resultant worldwide demand for fuel-efficient cars. The top civil servant during this period responsible for planning for the Tokyo Metropolitan Government, Tokue Shibata, told me this story with obvious relish.

Progressive mayors and governors were elected in a number of Japan's large cities. The election of Ichio Asukata as mayor of Yokohama in 1963 was symbolically the most important of these. Asukata had been a Socialist Party member of the Lower House in his fourth term when he decided to run for mayor of Yokohama. After the watershed Miike coal miners' strike of 1960, which the workers lost despite huge support organized by the left throughout Japan (something like the miners strike in the late 1980s that Margaret Thatcher successfully broke), and the antisecurity treaty battles of the same year, the leftist parties lost the national elections. Asukata was part of the wing of leftist politics that sought to return to grass-roots organizing through local electoral work and municipal government reform.

The first progressive government was in Kyoto Prefecture, where Governor Ninagawa was elected in 1950 and served in that post for twenty-eight years. Like the independent candidates who took office during the years of progressive government's ascendancy he, like Minobe in Tokyo and Kuroda in Osaka, could be characterized as a *bunkajin*, a "man of culture," an intellectual who commands wide respect in a community. [17] Such men led the electoral thrusts of progressive citizens' movements in the 1960s. All were one-time professors and respected intellectuals. They headed coalitions of movement groups supported by leftist political parties but independent and far broader in their support. By the late 1960s and early 1970s progressive local executives (not all former college teachers!) were found in jurisdictions where 40 percent of Japan's population lived. Rural areas remained in the control of traditional (LDP-affiliated) politicians and retained a patronage clientele politics based on personalistic control and the distribution of favors for support. In urban areas industrialization had produced a proletarianization of a formerly rural migrant population, and these urban voters were far more active and independent in their outlook. Disillusionment or at least dissatisfaction with the parties of the left and the trade unions led many to prefer social movement activism, a trend found elsewhere in the 1960s.

In Japan these citizens' movements were very actively involved in environmental issues, especially the ecological problems created by industrialism. Seeking compensation for victims and attempting to prevent the establishment of new polluting industrial plants, these activists were doing battle with Japan, Inc., and its philosophy of growth at all costs, which was supported by the giant corporations and the national government. Many of these struggles were fought against arrogant and stubbornly defiant companies and a procrastinating distant central government. The former actively attempted to steamroll the citizen movements. The latter stonewalled and delayed. The movements, therefore, also fought the notion of central control and administrative guidance from the center. The political culture of the citizens' movements was a determined, deeply moral, and driven perseverance. They stressed citizens rights to be involved and defended the U.S.-imposed constitution, which they believed offered support for their politics. The Ninagawa administration in Kyoto actually had thousands of copies of the constitution printed up and distributed. It hung a banner from prefecture office buildings, "Let's Make the Constitution Live in Our Lives," a move reminiscent of the Greater London Council's banners with messages from the grass roots that hung facing the Thatcher-dominated parliament building a decade later. [18]

The ideology of progressive localism was the practice of participation. [19] While the LDP politicians pursued votes based on their supposed "pipeline to the center," the progressives took pride in their "pipeline to the people." Organizations of artists and craftspeople, intellectuals, and religious organizations were the supportive base. Kyoto has traditionally been a bastion of progressive politics. It has been called the Japanese Bologna after that Italian city's leftist political culture and strong grass-roots support for historic preservation and democratic grass-roots–oriented economic policymaking. [20]

On specific issues raised by the environmental movements local governments generally sought ways of controlling pollution without getting into conflict with the national laws and the central government agencies. One method was the pollution control agreement between local government and industry that defined duties to the environment. The first such agreement was signed in 1964 in Yokohama with an electric power company that had planned a new coal-fired thermal power plant near a densely populated area. By national law the plant was exempt from local jurisdiction; however, popular pressure from strong grass roots organizations and the municipal government created the pressure for them to sign an epoch-making voluntary agreement. It was soon followed by similar contracts elsewhere. The one between the Tokyo Metropolitan Council (TMC) and the Tokyo Generating Company in 1968 included an agreement on a 50 percent reduction in sulphur emissions and the right of the TMC to enter and inspect power stations. [21]

Between 1971 and 1973 four major pollution trials ended in victory for victims of environmental crimes. [22] These cases established the principle that any industry could be sued and could lose in a Japanese court for offenses in the environmental realm. Progressive cities established compensation legislation that covered health care and living expenses (among such cities were Kawasaki, Amagashi, and Yokkaichi). In 1973 the central government established the Pollution Related Health Injuries Compensation Law based on these precedents, the first of its kind in the world. [23]

In the December 1972 elections the LDP suffered sharp losses and there were dramatic gains for the communists. In Japan's major cities communist strength was then at its highest level in history and the LDP was running scared, making concessions to popular demands on a wide front. By mid-1973 half of the Japanese people lived in areas where local government was led by socialists and communists. The dramatic jump in welfare state expenditures from 1972 to 1975 was the most impressive of the postwar period. The year that Japan's medical insurance and employees' pensions and insurance coverage introduced important extensions of state services was 1973. [24] Indeed, fiscal year 1973 has been called "the first year of the welfare era." [25] In February 1973 the LDP cabinet presented a five-year basic economic and social program, "For a Dynamic Welfare State," which deemphasized growth and put stress on housing, parks, regional development, and combatting environmental pollution. [26]

The year of OPEC's price shock was also 1973. The recession caused by the oil crisis caused a sharp drop in tax revenues. Bond dependence rose from less than 10 percent to over 25 percent of the national budget in the supplementary budget of fiscal 1975. Welfare-state spending was cut back and declined for a decade or more as a share of GNP after that date as leftist strength ebbed. The fiscal crisis at the local level removed badly needed resources and pulled the material base out from under progressive local programs.

The Second CNDP

With declining LDP strength in Japan's largest cities more attention had also been given to small provincial cities to shore up the LDP's traditional support. (Given the outmoded districting, rural voters hold a disproportionate electoral strength in Japan.) The official plan on which it was based—the *Shinzenso*, or Second CNDP (of 1969)—attempted to knit the nation more closely by extending networks by air, rail, and motor roadways in the hope that regional disparities would be overcome by spread effects. The plan called for the development of large-scale industrial complexes in remote areas so that the polluting industries, iron and steel, oil refining and petrochemicals, could be located in the periphery. The plan foresaw a division of labor among the regions and the construction of large-scale growth poles in the underpopulated regions of Hokkaido, Tohoku, South Shikoku, and Southern Kyushu, while administration as well as processing and assembly continued in the Pacific Belt.

Following the Shinzenso, a plan entitled "Building a New Japan: A Plan for Remodelling of the Japanese Archipelago" was put forward by Prime Minister Kakuei Tanaka. The two plans had a common root, but the latter was part of preparation for the national elections and so has generally been understood in such a political context. It promised to disperse generous amounts of public spending and facilitate the location of factories in the regions. The dispersal plan was successful in attracting voters, giving the LDP a major victory at the polls that year. The 1968 LDP party program statement, "General Principle of Urban Policy," can be read as a comprehensive statement of how to stimulate business, buy votes, pay off construction industry supporters, and do good. Public investment is part of the grease that lubricates the Japanese political system as much as securities companies instructing politicians which stocks to buy and when to sell them for maximal advantage and political protection of fixed commissions and other aspects of the Japanese financial industry's generous business climate. As adopted in public legislation it also had the impact of fostering dramatic speculation and rising land prices as overliquidity, which had made its appearance in the post-OPEC period, was channeled into real estate on a mammoth scale.

The large-scale development projects to move polluting industry to the periphery, as we have seen, met with resistance. A counterproposal was offered by progressive governors and mayors representing large-scale popular movements that stressed minimizing environmental disruption, civic participation, and preservation and enhancement of quality of life. Under such circumstances the second CNDP was officially "reconsidered" only two years after its announcement. While reconsideration was inevitable given the popular opposition that was cutting into LDP electoral support quite dramatically, an immediate shock provoking a change of direction was the Nixon New Economic Policy of 1971, which seemed to be aimed at Japan to a significant degree and the deep recession (for Japan) that followed.

The oil crisis of 1973 marked the end of the progressive era at the local level because of the effects of the economic crisis it precipitated: sharply reduced government revenues and the need for local austerity measures. The antigrowth politics of the previous decade could not be sustained, and inflation and recession compromised welfare-state–oriented local administrations, who were blamed for the huge deficits and charged with irresponsible spending. Delays in building and antidevelopment attitudes could also be more effectively criticized by the political right in the new economic climate. By passing environmental protection legislation at the national level the LDP also stole the progressives' fire. In the years that followed the move away from an emphasis on heavy industry as the engine of Japan's economic growth, which was necessitated by the higher energy costs, also meant a relatively cleaner environment and an end to construction of mammoth energy processing plants.

The Third CNDP

The *Sanzenso*, or Third CNDP, reflected what by 1977, when it was introduced, had become the need to "intentionally designate a united environment for a stable, healthy, cultural, human residence based on the historical and traditional culture with the best use of regional characteristics, where humanity and nature are balanced in harmony, on the supposition of limited land resources." The impact of the social reform movement and the widespread antipathy to large-scale industrialized zones is evident in the plan's language, but there was no budget allocation to meet these high-minded goals. The local autonomy movements had influenced the plan, and placed emphasis on self-reliance and meeting human needs through decentralization and better local area integration. This also meant cutting small and medium size construction companies after a period of giant projects which had concentrated contracts among the Big Five. The latter were looking more to overseas business in any case as large-scale building slowed in Japan. Post-industrial growth became the conventional industrial policy priority.

The new economic climate brought an even more single-minded focus on Tokyo. The regions witnessed depression as heavy industry and increasingly light industry as well moved to the newly industrializing neighbor countries, which produced a deindustrialization mild by the standards of the United States and the United Kingdom, but one that was significant and painful to many non-Tokyo areas. There had been a decline in the number of jobs in Tokyo in the 1970s along with the same sort of local fiscal crisis experienced elsewhere; overall, the economy of the city experienced decline. In the new internationalized climate of the late 1970s and 1980s, however, the city grew dramatically, fed by growth in the financial and corporate service sectors in a manner similar to that which New York and London were experiencing in the same years.

Heavy industry was moved out of Tokyo and many small manufacturing districts felt the pressure of rising land prices. While manufacturing employment in Tokyo peaked in 1961, however, it was still the city's major employer, a very different situation than in New York and London, which had grown almost entirely dependent on business services, above all else finance. Tokyo is a much more balanced city. The Kanto, the wider Tokyo region, is still the heart of Japanese manufacturing. The connections among research, the construction of prototypes and specialty production, and the large corporate sector is also greater because so much of Japanese industry is oriented toward new product and process innovation, and flexible production is integrated with other aspects of corporate management.

Depopulation in rural areas led to the collapse of communities. In some areas Buddhist temples, the emotional mainstay for local people, fell into ruin, and even ancestral graves were flown out to metropolitan areas (in a process referred to as "ultimate" depopulation). In the first half of the 1980s the population decreased in more than half the municipalities in the provinces of Hokkaido, Tohoku, Chugoku, Kyushu, and Okinawa. The only hope for these regions, a strand of the discussion picked up in the fourth CNDP, which will be discussed shortly, was officially said to be tourism, in which Tokyo-based firms would implant complexes importing inputs and employing limited number of locals in menial jobs.

In the receiving areas, following Mumford's usage of "factory slums" (to describe the English factory cities during the Industrial Revolution), Miyamoto speaks of Japan's "office-factory slums."[27]

> In Japan, many satellite cities are experiencing a complete desolation of the natural environment and are without any parks. These cities were originally built for residential use on farm land with little social capital, so the urban facilities such as the city water and sewer system, roads, schools, daycare facilities, and hospitals are missing.[28]

The loss to the natural environment in Japan during the years of high-speed growth were extreme. The shoreline of Japan was filled in and reduced to 40 percent of its former length. Around metropolitan areas the shore was nearly totally filled in. Beaches were lost, and swimming and fishing were made impossible as red tide and levels of pollution generally made these waters unsafe for living things. Mountains were cut flat for landfill, and green areas were decreased to make urban areas an unrelieved built environment. The human health damages and destruction of nature were on such a scale that some experts concluded that postwar industrial complexes in long-term perspective created net losses for the regions involved.

With hindsight and the experience of widespread environmental devastation, scholars reexamined earlier sites of the Japanese economic miracle and put together the research findings that had not been widely disseminated to get a clearer picture of the costs of growth. In the case of the Sakai-Senboku industrial complex in Osaka Prefecture, for example, the *kombinat* used 41 percent of the area's electrical power and 22 percent of its industrial water at its height, but employed less than 2 percent of the labor force and paid less than 2 percent (1.6 percent) of business taxes. Thus, despite the scale of the heavy industry complex and its deleterious impact on the quality of life for Japan's second largest city, small and medium businesses supplied 92 percent of Osaka prefecture's value added and over 98 percent of employment and business taxes. Today, in hindsight, a less-polluted environment and the retention of beaches and recreation areas would be of more value to the prefecture even in narrow economic terms. [29]

Mainstream public policy pronouncements did not really come to grips with the cost of the pattern of economic growth or their localized impacts. The economic sphere was taken almost as a given and redistribution policy discussion was limited to the venue of infrastructure spending, omitting the heart of national subsidies and planning, the support of particular patterns of economic growth, and expenditures to address the social costs of such growth. Thus, depending on medical care required by pollution hazards and diseases caused by industry are not measured costs, although, as we have seen, they influence public spending mediated through the political process. Thus, externalities are kept separate from growth accounting. This methodology is clear in the Third CNDP, which reflects Japan's moving into the neoliberal era.

By the 1979 Third CNDP social responsibility had been privatized. It had become an individual responsibility, not a collective one in which the state was to play the leading role. Policies emphasizing large-scale infrastructure projects in underdeveloped regions were replaced by appeal to what elsewhere was called "the magic of the marketplace," but which the plan called "regional independence" and "private sector vitality." The plan also came into effect as the unicentric development pattern focused national growth in the Tokyo area. Between 1980 and 1985 half the jobs created in the entire country were in the national capital region.

The Fourth CNDP

In the fall of 1985 the yen rose dramatically against the dollar going from 260 to 130 before the 1980s ended. Large enterprises, despite initial deep pessimism, did not experience devastating earnings losses. In part, this was because of intense cost-cutting measures (including offshore production), but, perhaps ironically, it was also because of huge speculative profits in real estate. The slowing down in manufacturing employment and the increase in information processing and finance in the context of internationalization, the in-migration of foreign corporate offices and the increased growth of research, increased the attractiveness of a Tokyo location and land prices soared. While the fourth CNDP sought a "multipolar dispersal land structure," political and economic realities spoke to even greater unipolar concentration. The fourth CNDP (the final draft of the *Yonzenso* was completed June 1987), while providing rhetorical support for a multipolar pattern of national land use, privileged the global city, Tokyo. As a result of political pressure from forces favoring the capital region, the Fourth CNDP kept decentralization to within 50 kilometers of the metropolitan area.

The Land Agency's December 1986 interim report addressed itself primarily to the problem of how to remodel Tokyo to better serve its role as world city. While the outcry from the rest of the country led to a dual focus in the final report on "correction of the unipolar concentration in Tokyo" and the need for "strategic high-priority development of the outlying regions," the Fourth Development Plan for the National Capital Region was very clear about the extent of decentralization that was contemplated—very little and not very far from the center. A multizone regional structure was proposed as a way to make continued unicentric development of the capital region work better.

When the CNDP report was about to be published Prime Minister Nakasone ordered a change in tone to stress the world city functions of Tokyo and the importance of its continued development to Japan's future.[30] At the same time the report retained the goal of forming a multipolar land structure by the year 2000, without creating overconcentration of population. It continued to speak of remedying the one-point concentration, but certain sentences were added to the report to satisfy Mr. Nakasone, including one that stated that it is not necessary to oblige offices to leave Tokyo or "to interfere with the promotion of the international role of our country." As a result Tokyo was considered "a special zone for consolidation," and this declaration was kept over the objection of representatives of other regions and advocates of serious decentralization of the capital region's functions.

As opposed to the industries of the high-growth era, which prospered by chewing up local ecologies, the Fourth CNDP speaks of cities as centers of a software- and service-oriented economy. It called for Integrated Local Settlement Areas, providers of urban services of commerce and culture, education, and medical care. Making good use of natural resources and providing a "soft" network of sponsored research, development, and information functions for active use in remote areas as well as preparing long-stay–type resort areas are discussed with an awareness of retirement needs for an aging, more affluent population. There is talk of rural high-tech smart buildings and international conference centers with teleport satellite uplinks.

The study is well aware that in Hokkaido, north Tohoku, parts of Kyushu, and in Okinawa there were many prefectures suffering serious employment and population loss induced by changing economic structures and new disparities emerging between unicentric Tokyo and the peripheries. The vision is one of the Japanese archipelago as a single stage for highly integrated human activities with a one-day access (the possibility for a person living in one area to have face-to-face contact with a person in another and return home the same day).

The significance of hypothetical one-day access is not considered in any depth in the report, perhaps because the positive nature of such a capability seems so obvious to the authors. One wonders, however, how meaningful face-to-face potential contact is now within regions given the closed circles of interest in hierarchically structured relations and non-intersecting roles as they now exist. Access is relevant for a management class while having less meaning for others. The same is true of information flows that in practice may be part of a new pattern of regional segmentation. Thus, one can read contradictory imperatives in the Fourth CNDP.

The stress on technological sophistication fits another initiative, for the development of technopolises that are spatial growth poles functioning to spread information and high-tech culture to the regions. This important regional policy was introduced by MITI, not by the National Land Agency. "Technopolis" appears (as a Japanese-English word) in a 1980 MITI report, "Vision of Trade and Industries in the 1980s," produced by the powerful Advisory Commission on Industrial Structure, which noted that "the Technopolis (the city of high technology) combines systematically the industrial and academic sectors mainly composed of high-tech industry of electronics and machinery with the residential sector in the same region." The Nihon Ricchi Center Technopolis 1990s Project Committee defines *technopolis* as a

> strategy to achieve two goals—knowledge intensification and heightening of value-added of industrial structure (creative nation-building based on high technology), and regional development headed for the twenty-first century—by introducing high-technology industry into culture, tradition, and nature of regional society, by accomplishing "town building" which is harmonious with "industry" (complex of high-technology industry), "academic center" (research institutes and experimental institutes), and "community facilities" (fertile and pleasant living environment).[31]

The Nakasone Administration's 1982 initiative to create nineteen technopolis sites to attract investment to areas of growing unemployment was inspired by the example of Silicon Valley in the United States and Science Park in the United Kingdom. The idea of a growth pole based on high-tech research was also a way to respond to the LDP's rural bastions, which were increasingly complaining about having been ignored in the new growth strategy of the post–heavy industry period. The decline of regional cities that were formerly dependent on shipbuilding or iron and steel had also meant a deteriorating situation for the regional construction companies that had serviced these sectors before the higher energy prices ended prospects.

While the technopolis idea represents a continuation of industrial policy thinking oriented toward generating economic growth, in the climate of the 1980s its regional policy aspect is endowed with a local initiative flavor. It is participatory in the sense that city officials, local bureaucrats, and private entrepreneurs are the area residents who are the actors. The central state is minimally involved by design. Local authorities, believing that a technopolis is the way forward for their region, tend to become overoptimistic, dazzled by the promise of the miracles of science and the high-tech cure to their problems. They spare no expense to invite enterprises with lavish inducements aware that dozens of other locations bid for the same prizes.

There was some appeal in the reliance on local participation and responsibility, yet the forces feeding unicentric development were so strong that without forceful state-led guidance of major actors it could be anticipated that the technopolis strategy would prove to be a high-tech, knowledge-based version of the industrial zone strategies of the 1970s. Without pressure from MITI, and absent significant resources from the central government, these grand proposals have been disappointing in their implementation. They become symbolism for good intentions. They also eat up local energies, displace anxieties, and prove electorally effective for sponsors.

Much that was written about the technopolis concept in the West, usually in the context of denouncing industrial policy, had a panicked quality to it, expressing fear that this was yet another tactic by Japan, Inc., to move ahead through state sponsorship of technology development. From a Japanese standpoint the proposal is quite similar to previous regional plans in its promise to bring jobs, education, and a better quality of life to the countryside. The "government" involved has been the prefectures and city governments in the local areas, who are in a bidding war to locate tenants for their parks. Even though the agencies were encouraged to draw up plans for decentralization, government practice was not to fight concentration where it was most efficient from a *zaikai*, or big business, viewpoint.[32]

The seemingly self-contradictory stance of the state reflected in this official's assessment of these issues reflects the need to mollify the regions while carrying out the preferences of capital, meaning in this case as in most the *zaikai*, the core power in corporate Japan. Such a perspective also qualifies much of what was said about economic theory earlier on in which we assumed economic policy set to maximize national well-being would operate very differently than by following the rules of the market found in the Anglo-American version of economic science. The Japanese developmentalist state, after all, is embedded in a socioeconomic formation of vastly uneven privilege and power. While the overriding goal has been to develop the nation this has generally been done in such a way that the powerful also benefit preferentially. This class dimension of Japanese society is likely to become more pronounced as Japan, having caught up with the West, debates new policy departures. We shall investigate this matter in the final chapter. The purpose here is simply to point out the limits to which available state power may be deployed when it is seen as against the interests of the most important interests in society to use it in a particular way, even if there is great popular support for that policy direction.

The peripheral technopolises did not attract population nor much research capacity. The subsidies did draw some assembly plants. Research continued to be carried out in the Tokyo region, and branch plants to be located on the periphery had a hard time given the strong yen competing with overseas locations. The firms that do locate, however, are not motivated by a burning desire to create local linkages and share technology with local firms. Few of the firms attracted become local, or resident, in the basic sense of Kokichi Shoji's clarification of residents as people who think of their region in use value terms and so are subjects living their lives based on appreciation of the ecology and culture of their communities. Residents in this sense are a different breed from those who seek maximum subsidies, have no local roots or loyalties, and function exclusively in terms of exchange relations.[33]

Many Japanese localities learned from the *kombinat* period the weak employment and local revenue-generating effects of these industrial complexes, their destructiveness of local agriculture, fishing, and general quality of life. Thus, many areas try to specify what they want from the new high-tech growth pattern in holistic development terms.[34] Beggars, however, cannot be choosers. It is not surprising that to be a successful technopolis required, it turned out, to be located near Tokyo. To underscore this point Yazawa suggests that we call the other twenty-five technopolis projects scattered across Japan "local technopolises." Those technopolises that are closely connected to existing production centers are successful. The difficulty of achieving success in isolated new towns, of attracting qualified researchers, successful firms, and the most promising technologies, is remote. Tsukuba Science City works because it was designed as an overflow center for nearby Tokyo. Having been given the national government imprimatur, forty-six national research institutes were sent to it. The Kanazawa experience is more typical of other technopolises. As Sasaki tells us, it "was launched with a flourish of trumpets, is confronted with fruitless results without achieving its original target. . . ."[35]

The most successful of the prefectures in attracting high tech was Oita, whose Governor Hiramatsu (a retired MITI official) had helped devise and implement MITI's restrictions on U.S. computer firms wishing to enter the Japanese market. The friends he made at the time returned the favors by locating facilities in Oita. Such *ongaeshi* is hardly the basis for generalized success of provincial technopolises. The Sony plant Oita attracted reflects the obligation, the *on*, Morita-san carries for his friend Hiramatsu, who forced Texas Instruments into a fifty–fifty deal with Sony a decade and a half earlier.

While there is some appeal in the reliance on local participation and responsibility, the forces feeding unicentric development are so strong that without forceful state-led guidance of major actors it would be anticipated that the technopolis strategy would provide a high-tech, knowledge-based version of the industrial zone strategies of the 1970s. Without pressure from MITI, and absent significant resources from the central government, these grand proposals have been disappointing in their implementation and impact. They become symbolic reassurance of good intention without material benefit. They also eat up local energies and displace anxieties, but prove to be electorally effective for sponsors.

As the 1980s became the 1990s a new emphasis was evident in regional policy planning, and leisure was to be the guiding goal of rebuilding the rural countryside and relieving urban tensions. The Japanese ideal of leisure, however, appears to be a worklike consumer activity. As so many of the other regional expenditure emphases, leisure represents a new profit center for Japanese capitalists connected to politically powerful decision makers. The government's Resort Law spells out the huge new market and expanding impact on the economy which is expected. The *Green Paper Plan Phase 2*, published in 1988, describes the new resorts as "a new basic industry for Japan."

A phenomenon of "reverse resort living" is becoming common in which the home village (our old friend the *furusato*) is redefined as the place outside the capital where the family lives while the salariman husband and father resides in a Tokyo capsule hotel between weekend visits. Further away, equally homogeneous resorts obscure locality and natural environment, reducing diversity and localism by creating artificial commodity spaces of ski resorts and marinas. Such developments are seen by critics as "irrelevant to the needs and problems of local communities, many of whom now see the whole process as a contemporary form of enclosure movement, in which public land, forest, mountains, and beaches are enclosed by private interests for corporate profit. While corporate Japan thrives, they say, the people suffer." The cost of affluence is still in a new dimension, made clear by the slogan *fukoku hinmin*— enrich the country, impoverish the people.[36]

Whether the Japanese yuppie in his womblike "Refresh Capsule," which allows total immersion via hi-fi tape recordings of the environment of murmuring brooks, the song of birds, and gentle breaking waves at the Brain Mind Gym Relaxation Salon at some new resort center, is a perfect substitute for the real thing, which may have been destroyed to build the resort, I do not know. The resort boom, and especially the construction of thousands of golf courses, where a frenzied game only remotely resembling its Western counterpart is played at clubs whose memberships are tradable commodities worth millions of dollars apiece, is another manifestation of the new leisure culture. A full 1 percent of Japan's woodland has been cleared for golf courses.[37] Environmentalists call attention to the three or four tons per year of herbicides, germicides, pesticides, coloring agents, organic chlorine, and the health abnormalities resulting from the carcinogenic and other toxic chemicals used and their impact as they run off into lakes and rivers. They question the wisdom of putting limited rural acreage to such a purpose.

Japanese resorts, as Gavan McCormack notes, "have little to do with leisure and recreation, much with the search for response to international pressures and the growing centrality within the domestic economy of construction and speculative capital."[38] Thus, the seemingly new policy departure, to stress of "quality of life," turns out in practice to be a continuation of long-standing urban and regional policies that have favored a core constituency of the LDP and a powerful interest group in the Japanese economic system. The widespread damage to humans and other living things has spawned new citizens movements to stop their spread and the devastation they bring. The commodification of place in ways that maximize developer profits at the expense of the larger society are not new. The logic is simple enough: The developer takes advantage of natural advantages of a site's surrounding area, imposing costs on neighbors; these costs are external to the decision maker, the profits are kept by the investors. When a significant state subsidy exists because of programs that present the process as socially desireable these profits can be impressive.

Overconcentration in Tokyo and Its Social Costs

As models of core–periphery, uneven growth, and dependency theories have all in different ways stressed, the value added in production tends to flow out of the areas in which it is generated to the head offices and to the ownership and managing strata. In Japan this tendency has existed going back to the days when feudal lords maintained expensive households in the capital, lavishly spending the surplus produced by the peasants in their fiefdoms. This phenomenon of centralization of surplus generated in the countryside continued into the industrial era. The tendency was strengthened from the late 1970s with the spatial restructuring and growth of corporate headquarters functions. According to Economic Planning Agency estimates, in 1983, 242 billion yen flowed to Tokyo from other regions of the country. The largest flows were from the Pacific Belt zones, such as the Tokai, Kinki, and Chugoku, although the amount from Tohoku and Kyushu, where industrial robot manufacturing factories and semiconductor-producing factories were generating large revenues, was also significant.

By the mid-1980s, 88 percent of foreign corporations were located in Tokyo. The city is responsible for half of all bank loans (and nearly 80 percent of checks exchanged) and 57 percent of information service sales. Such high densities in advanced global corporate services led to increasing population concentration so that today close to 10 percent of the country's population lives on 1 percent of the residential land. This is because of the premium on centrality in the Japanese system. As Kamo writes:

> Tokyo is somewhat similar to Toyota's "company town" system, which has been produced by its "just-in-time" system. In the case of Tokyo, in addition to the networks among manufacturing firms, the policy networks (connections) among politicians, bureaucrats, and business leaders, the information networks around corporate headquarters and high-level service sectors and so on all work together in its urban political economy. [39]

Tokyo, however, is far more than the center of decision making. Because it is also Japan's major production region, especially for high-tech industries as well for finance, as Hill and Fujita point out, greater Tokyo is also "Japan's version of the City of London, Silicon Valley, and the Third Italy all wrapped up into one dynamic region." [40] The geography of contemporary Tokyo is the spatial representation of the new neighborhoods of industry. Northwest of Tokyo is Tsubame City in Niigata Prefecture with its guildlike trade associations creating ever-new industrial activities based on small-scale firms with intense entrepreneurial drive. Among other specialties they make 90 percent of Japan's Western-style flatware there. Kanagawa approximates a Silicon Valley-type of industrial district, as Tsubame mirrors the Third Italy. [41]

The Tokyo Metropolitan Region has more than one third of all Japanese employees and 60 percent of information industry workers. For traditional Tokyo neighborhoods that still hold on, such as Tora-san's beloved *Shitamachi*, rising land values attack the fabric of the community as high-priced users invade.[42] If the *average* price of a condominium in Tokyo in 1990 was going for close to half a million dollars it was because so many Japanese felt the need to be there. In the early 1990s, when land prices finally began to fall as a result of the end of the bubble economy, MITI was finding a correlation between corporate spending on plant and equipment for firms to be closely linked to the value of their land holdings. For small and medium-sized companies the tail of land holdings was wagging the production potential of the firms.

Smaller companies without property in Tokyo are in a tight spot, unable to buy land for plant sites and offices. High land prices make it hard to start or expand businesses. A MITI analysis concludes that land-price inflation did more harm than good to small and medium enterprises considered as a whole.[43] In 1986 alone the major city banks increased their loans for real estate 50 percent, leading the chief of the Bank Bureau of the MOF to issue a formal warning in December 1987 that banks should refrain from financing apparently speculative real estate transactions. By bringing this period of seemingly endless self-levitation in real estate markets to an end, MOF also undercut the expansion of the entire Japanese economy, which had rested much more than people had been willing to think about on this alchemist-like creation of profits that had done so much to fuel the boom. The dramatic drop in land prices (averaging 20 percent annually in the early 1990s) brought a new set of problems. This sea change is the topic of the next chapter.

From the more limited perspective of urban quality-of-life issues, the expansion of Tokyo and the subsequent overpopulation made urban problems more serious.[44] The price of housing in the Tokyo metropolitan area (Tokyo, Kanagawa, Saitama, and Chiba) soared by 21.5 percent in 1986 and 69 percent the following year. Prices thus doubled in two years and continued to rise through the end of the decade. Traffic delays caused by congestion and overcrowding on subways and buses in Tokyo are most painful to commuters. The professional pushers, employees of the subway who force people in so that doors can close, are a familiar sight to Western television viewers. The exorbitantly priced "rabbit warrens" of the Tokyo work force is an equally stereotyped image. Both reflect a certain reality of growth at the expense of living standards that has been imposed on urban dwellers in Japan's largest urban centers. Let us add to this lore a recent report in a Japanese newspaper of an orthopedist in downtown Tokyo who says that ten people come to his hospital per month because of fractured ribs suffered in overcrowded commuter trains. The number of such patients has grown five times over the last decade.[45]

The 1991 annual White Paper of the Ministry of Construction calculates the cost of overconcentration in terms of wage levels in the Tokyo metropolitan area, which are 40 percent above the national average. However, if we also consider longer commuting hours and working hours as well as higher rent, then the wage level is only 8 percent higher than the national average. Given the job distribution in the capital region, average wages distort the situation. It is likely that most working people in the region are in real terms paid less than the average worker nationally. However, the Tokyo region is where over half of all new jobs are being created, and those seeking work are drawn to opportunities of employment even as they are then forced to bear burdens created by Japan's unicentric growth pattern. [46]

The overconcentration in Tokyo also created severe problems for Osaka, Japan's second city, as firms left for the capital region. Osaka, its residents increasingly the elderly and the poor, with the affluent commuting from its suburbs, faced fiscal crisis and a shrinking population, familiar inner-city difficulties, including a labor market mismatch. [47] Obsolete municipal facilities and a heavy welfare burden suggest that Osaka, like many Japanese and American cities, cannot hope to solve its problems on its own. In Japan's older cities and rural areas an unraveling of the social fabric is evident. From the suburban bedroom communities that are connected to rapid growth to the depressed factory towns and increasingly depopulated peripheral areas the lack of a coherent regional policy takes a toll. The cost of the opportunistic activity of speculators and political figures is undermining trust and stability. In the 1990s there are once again local social movements working to challenge these trends.

The Kanazawa Case

The dominance of Tokyo and the increasing branch plant character of the other Japanese cities may be inevitable. However, the hope of progressives in a more locally autonomous development in which residents actively shape their communities as use values and create synergies that generate economic surplus in a competitive world is not dead. One example of endogenous development in Japan is Kanazawa, a historic city far from the Pacific coastal zones favored by tourists, which does not have any headquarters of *keiretsu* firms, or even branch offices and plants in serious number. It has had a viable manufacturing economy based on small and medium-sized locally owned and operated firms in which production, research, and development involve interdependencies among these producers and are based on high value-added quality products that diversify and strengthen a network or web of economic activities with both a strong export component and local linkages. Some Kanazawa companies boast, "Small but National Brand." Their niche products enjoy a dominant share of the national market, even though the company is small. [48]

Long before the discovery of the Third Italy Kanazawa had moved ahead of competitors specializing in silk fabric for export, developing innovative textile machines to produce artificial silk and changing from rayon to synthetic fiber after World War II, creating a districtwide capacity of affiliated producers working with local trading companies to become a world-level production center of polyester fiber as local machinery makers realized still further high-efficiency innovations. Their profits went to diversify the industrial use machine business of a large variety small-lot types, which Masayuki Sasaki notes "adapted well to the spirit of traditional artisans as well as to the niche market which included big enterprises." Further, "these industries, though they are locally limited, have spirits of big enterprises which adopt constant innovation." The economy of Kanazawa can be characterized as a "flexible and self-innovative force."[49]

Historically, indeed since the Meiji Era, both textiles and textile machinery fed each other's growth in the city. Kanazawa has a system of local trading companies with developed sales, finance, and distribution capabilities of some power. As opposed to the branch plant cities, whose economies are run from Tokyo, Kanazawa has a contrasting independent urban economy that

> increased value added through roundabout production inside the region, prevented profits of total income produced in the region from outflow and kept it inside, realized constant innovation in medium-sized enterprises, and developed food and drink industry and various service industries which are characteristic of big cities. Furthermore, it brought about urban agglomeration of high quality through increasing universities and colleges, vocational schools and other academic organizations.[50]

I would not want to oversell this impressive case. The road is uphill for this alternative development model. In the organized society that is Japan the local trading companies that assist the small textile makers with technical guidance and financial help and keep profits recycling within the local economy by coordinating the small firms guided by knowledge of markets and cutting edge technologies are up against keen competition. Indeed, the success of Kanazawa's leading firms in automating production has resulted in excess capacity and loss of employment, which jeopardizes the city's economy.[51] The local trading companies and machine manufacturers have gone into crisis. Land speculation has increased dramatically as Tokyo-based developers tear at the urban fabric of historic Kanazawa.

An interesting citizen's movement has developed to protect the city. Financed in part by local businesses and old money imbued with civic pride, it has created a local think tank to develop analyses and counter-strategies to the Tokyo-dominated development pattern of the national plans. Politics has heated up over division as to the city's future as the Tokyo-based real estate interests threaten to change its traditional character. Whether the model of local production and resident citizenship is robust enough to survive in terms of the continued creativity of the local firms in a keen national and international economy, and whether the citizen's movement is able to beat back the exchange-value–dominated politics the city increasingly faces, are open questions.

My visits to niche producers, including one innovative firm run by the son of a local textile family that is making high-fashion company uniforms and doing exceedingly well, and other firms based on artisan traditions, and my discussions with local political figures give some grounds to be optimistic. The city has also sought to exploit its location, on the Sea of Japan looking outward toward Siberia, China, and Korea (and the prospect of a Japan Sea Trading

Zone, which local officials and universities are encouraging with research, conferences, and proposals to the central government).

Kyoto Then, Now, and Tomorrow

The continued despoiling of traditional Japan goes on apace elsewhere as well, even in historical Kyoto. Visitors to the famous *Kikokutei* Garden, to take one graphic example, look up from "Reflect-the-Moon Lake," where Emperor Meiji sipped tea and could raise his visage to view the full moon above the distant mountains, now raise their eyes to see "the towering grey and yellow hulk of a cut-rate love hotel, complete with a giant satellite dish on the roof. The effect is roughly the same that a Washingtonian might feel if a high-rise motel went up between the White House and the Washington Monument."[52]

The efforts by the Buddhist organizations to prevent the construction of an outscale hotel in Japan's historic capital is somewhat known from the widespread press reporting of this struggle. The organization of citizens in that city's neighborhoods to fight developers, building site by building site, has not received the same attention, lacking as it is in local color. Both are part of a struggle to preserve the environment and feel of this city of 3,000 temples and shrines that constitute the bulk of Japan's historical treasures. The city, spared by American bombers because of its uniqueness (and lack of military targets), contains beautiful neighborhoods of two-story houses with shops on the street level and owners' apartments above. These have been in the same family for many generations. In one such neighborhood, *Higashiyama Shiyakawa Tsutsum-icho*, the plan for a seven-storied-huge structure permitted by the militantly prodevelopment LDP city government, which had recently been elected by only a few-hundred-vote margin against the independent environmental preservation candidate, spurred the establishment of a neighborhood-based citizens' movement. After much organizing in this close-knit neighborhood a community charter was popularly developed and used as a basis to negotiate with officials over the right of area residents to preserve their living environment and the centuries-old physical character of the city. Kyoto is surrounded by mountains and part of the identity of local residents comes through being able to look up at the beauty of their surroundings. Most Kyoto residents today still enjoy a visual quality of life rare in the modern urbanized world. The activists in this particular neighborhood measured the offending site, calculated scale-dimension specifications, which, it turned out, were in fact illegal, and en masse brought their map and supporting evidence to officials. They eventually forced major concessions from the builder (and the city). When I visited with community leaders in 1991 they were proud that nineteen community chapters had sprung into existence around Kyoto's neighborhoods. Even a taxi driver bringing a visitor to the area knew of the group from media reports and supported its work.

The Kyoto case is one of stark contrast between a real estate industry mayor and the neighborhoods helped by local academics such as Shinya Katagawa of the National University in Kyoto, whose students built a scale model of the proposed outscale building described earlier so that neighborhood people could more fully visualize what it would mean to their lives if it were built. Lawyers contributed their skills on a pro bono basis as well. Citywide, thousands of residents identify with and many took part in developing "Our OWN Town Planning Scheme," which the preservation movement developed. It urges a living city for residents—not a dead museum city, but one respectful of, indeed grounded in, Kyoto's history and traditions. The fear is that the greed of developers are doing the work the U.S. Air Force refrained from undertaking. The candidate who lost the mayoral election by 242 votes is a living legend. Mampei Kimura is a retired teacher who exuded a quiet, intensely powerful rootedness in historical Kyoto. His platform is that no new building be built that is over four stories high. This would insure that within the fifty-year building cycle for new construction the traditional skyline would be reestablished as large aging buildings were replaced. When I left his traditional house on a "street" or passageway about four-feet wide and turned onto a main thoroughfare leading to the high-rise department stores also in the downtown area, I thought about how Japanese capital, which is capable of planning technological developments so carefully and carrying on transformations so single-mindedly over decades, has also been so irresponsible about the living environment of the country and the intricate antagonisms between speculators and community existence.[53]

Concluding Comments on Spatial Patterning

A final comment should be made about local finance in Japan. Some analysts have made much of the relatively high proportion of total government spending that takes place at the subnational level (80 percent in Japan as compared with a little over 50 percent in West Germany and the United States) and the much higher level of central government to localities in Japan. However, intergovernmental relations in Japan involve an exceedingly high degree of centralization. Despite recommendations of blue ribbon commissions to let communities have more say in zoning, approval of factory construction, and designating of new bus routes, Tokyo bureaucrats continue to control these functions. Strict central government control extends to the selection of school superintendents, the contents of textbooks, and even the size of school gymnasiums.[54]

The central government's vision for the 1990s, released in May 1990, stresses the development of domestic markets, leisure and vacation centers—the so-called silver industries targeted at an aging population—and an emphasis on basic research. There is awareness in elite technocratic circles that too many young Japanese are going into banking and finance rather than science and engineering and that creativity in manufacturing remains a core need of a dynamic Japanese economy. New technology is being foregrounded in environmental science in the hope that a country that now has such a bad reputation in this area in terms of the activities of its corporations abroad can make a major contribution to protecting and conserving the fragile resources of the planet.[55] Japanese companies favoring a multiple headquarters system are decentralizing production and increasing autonomy of their subsidiaries in the United States and Europe, producing more in the Asian NICs, and outgrowing their national economies. Whether these new global corporations will be able to pay less attention to citizen needs and problems of uneven growth in Japan now that they have a global reach is an important question.

The impact of these trends on regional developments in Japan are far from clear. While planners speak of increasing the integration of the country as a single spatial entity, discrepancies abound between ideal and actuality of uneven development. Even in high-income areas land cost pressures continue to price non-owners out of the possibility of home ownership. As Japanese have gotten richer and travel more, they have been able to notice the lack of urban amenities compared with cities in nations with now lower per capita incomes, to be aware, for example, that Switzerland, which is even more mountainous, has more attractive cities, and that Geneva devotes seven times more land per capita to parks than does Tokyo, or that Amsterdam provides fifteen times the per capita park space. Similar comparisons with other cities and for expenditures for publicly sponsored housing, for sewage, and for other urban amenities demonstrate costs of single-minded emphasis on narrowly conceived economic growth policies. Whether citizens in a rich Japan will be able to make claims on the social wealth to provide healthier regional growth patterns and more amenities in overcrowded urban areas will be an interesting question to follow.

8

Overaccumulation, Speculation, and Corruption

"'Everyone gets a part of the action when you corner a share, especially the politicians,' he complained. In return, the politicians were
able to introduce banking contacts to speculators. Suzuki noticed that
ruling Diet members Toshio Komoto and Entaro Itoyama conducted
two of the greatest corporate raids of the early 1970s. These were,
however, exceptionally high-profile instances of stock market killings
channelled into politics. The preferred route was a collusive arrangement among the speculators, politicians and a local bank manager who
provided a large line of credit. The speculator risked little or none of
his own capital, bought up stock, sold it back to the company at an
inflated price and paid back the bank, splitting the ill-made gains
among himself and his political friends."
ALBERT J. ALLETZHAUSER, *The House of Nomura*[1]

"Big business is not a separate interest group in Japan; it is the prime
beneficiary and virtual raison d'être of the Japanese system, as the
theory of the capitalist development state stipulates. For that reason it
is meaningless to speak of the role of big business in Japanese politics;
the two are indistinguishable."
MARK BORTHWICK, *Pacific Century*[2]

Performance of the Japanese model of capitalism in the postwar era surpassed
the Western version in a number of important respects. Its developmentalist-
state practices, labor relations system, and production regime were more efficient and led to Japanese triumphs in global competition. Yet, by the early
1990s the process of its decomposition was evident. Japan, having caught up
by emulating aspects of the U.S. system and improving on them, has also
followed the United States into financial excesses. This chapter recounts the
story of how in the 1980s Japan substituted financial overextension for the

198

unconstrained productionist drive of its postwar system. This did not occur because a conscious choice was made to abandon long-term growth of productive assets in favor of speculative excess. The production-driven strategy continued, but it encountered tough going. The global slowdown limited Japan's prospects for productive growth. Speculation and financial profit seeking was the result, not the cause, of this slowdown and increased global economic fragility. The corruption and excesses of the regime became more visible and the contradictions of developmentalist-state practices more evident and costly in the new era.

At the start of the last chapter I alluded to some of the ways politics as usual infuses urban and regional policymaking. These pork barrel carryings-on are not unfamiliar on the American scene or to one degree or another in most societies. What is more unique is the Japanese penchant for functioning in groups, which binds individuals to leaders and other members, infusing the country's politics with socially contracted dependence in a more structured system of exchange of favors and obligations than is commonly found elsewhere. *Gakubatsu*, the relationship based on university classmates, is an important influence, nowhere more so than the *Todaibatsu*, the University of Tokyo graduates. Todai's students monopolize the upper reaches of the prestigious ministries and of blue chip corporations. The networking, however, is widespread among the Japanese elite more broadly where one's *tsukiai* or personal network and the *on* one carries—the burdens to group members, obligations to reciprocate past favors granted (and those expected), and assistance received (and that to come)—makes for a tightness that carries advantages, but also disadvantages, for the system. Because of such "groupness" the prevalence and embeddedness of corruption in the Japanese system is understandable in structural terms. When made public, and the subject of popular domestic outrage and foreign condemnation, it can also threaten the stability of these long-standing arrangements. Because it privileges close working relations, consultation, and tacit agreements among key parties and reciprocity, the Japanese system creates more than simply a potential for abuse; it creates a likelihood.

The historical imperative to catch up and surpass the West produced a national consensus and shared outlook that put narrowly selfish acts (which did not also forward this overriding goal) in so bad a light. This limited and channeled avarice, harnessing it to serve the national purpose. As Japan has succeeded in its century-and-a-half quest the binding power of this overriding goal has weakened, privilege is more easily abused, and collaborative relations among the powerful have given way to a more greedy mutual aggrandizement at society's expense. At the same time internationalization has brought awareness that important foreign opinion is critical of many Japanese forms of accommodation. The great power of the Japanese developmentalist state and the informal behind-the-scenes dealings are increasingly questioned. Indeed, the issue of whether Japan is a truly democratic state is often raised given the ineffectiveness of public opinion to influence much of what goes on. The visible lawbreaking and profiteering that is revealed in collusion between politicians,

bureaucrats, and corporate wheeler–dealers, which is increasingly embarrassing, and led to the defeat of the ruling party for the first time in the 1993
election.[3] This purported watershed event, however, can be considered a new
modernization of ongoing politics. The older generation, which could not
make the adjustment to a more seemly public representation of self, gave way
to a smoother, media suave group of reformers led by LDP insiders who had
bolted from the discredited party. Indeed, it took five years of unrelenting
scandal before electoral change occurred.

Political Fallout

When Hiroshi Shinto, then eighty, former chairman of Nippon Telephone and
Telegraph, the largest firm in Japan, was sentenced to two years in prison
(suspended) for his part in the Recruit scandal, denied bribery charges, telling
the court he had just followed normal Japanese business practices, he was
stating the truth, as far as I can tell. We will probably never know the full
inside story of the Recruit Affair, which surfaced in June 1988 through the
resignation of Prime Minister Takeshita in June of 1989, brought down 150 or
so of the prominent politicians, bureaucrats, and business leaders, rocking the
Japanese system. By bringing down the mighty, including almost all LDP
politicians of the first rank, and forcing the party to tap a relatively unknown,
Mr. Kaifu, so far down the pecking order that there had been no reason to
include him in the lavish payoffs, the system seemed so shaken as to be ready
for real reform rather than a changing of the faces in the front row. When as
prime minister Mr. Kaifu actually introduced electoral reform legislation his
support evaporated, he lost his job, and things went on as usual. The old,
corrupt politicians, having humbled themselves sufficiently in public ceremon-
ies of repentance and feeling enough time had past, simply resumed their
front row seats.[4]

The LDP, when it encountered resistance from the auto and electronics
industries executives to anteing up sufficiently, warned them that tax cuts they
had received might be rescinded. We know this because a few corporate leaders, most prominently Takashi Ishihara, head of Nissan and of the *Keizai Doyukai* (the think-tank for top executives), responded to the pressure by openly
suggesting that they favored a breakup of the governing party into two centrist
parties. Ironically, there had been two centrist parties until Big Business forced
them to merge in 1955 so that they could more easily beat the communists and
socialists in elections and so that the pecuniary demands of the conservative
politicians could be better contained. Today, the thinking goes in some elite
circles that two parties would create more competition among such politicians
and increase the bargaining strength of the corporations in the political sphere.
This would allow Big Business to hedge its bets. When one party became
discredited in the public mind for its corrupt excesses, business could push the
other until the scandal's impact receded sufficiently to recycle the leadership
faces again.

The rebels who voted no confidence in the LDP, and after defecting comprised the core of the reformers, were themselves a section of the Kanemaru-Takeshita faction which had dominated the LDP. The most powerful player among the reformers, Ichiro Ozawa, was the former secretary general of the Liberal Democratic Party and its crown prince. Morihiro Hosokawa, who briefly became prime minister on an image of new face, bright young outsider, a governor from a southern prefecture, was a close confident of Kyoshi Sagawa from whom he had taken loans which he had evidently not paid back—as had a number of politicians involved in the far-reaching Sagawa Kyubin scandals that had ended other careers.

The reform, which supposedly would bring a new day to Japanese politics with the ousting of the LDP, seemed to critics more like a scrambling of all the mah jong tiles for a fresh start of the political game featuring most of the same key players. The opportunistic unity of all the opposition players (except the communists) was described by some bitter cynics as another *"yokusan"* system after the Taisei Yokusan-kai, the Imperial Rule Assistance Association, which brought together all of the political parties (again except the communists) to support a different vision of national unity by the ruling elite in 1940 under the government of Prince Fumimaro Konoe, Hosokawa's grandfather. Surely far less unity of purpose was involved in the opportunistic spoils-seeking reformers of the mid-1990s. There was also a tendency to misread what was happening. The firing of a powerful bureaucrat, which was seen as the reassertion of the power of elected ministers in 1994, and seen by some Western newspapers as a sign that bureaucratic power was being brought under control, for example, had more to do with the use of ministry power to launch a political career. The jockeying it reflected was among second and third generation bureaucrats and politicians for individual ends in the face of public loss of patience with the continuation of the very system that had put these men where they were. Prime Minister Hosokawa's family had been at the center of power in Japan for four hundred years. The iron triangle of powerful politicians, top bureaucrats, and big business maintains a corrupt hold even as the balance among the three and among particular players within each group changes. Revis-ions in the power balance should not be confused with reform of the system.

There continues to be a family nature within Japan, Inc., in the almost kinship networks and long-standing accommodations. There are often family ties among the key players. The Takeshita faction, or *habatsu*, had 106 members before the rebellions started, making it the largest in the Diet (Prime Minister Kaifu was widely regarded as a puppet of Takeshita-*ha* bosses and was forced to step aside when he exercised independent judgment).[5] This, as also noted earlier, is the faction of former Prime Minister Kakuei Tanaka, the powerhouse who built it up both before and after his own public humiliation.[6] Tanaka was able to remain the power behind the throne the same way Takeshita was after the latter was forced to stay in the backroom due to the Recruit scandal. The kingmakers change as godfathers age and younger men move up. The dance remains the same, only the dancers change. The accession of Mr. Miyazawa to the prime ministership by the hand of Shin Kanemaru brings to mind earlier transitions. In its inimitable style *The Economist* remarked of Mr. Takeshita's being chosen to head the Japanese government: "Mr. Takeshita's accession to the job was by Mr. Nakasone's hand, giving a new twist to one-man–one-vote elections. Mr. Nakasone was the one man with the one vote."[7] Takeshita and Kanemaru are in-laws. Takeshita's eldest daughter is married to Kanemaru's eldest son. The heir apparent, who masterminded Japan's "new politics" of the 1990s, is Ichiro Ozawa, former LDP secretary general, whose wife and the wife of Takeshita's younger brother are sisters. When Japanese speak of the passing of power to a younger generation, it is likely to continue to be within the clan. More broadly politicians hand down the family business (currently 40 percent of Diet members are the sons of former Diet members).

Power comes from spreading around money and money is mostly what factional politics is all about. Lower house members need $1 million or so per year just to cover staff and office expenses, and the government pays only 15–20 percent of that (a member needs about twenty staff members to be effective, the allocation provides for two). Another $1–2 million must be raised per election cycle, since the candidate is expected to pass around a good deal of money to his supporters. Being part of a lucrative *zoku* is a great advantage.

The Japanese system is based on personal relationships that are embedded in structural roles. Foreigners find this unfair. The collusive networks exclude them. Because bureaucrats both regulate and coddle informally through vague rules and interpretation of regulations that are handed down in private consultations to which foreigners are not invited, Americans and other *gaijin* are by definition outside the loop. The foreigners cannot hire former government officials and have no access to the *zoku*. When they complain that the bids on government projects, for example, are rigged, which they usually are, they can hardly appeal for justice to a political process in which everyone else is in collusion and key political figures are routinely cut in at fixed, though flexible, rates. Thus, to pursue this example, one rule of thumb is that 2.8 percent of all construction revenues are traditionally paid to the LDP construction *zoku*.[8]

Former Prime Minister Noboru Takeshita, as head of the construction *zoku*, oversees the $3 trillion worth of infrastructure projects promised for the 1990s. These projects, as discussed in the last chapter, are seen by some as demonstrating a new stress on improving quality of life, but such large-scale infrastructure expenditures are part and parcel of a payoff system of Japanese-style pork barrel politics. These funds are spread around to reward favored supporters and broadly because, as Muramatsu and Mabuchi have pointed out, "one-party dominance is maintained not by party strategy, but rather by absorbing the varied interests and opinions of society effectively."[9] When the LDP failed to do so it got into serious trouble with the electorate, as it did around both environmental and broader local area quality-of-life issues and through its failure to face up to the need for electoral reform and getting corruption under control.

Each Diet member has a local support organization (*koenkai*) that he personally funds out of payoffs. Other contributions come from *koenkai* members looking for favors. Each Diet candidate does battle with members of his own party, who run against him for the opportunity to represent the district. Local development schemes are the mother's milk of local politics. In the Japanese system, as Eisuke Sakakibara writes, the politician "is much like an executive treasury officer of various regional institutions who happens to be stationed in Tokyo."[10] That is, the politician's job is to wheedle as much for (again, usually his) local organized constituents from the public fisc as possible. Small and medium-sized local businesses make payoffs to the lawmaker's *koenkai*. Votes and money are exchanged for services—licenses, approval of projects, public funding. The mutual obligation can carry over from generation to generation. Indeed, close to half LDP Diet members are *nisei* (literally, second generation) politicians, the sons or close relatives of politicians. They inherited their *koenkai*. Thirty percent of the opposition, including the head of the socialist party, "inherited" their seats as well. Voters who knew a candidate's father or grandfather put young men in office who then gain seniority and have a fast track to leadership positions.

Because there is no primary election and so many candidates run, winners are chosen by far slimmer margins in Japan than they are in the United States, where only one candidate from each of the two major parties contest for a single seat. As a result incumbents lose more regularly. They therefore have to be more solicitous of constituents than do their U.S. counterparts and, given the nature of Japanese social customs of gift giving, they have to sponsor all sorts of events for their constituents to show their appreciation, from golf tournaments to flower arranging demonstrations. Under such burdens it would be surprising if they were not involved in perpetual financial scandals. It would be surprising, then, that politicians would not leave their empires to their heirs having played the system successfully. This is also why political reform has been so difficult, and only incompletely implemented in 1994 despite widespread public pressure.

The typical Diet member raises and spends an average of $2 million each two-year election cycle, about ten times the spending limit under Japan's Political Funds Control Law. The money does not go to TV ads, as it would in the United States, but in cash handouts to constituents. Companies send their ambassadors to *Nagatacho* with envelopes, briefcases, and even, as in the famous case of Hirohasu Watanabe, whose $4 million in 50,000 10,000-yen notes brought to Shin Kanemaru in large brown bags, required a shopping cart to deliver. Politicians are then expected to attend many funerals and weddings each week in their district, handing out hundreds of dollars in gifts, even thousands if the constituent is of high status. Gifts are also expected for hundreds of members of their booster club. When they return from trips abroad the politician might bring $100 Paris ties, for example, as presents. These gifts are spread lavishly among voters who take them as a sort of Robin Hood–like redistribution of what the big guys have taken from them.[11]

Many voters choose between candidates based on their political views as well as on an assessment of which candidates will be able to deliver on roads or hospitals the district needs. While such politics is essentially similar elsewhere, the Japanese structured groupism makes the relations clear. It is an organized society. Even crime syndicates in Japan have storefront offices, a presence complete with their banners and other corporate symbols on display, and interact in society based on rules of appropriate behavior, which they occasionally overstep.

There have been numerous scandals involving Diet members and almost all Japanese postwar prime ministers have been implicated in some sensational wrongdoings. [12] However, at the end of the 1980s, a decade of greed and sleaze in most of the advanced economies, as the bubble economy burst in Japan and the costs of speculation and corrupt dealings were widely perceived, public outrage grew. It is necessary to look at the material base of these events to see why citizens felt the betrayals more vividly than they might have in economically happier times. Before saying more about these scandals and their impact it is useful to consider why they seem so important. It is the context in which they are occurring that is new. The events to be discussed in this chapter triggered the first loss of control by the LDP in July 1993.

It was the failure of Miyazawa as party leader that led to voter outrage and loss of the support of the Establishment. For example, Takeshi Nagano, president of the Federation of Employers' Associations, predicted that the ruling party would lose the next election if it was not to credibly support political reform. A few days later Miyazawa was no longer prime minister. Nagano also said that he would not regret an LDP defeat. Business leaders were tired of paying for the ruling party and its increasing demands for funds. The loss of Nagano's support was indicative of what was happening. Corporate funding flowed to reform parties, and the LDP went down to defeat.

Whether the *Yomiuri Shimbun* (Japan's largest circulation daily) was right when it proclaimed, "Our country's political structure has undergone a sweeping transformation," depended on what one thought a sweeping transformation should involve. The new parties contained many of the same faces. Their vague commitment to economic deregulation and electoral reform were to be applied cautiously. The leader of the most successful of the new parties in the 1993 election, the Japan Renewal Party, former LDP Finance Minister Tsutomu Hata, when asked directly if he thought it was time to break the collusive "iron triangle" of business, politician, and ministry bureaucrats, answered, "Producers are consumers, too, and we cannot forget their interests." Hata is perhaps best remembered for his 1986 explanation while he was agricultural minister that "Japanese intestines are too short to digest American beef." The new Diet, the most thoroughly conservative in the post–World War II period because the socialists were the big losers, having purged their left wing in an effort at a pragmatic internal realignment, still lost sixty-four seats, about half their total, and had a new face prime minister, Morihiro Hosokawa, presented as a populist knight in shining armor. The real power was Ichiro Ozawa, the protege of Shin Kanemaru, the fallen leader of the LDP. Despite the "sweeping transformation" political continuity was evident. In a comment worthy of his mentor Ozawa brushed aside suggestions that he was the key player in the new coalition, saying "that never occurred to me. The mission of politics isn't about such petty questions, but whether we can accomplish the will of the people."[13] The key posts of ministry of finance and of international trade and industry went to former bureaucrats of those ministries. Continuity was also evident in Mr. Hata, the "new" foreign minister, who said, "I will carry on the usual diplomatic policies and develop them with my utmost efforts."[14] (Hata was to become prime minister after Hosokawa, tainted by bribery scandal, resigned in 1994.)

Reflecting on the results of the 1993 election Shoichiro Toyoda declared it a first step to a "healthy two-party system in Japan." He said the results showed "a continuation of the basic policies of the LDP."[15] From a business point of view two conservative parties were better than one. The LDP had grown arrogant and demanding with time and was less effective in delivering the goods while pacifying the public. Behind the electoral changes was a deeper reality. The systemic corruption visible in the early 1990s spoke volumes both to the structural nature of the postwar Japanese system and to the deep difficulties it was in.

The profit rate in Japan fell in the 1970s. By the end of the decade it was half of what it had been at its start. For the manufacturing sector the profit rate in 1979 was about one third of what it had been in 1970. Profit rates peaked earlier in the United States, but in Japan the fall had been proportionately greater.[16] Productivity gains slowed in Japan as elsewhere and there was less of a return to new investment in plant and equipment. The move to a speculative economy was the result of an end to the Golden Age of capitalist development. The statistics tell the story. In hindsight it was clear how really unusual the growth in the first half of the postwar period had been. Between 1950 and 1975 labor productivity in the developed nations grew twice as fast as ever before. The increase in the capital stock represented "an investment boom of historically unprecedented length and vigor," as one summary of the statistical evidence concluded.[17] For the world as a whole output in manufactures more than quadrupled and world trade in manufactures increased eightfold. These were remarkable rates of economic development and made the Japanese spurt much easier than it would be in the 1980s as world growth slowed.

In the 1970s and 1980s the turnover of funds in international capital markets expanded at twice the growth rate of world trade itself. A shift occurred in the nature of such financial flows as they were no longer primarily tied to servicing the international exchange of goods or even correspondence flows to overseas branch bank subsidiaries. With the lifting of nation-state restrictions on free capital movements, with successful European postwar recovery, and especially after petrodollar recycling following the 1973 OPEC price jump, offshore banking and proactive international finance more generally came into their own. The innovative new financial instruments by nonbank financial firms dominated the cutting edge of capital markets by the 1980s. Equity markets became international. Stock futures and other instruments caught on with investors around the globe. In the mid-1980s equity returns on Tokyo markets were five to ten times what they were in the United States. Other stock markets around the world also outpaced the American ones, setting off a worldwide search for yet higher returns. Investors began to move their money around the world more easily. This increasing global integration of financial markets had an important impact.

Until the 1980s MOF regulations kept interest payments to bank depositors at levels that transferred the equivalent of hundreds of billions of dollars to the banks. Consumers subsidized capital formation as the banks then made these funds available to Japan's large corporations at below market rates. It was not possible in the early 1970s to borrow to speculate in land or stocks on any significant scale. In the 1980s these funds were made available for such non-productive purposes.

Instabilities and the World System

In Japan through most of the 1980s money was available at low government-controlled rates. For decades, tight government regulation had virtually shut out foreigners. The MOF had strictly separated securities houses from banks and restricted every banking function imaginable—from the level of interest rates permitted to the hours automatic teller machines operated. In the 1980s while the United States needed to keep rates high to attract capital to under-write the growing U.S. debt, an interest rate advantage of half a percent was equal to a 5 percent price edge (according to Robert T. Winston, Westing-house's director of international trade policy).[18] Cost-of-capital disparity is of some importance in a world in which 2 percent lower financing equalled a 20 percent price advantage.

While difficult measurement and conceptual issues are involved in making such claims, as we discussed in Chapter 4, the perception of an important cost of capital advantage is grounded in reality. On top of this the "strong" dollar in the first half of the 1980s, of which President Reagan was so foolishly proud, gave Japan an additional 40–50 percent price advantage. It was no wonder the United States lost its lead across a range of important products. The Japanese had dramatically lowered capital costs and the seriously overvalued dollar over an extended period of time allowed the Japanese exporters a powerful edge.

The Americans had permitted the Japanese to maintain an undervalued yen throughout the postwar period as a way of helping to build up their economy as a bulwark against communism in Asia. Geopolitical considerations were uppermost. In the 1970s and especially the first half of the 1980s, with Japan's growing economic strength, this meant that we ran bigger and bigger deficits, which required the maintenance of high interest rates here to draw and keep loan capital to finance these deficits. This meant higher domestic in-terest rates and an overvalued dollar hurting our exports and overly encourag-ing Japanese imports by placing U.S. manufacturers at so serious a disadvan-tage. The "strong" dollar weakened America and led to a build up of a capital surplus in Japan. Japan became a new player in international financial markets.

It was not until the Foreign Exchange Control Law of 1980 that free interna-tional financial transactions became the norm rather than the exception. The move from net debtor to net creditor dates only from 1981. By the early 1980s, however, yen-denominated transactions swept past those in sterling and

Swiss francs and by mid-decade yen-denominated Eurobonds exceeded those issued in Deutschemarks. In 1986 an offshore banking facility was created in Tokyo. Higher interest rates abroad sucked out billions upon billions of yen. The context of these financial shifts is important. As in America, many Japanese firms in the 1980s also had high average returns on investment, but they judged net marginal returns from new ones to be too low to warrant investment of what became free cash flow. In the United States context mergers and acquisitions, leveraged buyouts, junk bonds, and other financial restructuring revolutionized corporate life. In Japan free assets went into real estate and stock market speculation. [19] The system of stable stockholders and more powerful stakeholders in Japan and the deregulation and lax supervision of financial markets account for very different reactions to realization problems in the two nations.

As long as the financial system is relatively stable most people's attention is centered on the real economy—the production sector, where they see goods manufactured and new technological breakthroughs that provide new and exciting consumer products. However, when the financial sector does go into crisis it can quickly move to center stage, as we shall see in this chapter. Direct foreign investment, which receives most of the attention in America, was perhaps one sixth of the total capital outflow since the mid-1980s, although a change in investment strategy was evident from the late 1980s as Japan's real yen return on its mammoth U.S. Treasury holdings turned out to be negative because of the continuing weakening of the dollar. (In this chapter the Japanese financial system is discussed. In the next chapter the topic of direct foreign investment will be taken up.)

By whatever criteria, the Japanese banks' strength (capital), soundness (capital–assets ratio), or performance (profit on capital or return on assets) took the top ten slots by the heady years of the bubble economy. This was not because they had done so well, but rather because Japan was so rich and because the more experienced global players, the risk-taking Western banks, had performed so disastrously. Leading U.S. banks were sadly represented among the bottom ten in pretax profits and their performance measures. By the early 1990s, however, the Japanese financial sector was in serious trouble. A crucial part of our story is an understanding of how the Japanese banking system and securities markets have functioned to bring about these dramatic disparities, how financial markets have been structured by the political system, and their relation to the "real" goods-producing economy that was the driving force of the Japanese rapid growth.

In the mid-1970s, before financial liberalization, there had been only a limited amount of negotiable debt and the virtual absence of a private capital market. The BOJ was the single tap through which virtually all important credit flowed. The BOJ was not simply the lender of last resort, it was "the sole lender." In order to guarantee their own lending capacities other banks "must therefore remain consistently sensitive to the Bank of Japan's overt and indirect policy preferences." [20] It is possible to trace this arrangement back to the Meiji era when the close relations established by Minister of Finance Count

Matsukata was based on tightly controlled specialized financial institutions as part of the targeted industrial policy of the day. By segmenting financial product markets and favoring large banks at the center of *zaibatsu* networks, the Japanese system guided subsidized capital to favored users and uses.

The system's interdependent aspects included overlending by the BOJ, which supplied Japan's leading bankers with funds, not necessarily large in absolute amounts, but part of a relationship that made these city banks sensitive to administrative guidance. Frequent examination of the composition of bank balance sheets and the *amakudari* practice[21] of placing MOF alumni into key executive positions at private financial institutions created a closed loop. Equity markets and alternative sources of financing were kept limited, and in banking, as in other sectors, the role of stockholders in both decision making and in terms of claims on potential earnings were subservient to growth as interpreted by managers and government bureaucrats. After liberalization it remained the case that Japanese banking remained the most centrally controlled among the world's major economies. The BOJ still maintains its close ties with the MOF and through informal guidance the banks. These came dramatically into play in 1993, as we shall see, when regulators moved to reverse the stock market plunge that endangered Japanese financial stability, and in 1994 when the Ministry tried to force the banks to become more competition-oriented.

Because of the high degree of leverage (the exceedingly large debt-to-equity ratios), the impact of monetary policy is more effective and can be targeted with precision through administrative guidance. The problem for the regulators, and the banks for that matter, is that as corporations needed to go to financial institutions, less lending opportunities had to be sought in riskier areas. Further, the system of bank financing at more or less fixed and subsidized rates controlled by the government and the relative unimportance of stockholders, which meant that dividend payout could be modest, created a bias toward growth and an ignoring of narrow profit calculations. These features were to bring problems at the end of the bubble economy. With financial deregulation and the possibility of interest swaps and other arbitrage techniques the Japanese system of segmented funding became obsolete. As growth slowed down there was thus the push into speculative activities from declining investment opportunities elsewhere and a new financial climate that did not prevent the spilling over of investment funds into such areas.

Zaikai, Keizaikai, and Zaiteku

The tangle of overlapping and competing peak interest groupings is clarified to some extent if we bear in mind the distinction between the *zaikai*, *keizaikai*, and *zaiteku*. *Zaikai* literally translated means "business world," but it carries the connotation of the back room and boardroom movers and shakers of Japan's corporate world (i.e., the big money folks who represent the collective interests of Japanese capital). They hammer out a consensus and communicate it (with detailed recommendations) to government bureaucrats and politicians. People who speak knowingly of the *zaikai* are inclined to smile at the exaggerated importance given to the bureaucrats by people who see only the *tatemae* (the pretense), their seeming importance in molding policy, and do not grasp the *honne* of the situation: Big Money calls the tune and the state officials find the tactical and even strategic means to carry out the goals the *zaikai* insists upon. The one is *omote* (in plain view); the other is *ura* (hidden from sight). The concept *zaikai* is different from *keizaikai*, or "economic world," which connotes an interest group representing some specific industry or business. *Zaikai* is concerned with the big picture, inclusive of social and political problems and considerations. *Zaiteku* (financial management) is a relatively new usage and reserved for the style of operation that had always been marginal to the Japanese system and became, as in America, the tail wagging the dog in the 1980s. The separation among these three ways of looking at Japanese economic activities is not watertight. The largest banks, for example, finance much of the most abusive speculative activities. It has been very profitable business.

There have been waves of speculative excess in Japan before, the boom years 1915–1919 and the expansion after 1931, among others, but the bubble economy of the 1980s was as dramatic as anything that Japan has seen and its full impact on the country's future is still to be measured. In the real estate industry, a cyclical extremist everywhere, declines in building and the collapse of leading property firms are the result of an overextension that gets carried away and cannot be sustained or even contained when the market peaks and the carrying cost of borrowed funds becomes unbearable. In Japan at the end of the 1980s, however, the case can be made that it was the government that pulled the plug on the speculators before the feared severe downturn had a chance to materialize on its own. The MOF moved to force the high fliers of the 1980s into bankruptcy, left the leading construction companies on the edge of insolvency, and lanced the bubble surgically to reduce the potential damage of greater infection.

The accession of Yasushi Mieno as head of the BOJ in November 1989 coincided with the end of the bubble economy. He resolved to wring out the asset inflation through higher interest rates and slower growth in the money supply supplemented by rigorous administrative guidance of the financial sector. Mieno, a career central banker, brought the period of easy money, which had lasted from 1985 to 1989, to a decided close. He proceeded further to bring down the high-flying property speculators and developers by forcing banks to dramatically cut their lending. A process of self-levitation was brought to a crashing halt. Between 1979 and 1989 the debt burden of nonfinancial institutions, government, and households had risen from $3.4 to $8.5 trillion. Then, as the bubble popped, liabilities in corporate bankruptcies shot up to $15 billion in 1990, $60 billion in 1991, leading to triple-digit losses. The MOF kept the banks, which had directly and indirectly underwritten the bubble, from going under, but it pushed the debt-pyramided property firms into liquidation. It tried to regain control of the financial system that it had lost when the cost of borrowing became essentially free (in real terms) in the second half of the 1980s. Serious dislocations resulted.

In just nine months, as Mieno took control of the BOJ, the money supply went from more than 13 percent growth on an annual basis to less than 2 percent, and the discount rate went from 3.75 to 6 percent. Some of Japan's highest-flying real estate developers were permanently grounded. The fallout in related sectors was also extensive. GSS Company, a trader in golf club memberships, went belly up with debts of about $2 billion. Obayashi and Tobishima, two of Japan's biggest construction firms, had 20 billion and 40 billion yen, respectively, in outstanding orders placed with them by Nanatomi, a property company, and one of many placed in receivership. In 1993 Muramoto Construction, which had built many a golf course, went under leaving billions in uncovered debts. The real estate industry at the peak of the bubble economy employed 800,000 people and generated an operating surplus almost equal to the entire manufacturing sector, with close to 15 million workers. As land values fell, the collateral held by the banks for their loan portfolios was devalued. Since land was the security for perhaps half of all city bank loans by the end of the bubble economy, this had a severe impact.

Something of the magnitude of the issue can be grasped when you consider that the land on which the Imperial Palace lies at the center of Tokyo at its peak was valued at enough to buy California. The market value of the city of Tokyo exceeded that of the entire United States with some spare change to buy Canada as well. These, of course, were paper values, but they fueled financial growth on a scale the world had never seen. For the year just before the height of the bubble economy, 1987, when Japan's GNP was 345 trillion yen, financial assets increased by 382 trillion yen and land assets grew by 374 trillion yen.[22] Such sizzling speculation could, of course, not be sustained, but the greater fool theory and the belief that the MOF would protect the players kept the pot boiling.

When the MOF decided to bring the speculation under control and called on banks to reduce lending to property companies, the question was: Could they move decisively to cut the speculators off at the knees and leave the rest of the economy standing? Bankruptcies mounted as interest rates rose and credit availability became constrained. Some called for an easing to restore growth, but, as Makoto Sataka, a business commentator, pointed out in the spring of 1992, "Take a look at just who is demanding measures to cope with the recession. They are real estate and related companies, companies that made huge profits through financial dealings, and politicians who made windfalls out of the bubble economy."[23]

The effort to sharply separate—even for analytical purposes—the impact of property speculation, rising stock values, and paper wealth from the "real economy" is doomed to failure. This is because so much of the liquidity of Japanese corporations came from their huge borrowing based on the security of the inflated value of land holdings and their stock portfolios, as well as because of their policy of reinvesting earnings in land and stock since, as the "real economy" slowed, available investable funds had no productive outlet. The wealth effect of the bubble economy prompted increased spending by the upper 30 percent, who did so well during these heady years. The new rich were heavily land owners.

In 1991 real estate corporation failures swept Japan. This immediately put severe pressure on the banks that financed them, and they were soon carrying billions in bad loans. Property values fell and vacancy rates in new office buildings soared. Owners were forced to grant serious rent reductions. The stock market fell by 50 percent in a year. Having lent to property and stock speculators, and having actively played themselves, the banks were caught in the downdraft. The banks had also financed purchases at the height of property markets from New York to London on deals that were also in trouble. Billion dollar resorts they had underwritten were also feeling the impact of the end of the 1980's bubble. While banks in Japan do not have to disclose the extent of problem loans, the nonperforming assets of the big eleven city banks were believed to exceed their set-aside reserves for bad loans by quite a bit. The banks' financial reports were more reassuring but widely understood to be misleading.[24] As of early 1994, Japan's 21 largest banks had declared that they had the equivalent of $123 billion in loans from which they had received no interest payments for six months or more. The financial press in Japan puts the actual figure at from $270 to $400 billion. The banks had in herd-like fashion overextended themselves in the 1980s and were being kept afloat by the MOF.

In 1980 Japan's banks controlled 4 percent of the international lending market with assets in its 139 overseas branches of $189 billion. In 1989 they had a 40 percent share of global lending with $1.4 trillion dollars in assets in their 327 foreign branches. Eighteen months into the new decade their share of world lending was down to 30 percent and was sitting on questionable assets valued in the tens of billions of dollars. Japanese banks had gained global market shares by accepting very thin margins to break into lending areas they knew little about, just as Japanese property developers went on a foreign buying spree, with their pockets loaded with newly appreciated yen. Dai-Ichi Real Estate, which owned the Tiffany Building in New York, among other properties, had trouble making payments on $10 billion in borrowed funds after the bubble burst. The Shuwa Corporation, which owned Arco Plaza in Los Angeles, had debts of a similar magnitude—bad news for Mitsui Trust and Banking Corporation, which had lent to Dai-Ichi, and for the Sumitomo Bank, a leading Shuwa creditor. Japanese banks learned expensive lessons as they innocently followed U.S. banks into extensive holdings of Third World debt. They had also bought into U.S. investment banks near the top of the market.

Recession ended Japan's headlong plunge into world financial markets leaving Japanese financial institutions with significant overseas exposure. Forty percent of Japan's bank assets were overseas and Japanese banks held 40 percent of all global lending. Sumitomo, Japan's third largest bank had large exposure to bankrupt Olympia and York, the Canadian-based global property developer. The Bank of Tokyo was taking major losses on its extensive Third World debt portfolio, and Mitsubishi Bank had big losses in connection with the falling California economy, where it had become a major player. Losses at home were also dramatic and frequently reflected bad business judgment if not outright criminal negligence and possible collusion in land scams. Thus, as the *baburu keizai* (the bubble economy) collapsed the relation between the healthy production-oriented Japanese economy and a supposedly separate speculation-driven greed machine became difficult to disentangle.

These developments in Japan were also integrally tied to government policies and market developments in the United States. The weak dollar following the Plaza Accord in 1985 is often credited with strengthening the yen and other major currencies in relation to the dollar. It is perhaps closer to the truth to say that this meeting recognized the futility and finally the counterproductiveness to all concerned of continued attempts to maintain the overvaluation of the dollar. Its fall permitted American exports a price advantage in foreign markets and discouraged imports, thus bringing the U.S. trade accounts into better shape. Because the higher yen made Japanese exports less attractive in American markets, the BOJ, to prevent a recessionary impact, lowered its discount rate in order to stimulate the domestic economy (to make up for the loss of U.S. markets). Lower interest rates meant availability of cheap credit that could be drawn on under liberalized financial market conditions to invest in equities and real estate. It was financial deregulation and easy money that created the bubble economy. By 1989 Japanese companies were flooding the market with new stock issues—$200 billion worth in new shares and equity linked bonds (about six times the amount U.S. corporations issued that year). Some of this money went into research and product development, new plants, updating equipment, and foreign investment. As much as 40 percent of the money the Japanese companies raised, however, was recycled back into the market and stock prices were driven even higher.[25]

The Japanese MOF, despite the very serious problems in the country's financial sector, was able to avoid the sort of bank collapses the United States experienced in these years and the huge losses that tax payers had to make up (e.g., in the Savings and Loan bailout). Heedless of the cost of American-style deregulation loud voices in Japan, influenced by the American model, denounced government intervention in the marketplace and argued that it is a passé phenomenon. Globalists, like Kenichi Ohmae, spoke of the borderless world[26] in which differences over industrial policy, immigration, investment restrictions, and trade barriers are a thing of the past. The only thing that matters in his "Interlinked Economy of the Triad" is that "IBM competes with NEC and Fujitsu." Ohmae and some other futurists see a world government or a UN-type fund collecting perhaps a third of our taxes and solving global environmental problems. Ohmae (a partner in the Tokyo office of U.S.-based McKinsey and Company) argues that "industrial development should be taken away from the central government and if done at all, go to local authorities."[27] Ohmae is especially peeved at the MOF "a dinosaur," designed for a time when Japan's financial industry was young and "believed" to need protection and encouragement. The major sin, according to him, is that the Ministry does not believe in the market. The MOF channeled savings to provide low-cost financing to industry, even forcing Japanese institutional investors to buy and hold hundreds of billions of dollars of U.S. government paper, a notoriously bad buy in the second half of the 1980s. They did this as a matter of pressure from the Japanese government in order to support the dollar, and out of fear that the bond market would collapse, along with the U.S. economy, triggering a worldwide financial panic. This was not an unreasonable reason for interfering. [28]

The demands, by Ohmae and others, for deregulation and free financial markets trouble many thoughtful Japanese, who do not see much to celebrate in the American way of banking. Japan has already adopted too many of these questionable practices. The U.S. financial system has made itself vulnerable. The cost so far in bailouts and the climate created by speculative excess are significant. Japanese financiers had been attracted to U.S.-style practices, and their banks were having trouble meeting the capital adequacy standards set by the Bank for International Settlements (8 percent capital-to-assets ratio by March 1993). The close to 50 percent peak through drop in the Tokyo stock market in 1990 was painful to the banks, both because of the damage to their own ample portfolios, and because the BOJ allows them to include 45 percent of the unrealized capital gains on their share holdings as part of their capital base. In addition banks that lent on the pledged security of stock holdings as well as on their outstanding real estate loans, which account for more than 100 percent of their capital (for some as much as three or four times more), were seriously affected by another new phenomenon in Japan: falling land prices.

Japan's eleven city banks, comparable to U.S. money center banks, together lost over $90 billion in "latent" value in their stock portfolios in fiscal 1991 on top of the growing burden of nonperforming loans. In the early 1990s most property developers in Japan were not paying interest on their loans to the banks. Some banks (Hanwa Bank Ltd. had 30 percent of its loans tied up in Osaka real estate, which dropped in value by 30 percent in 1991 alone) were all but bankrupt, although the MOF would not reveal much data on its problem banks and acted behind the scenes as it always had to prevent bank failures. [29] As the Nikkei fell bank stocks fell still faster. This was because so much of their capital was tied up in their own stock portfolios. Their capital ratios fell toward and in many cases below the 8 percent reserve level set by the Bank for International Settlements. [30] The depressed stock market thus meant lending curbs, lower corporate spending, and more economic decline. In the first eighteen months of the new decade the heads of five of Japan's largest banks resigned to take the blame both for poor performance and for questionable financial dealings. In the largest single bankruptcy, a local branch bank had lent an Osaka restaurant owner money on bogus securities. She left debts of over $3 billion.

Japanese officials could contain financial fragility in their own economy. Indeed, at the peak of the 1990 fear that the Japanese equity market's collapse would trigger worldwide depression, *Europemoney*'s cover story claimed the decline had been orchestrated by the all-powerful MOF and the BOJ, the world's most powerful financial regulators acting in concert to bring speculation under control. [31] Americans, however, saw the other side of the story and their criticism became more harsh and public through this period. In 1991 following a series of financial scandals in Japan that revealed the extent of collusion between the Ministry of Finance and the banks and securities industry (to be discussed momentarily), David Mulford, under secretary of the treasury for international affairs, linked Japan's unwillingness to "provide timetables" or to take "dramatic steps" to free financial markets (he was particularly incensed at refusal to open Japan's pension-fund management to foreign firms) with the current financial scandals. "Japan is at a crossroads," he said, "they either take dramatic steps to allow American financial institutions in on equal terms to their markets or perpetuate the atmosphere that breeds the current financial scandals." [32] What neither Mr. Mulford and the other Bush administration officials, nor the Clinton team which followed, who worked to get American firms access to Japanese financial markets, considered was the effect U.S.-style markets would have on financial instability in Japan. In keeping the Americans out, the Japanese were defending more than their own profitable cozy accommodations. The loss of ability to regulate markets that would follow such an opening was pregnant with potential disaster.

The internationalization of the yen was against the wishes of cautious Japanese, who do not want the exposure in the absence of tighter regulation of yen-denominated financial instruments. The loss of control was accelerated by the deregulation wave that rolled out of Washington as part of the new world order and Washington's effort to gain a greater share of the profit from Tokyo's emergence as a major financial center. Even in the absence of U.S. pressures, however, it would have been difficult for the Japanese financial sector not to pursue the short-term gain deregulation promised. [33] On a global scale there was simply too much money to be made in speculation for officials on either side of the Pacific to do much to reign it in. To some extent the dangers were understood. Former Prime Minister Nakasone, in a spring 1989 interview, said that in his view, "Japan's capitalism has become too heavily concentrated on *zaiteku*—financial management. It's becoming a casino economy. Observing this recent phenomenon of zaiteku financial management, I'd have to say that capitalism in Japan has degenerated." [34] The Japanese effort to resist the downside of domestic market liberalization thus encountered heavy going.

By the start of the 1980s finance had become more important than manufacturing, and the MOF the most desirable bureaucratic posting for the civil service elite to be. In 1987 Nomura, the world's largest securities firm and the world's most profitable financial institution, took over from Toyota as Japan's number one moneymaker. The auto industry had saturated its markets and the overaccumulation of capital in Japan, its domestic savings rate exceeding what could profitably be invested, sought speculative outlets. The resulting speculative boom centered on the stock market and real estate. The stronger yen resulted in increased overseas investment. Instead of addressing domestic social need, using the surplus to enhance the housing stock, ease urban congestion, or reduce average working hours, oversavings found their way overseas or into domestic speculation. The latter was troubling because it had something of a pyramiding scheme to it. Loans were made on the basis of property and stock and used to buy more property and stock. Albert Allentzhauser, who observed these events from his perch as a senior executive with a British investment firm in Tokyo, has written of the "black money" from speculative stock and real estate gains by gangsters and speculator groups generally, that on some days they accounted for 10 percent of Japan's trading volume. He also notes, however, that "the most dramatic source of capital, though, has been *zaiteku*. Companies themselves had fueled the market's rise in 1986 and 1987 by issuing new stocks and bonds and then putting the proceeds back into the market rather than spending the money developing their businesses."[35]

Japanese who love to gamble bet on everything from motorcycle and speed boat races to pachinko parlors and the stock market. Hundreds of billions of dollars per year are wagered on hunch, chance, and rumor. Securities are sold door to door by "middies," a force of middle-aged, middle-class housewives employed by the brokerage houses. Each week they come around armed with their buy recommendations (the same ones favored customers receive the week before). In the long bull market it did not matter, almost everybody was to some degree a winner so that it was hard to believe that the long run up could be over. The Nikkei Average had gone from 1,020 at the bottom in 1965 to 38,915 at the end of 1989. Then, in calendar 1990, the Tokyo Stock market lost over $1 trillion as the Nikkei plummeted. Into 1992 it lost another $1 trillion as it fell 50 percent from its 1989 high. In calendar 1993 Japanese economic "growth" was one tenth of one percent. In *Kabutocho*, however, the *kabuya* (the term for stock peddlers and a word that carries a tone of disdain befitting the disreputable reputation of the calling) the air had gone out of the balloon. The fuller implications of speculation became clear: One could lose as well as win. The contempt with which *Kabutocho* was held by hard-working nonspeculating Japanese seemed justified. The country looked at the harm the *kabuya* had wrought.

Nomura and the lesser securities firm rode this wave confident that their friends in government and in the bureaucracy stood by to help them. The MOF had not granted a securities brokerage license since 1968 and had allowed the favored existing firms to set fixed commissions at lucrative rates using its power to protect the industry from foreign competitors and the harsh winds of deregulation. In the light of scandals (to be discussed shortly), efforts were made to create an independent regulatory commission not under the control of the MOF. The idea was a U.S.-style Securities and Exchange Commission–like agency. One was in fact created during the U.S. occupation, but it disappeared soon after SCAP closed up shop. Indeed, of the twenty-three independent regulatory agencies set up under American tutelage only seven remain, and these tend to be toothless watchdogs. For example, Japan's Fair Trade Commission had taken administrative action against a securities firm in connection with a particularly gross cross-shareholding ploy for the first time in 1991. The Commission ordered Nomura Securities to cease and desist in contracts with stockholders in Nomura Real Estate. In taking such action the bureaucracy came under intense political pressure from Nomura and its friends in high places, setting off a contretemps that initially embarrassed the bureaucrats, but set the stage for their revenge.[36]

Nomura was alleged to have aggressively traded Tokyu shares for the leader of the *Inagawa-kai*, Japan's second-largest organized crime syndicate, and that created a major uproar. There were demands for strengthening Article 125 of the Securities and Exchange Law (which prohibits manipulation of stock prices). It was even suggested that the government agency enforce existing laws. A proposal that the Finance Ministry oversee a watchdog group on securities regulation was offered by the government. As a former Merrill Lynch executive in Japan said, "This is like naming a gang boss police chief. It's nonsense."

Extensive special accommodations made to powerful insiders continue to be part of the Japanese system. For example, in the early 1990s when the stock market collapsed, the practice of *tobashi* became known to the outside world. *Tobashi* translates literally as "flying." It is a scheme for privileged customers of the large Japanese brokerage houses that allows them to sell securities that have fallen in price to someone else at an unrealistically high valuation to avoid loss. The broker promises the new buyer a similar accommodation should the stock's performance not allow the buyer to recoup through an open market sale. The stock "flies" from account to account providing winnings where there should be losses until the market rises once again so that the last holder under the arrangement can make a profit selling at the market price. Rigged trading then stops. Everyone is a winner, but only insiders get to play the game. The practice, though common in a downswing, is illegal. Daiwa Securities, Japan's second-largest brokerage house, was unable to keep a deal of this sort going and the firm's president was forced to resign to take responsibility. The severe downdraft of the early 1990s also exposed Nomura and third place Nikko Securities' dealings with a leading organized crime figure as part of stock manipulation schemes.

Dozens of firms in the industry were forced to admit in parliamentary investigations that they routinely compensated important customers for stock trading losses. More than twenty Japanese firms admitted making more than $1.5 billion in improper payments to compensate favored clients for stock trading losses. The end of the bubble economy provided one of those windows through which the powerful figures of organized crime, politics, and big business could be glimpsed in the unsavory exercises of aggrandizement.

When Nomura's chairman, Setsuya Tabuchi, had been barraged with angry questions at the firm's annual stockholder's meeting he said that everything Nomura had done had been approved by the MOF. He was severely reprimanded for doing so by the minister of finance himself (even though, of course, the ministry did know and had allowed illegal loss compensations). When it became widely known that the ministry had indeed approved these dealings, the ministry responded that what the law forbade was *promising* loss compensation; it did not debar the actual payments. The brokers had not, the ministry and the brokers both agreed, made any promises and so no one needed to be punished since the law had not been broken. Other rulings by the ministry declared that the law of fraudulent trades did not apply because the trades in question were to the benefit of customers! In the past such legalistic sophistry would have been accepted with a cynical shrug since everyone understands that the ministry's job is to protect the industry and the industry's job is to provide lucrative sinecures to the ministry's top officials on their retirement from public service. In exchange for this accommodation they see that other members of the elite benefit from insider treatment. Everyone who is anyone in Japan, both individuals and institutions, makes money in the rigged markets, from corporate giants to government pension funds. The stock market is an important mechanism for giving money under the table to politicians who are brought in early on new stock offerings at bargain prices. That politicians are routinely paid off makes it seem less unreasonable that gangsters demand and get paid off as well.

The role of the *yakuza* in the Japanese political economy is not unlike that of organized crime elsewhere in the world where corrupt relations exist both with the police and with the corporate sector. Organized crime performs favors for respectable powerful interests and enjoys protection within negotiated boundaries. In many nations beside Japan the violence-prone extreme right and organized crime overlap, and both have been used to put down leftist movements. In the Japanese case, most accounts stress that since the early postwar years a close accommodation of this sort has flourished.

> The police realized they simply were not strong enough to control the forces unleashed by the country's devastation, particularly the once-violent communist movement. The *yakuza* were used as a shadow police force to throttle leftists. In return, they were left alone, as long as they left ordinary Japanese alone.
>
> "We haven't used our power only for doing bad things," insisted Mr. Takayama. "I myself personally wounded the head of the local Communist Party after the police asked us for help." [37]

The high profile of these mob connections is indicative of how visible the crisis of the old system has become and is worth some brief attention in and of itself. As leaders of the securities industry testified before Parliament in 1991 concerning illegal payoffs and stock manipulations, the overlap between the worlds of formal legality and openly criminal behavior were revealed. Because of the sharp downturn the Diet was forced to investigate criminal doings in the securities industry. This was something like the philandering members of the U.S. Senate's Judiciary Committee trying to ascertain whether Supreme Court nominee Clarence Thomas had engaged in sexual harassment. The high point of the Diet hearings was the appearance of the unfortunate Setsuya Tabuchi to explain how he had gotten mixed up with organized crime.

Mr. Tabuchi, the former chairman of Nomura Securities (former because he had to resign due to the scandals), testifying under oath (an unusual requirement in Japan in such instances, as the last sworn testimony that had been taken had been by former Prime Minister Yasuhiro Nakasone in the

Recruit influence peddling scandal two years previously) said, when asked how a notorious gangster had come to be accorded such special treatment by Nomura (his account had been handled personally by the head of their sales department and guaranteed against loss), that Nomura had first bought several million shares of a major company for the *yakuza* chieftain (in the process exceeding the legal limit for holding one firm's stock) and that then, after he held a dominant position, Nomura issued a buy recommendation to its other customers, causing the price to soar. Mr. Tabuchi flatly denied manipulation had taken place and said that he could not remember the name of the *sokaiya*, another type of gangster who specializes in corporate extortion, who had acted as a go-between: "I'm embarrassed, but up until yesterday I remembered his name, while today it does not seem to come to mind."[38] If pressed there were many names, including those of some who faced him that day, who he could undoubtedly have remembered in incriminating circumstances. The matter was not pressed, but Chairman Tabuchi's resignation to take blame for any acts which brought dishonor to his firm was hardly enough to end matters. Things had gotten out of hand. The public mutual recrimination between top MOF and securities and banking industry executives made matters still more difficult for the usual backroom deals to be made. There was "absolutely no trust between us anymore," as one top executive of a major broker told the financial press.

Hiroshi Ishizuki, director of the anti-mob division of the National Police Agency, told the press: "Looking at all the scandals we've had, people were becoming worried that if they allowed the *yakuza* to continue any further, the entire legitimate society would be swallowed up by them."[39] This was not an unreasonable fear. Susumu Ishii, perhaps Japan's most famous mobster, who was lent hundreds of millions of dollars by Nomura and Nikko Securities, had also had billions of dollars in loans and loan guarantees provided for him by some of Japan's largest corporations. High-profile socializing between Mr. Ishii and other underworld figures and leading corporate executives was beginning to challenge the old boundary understandings.[40]

The scandals brought the workings of the Japanese system to public awareness in an unfamiliar light. Governance in Japan rests on this three-legged stool: The *zaikai* (big business), the *seikei* (the LDP inner circle of politicians), and the *kankai* (the powerful bureaucrats). There is both a division of labor and a competition among them. There is also mobility between them. The scandals showed the collusive self-seeking that was usually kept private. In the late 1980s the dynamic propellant of the system was *zaiteku*, the money men of self-levitating finance. The enthusiasm with which speculation was embraced brings to mind a remark Marx made that "the industrial peak of a people [is] when its main concern is not yet gain, but rather to gain. Thus, Yankees over the English."[41] As Kabutocho merged with Nagatacho in the late 1980s, the main concern was clearly a narrow sense of short-term gain. In Kabutocho, Tokyo's Wall Street, and Nagatacho, its political center, speculation had displaced productive activities. In 1990 companies with less than 100 million yen in capital accounted for 99 percent of the nation's businesses and employed 80 percent of the work force.

Writing in *The Economist*'s survey of Japanese finance at the start of the 1990s Christopher Wood described Japanese speculative mania as "a form of collective arrogance."[42] Both the banks and the securities firms had given themselves to speculative undertakings with abandon. The Japanese banks were significant stockholders themselves and could legally count unrealized gains on their shares as capital against which they could lend. As prices soared, this created as close to a perpetual money-creation machine as one could imagine. The banking system in Japan, as was that in the United States, was holding bad debt and needing to raise its capital assets; it was in trouble as corporate borrowers, and lenders and individuals as well, found ways around the banking system in liberalized and internationalized capital markets. It welcomed these new profit opportunities. By the end of the decade, the twelve biggest commercial banks had made loans backed by real estate collateral equivalent to half of Japan's GNP. These loans also represented about half their loan growth in the period as well. Because the large corporations did not need to borrow from the banks in this period the banks were driven to real estate loans as the major source of profit. The rising stock market took care of the rest. It was the source of over 40 percent of the big twelve banks' own direct profits (from the securities they owned on their own account).

The casualties of the 1990–1991 scandal season included the fall of Ichiro Isoda, the chairman of Sumitomo Bank and the grand old man of Japanese finance (Sumitomo is the Citibank of Japan, the hard-driven innovator always pushing the legal limits of the system), and the chairman of the Industrial Bank of Japan (the nation's largest long-term lender) among other banks, the chairman and the president of Nomura, the president of Nikko Securities, and assorted other leaders of the financial sector were included in a rather large cast. The minister of finance left under fire. Efforts to calm things down called attention to the tight little island at the top of the system. The president of the Tokyo Stock Exchange, Minoru Nagaoka, was one of numerous former Finance Ministry officials with a post-retirement job in the industry his former subordinates continued to supervise. Indeed, his three immediate predecessors were all administrative vice presidents of the MOF (the administrative vice president is the highest civil servant at the MOF, running the ministry on a career basis while ministers, who are elected political figures, come and go, usually with little effect on what goes on in the ministry). He was, of course, a graduate of Tokyo University. When the press looked for evaluations as to how he was doing they went to Michio Takeuchi, his predecessor, as head man at both the Tokyo Stock Exchange and the Finance Ministry who, not surprisingly, perhaps, characterized his successor as a "person with a superb sense of balance."

It is interesting to note how much criticism the MOF received given the ministry's iron grip over anything in Japan vaguely related to money. Politicians, bureaucrats from other ministries, and powerful corporate leaders hesitate to say much since the MOF can, and does, remember at budget time who in government has been naughty and nice. The MOF sends tax investigators after whomever they want to punish, companies and individuals, and reminds others to watch what they say about the ministry in the future. Few need such warnings. While some commentators thought that MOF had gone too far and that the government-sponsored cartelized and bureaucrat-manipulated financial system would now have to change, I would not bet on its changing very easily. First, the power of the MOF, as noted, is overwhelmingly great. Second, without the MOF to hold the system together the shocks to the market (e.g., fallout from the October 1987 Wall Street Crash and wreckage littering the landscape from tightening the screws on the worst abuses of the bubble economy and so on) could easily lead to the sort of debacles we get in the United States, like the Savings and Loan fiasco and the rash of commercial bank failures. To this writing no bank in Japan has been allowed to fail in the postwar period by the MOF. There are surely pluses to a system of managed markets.

In 1993 MOF administrative guidance went into high gear to reverse the slumping stock market. Large institutional stockholders were discouraged from selling and government-controlled pension funds were told to pump tens of billions of dollars into the market to prop up prices. Government purchases of stocks and bonds in the spring of 1993 accounted for one third of all purchases on the Tokyo Stock Exchange. Private institutions managing large portfolios were told to start investing with a five-year time horizon and not on the basis of the volatile short run. When at the end of 1993 the stock market slumped, the Ministry of Finance called major brokers and asked for the names of big sellers. As word of the request spread the market temporarily turned around and headed north. The mechanism of this turnaround is of some interest. One difference between the Japanese and the American systems is illustrated by the different role of Fed watchers in America and MOF-tan in Japan. Fed watchers study the Fed looking for signs of what it is up to and will be doing as it affects markets. MOF-tan also watch full time but they are also conduits for regulators to pass administrative guidance informally to banks and securities companies. MOF-tan seek special favors from the Ministry of Finance and are responsive to its wishes. To try and prop up prices the Ministry, for example, prevents firms from not only unloading their stock holdings but also prevents them from issuing new stock when it doesn't want weak markets depressed.

Growing Financial Tensions

Cause and blame are of course the most subjective of concepts. Japan, once praised for its role in bailing the United States out from financial problems, was accused of causing them. For example, when the Continental Bank of Illinois collapsed in 1984, its failure was generally taken at the time as a result of unwise overextension and bad loans. A new spin was put on these and other financial panics of recent vintage. R. Taggart Murphy, managing director of Japan Private Placements at Chase Manhattan, is typical of such a revisionist perspective. He writes,

> Continental collapsed in Tokyo when Japanese money managers, acting on the basis of a mistranslated press report and without the knowledge of their regulators, pulled their funds out of the bank. This small group of money managers triggered the failure of the seventh largest bank in the United States.[43]

The gnomes of Tokyo were surely not the only ones to pull out their money, nor were all reports that Continental was in trouble the result of translator error. It is in the nature of high finance that fears prompt bank runs. This is why strong regulation and quick intervention by more powerful monetary authorities rather than more deregulation can be a good thing. Private players will surely not wait to take action upon which huge profits or losses may result—unless *not* first asking permission of regulators is seen as more costly. Absent such regulatory clout they will move quickly. Moreover, the regulators, who needed to be more on the ball in this case, were those in Washington, D.C. The projection of American failure onto the Japanese in such instances is part of an emerging pattern, but it contains a serious dose of projection.

When bankers and others conclude with Nicholas Brady, who carried out the official U.S. government investigation of these events, that the "real trigger" for the October 1987 stock market collapse was "that the Japanese came in for their own reasons and sold an enormous amount of government bonds . . . ," we should not confuse trigger with cause. A capitalist system is structured so that investors for their own reasons put in money and take it out. We have had years of warnings that foreign borrowing and lending leaves the United States vulnerable to just such a shock. Unless some sort of reregulation suited to the new climate of internationalization is worked out, they will be even less able to act successfully in the future, a prospect officials at the BOJ worry about.[44]

Indeed, as the damage of reckless speculation became clear in the early 1990s and Japanese banks, while they continued to sit on huge assets, were at the bottom in profitability and little but the regulator's safety net kept many of the biggest as well as their smaller brethren from bankruptcy, the seemingly unstoppable Japanese onslaught seemed to turn on a dime.

Scandals at Nomura, involving bribes to public officials to obtain contracts to manage municipal pension funds, and others, discussed earlier in this chapter involving rebates to make up for losses to major players, cast new light on a securities market that was the cloistered playground of a handful of wealthy speculative investors until only a few years before.[45] Rapid growth and internationalization of financial markets brought exposure of long-standing practices. Because Nomura and the other brokerage firms accounted for perhaps half of all funding received by the various LDP factions,[46] they felt that the politicians would protect them from their bureaucrats. When the MOF challenged payoffs to the well-connected client, the industry assumed that it had the clout, and so behaved arrogantly toward the bureaucrats. They paid a high price. The freewheeling (and spending) financial sector underestimated the cohesion of the developmentalist-state system's powerful bureaucracy.

The international context has made the developmentalist state more aggressive about bringing usual accommodations under control. Many Western experts had assumed that in the wake of the series of scandals Japan would have to harmonize its financial regulation system with those traditional elsewhere (i.e., copy the framework prevalent in the United States). Japan, however, undertook financial reform in its own way. In the summer of 1991 as the Japanese financial industry was feeling the heat, the man in charge, Vice Minister of Finance Tadao Chino, promised a more open version of administrative guidance in place of the unwritten instructions that were not based in specific legislative authority, were typically given orally, and were disseminated and enforced in a secretive manner that kept foreign firms in the dark as to what was going on. While bureaucrats spoke of reform, however, the reality remains and the bankers themselves are hardly willing to give up guidance for an uncertain freedom. As Osamu Sakurai, chairman of Sumitomo Trust and Banking Company, remarked of these efforts to change *gyosei shido* procedures, his industry benefitted from the way things worked. "Some people," he said, "call it collusion, but I don't think that is wrong."[47]

Under this system financial institutions were expected to follow "suggestions" scrupulously. In exchange, they were granted lucrative favors (including overlooking and even encouraging practices that would not easily withstand outsider scrutiny). Even in its "reform" version the system was not to be very different. Mr. Chino made clear to Western reporters "that people should not forget Japan's special history, and the fact that the current system had worked well for most of the postwar era." He said that Japan did not want a system like that in the United States, where there were too many regulators and it was too easy to get into the securities business. "I don't like a society that requires so many people to watch everything," Vice Minister Chino said, "I like a more cooperative society with a smaller number of regulators."[48] Administrative guidance was to remain strong and competition modified in ways that served state-designed ends and bureaucratic designs were to continue to be controlling. Indeed, the banks' weaker positions strengthened the hold of the ministry.

The issue the Americans raised—an open and fair financial market so that foreign firms have an equal chance to make money—is a very different one than that which concerns the Japanese bureaucrats, which was how to preserve regulatory powers in an increasingly deregulated and unstable internationalized financial market. Bureaucratic control of financial institutions served Japan well in the past. It is not clear that it would not continue to do so in the future, but Japan is faced here with a serious contradiction. The strength to regulate effectively is also the power to reward friends and punish those out of favor, which will always include foreigners. If Japan moves to a more open system it risks losing its effective regulatory powers. If it plays "fair" and establishes what the United States considers free markets, then that power is largely gone.

The choices facing Japanese regulators were increasingly unappetizing. As the crisis persisted, Governor Mieno increasingly and in no uncertain terms criticized the banks for their pack mentality and inability to evaluate financial risk and for their unwillingness to innovate. In effect he acknowledged that MOF coddling and overprotectiveness was a problem and was not simply the result of a cyclical downturn but also the lack of realistic risk assessment of borrowers and failure to take corrective action in the face of nonperforming loans. His call for bank deregulation was taken by some as an admission of the failure of the bureaucratic control model.

Because the Ministry of Finance had been prepared to keep even the most ineptly managed banks from going under, overwhelming moral hazard problems had been created. Banks could lend recklessly, ignoring severe adverse selection problems, because they seemed to have few consequences. The government never let a bank fail. Therefore there was often not even the most rudimentary evaluation of potential borrowers or of how loans were being used. More is involved, however, than overregulation and bad management. The issue should not be seen as a once and for all choice between regulation and free market banking. Through the postwar recovery and catch-up phase the Japanese system of artificially holding down interest rates and channeling investment to selected industries, switching priorities as the economy grew more sophisticated in its capacities, and preventing capital investment abroad until Japanese industry had matured, worked quite well for the most part. Only with overaccumulation did the model need to be changed. Unfortunately the free market was allowed to allocate resources that went to speculative activities underwritten by statist guarantees (not unlike what happened with the savings and loans in the same period in the United States). One can blame the bankers for their herd instincts and lack of risk assessment capacities. One can blame overregulation and misguided bureaucratic guidance. One can also look at the structure of financial markets as they have operated for centuries of capitalist development. To omit the last would be an incomplete evaluation of these events as economists from Marx, to Keynes, to Minsky have known. The lure of lucre promotes such an outcome unless there is a degree of independent regulation well beyond any that existed in Japan. The system of private-governmental collaboration that had worked so well to bring historically unprecedented success to Japan also, in new circumstances, brought disaster and prolonged crisis. The overhang of bad debt would heavily burden the Japanese economy for some time to come.

In 1994 the Finance Ministry permitted the banks to begin to write off their losses on loans to the non-bank banks (which officially amounted to $126 billion, but were perhaps over $400 billion). By allowing banks to sell off bad loans and enjoy a tax deduction for the losses, the Japanese taxpayer would provide funds for the banks to engage in new lending.

Globalization as a market process, in an increasingly deregulated climate, means that capital can flow quickly and bring destabilizing change. Fraud and abuse flourish outside of the narrow boundaries of local regulation. Misjudgment can lead to overextension and then to collapse, with wide-scale ramifications. Because of the interpenetration of ownership of finance, and the dependencies of commodity chains, conflagration can spread quickly. Between the law of value working itself out on a global scale within a system of market freedom (or anarchy) and the planned expansion of the Japanese system is a dialectical tension of world-shaking dimension.

As to the politicians, the LDP had held power by periodic symbolic self-purification. When a particularly bad scandal occurs, it changed the faces of the front bench. Changing faces while not changing its ways has served it well. While editorial writers denounce such political sleight-of-hand, denouncing the party's corruption, business continues as usual—the big development projects, the payoffs, and the backroom deal making. The socialists have seemed a possible threat from time to time, although as we have seen, far more at the local government level than at the national one, where money politics and a general fear that if anyone but the LDP ran things the economy and foreign policy might take unpleasant turns. It was not until 1986 that the Japan Socialist Party gave up class struggle and commitment to the revolutionary road, accepted a free-market economy, and pledged to seek reform within the existing system. Its public professions of what was really a long-standing revisionism, plus the Recruit Scandal, and the particularly attractive figure heading the party ticket, Takako Doi, propelled the party to a high-profile challenger position. In the upper-house election in 1989 the LDP won only 40 of the 126 seats at stake. The large number of new faces, who also happened to be women running on the socialist ticket (dubbed "the madonna strategy" by the press), seemed to some to be a harbinger of a new politics in Japan. Twenty-two women won seats in the election of 1989. Half of them were socialists, so that one third of the Japan Socialist Party winners were women. These gains, however, were reversed in the next election.

When the LDP was dethroned in 1993 it was not at the hands of the socialists; indeed, they were the biggest losers in that election. Rather, it was at the hands of a new Morihiro Hosokawa, prime minister of the seven party coalition government, promised deregulation and reform. He was compared to Bill Clinton, also presented as an outsider. He, too, was a modernizing governor from a small southern prefecture with a practical centrist politics and a desire to turn around a central government that had grown out of touch with the people. Hosokawa, by Japanese standards charismatic, even Kennedyesque, and, if not quite a "policy wonk," he had written a best-selling book with a program for the reorganization of Japan. He had called for transparency of bureaucratic functioning, deregulation, and for local government autonomy. Most of all he had called for electoral reform. In a basic sense, as we'll see subsequently, he called for the modernization of the Japanese system so that it would be compatible with a greater role for Japan, and its increasingly global corporations, in a new world order.

9

Trade Antagonism and
Industrial Policy

"The Germans somehow evoke little American bitterness because we understand their culture, establish American plants there without hinderance. The Japanese provoke American wrath because they are a locked and closed civilization that reciprocates our hushed fear with veiled contempt."

THEODORE WHITE[1]

"As things stand now, Japanese companies might capture 100 percent of the world market."

GAISHI HIRAIWA, chairman Keidanren (upon creating a committee to seek ways to better cooperate with foreign enterprises)

There is little doubt that Japan acted as a discriminating monopolist selling in their domestic market at higher prices and using the profits to improve capacity to sell at cut-rate prices abroad. Since they could close their domestic market to foreign competitors and sell in competitors' markets at lower prices, they could pick up market shares where they faced competition. This, of course, is exactly what Germany and the United States had done to free-trade England a century earlier.[2] Contemporary arguments concerning the continued extent of such practices have dominated questions of trade policy to a great extent, but they are an inadequate way of looking at matters. Over the 1980s evidence mounted that a large proportion of the exports of Japanese corporations from Japan had been replaced by the output of their overseas affiliates and subsidiaries. This transnationalizing of production puts a more complex light on competitiveness. Cross-subsidization by large Japanese firms of research and development expenses and state policies to encourage technology development through cooperation and underwriting have also been important. The next chapter deals with the issue of overseas production by Japanese firms. I would point out here that while Japan gives up some domestic production and abandons certain industrial policy instruments, it continues to promote industries (e.g., biotechnology, communications, and materials science), resisting trade liberalization in these areas so that it can capture leadership in emerging sectors of high promise. Japan pushes up the value added hierarchy while increasing indirect exports to the United States by producing in and exporting from other nations.[3]

When Americans look into the Rashomon mirror at our economic relations with Japan, three ways of seeing are most often reflected. The first of these is the competitiveness discourse. It usually carries rhetorical trope, such as, "When will the Japanese remove this or that trade barrier? Really remove them and stop stalling?" It is an "us versus them" view of the world in which trade disputes with Japan replace the Cold War with the Soviet Union as the central contest of our times. The *competitiveness discourse* is a divisive framework in that it assumes a negative sum game. The second view is the *transformational perspective*. It is as old as Adam Smith's discussion of how technological and organizational innovations drive capitalist development through a quest for higher profits. The transformational perspective is a positive sum growth-oriented view in which progress is the leit motif. A third approach is *globalization*. It examines economic change from the world system vantage point, in terms of nations and regions, seeing growth as a process of combined and uneven development.[4] The emphasis shifts to considerations such as commodity chains that combine venues at different stages of the production process and the shifts in location that leave some regional participants better off, and others left behind. In its general meaning globalization is clear enough. It is a consideration of the tendencies in the world political economy toward an interpenetration of distinct national economic entities. As a trend it is many centuries old, although it is argued here that the degree of contemporary interpenetration denotes a qualitative change from the earlier international economy.

These three levels of analysis overlap and in the policy debate we can see them as cross-cutting at odd angles confusing matters by eliding one set of issues with a perspective grounded in different concerns. This leads to a good bit of talking past each other in classic Rashomon style. The matter of national location is on top of the confusion of levels of analysis. Within the competitiveness debate, which is the most prominent of the three, Americans and Japanese tend to begin from very different assumptions. Stepping back, and looking from transformational and globalization points of view, the tempest over trade policy is an exceedingly narrow formulation. Competitiveness is typically formulated in static terms. Since preservation of past advantage is at issue the discussion can have a backward looking quality to it.

Disaggregating the effects of various aspects of the Japanese system is an academic growth industry. I have suggested that such price effects as exchange rates and capital costs have been important and that it is necessary to consider them in a larger political economy context that is historical and institutionally grounded. I have discussed the social entrepreneurship of the developmentalist state affecting the constraints and incentives under which individuals and corporate entities make choices, but the balance between administrative guidance and corporate self-initiative remains problematic. Matters are complicated by the way rules of international competition are decided, and by the extent to which they are binding on governments and corporations.

On the larger canvas there is not a presumption of unresolved conflict, as in the competitiveness discourse, nor the benign optimism of progress, as in the transformational perspective. There is a double movement—toward freer trade and also negotiated accommodation—to soften adjustments and integrate economic policy making and international rules. A tendency is evident in the process. The movement away from mercantilist industrial policies by the Japanese is a function of their greater stake in an open world system. Having caught up in many areas Japan no longer needs old-style industrial policies. How corporate and political figures in various nation-state locations maneuver among these three perspectives reflects their current appreciation of self-interest.

The issue of how important trade has been and is in terms of Japan's success and the extent to which Japan's trade patterns are fundamentally different from those of the other advanced capitalist nations are matters of some debate. Japan has a remarkably *low* dependence on exports. In 1990 its ratio of exports to GNP was 10 percent, about what it was at the turn of the century, and far below that in Europe and for most other nations in the contemporary period. The only country with a lower dependence on exports is the United States, with a 7 percent export-to-GNP ratio for that same year. Japan, far less generously endowed with natural resources than the United States, has to export to obtain needed raw materials that the U.S. produces domestically. In the 1980s Great Britain, France, and Italy, with combined populations and GNPs larger than Japan's, imported less from the United States than did Japan. Overall, it was the world's largest importer in the early 1990s. Even in terms of manufactured goods Japan has taken more and more of the production of other nations. Manufactures that were only 20 percent of its total imports in 1975 were 50 percent of the total in 1990. Measured in dollar terms its imports rose by 84 percent between the 1985 currency revaluation and 1990. What was the problem?

The matter, of course, was the huge trade surplus Japan was running with the United States. In 1990 Japan's per capita imports of $1,960 exceeded those of the European Community ($1,770) and were only slightly less than those of the United States ($2,060). However, Japan's per capita imports from the United States and the European Community were $360 and $171, respectively. Japan's imports of all goods in the 1980s were estimated to have been between 25 and 45 percent lower than they "should" have been based on criteria of the country's industrial structure, size, and level of economic development. Further, depending on the year in question and the researcher, the prices of traded goods in Japan have been estimated to be as much as 86 percent higher on average than they were in the United States. Trade barriers may not be obvious. They do not take the form of tariffs and official quotas, but they are significant.[5]

There remains considerable disagreement over what the basic "facts" are.

In terms of importing of manufactured goods, leading experts' views clash jarringly. Robert Z. Lawrence estimates that after adjusting for resource endowment and location Japan imported only a little more than half as much manufactures as one would expect.[6] On the other hand, Gary Saxonhouse's reading of the econometric evidence suggests to him that "after allowance is made for Japan's distinctive national endowments, particularly its lack of natural resources, that there is relatively little that is really distinctive about Japan's trade structure."[7] I am not at all sure that econometric evidence will resolve the nature of the differences in the two economic systems.[8]

The Competitiveness Discourse

Trade frictions between the United States and Japan surfaced in the 1960s when domestic producers felt the effects of rapidly rising imports of textiles from Japan. Then came steel and TVs, machine tools, and video recorders. By the 1980s construction, financial services, and telecommunications were areas of contention. In the 1990s, Clinton Administration negotiators had added insurance and medical services, zeroing in on any product class in which U.S. sales in Japan were significantly lower than our market share in neutral markets (Europe was the typical benchmark). To many Japanese it looked as if the United States had given up on free trade—when it could no longer be master of the international marketplace on any other basis, it demanded negotiated concessions, affirmative action for a weakened superpower. There seemed to be little that traded freely—certainly not textiles, steel, electrical appliances, or automobiles. The fact that the United States insisted on calling the restrictions it forced on Japanese exports "voluntary" added insult to injury.

Under free-trade conditions, Japanese industrial policy planners think there are winners and losers, yet the United States, because "it cannot bear to lose, has concluded that free trade means arranging things so that you can't lose." As Osamu Oshimomura has said, and he speaks for others, "America believes that by rights it ought to be stronger than Japan; since it cannot be, it tries to hold Japan back."[9] This is from a noted commentator, an economist, and a graduate of the University of Tokyo who served in the MOF and the Japan Development Bank. In attacking core Japanese institutions, the Americans were also taking a fairly ineffective bargaining stance. Foreign Minister Watanabe said, "We will amend the way we do business if there's something wrong with it." He said, however, that the Japanese cannot change who they are, "even if it upsets others."[10]

The conventional wisdom in Japan was that the United States needed to get its own house in order, reduce its deficits, save and invest more, spend less on consumption, work harder to make better products, and get serious about quality and work effort. America lacks the will, many Japanese said, sadly and increasingly in anger at being scapegoated for what they saw as problems "Made in America." There were a good many Americans who agreed. We may call them the free-market internationalists. Their views can be contrasted to those who have been characterized as protectionists, who assumed that the United States could not compete with Japan's methods and so ought to be sheltered from the competitive storm by imposing restrictions on the Japanese, and to the declinists, who see the need for America to restructure its economic institutions to restore vitality.

The internationalist viewpoint is a free-market stance that accepts the concept of economic efficiency central to mainstream economic theory. In its ideological presentation it deprecates two aspects of competition that I take to be crucially important: the social costs of narrow market efficiency criteria and the possibility that developmental states can pursue policies that, while not always successful, can shift a nation's economic performance trajectory by framing incentive structures and offering guidance to private actors, advice that differs from the short-run preferences in a "free"-market environment, but which may reinforce long-run market success. The Rashomon Mirror being what it is, the viewpoints of internationalists, protectionists, and strategic economic pragmatists reflect different realities. All see different Japans. There are also counterparts to the enlightened internationalism of such Americans in Japan as there are to our protectionists and strategic pragmatists. The internationalists can claim to have history on their side in the sense that globalization is a secular trend. Yet, in the past, strong state formations have mediated the process in determinative ways. As a triadic global trading bloc structure emerged they were joined by strategic pragmatists in stressing a politically accommodating stance, to some degree, of assisting a weakened United States while insisting on the primacy of market forces within the context of a new regionalism.

American and European fears of its successes created pressure on the Japanese to change. Japan recognizes that it could "no longer get away with mercantilist, export-led economic polices," Hideo Sato declared.[11] He went on, writing in a generous tone:

> After World War II the United States, then the paramount world power, worked single-handedly to bring prosperity and peace to the rest of the world. Japan was the greatest beneficiary of America's largesse. Today, the American eagle is wounded both economically and spiritually. In its pain, it is lashing out with apparently arbitrary demands. Instead of simply registering emotional protest and presenting statistical evidence in its defense, Japan must come up quickly with a concrete plan for aiding the wounded eagle.[12]

Sato, who did his graduate work at the University of Chicago, has been a researcher at the Brookings Institution, the premier Washington policy think tank and an associate professor at Yale, is now back in Japan at Tsukuba University. Unlike most of those writing on Japan–U.S. economic relations in the United States, he has a most intimate understanding of "the other." American internationalists share the good will, but often lack the intimate knowledge. They therefore tend to underestimate the extent to which the Japanese system really is different. The Japanese internationalists often operate within an environment that combines advocacy of free trade abroad with developmentalist-state policies at home aimed at helping to insure that Japanese industrial performance is successful.

Traditional measures of comparative efficiency can be misleading. Some American economists take comfort in the statistic that Japanese workers produced on average, in the early 1990s, about 70 percent as many real goods and services as American workers did. The average figure is misleading because it obscures important compositional differences. The average figure is heavily weighted to the domestic sector production where the Japanese are much less efficient than they are in agriculture and retail distribution. Overall, the two countries use their potential work forces differently. In Japan many workers, especially older workers, are employed in low-productivity jobs. In the United States much of the potential labor force is classified as not in the labor force and so not in the denominator of the productivity calculation. They are either unemployed or not considered part of the labor force.

Social efficiency has a number of dimensions that are all part of competitiveness, but which are not addressed in a discussion of industrial policy stuck on whether the U.S. government is capable of picking winners and usefully subsidizing their growth. To compare the performance of the two economies in terms of their utilization of human resources it would be better to measure real social productivity, which is about the total efficiency, with what a country uses for its potential. In Japan, to take a different sort of example, shoplifting and stealing from your employer are not the major activities that they are in the United States, so rent-a-guards, monitors, and other security personnel do not make up a large employment category. Suspicion between employers and employees does not result in output-reducing tensions to the large extent that it does in the American system. Drugs do not have widespread devastating effects. On average, schools produce a higher quality work force. By the time of the Clinton administration, Washington seemed ready to a greater extent than ever before to redefine competitiveness comprehensively, but floundered when it came to any program that was perceived as too costly or an act of favoritism to one competitor over another U.S. firm. [15]

Staying Ahead in Hard Times

For over a century Japan had followed conscious nationalist policies to try and outrun the grasp of Western powers, who they saw, not without good reason, as wanting to impose sovereignty over them. At the start of the Meiji Restoration, as we saw in Chapter 3, Japan began a long-distance race with a belief that the stakes were so severe that it must never let up. In the 1980s, having caught up and seemingly surpassed the West, determination gave way to hubris and making money-making an end in itself. Unable to continue growth on the postwar model of accumulation, speculation overcame productive growth and collaboration turned to collusive rent-seeking.

In the present period differences in attitude toward the public role in shaping competitiveness are played out in the way financial deregulation is seen as the cure by free marketeers and as creating deep problems by believers in the regulatory powers of a developmentalist state. The finance–production tension has historically taken many guises, from Veblen's engineer versus the price system, to the debate between those who believe the binge of mergers and acquisitions of the 1980s in the United States was essentially a way to increase efficiency (by providing a market for corporate control), to those who see the need for patient capital and some form of industrial policy based on longer-term thinking.

In Japan the driving desire to stay ahead privileged, at least until the 1980s, an almost Veblenesque attitude, a desire to control those who would let short-run financial profit undermine innovative technology. It is embedded in the pattern of Japanese manufacturing investment. With half the population Japan invests more in new plant and capital equipment *and* commercially driven research and development in absolute terms than does the United States. The composition of its investment is future-oriented as a matter of built-in design. Approximately 30 percent of capital investment goes for developing new products and services. Another 30 percent of new capital investment creates means of product development, design production, and distribution. The remaining 40 percent is for expansion of capacity. Half of this is going to produce products, which, as Kenneth Courtis writes, "didn't exist five years ago."[13] Such investment patterns reflect the drive of the Japanese production system. Among American corporate leaders in the 1980s such awareness became commonplace. The need to constantly reinvent the company, or "re-engineer" it, in the contemporary management parlance, meant organizational evolution and product revolution. Hewlett Packard officials explained in the early 1990s that they want, indeed need for their company survival, to "turn markets upside down." They spoke of being after "destroyer products," the kind that "will put an old industry instantly out of business." The spokesman saw HP as an "almost totally different company 10 years from now."[14] Professor Schumpeter would be happy.

Economists are not generally very good at discussing such changes. But we know it can't hurt when KMart gives Black & Decker access to how fast different products are selling and when software manufacturers in America move from vendor-proprietary software to open software standards to speed the flow of interoperative systems. What was a decade earlier a Japanese pattern is standard operating procedure among forward-looking corporations everywhere.

While unforeseen events can always mock forecasts and visions, plausible scenarios have long been constructed by MITI and in corporate board rooms in Tokyo. Japanese "targeting" (one is drawn to place the inverted commas around such a now loaded word) succeeded in sector after sector as Japan moved from the basic industries engine of postwar recovery to the cutting edge sectors of the post-postwar world economy. Allowed to export to American markets the Japanese used our laissez-faire presumptions and their own developmentalist state to gain strategic advantage. Science Technology Agency statistics show Japanese exports of high-tech products (as defined by the OECD) increasing from a little over $1 billion worth in 1965 to about $700 billion in 1986, when they exceeded U.S. exports of these products for the first time.

High-Tech Competition

There are many understandings, both contradictory and overlapping, of how the Japanese caught up to, and in a substantial number of product areas surpassed, their American competitors. One of the most important and also well studied is the semiconductor industry.

American computers began to arrive in Japan in 1954. In 1955, MITI organized a research committee to study how to make Japan a competitive producer of computers. By 1957 the Electronics Industry Provisional Development Act had authorized research cartels (exempted from the antitrust law), and was directing low interest loans, directing subsidies and tax incentives to the industry. In 1960, when foreign producers held 70 percent of the market, the Japanese government raised tariffs on computers from 15 to 25 percent and, perhaps more importantly, restricted access to foreign exchange for firms that wanted to use the money to import computers. The Japan Electric Computer Company (JECC), a "private" firm created in 1961 by six major computer firms and Matsushita, was set up to lease computer hardware and in doing so acted as a vehicle of industrial policy to promote the industry. It was privately funded and managed but created at the initiative of MITI, and the Japan Development Bank made large amounts of low cost capital available to it. The JECC played an "indispensable role" in the growth of the Japanese computer industry.[15] By the 1980s, the American semiconductor industry was accusing the Japanese of dumping computer chips (that is selling them below cost of production). Indeed, the Japanese *were* selling them below cost, in the United States and elsewhere around the world. To the Americans, this was anticompetitive behavior. Why the difference in understanding?

Japan's *forward pricing* (pricing under current costs but in anticipation of later economies of learning), is a policy also followed by American firms in technologically dynamic fields. The dumping standard applied to the Japanese by the Commerce Department could just as easily be applied to American companies by other nations, or domestically, for that matter. The U.S. policymakers had used ideological neoclassical arguments in pursuit of short-sighted self-interest. Kenneth Flamm makes the point cogently:

> U.S. chip makers did not allege that Japanese chips were being sold in the U.S. market at prices below those prevailing in the home market, the standard notion of dumping. Instead, they accused Japanese producers of selling all their chips, worldwide, at prices that did not cover the full average cost of production, a practice that technical changes in U.S. trade law during the 1970s had also made actionable as dumping.[16]

The neoclassical illusion strikes again.

In the early 1970s MITI prevented lower-cost American chips from taking over Japanese markets. The share of imports in Japanese integrated circuit markets actually peaked at 40 percent in 1974 because MITI stopped Japanese companies from buying the cheaper and better chips available from American producers. Sharp, which had been the leader in importing U.S. chips, was denied licenses for importing chips. The other companies learned the lesson: MITI wanted domestic production. When American companies tried to hire Japanese semiconductor industry executives to sell their chips, MITI stepped in to dissuade prospective ship jumpers that such a move would be unwise. (Is it any wonder that former Japanese trade negotiators never end up lobbying for American interests?) At the same time the (then) nationalized telephone company refused to buy higher-quality foreign equipment and underwrote domestic development of new systems. MITI paid research and development costs, and the private Japanese companies involved and their work teams, suppliers, designers, and distributors all gained essential experience, consumer good will, the ability to function together under stress—the list of benefits of administrative guidance and state development subsidies and encouragement are impressive. The Japanese view was that to sit out the development of new technological possibilities and allow free markets and comparative advantage to dictate outcomes is to invite extinction as a global player.

For the most part the American government left our individual companies to the mercies of coordinated attack by the Japanese developmentalist state and *keiretsu* giants. Preferring an open market and a hands-off attitude, the United States had spent decades trying to get the Japanese to do it our way. MITI's VLSI (Very Large-Scale Integration) subsidies exceeded 40 percent of the Japanese industry's funding of integrated circuits through the latter half of the 1970s and helped develop a whole new generation of semiconductor production technologies while Silicon Valley scratched for venture capital. The U.S. share of world semiconductor sales peaked by 1980. For the rest of the decade Japan's rise mirrored American relative decline in world market shares. The X marked the result of national industrial policy stances. In the early 1990s the situation changed once again for reasons that will be discussed subsequently.

It was the Japanese skill, from long years of practice of combining competition with cooperation, firm initiative, and state encouragement, that gives them the continuing advantage. The specific techniques of assistance do not remain the same. The total level of help, while difficult to measure, is not constant. Japanese producers can now stand on their own, although, of course, they do not have to—there are always new mountains for the government sherpas to assist the Japanese corporations to climb. However, some traditional aspects of the government role can be dramatically reduced. Indeed, as there shall be occasion to emphasize later, the large transnationals, Japanese and Western, now have reason to collaborate in strategic alliances in ways that to a significant degree are breaking down national boundaries and requiring such rethinking as to the proper role of state-developmentalist policies. As we shall also note the concentration of production in the hands of the giants still left niche production specialties in which nimble American produc-

ers could continue to do quite well and in which innovative American entrepreneurial startups often scooped key market segments.

Learning economies made the initial American reaction less than optimal.
The United States responded to Japanese developmentalist-state gambits by
forcing the Japanese producers to charge more for their now cheaper chips.
The result of this 1986 agreement, in which the U.S. forced the Japanese to
accept a minimum floor price under dynamic random access memory (DRAM)
chips was that the American users had to pay more. Electronics firms in Japan,
their competitors in computers and communication systems, did not. Higher
profits for the Japanese semiconductor industry funded the next round of chip
development and more competitive electronic products from Japan.

A further impact of the agreement was that in order to monitor its restrictions, MITI regulators, who had played a smaller role in administrative guidance in the semiconductor industry, were forced into greater interventions to
police the American restrictions on Japan. These limits on imports to the
United States also helped push Japanese producers upscale to higher value
added products, where they could make more money shipping fewer units.
The American measures also undercut competitive pressures among Japanese
producers who, under government guidance, enjoyed cartel-like higher profits
and protected domestic markets. To sell in Japan, U.S. firms were forced into
joint ventures, sharing a substantial part of the profits with their Japanese
partners. The only alternative they were given by MITI was to stay out of the
lucrative Japanese market entirely.

When the American government did intervene it was often a piecemeal and
ill-thought-out action. Japan was increasingly willing to retaliate and other
American producers often sided with the Japanese because they had become
dependent on imported supplies that are more expensive and less reliable
domestically. To take one such case, in the fall of 1991 Japan retaliated for a 63
percent surcharge imposed on its computer screens. Toshiba said it would be
moving its manufacturing operations, which it had located out of the United
States (since the screens faced the high tariff, the completed computers did
not). "Our policy is manufacturing as close to our customers as possible," the
company's spokesman said, and, "if the tariff is removed, we will produce
again in the United States." As interesting, IBM, Apple, Compaq, and other
large American companies fought the duty, too, because they were dependent
on Japanese suppliers for the computer screens that were part of their finished
products. These U.S. companies argued that it was pointless to impose duties
on imported screens because the American flat-panel screen industry did not
have the financial strength or manufacturing capacity to supply them. The
tariff on liquid display terminals followed an extended period over which
Sharp and other Japanese companies had pumped money into LCD technology while U.S. companies, including GE, IBM, and Exxon, were getting out of
the field.

The same familiar elements are present. The American producers of a technology with significant potential were being undercut by larger Japanese producers. The advanced flat-panel displays were a small part of the market, but

they were widely considered the wave of the future. Whether small firms, however, like OIS Optical Imaging Systems of Troy, Michigan, or Standard Industries of Lake Mills, Wisconsin, make it against Toshiba depends on whether American buyers will pay what the U.S. Commerce Department considers fair market price in the short run. There is little or no effort to help strengthen the U.S. producers, to help them innovate, and bring down their prices. In terms of jobs the matter is complicated because, for example, IBM turned down the idea of developing and producing its newest laptops in Japan and some Japanese producers moved assembly to the United States as a goodwill gesture (and to avoid potentially being cut out of the market or made to pay tariffs on their products). The tariffs that were imposed on the screens put them at a cost disadvantage since the prior 100 percent duty on finished computers was revoked after the 1991 semi-conductor accord, making it as cheap to export laptops from Japan as to build them in the United States. With the imposition of the tariff on screens it became significantly less costly to move production to Japan. Good will was lost, and so were jobs. In 1993 the Commerce Department revoked its 63 percent antidumping duties on imports of active matrix displays, the most advanced flat panels.

At the encouragement of Kenneth Flamm, the Brookings Institution economist who had been brought on board by the Clinton Administration to look at dual use technology, the Defense Department in April, 1994 announced plans to spend up to a billion dollars over ten years to subsidize research and development on flat screen panels, finding companies that committed themselves to build full scale factories to produce flat screens. While the Pentagon was likely to account for only 5 percent of the market, the use of flat screens for laptops and goggles for visual reality videogames, as well as in aircraft cockpits, made the subsidy a natural for the Clinton team's desire to develop a more active industrial policy.

The fear of the strategic trade mavens was that the Japanese *kereitsu*, since they made not just flat screens but the telecommunications and computer products which use the display screens, would employ transfer pricing to raise screen prices that would translate into cost advantage in products using the screens and put American competitors, dependent on Japanese suppliers, at a cost disadvantage. The same problem had arisen a decade earlier with DRAM chips. It is possible, that as in the case of DRAMs, where the South Koreans came to America's rescue by entering the market and driving down the cost of the chips, the South Korean firms would successfully produce flat screens and turn them into low cost commodities in the same way as they had for the DRAMs. Both Samsung and Goldstar in 1995 moved to gain market shares even if this meant selling the screens at a loss at first. It is unlikely American firms would embrace such a strategy. America's hope was in leapfrogging Japan by coming up with alternative technologies that would be profitable.

Having been driven from basic chip production by the lower-cost Japanese, and having been saved by the new standard chip capacity of the South Koreans, American competitiveness with their greater expertise in design capacity had come back at the upper end of the market. By 1992 the United States was once again supplying over half the world's semiconductors and by 1993 the U.S. was outspending the Japanese in capital investment by chip makers. Intel expanding production with U.S. made equipment (where a few years earlier it had relied on Japanese suppliers) credited Sematech with "helping the turn-around."[17]

Sematech (one of America's few ventures into industrial policy) achievements include setting standards and getting customers and suppliers to cooperate with semiconductor manufacturers. Sematech was one of the few instances of a more interventionist stance by the federal government during the Reagan–Bush years.[18] It helped open markets for U.S. semiconductor firms in Japan and contributed to the United States taking back the global lead in semiconductors. However, given strategic alliances between Intel and Matsushita and IBM and Toshiba, the way score will be kept in the competitiveness arena is bound to change and different understandings of industrial policy will have to be developed to fit twenty-first-century capitalism.

Most Japanese government-led joint ventures to develop new technologies have involved fewer than a half dozen members from different industries with complementary interests. The cross-fertilization of ideas as well as a division of labor in developing new technologies from biotech and new materials products to "thinking" computers and commercial aircraft rely on member companies for research facilities. The research and development associations get tax exemptions and easy access to government funds that must be combined with industry contributions. The consortia are often managed by former government officials who retain access to their agencies. Japan will be able to continue this sort of thing because of the absence of American firms.

Whether new consortia for machine tools, for example, or for robotics, will follow remains to be seen, but there are those who accept that if the United States is to compete it will have to learn to mimic Japanese corporate form and institutional arrangements. The Defense Department, long concerned that American capacity to make anything out of metal depended on foreign machine tools, had in fact taken a strong interest in rebuilding the industry. Could the country accept a broader rationale for industrial policy?

Three issues are strikingly evident. The first is that the closed nature of the Japanese domestic economy persists despite some changes. The second is that American firms in some market segments have been quite innovative with little or no government assistance and are informally and without state coordination making linkages among firms with complementary skills building the functional equivalent of *keiretsu* network contracting. Third, strategic alliances are becoming routinely international, thereby eroding national articulation. It is not clear how industrial policy comes to be conceptualized in the U.S. context under such conditions. Initial indications were that leadership would come from the private sector in specific industries that had the capacity to design cooperative alliance forms. America's capacity for product innovation continued to help the U.S. industry rebound.

The American strength in programming and innovative design meant that new systems continued to come from the U.S. producers, often revolutionizing the industry and over remarkably short life cycles upsetting existing patterns. American success in building custom chips in the early 1990s, putting entire systems on silicon chips, integrating software and hardware (or plasticware) and building complex systems quickly and creatively, and merging TV, computers, and telephone are revolutionizing the industry; indeed, they are merging industries and shaking up giants and restructuring information processing. Which producers are most successful in the short run and longer run depend in part on what type of innovation dominates and for how long. It may well be that American and Japanese competitors accept the better parts of the other's system.

The American strength was perhaps the result of the intensively competitive nature of what had never become a stable oligopolistically structured industry. Shifting patterns of competition and cooperation set the sector apart. Major American firms—Apple, IBM, and Motorola—like their Japanese counterparts, could compete and cooperate (e.g., joining together in the early 1990s to produce a Power Chip for PCs to challenge Intel's dominance). The consortium assigned people from their own firms and signed up chip designers from Intel, Digital, Texas Instruments, Hewlett Packard, and others to form a 300-member design team eager to work fifty to ninety hours per week on a breakthrough project. Whether a new industry standard would be forthcoming would be important to the future of the industry. For our purposes, it is of interest that the American industry was developing new organizational forms of institutionalized entrepreneurship without government aid. American companies had found in strategic alliance building a functional equivalent to the *keiretsu* version of network contracting.

The Japanese system is more methodical. It excels where there is an established standard that can be continually *kaizen*ed (incrementally improved in countless ways). To the Japanese there is a learning curve (a learning by doing that lowers cost with experience). This insures that the cost of production of chips, or any other product that involves such learning and constant innovation, quickly falls as more new units are produced. Indeed, in computer products the same power system and products fall in price by about 25 percent per year or more as production costs fall and improved products come onto the market. Selling fast and in high volume is the best competitive strategy in such industries. Also, success in one round positions a player to do well in the next round. Even if the Japanese sell at prices that do not allow full recovery of costs over the product's life cycle, they gain economies of learning that are worth this price to them because they move up their learning curve faster than do their rivals, and they are better positioned for the next round. This does not happen in neoclassical textbooks, where learning economies are an odd case, if they are mentioned at all. Above-normal profits should induce entry. Indeed, they will, but only by firms that can expect to compete successfully over the long haul.

Such cases continue to claim the attention of technologists concerned with competitiveness. For example, scientists are discussing the uses of scanning probe microscopes (SPMs) that create three-dimensional images of atoms and allow the study of the properties and behavior of matter. The field, nano-science, will help engineers shrink chip circuits, for example. Scientists can watch living cells at the molecular level. Japanese electronics makers were among the first to grasp the instrument's potential, and at this writing Japan is ahead of other nations in the field. In January 1993 a Japanese government $0.75 billion-funded project had brought together thirty companies in an Atom Manipulation project. It is interesting that Motorola and Texas Instruments, both strong presences in Japan, were members. How the industry will develop cannot of course be known, but experts see the risk that large Japanese manu-facturers will throw a lot of resources into knocking out the creative U.S. startups, which are at present doing quite well in the emergent industry, once a large enough market for SPMs develops.[18]

The short-term time horizons of our standard large U.S. firms make this decision to enter, take low or no profits for some time, and exert effort to win market shares, gain experience, and, in the future, one hopes, turn a profit, inconsistent with the payback profit hurdles that are the dominant rule of thumb. The growth-oriented new American firm, which understands itself to be engaged in global competition over a dynamically changing market, understands that betting the company on product development is the require-ment of continued existence. Smaller startup firms in which entrepreneurs were also the major stockholders and performance pay was the rule provided Silicon Valley competitors an alternative and more nimble model. The strategic alliances represented by the super chip Summerset project described earlier represent a new strategy for established competitors.

American industries represent a mixture of responses to intensified compe-tition. In the context of serious unemployment and less success in some indus-tries Congress moved to protect American producers and their workers. Lack-ing appreciation of the benefits of comprehensive coherent industrial policy and in the cultural economy of obeisance at the shrine of the ethereal digits there was the tendency to believe as an article of faith that if America, the nation God chose to lead, appeared to be losing out to foreigners, then it must be because they were deceitful and would not play by the rules. That these were our rules and not ones they chose was not considered in the halls of high-profile political posturing.

Restraining Trade

As early as 1968 the United States had requested and Japan had imposed "voluntary" export restraints on fifty-one items. What the United States saw as dumping, the Japanese considered building market position. As we have already seen the Japanese have been willing to take low initial profits to build long-term market shares. The U.S. Department of Commerce, however, de-clared that a foreign company earning less than 8 percent on sales of a product in the U.S. market to be illegally dumping on the assumption that that is the "normal profit" rate here and so must therefore be the objective of foreign firms as well. Japanese firms, however, were also willing to earn little or no short-run profit to build market shares at home.

The U.S. Congress, which tends to be responsive to national producers and local interests, has never been able to get the executive branch to fully enforce existing GATT and U.S. trade laws. While Section 301 of the 1974 Trade Act allows the president to retaliate against foreign trade restrictions on U.S. exports the White House has generally been more responsive to the large transnational companies' argument that such action would risk retaliation and is not in the best interest of U.S. companies that retailed imported goods as their own brands. These companies responsible for marketing so many of these "unfairly" produced products could profitably favor free trade while their competitors might demand protection from foreign products. It is also the case that Article 301 did not have GATT approval. Its application is based only on the U.S. government's judgment and is viewed by other nations as a wanton exercise of unilateral power by the United States. Not satisfied with the original act Congress moved to strengthen its retaliatory fire power. By imposing penalties on products that are completely different from the ones allegedly involved in unfair practices it allows the United States to "nuke" other nations and force them to see things our way. Because the United States always believes virtue is always on our side, Super 301 (article 301 of the 1988 Omnibus Trade and Competitiveness Act) is looked at as a way of forcing compliance to our just demands—something like the use of gunboats in the hands of Teddy Roosevelt.

In May 1989 Congress invoked Super 301, which levied penalties on trading partners who have failed to improve on their "unfair trade practices" as unilaterally defined by the United States. The "super" part denoted that it was not a particular trade practice or industry that is cited as "unfair," but an entire nation (a provision of very dubious international legality). In September of that same year the other face looked at Structural Impediments Initiative talks held in Tokyo between the United States and Japanese representatives as a way to defuse the tensions by moving to the root causes of these imbalances. I shall have more to say about the nature of such negotiations and the slow movement from a competitiveness discourse to consideration of transformational strategies for the United States embracing industrial policy thinking to a globalization discourse in line with the direction implicit in the Structural Impediments Initiative–type thinking.

The United States itself maintained trade barriers on a wide range of products including wool, sugar, and cotton, and even rice! At the same time it preached free trade to the less-developed nations and to the former communist nations, denouncing state interventions of the sort the Japanese had used with such success. It is not the protectionism, however, that does the trick. Corrupt use of subsidies and trade barriers have been used to support privileged domestic groups without creating strong economies. Local conditions matter. Protection needs to be part of a holistic development strategy.

This was surely not the case in the United States, where protectionism was won by those with political clout and never as part of a larger restructuring strategy. As the U.S. economic performance worsened demands for protection from foreign competition grew. MITI strategists, faced with continued U.S. demands for more concessions that violated free-trade norms to create benefits for the Americans at Japan's expense in the early 1990s, sought to refuse bilateral negotiating and instead to refer disputed issues to the GATT. If this were to work, Japan could move away from further bilateral rounds of what MITI saw as unreasonable pressure on Japan to accept still more severe "voluntary" restraints. Indeed, in a stronger position, Japan could demand truly open markets, an end to U.S. "Buy American" laws, and force the United States into the hard adjustments needed to balance its foreign trade. As Ryutaro Komiya has written, "No country except the United States has ever requested other countries to take actions to correct its own balance-of-payments deficit."[19]

From the U.S. perspective, GATT procedures demanding lower tariff and nontariff barriers to trade were not of much help. By the 1990s Japan was in a position to comply more fully than other nations, including the United States. The institutional structures of Japan remained less permeable than elsewhere, and in the areas that counted GATT was of little help. Foreign firms tended to flounder on the margins and sell only on Japanese terms. Corporate decision rules, relational contracting, and bureaucratic support by the state set Japan apart. In fact, GATT was pretty much irrelevant to the remaining barriers to trade that Japan had. Variation in institutional structures remained the key to Japanese advantage. Given Japan's economic strength and its flexibility in positioning itself in high value added new products it was able to proclaim its virtue as a free trader and a better follower of the GATT rules than the United States. Indeed, as far as the existing rules of trade it was the United States that could be held to be the greater lawbreaker.

In the summer of 1992 a detailed 200-page report ws released by MITI. It was the product of a subcommittee of the Industrial Structural Council, a MITI advisory body. Before this report Japan had as much as possible publicly refrained from discussing trade disputes. This report directly confronted charges made against Japan and counterattacked. It did so first by observing that the United States arbitrarily brands any foreign trade practice "unfair" if it is contrary to U.S. (and not internationally agreed upon) trade provisions. Second, the report pointed out that a nation's trade surplus or deficit is determined basically by its macroeconomic policy mix and industrial structure, not by the number of its unfair trade practices. Third, MITI argues, the United States was to blame for many restrictions that, while formally imposed by Japan, were at the request of the Americans. As one young MITI bureaucrat said in support of the ministry's decision to gather and release the report, "Japan's voluntary restraints on car exports to the United States were an unfair act that was carried out due to U.S. protectionist pressure. We had not been able to speak our minds about this before."[20]

The American insistence that others play by the rules of the game may lead to rules that nobody ends up liking. The Dunkel text, the result of half a dozen years or more of negotiations that began in Punta del Este, Uruguay (and are named after GATT Director General Arthur Dunkel), created in 1994, among other things, a Multinational Trading Organization that can strictly enforce global trading rules. It partially fulfills the initial design for an International Trading Organization first proposed in the first GATT after World War II, which the U.S. Congress rejected. America considered such an organ a threat to U.S. national sovereignty. Nearly half a century later a similar regulatory mechanism is more badly needed since the United States is far from being able to offer the sort of leadership it gave during the Bretton Woods era. The United States, however, is still not ready to let an international body "tell us what we can and cannot do."

The problem can be seen as removing sovereignty from democratic control, but in different ways perhaps than the Congress and the president fear. Would international technocrats respect strict environmental protection legislation covering some small nation that interfered with growth as traditionally measured? Would they, in their free-trade zeal, ride roughshod over workers' rights? Might they be the principled enforcement agents of global pollution laws and health and safety standards? Would they do the bidding of the transnationals or be the vehicle for their regulation in the interest of workers and consumers? Isolationism is impossible and the possibilities span a wide spectrum, but these are not the questions being raised by policymakers or advisers. America, the remaining superpower, seemed intent on playing hardball on trade and other matters as it created a New World Order after the fall of communism.

Internationalization received another setback in 1992 when the U.S. Justice Department decided to apply American antitrust laws to business practices beyond the border of the United States. As applied in Japan such a decision declared illegal actions that were accepted practice in Japan under Japanese law. The Justice Department action could be seen as symbolic pique since it was not practically possible to enforce. Unlike kidnapping Panamanian heads of state to put on trial in Florida, the move against Japan only brought that country and the European Community together against American posturing. American frustration was understandable. By U.S. standards Japan's major corporations appeared guilty of stealing intellectual property. In the much publicized Fujitsu-Texas Instruments and Minolta–Honeywell cases involving Japanese corporations allegedly stealing key technologies the Japanese were generally conceded to have violated American legal standards. After five years of litigation Minolta reached an out-of-court settlement in which it agreed to pay well over $100 million for the use of Honeywell's autofocus technology. Japan's major video makers, Sega and Nintendo, have also been sued by Americans for patent infringement. However, the shoe increasingly came to be on the other foot. Matsushita Electric opened offices in Washington, D.C. (as well as Munich and Singapore), solely to protect Matsushita's intellectual property abroad.

The Shifting American Position

Despite executive branch opposition through the beginning of the 1990s the science policy bureaucracy in the United States found ways to act on its own. The National Science Foundation added to its mission by sponsoring joint industry–university research with commercial applications. For example, Columbia University's Center for Telecommunications Research received a long-term $14 million grant in 1991 to work on fiber optics projects co-sponsored by Bell Communications Research, GTE, Phillips NV, and other high-tech–oriented companies. Most states have industrial extension programs modeled on the agricultural extension model they pioneered over a century ago and which were so instrumental in disseminating and developing farming.[21] The emphasis of such programs has been diffusion of existing technologies to small manufacturers. This is a task that is performed in Japan by parent corporations for their suppliers. In the United States large firms stand apart from their suppliers, cutting off those who fail to meet their immediate expectations. Yet, the health of these suppliers is essential to the nation's economy. Better parts would improve final products and deter sourcing abroad (which both reduces American jobs and is often a step on the road to producing competent competitors in final product markets).

The election of the Clinton–Gore team in 1992 was said (by Erich Bloch, former director of the National Science Foundation) to be "a paradigm shift in terms of the government's role in technology."[22] Clinton certainly made clear his orientation in this area of economic policy: "Civilian industry, not military, is the driving force behind advanced technology today. Only by strengthening our civilian technology base can we solve the twin problems of national security and economic competitiveness."[23] Indeed, early in the Clinton Administration senior Pentagon officials offered to trade military research and development project results for technology that could be used primarily in non-defense fields.[24] Vice President Al Gore took over responsibility for overseeing the transition of funding from Pentagon spending to civilian research and development targeted to increasing U.S. technological prowess in internationally traded goods. The stakes are high. New materials—from custom-made ceramic superconductors to ultrastrength plastics, metal alloys, intermetallics that allow planes to be lighter and fly faster and higher (perhaps incorporated into the proposed aerospace plane, which would enter into low orbit during a two-hour trip from New York to Tokyo, even faster than the hypersonic model touted earlier)—hold promise to be a multibillion-dollar business in the not-so-distant future.

Incentives, the Japanese model suggests, need to be tailored to accelerating industry's structural transformation. While some feared (rightly, I think) that targeted incentives with requirements of plan compliance from the private participants as the condition for government aid—in the U.S. institutional-political context would be subject to pork barrel political pressures—the "throw money at the market" solution was a failure whose costs would constrain growth prospects well beyond their demise. The antigovernment ideology that they inflamed also made constructive state action more difficult. The Clinton stance represented the first tentative and in practice contradictory steps toward embracing a self-conscious industrial policy.[25]

When the president unveiled a $17 billion technology spending program shortly after taking office it was a plan that had been worked out in close consultation with leading high-tech executives. It included expanding the role of the National Institute of Standards and Technology and cutting dubious projects in some military research areas. In transforming the Commerce Department agency to serve as an incubator–coordinator for advanced technologies, stressing partnership with key sectors of the private economy, and turning down the military spending spigot, Mr. Clinton spoke of his goal: "to adjust America so we can win in the twenty-first century."[26] His initiatives prompted a reassessment of the American industrial policy debate of the previous two decades. President Clinton, however, while he held the White House, was outmaneuvered by a majority alliance of conservative Democrats and Republicans in the Congress.

The Debate That Will Not Go Away

There has to be a sharp distinction made between arguments for and against regulation and arguments over methods of regulation. Those who are against government efforts to regulate the economy in any way represent a free-market libertarian position. This extreme view is in a distinct minority when stated in this form. Are we really against traffic lights? All taxation? Child labor laws? There are, however, those who say that they are against regulation but who really mean some regulations. It is important for them to be specific about which they like and dislike. Similarly, those who favor industrial policy are not for each and every type of possible intervention.

The American debate on industrial policy that developed in the second half of the postwar period as the growth rate slowed was about a particular form of targeted government intervention. It involved a campaign to reindustrialize the older manufacturing belt, which, and this was centrally significant to the debate, voted Democratic, was the home of strong trade unions, and wanted national resources spent in ways that may or may not have helped the nation in the long run but would have helped their region (and the Democratic Party) preferentially. Thus, the Republicans and Sunbelt regional representatives generally came out against the very idea of industrial policy first and foremost out of a narrowly conceived sense of self-interest. Ideological objections were strong, yet it would be possible to conceive of a form of industrial policy that would have been more widely accepted as good for the country as a whole. The debate also came at a time when the more internationalist corporate interests were opposed to such restructuring. Their interests were in a globally articulated production system in which national restrictions to the short-run free flow of capital were seen as harmful. Domestic politics and the internationalist interests of U.S.-based transnational capital seemed to doom industrial policy in America time and again, only to see its phoenix-like rebirth in the next firestorm of competitiveness decline.[27]

From a Japanese context industrial policy is about a different sort of discussion. As Hiroya Ueno writes:

> Unlike traditional fiscal and monetary policies, industrial policy demonstrates no clear relationship between its objectives and the means of attaining them. Its conception, content, and forms differ, reflecting the stage of development of an economy, its natural and historical circumstances, international conditions, and its political and economic situation, resulting in considerable differences from nation to nation and from era to era.[28]

In a Japan ruled by a cohesive capitalist leadership, the LDP, and the developmentalist state planners, without much meaningful opposition, such industrial planning could be a flexible tool. Tactics differ over time and between situations. They are influenced by shifts in ideological currents that blow in from the West and increasingly by electoral turbulence. The goals of industrial policy, however, remain as constant as those of monetary and fiscal policy. Continuity of purpose and coherence of governance are central. The tools and the specific actions are time and situation contingent. Japan, as it sought a place in the sun, was protectionist. The Japan that has reached parity can be more favorable to free trade. A Japan that seeks to build productive capacity in its major markets around the world can be more Catholic than the Pope, advocating free trade and even practicing it far more rigorously than the United States itself. Industrial policy is about increasing international competitiveness. International competitiveness is about "organizational inventiveness."[29] Industrial policy properly conceived is about developing new and better forms of organization. The peeling away of old forms of MITI guidance and allowing freer markets in some areas should not be taken as abandoning long-standing strategic orientation; rather, it should be seen as a change in tactics, one that is exaggerated for foreign consumption.

There remains disagreement on what the essential elements of Japanese industrial policy have been and how well the state has performed as a developmentalist agent. More broadly there will always remain great disagreements over the proper industrial policy for any specific nation. In my discussion I have described how Japan has protected its domestic markets, allowed cooperation and encouraged competition among its firms, provided low-cost financing and export subsidies, research and development funding, and offered other forms of assistance. The particular forms of proactive developmentalist policies are not integral to a definition of industrial policy.

Kaizuka in 1973 offered the classic, but I think misleading, definition of industrial policy when he wrote, "With little sarcasm, I would define industrial policy to be the policy that MITI implements."[31] Such a definition does capture part of the story. The policies MITI implements constantly undergo change. The Japanese industrial policy of the 1950s and 1960s was not relevant at the end of the century because in no country, including Japan, can it be expected that control over foreign exchange and the item by item control of imported technologies be maintained in an era of globally integrating markets. The ability to dispense preferential financing and tax privileges while still possible is more complicated since targeting benefits in a more politically charged environment is exceedingly difficult. Creating domestic cartels and national champions is possible, but international strategic corporate alliances present serious complications and undermine the contained effectiveness of such approaches. Short of nationalizing enterprises and exercising exceedingly tight statist control, undoing such interrelationships among global firms is an impossible task. Given the importance of knowledge developed elsewhere, blocking or attempting to block its flow is probably counterproductive to those who would close themselves off. Nonetheless, there are relevant lessons to learn from the earlier phase of industrial policymaking.

The Japanese bureaucrats self-consciously built, as Naohiro Amaya, one of the greatest of these pioneers, wrote: a "science of the Japanese economy" rather than following accepted "economics in general." He knew that economics has distinct national grammars and it is important that practitioners work within the relevant parameters of their own situations. Most mainstream economists in Japan, as in the West, take exception to such views. The distinguished quartet of Motoshige Itoh, Masahiro Okuno, Kazuharu Kiyono, and Kotaro Suzumura write approvingly: "In postwar Japan, at least from the academic standpoint, the most commonly held view was that there was no positive role for industrial policy to play."[32] Orthodox trade theory, however, as these authors are well aware, has not adequately analyzed the relationship between industrial structure and the gains from trade and so has a limited appreciation of the mechanisms of the industrial development.[33]

The revolutionary nature of what MITI achieved in the light of received doctrine is hard to overestimate. MITI protected nearly all modern industry using reasoning that defied the theory of the international division of labor and went beyond even the infant industry rationalizations for intervention by so great an extent as to propose a new theory of economic development. Government policies were used to create dynamic comparative advantage over a decade or more planning horizon rather than by taking existing endowments and maximizing in the short run. "Ironically," Miyohei Shinohara writes, "Japan's industrial policies achieved unprecedented success by going against modern economic theory. Whether it was steel, petrochemicals, or other industries, dissenting voices were raised claiming that the development of capital-intensive industries was irrational."[34]

In attempting to minimize the role played by MITI, some economists point to the small share of the national budget at the ministry's disposal. How could it be responsible for much under such conditions, they rhetorically ask? MITI does get to spend very little of the national budget, about 1 percent compared to 5–7 percent for the Ministry of Construction and of Agriculture, Forestry, and Fisheries. Even the Ministry of Transport has a larger budget appropriation. Spending levels, however, while significant, are hardly the whole story. The MOF budget is relatively small, but it controls how much other agencies spend, regulates the financial system, and carefully audits the tax returns of anyone who criticizes its judgments. No one would use its own monetary spending level as an indicator of its influence. So it has been with MITI.

Budget figures are especially misleading when considering MITI's impact on industrial development in the 1990s. Japan's government spends about one third to one half of what other major industrialized nations do as a percentage of total national research and development expenditures, but the Japanese government plays a much more significant and effective role in initiating and coordinating key research projects even though it may offer them only limited financial aid. This is all despite the fact that private research and development spending in Japan has increased at a much higher rate than it has in other advanced nations since the 1970s and, as Shimada has written, "much of this is due to government policy."[35] As in so many other areas touched upon in this study, the idea here was imported. MITI's efforts to promote commercially optimal technology through bringing competitors together into technology research associations (TRAs) to conduct joint research and development with the help of government subsidies is an idea imported from the United Kingdom in 1961. A key difference is that the Japanese organizations are set up to solve specific technology challenges and are temporary organizations dissolved after a stipulated period. Such TRAs do basic research from which all members benefit and compete to bring to market. They work if members have complementary interests.

The importance of the structures in which individual and firm behavior is embedded is recognized in the changing nature of the negotiations between the United States and Japan that began at the end of the 1980s with the Structural Initiative talks. It is not a question of particular products that are protected, but the ways each society establishes the givens, the context in which firms compete. These include everything from the size of the U.S. government deficit to the Japanese system of retailing. Whereas the United States turned its back on social engineering in the domestic realm, it joined in establishing the historic precedent to negotiate international differences and seek rules for structural accommodation not unlike the approach taken, if in a more encompassing manner, at Bretton Woods. There is the glimmer in the present instance of an understanding of the need for a stable international regime, a set of rules for nation-state behavior in the realm of trade and investment that includes harmonizing domestic policies. There is awareness of the costs of allowing harmonizing to be a process of leveling down to the lowest common denominator, as tends to be the case under the force of unrestricted market forces and the desirability of a leveling up that necessitates an international social contract.

It should be clear why the concept of industrial policy is so charged in the American context. It implies just the sort of strategic goal-oriented approach to the construction of an economy that American ideology has for the most part rejected. It involves a strong state with developmentalist priorities and a bureaucracy capable of effectiveness in achieving its goals. In an article published in 1970 Robert Ozaki could write that it "is an indigenously Japanese term not to be found in the lexicon of Western economic terminology."[30] Since then, the lexicon of Western economics has been revived. There has been greater awareness that some European nations have also had coherent industrial policies, as more recently have some other East Asian nations, and it is suggested even the United States has had an unconscious industrial policy. In the wider usage policies that promote industrial industries, adjust the structure of the economy in response to or anticipation of external and internal developments, acting to promote the national interest in the economic realm, count as industrial policy.

In such a usage the Department of Defense is sometimes said to have been the American MITI underwriting the development of the commercial aircraft and the computer industries, to take two prominent cases. The Department of Agriculture's extension service and subsidization of research and American land policies in the nineteenth century would also qualify as changing our productive capacities. Alexander Hamilton and Henry Clay, with their advocacy of federal assistance for manufacturing and subsidies for roads and other internal improvements, may be thought of as the fathers of American industrial policy. Today, industrial policy at the micro level, means rationalization of enterprises, encouragement of the adoption of more efficient techniques, quality control, cost reduction, and innovation. At the macro level it means the rationalization of the environment of enterprise and encompasses education policy and incentives to shape private decision making to accord with national developmental goals.

Before turning to the issue of the political problems that adopting an industrial policy in the United States would entail, it would be useful to round out the economic approach I have taken earlier with a brief political discussion of policymaking in Japan. Looked at in terms of an internal internationalized sector and internal national sector we can see why the governance structure of Japan seems both supple in the ways bureaucrats promote competitiveness and rigid when it comes to reforms that impose costs on powerful domestic interests. Domestic politics is based on mutual advantage-seeking in which there is no central power or group that imposes its will on other strong vested interests. The political cost of changing existing policies in such cases is extremely high, as the LDP found out when it introduced a consumption tax, moved to liberalize agriculture, or open bidding on major construction projects. The system works through marginal changes. Even the electoral loss did not mean the reformers could fundamentally change the collusive regulatory structures that had so long defined the Japanese political economy. In 1994 Prime Minister Hosokawa began to hear from the consensus-building commissions he had appointed to gain acceptance for basic change. (The most radical of the deregulation studies Hosokawa commissioned called for dismantling 15 of Japan's 21 government departments.) But even the more moderate proposals for change were accepted only in the vaguest terms by the bureaucracy that continued to dominate. While many Western commentators saw this as a victory of the bureaucrats to deny freedom to Japan's private sector and real control to elected representatives, the story is more complicated.

Special interests grease the wheels of a remarkably responsive political machine. As Sakakibara writes: "[T]he frequent contacts and interaction between *zoku* representatives and ministry bureaucrats closely resembles those of business partners. *Zoku* representatives essentially chase after votes and political contributions while the ministry seeks more funding and influence."[36] The party bosses direct traffic. The extent to which elected representatives can raise enough money not to have to depend on these bosses for cash depends on their own skill as independent money raisers. They can go their own way pursuing their client interests acting as feudal lords in their own right rather than as vassals of the party leaders. Given the strength of the vested interests any change in ongoing accommodation is difficult. The proportion of the public works budget, for example, is essentially fixed. Spending by category—fisheries versus sewage or irrigation to road construction—would be difficult to achieve no matter what an objective observer might think of the changed needs of the country. As a result while the economy continues to metamorphosize, public works spending by category remains stubbornly fixed.

When reform does occur it is often difficult to know where shifts are initiated and who is pushing them through. Understanding what is going on in the sense of grasping the extent to which putative decision makers are in fact complying with the wishes of those who really hold power is often difficult, and the opinion of observers in these matters often differs. Samuel Kernell, for example (contra Chalmers Johnson's earlier stress on the role of the MITI bureaucracy), suggests that "the bureaucracy has so thoroughly accommodated the priorities of the long-standing governing party in its training and advancement practices that the LDP rarely has to undertake a major intervention."[37] Kernell goes as far as to declare that the bulk of MITI's administrative guidance decrees may represent little more than the codification of LDP-endorsed "implicit understandings" among affected businesses. He thus gives a different weight to the power of the codifiers. Other more market-oriented observers see administrative guidance as simply reflecting the demands of those being guided. In attempting to allocate power in these ways each perspective captures a partial if seemingly mutually incompatible truth in classic Rashomon mirror fashion.

For our purposes Daniel Okimoto's term *network state* steers us to a relation between public and private decision makers that stresses mutual interdependence.[38] In terms of industrial policy the key formal networking instrumentality is the legally established deliberation council (*shingikai*). There are hundreds of these instruments of consensus formation at the national and local levels. The most important players are brought together in councils, subcouncils, committees, and sectional meetings to work out in some detail accommodations in particular policy areas. The governmental agency with authority in the particular responsibility plays a secretariat role, and while it often works to guide outcomes, it is itself limited by the will of other powerful participants. The decisions of these bodies, while not legally binding (and, indeed, may not become embodied in any new law or formal regulation), are generally accepted by participants in the consensus-formulation process. This is because once the positions of the network members are clarified, the costs and benefits each attaches to various courses of action shared, and given knowledge of the power standing of each, the calculation of possible reaction against those who violate the consensus can easily be estimated. Rationality dictates compliance. Those who "lose" in any one round know they will receive special consideration in the next. A balancing and a mutual accommodation rules, based on overall interests and the particularistic claims of powerful participants.

While the insights of such views are not to be denied the competition among interest groups means that skillful bureaucrats can often play off rivals and skillfully build coalition support in the Diet to offset opposition to their plans. The ministries themselves act as oligopolistic competitors that are always rivals, but who also have a common interest in bureaucratic supremacy. The politically appointed ministers come and go, the bureaucracy remains, and if individual lower-ranking bureaucrats may not be able to go against the stream, then senior officials navigate the current with great skill and powerful strokes. The politicians' influence is often on a different level. They can mediate with the bureaucracy on behalf of powerful constituents. Key figures swing contracts to favored companies and projects to home districts, as we have seen. The execution of government policy is flexible in these ways. The symbiotic relationship among bureaucrats, Diet leaders, and the business community, because it is far less formal than corporatism in the European sense, appears more obscure. It is a family matter negotiated in private to a great degree, and this keeps outside observers guessing as to where power lies. I think the answer is more fluid than the deterministic specification of any one leg of the three-legged stool. [39]

For our purposes it is enough to say that in Japan the primacy of accumulation has dictated the priorities within which other accommodations are forthcoming. A conservative government, an activist bureaucracy, and powerful industries have had a common interest in collusive solutions to problems seen pretty much from a common perspective. Differences are secondary to the power of the growth consensus. It is the structural accommodation of the system that is so remarkable from the perspective of the American system. The bureaucrats and politicians broker in different ways. The former are more farsighted. The latter take care that the most powerful are not slighted in the passing out of favored treatment.

An Industrial Policy for the United States

It would be difficult to exaggerate the depth of the changes that would be required for the United States to develop a successful set of policies that would allow us to approximate, in our own cultural economy, measures that would be as effective for us as Japan's developmentalist state is for that nation. The changes in consciousness, politics, sense of national purpose, training and education, and an inclusive and cooperative stance toward community would be involved. Most experts are skeptical. They believe we could never do it. Some argue we would not want to have such an elite controlled system of "planning." Some claim we already are doing as well as we can and it would be foolish to change.

Much of the most often repeated responses by economists, policymakers, and others is not justified by evidence. As Wade writes, "The popular belief that government cannot 'make winners' rests on remarkable little empirical research into the record of different governments in selective industrial promotion." His impressive investigations of East Asian industrialization certainly show success of developmentalist states in "governing the market." There can be little doubt that in Japan MITI's approach "ran counter to the basic principles of modern international economics,"[40] but so much for the conventional theory. In fact, even the most conventional of trade theorists have been forced to begrudgingly grant that economists' traditional trade-policy views need to be modified to accept some new ideas.[41]

The usual sense of the unfairness of what the Japanese do at the same time ignores the totality of the Japanese model, which extends to labor relations, education, a production system that combines cooperation and competition differently, and the other factors we have discussed in addition to transfer of resources to corporations through tax policies, protection, and subsidies for research and other purposes. Moreover, it ignores the centrality of what must be the core of successful industrial policy, a national consensus and unity. Without this cohesive sense of purpose and essential agreement there cannot be a working industrial policy.[42] In the context of a democratic America such a real consensus would have to include a pattern of growth sensitive to environmental concerns, issues of social justice, matters of racial harmony, and respect for local preferences. These important issues, however, are secondary to a more fundamental problem. As Komiya has written, the United States "tends to believe that its social, legal, and administrative institutions are universally superior and should be adopted by other countries. This belief often leads to an imperial or imperialistic manner in economic negotiations with different cultural traditions."[43] Komiya makes the comment in the context of noting that such an attitude interferes with our marketing successfully in Japan and in negotiating with that nation. It is also the case, however, that such an ethnocentric stance keeps us from learning from the Japanese and others and changing our own system where it would be beneficial—at home.

There is a totality to industrial policy as a developmentalist strategy that goes beyond the begrudging piecemeal efforts of the United States, although it is certainly true that those industries in which this nation does enjoy advanced standing—from aircraft to communications satellites, from agriculture to bio-technologies, the U.S. military, and even our land-grant college research and agricultural extension work—played a major role. Government subsidies have led to the success of our major export sectors, usually through the military budget. This continues in categories as diverse as high-capacity microchips to new materials and high-temperature superconductivity.

The realists say leave research and development with the Pentagon, noting that between 1975 and 1990 defense-related research and development expenditures tripled in constant dollars while government sponsored civilian research and development was cut back. The Japanese saw President Reagan's call for an ambitious Strategic Defense Initiative (his "Star Wars" proposal) as an industrial policy offensive. Indeed, the only ideologically acceptable way to fund research seemed to be through a military cover. DARPA was founded in 1958 in response to the Soviet Sputnik space launch, and it was DARPA that was the vehicle for the Bush administration's multibillion dollar program to develop a nationwide supercomputer network. While the network has strategic military applications, it also has tremendous potential for business applications. It took the demise of the Cold War to clear the way for America to think about an industrial policy based on nonmilitarist conceptions of the national interest.

The decision to identify specific firms as national champions in, for example, commercial aircraft and electronics in Great Britain and France, were strongly influenced by the issue of enhancing military capacity. The Gaullist desire for independence was especially costly to France, and Great Britain's failures are well known. The causes of the failure of industrial policies in such nations, however, need to be theorized carefully. As Eads and Yamamura, reviewing the postwar British case, remark, perhaps it was inevitable, but they write, "We are, however, less than fully satisfied with the neoclassical assessment of this failure. We are much more comfortable with an assessment that considers institutional and social factors. If these considerations are absent, the British lesson is likely to be misinterpreted."[44] Politics in the widest sense, which includes struggles to shift the cultural economy of a nation, is integral to its economic performance.

The real case against industrial policy is not the difficulty of picking winners. As numerous wags have commented, we could just use MITI's and we would have a pretty good list, but rather that the American political system is ill-suited to adopting a coherent industrial policy. Congress, it is feared (not without good reason), would spread around the subsidies in pork-barrel fashion, organized constituencies in declining sectors would be better situated to muscle support than potentially more important industries that do not yet exist as a powerful constituency. Particular firms would no doubt lobby for special favors and powerful congresspeople would favor companies located in their home districts.

By the time the United States sorts out these issues and overcomes its ideological biases it is likely to face a very different economic world than the postwar world in which Japan was able to pursue the developmentalist-state policies. The internationalization of research and development undermines certain forms of developmentalist-state policies to a significant extent. The Japanese realized, surely by the early 1990s, that to compete at the cutting edge they were better off having a substantial research presence in the United States. This was especially true in software, where they lagged, and without which their strength in manufacturing would be less valuable. From a marketing point of view they had also realized that localization of all aspects of operations from research to manufacturing and customer support made sense, to meet local tastes better and to allow for quicker delivery and a clearer sense of ongoing developments in this market that would allow them quicker response time and more accurate information. Political factors also play a role. Komatsu, for example, is probably aided in its rivalry with U.S.-based Caterpillar by moving some of its production to Tennessee in a joint venture with a major American firm. The CEO and top management of the Tennessee entity are all Americans. With half the equity, Komatsu limits itself to only two seats on the board of directors. Such a company can be perceived as American enough to avoid anti-Japanese ill-will or governmentally sanctioned disadvantages.

Some Japanese companies are well on their way to becoming global entities. Sony was the first Japanese company to produce in the United States. It located a plant in San Diego in the early 1970s. By the early 1990s only a third of Sony's sales were in Japan. In pursuit of truly global status Sony produced, marketed, and carried out research in the United States as well as Europe and East Asia. Honda, like Sony, is not a dominant player in the Japanese market. It, too, moved overseas early as an alternative to butting heads with larger domestic rivals. Honda moved to Malaysia in the late 1960s and has had a network of production facilities from Taiwan to India, and was the first Japanese auto producer to come to the United States. It is now the most integrated Japanese producer in North America, as noted in Chapter 5. Such Japanese firms, once the exception, are becoming prototypical of the new internationalized Japanese corporation.

In concluding this discussion of industrial policy it is necessary both to position it in the context of the changing globalization process (as I will do in the next chapter) and to say a bit about the transformational issues raised in the last chapter by the rise of financial speculation and its relation to the productive economy. To do this let me return once more to the powerful impact of Chandler's contention that the modern business enterprise took the place of the market mechanism in coordinating the activities of the American economy in allocating resources. It would be difficult for Japanese (apart from neoclassical economists there) to understand why this revisionist view made such an impact. In their country the developmentalist state and *keiretsu* organization are premised on just such conscious planning of markets. In contrast to the dynamic American corporation of the postwar era, which bought and sold divisions, closed plants, and fired workers wholesale, all according to short-run financial criteria and operation as a holding company, the Japanese corporation could better be described in the terms Chandler used for the American corporation in its ascendancy that

> took on new products and services in order to make more complete use of its existing facilities and personnel. Such expansion, in turn, led to the addition of still more workers and equipment. If profits were high, they preferred to reinvest them in the enterprise rather than pay them out in dividends. In this way the desire of the managers to keep the organization fully employed became a continuing force for its further growth. [45]

If managerial capitalism replaced family capitalism in the United States between 1840 and World War I, the years of Chandler's story, and the Japanese capitalism of the developmentalist state and the *keiretsu* improved upon the American model, then a new dominance of a different kind of financier was asserted in the 1980s. The future will tell whether the short-run financial considerations that came to dominate Anglo-American business organizations will continue to prevail and how far Japanese capitalism will go following this trajectory. Industrial policy must cope with such questions. Globalization factors and new forms of transnational corporate development that span national boundaries in the ways they integrate commodity flows, including strategic alliances with competitors in other regional blocks, must, however, be considered in new ways in any discussion of industrial policymaking in the contemporary period.

It must also be said, however, that the discussion of industrial policy is itself a limited one. It presumes that more competitive national champions will bring good, high-paying jobs to a country's workers or that foreign-owned firms can be enticed to locate so that the private sector will create desired levels of domestic employment. This need not be the case. The irony of industrial policy discussion is that it is about increased profitability at a time of hypermobility of globalized capital, of overaccumulation, and the marginalization of millions in both the underdeveloped and the advanced nations. It is presumed that helping "their" companies will help them. Matters look somewhat different from an internationalization perspective.

It is too early to speak of global progressive taxation and anything but the brief rudiments of international redistributional justice. It is worth noting, however, that transnational capital as the main shaper of our world and generator of innovative growth should be subject to unit taxation—each company should pay a tax based on the amount of business it does in each nation. This would avoid transfer pricing and the playing off of one location against another to the detriment of all. The particulars of such an international tax treaty, whether based on value added, sales within each jurisdiction, or some other formula can be debated. That the main force of accumulation should increasingly move beyond the tax collectors in an era in which the social costs of capitalist transformation are so severely felt should in fact be central to thinking about a comprehensive industrial policy. Other extensions of familiar principles should also be part of the discussion. Vesting, the idea that after a worker has been on the job for five years or some other agreed upon period they are entitled to keep the pension benefits employers have committed even if they do not stay with that employer until retirement, can be extended. Communities should have vesting. The social cost of plant relocation should be internalized and made part of the real total cost, part of the company's balance sheet calculation.

Competitiveness is a lens of profitability and must, if we are to talk of the best government policy, be considered as part of the larger questions of living standards, fairness, strengthening the social fabric, and so on. It is clear that these are difficult issues and that business people may be forgiven for not paying them sufficient attention. Public officials have a different charge than simply maximizing private profits. Nowhere have they really begun to think comprehensively about the interrelations between private efficiency and social efficiency. They have hardly been helped by academic researchers who leave such nebulous considerations to others or believe they are unimportant, a touching faith in the ethereal digits. As costs rise environmental concerns have moved to the fore, as crime and drugs change basic social expectations, and the 34 million unemployed people in the rich industrial countries (who would stretch from New York to Sydney and back again if they stood in line, or so the *Economist* told us in the spring of 1993) weigh on the promise of these democracies. The hundreds of millions in the poor nations desperately seek survival, and the appeal of hate and divisiveness grows. Such issues take us beyond our already overly ambitious project, but it should not be forgotten that they are the reason the answers the richest and most powerful choose are so important.

10

Economic Transformation and the World System

"When I was twenty I realized that I play a part in my local state. After I was thirty I realized that I play a part in the affairs of the nation. After I was forty I realized that I play a part in the affairs of the entire world."
SHOZAN SAKUMA, Nineteenth-Century Confucian Scholar[1]

"Japan is worth particular notice. The Japanese scientists, technologists, technocrats, have shown skills and originality in all this electronic apotheosis which quite outclass the West's. This ought to surprise no one who has given the most perfunctory attention to Japanese visual art or literature or to pure science. For hundreds of years, the culture has been wildly original, something oddly different from any other among the sons of men. It was an instance of Western blindness not to discover that simple fact."

C. P. SNOW, *The Physicists*[2]

There are, of course, those who believe that Japan has never been different in any theoretically significant way from other capitalist nations. Given the detailed, though contested evidence, some neoclassically oriented economists suggest that whatever might have been true in the past, and they concede nothing, Japan today is becoming more like other capitalist nations. In the world system convergence is thought to be inevitable; indeed, it is seen as the result of market forces working themselves out. In this chapter the issue of convergence will be explored in a globalization context. It will be suggested that some of us in the United States may be turning Japanese, at least as much, if not more, than Japanese are being truly converted to laissez-faire thinking. Indeed, the rhetorical acceptance of Western economic ideology is partly the result of corporate Japan having outgrown the need for many types of industrial policy support and partly serves a tactical function of further disarming the ideologically hardened sons and daughters of Adam Smith.

255

The continued evidence for Japanese exceptionalism (as compared with the U.S. norm, but not, however, to other late industrializers) is evident in the manner of global insertion of the Japanese corporation and in the more sophisticated developmentalist-state strategies. Accepting the outcome of free markets has always been the economic ideology of choice among the strong. As Japan has increased its comparative strength across a widening array of product lines it has a greater investment in open world markets. This does not mean, however, that it has abandoned planned marketing and coherent competitiveness strategies.

I have made the distinction between the competitiveness discourse that is an "us versus them" discussion, a transformational framework that stresses the new production system that increases efficiency and so potentially the living standards of all who adopt it, and the globalization trend, the integration of the world economy through commodity chains and complex webs of production that transcend national boundaries, weaving disparate parts of the planet into a single market. To repeat, these approaches are complementary; they are ways of describing different aspects of a complex process. In this chapter, as Japan's direct foreign investment patterns are discussed, the focus is on the unique role Japanese corporations and state policies have on the reshaping of the world political economy. The extent to which the Japanese companies and the state approach the internationalization process differently than in the American case brings possible transformational issues into the discussion.

The question of whether Japan's groupism means that their firms abroad would set up closed networks that exclude others from participating in their transaction networks was not only an American's worry. Australians, for example, have noted that when Japanese property developers go abroad they organize things through their own financial and construction affiliates, entering strategic local partnerships only when they find some special access advantage. Japanese tourists fly Japanese airlines to foreign countries, where they stay in Japanese hotels, use Japanese buses, eat in Japanese restaurants, and shop in Japanese department stores. Australians, who see some of their holiday areas increasingly dominated by the Japanese rich, grumble imperialism, while others point to how much money is in it for Australia. The *Australian Financial Review*, summing up the way the wind was blowing in their country at the end of the 1980s, wrote, "The lesson is: watch the Japanese. Only buy or build assets that the Japanese like, because they are your market. Real wealth over the next decade is unlikely to come from any other source."[3] The business community in other countries came to similar conclusions. From the standpoint of local consumers, however, being priced out of the home market by foreigners has not been a pleasant experience, and the dislocations resulting from rapid foreign penetration and unplanned resulting growth can be immense.

The Growth of Japan's Investment in Asia

In the 1950s and into the early 1960s, as Japan successfully rebuilt its economy and was once more able to export, Asia was its largest market. The pattern of trade was that of a semi-periphery social formation. Japan imported complex manufactured goods from the West, primarily the United States, and exported simple manufactured goods to countries less developed than itself. As an immature industrializer Japan had trouble competing in more sophisticated core markets and ran a sizable trade deficit with the United States. Japan's pattern of rapid growth, as discussed earlier, was one of moving continuously upscale to more sophisticated process technologies and product mix. Wages did not keep up with productivity, but they did rise substantially. For example, in 1960 Japanese workers on average earned some 15 percent less than did their Philippine counterparts. By 1970 they were earning four times as much.[4] As wages in Japan increased there was pressure on manufacturers to source from abroad.

Significant Japanese direct investment in Asia was initiated in the early 1970s by medium-size companies. The largest Japanese companies only moved in a planned way into Asia with the oil crises and then, in a dramatic spurt, after the yen appreciation of the mid-1980s. The independent producers were at first looking to these countries for their domestic market potential. After 1985 low-wage labor was a more crucial consideration. Japanese producers were also drawn to overseas production during these years by the strong yen, which drove up their domestic costs and made foreign investment less expensive. In Japan labor costs were an issue, but so were labor shortages and the pressure of the huge bilateral trade surplus. The small and medium-size Japanese companies that went abroad (while small and medium-size U.S. corporations of the period knew nothing of foreign markets and had little help should they wish to find out), were given indispensable assistance by the Japanese government and the large trading companies. The government provided financial assistance; it used its foreign aid to ease entry into new markets and to soften possible resentments against Japan in developing countries. The information-gathering and dissemination systems of the trading companies were crucial.

The large Japanese corporations were initially less drawn to produce overseas than the Americans because their production system, the just-in-time delivery system, and their close relations with subcontractors did not lend itself to overseas production. Also, Japanese productivity was based in significant measure on the close working relation between engineering and the constant improvements developed on the line. This depended on attitudes and work habits of Japanese labor and were not easily developed abroad. Still, because of U.S. pressures the Japanese learned to export to the United States through third countries, and to produce in the United States itself. It was in these years that the Japanese system became internationalized. It did so, however, in a way consistent with the underlying Japanese model and in a manner that stands in contrast to the globalization strategies of U.S. transnational corporations.

In October 1980 Japan's foreign exchange and foreign investment laws dramatically changed from "prohibition in principle" to "liberalization in principle." Foreign direct investment increased dramatically. The "real" increase in Japanese influence in the East Asian economies was, and is, far greater than the data show because, as Shojiro Tokunaga has written, "The essence of FDI . . . is related not necessarily to acquiring the 'ownership' but to exercising effective influence on the management of a foreign-located firm."[5] Still, the data show that in 1984 Japanese manufacturing subsidiaries abroad produced an output of only 4.3 percent of the total manufacturing that was then taking place within Japan itself. The comparable figure for the United States was 17 percent. This was in large part because even with rising domestic costs and given exchange rates the advantages of home production were substantial. However, Asian labor costs fell in real terms with the appreciation of the yen.

As the United States increased pressure to reduce Japan's bilateral trade surplus, investment in North America and indirect exports from Asian subsidiaries grew far more attractive. Even so, only 9 percent of Japan's manufacturing capacity was located outside of Japan in 1992 (the proportion for the United States was two or three times as large), and Asia accounted for less than 20 percent of Japan's total. This percentage will undoubtedly grow. As of a year later 40 percent of the outstanding loans of Japanese banks was to Asia, more than to the United States or Europe (Japanese banks had seventeen branches in China alone in 1993). Some sectors were experiencing particularly high rates of Asian investment. In 1993 Matsushita had 61 percent of its overseas production in Asia (up from 49 percent in 1985), and Aiwa built two thirds of its products overseas and planned the figure to be three fourths in the near future.

Nations that are currently backwaters, such as Vietnam, are experiencing major flurries of attention. A Japanese consortium was spending $150 million to upgrade Haiphong's port. The Japanese are opening banks in Ho Chi Minh City and scheduling regular flights to Tokyo, and careful, detailed proposals are being made to the Vietnamese. A 1992 report by the Mitsubishi Corporation, "The Master Plan for the Automobile Industry in the Socialist Republic of Vietnam," is one strand of a longer-standing involvement that sought to take advantage of Vietnam's hardworking, well-educated 33-million member work force. With a population twice the size of South Korea's, abundant natural resources, and a reforming, if still nominally communist, government Vietnam was attractive to farsighted foreign investors. The Mitsubishi Plan is about selling cars. There are breakdowns by type of vehicle (three categories of trucks, vans, passenger cars, etc.) with forecasts of changing consumer demand and so on over a thirteen-year horizon, but such details are embedded in a larger vision of a Vietnam developing machinery, electronics, and petrochemical and processed agricultural industries. Along with their own plants would come, Mitsubishi suggests, Bridgestone for tires, Asahi Glass for the windshields, and other specified suppliers (Nippon Denso for nuts and bolts, Aisin Seiki for pistons, Riken Corporation for piston rings, and so on. American firms were discouraged from entering the market by domestic concerns.

The dramatic upsurge in Japan's direct foreign investment in the second half of the 1980s did not hollow out their own economy, as some had feared.

In the late 1980s Japanese domestic spending on plant, equipment, research, and product development equaled a quarter of the GNP, and was more than three times the comparable proportion for the United States. Thus, Japan preserved their lead, keeping Asians dependent upon technology imports from Japan. At the same time, Japanese enterprises, especially multinationals assigned the countries of Asia places within their enterprise strategy.[6] Japanese corporations in the late 1980s had established more sophisticated textured patterns of foreign investment.[7] These were discernable in a new-wave co-prosperity sphere, based on the incentives of mutually advantageous growth combining Japanese capital, technology, and marketing to Asian low-cost labor and abundant natural resources.[8] Despite the ecological violence of many of these extractive projects and the intensely exploitative if scientifically efficient factories with near-zero wasted time work organization, such investments are attractive to poor economies—certainly to their elites wishing to modernize.

Ariyoshi Okumura of the BOJ likened the Plaza Accord to the arrival of Commodore Perry in 1853 in its impact on Japanese manufacturing. Following the agreement by finance ministers and central bankers of the leading industrial nations in September 1985, the yen appreciated in an unprecedented fashion, nearly doubling in value as against the dollar. In 1984 the strong dollar had accounted for two thirds of that year's $37 billion merchandise trade deficit between our two nations. As the dollar weakened, segments of Japanese manufacturing moved offshore in search of lower labor costs. This sped up a process that had long been underway. The Japanese relative growth in productivity was so strong that it was able to overcome 70 percent of the initial disadvantage of the yen appreciation between 1986 and 1990 by retaining market shares through advancing its technological frontier. As for U.S. manufacturing, exports did pick up, as noted earlier, but this was not enough to spark a serious domestic recovery.

In the key second half of the 1980s as the yen strengthened and real interest rates came closer in line (with the financial deregulation in Japan), many U.S. firms took advantage of windfall gains to increase their profit rates. They did not reinvest revenues in productive capacity to the extent the Japanese continued to do out of a smaller profit stream. The Japanese companies cut their operating profits, while U.S. companies increased theirs. Japan's sales continued to rise in the United States, while these American companies increased their profit margins and dividends. Many U.S. firms if they could not meet the profit hurdle established by management withdrew from an area of competition.[9] In some areas the U.S. moved to source the product abroad from lower cost areas such as Korea or Singapore, putting the U.S. brand nameplate on the product before final sale. In this way the Asian newly industrialized countries developed the capacity to meet the needs of the U.S. market, and they soon sold under their own brands as well. Other American firms, both before and during the period of opportunity afforded by the export strength the lower dollar provided, adopted aspects of the Japanese system, some with significant success.

The Peaceful Co-Prosperity Sphere

In the late 1940s Kaname Akamatsu suggested what has come to be known as the "flying geese" theory to indicate how the structure of exports was related to the product cycle. In late industrializers like Japan a product initially imported first went through the stage of import substitution. As domestic manufacturing rapidly expanded it was transformed into an export item. The nation's imports shift to more sophisticated products and old exports are passed on to less-developed economies. The wedge-shaped pattern in which the product goes from the import to the export side was pictured as resembling the pattern of geese in flight. In the late 1950s Kiyoshi Kojima used Akamatsu's model, combining it with a dynamic comparative advantage stage description of Japan's changing export pattern. Going beyond Western product cycle literature Kojima showed how each wave of industrial development leaves Japan with a more sophisticated export structure.

Such shifts in comparative advantage bring forth a higher wage employment structure as well as an expansion of the domestic market for sophisticated manufactured products. It is just such linkages that those economists who argue that it does not matter what kind of production mix and export products a country has deny. For our purposes here it is a second usage of the image of flying geese that is relevant: Japan as leader of the flock, with the newly industrializing nations of the region following along its path, picking up the discarded lower-technology manufactured goods that Japan has outgrown. The usefulness of this usage, however, can be questioned to the extent that it implies independent autonomous national growth patterns. It is Japanese guidance and investment that has structured the prospects for industrialization in the region to a significant degree.[10]

The inferences drawn from the product cycle notion have been a matter of some contention. As early as 1970 MITI Vice Minister Yoshihisa Ojimi told a gathering of the OECD that Japan favored "progressively giving away industries to other countries, much as a big brother gives his outgrown clothes to his younger brother. In this way a country's own industries become more sophisticated."[11] Kojima wrote in the late 1970s that Japanese investment in East Asian nations would "eventually" enable these countries to "raise their economies to the level and quality of Japan's."[12] In the 1980s some Japanese economists wrote about an expected "boomerang effect" as Japanese investments in Asia came back to displace domestic production and cause severe dislocations. There are inevitable tensions between the flock and the head goose.

From their perspective, Asians outside of Japan have viewed the concept skeptically. The formation of geese, it seems to many of them, is unlikely to close ranks any time in the foreseeable future. The image is a rationalization for why Japan should always be in a position to determine what they are allowed to do. "These concerns have mounted amid evidence of a growing— not shrinking—technological gap between Japan and its neighbors."[13] In any case the better image is not this popular one of "flying geese" nations, with

Japan at the head followed by Korea and Taiwan, Singapore and Hong Kong, then Thailand, Malaysia, and so on. Rather, an international division of labor has been set up by the Japanese, who restrict licensing of key technologies while at another level much of Asia is already part of the Japanese economy from the massive hydroelectric and aluminum smelting facilities in Indonesia to the strip clearing of huge virgin forests in the Philippines. The national unit is not an unimportant one, but it is the regional system of development that merits primary analytical attention.

The implicit assumption that successful newly industrialized economies have grown autonomously, when in fact they rely on transnational corporations for technology and marketing (among other things), it is a misspecification tied to a traditionalist way of seeing international trade. In the extreme case of Singapore, where transnational corporations employ 70 percent of the labor force and account for well over 90 percent of the city-state's exports, dependence must be judged to be high. Unlike the predictions of many theorists such dependency has coincided with incredible increases in the average standard of living, and to economic and social development that exceeds that of many first world nations, in Singapore's case on average exceeding its former masters, the British.

While attention is focused in much of the transformational literature on foreign penetration measured by direct foreign investment (defined as control of firms through ownership), the Asian patterns include minority shares, long-term contracting, and international coalitions without juridical ownership claims. Foreign influence elsewhere is also being increasingly perceived as a more subtle exercise as company strategies on subcontracting, marketing, and technology diffusion represent an extent of interpenetrating influence that far exceeds that captured in the statistics on direct foreign investment and patterns of cross-border sales of goods.

In textiles, the first industry of significance to move production from Japan to East Asia, for example, quite a fine intra-industry division of labor has developed between Japan and the other nations of the region and among production processes and types of product lines. These linkages are not primarily within single enterprises, although Asian subsidiaries of Japanese firms are significant, as MITI surveys show.[14] Such intraregional division of labor had proceeded by the late 1980s to the point where the Seibu Department Store and its subsidiary the Seiyu supermarket chain could set up special departments nicknamed "NICSONs" (as in, "Son of NICs or Newly Industrialized Countries) to display TVs, stereos, watches, and other products that sold well below comparable Japanese-made low-end goods. As the yen grew stronger such products, often made by subsidiaries of Japanese firms, increasingly found markets in Japan. The increasingly articulated regional economy represents a new stage in global economic development.[15]

As noted, wage differentials did induce Japan to let labor-intensive products well advanced in their product cycle go to lower cost production sites elsewhere in Pacific Asia. Yet, Japan's balance of trade with the countries of the region continued to soar as these nations bought more sophisticated Japanese exports. The Asian new industrialized economies also depended heavily on Japanese semiprocessed inputs for their own production of export goods. Korea exports fax machines, but imports all its thermal printer heads from Japan. Its printer makers are also dependent on Japan for the key component, dot matrix impact heads. Korea's important television export industry depends on Japan for its electron guns and integrated circuits. Hyundai's export success is built on Mitsubishi-constructed factories and the import of its technologically advanced automobile components. In 1993 Japanese officials, Chuh Young Souk, vice chairman of the Korea–Japan Economic Association said, "have this model in which Japan controls everything, and they are just applying that model to a new area, Asia." [16]

In 1992 Japan was running a surplus of $42 billion with East Asia, almost as much as with the United States ($44 billion that year). The Asian industrializers could run a large deficit with Japan because they had a $36 billion surplus with the United States and a $10 billion with the European Community. A similar pattern was evident with the ASEAN nations. Both cases indicate strong indirect exports by Japan to the United States and the European Community that do not show up in the data as exports from Japan itself. With the success of economic development efforts in the wider Asian Pacific the region became a major market for sophisticated consumer goods produced in Japan and increasingly by Japanese companies producing locally for these markets.

In 1970 Japan had accounted for only 12 percent of foreign investment in Southeast Asia and the United States for over half. By 1990 the U.S. share was down to 20 percent and Japan's was nearly 40 percent of the total. Similarly, 24 percent of Japan's exports in 1970 went to the United States, 40 percent in 1985, but by the end of the decade the U.S. share was down to 31 percent and East Asia's share was up to 19 percent and rising fast (by 150 percent over the second half of the 1980s compared with an increase of 39 percent for exports to the United States).

Japanese direct foreign investment in Asia jumped from $2 billion in 1987 to $8 billion in 1990, according to MOF figures. It was double or triple U.S. direct investment in the region by the latter date (depending on method of valuation). Japan's trade with Asia was increasing fast and was already greater than its trade with the United States. A Bank of Tokyo survey presents comprehensive data for 1988 showing that total foreign investment in four ASEAN nations—Thailand, Malaysia, Indonesia, and the Philippines—had increased threefold in the previous year. In Thailand 10 percent of the industrial work force was employed by Japanese companies. By 1992 15 percent of Thai manufacturing jobs were with Japanese companies. Japan provides half of Thailand's foreign investment each year. The United States is well behind, investing less in Thailand than do Taiwan, Hong Kong, or Italy. As Japan imports more, the main beneficiaries are close to home, not across the Pacific.

Consider the example of MTV in Malaysia (connoting Matsushita Television not music video), the main producer of color TVs for markets throughout Asia and well into the Middle East. In 1994 Matsushita alone accounts for more than 4 percent of the nation's GNP. Every morning its thousands of workers put on their uniforms, which are close approximations of those worn by the company's labor force in Japan, and sing the Matsushita song (in Malay) before their morning Japanese-style discussions with management and the start of a new day on the assembly line making products, many of which reach the U.S. markets counted as Malay, not Japanese, products. The re-Asianization of Japan presents a significant shift in the power balance of the world's political economy. Malaysian officials already tell visitors that the Japanese triggered the postwar independence movement. In Thailand, where Toshiba's Bangkok subsidiary produces refrigerators and air conditioners for the Asian market, officials point out to visitors that Thailand was allied with Japan against the West during World War II.

By the 1990s Asia was a maturing market as well as a production site and a new complex regional pattern of production and distribution was evident. Sanyo Electric, for example, with three plants in Korea, six in China, two each in Taiwan, Hong Kong, Singapore, and Malaysia, and one in the Philippines, Thailand, and Indonesia was exporting and importing parts from its facilities in the region, and assigning a specific role to each (depending on wage and skill levels, degree of political stability, transfer costs, and so on) within a dynamically flexible, but coherent, strategic plan organized and administered from Japan. In contrast to the Japanese holistic production chains in Asia— from raw materials to final marketing of manufactured product and customer service—the United States had a more arm's-length market approach.

The new booming Asian economies depend on Japanese capital, technology, and strategic guidance. Whether one talks about a new interdependence or a new colonialism, and whether recipients welcome Japanese investors with incentives and optimistic expectations, or are wary with memories of a brutal occupation fifty years ago, there appears to be no other alternative. The offer to be incorporated in a new co-prosperity sphere this time around seems the only game worth playing and, as Tessa Morris-Suzuki has remarked, [17] familiarity can breed indifference. Japanese brand presence is even more important in some of these East Asian nations than it is in the United States. Even efforts to balance Japanese influence by attracting American and European investors seemed fruitless as the United States gave priority to military adventures while its recession-prone economy and fiscal excesses put new investments on hold. The Europeans turned inward or looked to reincorporate their Eastern periphery. With the Bush administration's East Asian policy on autopilot, Japanese exports to East Asia and its investment in the region in the early 1990s were both twice those of the United States. The Clinton team, determined to do something about these developments, initiated a hardball game played by internally inconsistent rules as U.S. policymakers strove to catch up both in terms of actual economic outcomes and in the building of developmentalist capacities within the executive branch.

East Asia emerges as a loosely coordinated manufacturing bloc. Tokyo planners think out location decisions, country by country, industry by industry, and even product by product. MITI, in conjunction with Malaysian planners, was hard at work to make their less-developed neighbor one of the world's foremost producers of word processors and of fax machines. Indonesia was targeted for textiles and plastics. In such matters, "laissez-faire can't be recommended," as Nobuhito Hobo of the Ministry of Foreign affairs sees it, representing the views of his peers, "Careful utilization of market forces is always ideal."[18] While investment decisions by Japanese companies are based on private calculations, host governments and ministries back in Tokyo influence the climate in which these decisions are made.

Labor costs and skill levels, political stability, and market potential are carefully analyzed in Tokyo and technologies and products are matched with locations over the relevant time horizon. Planning does not replace the profit motive, but is its agent. As in the case of domestic industrial policy, coordination "plans markets" in ways consistent with promoting the long-term success of corporations using techniques sensitive to a constantly changing external environment. All this gives the Third World demand for appropriate technology a new twist. By investing for the long haul, the Japanese have won important concessions such as the way local content laws are interpreted to allow regionwide divisions of labor. Parts requiring different skill levels are produced in different countries, minimizing cost, but also increasing the dependence of each nation on a monopsonistic buyer—Japan. This pattern of regionally articulated development, of course, is an assault on traditional understanding of national sovereignty and the development strategies of the autonomy-minded Third World dependency theorists.

The pattern in the Asian regional economy is a complex pattern of cooperation and competition. Korean and Taiwanese firms have also gone abroad to lower-wage neighboring countries. They are increasingly caught between the high-tech edge of the Japanese and their own rising labor costs vis-a-vis Asian neighbors. South Korea's largest producer of running shoes has facilities in Indonesia and Thailand, where it produces millions of pair of shoes per year. Singapore businesses have long produced in Malaysia, and Hong Kong and Taiwan have done so in China. (Historically, much of Taiwan's mainland Chinese investment has been routed through Hong Kong due to political concerns and restrictions.) Indeed, in my discussions with economists in Hong Kong there is a predominant feeling that it was all well and good to talk about Japan if what concerned us was the next fifty years or so, but after that the dominant force shaping the world economy would be China.

Much of the neoclassical-influenced development literature represents the growth of the Asian newly industrialized countries as a result of their adopting a free-market orientation. This is a serious misreading of what in Korea, Taiwan, Singapore, Malaysia, and Thailand have been activist government promotion efforts. It would be accurate to say that these new-wave development strategies are both profoundly interventionist and promarket. The government interferes with markets to restructure incentives that promote long-run development. This, of course, is the approach the Japanese developmentalist state pioneered. The neoclassical models are also misrepresentative to the extent that they treat each of these nations as an autonomous unit of analysis. It is not each nation separately that adopts correct policies and autonomously grows by its own efforts combined with opening its markets to foreign investors who then react simply to market signals in a series of individual investment choices and market contracts.

As I have noted, to view things from the perspective of individual nations is to miss the driving developmental dynamic. Rather than the transformational perspective with its stress on internal nation-state economic development we need a regional approach to globalization: that is in the triad world in which Germany looms large in a unifying Europe, the United States spreads its free-trade community both north and south in the Western Hemisphere, and Asia comes under Japanese guidance. While there are fears of a revanchist Japanese imperial state the primacy of the market (Japanese-style) over the political is likely to remain the source of Asia's regional order.[19] In any case the Asian nations are at vastly different levels of development and encompass a much greater range of political styles than found in the European Community of 1992. Indeed, from Japan's point of view there is little to be gained from political intervention and formally assuming responsibility for regional development. Over the coming years, however, Japan, like Europe, may find that destabilizing developments in nearby countries may force a preemptive political engagement in their affairs.

Some economists, perhaps optimistically, project that by early in the twenty-first century the East Asian economy (without Japan) will be almost as big as that of Europe or the United States, and that the Asian GNP (with Japan) will be about half that of the entire world by 2050 (it is currently about 20 percent). Given the stakes, the Japanese, while still sensitive to local feelings, now see "the question is not whether or not we can avoid any suggestion of interference in domestic politics, but rather what level of mutual interference is acceptable and how we can most equitably share the costs that such cooperation entails," as Saburo Okita, long-time chair of the Japan National Committee of the Pacific Economic Cooperation Conference, puts the matter. Of course, any possibility of Thailand interfering in the domestic politics of Japan must be judged remote. Japanese pronouncements may soon come to resemble those of the United States addressing its economically diminutive allies in a better time. The country that carries the thick wallet, controlling technology and markets, finds it natural to speak of "cooperation."

The only other important economic force in the region is the Chinese. Indeed, in the early 1990s Hong Kong and Taiwan together were outinvesting Japan in Indonesia, Malaysia, and the Philippines. They were also reconquering China itself by capitalism starting from Guangzhou province and moving north. Overseas, Chinese in Singapore are also a regional force. It is not too far-fetched to expect these personalistic businesses in which networks and loyalty are crucial to form *keiretsu*-like arrangements in the future. The overseas Chinese, however, have thus far concentrated outside of the areas of Japanese strength in hotels, construction, and other real estate and infrastructure building. High value added markets are still Japanese or dependent to a considerable extent on Japanese technology. Japan is likely to play an important role in the emergent Shenzhen–Hong Kong–Taiwan regional economic formation and a Korean–Shandong integrated area. Most interesting is the prospect of a mainland China open to the world economy, given its vast workforce and potential productive capacity. Those economists in Hong Kong may be proven right before half a century has passed.

Yet the available statistical data and casual evidence of growing powerful ethnic Chinese corporate growth in the region must be examined with some care. Behind Chinese minority ethnic firms in Malaysia, Thailand, and Indonesia are often Japanese companies. The Liem group assembles cars with Mazda, Suzuki, and others. It is involved in real estate projects of some scope but in alliance with Marubeni. Another leading ethnic Chinese group Astra has joint projects with Toyota and Daihatsu. It manufactures auto components, but with the key aid of Nippondenso. It distributes for Komatsu and Fuji.[20] The extent of such relations is vast and undercuts assertions that these companies represent an independent, emergent manufacturing Chinese capital.[21]

Japan as a Regional Power

The Pacific Rim development strategy of an open and stable trading system with more highly developed regional specialization dates back to the pre–World War II efforts by Japan to establish a Greater Co-prosperity Sphere under its control. In the postwar period the 1967 Pacific Basin Economic Council was perhaps the first formally organized effort at a different model of regional integration. It was formed by corporate executives from the United States, Japan, Australia, Canada, and New Zealand. The focus on the settler nations plus Japan continued in the Trilateral Commission's vision of a Pacific Rim strategy presented at its 1975 Kyoto meeting. Japan and the United States would supply the capital and technical leadership for the region, the managers and coordinators, and the sophisticated consumer and producer goods. A second tier, Canada, Australia, and New Zealand, would provide minerals, energy, and food stuffs. The third tier, East Asian and Latin American nations, would provide labor-intensive manufacturing and agriculture. The socialist nations of the region, the "dropouts," were a fourth tier. In fact, as things have turned out, the nonwhite Asian nations, especially those in which ethnic Chinese predominate, have been more dynamic and the East Asian Industrial Belt is led more by the Japanese and less by the Americans.

Organizations such as Japan's Choice Study Group and the Asian Forum Japan, with a membership drawn from political, academic, business leaders (typically chief executives from trading companies and major banks), foster technical assistance to Asia, promote Asian language studies, support foreign students wishing to come to Japan and Japanese interested in volunteer service in Asia. Japan's Export-Import Bank since the latter half of the 1980s worked as a foreign direct investment financing institution. Kedanren promoted a Japan International Development Organization, which was set up in 1989, to underwrite cooperation related projects. As investment in China boomed in the mid-1990s, Keidanren urged formation of the Japan-China Investment Promotion Organization. There is also the Japan–ASEAN Investment Company.

There are a number of new types of investment companies and quasi-government or mixed form go-betweens promoting Japanese interests in Asia.

Japanese foreign aid is an integral part of economic policy (just as American aid was and remains integral to its geopolitical foreign policy designed on Cold War premises). The bureaucrats who allocate aid offer administrative guidance on capital outflows so that, like foreign aid, they, too, contribute to strengthening Japan's economy and support whatever strategic designs the officials are pursuing. Japan uses its aid as seed money to attract Japanese manufacturers to particular foreign direct investments by creating a more attractive business climate for them in a particular aid-recipient nation. War reparations to Southeast Asian countries were also in the form of tied loans and export credits calculated to be of assistance to Japanese businesses in regaining their influence in these nations.[22] The loans are typically for infrastructure development to facilitate trade with Japan. These projects also create jobs for Japan's giant construction and engineering companies. The president of the regional multilateral lending facility, the Asian Development Bank, which strongly influences the pattern of such expenditures, is "by custom," as they say, always Japanese.

The government of Japan makes clear to the potential aid recipient the sorts of domestic economic policies that will bring forth generous assistance. The United States has generally used foreign aid to win friends and shore up governments that it finds attractive, yet the difference in criteria used is important. For the United States aid was traditionally a foreign policy global power struggle among superpowers and "ways of life." For the Japanese it is more narrowly a matter of business, of creating a stronger, tightly linked Japanese system on a global scale, one that is seen as good for everyone involved. Such cooperation means that billions of dollars will potentially flow in private investments from Japanese transnationals, not simply that foreign aid is granted. The bureaucrats work closely with the *keiretsu* to increase exports from particular countries of particular products to specific markets. Rather than dismantling the *keiretsu* form, as the Americans asked them to do, Japan extends its system of cooperation among the giant families that dominate the domestic economy and of state guidance to a global level.

Japanese planners envision the export of technopolises to the emerging Eastern Asia Corridor (Seoul to Hong Kong) and the Southeast Asia Corridor (Chiang Mai in Thailand to Bali in Indonesia). These would act as growth poles stimulating foreign investment and defusing technology. The Australian geographer Peter Rimmer even raises the prospect of a merging of East Asian cities into a transnational technobelt.[23] Whatever form Japanese coordination of the new international production regime takes, however, it is sure to offer a serious challenge to Western economies.

Japanese investors at the height of the bubble economy with the strong yen behind them looked toward Europe and North America. Everything, from Monets to office buildings, seemed like a bargain when calculated in yen. The European Community's plan for a true common market by 1992 provided an incentive to get in under possible "Fortress Europe" walls by establishing production facilities there. Japanese banks and insurance companies moved quickly, too (too quickly, as we saw in Chapter 8). Japan found it increasingly natural to think globally, much as the United States and Great Britain had come to do in their years of ascendancy. The absolute rate of Japanese investment was enough to sustain increased productive capacity at home and to build up a more significant presence in Asia, Europe, and the United States as well.

In absolute terms Japanese investment in new plant and equipment surpassed that of the United States in 1989 after decades of a more rapid rate of increase in capital investment per worker (a rate four times as rapid for Japan compared to the United States for the twenty-year 1964–1984 period). A significant aspect of the new globalization of Japanese industry was the shift from portfolio investment, heavily U.S. Treasury instruments, to direct control of productive assets in the United States. While the Americans have never really succeeded in gaining a serious presence in the Japanese economy, Japan was on its way to being a major player in the United States. At the same time, while manufacturing in Japan fell as a proportion of GNP by 6 percent between 1965 and 1985, this was far less than the 30 percent decline for the United States.

In early 1989 Australian Prime Minister Bob Hawke proposed the formation of "Asia-Pacific Economic Cooperation" (APEC), an intergovernmental forum limited to Western Pacific countries. Interest from the United States and Canada, which did not want to be left out, led to the formation of a twelve-nation group (the six ASEAN countries, Australia, Japan, Korea, New Zealand, Canada, and the United States). In 1991 China, Hong Kong, and Taiwan joined the annual conference forum and affiliated lower-level working groups. Its evolution has not been toward a European Community form, but rather an OECD one in which information and opinion sharing rather than supranational governance is the goal. APEC, for the United States, is part of a regionalist strategy of triadic global participation in which the United States insists on a presence in fora in all regions—Atlantic, Pacific, and Western Hemispheric. The New World Order the United States desires is one in which it is the only nation to participate in all three regional institutionalizing arrangements. America seems to see itself as the stabilizer in each region, the only player with a truly global reach.

In March 1994 two meetings took place, each historic in its own way. The juxtapositioning of the two was poignant in the conjuncture of rapid Asian growth and European stagnation. The United States was key to both. The first was the APEC forum in Honolulu that brought together finance ministers. It suggested the birth of a new alignment that would replace the Group of Seven as the world's most influential economic-political club. Reporting from the gathering Thomas Friedman wrote, "American officials do not want to say it out loud, but the conclusion is obvious: the Group of Seven increasingly seems like a relic of the cold war. The Asia Pacific group reflects the transformation of its region into the economic center of the world. It is about the future."[24] In Detroit, labor ministers from Europe, the United States, and Canada gathered at the same time to discuss what could be done to address stagnation and unacceptably high levels of unemployment in the old core of the world's economy. As one Administration official put it: "The G-7 jobs summit is about what is going wrong. APEC is about what is going right."[25] By the mid-1990s APEC emerged as an important forum for trade liberalization and open regionalism.[26]

There is a consistent difference among the three regional groupings in the way integration is taking place. In Asia, regional elites have not wanted to openly politicize a process that has included a social contract and distributional justice issues in Europe. The class dominance of capital in the Pacific allows a greater backroom regionalism. Asian nations have shown little enthusiasm for the creation of a formal regional governmental body like the European Common Market preferring informal and flexible market-driven ties. There is a Pacific Economic Cooperation Conference (PECC) based in Singapore that is a government-supported nongovernmental framework for pursuit of such discussions. As Mark Borthwick, the U.S. executive director of PECC, notes, however, "The early stage of Asian regionalism proceeded without the enthusiastic support or even the knowledge of major domestic constituencies."[27]

The United States remained a key power in this emergent East Asia Pacific Region, but America's long-term commitment and continued presence could no longer be taken for granted. The Defense Department's Office for International Security Affairs April 1990 Report to Congress[28] suggested that America's role should be that of a "regional balancer, honest broker, and ultimate security guarantor." Our role was as "an irreplaceable balance wheel" able to play "a unique and central stabilizing role." Nearly a century earlier Secretary of State John Hay had pronounced an "Open Door Policy" to prevent others from laying fixed claims to areas of the Asian Pacific. This time the United States would be guaranteeing an open region for our investors by offsetting the emergence of any regional hegemon or local wars that would undermine the economic stability and continued integration of the region.

The new strategy was a version of Secretary Hay's intention. This time around the United States would broker a Pacific regional economy that in the twenty-first century would put the United States as an integral part of the emergent Pacific Economy as we had been part of an Atlantic Economy in the nineteenth century. By maintaining a military capacity in the region the United States would support a political base capable of extracting economic advantages. The expectation of continued eruptions in regional hot spots, which could not be predicted with precision, led many Asians to welcome such an accommodation. The United States promised a security blanket under which others could continue to go about their business in exchange for only modest side payments and the limited inclusion of the Americans in regional development strategies.

The big winner in the new regional accommodations was Japan. In 1988 Japan moved ahead of the United States to become the world's largest direct foreign investor (as a later starter its absolute foreign holdings still lagged behind those of the United States and Great Britain). Japan had moved from the stage of using direct foreign investment mostly to procure raw materials through a second phase of manufacturing abroad based on local labor costs and access to local markets, to a third stage, a global strategy in which Japan becomes primarily a headquarters economy in a worldwide web of production and distribution inclusive of joint activities and sophisticated subcontracting as well as direct control of subsidiaries. Japan became more like other nations by admitting a degree of intraindustrial trade it had not known previously. As noted earlier, when the yen grew stronger such products were accepted by Japanese consumers. Matsushita produced all of its audio products, which retailed in the early 1990s for under $100 or so in Taiwan or Singapore, and as costs rose there to move whole assembly plants and other operations to even lower-cost venues. This zone continues to expand and a number of overlapping configurations are possible. One goal is a Sea of Japan Economic Development Zone with ties to the Koreas, Pacific areas of the former Soviet Union, and China. By the early 1990s some two and a half million workers were employed by 30,000 Japanese companies at plants in South East Asia at wages a tenth to a quarter of those in Japan, and far more were employed indirectly by contractors.

The yen, while it is still a minor part of official reserves held by Asian nations, represents a growing share of the total. Yen-denominated trade is expanding rapidly, and the trend extrapolated is for a de facto yen bloc in the early twenty-first century. The implications of such developments for the dollar and for the U.S. economy more broadly are significant. At present dependence on U.S. markets and fears of Japanese control make most nations of the region wary of Pan-Asian cohesion under Japanese leadership. There is a tension, however, among the region's leaders. Some, such as Malaysian Prime Minister Mahathir bin Mohamad, who proposed the formation of an East Asian Economic Group, welcomes Japanese dominance in a more tightly coordinated regional entity, but most prefer pan-Pacific forms of organization with the United States as a member and counterforce.

The consequences of such developments for America are significant. The Western Pacific (defined to include Japan, the newly industrialized economies, the ASEAN nations, China, Australia, and New Zealand) is a bigger market for foreign products than is the United States. Imports to the Western Pacific are about 20 percent greater than are those bound for the U.S. market. On recent trips to Hiroshima and Kanazawa, cities on Japan's western coast, I heard of meetings and conferences with Siberians, talk of Soviet Asia as a potential part of this Western Pacific economy. The normalization of relations with North Korea, the Japanese foreign minister's trips to China, and new attention by the prime minister with trips to the ASEAN nations, all represent a stepped-up interest and activity in a region of diminished U.S. presence.

While in their decline hegemons rely more on force and rent seeking than on their competitive prowess, a rising economic power is more willing to enter markets on a small scale wherever they are to be found and to nurture them with patience. Japan's longer time horizons proved valuable. For example, the markets in Thailand or in Malaysia in the 1970s were not worth the trouble for Americans, but the Japanese went in, cultivated local governments, and set up plants. Technology was controlled, not transferred, and a mutually advantageous dependency was established. Critical parts come from Japan, which also markets any exports. As these markets have matured Japan has reaped the benefits of its long-term thinking and patient investment strategies.

Autos are the most dramatic case, with Mitsubishi's production of the Malaysian national car, the Proton Saga (complete with that country's flag on the hood), to Korea's Hundai, with its key parts coming from Japan to be reexported to the United States and Canada. The Korean miracle more broadly depends on inputs from Japan, with whom Korea runs an enormous trade deficit, as does Taiwan and other intermediate-technology newly industrialized countries. Japan is thus able to squeeze them from the top and bottom, providing essential parts, components, and machinery while producing high value-added final goods in Japan and labor-intensive ones in the lower-wage countries of Asia. While bureaucrats in Tokyo plan out where the world's goods will be produced in coming years, U.S. firms have taken a shorter perspective on investments and sourcing. For example, car sales in Thailand were increasing by 35 percent a year in 1993 and 1994. Japanese automakers held 90 percent of that market, no small matter. Thailand was Toyota's third largest market area outside of Japan. Auto sales were projected to account for two-thirds of the growth in global demand for cars in the 1990s.

The difference between an imperial state and a developmental state can also be seen in their foreign aid policies. U.S. assistance goes primarily to client states perceived to be of geopolitical strategic importance (Israel and Egypt foremost). Japanese aid goes overwhelmingly to cultivate economic relations. China comes first (because Japan takes the long view and has a sense of economic potential and proportion), followed by resource-rich Indonesia and the Philippines, and to Thailand. All received over $1 billion in 1989, the year Japan surpassed the United States as the world's largest aid donor.[29] Within the Pacific-Asian region Japan's foreign aid was more than double that of the United States, and Japan's aid has been equal to 15–20 percent of the official government budget in virtually every Asian nation.[30]

The Japanese favor the use of economic carrots to influence the behavior of nations in which they have trade and investment interests. The United States tends to rely on the stick of negative sanctions, overt and covert destabilization, and military intervention. Some analysts see a new kind of world power in this difference.[31] Foreign aid flowed overwhelmingly to East Asia, not to Eastern Europe as the Americans had asked in the twilight of communism, because of ministerial designs to consolidate a low-cost manufacturing base there, an integral part of Japan's industrial strategy. Japan consistently used its balance of payments surpluses to increase its economic power. ("The purpose of recycling," said Stanford-educated economist and Vice Minister of Finance Tadao Chino, Japan's top policymaker in this realm, "is to stimulate and assist private capital flows."[32])

Japan and the United States

Japan has been under pressure from the United States to pull its weight internationally, which seems to mean subsidizing U.S. global priorities. Such pressures had mixed results and carry a mixed message. When Japan committed $13 billion, no small account, to the U.S. war against Iraq it received scant thanks. Rather, it was roundly criticized in the United States for not sending troops and being more actively enthusiastic about the use of military means to settle differences with Saddam Hussein. It was accused by Mr. Bush's secretary of state, James Baker, of simply practicing "checkbook diplomacy." The Japanese were stunned. They pointed that out Article 9 of their constitution, put there at General MacArthur's insistence, foreswore their use of military means to settle international disputes. They were also taken aback at the U.S. insistence when it came to deciding policy they were not to be consulted yet forced to play the role of an automatic teller machine.

The final chapter returns to this issue of Japan's global role. It can be noted here, however, that the stronger Japanese global position creates the material base for a Japan that can say *no*. In an interesting milestone, Japanese officials in the spring of 1991 reneged on promises of loans to Poland and Egypt in the wake of announcements that the United states had forgiven the debt obligations of these nations.[33] Japanese officials were furious that politics blatantly guided U.S. loan policies, putting pressure on Japan to violate standing agreements among lenders that only economics considerations should be applied. The Japanese, having made their point, then proceeded to extend billions in aid to Eastern Europe at the behest of the Americans despite no real interest in the region. A transitional readjustment between the good follower and still loyal if somewhat more assertive Number Two and a more confused and less secure USA Number One was in evidence.

By 1993, when the Clinton administration took office, key figures in the Japanese power structure spoke of Japan's emergence "as an equal partner" with the United States (the phrase was used in public pronouncements by the Foreign Ministry's chief spokesman, Masamichi Hanabusa and the director of the North American division of the Foreign Ministry, Yukio Satoh, one of the chief architects of Japanese foreign policy toward the United States). It was hoped that the Clinton administration would take Japan seriously as an ally rather than see it only as an economic threat. (It was noted that James A. Baker, 3d, as President Bush's secretary of state, had spent more time visiting Ulan Bator than Tokyo.) American foreign policy under Clinton paid more serious attention to the region. The Clinton Administration did pay Japan more attention, but its aggressive unilateralism was seen by Tokyo as whining and an effort to bully where it could not win markets any other way.

Prompted by the largest bilateral deficits to date and in accordance with its campaign rhetoric, the Clinton administration negotiated hard for numerical quotas like those which the Japanese had acquiesced under the 1986 semiconductor agreement. Asking for numerical targets for auto parts, insurance, medical equipment, and in telecommunications, the United States moved to revive Super 301 sanctions under the 1988 Trade Act which had expired in 1990. These provided for the establishment of a list of nations deemed to be erecting barriers to U.S. exports and authorized the U.S. trade representative to impose up to a hundred percent tariffs in retaliation on the exports of such countries if they did not satisfy American demands. The head of GATT, Peter Sutherland, called the move "misguided and dangerous." The Japanese who remembered how the semiconductor industry had overexpanded in the 1980s on MITI's promise of support only to have the Americans coerce the market surrendering agreement that MITI then forced them to swallow, saw no reason to accommodate the Americans, especially at a point of rising unemployment and falling profits in what was the longest Japanese postwar recession.

Clinton's hang tough negotiating stance was applauded by much of the American public and many business leaders. George Fisher, the chairman and chief executive officer of Eastman Kodak was typical. "It's time the Japanese understood that this chronic deficit is intolerable," he said.[34] Indeed, his company is a good case for why numerical targets might be necessary to crack many Japanese markets. The reason Kodak sells so little film in Japan is that it is typically sold through camera stores and small kiosks that are tightly linked to Fuji. I remember interesting discussions buying film in Japan where it was assumed of course I would want Kodak (as a presumably loyal American). Sometimes the establishment refused to carry it. Others had it, but not on display. One had to ask for Kodak by name and only then was it produced.

Not all Americans agreed with President Clinton's approach. Mainstream economists saw it as an unreasonable move away from free trade to negotiated trade. Democratic Senator Bill Bradley accused Mr. Clinton of "gratuitous brinkmanship" and "Japan bashing." He said the debate was tinged with decades of anti-Japanese sentiment and that the idea of quotas had a "historic resonance" with the early period of Japanese immigration.

In Japan, Morihiro Hosokawa entered the history books as the first Prime Minister to say no to an American president. Rather than papering over basic disagreements both Hosokawa and Clinton had accepted a breaking off of their 1994 negotiations, each gaining political points with constituents. Importantly, when the prime minister spoke of a "relationship between grown-ups," he struck a far different pose than his predecessors, who unlike Hosokawa, had come of age politically under the U.S. occupation. Hosokawa, the first post-postwar Japanese leader showed not a hint of inferiority complex in dealing with the Americans. He could afford to stand firm against them in part because the *keiretsu* had solidified so many strategic alliances with U.S.-based corporations that it was unlikely that sanctions could be devised that did not hurt American firms which were not shy about going to Congress for protection from the Clinton proposals. Moreover, since more than half Japan's exports to the U.S. were intermediate goods, higher tariffs would make a wide range of U.S. products less competitive, and raise prices for domestic consumers. Americans grew more skeptical about protecting "their" transnationals which did not seem hesitant to move jobs abroad. The interpenetrating presence of Japanese companies in America had proceeded to a point where attempting nationalist resistance had become far more complex.

Japan and America

The Japanese global corporation is not a holding company like the American giants that buy and sell divisions and contract out production on a lowest bid basis. They represent internationally the same patient capital attribute that they manifest domestically. Local suppliers are sponsored, frequently by bringing first-tier companies from Japan, who may in turn bring second-tier suppliers, who are asked to open plants. Ownership is a secondary consideration to the establishment of dependable quality input linkages. Japanese firms do not always do this well in practice, especially in East Asia, where memories of the Japanese occupations of the World War II era are strong, where styles can clash, and the kind of obedience and "voluntary" enthusiasms expected may not be forthcoming. Over time, however, they have learned to work with local suppliers and state officials. The "ugly" Japanese image is not absent, but the long-term nature of relationships forged to some extent disarm criticism.

The impact of transnational corporate behavior on their nation of origin may be another area in which the two systems differ. The top U.S. multinationals account for 85 percent of U.S. exports. Yet,

> When it comes to the yawning trade deficit, America's multinational corporations are as much a part of the problem as they are part of the solution. Sure, these multinationals are the country's biggest exporters. But they're also the nation's biggest importers, often bringing more into the U.S. than they ship out. . . . The plain truth is that U.S. multinationals have a major stake in keeping much of their production overseas. They manufacture and sell nearly three times as much abroad as they make in and export from the U.S., and by now they have set down deep roots abroad. The view that U.S. multinationals will quickly move big portions of their operations back to the U.S. because of a drop in the dollar is mistaken."[35]

In terms of the global patterns of production Kiyoshi Kojima has argued that U.S. and Japanese direct foreign investments were quite different. The United States, he asserted in the mid-1980s, as often as not went after industries that could be operated with comparative advantage at home. The American practice made it difficult for U.S. domestic advanced industries to export from the United States. U.S. direct investment in developing countries is export substituting and creates obvious problems for the U.S. trade balance. It also contributes to lost opportunities in the developing countries to pursue development based on their "real" comparative advantage. Japan, in Kojima's view, pursues the "correct" policy (from the viewpoint of global efficiency) of investing overseas in industries that have lost or are losing comparative advantage in domestic production and which should be spun off to the lesser-developed countries (those that are labor and resource intensive). Japanese investment policy is "trade oriented" in this view. It is advantageous to everyone: to Japan, which moves into more appropriate exports, and to the developing countries, which pick up production in proper product cycle fashion. The U.S. type of overseas investment "serves the interest of specific investors in maximizing their profits, [but] will only play a negative role in overall global welfare."[36]

From 1965 to 1985 the share of U.S.-based multinationals in world exports increased slightly on trend while the United States as a country experienced more than a 20 percent drop in its share of world exports. Within these multinationals the share of exports by their major owned foreign affiliates drifted upward so that by the late 1980s they accounted for over half of the firms' exports.[37] After 1985 the weak dollar helped U.S. exports. Indeed, overseas trade was responsible for 30 percent of the real growth in the economy in the second half of the decade. Our share of world trade increased from 15 percent in 1985 to 18 percent in 1991. This helped strengthen the constituency in favor of free trade and internationalization of the economy.

In the years of the overvalued dollar there has been a hollowing out of many large U.S.-based multinationals that has worried some Japanese, who fear such a development prefigures a similar trend for Japan as the yen strengthened. To date, however, their offshore relocations have been of low-technology content and unskilled tasks. Their impact has been significant for some branch plant cities and in peripheral regions, but corporate employment in the Tokyo area has continued to grow. The impact on the corporations themselves has not been to turn them into retailing outlets, firms that put their nameplates on products manufactured abroad. They do not suffer from corporate anorexia, the lack of capacity to do their own manufacturing, which characterizes many U.S. companies. Between 1979 and 1991 employment in America's Fortune 500 dropped from 16 to 12 million. This was not all the result of technological change, plant closings, and moving production abroad. More work was contracted out and many former workers became independent contract workers as the number of core employees of many large American corporations was significantly reduced. A more intense dualism characterized the American economy, bringing it closer to the Japanese pattern. The change toward the Japanese structure was generated by a very un-Japanese abandonment of employees with what was once thought to be lifetime employment.

The U.S.-Japan bilateral trade gap for the 1980s peaked at $52 billion in 1987. In the following three years American exports, aided by the strong yen, grew by over 70 percent (from $28 to $49 billion). By the start of the 1990s the United States was exporting more, but it was also running two thirds of its larger foreign deficit with Japan. The Japanese, it appeared, had adjusted to a remarkable degree to a weaker yen and had reorganized their economy in a way consistent with continued strong export performance. Masaya Miyoshi, president and director general of *Keidanren*, expressing fear that Japan's success was turning his country into a global pariah, told his compatriots, "We can't overdo it. Defeating our competitors means we'll defeat ourselves."[38]

Japan's achievement was even more impressive because it had been achieved against the severe obstacle imposed by the dramatically higher yen.

A White Paper presented to the Japanese cabinet in May 1991 summed up the situation, suggesting that despite some short-run improvements in manufacturing performance "these indicators of improvement should not lead us to be too optimistic, for a number of problems still remain, such as the economy's deep-rooted reliance on imports, the sluggish growth in R&D investments and capital stock, and the slow-down in investment for strengthening productive capacity." Japan was advised to continue to diversify away from dependence on U.S. markets[39] and especially to increase involvement in Southeast Asia. This was partly a matter of narrow economic considerations and in part a reaction to rising U.S. protectionist sentiment. The shift was fairly dramatic. In 1985, Japan had exported a third more to the United States than to Asia. By 1993 Japan exported a third more to Asia than it did to America.

In Chapter 9 the case of Toshiba and its threat to move its manufacturing activities out of the United States in protest over the tariff the United States imposed on advanced technology computer screens exported from Japan was discussed. There have been other more serious flashpoints since. A Japan that can say *no* is unlikely to take such unilateral American actions without retaliating. Further, the U.S. market, while still important, counts for much less in the total scheme of things. The Pacific Asian region especially has become a major venue for lower-cost production and a market of great significance.

Despite criticisms, Japan's import of manufactured goods in fiscal 1989 were over half the value of all Japanese imports. This led Isao Yonekura, chairman of C. Itoh, to declare, "It is possible to say that the imports and exports of manufactured goods forms the core of Japan's trade activities with various foreign countries and that Japan has now achieved the basic framework of a so-called 'Horizontal Trading Nation.'" There is good reason to doubt such a formulation. It is true that Japan's imports of manufactured goods have increased by 30 percent each year from 1985 to the end of the decade; indeed, by the early 1990s the average Japanese consumer bought twice as much in U.S. products as did the average European Community buyer. While it still ran a huge trade surplus with the United States, Japan was also *indirectly* penetrating the U.S. market through other Asian nations.

The raw trade figures do not tell us all that much about what was going on when, for example, half the value added from Korean car exports consists of components imported from Japan and the explosion of electronics goods entering the United States from Thailand is from Japanese factories, as are most of the imports to Japan itself. In the discussion of these patterns earlier it is clear that the much-vaunted figure that exports of manufactured goods from Asian neighbors doubled in the three years to the beginning of the 1990s fails to give weight to the fact that this was almost entirely from Japanese overseas plants.[40] Japan's direct foreign investment totaled $50 billion in 1990, up from $20 billion in 1987. Export growth from Japan has slowed because Japan produces most of what it sells in foreign markets outside of Japan, increasingly in the nations in which it sells. Thus, Japanese strength abroad increases, but is not reflected in its visible trade balance. Current account surplus and long-term capital outflow may in fact fall. Government officials feeling foreign pressure have offered administrative guidance that has been integral to bringing about these results.

Japanese Investment in the United States

I have stressed Japanese investments in Asia, and the emergence of an increasingly integrated and powerful Asian Pacific economy because its long-term consequences for the world are enormous. Americans, however, were more concerned that Japanese investors were buying up high-profile assets in the United States, such as Rockefeller Center and Columbia Pictures. By the early 1990s, however, Japanese companies partially or completely owned 600-odd factories in a variety of American industries. Many were ones the local owners had given up on either because of a "troublesome" labor force, outmoded technologies, aged plants, or all three. Japanese management saved American plants such as the former GE special alloy plant in Michigan, which had been declared a failure before two years' work by new owner Hitachi Metals (with the same unionized work force and plant manager) made it a success, and Sanyo's bringing color TV production back to the United States is another celebrated instance. Japanese plants continue to challenge the conventional management wisdom in America.

In 1981 the investment by Japanese companies in the United States became larger for the first time than that of U.S. companies in Japan. Through the 1980s that gap continued to widen. In 1991 the report of the U.S.-Japan Structural Initiative talks argued the need to raise the level of U.S. corporate investment in the Japanese economy as a way to facilitate a more balanced mutual interdependence. While there is a tendency to view such pious sentiment on the Japanese side as so much window dressing, a subterfuge for their continued effort to dominate America, such thinking represents an important tendency in Japanese policy circles that suggests that Japan would be more secure if the United States was doing better. In this view, it would be to the long-term advantage of Japan if interdependence was perceived in the United States more as a two-way street. Japan would be more secure and more prosperous as well. For true internationalists the prospects are breathtaking. Fusion offers the ultimate advantages of comparative advantage in total market freedom.

Many Americans did not view matters this way. It was not that Japanese direct investment in the United States was very great. Its book value—$83 billion in 1990—was only 21 percent of total foreign direct investment in the United States. Even in manufacturing it was only $15 billion, compared with $53 billion for the United Kingdom[41] The Japanese capacity to dominate markets upset Americans; and perhaps, it was feared, the domestic U.S. economy as well. It was this threat, not the actual numbers, that exercised many Americans. Japan bashing was a comfortable escape valve for pent-up economic fears for which no other logical explanation could be found. From my own perspective, increased Japanese ownership, while growing, is hardly the problem.

Half of the American-based companies involved in consumer electronics are foreign owned, overwhelmingly by Japanese. The Mitsubishi television bought in America is likely to have rolled off the assembly line in Santa Ana, California. In 1990 more than one quarter of American exports carried the label of a foreign-owned company, 10 percent were Japanese. The fears of foreign takeover lagged the reality of a no-longer-national American economy. It was the globalization of production that pulled American workers and those in other nations increasingly into competition with each other, and it was the growing political power of internationally mobile capital to limit efforts of locally rooted workers movements seeking to protect and improve their wages and the social wage through collective activity that was key. The workers of the world had not learned to unite; globalized capital had. The desire to level living standards upward through public governance was not yet on the agenda. Nationalist politics, protecting "our" jobs, led to a narrow and self-defeating focus.

While questions raised by increasing interdependence and interpenetrating ownership would continue to be important, the deflating of the Japanese financial bubble gave the world some breathing space. While Japanese direct investment in U.S. manufacturing increased six fold between 1985 and 1990, the upward trend broke in 1987 when Japanese long term foreign investment peaked at $136 billion. The figure was only $28 billion in 1992.[42] I think the objective financial conditions were determining but Japan's enthusiasm was no doubt also slowed down by American opposition to Japanese ownership.

There were numerous instances of xenophobic reaction to the Japanese presence. Sports fans will recall the reaction to Nintendo America offering (along with other Seattle area businesses) to buy the Mariners, the local major league baseball team threatened with removal to Tampa, Florida. Nintendo employed 140,000-plus Americans. Its management, far from trying to take over America's pastime, was being a good local citizen, which is how most people in Seattle saw it. Anti-Japanese fever elsewhere rose a notch or two at this new provocation. Zero sum nationalism is unproductive. The question was how long would it take American workers, and indeed those in Japan and elsewhere, to develop a consciousness of common interest that would support international regulation that made country of origin secondary to socially responsible behavior.

Rather, it is the closed nature of decision making that should command popular concern. For example, in 1990, as Mitsubishi and Chrysler were producing automobiles together at Diamond-Star Motors Corporation in Illinois, their plant was being supplied by such firms as Mitsubishi Electric in Ohio and Mitsubishi Heavy Industries in California. Five Mitsubishi companies teamed up to buy a cement factory in California helped out by Mitsubishi Bank, Mitsubishi Trust, and the Mitsubishi Corporation in putting together the deal, suggesting a local recreation of the keiretsu-style linkages. One year later Chrysler, hard pressed for cash, sold its share of Diamond Motors to Mitsubishi. The

Mitsubishification of the world moved on. Many of these U.S. subsidiaries tend to have their offices in or near Rockefeller Center, recently purchased by a Mitsubishi division. They get together in restaurants affiliated with Mitsubishi. Mitsubishi-America company presidents golf together at the Japanese-owned Canyon Club north of the city. The trust relation and linkages between these legally independent companies gives them a business edge. By dominating a commodity chain, and with privileged access to linked inputs, Mitsubishi competes in a different manner. Because Mitsubishi is a leading presence in major industries from coal mining to chemicals and functions around the globe, each member firm can draw on the basis of secure knowledge in the competence and trustability of the firms it needs to deal with over a range of connections. It has potential suppliers who are high quality and dependable for nearly anything it may need.[43] Such corporate governance mechanisms have certain advantages over arm's-length market exchange, which has contributed to *keiretsu* success. At the same time such a concentration of market and political power has had serious redistributional consequences, as we have seen.

Does the *keiretsu* form of organization violate U.S. antitrust laws? In general, these firms compete in different markets. Their goal is not to gain market dominance in one industrial classification (through merger or setting up a number of firms in that one industry); rather, it is to grow successfully and win in competition through internal improvements in performance, which is to some degree based on access to other firms on a favorable basis. Market power comes from informal linkages that do not violate U.S. laws. Little, if any, evidence is likely to be uncovered that they conspire to limit competition in the manner of, say, U.S. Steel or Standard Oil in their heyday. Yet, together their structure is a formidable competitive weapon that gives them a decisive advantage, not one contemplated by those who designed U.S. antitrust laws. Perhaps something of the global oligopolized future can be gleaned from the way Sony's Columbia Pictures, CBS records, and its video games and Mini-Discs units collaborated in cross-marketing products around the Arnold Schwarzenegger movie, *Last Action Hero*, which showed its star making calls on a Sony cellular phone, listening to Sony artists' music on a Sony MiniDisc player, and encouraging viewers to do the same, suggesting the world's first $60 million commercial.[44] An interactive videogame using some of the film's footage could be played at home. Competitor Matsushita over at MCA was creating similar synergies.

The social regulation of capital will eventually have to be put on the agenda at the international level. This is some way off because democratically responsive globally encompassing governance institutions seem at this point too far a stretch even conceptually for most of those who discuss these matters.

There are two distinct if interrelated issues here best discussed together. The first is that the individualistic U.S. competitive model in the postwar period has simply been a less-competitive system of capitalism, using competitive in the sense of what it takes to win. A society, of course, has the right to say that certain patterns of corporate ownership and organization will not be permitted in the interest of some greater good. The American antitrust tradition has favored, in theory surely if not always in practice, a definition of competition that stresses ease of entry and exit and the preservation of a sufficiently large number of firms so as to avoid the collusion possible when only a small number dominate a field. We have not yet had the kind of careful study of the sources of *keiretsu* advantage to say with any assurance how much of their success is based on market power and cross-subsidization, which is inefficient in neoclassical terms for the system as a whole, and the extent to which synergistic reduction of transaction costs, the savings from freer internal information flows and greater trust, bring economies that raise dynamic efficiency for the system. Most important, the *keiretsu* structure has functioned in the context of keen inter*keiretsu* competition and the presence of important free-standing and highly dynamic competitors.

The second issue has to do with the potential for abuse of power. The *Mitsubishification* of the world brings with it an awesome concentration of power. If the world economy of the 1990s approximates in some general sense where the United States economy was a century earlier, and I would argue that it increasingly does, then the intense competition among large transnationals may give way to an oligopolistic interdependence. Global overcapacity today approximates the conditions that led to the first Great Depression of the last quarter of the ninteenth century during which strategic alliances were developed, mergers consummated, trusts divided markets, and other accommodations to restrict ruinous competition were reached by companies that had much to lose from head-to-head competition. At the national level a century ago such developments led to a public outcry and to antitrust regulation to promote competition. On a global scale developments should take us in this direction, but accommodation among politically independent states will be more difficult to reach. That in the relatively early stages, more intense competition, rather than *Mitsubishification*, seems the dominant moment should not lull such concerns.

International coordination of policies toward transnationals is difficult. Even in our own country there is interstate competition in offering subsidies to attract investment that reduces taxes and social expenditures. Japanese corporations today are being assisted in building a parallel economy in the United States by generous subsidies from subnational governmental units, assistance offered to lure them to one state over another. Cash handouts by the fifty states to profit-making corporations, according to the National Association of State Development Agencies, exceeded $16 billion in 1991. The country as a whole loses out. The assistance sometimes proves cost ineffective even to the jurisdiction involved, occurring because the company is in the stronger bargaining position and the country's locational incentive programs are not harmonized at the national level. These are also benefits existing firms, often burdened with an older, perhaps higher cost labor force with long-standing work rules and customs do not receive. The Japanese plant, often shipped from Japan and modeled on one successfully operating there (thanks to the stronger yen and historically lower capital costs), often starts life with significant advantages in its new site. Included among these is the employer's ability to pick and choose in assembling a work force with the skills, aptitudes, and attitudes it finds congenial. It is difficult for older firms that have become encrusted in a set of tax, wage, and benefit accommodations to compete with newcomers. This is true whether the companies involved are foreign owned or domestic, or are accorded more generous terms. Attracting new investment leads more generally to a lower corporate contribution.

There are differences, however. These involve a strategic orientation in which the long-term developmentalist proclivities of Japanese capitalism clearly emerge. Although Japan is buying more from America, purchases are carefully selected for maximum strategic benefit. Assets are still often sold in the form of technology sharing. When goods are shipped from the United States to be sold in Japan, it is typically through a Japanese partner who controls distribution. Things are not evening out. America's Japan problem is likely to remain. As the Japanese overseas economy grows stronger it is also likely to build support in the communities in which it operates. Americans who already work for the Japanese form a local support network for equal treatment for foreign-owned companies. If the Japanese economic system continues to grow faster than our own the real fear may not long be of Japanese investment; rather, it will be that the Japanese will not invest or invest as much as we would like to ensure jobs and dynamic growth. The discussion here is in terms of the advantages the Japanese business groups may enjoy. In slow growth they may appropriate gains from monopoly power, but they also carry weight of less-competitive divisions of the larger group.

It is necessary to reiterate three dimensions of this political discussion. One concerns Japanese versus American ownership and the costs and benefits to Americans and others of different ownership patterns. The second surfaces in a period of slow growth. It is the freedom of owners, American or others, to move capital, create and destroy jobs, and impact on the tax base of jurisdictions to an extent that undermines their ability to meet the basic needs of their citizens. The exertion of bargaining power by the transnationals in these respects must be constrained if government is to be able to play an effective role in rebuilding local, regional, and national economic coherence. Whether the U.S. economy will incorporate the millions of unemployed and underemployed, the labor force dropouts and all the other potential workers who are not in a healthy relation to what is hardly an economy ready to incorporate them, depends on political constraints, not on juridical ownership. Just as U.S. companies' short-term orientation may lead them to lose out to the Japanese the United States as a society may lose out because of individualistic notions of society that allow blaming the victims of larger economic restructuring and abandoning them to their fate. A larger number of Americans have fallen into a none-too-productive relation to the economy. This imposes suffering on them and significant social costs on the society. The real problem is the U.S. cultural economy and a politics of individualism and division. The neoclassical view of how competition should work to maximize profit comes to be understood as part of the problem when the economy does not provide expanding opportunity. The third dimension of the problem is the international regime itself. Can a new system of rules be designed internationally to help all countries and groups participate, to share in and cooperate in the building of a set of social relations that is designed to level up and not down? At the national level the welfare state and Keynesian fiscal policies attempted such a trajectory. Intensified internationalized competition has undermined the security and seeming influence on growth rates to which this model aspired. Can a new international regime be designed to achieve these goals on a global scale?

The Japanese political economy will play a more important role in the discourse of each of these dimensions. Japanese neocapitalist groupness offers their companies a different understanding of how best to compete. The social cohesion the society demonstrates remains an important source of economic success although given global instability it is necessary to offer a constant warning. The Japanese, of course, must function within the context of the larger global political economy. At the end of the postwar era they, too, were faced with overcapacity, stagnant markets, rising debt, and other economic ills. Unable to maintain their highly leveraged asset structures they were forced to pull back from many anticipated investments at home and abroad. With global stagnation, the hard-driving Japanese became something of an international pariah, and frightened Japanese leaders looked for ways to accommodate their system to international norms. The advantage of the *keiretsu* form may prove insufficient when the strong *keiretsu* members have to assume too heavy a burden of holding up sinking affiliates. Under such conditions the temptation to jump ship and the advantages of smaller, more flexible stand-alone innovative competitors changes the structural advantage picture dramatically.

Becoming More Like Everyone Else?

As the world was striving to copy Japanese practices thought to induce economic growth, important voices in Japan were engaged in a new debate. The debate began in earnest in the early 1990s over creating a national lifestyle standard appropriate to the world's second-largest economic power. In an influential February 1992 article in the popular magazine of opinion and commentary, *Bungei Shunju*, Akio Morita argued that Japan must become more like other countries and play by similar rules.[45] He also said Japanese workers should be paid more. He was quickly answered by Takeshi Nagano, president of *Nikkeiren* (the Japan Federation of Employers' Organizations), who publicly wondered whether Sony workers were not paid enough. Nagano said Japanese companies needed the surplus for investment to increase productivity and maintain competitiveness. *His* critics, in turn, said it might be a good idea to actually invest less given the context of international climate that prevailed. Sadahiko Inoue, a researcher for *Rengo*, expressed organized labor's view in saying that "the Japanese have forgotten the purpose of economic advancement as they went along."[46]

Morita proposed, before the Trilateral Commission meeting in Lisbon, that

Japanese, Europeans, and North American producers set up mutually acceptable parameters to guide corporate decision makers so that dividend ratios,
working hours, pay scales, and so on could be harmonized within an acceptable range. By subscribing to such norms, Japan could take some of the heat
off itself by working fewer hours, paying out higher dividends, raising profit
margins, reinvesting less, and not going after unlimited market shares. This
new togetherness or *kyosei* (living together, symbiosis) among global capitalists would both present a united front and reduce, it was hoped, hostility
toward Japanese capital.

A few weeks before Morita's article appeared, Prime Minister Kiichi Miyazawa, in his keynote speech opening the new year's session of the Diet, declared that Japan must shift from a producer-oriented society to one in which
the priority was given to consumers and ordinary citizens. Japan, he told the
parliament, must change from "an emphasis on efficiency to fuller consideration of fairness." He advocated a priority to better housing, less time commuting and on the job, and more balanced regional growth. While none of this
was new, politicians with elections coming up find such themes good ones to
raise. At the same time a series of important documents had also been coming
from the permanent government stressing these themes in ways that suggested a seriousness of intent.

MITI's *Industrial Structure in the Year 2000: The Perspective of Industrial Policy
Beyond the Economic Efficiency-Oriented Policies*, had asserted in 1990, "It is very
difficult to say that the profits of economic growth are returned enough to
improve the standard of living of the Japanese nation."[47] In MITI's vision
document, *Vision of International Trade and Industrial Policy for the 1990s: Creating
Humanitarian Value from a Global Point of View*, similar sentiments were offered
concerning the need to offer "self-criticism of the so-called companyism society." Such documents stress the social cost of the Japanese developmental
model's privileging of growth so far above quality of life as to deny the benefits
of Japan's achievements to its citizens. It is left to the final chapter to discuss
how likely it is that such goals will be achieved.

MITI historically has a good record of accurately calling the turns of Japanese economic developments over which it has had so much influence. It has
provided new visions for each decade. Their purpose is to keynote the new
period, demarcate the emphasis of growth, and outline the direction the economy and society are to take. In the 1960s the vision statement was, "Promotion
of Heavy and Chemical Industries." In the 1970s it was, "Seeking a More
Knowledge-Intensive Industrial Structure." In the 1980s the vision statement
was titled, "Fostering More Creative Knowledge-Intensive Industries." The
1990s theme, "Toward Creating Human Values in the Global Age," seems
fitting. The 1990s vision statement, prepared as in the case of previous ones,
by a ministry council whose members represent industry, government, and
the academy has contributed to building a national consensus around concrete
goals, but unlike past statements the one for the 1990s calls on companies
to more profoundly change their internal philosophy, by moving away from
companyism, the total concentration demanded by companies on their work-

ers' time and energies and the promotion of shorter working hours and a consumer society. This was quite a challenge to Japan in a period of intensifying international competition and slow growth. Whether a domestic Keynesianism would work remains to be seen. If it does, and especially if Japan moves from its role as the international rate buster, it will provide breathing room for everyone else. Whether the new emphasis will be attractive as companies face declining profits, however, is another matter.

11

Japan and the New Competition

"The difficulty with the Meiji Westernizers, was copying everything they knew of the West. Instead, they should increase their knowledge of the West tenfold, and then select only those things which are suitable for Japan. To do this selection and adaptation, however, they must also know Japan, but such people did not know their own country either."

SHIGEKI NISHIMURA, nineteenth-century scholar[1]

"Theory building" carries with it an imagery of the careful construction of layers of generalization, firmly cemented together by accumulated empirical observations. How far such a view is appropriate even in the natural sciences might justifiably be doubted. It is naive to suppose that it has much relevance to social science."

ANTHONY GIDDENS, twentieth century scholar[2]

In looking at Japan we have considered social facts as they exist in a matrix of pervasive attitudes, belief structures, loyalties, acceptance of authority, and hierarchy. Japanese definition of property rights and forms of collective discipline have been examined. These attitudes and norms are embodied in the rules and procedures of governance mechanisms and institutions were also examined in some historical detail. At the start of the book it was suggested that culture is created through human response to situations and structure perceptions of the world around us. Elements of the cultural economy can be signaling instrumentalities and communicate attitudes reflective of, and intertwined with, institutional behaviors economists and other social scientists seek to understand. If bringing culture into any study of economic development has been emphasized, so, too, the ways we have to look carefully at the economic theory that we apply to our specific problematic have also taken a great deal of our attention. To look at the political economy of Japan it has been necessary to mold appropriate tools of economic analysis.

This penultimate chapter will examine why this is so by once again considering the corporate form in the Japanese context. As I have done in earlier chapters, I will draw on some of the literature of organizational economics in an effort to sum up a relevant microeconomics connected conceptually to institutional embeddedness. The second part of the chapter will initiate a discussion that will be continued in the next of the forces that threaten to undermine the accommodations of the Japanese system. Such factors include the growing labor shortage Japan was experiencing, its impact in changing capital–labor relations and on the intense loyalties and driven involvement of Japanese workers in their companies. The labor shortage also brought about an influx of foreign workers (mostly illegal), and the higher cost of Japanese labor and the ongoing trade surpluses have led to a redeployment of Japanese productive capacities. These trends are likely to continue forcing the Japanese to come to grips with their relative ethnic exclusiveness by forces of globalization.[3] Other issues that will be of importance to Japan's future involve the breakdown of the 1955 System, the political accommodation that governed Japan for most of the period since the end of World War II, and the revision of Japanese thinking about its role in global politics, including a military presence, will be discussed in the next chapter in the context of macroeconomic restructuring questions.

Japanese groupism is hardly an ideal system. It is a possible starting point, however, for exploration of how more people- and nature-friendly forms of collective orientation could foster more equitable social efficiency than either the Japanese or the American systems as presently constituted have done. The normative issues of what sort of societal arrangements are desirable need to be separated from the analytical descriptive moment, but never far removed; otherwise, value judgments built in to existing arrangements implicitly claim a legitimacy to which they may well not be entitled. It is important both to learn what works in other contexts as well as to interrogate that working so as to consider its flaws in its own context and how the best aspects of foreign practices can be enculturated given our own values. Unnuanced celebration of the other is no more a healthy response than is fear and hatred of their economic culture and practice.

Specifying Historical Context

The economics and management literature that stresses the commodity *information* places its emphasis differently than do those who foreground social practices as involving interaction and persistent reexamination of ongoing processes that admit conflict and power relations into the analysis. To reduce learning, a socially complex problem involving the organization of human agents, to accumulating and spending the commodity information misses the substance of what is going on over time in terms of social relations and in relation to spatial patterning. Competitive success is about learning capacity located in concrete agents and communities of work relations, and not simply about "information."

In Japan, the *keiretsu* rely on the larger national cultural economy to foster group loyalty, teach, and reinforce corporate discipline. The Italian industrial districts, with their small interdependent firms that contribute so much to the nation's development as to be designated as the Third Italy, to take a compatible non-Japanese example as a comparison, rely on the rootedness in their local communities of workers and managers, who have known each other over long periods and share a common culture, knowledge of each other's character and trust level that allow them to build complementary relations in a localized commodity chain or in subcontracting finished pieces when orders exceed one firm's capacity. These have to do with local realities including class configuration and cultural economies. In the Third Italy model, dynamism comes from decentralized and autonomous design capacities. In industrial districts economies of scale in information generation (concerning available technologies and markets) are provided by local governments.

In Japan, hierarchy and centralized coordination play a large role in molding consensus, which then permits flexibility and encourages institutional entrepreneurship and structures innovation projects. In the Third Italy case and in similar localist models skilled artisans and craftworkers have the option of starting their own enterprises, and employers are under pressure to reward such people sufficiently to prevent them from leaving and becoming rivals. In corporate Japan quitting jobs in dominant firms is rare and any spin-off is generated by the company, not the employee. Teamwork is central to both models, but a different culture and institutional framework prevails in each. It is simplistic to lump the two into one category, "flexible production," even if both are instances of a wider phenomenon. In most considerations of the American case there is a less-nuanced discussion or consideration to even recognizing what is unique, for better or worse, about our own historical specificity. Rather, there is a faith that whatever exists is a product of market forces and hence essentially a beneficial arrangement.

The outstanding success of the Japanese system by the 1970s created questions concerning cherished Western assumptions about markets and the most efficient means of organizing production. The developmentalist state generated uncertainty about the best role of government in the capitalist economy, making obsolete much of the conventional wisdom in defining the regulatory role of the state. This debate had been heating up for decades. It is interesting that both Schumpeter and Deming, decades before the approach became popular, argued that breakthrough innovations come from large monopolistic firms, not from small competitive ones. Their view remains less popular in the United States, but is the conventional wisdom in Japan. Innovation by firms rely on appropriate corporate cultures. Economists, whether neoclassical mainstreamers or orthodox Marxists, have been suspicious of culture as a category either to understand the nature of the firm or the larger political economy. To understand the multiple identities of Americans and Japanese in gender and in work roles, as members of communities of self-identity and geographical proximity is not, however, irrelevant to comprehending economic relations. We can speak of building a new macroeconomic awareness on microfoundations, then, in a mode quite different from that of neoclassical theorizations.

Individuals experience multiple realities and, while economics exerts a standardizing pressure, its force comes up upon cultural differences that are the result of both national histories and of group identities. William Lazonick is right when he suggests that "the advantage of Japanese organization over American organization is not that it is fundamentally different in its conception of planned coordination but that it is able to put conception into operation subject to much less individualistic political and cultural constraints."[4] The advantage had proven formidable.

Researchers have been able to find instances of failure by the Japanese state, interventions in which the market has triumphed in spite of bureaucratic hubris and error. Others have chronicled the wise vision and multifaceted, often subtle, often bold, remarkable and flexible mix of incentives and restrictions employed by government officials to spur economic growth. It is as if one can choose one's window and look at the Japan of one's choice. Economists who choose the former are almost always those who lean toward the laissez-faire ideal. The latter researchers, in general, favor industrial policy or other forms of corporatist coordination to address shortcomings in the market. Our seeings through the Rashomon mirror have to some extent supported aspects of contending viewpoints. It is time to put the pieces together.

Japan's Economic System is Different

In the early phase of developmentalist-state entry into an industry, resources are thrown at problems and regimentation of labor can lack the finesse evident at a later stage. Over time, depending on the sector, the Japanese system's human relations approach changes as more sophisticated responses need to be elicited. This does *not* necessarily mean a growth of employment in the core sector. Technical sophistication is nowhere coterminous with the creation of good jobs. With the growth in demand for software there may be an upgrading of programmer conditions within primary sector firms, but there may also be subcontracting to small sweatshops for standardized production. In many parts of the Japanese production system Taylorist methods prevail for the army of secondary workers and Theory Z[5] at the top.

The move from Fordist to post-Fordist production regimes has a lot to do with the way labor is employed in the two systems. When Henry Ford introduced the assembly line, he reduced labor time per car in production by 80 percent in two to three years at a time when manufacturing was a very labor-intensive procedure compared with the present period, in which direct labor is less than 15 percent of total labor cost in manufacturing. The place many companies today continue to look to cut cost—production worker wages—is often the wrong place to find large savings. Indeed, in such high-tech sectors as manufacturing semiconductor memory chips, 70 percent of the cost is in research, development, and testing. No more than 12 percent is in direct labor. As social knowledge becomes more dominant and the 2.5 sector grows—manufacturing with lots of service component built into the production, and ongoing servicing, the incorporation of microelectronics into product servomechanisms, and so forth—social knowledge comes to dominate the cutting edge of development.

The Japanese system obtained the benefits of the British and American models while avoiding many of their shortcomings. Japanese worker skills are tapped and their creative energies made use of without ceding to the workers any real power to pursue actions counter to corporate interests. Similarly, by reducing the communicative distance between levels and using team approaches, the rigidities of U.S. corporate hierarchy was avoided while large-scale organization was strengthened. If these essentials of Japan's development teach us anything it is that more than one version of a market-driven economy is possible. Such an awareness helps economic theorists recognize that institutions are an important variable, that they are created by human agency rather than by divinely given markets. Indeed, markets have histories that are embedded in cultural understandings and are shaped by political interests. Their workings change over time with developments in technology and consciousness.

A Newer Institutional Microeconomics

The problem is not with "theory," but rather with the need to integrate theory and history.[6] It is the excessive abstraction that needs to be continually criticized. "The problem of theorizing," as Stephen Marglin says, "is to trade off the potential generality of the theory, which leads one to institutional spareness, against the need to say something specific about specific problems in specific historical circumstances."[7] My task here is not the reconstruction of economic theory, but through looking at Japanese development to raise questions and to suggest points that need to be internal to any political economy worthy of its founding traditions. In my own reflections on Japan I have tried to study the historical evolution and transformation of what I have called the "postwar Japanese system," a social structure of accumulation, a mode of regulation within a larger analysis of how that nation-state fits into the larger global political economy. It included a strong mix of industrial policies implemented under the leadership of the powerful bureaucrats of the Japanese developmentalist state. Mainstream economists continue to give primacy to the individual actor—the chooser, not the institutional and cultural setting in which choice takes place.[8]

Because our norms of efficient competitive behavior are so different I am concerned that when the United States comes with much kicking and screaming to some sort of agreement that an industrial policy is needed for this nation, the resistance from free-market-oriented thinkers and interest groups will be so strong that the sort of industrial policy we get may be like the kind of national health care system America initially adopts. Both will be so compromised by the demands of powerful producer groups that they will be far from optimal from a societal point of view. The inefficiencies of each will be made evident in a comparative analysis to more effective systems elsewhere.

The grounds for agreement that we must "do something" in these areas is overwhelming. As William Spencer, president of Sematech, the government-backed alliance of companies in the semiconductor industry, discussed earlier, has stated:

> We're faced with a situation now where the rest of the world takes it as a standard method of operating for industry and government to cooperate on what they consider to be critical industries and technologies for their country. That's happened in the Pacific Rim countries since World War II, and that's happening in Europe. The U.S. will be at a disadvantage in world competition if we don't find an American way of working together.[9]

While the debate was whether we should have an industrial policy the important issue was the changes necessary in our economic and social institutions into which a successful set of policies could be fit. The narrow, shortsighted, and deceptively pragmatic stance of American experts and decision makers has insured only the most limited discussion and the narrowest framing of the issues down to the Clinton administration. I will say more in the next chapter about the macroeconomics of globalization trends in the world political economy that make the nationalistic industrial policies of earlier decades, if not completely irrelevant, then in basic ways inadequate, and in some regards counterproductive to the interests of most citizens.

Agreeing that the United States needs an industrial policy is not the same as devising a set of instrumentalities and institutional processes, setting in place technical competencies and democratic accountability that are able to grasp the nature of the global economy, knowing when and in which ways to accommodate to competitive pressures, and when and in what ways to modify the global rules of the game in pursuit of the best interests of America's people. A positive sum game that does not attempt to beggar one's neighbor, and does not force adjustment costs on to the weak at home or abroad, is part of a very different utility function than the one trade negotiators now maximize.

Central among the features that need reexamination is first, an awareness that governments can function as economic agents seeking to promote prosperity and capable, though not preordained, to succeed in this endeavor. Second, I am concerned with the meaning of community, institutions, and the wider culture. The methodological individualism of the economist's approach alerts them to the powerful interest individuals acting alone and in coalition have in subverting the impulse toward the public good. Government can misallocate resources generating private benefit under the mantle of state regulation undertaken in the general interest. This does not mean that we should conclude that the most benefit to the largest number comes from reliance solely on the market.

The Japanese case strongly calls our attention to the extent to which state power is capable of constraining individual choice, of shifting the incentives to provide a different calculus to the actors that maximize economic growth and societal integration as compared with a different set of constraints that favor short-run profit-maximizing behavior and atomistic uncontrolled forms of competition. In counterpoint to the individualistic assumption that presumes atomistic construction of society I have stressed the centrality of informal and formal rules, laws, and defined property rights that make up an important part of the sum of constraints that shape choices. The pervasiveness of informal constraints, their social transmission, and the institutional structures designed to reinforce attitudes and coerce certain responses that characterize the Japanese social formation are important determinants of its economic performance. Individuals in a specific culture are cued to acceptable behavior and rewarded for choosing appropriately. The legitimated standards are internally enforced and appear to be freely chosen. Self-interest is constrained and shaped. Such conditioning informs market participation in any society we study, surely in Japan and the United States.

Whether we call it relating, transacting, or social interaction, the rules we follow in life hardly exist in some finished form. When people trade or cooperate they do so within a web of precedents and understandings. Arm's-length market exchange between atomistic individuals is involved to a much lesser extent than economists tend to think. This is true even in presumed market exchange itself. Because of the unknowability of many specifics, contracts covering all contingencies are not easily written, indeed even in America's legalistic and litigious economic culture, efforts to draw up iron-clad agreements often flounder. Constant contract revisions can turn out to be expensive. Costs arise in measuring the acceptability of performance, the honesty of new changes, penalties for lateness or lack of performance agreed to, and in how to divide responsibility for agreed upon failure. These features make lawyers in the United States rich and account for the increase of their tribe fatted on transaction costs. The Japanese system, which relies on maintaining good relationships over time in which reputation and shared standards play so large a part, seems closed to outsiders. This leads the Americans to sue. The Japanese system presumes that good relations emerge from repetitive interactions over a lengthy time horizon. There is little reason for Japanese to expect that the Americans are interested in establishing long-term relations of trust since our historic "let the buyer beware, play it close to the chest, and make the best effort to screw the other guy" mentality. A reputable Japanese businessperson will not throw over established relationships to save a nickel a unit on a new order and is unlikely to stiff a business associate for a one-time windfall gain. (This does not mean that outsiders with whom there are no existing patterned relations of reciprocity will be accorded fair treatment or even that individual Japanese outside of their constraining home environment will act in responsible fashion.)

Such a stark contrast is admittedly overdrawn. American firms have not all embraced such attitudes and practices, and many do accept standard operating procedures close to the Japanese way of relational transacting as noted in the introductory chapter to this book. The Japanese system also involves significant elements of coerced relations based on unequal power, which can be used to squeeze subordinates; one simplifies to generalize at some peril. Still, generally speaking, within the Japanese system the risk-discounted return to opportunism, shirking, and cheating can rise in complex organizations and social formations when informal constraints against such behavior are not strong. As two corporate entities in different types of social formations come to interact accommodations are worked out through praxis. It may even be that over time cooperation wins in the market test over naked greed. Economists are increasingly figuring their payoff matrices to show that the optimal strategy is in fact to cooperate. Some pure theoretical models (non-economists may wish to imagine these as sort of Pac Man game-controlled environments) show how a colony of cooperators, if sufficiently large, can invade a world of mean-strategy opponents and drive them into submission. [10]

As Robert Alan Friedman, a vice president at Salomon Brothers concludes about *keiretsu*, "Even though members of a cooperating group tend to have lower average scores than some clever but mean opponents, they still thrive in the long run." [11] I would add three points, however, to such an observation of real-world practices. First, as growth slows and a competitive framework that levels earlier Japanese advantages erodes, the Japanese cooperators come under greater pressure. The cost of holding up less-productive group members increases and conventional profit squeeze changes the environment in which these firms operate, and so their behavior. Second, the *keiretsu* players can combine cooperation with hardball play in creative ways that allow them advantages from both sides. Third, as a globalized economy comes into being there is no reason that cross-national strategic alliances and then outright mergers will not erode the strictly national character of so-called transnational corporations, creating a merged international corporate culture alongside— partly in competition with, partly accommodating to—distinct national cultural economies and subcultures. The *tao* of competition is not a simple either/or of mean and lean competition or long-term cooperation.

The focus on individualism also influences the attitude of Americans as social and economic agents. Indeed, we have the expression, *Attitude*, as in "attitude problem," to an extent summed up on a T-shirt motto, "I love (as in a heart ideogram) my attitude problem." The issue is a complex one involving working-class rebellion and youth culture. At another level, however, Merry White is surely correct that Americans "confuse self-expression with creativity, placing the greatest value on spontaneity rather than on taking pains." [12] Everyone wants to be a star rather than appreciating the extent to which they must be competent first or the benefits of working cooperatively to meet common goals over extended horizons on the basis of mutualism. By privileging individual achievement team players are devalued on the one hand, and the amount of work and training it takes to be good is not widely appreciated by those who are taught to want the moon, but do not receive the skills needed for stable employment and the collective nature of complex tasks.

Some Americans have looked down on the rigidities of the Japanese way, the precise imitation of the master as a mode of learning the possibilities and limits of one's metier. As a norm for the Japanese, concentration on a task is valued; in America it is boring. Such cultural differences are embodied in conventions, expectations, and institutions. American society too often does not value disciplined training. There is less appreciation that our future as a society depends on the depth and breadth of collective effort. The bottom line, however, remains that as individuals we react to incentives. Many, perhaps most, Americans face hostile authority on the job and more generally that, rather than offering assistance to "be all you can be" (indeed, this is only promised to those for whom enlisting in the army is their best opportunity to learn marketable skills), creates a sink or swim environment that is not supportive. Some people do thrive in a rat-race environment, but the society as a whole is divided and at war with its own best instincts and the winners too often seem to be the biggest rats. For all the talk of new work relations and attitudes on the part of corporate leaders in the United States, the Commission on the Skills of the American Workforce reports that relative to other benchmark nations 95 percent of major American companies cling to traditional work organizations, although they find the most successful share characteristics consonent with the ideal type Japanese model described here.[13]

Looking at Method

Such considerations lead me to argue that one of my profession's most cherished images, Adam Smith's metaphor of the invisible hand, set economic thinking back in significant ways. If the form markets take, the way economic entities are shaped by conscious, and unconscious, human agency and the institutional context in which decisions are made is the subject of investigation, then the founder of the scientific study of economics got us off on a wrong foot. Actually, it would be better to say the mainstream of his followers did this deed. Smith himself was an acute observer of actual people in the real world. Many of his contemporary followers have a more mechanical view of people and markets. In this regard they substitute the magic of the marketplace for the hand of God. As a secular view of causation they replace a "God determines the fall of each little sparrow" with a new physics-like supply-demand equilibrium determinism. The distance between the two perspectives, at least as far as a clearer understanding of how markets are created, modified in their operation and superseded by social activity, was far less than mainstream economists tend to think. We need to have a greater appreciation of the social construction of markets and in encouraging participation rather than their virgin birth as the immaculate conception spawned by the ethereal digits.

In looking for assistance from the teachings of classic political economy, the field that existed before the divisions created by dissatisfaction with the neoclassical revolution and the academic disciplinary boundaries we have inherited, it is necessary to draw from related fields of inquiry. Unfortunately, little comes readymade for appropriation. Within the academic discipline of sociology there is a long and continuing tradition going back to Max Weber, which speaks to a subject area designated as "Economy and Society." Defining contours of both economy and society, rather than taking them as existing fields within which one asks questions, leads to a consideration of cultural embeddedness. The cultural economy, as I have used this term, is the problemetized arena in which economic development takes place. Its contours shift

with important consequences for economic evolution. The necessity of con-
necting economic relations of and in production to other institutions and value
beliefs that structure and define society then becomes difficult. A major function of the rejection of totalizing discourses is to deny the possibility of such
understanding. Yet, it is just such understanding we seek. The cultural economy is used here as a way of affirming such connectedness, a connectedness
that is clarified by considering economics as embedded in culture and of seeing
cultures built on economic foundations. In trying to build connectedness between understandings of culture and economy we can draw on some unlikely
analytic sources. [14]

The fashions of the day call for rejecting any framework smacking of anything as vulgar as Marxism and distinguishing between base and superstructure, even analytically as moments of a totality. In Marx's image of base and
superstructure he is pointing out that some types of structures cannot be built
on certain particular foundations while others can. He does not claim that
only one sort of architecture is possible in constructing superstructures, one
outcome foreordained, but rather that there need be consistency between the
two if buildings are going to stand and intellectual constructs are not to buckle
under the strain of the weight we put upon them. The denial that economic
foundations determine—in this sense, superstructures—and, we would quickly add, are determined by them as well (to draw on another period expression), is throwing the baby out with the bath water. Rigid determinism is
not the same as dialectical connectedness. Agency intrudes, indeed pervades,
history in the choices people make within the structures they inherit. Merely
recounting these choices without discussing the larger structures that constrain
options would be as inadequate as to claim that agency is absent. Historical
theory alone would be structuralism and historical data piled on top of more
detail would be simply narrative. The reasons for human action are both in the
contingencies and the institutions, the specifics of situations and the structures
in which choices are constrained. [15]

The dialectic aspect of social change is never easy to analyze. Within Japan
there are a number of contradictory processes. How they are resolved or
transformed alters what analysts will be able to take as givens in the next
conjunctural investigation. Bureaucratic guidance, the particularities of patterned group loyalties, and the social construction of meaning, shared understandings that exist at a point in time as seeming consensus, are always laden
with internal contradictions. Interests are defined, created, contested, and negotiated. We need to remember, as Karl Polanyi has done much to teach us,
that "regulation and markets, in effect, grew up together." [16] Markets, whether
for labor, products, technology, or ideas, are not given by some unique and
prior set of individual preferences. They are shaped in the crucible of explicit
interactions.

There are other governance structures. Some of these are within the state
sphere and differ among social formations in their specificities. Others are
internal to corporate governance and include cooperative work teams and
hierarchy. There are patterns of quasi-permanent informal contracting among

juridically independent firms that exhibit substantial stability.[17] As production webs have grown more complex and scholars trace commodity chains and explore mechanisms used to coordinate them, economists have come to appreciate the complexities of transaction forms. While actors collectively "choose" the specifics of their market relationships they do not do so systematically or always consciously. When they do act instrumentally as institution builders outcomes may depart substantially from intent. In any social formation those with greater resource endowment typically have more influence on market outcomes. Those with little to sell and scant resources to fall back upon have slight bargaining power in any market. Economists tend to privilege markets to the exclusion of other exchange and allocation mechanisms.

To understand the cultural economy, economists need to address some of the uncomfortable silences within mainstream thinking and explore what is the absent center of its allocative emphasis—the nature and causes of the wealth of nations that are embedded in the daily life and historical processes of a social formation, the non-economist's realm of a larger structuring context that I have called the cultural economy. It is the place in which choices are constrained, behavior is rooted, and institutions are grounded. Failing to explore the cultural economy of a social formation contributes to failure to understand how political economy can operate in other institutional contexts.

Institutions, Transactions, and Theories of the Firm

There has been a separation in the professional literature between those who study the evolution of the corporate form and business behavior, students of the national state and economic policy, and those who study the world system. Such a division of labor is perhaps inevitable if we are to make progress in understanding these important subjects. Yet, those interested in the Japanese and American trajectories must connect and integrate these discourses. If we are to consider the progress of our nations, the role the state has played, the development of the corporate form, and the economic analysis that is used to theorize these relations, then there must be a good bit of translation between the two models of capitalist development. We also need to confront differences in basic economic philosophy that influence economists' perceptions. This is nowhere more evident than it is in theorizing the relation between the firm, the market, and the state. In this section I will draw some conclusions concerning these matters that suggest the need for economists to change the focus of their investigations of these topics that follow from what has been said.

In describing the evolution and operation of the Japanese system, to take an example that has figured prominently in this study, much attention has been given to the role of government bureaucrats, a class of people quite marginal in the American case. In Japan, where economics is socially embedded in a different cultural matrix, one studies bureaucratic guidance as an interactive social construction, a product of the Japanese system writ large, and a force molding and changing that system. Individual interests are perceived within the penalty and reward structures of bureaucratic power that is limited by the sanctions at their command and may vary over time with the independent strengths of those they seek to guide, the sanctions that can be exercised, and the larger ideological norms. Social ideas act as a force along with more material resources. It is this dialectical process, rather than the one-way "this causes that" sort of world that much of modernist social science assumes more closely resembles the life world we wish to understand. It is necessary to study repeating performances that are not unchanging. Social practices are given in a historical sense, "coerced" situationally, and evaded to some extent through the initiatives of agency. As the process unfolds communities are modified and this (re)forms institutional relations.

The nature and purpose of the state and of firms, how they function in a market economy, are basically different in the American thinking than they are in the Japanese. The classic article in the American literature on the contemporary approach to the theory of the firm, by Alchian and Demetz, explains that "the firm serves as a highly specialized surrogate market." If so, then it has been the planned market in the case of the Japanese. The tradeoff of producing internally when it is difficult to get accurate information on potential suppliers (the reliability, quality factors) is not the same calculation.

Transaction cost analysts who see firms indifferent to organizing an activity within a firm and between firms, adopting one or the other depending on the transaction cost of each alternative, miss the dynamic nature of strategic choice. Even the source of transaction costs in Oliver Williamson's work, opportunism ("a condition of self-interest seeking with guile"), builds on a model in which there is seriously incomplete or distorted disclosure of information between individuals or firm surrogate individuals. Japanese parent firms, however, have the cost data of their contractors and it is difficult to mislead them. The relation is one of more than market exchange; it is the embeddedness of the transaction that is worth studying. The working assumption in the American literature of a dualistic market exchange versus firm specific hierarchical production is a incomplete choice set. [18]

Alchian and Demetz reject any notion of a firm characterized by authority to discipline others: "It has no power of fiat, no authority, no disciplinary action any different in the slightest degree from ordinary market contracting between any two people." [19] The generalizations of such a perspective are suspect on ideological grounds, and they can lead to faulty generalizations based on weak theorizing. Ronald Coase, in his foundational article on the theory of the firm, is led to generalize that "all changes which improve management technique will tend to increase the size of the firm." Lean production with its extensive spinoff webs of subcontracting suggest that economists who see corporations as organizations defined as mechanisms for overcoming market failure underestimate their ability to organize markets. To explain such economic activity instead in sociological terms that capture the complexity of these relations and more accurately describe and theorize their nature suggests that the absent center of a wide category of economic phenomena may be outside the terrain of the profession's self-definition. To take another example from Alfred Chandler's story, it is the manager whose view is the long-term one. The owners of these large turn of the twentieth century corporations are the short-run profit maximizers, especially when owners are no longer active managers, but are simply large stockholders. What can such historical findings or examinations of Japanese corporate behavior in the present period tell us about agency problems and the other acontextual theorizings of free market oriented economists?

The neoclassical economists may be formally correct, to draw on the wording of the preeminent statement in this tradition on the nature of the firm, that "a firm will tend to expand until the costs of organizing an extra transaction within the firm become equal to the cost of carrying out the same transaction by means of an exchange on the open market or the costs of organizing another firm."[20] Such "theory," however, tells us little about the real-world differences between the traditional American firms' relation as compared with the Japanese. The theory is an "empty box."[21] Like many theoretical boxes in economics, it may be empty primarily because they are not built in such a way that they can hold reality. Indeed reflecting reality at the level of accurate description is said by some methodologists, following Milton Friedman, to be irrelevant. The test for them is prediction under the assumptions of the model. The ahistorical generalizations of such economic theories are disappointing as we try to come to grips with why and how Japanese firms perform as they do.

The Anglo-American enterprise discourse presumes that markets provide the most economically rational, and indeed optimal, distribution of resources. The best market is the freest market. It is precisely this contention that the Japanese experience brings into question. The Japanese insistence on the benefits of planned markets for optimal outcomes flies in the face of dominant neoclassical presumptions. If our first principles are called into question, how much more of the mainstream economist's way of seeing and understanding the social world stand in need of interrogation? By asking what another cultural setting is about thus carries the potential for unexpected insight, and, as Anthony Giddens informs us, the practical implications of this "anthropological moment" of social research should not be underestimated. This is because "The most far-reaching practical consequences of social science do not involve the creation of sets of instrumental controls over the social world. They concern instead the constant absorption of concepts and theories into that 'subject matter' they seek to analyze, constituting and reconstituting what that 'subject matter' is."[22] The formal rules, laws, and defined property rights make up an important part of the sum of constraints that shape choice. In calling our attention to the pervasiveness of informal constraints and their social transmission we are drawn to categories of culture and to the contribution of anthropologists to explain how in different settings communities operate with a set of rules or standards deemed appropriate in defining acceptable or desirable behavior under a variety of circumstances.

Institutions[23] determine the cost of acting in various ways. They constrain and guide the way humans cooperate in social settings and can, as is often the case of Japan, offer security and reduce risk of unexpected outcomes. If an investment is favored by the developmentalist state, then the path is eased for company success. Similarly, an individual is part of a group or groups that offer support and networks of access. Thus, the Japanese can be both cautious and bold. Of course, all institutions structure incentives. In the Anglo-American tradition, and surely in our economic theory, "economic man" is an individualist. Constraints or prohibitions are viewed as negative impediments to freedom. In Japan the social unit is not atomistic man, but rather molecular bodies, groups of individuals bound together by a common identity and/or objective.

In one system organizations give pride of place to the group, and organizational learning by doing brings status to all members, who gain from such organized capacities of a successful group. They are unlikely to leave it and so its organic life is more important to them than it is for analogously situated Americans. The specifics of team organization—that people stay together over the life of a project, that specialists work together rather than in functionally distinct departmental locations—are strategies to increase organizational density. It is in this context that we are to understand Japan's famous "harmony." It is more accurate to say that the Japanese system rests on reciprocal consent developed after hard negotiating typically by parties with unequal bargaining power. The Japanese structural arena for conflict resolution is one in which negotiation and bargaining are first informal, after agreement is reached the formal discussion can proceed smoothly.[24] This occurs because players can see likely outcomes many steps away and because the costs that can be imposed on noncooperators are typically high.

Agency problems do not arise in the same way in the context of the constraints of the Japanese corporate system. Less resources are spent on the formal measurement of exchange costs in each instance, whereas more are spent on building relations of trust and also of submission to superior strength, which signals a willingness to limit its demands in exchange for continued cooperation. Different kinds of exchange can take place in the two systems, although there are clearly large areas of shared practice, and the Americans have learned to mimic and adopt Japanese norms. In the Japanese-style agreement measured costs of transacting can be low because of a dense network of interactions that remain in place over an extended time horizon. In a sense there is no escape from continued cooperation that does not imply substantial cost. This continuous basis of relating places a premium on good behavior. Shirking and other individualistic forms of cheating have less potential payoff and greater cost than in the American "lean and mean" model, where winners in a sense demand too much for further rounds to be played without greater animosity. In the American corporate jungle any sign of weakness or generosity invites being taken advantage of and does not in the normal case elicit reciprocity. Participants expect adversaries to press their advantage and not to make strategic concessions in the interests of better relations in replays.

In the U.S. traditional environment enforcement costs are high and resort to legal redress is frequent. In the Japanese norm of transacting it is possible and indeed normal not to contractually specify outcomes in great detail or perhaps at all. Consensus is reached as the product is developed and produced. Where uncertainty prevails and costs cannot be accurately known trust is a kind of insurance for both parties. Without trust information and cooperation are more likely to be withheld to the mutual disadvantage of both parties. Fairness and reliability are assured by mutual interest in an ongoing relationship. Altruism is not involved, nor is egalitarianism assumed. The relative power of the parties sets the bounds of gain sharing. The superordinate party knows that destroying those they would wish to work with again is not good policy. In some cases the exploitation involved may be extreme, but like a slave owner who keeps his slaves adequately fed, even the most hard-driven relational contractor thinks of his interest in the other party over an extended time horizon.

The relationship between transaction costs and institutions is a direct one. It is the prevalence of measurement and enforcement costs that are the source of both economic institutions and of political and social ones as well. Considering Japan and its different institutions allows us to examine ways we may better reduce the vast resources this country expends in transacting. Exchange is relational, and governance structures are institutionally distinct and historically imbricated. To change incentive structures as outsiders demand would influence transacting costs significantly. Cross-national negotiation is often frustrated because these difficulties are underestimated.

One attempt to measure transaction costs incurred in operating the American economy by Wallis and North (who include banking and insurance, wholesale and retail trade, and involve the labors of lawyers and accountants among others) estimates that 45 percent of our GNP went to "transacting."[25] A century earlier, by their calculations, it was only 25 percent. Thus, economies in transacting would appear to be an important potential source of huge cost savings. If the Japanese system over the same 100 years has been able to define, protect, and enforce property rights and coordinate exchange of factors of production and commodities more efficiently than under our free-market style of capitalist development, then this may account for a significant part of Japan's rapid growth. Looking at property rights structure constraints in a positive light, the Japanese cultural economy has elicited sacrifice and nation-building behavior of impressive dimension.

The preceding discussion of economic transactions implicitly makes a number of presumptions about the interests of companies and workers. Foremost is that they have a common interest in cooperation. Just as companies combine cooperation and competition in their dealings with each other, however, so, too, do workers have an interest in cooperating with "their" companies only to the extent that they accept the compensations they receive (over their expected working life at the company discounted to present value) as adequate or the cooperation as unavoidable due to the greater power of "their" company. It would be well if we could overcome the deep separation between discourse of modes of organization and transacting and the labor process literature that stresses the consciousness and autonomous motivation of workers as individuals and as members of a class formation. A better approach to building theories of economic development would require consideration of just such issues and a bringing together of what have been separate discussions. We are reminded how difficult such theory building is when we also try to deal with the changes in the givens that are taken for granted in a particular historical conjuncture.

Cracks in the Mirror

Serious strains in the older accommodations are visible as changes in the forces of production engender class recomposition in Japan. Old core constituents of the ruling consensus, the small farmers and shopkeepers, are increasingly less central and find state protections diminishing. Conflicts between state bureaucrats and increasingly independent-minded elements of the business and financial communities is evident, and politicians are asserting themselves more with regard to the autonomy of agency staffs. For one thing, Thatcher–Reagan conservative politics seems congenial to some Japanese. Market-oriented liberalism is more appealing to winners, and Japan is now in a position to embrace such an attitude. The combination of the celebration of high-tech and traditional values would seem an attractive political gambit in Japan as elsewhere. Smaller government and a reduction in transfer payments seems a viable politics in Japan in the face of mounting deficits. These in turn come, as they do elsewhere, from slower economic growth and incite movement away from progressive taxation. The costs of older forms of market sheltering became greater and the benefits too narrowly focused for a constituency to rally successfully around their defense. At the same time nationalism is on the rise and appeals to traditional values signal a digging in of the heels in an effort to slow the pace of disturbing changes. The opening up of national markets also enforces a new norm of business on people at the top. The comfortable accommodations of the closed system are challenged and there is pressure for dramatic change and political realignment.

The stable stockholder-interpenetrating *keiretsu* structure is also under pressure. As in the United States, where old-line manufacturing firm executives, weakened by the Japanese onslaught, were more receptive to industrial policy in the 1970s than were the up-and-coming high-tech entrepreneurs, so in Japan in the 1990s are the younger generation of cutting-edge companies less patient with the desires of the CEOs of yesterday's industries who still hold to the presumptions of leadership within the *keiretsu* based on the status of their firms and their seniority. In the vertical *keiretsu* some suppliers have gained competence to the point of being able to guide parent firms and have thus increased their bargaining power. Some suppliers have always been able to sell to more than one major customer. This practice has increased as niche producers are able to capture economic rents needing to surrender less of the value added they produce to the giants.

There is a tendency to see a diminished ability to run an effective industrial policy because of foreign pressures, more open financial markets, and the independent resources of strong Japanese transnationals. Regulators have approved various speculative instruments for trading intangible products such as commodity index futures and other derivative instruments. It can be argued they had to do so since futures have already been widely purchased in the Grand Cayman Islands and elsewhere on behalf of Japanese investors, and U.S. futures firms have been bidding business away from Japanese firms. The scandals discussed in Chapter 8 are part and parcel of a deregulated financial sector, a source of dangerous international instability.

Whether the postwar system is able to reproduce itself on some modified basis that takes into account globalization trends in the post-postwar political economy or not will depend in part on its institutional flexibility. There are certainly important issues of governance—will the 1955 system that led to the uninterrupted rule of the LDP created that year out of the two rival conservative parties be supplanted by a U.S.-style two-party system? Will the lifetime employment system for primary workers give way to greater job hopping and employment uncertainties? Will the administrative guidance system undergo transformation in the new conjuncture and be seriously undercut by the internationalization of strong Japanese corporations? Will strategic alliances and regionally based production change the nature of the *keiretsu* themselves?

There are also questions of popular consciousness and social reproduction. The most prominent "containers" of this latter issue are labor supply and the educational system, which in Japan, as in the United States, is undergoing prolonged scrutiny and is the focal point of disagreements over social philosophy and the broader concerns of national purpose and direction. Labor supply becomes problematic for Japan in the 1980s as forecasts of likely implications of a rapidly aging population on economic development prospects, the need to draw on foreign workers, and increased need to care for the aged with implications for the government's budget. For the first time since the early 1950s, when class-conscious trade unionism was decisively defeated and a stable industrial relations regime was put in place, the perception of labor shortages raises a host of questions. Since work effort has been so central to Japanese achievements the issue deserves extended treatment. What will happen when a better-educated younger generation that has grown up with the assumption of affluence comes of age? Will they work as hard? Will they accept the old education system's demands? Will their expectations be disappointed? If so, how will they react?

Concerns about education in Japan are quite different than they are in the United States and the contrast tells us something about our two societies. The Japanese work at education, at least until they are accepted into college, the same way adults work at their jobs. In Japan 4.5 million students are enrolled in over 50,000 after-school cram programs to help them get a leg up on the competition for the relatively few good slots in the system. They include one half of all students in the seventh through ninth grade, and both the time these students spend in *juku* and the money their parents spend is growing. Programs range from preschool *juku* for two and three year olds (where students learn colors and shapes so they have a better chance to get into the more prestigious kindergarten programs) to cram programs mentioned earlier, which help older students succeed on the law exams. There are chains of *juku* that have worked out systems to break information down into digestible bits and franchise the technique. There are charismatic *juku* teachers whose lecturing prowess puts them in the upper ranks of the country's income distribution. Indeed, the most successful cram schools have their own entrance examinations.

Children sacrifice playtime and sleep to get past exams so that they will get into better schools and so be accepted into better jobs. Learning to work doggedly at senseless tasks of rote memory and getting by on too little sleep also prepares them for the world of work they will enter. The more they all do the worse the competition to get through the same narrow gate becomes. Critics like Hiroyuki Tsukamoto of the Japan Teachers Union say that "*jukus* are raising a generation of kids who can only pass entrance examinations. But the most important educational purpose is giving children the ability to live in society. That is being left out."[26] The truth, as I have suggested, may be just the opposite. The educational training is in fact preparing children for exactly the kind of society in which they will live.

Merry White, an educational specialist on Japan, argues that a very positive aspect of the system is that children learn that they must "cheerfully conform to the community's expectations and yield some exercise of free choice to the necessary constraints of society." While such phrasing may bring to mind the "be happy in your work" injunction of the prisoner-of-war camp commandant in the film, *Bridge on the River Kwai*, she argues;

> If "society" is simply to be seen as the social environment in which the child is nurtured and developed only as an individual, the child's active participation in and responsibility toward it is less important than if his social environment is a "community" in which his identity and future life chances are embedded.[27]

Whatever valence one places on this core aspect of education it is surely the case that Japanese learning is as much about relationships as facts and those who see only cramming and rote learning miss this.

The life of the group comes first and foremost. Schools teach the internalization of norms; in Japan, of consensus and respect. They also teach that individual achievement is based on hard work. Education in Japan is also seen as key to economic development. Cultural continuity, character building, and being competitive as a nation go together. Learning to read music and play an instrument, which every Japanese grammar school child can do, and a focus on physical fitness, extensive regular exercise and the seriousness of "sports day" in which all participate, are part of a regime that hardens and rounds students through communal activities.

When Americans learn of a best-selling home-study desk for children that shields the child on three sides from any distraction and, in addition to an electric pencil sharpener and built-in calculator, has a button connected to a bell mounted in the kitchen so that the student, who by high school is doing five or six hours of homework per night, can summon his (or even perhaps her) mother for help or a snack, the reaction is often that the Japanese carry things too far. When one hears the exhortation "Pass with Four, Fail with Five" (if one sleeps five hours rather than four one will fail the exams), one begins to imagine the kind of training and endurance that is required to make it to the best Japanese universities. This perseverance is taught in the Japanese system. It is the process of work, its intensity and focused concentration, not simply the end product that counts. One does not cut corners. One does it right on each occasion and learns to see small improvements over time as their own reward. Work is ideally always done cleanly. It is not rushed. There is no cachet to quick brilliance and seemingly effortless achievement as in the United States. Rote learning is necessary, like musicians' fingering practice so that they will eventually fly to the right notes automatically and only then allow concentration on expression—after technical virtuosity is achieved. In the same way diligence is part of the problem-solving skill in other realms.

The "education mama" of Japanese lore still brings her child food and drink as he studies late into the night wearing a headband inscribed with "Certain Victory" (or some other inspiring message) to pass the exams that will determine the child's future. Japanese parents, however, are also said to overindulge their children. Elders fear that the younger generation is soft. The Japanese language develops terms for such phenomena. In this case it is *shinjinrui*, the new breed, young people who reject their parents' values of obligation, self-sacrifice, and deference to superiors. Such labels aside, it is hard to imagine what the next generation will be like, but those who fear or hope that they will lose the work ethic may underestimate the hold of the cultural embeddedness of attitudes toward education. As the Ministry of Education tried in the early 1990s to slowly do away with the six-day school week (Japanese students are in class 25 percent longer than are American children each year) they were met by resistance of parents who did not want to see their children "fall behind." Some schools make up the missed time from the one Saturday off per month the government imposed with longer sessions on the other days. The long hours of school, like the dress code, are seen as preparing children for life in corporate Japan.[28]

When schools try to organize after-school programs their problem is that parents complain that sports and hobbies get in the way of their kids putting in time at their *juku*, not that the school boards cut their funds. Successful *jukus* give tests at 8:00 A.M. Sunday morning followed by three-hour review sessions that parents attend so that they can better help their kids. Many Japanese parents buy an additional set of textbooks so that they can keep up on lessons and better assist their young scholars. Leona Esaki, a Nobel laureate in physics and the president of Tsukuba University speaking of the crisis in Japanese education told the *Asahi Shimbun*, "Seeing what high school students put themselves through to get into 'good' universities, I am not surprised at all that they fail to develop into mature, balanced persons."[29] Once again different observers will choose to stress different aspects of the reality. For many Japanese the only educational crisis is that "the young aren't working hard enough, not like we did." If the public opinion polls are to be trusted, then these elders are correct. The young are decreasingly willing to put their companies before their families and finding their own meaning in life.

Because educational success is *the* route to personal advancement stakes are high, pressures are great. At the same time the achievement of the average student shows the results of this focus on excellence and the system benefits from a well-educated and disciplined work force. Amid the criticism of the regimentation and conformity it is easy to forget that the average student's performance is so very impressive. "It is as if Japan accomplishes for 70 or 80 percent of its youth what American education is able to accomplish in its suburban public and elite private schools for the top 10 to 20 percent."[30] It is the expectation that any child that is properly taught and works hard will do well, which sets the Japanese and the American systems most apart.

The issue of labor shortage raises the question of the younger generation and the *shinjinrui*, who is said by some of his elders, to be almost a Westerner. I have noted the fear among the older generation that the kids will not want to live for the company, will move if they get a better job, and will not be loyal to the old ways. They mark the end of traditional Japanese discipline and signal the collapse of the Japan we have known. Maybe. Maybe not. One can certainly understand the fear of a generation that has worked and sacrificed that in their old age the kids will eat up the seed corn and lack respect for their elders.

It is certainly true that for a substantial number of young Japanese employees a chance to slave away their lives for the good of the company just does not sound like such a great deal. As a result they are demanding and often getting more interesting work when labor shortages force a change in employer attitudes. One young man explaining the system and his attitude toward it says:

> I don't know what a company really does before I go for an interview.
> A company is like a cave that you can't see inside, and when you enter it,
> you can't complain, no matter how the company treats you. That's why I
> tell them straight off that I'm only interested in working in the planning
> department.[31]

The most popular jobs among graduates in the liberal arts, at least, are in planning, international relations, and public relations—jobs that allow travel and getting out of the office.

The most highly valued interviewees can afford to be picky given the openings available to them. Employment advisers at the nation's prestigious schools receive visits from young alumni who wish to change jobs. Indeed, companies in the early 1990s began to run talent sweeps to attract job hoppers. The Ministry of Labor started conducting surveys of "second graduates" in 1992. To get to this charmed circle, however, still requires almost superhuman endurance and perseverance in learning the minutia of arcane test fact knowledge. The old system will not change easily or as quickly as some optimists are suggesting. There is, however, another sort of pressure involved. Having increasingly caught up with the West, Japanese are called upon to be more creative and the aspects of the education system involving rote learning for tests is being questioned.

Other changes were brought about by the labor shortage in the late 1980s. Women were getting better jobs. More women are refusing to get married and have children. Fewer births means a greater labor shortage in the future. Women able to ''select a life style'' in the parlance of the times had options their mothers did not. Disregard by the government of adequate daycare and the high costs of educating children and housing also mean fewer children and fewer future workers. Failure to give child care leave means wasted women-power for corporate Japan. Women's rights groups begin to receive a different kind of reception from the patriarchs. Change, however, does not come easily.

In Chapter 6 the first landmark victory in a sexual harassment case in Japan in 1992 was noted. At Hitachi, Sumitomo, and other giants of Japanese industry groups of women are suing over delayed promotions and are organizing against second-class treatment. Only 3 percent of professional positions at Japan's large blue-chip companies are filled by women, and promotion of these few appears very limited. Yet, the challenge is being felt. There are also questions about how long the uniformed smiling office ladies who bow politely and make tea for visitors and male employees will continue to outwardly conform to the stereotyped limited roles prescribed by corporate patriarchy. One would not want to exaggerate, but gender relations are in flux and the young are not accepting traditional roles quite so easily. Indeed, many are finding their own way; unfortunately, the global slowdown in the 1990s led to a great deal of backsliding as leading Japanese corporations turned away from recruiting even token numbers of qualified Japanese female graduates. The possibility of a wide sweeping attitude change however is still present.

There are other aspects to the generational shift. In the 1960s Japan had a counterculture that was not unlike that which developed at the time in the West. In the 1990s there are also stirrings of a new generation that is not terribly revolutionary, to be sure, but is thoughtfully and creatively expanding the limits of tradition. This development is most obvious in the arts.

In his centuries-old home in Kanazawa, the fourteenth Ohi, a young ceramicist, explained to me over tea, served in the traditional fashion by his kimono-clad wife, how he tried to combine tradition and his own innate creativity. He had at one point in effect run off to America to do pottery in a place tradition did not bind him and the expectations of others concerning his work were not fixed and had returned able to accept his inheritance as a gift not a prison. Other creative Japanese have pursued similar paths combining their patrimony and their own unique gifts aided by a welcoming openness to other cultures from the solidity of their own core. Ennosuke Ichikawa (the third of that name), to take another example, has challenged the closed world of *kabuki* He can do so because his ''family'' lineage gives him the status to do so. He has introduced daring special effects, quick costume changes, and stylized sword fights to this nearly 400-year old dramatic art. He has also directed Strauss in Munich. Tamasaburo Bando (the fifth of that name), *kabuki*'s superstar *onna-*

gata (a male actor who plays female leads), has played in various Western plays including Desdemona in *Othello*, and directs his own dance troupe. There are other classically rooted artists who have defiantly broken with traditional boundaries and conventions. I also think of the lively emigré or binational arts culture of young Japanese in lower Manhattan who have come seeking inspiration and to compete where there is perhaps a freedom and a vibrancy they have not felt at home and which their presence enhances. These talented young people will contribute to the development of world culture combining their own heritage with the stimulating inputs they absorb from experiences of encounter with other cultures. The spread effects to mass culture in Japan are not yet large but there is new yeast in the *salaryman* system.

Importing Secondary Workers

The number of job seekers and the number of job offers recorded on Ministry of Labor graphs look like an X, with the number of job offers considerably less than the number of job seekers until 1987. They then cross in 1988, and the gap then widened until 1992. A consumer slump in the early 1990s, Japanese-style, cut back sales of Rolls Royce imports and old masters. Expensive restaurants suffered, as did other upscale businesses. Mass-market products felt the downturn far less because few workers were laid off by the *keiretsu* even as profits suffered. Their workers were given first two, then three Saturdays off per month while continuing to receive 90–95 percent of their regular monthly wages. The companies used attrition and an active transfer program to minimize the pain of trimming payrolls. The presumption of long-term labor shortage helped maintain the system. By 1992, however, the jobs per worker ratio had dropped to only 1 : 1, and for the first time since recovery from World War II the prospect of prolonged stagnation raised the specter of job shortages, not labor scarcity. The number of *kigyonai shitsugyosha* (in-house unemployed) rose (estimated by Labor Ministry researchers at about 1 million in early 1993), yet labor hoarding continued, given a belief in long-term labor shortage being the expected norm for the Japanese economy.

The industrial relations system, with its implicit employment contract for primary workers, is premised on an underlying material base that the suppositions of the postwar Japanese system were shaken, but for the time being at least remained in place. *Unless* offshore activities grow at a rate beyond the capacity of domestic demand to generate replacement work and global economic slowdown persists, then Japan cannot escape labor shortages, unless economic stagnation becomes a continuing feature of its economy. Even then, competitive pressures and an awareness of foreign practices may lead to a reliance on foreign workers to cut costs. How the domestic economy would cope with the expected labor shortages will say much about the kind of country Japan will be. This crucial issue is closely linked with Japan's sense of identity and national uniqueness because of the role immigrants or guest workers will have.

Illegal foreign workers in the 1980s already played an essential role in the

Japanese economy. By the year 2000, one prediction is that Japan will have a labor shortage of nearly 6 million workers unless productivity rises faster than projected. [32] A more cautious estimate by the Ministry of Labor is for a labor shortfall approaching 2 million by the year 2010. There is no doubt that immigrants, now almost all illegal, will continue to find their way into Japan. Many are brought by gangster elements to work as bargirls and prostitutes. Even in remote rural areas illegal workers are found in these and other occupations. Many were promised proper work and are forced into prostitution by unscrupulous criminals who withhold their passports. While the problem does not officially exist, there have been studies of different aspects of the situation.

The number of undocumented workers at the end of the 1980s was estimated to be between 100,000 and 300,000. Most of these people slept crowded together in small airless rooms, cooking for themselves because even the cheapest noodle shops were beyond their means. They were employed at the three Ks—*kitanai, kikenna,* and *kitsui*—which translate into the three Ds in English—jobs that are dirty, dangerous, and difficult, the sorts of jobs young Japanese will no longer do. The contradiction between this need and the unwillingness to include non-Japanese in the society will become more severe as Japanese age and labor shortages grow. There are already strong indications that Japan will not handle incorporation of "others" very easily into their tight island society.

The Japanese also show insensitivity to the Korean minority, people whose families in some cases had been in Japan for four generations, first brought to do forced labor by the imperialist state in the pre-war period. The current descendants are pariahs in the only country they have ever known. Even though 85 percent of them were born in Japan they can be deported to Korea. The harsh Alien Registration Law and fingerprinting requirement, deportation provisions, and so on are modeled on the U.S. Alien Registration Act of 1940 and the Internal Security Act of 1950. Militant civil rights activities can brand people as criminals and subject them to deportation. The Koreans brought by force during Japan's brutal colonial rule (Japan forcibly annexed Korea in 1910) were forbidden to speak Korean and were required to take Japanese names. Many Japanese still show the attitude of former masters and look down on the Koreans in their midst, keeping them out of good schools and the better jobs. Foreign students from Korea studying in Japan find that officials list their home town on alien registration cards using the Japanese names (i.e., *Keijo* instead of Seoul) even though Japan's colonial rule of Korea ended more than a half-century earlier. Current law and officially condoned practices perpetuate mistreatment. More recent immigrants from the Philippines or Sri Lanka face even worse treatment and the disdain of a racially superior Japanese attitude. Even Japanese who do not come up to acceptable norms of status—both the Japanese version of the untouchable caste, the *burakumin*, and poor day laborers—are treated with contempt as others within their own country. Such ethnocentric arrogance augurs ill for a future in which internationalization of labor will be part of Japanese reality and Japanese business penetration of Asian neighbors offers greater occasion for migration to Japan.

America

In the United States, too, the new immigrants, many coming with entrepreneurial experience in their home nations, a drive to educate their children and see them succeed, may invigorate our country as generations of newcomers have in the past. The legacy of racism, however, casts a long shadow over America. The problems Japan has in absorbing non-Japanese, and these are likely to continue to be significant, pale to those the United States experiences in its ongoing racial conflicts. The impact on competitiveness is enormous. While it may be possible to form an enclave successful economy in the territorial United States, which excludes an exceedingly large part of our population from its benefits, the reality of such a solution of class and racial apartheid needs to be looked at unflinchingly and a different sort of societal debate undertaken. The analysis earlier in this chapter of transacting needs to be extended to embrace the larger social fabric in which individual and corporate choices are structured.

In Japan, long-term employment and the built-in incentives against changing jobs increase the returns to investment in human capital by the firm and the individual worker, in both general and firm-specific forms. Our society, like the Japanese, has a significant interest in the preparation of young people for participation in the job market. The number of potential workers who do not come into a productive relation with the economy are a measure of policy failure and impose costs of different kinds on the society at large. There is the matter of forgone output, as well as the cost of transfer payments, social disruption, and dislocation (from crime to homelessness and the antagonistic contestation over public space, which may set whole areas of our cities off limits for visitors and are less than hospitable for their residents). The obvious costs to national competitiveness is only one concern generated by social distancing and alienation.

Employability is a function of the interaction of the quantity and the job structure of effective market demand for labor and on the other side the capacities of the labor force. In turn, the capacities of the labor force are not simply a matter of the worker's choice to invest in human capital, as the individualistic neoclassical model would have it. Rather, they are a function of schools, family life, and the cultural environment more broadly. It is also a matter of the larger accommodation, or the lack of one between capital and labor. Many of the efforts companies expect under such accords require greater exertion on the part of the workers, as noted in Chapter 6. Labor may be unwilling to perform as corporations wish them to and be able to resist capital's efforts to coerce them. The specificity of situation is important to such discussions as well as consideration of the abstract advantages potentially involved for all parties. To enter this terrain is to embark on a discussion that takes us beyond our immediate subject. To tell ghetto kids, potential workers, to stay in school, however, while certainly not a bad thing to do, should be part of a societal commitment that is serious all the way down the line, committed to giving the young people good schools in a secure living environment and paying the bills, creating a receiving job market that is welcoming and promises wages that will rise with experience and performance, and employment that is relatively secure so that their kids can be raised in a supportive environment as well. The classic liberal individualism in which, as Robert Nozick has put the matter, it is "from each as he chooses, to each as he is chosen," is in my view an abomination. It is to blame dropouts for causing their situations when no one chooses to hire them after a cursory preparation of a type and quality decided by the (ir)responsible adult community. This perversion of the notion of freedom of choice serves to perpetuate injustice.

On a more narrowly self-interested basis it is also the case, as Lester Thurow has been prominent in arguing, that the "smartest 25 percent" of the labor force may invent the new product, but it is "the bottom 50 percent" that produces it. The education and training of the latter group becomes important if the breakthroughs are to be manufactured in your country. If the "bottom 50 percent" cannot learn what they must learn, new high-tech processes cannot be used. Sustainable comparative advantage depends on work force skills. There are surely lessons to be learned from Japan in this area. "Unless some new policies or practices intervene to commit them to retraining of their existing workers, U.S. firms seem to be heading toward a mode of operation in which they periodically replace their work force," reported the MIT Commission on Industrial Productivity in a 1989 study.[33] They contrasted the American approach to the frequent retraining of a work force that is seen as a necessary part of a nation's economic practice. The latter approach is good for the worker, the companies, and the country, these experts thought. As we saw earlier Japanese blue collar steelworkers have become programmers, and engineers in the industry are moved to biotechnology projects. As the MIT group comments on another aspect more prevalent in Japan, "rotations create a multiskilled, flexible work force prepared for change by creating a mind-set for learning."[34] There are some lessons here, but they must be absorbed in the context of the historical specificities of American realities.

In America the workers who will account for more than half of the growth in the labor force at the turn of the century were expected to be members of minority groups, many of whom are poorly equipped for the better jobs of the twenty-first century. Employers complain about the preparation of job-market entrants and, at some level perhaps, see the connection between their own efforts to avoid taxation and abandon the inner cities. Endless blue-ribbon commissions detailed the poor performance of America's schools and the impact for the nation's future. "Since we're doing such a lousy job providing these young people with education and training now, it simply implies a lower standard of living for all Americans, not just blacks and Hispanics," said Bill Brock, a former secretary of labor who chaired a high-level commission on the skills needed in the workplace of tomorrow. In a similar vein said Senator Bill Bradley:

> Children of white America and their future will depend increasingly on the talents of nonwhite America. If we have fewer people with sufficient

skill levels we won't compete as well against other national economies. Children of white America will have a future where their economic prospects will be less than they might otherwise be. This is a matter of real enlightened self-interest. [35]

Matters are far more complicated than these good sentiments reflect. For many white working people, who must compete or their kids will compete with minority kids for limited numbers of not such great jobs, racial privilege is all they have going for them. Racial equality in existing labor markets will initially come at their expense. This is not an altogether unreasonable fear. Nor is staying in school a guaranteed ticket to anywhere. Completing high school for many Americans did not insure earnings sufficient to raise a family out of poverty. Many young people will continue to make choices that seem rational to them, but which have antisocial results and will be condemned by society for the lives they "choose" to lead.

In the drama that took place "In the Grove," Tajomau, the bandit, when brought before the officials who were to judge him, offered his own truth: "Am I the only one who kills people? You don't use your swords. You kill people with your power, with your money. Sometimes you kill them on the pretext of working for their good. . . . "[36] Who is to say that these officials were any less honorable than their contemporary counterparts or that they were any more able to see things from the point of view of those they call the underclass and of the working class? This class aspect of the Rashomon Mirror's distortions is the uncomfortable absent center of a discussion that we prefer to see in terms of only the positive side of the transformational potential of capitalist development.

When we move from the level of organization theory to the lived experience of Japanese workers, students, and migrants we can see the way the life world of Japan and in America are changing, modifying the cultural assumptions within which the economy will function. Another set of changes are being forced on Japan from the outside. We turn to these in the next, and final chapter.

12

Through a Rashomon Mirror Darkly

"Either the well was very deep, or she fell very slowly, for she had plenty of time as she went to look about her, and to wonder what was going to happen next . . . She tried to look down and make out what she was coming to, but it was too dark to see anything."

LEWIS CARROLL, *Alice*

"Gone is night's dream this morning.
How sweet, how dear! All this pining.
Unnoticed, the snow deepens."

TRADITIONAL *Nagauta* BALLAD

Every nation-state should play a strong self-aware role in setting the terms under which the country's insertion in the world system takes place. It should contribute as well to the working out of an international regulatory regime in which social costs are minimized and benefits are spread widely and inclusively. The latter task moves us into relatively unchartered waters. It is clear that government roles in the latter process will be related to the cultural economies, domestic regulatory regimes, and historical specificities of the individual nation-state formations, especially of the economically, politically, and militarily most powerful governments. For this reason it would be well if Americans understood more about changing politics, class recomposition, and strategic corporate planning in Japan. Japan's more self-referential national developmentalist model has undergone modification and in important ways has been eclipsed by bold new departures as Japan assumes global leadership responsibilities. The Japanese have made clear their view that they (and Germany) should be given permanent seats on the United Nations Security Council and that the United Nations should be strengthened in the direction of building an effective global governance organization. This means that the UN Security Council will take on a more activist role in anticipating conflicts. The Japanese also want a permanent UN standby military unit for quick deployment, and a closer working relation with the G-7 economic powers so as to integrate global economic development and peacekeeping. As one influential report by an important Japanese establishment organization suggests:

> Many of the global woes we are now surrounded with are far beyond what individual nations alone can solve. In some areas, we should accept these limitations, and prepare to cede at least part of our national sovereignty to an appropriate international organization. Coordination among nations when setting tariffs or making fiscal and monetary policies, the two most typical areas of national sovereignty, is no longer something unusual. And national borders will increasingly become less defined in the future.[1]

Key Japanese decision makers look to a future in which their government is ready to accept greater responsibility in international affairs and in designing new governance structures that greater interdependence and economic integration require. In important respects the Japanese seem more ready for such a world than Americans have been. The debate in Japan is likely to be similar, however—between reassertion of nationalism and acceptance of a new internationalism. The former resists homogenization and loss of traditional identity, and of autonomy. The latter seeks mutual accommodation on favorable terms and the smoothing over of conflicts among localist interests.

These two perspectives—the former protecting existing status relations and distributional claims, the latter promising more for everyone in the long run after some temporary sacrifice—present from a working-class perspective a Hobson's choice. The debate is posed as "accommodate to restructuring now and accept cost of displacement in the short run or try unsuccessfully to hold on to the status quo and lose more later." Sacrifices now hurt, but there are no guarantees about later. One "chooses" to accommodate without real choice over the terms of that accommodation. Are there lessons to be learned from the experience of the Japanese model in the postwar era that will help make the internationalization transition less painful and reduce the pressures toward defensive nationalism and separatist identity politics?

In the discussion of industrial policy in Chapter 9 the argument was made that conventional protectionism is unlikely to work. Neither is the building of national champions. Both changes at the level of the corporate redefinition in global and strategic alliance terms and the political consensus that some form of coherent world governance is necessary suggest major changes in the context of macroeconomics. It is difficult either to preserve old production regimes or to close oneself off and attempt to duplicate the sort of industrial policies that have been described as having worked so well in past decades. When Apple and Toshiba are jointly developing equipment that combines text, graphics, video, and audio for multimedia products, and Kawasaki, which started to manufacture motorcycles in Nebraska in the mid-1970s, is a local producer of rolling stock in Yonkers, New York, robots in Farmington Hills, Michigan, and machinery in Newman, Georgia, is it smart to assist "American" companies?

A corporation like Toshiba, which operates an information systems lab in

California and an Advanced Television Technology Center in Princeton, New Jersey, or Fujitsu, with a plant in Oregon and subsidiaries in Colorado, also have extensive strategic alliances with American producers. Kawasaki is a major collaborator with Boeing on design and manufacture of the mainframe for the B-777 aircraft. Matsushita has been operating research and development labs in North America since the mid-1970s. Its work focuses on speech recognition and synthesis in Santa Barbara, on software developed for retail industry equipment in Illinois, on home automation in New Jersey, and on satellite communication in North Carolina's Research Triangle. Should these facilities receive subsidies from state and federal agencies wishing to enhance high-tech growth in this country? How could building a closed national economy work under such conditions?

What about IBM, which, in a landmark strategic alliance to develop a revolutionary new microchip with Toshiba and Siemens, will use technologies developed in part thanks to U.S. taxpayer subsidies? In announcing its global chipmaking alliance, IBM's President Jack Kuehler explained that "companies need to be able to compete globally to survive." For IBM, he said, "survival is the first priority. Nationalistic factors are second priority."[2] These interlinks and strategic alliances undermine much of the logic of a simple-minded, subsidized American corporate development of new technology thinking.[3]

U.S. industrial policy has been most extensive and effective in the microchip industry. Between its founding in 1987 and 1992, the year of the IBM–Toshiba–Siemens pact, Sematech cost the U.S. taxpayer $0.5 billion. The Sematech consortium helped the United States rebuild its chipmaking technological base. The question at the end of the twentieth century was not whether the old way of thinking could survive—it could not. As Sematech's chief executive himself said, "We're entering an era when nationalistic issues will continue to decline. Sematech gradually will become an international organization."[4]

How does U.S. industrial policy move to protect the U.S. electronics industry when half of the American-based companies involved in consumer electronics are foreign owned? The Mitsubishi television sets bought by American consumers are likely to have rolled off the assembly line in the company's Santa Ana, California, plant. The Mitsubishi automobiles sold as Chryslers may also have been made here; of course, they could also have been assembled in Thailand. On the other side, in 1990 more than a quarter of American exports carried the label of a foreign company; 10 percent were Japanese. If these foreign employers offered greater job security and better long-term prospects for workers than U.S.-owned counterparts, spent more on training blue collar employees and on research and development *in the United States,* as many did, why should industrial policy be used to favor U.S.-owned companies?

The United States is likely to come to acceptance of industrial policy too late and may embrace an approach that does not speak to the relevant core issues effectively, or at all. Its contours may be shaped to fit a situation that has passed. The industrial policies embraced by developmentalist states in the 1970s and 1980s may do some good in the twenty-first century, but they are also likely to be of limited value to the extent that the country's largest (and also smallest) companies have entered strategic alliances with the foreign competition. The fear of adopting an outmoded industrial policy, however, should not prevent us from consideration of the type of policies that could effectively make a difference to the quality of life in America.

Japan in the World

While there are increasingly influential voices urging Japan to deregulate, to dismantle the developmentalist-state guidance system (which, by eschewing a role in international politics, has been instrumental in carrying Japan to economic superpower status), others urge Japan to take on globalist political leadership, to become more like the United States by assuming greater leadership in world affairs. Eiji Suzuki, chairman of the Japan Federation of Employers' Associations, for example, urges Japan to reduce government meddling and to become more actively involved in the development of a post–Cold War World Order. [5]

Should Japan deregulate its developmentalist-state accommodations and build up a political and perhaps military power commensurate with its economic position? Having watched the plight of the United States as it sought to project a continued superpower dominance, Japanese were well aware of the Paul Kennedy question of whether declining hegemons get into trouble from an overconfidence and blindness to the seriousness of the external challenge and succumb to an imperial overreach as its military extension exceeds the grasp provided by its diminishing underlying economic strength. [6] Kennedy's book was a best seller in Japan. Its argument of imperial overreach makes good sense to the Japanese (and also to the Germans). The emphasis of both these former imperial states this time around on gaining economic advantage through statist policies—underwriting research and development, protectionist devices, and the underwriting of foreign market penetration through export subsidies—is a more efficient version of imperialism when put up against the U.S. postwar system's imperial state's monomaniacal engagement in military interventionism and a CIA view of national mission to destabilize ideologically unacceptable governments.

Developing a new international regime appropriate to twenty-first century economic conditions will be an interesting process. The role Japan plays will in part be determined by how its domestic battle between the forces of transformation, embodied in what we have called the postwar Japanese system and globalization pressures to dismantle it, are played out. If the latter forces triumph Japan will not turn out to be the future of America, but its past. Much will depend on the growth rate and whether financial disaster overtakes Japan. The growth of industrial capacity, which increased by over 14 percent per year in the 1960s, was only 3 or 4 percent in the 1970s and 1980s. In the early 1990s Japan's economy went into serious recession.

Under such circumstances Japan was not in a position to lead even if it had wanted to, and it was clearly unprepared and unwilling to attempt much of a role in any case, in large measure because the United States continued to make it clear that it would not tolerate an independent role on Japan's part. Simply underwriting America's choices was an increasingly unattractive option. A free-market oriented departure of the sort the United States had urged on all nations during the 1980s ironically seemed a plausible answer in dealing with the Americans. "The magic of the marketplace" favored Japanese exporters and cut against many of the negotiated trade and investment concessions the United States continued to demand.

Such movement to greater market freedom is in my view temporary. Rather than abandoning "planned markets," a new international regime will eventually emerge that places a stable economic environment high on its agenda. Rather than each nation going its own way against all others, policies need to be harmonized within a new international regime. To be effective and allow coherent reinforcing positive actions among nations national policies require a globalized macroeconomics that has to be rooted in turn in an awareness of institutional interdependencies. Its policy levers need to be appropriately international in reach. Its coordinating mechanisms best legitimated by inclusive international treaties for successful policy intervention need to be global in their coverage. At the same time separate nations will have the key role to play in their own well being for some time even as globalized negotiations in the policy area become more mature.

Accommodating to History

The Japanese, having succeeded by holding down domestic consumption and fostering investment through conscious policy measures, faced a world by the early 1990s that was not growing very fast and was increasingly resistant to continued large Japanese balance of payments surpluses. Growth would depend on stimulating domestic markets and imports to bring Japan's trade into a greater semblance of balance. There was ample ground for raising wages at the expense of slowing investment—for a shift in wage–profit shares. Economic Planning Agency data shows that in 1989 labor's share of national income was only 76.5 percent of national income, compared with 80.1 percent in the United States, 81.2 percent in Great Britain, and 82.8 percent in France.[7] For Japanese manufacturing labor productivity more than doubled between 1975 and 1985, but the index of real wages increased by only 6 percent in this ten-year period, and while a gap between productivity growth and real wage growth is common among advanced capitalist nations, nowhere is it as great as in Japan. From a macropolicy perspective Japanese production was being limited by a lack of markets. Increasing wages would create a domestic expansion. While higher wages would impose a higher cost structure on producers already faced with a dramatically appreciated yen, and greater social spending adds to an already large deficit, yet given foreign pressures there seemed to be little choice.

The Maekawa Report (named after its senior author, Haruo Maekawa, a former BOJ head and officially "The Report of the Advisory Group on Economic Structural Adjustment for International Harmony" submitted to Prime Minister Nakasone on April 7, 1986) is a pivotal document. It recommended a reorientation of Japan's growth strategy away from export dependence to a domestic-led growth. In one stroke it spoke to the complaints of both the Americans with whom Japan runs a huge trade surplus and of ordinary citizens who complain of "Rich Japan, Poor Japanese." The ordinary citizens' demands for a better quality of life through a domestic Keynesianism potentially provide the market no longer available to Japanese products abroad. The document was a transitional one. It represented a departure from "growthism."

Japan moved to comply with the spirit of American requests. Even the Structural Impediments Initiative demands are being met with what one can consider to be, by historical standards, all due speed. Domestic opposition to some of the liberalizations demanded remains heavy, and it is not clear whether any American administration could do better on changes that would cut as deep. In fact, the United States had not kept its promises on reducing budget deficits and was not doing much to upgrade American education nor on the other "concessions" the Japanese were so kind as to suggest needed our attention. For example, Japan pledges to spend over $3 trillion in ten years on infrastructure. It expends over 6 percent of its GNP on public investment, compared with about 1 percent that is spent by the United States. It is ironic that the United States has pushed more *infura* spending on the Japanese. Japanese infrastructure spending is setting records, despite the labor shortages and the stretched construction industry capacity. The LDP's strongest financial supporters in the construction industry, acting like patriots and the politicians doling out the largesse, stagger under the load of carrying symbols of their patriotic duty well done off to the bank. Whether they were doing more than paying lip service to the familiar complaint that the in group nature of Japanese business dealings prevents foreigners from getting fair consideration or whether the interrelated restructuring of the Maekawa Report and the Structural Impediments Initiative agreements signals adequate enough change to satisfy the United States is another question.

In 1991 the Commission on National Living, an advisory body to the prime minister, in its report, "Looking to a Society Giving Priority to Individual Life," pointed out the reason the Japanese people were unable to lead an affluent life, one commensurate with the great economic power of the nation, was that Japan is a "companycentric society" that emphasizes only economic efficiency and growth. That leading sectors of the Japanese elite recognize the costs of the Japanese system is encouraging. However, such statements were met with skepticism by those who would like to see a more people-oriented economy. The Japanese government has long issued pronouncements of this sort. What Japanese policy influentials sought was a basis for continued growth under new circumstances.

The headline writers taken by Morita's call for higher wages for Japanese workers and the creation of a living standard appropriate to the world's second-largest economic power, which was mentioned earlier, did not fully understand Morita's critique of the Japanese system. He criticized Japanese companies for relentlessly pursuing market shares by accepting razor-thin profit margins that no Western company would tolerate. He said the Japanese should take it easier, pay workers more, and raise stockholder's dividends. Japan, he said, must "reinvent itself to blend with the prevailing attitudes and practices of international business."[8] The pressure for such a fundamental change in strategy was not solely a matter of good international relations in an immediate public relations sense.

Morita offered a six-point plan that outlined areas in which Japanese industry needed to apply new thinking because it was out of sync with Western norms: salary levels, work hours, stockholder dividends, community involvement, subcontractor relationships, and environmental management. Morita divided areas of corporate activity in two; those that should be driven by competition and those in which cooperation and harmonization should be the focus. He told a Lisbon Trilateral Commission gathering in 1992, in remarks that were already referred to, that economic competition should take place on, and perhaps even be limited to, "the playing field of creativity." "By that I mean," he added, "corporations should focus on areas such as technological innovation, product planning, and marketing," the "three creativities," as Morita called them. The six areas noted should be taken out of competition to the maximal extent possible. "Target zones" would be agreed upon by decision makers. He thought this might first be done within the Trilateral Commission itself and then passed on to governments for further discussion and ratification. There would be controls of chief executive compensation. Minimum wages and dividend ratios would also be harmonized. Morita's goal is to make the rules of capitalist global competition "clearer, markets more transparent, and mutual suspicion a thing of the past." This dream of orderly competition and harmonious class relations that would allow all concerned to have a voice in debating the optimal balance between areas of competition and areas of economic harmonization is as old as the system itself.

It is easy to be cynical about its chances and even to point out that more leisure, higher dividends, and so forth are just what a consumer electronics firm with all sorts of new diversions to fill time freed and absorb higher incomes, needs in this world. One hundred years ago the leaders of American economic life worked out gentlemen's agreements that proved ephemeral and merged competitors after strategic alliances proved insufficient to regulate competition. They sought collaborative relations in the Trilateral Commission of its time and place, the National Civic Federation. At the end of the twentieth century, as markets in the advanced economies become saturated and the global economy reaches the stage of relative maturity that the individual advanced economies of the late-nineteenth century experienced, observers can be excused for suspicions of accommodations worked out under such exclusive auspices, Morita's view notwithstanding.[9]

The need to slow down the Japanese production system was not simply a matter of needing to respond to the increasing pariah status in which the Japanese found themselves. It was also the actual global economic situation that underlay the growth of hostility. By the early 1990s even Japan's most successful firms could no longer justify the costs of the standard breakneck race for new products and the proliferation of models. The market was just not there to support the high costs of product development and extensive product lines. Toshiba, for example, which had been bringing out a dozen new laptop computer models per year, slackened its pace. It entered joint ventures with IBM to build flat-panel displays and joined in other strategic partnerships, as noted. Other major corporations likewise slowed their introduction of new models and sought international alliances.

Japan was a relative latecomer to working in foreign cultural contexts. Some analysts argued that its own powerfully cohesive internal culture would be a disadvantage in the twenty-first century because the need to integrate foreign managers and professionals as equals within Japanese companies would be difficult to achieve. Foreigners would not have a chance to get to the top in the closed Japanese corporate culture, and even at lower levels they would lack mobility within the corporate structure. Largely because of this (and because the United States has allowed our education system to atrophy and because it seems unable to get its fiscal house in order) Lester Thurow gives the nod to Europe in the three-way race. [10] Jacques Attali, advisor to the French president and Europeanist guru, agrees. In counterpoint, Ishihara saw Japan's unique culture as its strongest asset. He saw America as Number Three (becoming a granary to Europe much like Poland was to Flanders in the sixteenth century). He saw the United States, having lost its lead, turning inward. The futurists differ sharply and for some thinkers patriotic hubris seemed to play a large part in the analysis and choice of victor. To Attali, Europe would once again be the power; for Ishihara, Japan would lead. Contemporaneously to books by these individuals Henry Nau wrote about *The Myth of America's Decline*. One could choose one's mirror not only as to the identity of "the winner," but of the optimal cultural economy. Uneasily combined commitment to individualism and free enterprise, a suspicion of central authority, and the forces of Big Government and Big Business, the cultural economy of the United States could be viewed a powerful obstacle to economic restructuring based on state-led development. Japan's greater cultural homogeneity may be more of an advantage in a slow-growing world economy even if it might be a disadvantage in the ways Thurow suggests.

Along with the tendency for regional blocs to form and a global economy to emerge there are also disturbing centripetal forces at work. In the discussion of the power of the global economy to set terms of incorporation for nation-states and regional economies, the importance of the cultural difference is typically underestimated. Individuals and communities seeking shelter from internationalizing forces, which are perceived as threatening their well-being, turn to narrow nationalisms based on ethnic claims or religion, leading to powerful separatist movements and demands for local independence, the power of which economists tend to underestimate.

Popular Tensions and Identity Politics

I am convinced that ethnic and nationalist narrowness will continue to be a severe, indeed determining, problem around the world over the extended future we face, especially if national competitiveness takes the form of a negative sum game in which insecurity increases for a large part of each country's citizens. In Japan, the other side of cultural homogeneity has become a destructive chauvinism in periods of stress. As Hall has written:

> What makes Japan fundamentally different is that its racially based national consciousness and exclusivity, far from being the objects of attack, disdain, and efforts at amelioration, are openly sanctioned by the intellectual establishment, public consensus, and government policy. . . . The problem, in short, is an ideological one—in the end the product of artificially willed, intellectual constructs running the whole length of Japan's 120 years of post–Meiji Restoration modern history. [11]

I am also troubled. Living in a glass house called the United States of America I am unwilling to throw stones without also reflecting on our own practices. Nor would I think Europeans would have much left to throw that they had not hurled at each other and at foreign residents in their midst. This is not to say that Hall does not have the essence of the Japanese side, yet the institutional racism that perpetuates a separate but unequal life space for the overwhelming majority of Americans of color needs to be faced and it is not now being honestly confronted. The emotional core irrationalities of identity politics and their material base in scarcity and uncertainty can erupt. It is for this reason if no other that stabilizing accommodations to globalization need be sought.

In a slow-growth global economy it is possible that Japan's developmentalist state may get a new lease on life as its management abilities are seen as still essential in such an uncertain international context. The macro-context will play an important role in nation-state level decision making. It would seem of limited value to speculate on such matters, but what they do raise is the relation between how Japan will adjust to globalization as it develops in a world of slower growth in which productive capacities outstrip ability to sell potential output. The examination of Japan's institutional development and transformation in the postwar era took place within the context of remarkable global economic expansion. In such a positive sum situation competitiveness could be examined ignoring system stability issues. The expansion of the Japanese production system and even the attention paid to the overextension and fragility of the financial system do not give sufficient weight to tendencies to overaccumulation of the means of production on the one hand and the inability to meet basic needs of a large part of the global population on the other. Without the kind of high-wage-led development in Japan and the West more generally the world risks a global Keynesian crisis. Everybody cannot succeed by exporting more than they import.

The United States, Japan, and other nations found themselves in the early 1990s with excess capacity, large public debt, and increasing problems of governability as incumbency became a burden and voter dissatisfaction grew nearly everywhere. The global economic slowdown exerted a strong pressure on governments that they were unable to meet. With slower growth, living standards did not go up as people had come to expect. With larger deficits governments were unable to make side payments to reduce interest-group discontent. Internationalization itself seemed to be responsible for growing inequalities within nations as those connected to globalization, selling their products and talents on a world market, seemed to outpace those tied to national or local economies.

The new competition works far better in an expanding macro-context. The promise of rapid innovation, rising productive potential, and unleashing continuous growth is undercut in a stagnant global economy. For the individual producer the game is competing, surviving, and prevailing no matter what the larger context. For government decision makers and citizens, however, the question of stability looms large. The assumption that a new mode of accumulation will simply expand until it absorbs workers still trapped in older regimes of accumulation is flawed on several grounds that should be clearer in an era of slower economic growth. First, slower growth highlights the large segments of the economy that are not part of the dynamic sector. The new model of flexible specialization relies on the continued existence of Fordist producers for much remaining standardized production (who employ only part of those needing work). Second, its flexibility depends on large numbers of contingent low-paid workers without social benefits or employment security. The number of such individuals is likely to grow in a period of economic stagnation. Third, the new mode of accumulation thinking presumes a dynamic Say's Law. Rising productivity fuels market expansion to absorb potential output increases. This is unlikely in a period of slow growth. Attention must be paid to traditional Keynesian concerns, but in a new global economy context that complicates policymaking.

The trajectory of globalization on this model is for international agency technocrats to ride over local interests to enforce internationalization-oriented accommodations among transnational corporations. I think it likely that as first regional blocs and then a global institutional regime is formed, the policy debate will be an expanded version of the same three-sided affair as it has been at the national level. The three main positions in response are: a free market, deregulation, privatization thrust along Reagan–Thatcher lines; second, a bureaucratic regulationist one, approximating corporatism in which the peak organizations of government, large capital, and organized labor work out some form of planned markets; and third, a democratic participatory model of localizing governance that attempts to move the locus of decision making downward so that people can have more say over the decisions that control their lives. Each of these three approaches has strengths and weaknesses.

From the point of view of the most internationally competitive in each nation-state formation an openness on the part of government to the internationalization process is advantageous. Efforts to subsidize "losers" comes at their expense, and in a competitive situation any taxation or regulation of market freedoms can be seen as undermining competitiveness of locally domiciled actors. The downside, of course, is the abandonment of many citizens to economic hardship and the undermining of national community. Movement toward a global corporatism promises a smoother transition and a governance structure in which difficult trade-offs can be made among interest groups and some form of planning to ease otherwise destabilizing changes being institutionalized. These decision makers, however, will also be remote from the voters in each country, who may find them unresponsive to their desires, favoring instead more internationalized interests and the bidding of the most powerful states in the world community at the expense of the environment, workers, small businesses, local governments, and the unique concerns of these less-powerful interests.

The bottom-line politics in the United States and Europe at the end of the postwar era was a Japanese-style accommodation to corporate priorities. Stephen Gill has called this development the discourse of the new constitutionalism, by which he means "the move towards construction of legal or constitutional devices to remove or insulate substantially the new economic institutions from popular scrutiny or democratic accountability."[12] The fear raised is of technocratic solutions by distant bureaucracies, the very sort of structure that the Japanese have developed so successfully within their domestic political economy and which is so partial to corporate perspectives and to the imperatives of accumulation. Such dominance creates a norm in which current working-class consumption and the provision of social welfare goods and services takes a back seat.

The developmentalist state in this regard acts in the interests of capital accumulation so as to act, to coin a phrase, as the executive committee for the ruling class far more completely than under more democratic governance forms. As Stephen Marglin has argued, and the point can be extended to a developmentalist state, "By mediating between producer and consumer, the capitalist organization sets aside much more for expanding and improving plant and equipment than individuals would if they could control the pace of capital accumulation."[13] If the social function of hierarchical control can be said to provide for the accumulation of capital, then we may say that the Japanese model of capitalism has pursued accumulation with a singlemindedness that has proven more successful than other variants. It has done so by combining a high-investment rate with rapid innovation of product and process. To a substantial extent its success has been predicated on holding down labor's share and governmental social spending.

Contemporary orthodoxy from the International Monetary Fund's prescription for the poorest of debtor nations to the hard-headed realism of politicians in the advanced nations calling for passage of balanced-budget amendments and cutting taxes and spending is that austerity will solve economic problems. The game is to compete more efficiently in the global economy by being a low-cost producer. This is a game that some can win relative to others, but which many more will lose as stagnation overtakes a larger and larger portion of the world's people. The macro-context, on the contrary, must be one of coordinated expansion within which a positive sum competition can take place. In such a macro-context some of the lessons being drawn from the Japanese case are legitimate.

Many thoughtful Americans looking at the Japanese success have come to see our problem as one of creating institutions of governance "that can pursue policies of sufficient coherence, consistency, foresight, and stability that the national welfare is not sacrificed for narrow or temporary gain."[14] While I am sympathetic with the need for such coherence, consistency, foresight, stability of policy, and the creation of governing arrangements that can pursue such policies, I also worry about the accumulation bias that privileges growth efficiency over distributive justice and equity on the lame excuse that we can always attend to such matters out of the growth dividend. There is no reason to think that there will ever be "jam today" on such reasoning. Indeed, by overriding the checks and balances and further centralizing authority and removing it from democratic pressures there is no assurance that such a streamlined governance structure would not be a vehicle for social discord and greater inequality (even if it did make the economy "more efficient").

Participatory democratic forms of decentralization, while they address the problem of overcentralization and the absence of sufficient responsiveness, may lack a cohesiveness in which truly global questions can be decided and necessary choices among interests made. Given the mobility of capital, decentralization may not be the most effective form of governance. Global governance structures are important, but if they are to be democratically responsive they must be inclusive, capable of response to democratic pressures to place living conditions high on the priorities of the society. It is no easy task to develop such a democratic structure.

Worker Involvement and Social Citizenship

It has been suggested that workplace participation may be just the vehicle called for because by involving employees in the governance of their company they gain experience and broaden their understanding of the realities of economics. Here again there is an appeal to the Japanese experience. Groupism is seen as a step to greater citizen participation in the decisions that affect people's lives. This represents a serious idealizing of what actually takes place in Japanese industry. Companies are not run democratically and participation is limited to improving the competitiveness of the firm. Changes that would benefit workers but not increase bottom-line productivity are not usually considered, and group processes are closely controlled by the company. Second, the extensive participation is based on implicit threats on the one hand, and the long-term employment cooperating workers are guaranteed on the other. Yet, should American firms move further in a Japanese direction, they do so in a period in which job security has become tenuous for most workers. In our context an institutional form responsive to worker interests may provide the needed participatory link.

While the American literature of the 1970s and early 1980s showed a person who had persisted in the same job for a few years was likely to continue employment in it for a long time to come, job tenure seemed far less secure by the early 1990s. The lower-wage solution to competitive pressures and a downsizing, contracting out, and greater use of temporary workers also approximates the dualistic structure of the Japanese economy. It brings intense exploitation of such secondary workers, who are not able to achieve a middle-class living standard. The intensification of workers in primary-sector jobs is also replicating the Japanese pattern. While one may say there is nothing to be done except expect such market pressures, it is the rare person who sees such increasing polarization on the one hand, and work intensification on the other, as good per se. Can the United States find ways to adopt the positive aspects of Japanese-style industrial relations while avoiding its negative aspects? Given increased foreign competition a more productive work force is surely essential.

Many large firms in the United States attempt to combat alienation, absenteeism, and an antagonistic capital–labor climate through use of employee-involvement programs of various kinds. The costs of the Taylorist dispensation, with its separation between the management that controlled workers through layers of supervision and detailed direction and a work force that was told to check their heads at the door and just follow orders, increasingly recognized and steps were taken to follow Japanese-style cooperative labor relations practices. In one study of ninety-two unionized manufacturing plants of employee participation programs in place in 1986 it was found that over 90 percent had been established after 1980.[15] The evidence on the effectiveness of these programs was mixed. They do seem to positively influence perceptions of both employees and employers that workplace conditions and relations have improved, but tangible, measurable gains have been elusive in the main. Although some studies have claimed much for such programs serious methodological questions lead one to take such enthusiastic findings with a large measure of salt. In a rather pessimistic evaluation Kelley and Harrison write,

> [R]ather than being a vehicle of liberation from bureaucratic structure, LMCs [labor management committees] may simply have become another grafted on layer of bureaucratic structure itself which helps sustain commitment to the status quo. By taking precious time away from productive activity, and by failing to generate radically new, more productive methods EI [employee involvement] just *adds* to cost.[16]

The American corporation is moving toward the Japanese pattern in establishing ex ante risk-sharing agreements that promise that if the firm succeeds, then the worker will in effect be treated as a partner in the enterprise. Without some mechanism of countervailing force the worker may find the company only a fair-weather partner. Independent trade unions have traditionally been the device for assuring the workers a collective voice and the solidaristic strength to bargain and negotiate on more equal terms with their employer. Yet, because companies have seen unions as their enemy they have pursued a two-pronged attack—trying to destroy independent unionism and attempting to win employee loyalty. Efforts at worker involvement have increasingly been attempted as an alternative to unionism, and even where unions persist they come to more closely resemble Japanese-style enterprise unionism. While it is at the plant level that work processes, labor relations, and compensation are negotiated, in the U.S. case this transpires in the context of constant fear of plant closings, outsourcing, and layoffs, all of which are absent for core workers in Japan, who face the realities of the competitive environment as part of a corporate family that will stay together. In the American case the company is always ready to say goodbye to their labor partner. This lack of countervailing force in the contemporary U.S. system is a problem for its effective operation.

Individual American companies will continue to seek ways to make employee involvement work, but they are up against serious obstacles. Many are unwilling or feel unable to provide the quid pro quo of employee security and gainsharing with their employees in any meaningful way, as the massive layoffs in the early 1990s by IBM, General Motors, and other giants of American industry demonstrated. The efforts to become a mean and lean competitor undercut the basis of "a one big family, we are in this together" proclamation. If these companies had difficulty maintaining their commitment to their workers most smaller companies could not even attempt new labor relations. The failure of macroeconomic policy to provide a stable full-employment economy and the absence of *keiretsu*-style relationships that would allow for labor redeployment and the claims of stockholders on corporate profits, which prevented the high degree of labor hoarding by the firm in periods of downturn, means American companies do not provide for their employees as do their Japanese counterparts.

In an economy in which mobile workers can sell their labor power as they choose and to job hop, companies are less able to capture investments in training since their ability to discount over the long-term relationship assumed in Japan is tenuous at best. A firm that offers portable education and training in a competitive labor market finds itself with higher costs and a less-desirable work force as its best employees seek to cash in their skills since they command higher compensation by taking advantage of short-term employment at the skill-providing firm before moving on to employers willing to pay a premium to bid them away. Such shortcomings suggest the importance of public investment in education and training, active labor market intervention, and stronger effort to maintain full employment to preserve the value of these investments in human capital in the context of bringing the bottom half of the labor queue up to international standards, and finally, stronger rather than weaker unions.

This last prescription, reinvigorating the concept and the institution of unionism, goes against the tide of the late 20th century. In one of the few empirical studies to examine unionized and nonunionized companies over a range of sizes through extensive surveys Kelley and Harrison have also found that what makes employee involvement work in the sense of measurably increasing productivity is the presence of independent trade unions. The protection and "voice" a union provides for individual workers create the context in which trust has a materially solid base and cooperation is effectively forthcoming. The residual apprehension workers feel without their own organization (separate from management) is well advised. Changes in top leadership, market pressures, and opportunism on the part of the corporation are all very real issues. Even with stronger independent trade unions some institutional innovation, perhaps along the lines of Germany's Work Constitution Act (which instituted works councils in 1952), may be in order. [17]

The reconstitution of viable unionism in the U.S. context or some other institutionalized collective solidarity organized form of worker cooperation may be essential for social stability. A "free" market for labor just has too many severe social costs. It would have to be an inclusive form and would require greater employer commitment to job security and, in turn, reflect greater willingness on the part of workers to participate. Their union would be a vehicle through which they could claim a fair share of productivity gains within the constraints of the larger economy in which their employer must function. The workers in a unionized environment who are unhappy have a voice—their union. [18] There is now an extensive literature arguing the efficiency benefits of trade union voice that treats unions as institutions that give collective expression to labor's concerns enhancing communication and providing management with valuable information, thereby adding substantially to the bottom line of firms able to listen. [19] At the same time there is a need as well for an expanded role for social citizenship so that people are not only part of workplace organizations with their narrow job focus, but for work issues to be considered in a societal context.

Labor unions have to fundamentally change if they are to survive and protect their workers. They will have to accept a threefold responsibility. [20] They need to participate in increasing company efficiency and innovation even as they bargain over sharing gains, and they must never lose sight of their first mission, protecting the interests of their workers, to do this. They must also learn to act as conscious agents for class-inclusive structural change. This calls for a long-run view on the part of labor in the context of maximum job security and exacting severance procedures, as well as a social conception of investment decision making. Coherent flexibility might be a good description of such arrangements, which provide for maximizing healthy economic growth and the worker's well-being, but not at the expense of excluding others from equal consideration. An inclusive social policy would need to contest the movement toward economic dualism with a commmitment to building new and empowering societal institutions of inclusiveness. [21] The state role from such a vantage point would be to provide freedom *from* external coercions, not merely freedom *to* lead a better life, through positive activities of an empowering government working in a participatory responsive fashion as close to the local community as possible while structuring national and global constraints in ways that allow for and support individual and community development. A final constraint would also be necessary. The idea that some stockholders are entitled to maximum profits at the cost of all other stockholders needs to be challenged. The Japanese did this, as I have noted earlier, with profoundly important implications for improving the efficiency of their economic performance in the postwar era. Even more dynamic social efficiency gains are possible but require new global level governance structures.

The Japanese system is in need of substantial modification from this social efficiency perspective. The speedups and extreme exploitation (by international standards) of the Japanese system needs to be addressed. Enterprise unions put workers in each plant into intense competition against workers elsewhere and seriously limit what the union is able to contemplate as in their members' interest. Industrywide bargaining, international labor accords for regulation to enforce workplace safeguards, limit the working day, and establishing norms for vacations and other benefits are essential. There can only be a leveling up that will provide security for the workers of the world through a globally binding accommodation. Such regulation comes as the fruit of strong local and national organization. To protect their members labor unions must be part of a social movement serving consumer, environmental, and other quality-of-life concerns that would otherwise be ignored in a market economy. Whether or not this leads to some further variant of the social control of industry as some hope and others fear is a different question from the need for socially desirable constraints on greed being firmly guaranteed in a democratically responsive institutional setting. If capitalism cannot guarantee basic human rights of a social and economic kind, then it has a weak claim on worker and community loyalties.

Democracy in the Global Marketplace

The predominance of a meaningfully democratic movement is crucial because left on their own corporations and bureaucrats will pursue accumulation and to a great extent overlook distributional questions and important social costs. In the past it has always been an aroused and informed citizenry that has proven capable of preventing such abuse by the powerful. If meaningful democracy by an involved citizenry is in charge, markets and statist regulations will be structured quite differently than in their absence. Efforts by the powerful to limit such participation lead to a striking-out by ordinary people who feeling powerless tend to say no to the system in whatever way they can. The negation of the negation, however, is not a positive vision, as Hegel and Marx surely should have taught us.

At the present stage we are more likely to see benign internationalism pushed aside by nationalist fears. Tension at the international level easily develops so that friends may act in their own self interest at the expense of their erstwhile allies. As Kazuo Chiba, former Japanese ambassador to the United Kingdom and former chairman of the GATT Council, told the 1991 Tokyo gathering of the Trilateral Commission, "[T]he biggest concern for the Japanese is that the Americans and the Europeans will get together and stab us in the back. The biggest concern for the Europeans is that the Americans and Japanese will do this to them."

I would suggest the possibility that the world today is where the United

States was 100 years ago. In the 1880s and 1890s there was overcapacity in relation to existing markets to absorb output. The large corporations could not all keep growing. The merger movement at the turn of the century consolidated smaller (though of course quite large) competitors into monopolies and oligopolistic giants. The strategic international alliances today seem to me to auger a similar development in a global context representing an analogous phenomenon. (The continued existence and indeed place in the new scheme of things for smaller, flexible niche producers and the rise of newcomers to global status would not belie the centrality of this tendency.) There is surely no reason to think that existing antitrust laws of individual nation-states or regulatory mechanisms are capable of addressing such a development. The concentration of economic power a century ago gave way to a countermovement by farmers, industrial workers, and middle-class reformers to the growing arrogance of wealth and power. Today nationalisms complicate matters, but the forces may play out in response to similar pressures. I cannot pursue this speculation here, but if I am right these matters will affect Japan's trajectory as well as our own.

Identity Political Conflict and a New Internationalism

While in the past Japan saw internationalization as a way to better preserve its isolation—sending personnel abroad to learn, inviting experts for short stays, and the export and import of goods and not a mixing of peoples—in the new world insularity is being challenged. How the Japanese respond will not be within the control of the sophisticated West handlers whom we have grown used to seeing on our televisions speaking English, with their intimate grasp of who we are, and their clear agenda of what they want us to think about Japan. The future course of events will be decided by domestic politics and consciousness of more typical Japanese, and we do not know them very well.

The images that come to my mind are of frightened and insecure groups on both sides of the Pacific. I remember a chance encounter with one of Japan's popular comics, an all-smiling, laugh-a-minute Shecky Greene Borscht Belt vaudevillian who regularly has Westerners on his popular TV show. The *gaijin* typically lack a command of Japanese, which makes it easy to subject them to in-the-face ridicule. The day I encountered him by a famous ancient gate in Tokyo his flacks had rounded up hungry Westerners, black and white, Europeans and Americans, all of whom towered over their host (who nonetheless controlled them all). They were about to engage in an eating contest, to make fools of themselves for a fist full of yen in prize money. The rubes I spoke to in the group knew what was going down, but "hey man, trying to make a living in Tokyo is tough." The subtle and not-so-subtle interplay of getting back at the West, showing Japanese superiority, and "good clean fun" was disgusting. The local audience loved it. I think of visual racist presences, fixed in my memory, as in a Christmas Santa I saw outside a Hiroshima department store, a huge fat Black Santa with enormous exaggerated lips and bulging eyes wishing passersby a "Many Christmas." Such examples can easily be multiplied. They manifest Japanese fear of the other and an arrogance of racialist superiority.

The powerful voice of Japan's uber-rightist Shintaro Ishihara, whose book, *The Japanese Who Can Say No: Why Japan Will Be First Among Equals* (co-authored with Sony's Akio Morita before Morita embarrassedly withdrew his name when a bootlegged English version of this initially Japanese-only text began to circulate in Washington), created quite a stir in this country for its "frankness" urging Japan to stand up to Americans. He defends Japanese purity and condemns Americans as "virulent racists." He tells interviewers things like the 1937 rape of Nanking never took place. "It is only a story," he says, "concocted by China to make Japan look bad."[22] The Japanese media, while it covered the international storm that followed the statement, did not question the accuracy of Ishihara's contention. Indeed, Japanese generally know little or nothing of the realities of Japanese imperialism, seeing themselves as the victims of white racism even as they take a superior attitude toward blacks and Asians. As Japan grows more powerful such attitudes will have far-reaching impact.

Ishihara's position includes an understanding of historical truth that while offensive in many ways contains elements that Americans need to hear. Ishihara believes that "the war was an American set-up and that Japan was trapped into it. In other words, the Japanese attack on Pearl Harbor was an American *coup de main*." Why should Japan and Germany be forced to apologize? "No one has ever heard apologies from America, Britain, France, and Holland for their imperialist pasts. Yet these nations," Ishihara goes on, "were all guilty, at one time or another, of plundering their colonies and treating their people inhumanely." As he sees it, speaking like some latter day Stalinist discussing ambiguous legacies that nonetheless are deemed "historically progressive," there is good and bad in Japan's imperial past. Japan was the only "colored" nation among the great powers. The colonial war in Asia should be viewed in terms of Japan's role in freeing Asia from the Westerners and encouraging the liberation movements of the postwar era "seeking exploitation from their white colonial masters."[23] These differences in viewpoint represent a continuing tale of Rashomon Mirror foreign affairs.[24]

I would expect as the Pacific Economy grows more powerful in relation to the Atlantic one, there will be a revisionist accounting of the colonial period in Asian history in which the Western powers will not come off as well and the example of Japan standing up to the whites will be privileged (maybe by Hollywood studios under new ownership). The John Wayne version of *Back to Bataan* may not in the future be as acceptable as it once was. In time much of the real story of Western imperialism in Asia may become known in the United States and Europe, although we may be expected to continue to undercount the costs of colonialism to peoples of color. The atrocities committed by the Japanese in the Pacific are now, and are unfortunately likely to remain, mostly unknown to the general public in Japan. For three decades historian Saburo Ienaga has had a civil suit disputing the Ministry of Education's attempt to force him to rewrite a high-school text (if it was to be allowed in the schools).

The Ministry of Education has a long and odious history as a Ministry of Truth forever doing battle with the leftist teacher's union to reinstitute strict discipline reminiscent of prewar state Shintoism, "moral purification," respect for the emperor, the *Hinomaru* (the imperial rising sun flag), the former national anthem, and so forth. They want to show Japanese actions in World War II in a more patriotic, but less historically accurate, light.

The forces of the ultra-right are a significant presence in Japan. The threat, and actual use of violence by Japanese "patriotic" organizations to enforce conformity is a part of Japan's political landscape. In 1990 there was the famous attempt to murder the mayor of Nagasaki after he had the courage to say publicly what most Japanese perhaps knew but were afraid to say—that Emperor Hirohito bore some responsibility for the war. There remains a coerced historic amnesia over the Japanese brutalities during the Pacific War. There are the pilgrimages to the shrines of Japanese war dead by leading political figures to which so many Japanese object because such places are symbols of unrepentant Japanese imperialism (e.g., the *Yasukuni* Shrine's "Memorial to the Heroic Martyrs of the War Crime Trials," which celebrates those who "were executed, committed suicide, or died in prison, their innocence unrecognized, due to the one-sided trial conducted by the victorious nations of the Great East Asia War"). These and other instances remind one of the ongoing efforts to revive Japanese militarism and to intimidate those committed to the Japanese constitution.

The constitution is a symbol of great moment. It was imposed by General MacArthur on the Japanese. Because of this some think a new indigenous one should be written. Others, having come to accept the wisdom of the peace constitution adopted in 1946, think it would be to "raise the lid of hell,"[25] to unloose the demons of reaction, to open the question of the basic direction of Japan to the dangers of a new constitution-making process. The constitution rejects Japan's past in decisive terms. Article 20 requires that "the state and its organs shall refrain from religious education or any other religious activity." It was under this article that many objected to the traditional Shinto enthronement of the new emperor with the subservience of state officials, and so forth. Most famous is Article 9 with its well-known words, "The Japanese people forever renounce war as a sovereign right of the nation and the threat or use of force as means of settling international disputes," followed by, "In order to accomplish the aim of the preceding paragraph, land, sea, and air forces, as well as other war potential, will never be maintained. The right to belligerency of the state will not be recognized."

Even though Japan spends only 1 percent of its GNP on the military, 1 percent of the world's second-largest GNP was the world's third-highest spending level on a national military capacity (in the years when the Soviet Union was still a game Number Two). Even though the Japanese armed forces' numbers rank them twenty-fifth or so in the world (tenth in Asia), size, as we know, should never obscure quality and efficiency. The potential performance of Japanese technology in an age of high-tech warfare should give pause to those in the United States clamoring for Japan to more fully rearm. There are also some loud voices within Japan demanding the reconstitution of Japanese militarism. The sound trucks that proclaim the need to restore the emperor to his rightful place may be ignored by most people on busy downtown streets, but that they are allowed to operate there is a result of policy complicity. Analogous ultra-leftist activity would draw police countermeasures.

The majority of Japanese remain opposed to upgrading the armed forces and most strongly support no use, manufacture, or presence of nuclear weapons on Japanese soil. The embarrassing failure of the ruling faction of the LDP to gain acceptance for a Japanese presence in Kuwait in 1991 is indicative of the strong pacifism of the Japanese public. Japan's Defense Agency Director General Sohei Miyashita himself emphasized in the Diet debate the need to let each soldier decide for himself whether to use his weapon to defend himself if attacked! Elements of the Japanese ruling elite also fear militarism as bad for business both because of the reaction within Asia and acceptance of the argument that the road to national decline is paved with military pretensions. Yet, over the years, and under American Cold War prodding, a mighty "Self-Defense Force" (SDF) was established, and after much rangling in 1992 the Diet passed a law allowing the SDF to go overseas to take part as noncombatants in UN peacekeeping missions. [26]

Japan's first overseas deployment of the new era was to Cambodia in 1992. Yasushi Akashi, who headed the United Nations Transitional Authority in Cambodia (UNTAC), made clear the extent to which this operation represents a new departure in the minds of Japanese policy officials:

> The UNTAC mandate goes very deeply into the area of traditional sovereignty. The UN has never been given such extensive authority in a noncolonial situation, in an independent country. . . . I do not want you to think of our Cambodian operation as simply a peacekeeping operation. In fact, it is the civilian part which is most remarkable and extensive. We have a civil administration component in order to assure a neutral political environment. We have direct control over foreign affairs, national defense, finance, internal security, and information. [27]

In this nation-building project Akashi spoke of the need to redress harm done by Thai and Singapore capital, which had swept into the country to take advantage of privatization of state enterprises for the quick buck, the need for long-time horizons.

Akashi saw Japan's involvement and the use of the United Nations as the umbrella for consensus interventions in failed nations to building new cultural economies supported by developmentalist institutions of governance as a way of decreasing global tensions and establishing a new international order in which people everywhere would come to have an interest in being part of the expanding division of labor in an integrated, cohesive world system. This would be an internationalization of the Japanese system of social relations, cooperation that respects hierarchy and order in which the benefits of accommodation come to be seen as more desirable than antagonistic efforts to achieve advantage through antisystemic violence. [28] Michio Morishima has called the focus on diplomacy and cultural exchange the software approach as opposed to the hardware approach of using tanks and missiles. While the generalization of software's growing importance over hardware may carry over into international politics the reality in any specific instance could be quite different (e.g., on the ground in Cambodia) where the killing continued and the software seemed to adjust to functioning under local restraints.

UNTAC, criticized for promising too much, was mired down by the corruption of both Cambodian and UN officials. The country's prime minister, Hun Sen, had been among the main beneficiaries of privatization and was personally collecting outlandish rents by UN personnel for housing and office space. The UN bureaucracy, which received huge salaries and expense accounts (many earnings more in a day in Cambodia than a normal month's salary back home) and those arranging multimillion dollar supply contracts to mysterious firms whose owners were not disclosed, bring to mind the early days of the Alliance for Progress as another seemingly idealistic nation pumped money into Latin America to restore stability to a region, only to be defeated by the progressive imperial technocrat's innocence and the realities of belligerent's self-interest. As Japanese peacekeepers were killed by the Khmer Rouge, who obviously did not want peaceful elections and a transition to a new accumulation strategy for Cambodia, Japan was forced to confront the difficulty of encouraging such a model of social reconstruction. The Japanese can hardly count on employing large numbers of Cambodian workers any time soon.

There has been a long-standing split within the LDP between business-oriented and military rearmament views. The polls of the mainstream LDP debate are set by Kiichi Miyazawa, who puts economic power first and sees a military buildup as dangerous to Japan's acceptance in the world and therefore as costly to its bottom-line interests, and Yasuhiro Nakasone, who urges Japan to rewrite its constitution and take an activist role in world affairs, including a military one. While Miyazawa supported the pacifistic Yosida Doctrine, named after the postwar prime minister who urged the policy of a nonmilitary role in the world, the foreign minister in Miyazawa's cabinet, Michio Watanabe, holds views similar to Nakasone's, as does Ichiro Ozawa. Ozawa was three years old at the end of World War II and sees a military role under the UN peacekeeping aegis as part of being a responsible participant in world events.

Naohiro Amaya, a leading figure of Japan's postwar economic restructuring as the innovative vice minister for international affairs at the MITI, captures much of what is driving Japan against its will to a higher-profile role in world politics when he writes that the Japanese can in effect hide behind their peace constitution if they want, ''but they must be prepared to endure a considerable amount of humiliation from the world community, similar to a hard-nosed merchant who will gladly endure being spit upon with contempt so long as he can amass his fortune.''[29] He asks if this is really the way Japan wants to be perceived. Even though Japanese politicians, in Amaya's view, care little intrinsically about the rest of the world, which does not generate any votes, he thought Japan should seriously consider what role it can play in the world and make sacrifices, which are necessary ''if it wishes to survive.'' This is strong stuff, but not untypical of far-sighted Establishment figures and representative of a response that has begun to creep into official pronouncements by Japan's political leaders now as well. In the West we may ask whether the voices of Washington policymakers hell-bent on rebuilding Japan's military capacities represent our best interest.

While some suggest it is the better part of wisdom to adapt to the Western sense of what Japan's role in the world should be (at least the consensus Western policymaker view whose wisdom I question), other voices argue for a greater confidence in the route Japan has taken under MacArthur's prodding in giving up the normal ways of big powers. Japan, having been an aggressor and an imperialist much like the Western powers, is now able to offer a different vision. Japan could lead the way in international diplomacy by urging that problems be resolved peacefully and that other nations deescalate, disarm, and think of accommodation and mutual respect rather than solving disputes through violence. A revival of Japanese militarization would be quite tragic. Japan has the potential to help the world toward a different form of conflict resolution. The issue is far from settled and it is still possible that Japan may become a new kind of superpower, one that does not settle disputes by armed might. Cynics may point out that Japan could use its substantial economic might to coerce others, using economic incentives in place of military intervention to work its will. Yet a *nemawashi*-based process of mutual accommodation, even if it did favor the stronger party, would be a step up from current violence. The Japanese interest in doing business in a stable climate promises long-term accommodations that aim at harmonizing relations. Remilitarization would bring out a very different side of the Japanese character.

Somewhat the same tension between announced good intention and ambitious program on the one side and the objective conditions and self-interest of key participants is also evident in a second key area that the Japanese have singled out for major involvement—environmental policy. The targeting of environmental issues by leading Japanese policymakers as a priority has been a significant development. They urge Japan to take global leadership using its impressive research capacities to find solutions to global environmental problems, thus producing international public goods and winning friends in a peaceful and profitable area. In 1992 former Prime Minister Noboru Takeshita sponsored an international meeting in Tokyo to discuss how to pay the estimated $125 billion annual cleaning bill for the globe in the decade ahead. This politically correct issue played well' at home and abroad, although it was not an uncontested concern. Japan's Environmental Agency, long a lapdog to industry, had been stopped from distributing a report on industrial pollution in Japan at the London Group of Seven's London meeting in 1991 by MITI and Foreign Ministry officials. The report, produced by the agency's young turks, had, among other things, documented the damage payments due to victims of Minamata disease (mercury poisoning) and *itai-itai* disease (cadmium poisoning) and concluded that Japan paid dearly for failing to take proper cautions to prevent industrial pollution. The paper was handed out after some political maneuvering and the intercession of then–Finance Minister Ryutaro Hashimoto.

Hashimoto went on to head a fourteen member committee of the LDP to study basic environmental problems. The committee's senior advisers included Takeshita and former Prime Minister Toshiko Kaifu. As Takeshita said, "Diet members are beginning to take interest in environmental problems. Any politician who ignores these issues deserves to be called a nitwit and a coward."[30] Cynics suggested that Takeshita was simply trying to ride an apple pie issue back to power. He had a longer track record, however, having been active in passing the fourteen pollution-control laws in 1970 and special UNCED adviser. He had made the Earth Summit in Brazil a priority. Takeshita was also the head of the LDP's *zoku* concerned with the global environment.

While U.S. President George Bush, "the environmental president," stunned the world by seeming to put U.S. business interests ahead of efforts to preserve biodiversity and set timetables to reverse environmental damages, MITI was working out the details of 100-year plan to restore environmental integrity, a serious effort complete with decade by decade specifics and a coherent approach to the science and economics of the monumental tasks involved. The Japanese hope to undo the damaging image their multinational corporations and past government pollution-producing policies have brought upon the nation, as well as to make quite a lot of money by developing the expertise they can sell when the world comes to agree on the importance of concerted global action. As environmental constraints to traditional patterns of economic growth become more binding and increasingly visibly important the Japanese are likely to be in a position to foster their own national interests even as they offer statesmanlike leadership. The Clinton administration, and especially Vice President Al Gore, showed serious interest and knowledgeable commitment in this area, but had trouble building consensus in Congress for a similar departure from existing policies.

It is likely that with Japan's importance to the rest of the world widely acknowledged there will be greater attention paid to its internal politics and less stress on a single undifferentiated Japan, Inc. In terms of the issues that have been discussed serious tensions remain. The acceptance of a very limited SDF detachment that will go unarmed overseas for humanitarian work as part of UN peacekeeping missions did not give Ozawa and others acceptance of the military mission they wanted, but it was a start. Resistance to serious limits being placed on Japanese corporations despoiling the forests of Borneo and the Philippines and other ecocide has not disappeared. The rhetoric of global citizenship covers a multitude of narrower economically destructive interests.

As for economic tension, Ishihara is again a good point man for a troubling perspective. Most troubling about his views, perhaps, is that he says out loud and with confidence things the West is not used to hearing. Ishihara voices the concern that the West once again cannot be trusted—that it should get off its high horse, accept its imperialist past, and understand the way it continues to use violence and the threat of force to coerce what it cannot rightfully claim on the merits of the case. In the postwar period the Japanese accommodated public utterances to American sensitivities. Ishihara, unlike many Japanese who may in fact agree with him, is bold in his challenge. He is spokesman for a self-assertive nationalism among businessmen who want to ride over their foreign competitors. For these reasons he is worth quoting at length concerning both his reading of the past, and of the future as well. His is only the loudest of many New Right voices that are being raised in Japan. He has said:

> If someone cannot be open minded enough to introduce a system that is clearly better than the current one, he lacks freedom of spirit. If that someone then goes on to condemn the other merely for being different, he shows barbaric arrogance. As in a sport, you cannot make excuses in economics, because the results show up in the scores, Every high jumper used to do the straddle—a face down belly-roll—to get over the bar. But as soft rubber replaced sand to cushion the jumper's landing, athletes could do a back-flip over the bar without fear of injury. The result was that the high-jump record went up. No athlete today would dream of using the straddle.
>
> The same should surely be true of management. The success of Japanese companies in overseas markets—and the high marks those companies earn from their own foreign staff—should be proof enough that the corporate values and techniques fostered within the Japanese religious and cultural milieu are frankly superior. Japanese-style management ought to have replaced Western-style management everywhere—just as the back-flip has replaced the straddle. [31]

Whether a new wave of history is upon us and the cultural order he calls modern Europeanism has collapsed, brought on by the final fall of colonialism, as Ishihara contends, will be settled by history. Like so many of his provocative statements, however, this one has enough truth to be painful. On reflection, however, it is also clear that high jumpers and other athletes compete under internationally negotiated rules. To continue the parallel, if leading athletes allowed Japanese to use rubber mats while they continued to jump into sand, perhaps because they felt magnanimously toward the diminutive Japanese and knowing they could never win allowed them this advantage while continuing themselves to play by traditional rules, we would be closer to the truth of the manner in which the Japanese learned to compete more effectively. It was in fact the hubris of the Americans who opened their markets to the Japanese while Japan's markets stayed closed to U.S. products and direct investment until, through a truly innovative system, they had created better products and a better-conceived economic complex for the international competition. The larger point is that it is not only from Japan, but from Maylaysian, Singaporean, and Chinese leaders, that the United States is hearing that it will no longer be able to presume that its way is always best. The days of American preaching to Asia are over, they loudly proclaim. The balance between Japan and the increasingly powerful Asian region on the one hand and the United States on the other will continue to undergo shifts. Asians remain wary of

Japan and so while they do not want to be bullied by the United States, most desire a continued United States presence.

There is a perception held by many close observers that the Japanese have a hard time with horizontal relationships among equals. Ivan Hall, a long-time American expatriate law professor living in the country, has expressed the not uncommon fear over what a confident Japan might be like.

> A Japan that is both powerful and insular minded would be less worrisome if we could at least feel that democracy, individual rights, and freedom of expression were firmly rooted within Japan itself. But I find quite unattractive the prospect of an increasingly direct penetration of my own country's economy, politics, and internal discourse by a Japan that still refuses to come to terms with its own dark past, that avoids serious dialogue over criticisms directed at it from outside, that responds to its own newly felt powers with the reassertion of an outmoded, regressive, race-centered, particularistic national consciousness. [32]

When one thinks about the very real danger of what Hall calls the New Old Right, which continues to assert the unique Japanese character as a people set apart from the rest of humankind, I am troubled but also reminded of the influence of analogous groups in the United States. It behooves us as we look critically at the Japanese to use the same standards on our own political culture, something that is rarely done in such discussions.

The optimism of nineteenth-century modernism, confidence in progress, science, and material advancement, is now most viable in Japan. Yet, even there the disturbing postmodern fragmenting and potentially disastrous social costs of the environmental costs of growth, the yawning gap between the ostentatious affluence of some and the homelessness and treatment of the less fortunate, and the emptiness of lives that do not share in the gains or participate in any positive sense in community are the powder kegs of the contemporary era.

The Americans and Japanese are part of a world system that has experienced slower growth over recent decades. The stagnation is not offset by the growth of huge transnationals, the concentration and centralization of capital, the bright spots of successful niche producers, and other signs of success are no substitute for an inclusive pattern of economic growth. The global Keynesianism that is required should have human resources and a social infrastructure orientation. There is much agreement on these points. Implementation is another matter.

The U.S.-based transnationals, which continue to hold their own in world markets by producing more and more outside of the United States, play tax jurisdictions off against each other, and those which egg on taxpayer rebellion undermine the social fabric and stability of their home nation. Given the nature of a competitive system it is unrealistic to think they will change their behavior without a great deal of administrative guidance by national and international regulators who understand the nature of social costs and the dynamics of sustainable growth. Such reforms will require reenergized popular social movements. There must be global governance mechanisms and institutional innovations that are more than tools of globally oriented capital.

A coordinated global Keynesianism, stimulating economies simultaneously and spreading benefits on a politically acceptable basis, would not be easy and involves considerations that would take us far beyond even the broad canvas of the present work and into a new institutional macroeconomics that makes environmental constraints endogenous, measures growth inclusive of social costs, and benefits in policy decision making, and which balances nations as sectors of a larger global system. Such issues will be made more complex by the emergence of new industrial powers in Asia. Late industrializers are less likely to want to follow rules established by others that may limit their own development. If we learned nothing else from the history of Japan's relation to the West in the 1920s and 1930s we should have learned this.

Through a Mirror Darkly

Japanese economists are increasingly contributing to these debates. Tokyo University Professors Hirofumi Uzawa and Yasusuke Murakami have written on the maladies of industrial society and the economic limits imposed by the earth's natural resources, of the need for changing values and understanding growth in new terms. Kenichi Miyamoto has taken these critiques further and has challenged the social cost of the model, which is so deeply embedded in the drive to accumulate, of Japanese capitalism itself. Some of the leading figures of mathematical growth modeling, like Michio Morishima, have concluded that abstract and sterile models that are not grounded in historical experience are part of the problem, not part of the solution. Takamitsu Sawa has developed an understanding of economics as "a cultural product whose development can be understood only by a careful examination of its technological, social, and political context."[33] Sawa's work on the information economy and the shift from "a stock society to a flow society" offers insight into what counts as a productive resource in an age in which fixed assets becomes less important compared with soft-knowledge commodities. One of the very positive developments in the globalization process is that we come to learn how many others are working in different cultures toward goals we share in ways we can respect and from which we have much to learn.

The Japanese have always worried about the future. They then proceed to do something about it. Today, MITI's vision statements (for the 1990s) promise a sharp departure from the narrow economic efficiency goals in production terms of the past and a new amenity-oriented pattern that will directly improve the living standard and spread benefits of traditional and noncommodified forms of growth more widely. The surplus is finally to be invested in the people who produced it rather than simply being plowed back only into further accumulation. Many are skeptical, but with foreign markets stagnant and other nations objecting to the perpetually large surpluses on its balance of payments, Japan looks within for sources of growth.

Blaming the external "other" is the most attractive course when internal contradictions become contentious and hard to contain. In the past this has meant foreign adventures, wars to restore national pride, sense of purpose, and cohesion. In the present historical moment cultural wars with very real victims are as likely (i.e., hate campaigns, formal or informal, that allow letting off steam and focusing anger and violence outward). This is why it is so important to understand that we look at Japan through a *Rashomon Mirror* to see what is to some extent an image from within our understanding of ourselves, of America as a nation, as a people, as a scared hegemonic power fearing decline and even domination by a new "other" of history. The nationalistic chauvinism of much of the discussion continues. As I have argued it is relevant to only a small part of what is going on. The narrowness of our ways of seeing have blinded us to larger realities, and our lack of vision can cost us greatly.

A new globalized economy is taking shape. Measuring how well "we" are doing is to narrow a formulation. The "we" that benefits from the globalization process, the expanding markets, the reorganization of production, the intensified competition to produce better products at lower costs, is doing quite nicely. Those Japanese, Americans, and others who are in the backwaters of the process are not, and they are resentful. The contemporary process of economic transformation over physical space brings with it a complex class recompositioning. Nationalism in a globalized world takes on new meanings. Who "we" are, ever a contested question, becomes more difficult. Many images are seen in the Rashomon Mirror and contestation over their interpretation remains a powerful force in the postmodern world.

Notes

Preface

1. Edward W. Said, *Orientalism* (New York: Vintage Books, 1978), p. 20.
2. Richard Rorty, *Contingency, Irony, and Solidarity* (Cambridge: Cambridge University Press, 1989), p. 5.

Introduction

1. T. B. Macaulay in Eric Stokes, *The English Utilitarians and India* (Oxford: Clarendon Press, 1959), p. 43.
2. Alfred Marshall, *Industry and Trade* (Chicago: Augustus M. Kelley, 1970), pp. 161–162.
3. Marilyn Ivy, "Critical Texts, Mass Artifacts: The Consumption of Knowledge in Postmodern Japan," in Masao Miyoshi and D. H. Harootunian, eds., *Postmodernism and Japan* (Durham: Duke University Press, 1989).
4. Peter F. Drucker, "Trade Lessons from the World Economy," *Foreign Affairs*, January/February 1994, p. 105.
5. Richard Beason and David E. Weinstein, "Growth, Economies of Scale, and Targeting in Japan (1955–1990)," Harvard Institute of Economic Research, Discussion Paper #1644, October 22, 1993, p. 1.
6. Mark Mason, *American Multinationals and Japan: The Political Economy of Japanese Capital Controls, 1899–1980*, Harvard University Press, Council on East Asian Studies, 1992.
7. James Sterngold, "The Men Who Really Run Fortress Japan," *New York Times*, April 10, 1994, Section 3, p. 1.
8. See Alain Lipietz, "Questions of Method," in *Mirages and Miracles: The Crisis of Global Fordism*, Verso, 1987; and Samuel Bowles, David M. Gordon, and Thomas E. Weiskopf, "The Rise and Demise of the Postwar Social Structure of Accumulation," in *After the Wasteland: A Democratic Economics for the Year 2000* (Armonk, New York: M. E. Sharpe, 1990).
9. Solomon Fabricant, *Economic Progress and Economic Growth* (New York: National Bureau of Economic Research, 1954).
10. Zvi Griliches, "Productivity, R & D, and the Data Constraint," *American Economic Review*, March 1994, p. 10.
11. See for example the discussion as part of a symposium on new growth theory, Howard Pack, "Endogenous Growth Theory: Intellectual Appeal and Empirical Shortcomings," *Journal of Economic Perspectives*, Winter 1994.
12. Elise S. Breziz, Paul Krugman, and Daniel Tsiddon, "Leapfrogging in International Competition: A Theory of Cycles in National Technological Leadership," *American Economic Review*, December 1993, p. 1218.

Chapter 1

1. Roland Barthes, *Empire of Signs* (London: Jonathan Cape, 1982), p. 3.

2. Walter Lippmann, "The World Outside and the Pictures in Our Heads" from *Public Opinion*, 1922 in *Images of Man*. ed. C. W. Mills (New York: George Braziller Inc., 1960), p. 28.

3. Peter Tasker, *Inside Japan: Wealth, Work and Power in the New Japanese Empire.* (London: Penguin Books, 1987), p. 6.

4. Peter F. Drucker, "Trade Lessons from the World Economy," *Foreign Affairs*, January/February 1994, p. 105.

5. Arthur MacEwan and William K. Tabb, "Instability and Change in the World Economy," in *Instability and Change in the World Economy*. eds. A. MacEwen and W. K. Tabb (New York: Monthly Review Press), 1989.

6. Tasker *op cit*. pp. 4–5.

7. Chalmers Johnson, "How to Think About Economic Competition From Japan." *Journal of Japanese Studies*, 13(2), 1987.

8. The excerpt is from Volume 14 of "Foreign Relations, 1952–54," a State Department compilation as cited in the New York Times after its declassification. The date of the text quoted is August 6, 1954. Whether there was awareness of the importance of that data—August 6 the anniversary of the nuclear bombing of Hiroshima—is not clear in the report.

9. As quoted in Alan Riding, "Anti-Japan Din in France Softens a Bit," *New York Times*, July 24, 1991, p. A13.

10. Henry Kissinger privately derided the Japanese as "little Sony salesmen" as national security adviser to President Nixon. See Alexis Johnson, *The Right Hand of Power*. (Englewood Cliffs, New Jersey: Prentice-Hall, 1984), p. 52.

11. Nakasone also envisioned the emergence of a new Japanese character, a personality change that would allow a more substantial role in world affairs. Much of the discussion of a new Japanese assertiveness at the end of the Cold War era dates from his effort at redefining Japan's relation with the United States into a more active partnership than his deprecating remarks would suggest. See the essays on Nakasone by Kenneth B. Pyle and by Michio Muramatsu listed in references.

12. It is also premised on an appalling degree of ignorance. An October 1991 survey of American views of Japan's form of government, for example, found that 35 percent thought of it as being freely elected, 20 percent believed it was "run by the emperor," another 20 percent declared it a dictatorship, 13 percent placed it under military rule, and 17 percent said they had no idea. *Japan Times*, January 7, 1992, and summarized in Gavan McCormack, "The Emptiness of Affluence: Vitality, Embolisms and Symbiosis in the Japanese Body Politic," Institute for European and International Affairs, Luxembourg, 1992.

13. See for example, Kozo Yamamura and Yasukichi Yasuba, "Introduction," *The Political Economy of Japan, Volume I, The Domestic Transformation*. eds. K. Yamamura and Y. Yasuba (Stanford: Stanford University Press, 1987), p. 1.

14. John Bresnan, *From Dominoes to Dynamos: The Transformation of Southeast Asia* (New York: Council on Foreign Relations Press, 1994).

15. Gish Gen, "Challenging the Asian Illusion," *New York Times*, "Arts and Leisure," August 11, 1991, p. 12.

16. Stephen Holden, "Humiliation as a Gauge of Identity," *New York Times*, July 30, 1993, p. C12.

17. The MITI vice minister as I'll discuss more fully is the highest civil servant in that organization. He runs industrial policy making while ministers, politicians, come and go and leave far less impact on things. The Mitsubishi Corporation is the first among equals of the Mitsubishi family of interlinked companies which is the largest *keiretsu* grouping in Japan. The man's views on culture are thus not unimportant.

18. Howard Hibbett, "Introduction" to Ryunosake Akuntagawa, *Rashomon and Other Stories*. (Tokyo: Charles E. Tuttle Company, 1952), p. 11.

19. See Eric R. Wolf, *Europe and the People Without History*. (Berkeley: University of California Press, 1982), p. 9.

20. Clifford Geertz, *The Interpretation of Culture*. (New York: Basic Books, 1973).

21. Edward W. Said, *Culture and Imperialism* (New York: Alfred A. Knopf, 1993), p. 15.

22. Emile Durkheim, *The Rules of Sociological Method*. (New York: The Free Press, 1964), p. 3.

23. Thomas Rohlen, *Japan's High Schools*. (Berkeley: University of California Press, 1983), p. 314; cited by Merry White, *The Japanese Educational Challenge*. (Tokyo: Kodansha International, 1987), p. 25.

24. White. *Ibid.*, p. 48.

25. Quoted in James Sterngold, "Intractable Trade Issues With Japan," *New York Times*, December 4, 1991, p. D4.

26. Quoted by Leonard Silk, "A Time of Peril For World Trade," *New York Times*, January 17, 1992, p. D2.

27. The point is well taken yet it would seem here she is forgetting our wars with native Americans.

Ruth Benedict, *The Chrysanthemum and the Sword: Patterns of Japanese Culture*. (Boston: Houghton, Mifflin Company, 1946).

28. See former Prime Minister Noboru Takeshita, *The Furosato Concert: Toward a Humanistic and Prosperous Japan*. (Tokyo: Simul International, 1988).

29. See Harry Magdoff, "Globalization—To What End? Part I," *Monthly Review*. (February 1992), Table II, p. 9.

30. This is another one of those subgenre growth areas. See particularly: Paul Bagguley, "Post-Fordism and Enterprise Culture." *Enterprise Culture*. eds. R. Keats and N. Abercrombie (London: Routledge, 1991) and Ash Amin. "Flexible Specialization and Small Firms in Italy: Myths and Realities. *Farewell to Flexibility*. ed. A. Pollert. (Cambridge: Basil Blackwell, 1991).

31. Robert E. Cole, "Some Cultural and Social Bases of Japanese Innovation: Small-Group Activities in Comparative Perspective," in Shumpei Kumon and Henry Rosovsky, *The Political Economy of Japan Volume 3, Cultural and Social Dynamics* (Stanford: Stanford University Press, 1992). Cole usefully distinguishes cases of participation and cooperation in three national settings in his *Strategies for Learning: Small-Group Activities in America, Japanese, and Swedish Industry* (Berkeley: University of California Press, 1989).

Chapter 2

1. J. J. Servan-Schreiber, *The American Challenge* (New York: Avon Books, 1969), p. 31.

2. Shinya Arai, *Shoshaman: A Tale of Corporate Japan* (Berkeley: University of California Press, 1991), pp. 178–79.

3. On "textbook orthodoxy," see Sidney G. Winter, "On Coase, Competence, and the Corporation," in eds. Oliver E. Williamson and Sidney G. Winter, *The Nature of the Firm: Origins, Evolution, and Development*. (Oxford University Press, 1991), pp. 179–81.

4. For a discussion of "obligated relational contracting" as an alternative to mainstream economics on this topic, see Ronald P. Dore, "Goodwill and the Spirit of Market Capitalism," *British Journal of Sociology* 34:4 (1983).

5. The literature on this topic is vast, but see Masahiko Aoki, *Information, Incentives and Bargaining in the Japanese Economy* (Cambridge: Cambridge University Press, 1988), and Ken-ichi Imai and Hiroyuki Itami, "Interpenetration of Organization and Market. Japan's Firm and Market in Comparison with the U.S.," *International Journal of Industrial Organization* (December 1984).

6. Alfred D. Chandler, Jr. *Strategy and Structure: Chapters in the History of the Industrial Enterprise* (Garden City, Anchor Books, 1966), p. 476. (First quotation.)

Alfred D. Chandler, Jr., *The Visible Hand: The Management Revolution in America* (Cambridge: Harvard University Press, 1977), p. 1. (Second quotation.)

7. Agricultural did receive sectorial aid for political reasons unrelated to its economic development potential as did the arms industry.

8. The bureaucracy plays a leading role, but there is in many accounts a tendency to accord too great an autonomy to it. As Upham has written, the bureaucracy "tries to gauge the fundamental direction of social change, compares it with the best interests of society from the perspective of the ruling coalition of which it is a part, and then attempts to stimulate and facilitate the creation of a national consensus that supports its own vision of correct national policy." Guidance is in part a matter of preserving harmony and an elite consensus. The government is facilitator and mediator, a manager of conflict, as the state tends to be in any social formation, but the informality and unaccountability of Japanese bureaucrats comes from a networking and interpenetration of governance institutions, private as well as public, that is unique.

Frank Upham, *Law and Social Change in Postwar Japan* (Cambridge: Harvard University Press, 1987), p. 21.

9. Dan Clauson, *Bureaucracy and the Labor Process: The Transformation of U.S. Industry, 1860–1920* (New York: Monthly Review Press, 1980).

10. Frederick W. Taylor, as quoted in Harry Braverman, *Labor and Monopoly Capital* (New York: Monthly Review Press, 1974).

11. John Bellamy Foster, "The Fetish of Fordism," *Monthly Review*. (March 1988).

12. Maryellen R. Kelley and Bennett Harrison, "Unions, Technology, and Labor-Management Cooperation," *Unions and Economic Competitiveness*, eds. L. Mishel and P. Voos (Armonk, New York: M. E. Sharpe, 1993).

13. Harvey Leibenstein, "The Prisoners' Dilemma in the Invisible Hand: An Analysis of Intrafirm Productivity," *American Economic Review, Papers and Proceedings* 72 (May 1982).

14. The advantages of such an approach have been brilliantly documented in the case of the auto industry by David Halberstam, *The Reckoning* (New York: William Morrow and Company, 1986).

15. Anthony Woodiwiss, *Law, Labour and Society in Japan: From Repression to Reluctant Recognition* (London: Routledge, 1992), p. 2.

16. Upham, *op. cit.*, p. 17.

17. See Gavan McCormack, "Crime, Confession, and Control in Contemporary

Japan," *Democracy in Contemporary Japan*, eds. G. McCormack and Y. Sugimoto (Armonk, New York: M. E. Sharpe, 1986).

18. For a discussion of Japan's alleged litigation-free society, see John Haley, "The Myth of the Reluctant Litigant," *Journal of Japanese Studies* (Summer 1978), and J. Mark Ramseyer, "Reluctant Litigant Revisited: Rationality and Disputes in Japan," *Journal of Japanese Studies* (Winter 1988).

19. W. Carl Kester, *Japanese Takeovers: The Global Contest for Corporate Control* (Boston: Harvard Business School Press, 1991).

20. Michael L. Gerlach, *Alliance Capitalism: The Social Organization of Japanese Business* (Berkeley: University of California Press, 1992), p. 129.

21. How much less binding is a matter of dispute. Komiya believes they "have little more than monthly meetings which are primarily of a social nature, with little fundamental significance." In his opinion, "these industrial groups are, therefore, more imaginary than real." Gerlach, on the other hand, sees much of the scholarly discussion concerning Japanese business organization as having gone too far in such a direction "leading to an underappreciation both of the overall significance of the *keiretsu* and of their continuing viability in the contemporary Japanese economy."

Ryutaro Komiya, *The Japanese Economy: Trade, Industry and Government*, University of Tokyo Press, 1990, and Michael L. Gerlach, "Twilight of the *Keiretsu*? A Critical Assessment," *Journal of Japanese Studies* (Winter 1992), p. 81.

22. Michael E. Porter, "The Competitiveness of Nations," *Harvard Business Review* (March–April 1990), p. 78.

23. Michael H. Best, *The New Competition: Institutions of Industrial Restructuring* (Cambridge: Polity Press, 1990), p. 2.

24. William Abernathy et al., "The New Industrial Competition," *Harvard Business Review* (September–October 1981).

25. Lester C. Thurow, *Head to Head: Coming Economic Battles Among Japan, Europe, and America* (New York: William Morrow and Company, 1992).

26. See Zenichi Shishido, "A Texan Raid on a Japanese Company," *Japan Echo* (Winter 1989).

27. Michael C. Jensen, "Agency Costs of Free Cash Flow, Corporate Finance, and Takeovers," *American Economic Review, Papers and Proceedings* (May 1986).

28. Gerlach. *op. cit.* pp.78–79.

29. Jeremy Bulow, Lawrence H. Summers, and Victoria P. Summers, "Distinguishing Debt from Equity in the Junk Bond Era," *Debt, Taxes and Corporate Restructuring*, eds. J. B. Shoven and J. Waldfogel, (Washington, D.C.: Brookings Institution, 1990), p. 145.

30. Masahiro Okuno-Fujiwara. "Interdependence of Industries, Coordination Failure and Strategic Promotion of Industry," *Journal of International Economics* 25:1 (1988).

31. J. A. Bander, "Rationales for Strategic Trade and Industrial Policy," *Strategic Trade Policy and the New International Economics* ed. P. Krugman (Cambridge: MIT Press, 1986).

32. Arman A. Alchian, "Uncertainty, Evolution and Economic Theory," *Journal of Political Economy* 58 (June 1950).

33. Joseph A. Schumpeter, "Economic Theory and Entrepreneurial History," *Joseph A. Schumpeter: The Economics and Sociology of Capitalism*, ed. R. Swedberg (Princeton: Princeton University Press, 1991).

34. Chalmers Johnson, *MITI and the Japanese Miracle: The Growth of Industrial Policy 1925–1975* (Stanford: Stanford University Press, 1982), p. 81.

35. Pavel Pelikan, "The Formation of Incentive Mechanisms in Different Economic Systems," *Incentives and Economic Systems*, ed. S. Hedlund (New York: New York University Press, 1987).

36. Schumpeter's own view of the process can also be criticized for making entrepreneurial activity something that is carried on "offstage and out of sight. Invention comes onto the Schumpeterian stage already full grown," Nathan Rosenberg has written, "and not as objects or processes the development of which is a matter of explicit interest; nor are subsequent improvements or modifications of the invention typically treated as significant." As the writing of Japanese theorists of the entrepreneurial process, such as Kenichi Imai (upon whose work I have drawn in the text) have amply demonstrated, it is possible to theorize the entrepreneurial group process of innovation "without excessive reliance on individual personal qualities."

Nathan Rosenberg, *Perspectives on Technology* (Cambridge: Cambridge University Press, 1976), p. 67, and Ken-ichi Imai, "Japan's Corporate Networks," *The Political Economy of Japan; Volume 3, Cultural and Social Dynamics*, eds. S. Kumon and H. Rosovsky, (Stanford: Stanford University Press, 1992), p. 203.

37. Richard R. Nelson and Gavin Wright, "The Rise and Fall of American Technological Leadership," *Journal of Economic Literature* (December 1992).

38. On the historical case of Great Britain, see R. C. O. Mathews, Charles Feinstein, and John Odling-Smee, *British Economic Growth, 1856–1973* (Stanford: Stanford University Press, 1983).

39. Jean-Jacques Servan-Schreiber, *The American Challenge* (New York: Penguin Books, 1969), p. 210, as cited by Robert B. Reich, *The Work of Nations: Preparing Ourselves for 21st Century Capitalism* (New York: Vintage Books, 1992), p. 66.

40. Richard Morin, "Maybe We're Chasing After the Wrong 'Evil Empire'," *The Washington Post National Weekly Edition*, May 16–22, p. 34.

41. Susan Chira, "Poll Blames U.S. on Japan Trade: American Viewed as Seeking Scapegoat for Problems," *New York Times*, August 13, 1985, p. 1.

42. S. R. Saunders, "Poll Shows America's View of Japanese is on Negative Trend," *The Japan Times*, September 13, 1990, p. 1.

43. By the end of the 1980s, the most difficult postwar decade yet for U.S.-Japan relations, *The Brookings Review* could carry an article titled: "Japan, the Enemy?" which asked rhetorically, "Is it time for the Pentagon to draw up plans for an eventual war with Japan?" Fortunately, the conclusion was *no*, but the fear of Japanese prowess the appearance of such articles demonstrate is palpable in the United States of the 1990s. The author of the piece is Philip H. Trezise, and it was published Winter 1989/90.

44. Russell Keat, "Introduction: Starship Britain or Universal Enterprise?" in eds. Russell Keat and Nicholas Abercrombie, *Enterprise Culture* (London: Routledge, 1991), p. 11.

45. Anna Pollert, "The Orthodoxy of Flexibility," in ed. Pollert, *Farewell to Flexibility?*, (Oxford: Basil Blackwell, 1991), p. 7.

46. Ronald Dore, *Flexible Rigidities*, Athlone, p. 96.

47. J. McIlroy, *Trade Unions in Britain Today*, Manchester University Press, 1988 as cited in Richard Hyman, 'Plus ça change,' The Theory of Production and the Production of Theory," in ed. Anna Pollert, *Farewell to Flexibility?* (Basil: Blackwell, 1991), p. 269.

48. Makoto Itoh, pp. 202–3, in "Japan in a New World Order," in Ralph Miliband and Leo Panitch, eds. *Socialist Register* 92. (London: Merlin Press, 1992).

49. Russell Keat, *op cit.*, p. 3.

50. Emile Dirkheim, *The Rules of Sociological Method* (New York: The Free Press, 1964, p. 90).

51. On the British system, see eds. Bernard Elbaum and William Lazonick *The Decline of the British Economy* (Oxford: Clarendon, 1986). See also Lazonick, "Competition, Specialization, and Industrial Decline," *Journal of Economic History* (March 1981). This discussion of the British auto industry draws from Lazonick's work.

Chapter 3

1. On the ambivalence toward the West, its technological riches and its threat to national identity, see Bob Tadashi Wakabayashi, *Anti-Foreignism and Western Learning in Early Modern Japan: The New Theses of 1825* (Cambridge: Harvard University Press, 1986).

2. As Alexander Gershenkron has taught us:

"To break through the barriers of stagnation in a backward country, to ignite the imaginations of men, and to place their energies in the service of economic development, a stronger medicine is needed than the promise of better allocation of resources . . . " *Economic Backwardness in Historical Perspective* (Cambridge: Harvard University Press, 1962), p. 24. Even as we marvel at such nation building by the elite of the modernizing society, however, it is well to also remember, as Borthwick has written of nineteenth-century Japan, "The virtues of hard work, thrift, self-discipline, obedience, and selfless service has been instilled in the Japanese people by the edge of the sword" (*op. cit.*, p. 158). In the morning of capitalism's rosy sunrise in all times and all places both moments are present.

3. In Jansen, *op. cit.* p. 12.

4. See Almond and Coleman, *The Politics of Developing Areas* (Princeton: Princeton University Press, 1960), p. 52.

Much of postwar U.S. scholarship has seen Japanese economic development in a modernization framework that can be highly selective. For a critique of this perspective see Shigeki Toyama, "The Meiji Restoration and the Present Day," *Bulletin of Concerned Asian Scholars* (October 1969) for a linking of the issues of modernization in the postwar period with interpretations of the Meiji Restoration, the subject I will turn to in the latter part of this chapter.

5. While the English translation *restoration* is too ingrained to be modified, Edward Seidensticker, that most gifted of Japanese to English translators and holder of the title for longest subtitle in a title of a major publication concerning Japan, argues that " 'Restoration' is actually a bad translation of the Japanese *ishin*, which means something more like 'renovation' or 'revitalization.' "

Edward Seidensticker, *Low City, High City: Tokyo from Edo to the Earthquake: how the shogun's ancient capital became a great modern city, 1867–1923* (Tokyo: Charles E. Tuttle Co.), p. 11.

6. See Marius B. Jansen, "Introduction" to Part II of his *Changing Japanese Attitudes Toward Modernization* (Tokyo: Charles E. Tuttle Co., 1969), p. 93.

7. Walt W. Rostow, *The Stages of Economic Growth* (Cambridge: Cambridge University Press, 1960); see entry in John Eatwell, Murray Milgate, and Peter Newman, eds. *The New Palgrave: Economic Development* (New York: W. W. Norton & Company, 1989).

8. William Lockwood, *The Economic Development of Japan: Growth and Structural Change 1868–1938* (Princeton: Princeton University Press, 1954) is a good basic

account. See also William G. Beasley, *The Meiji Restoration* (Stanford: Stanford University Press, 1972), and *The Cambridge History of Japan: The Nineteenth Century,* ed. Marius B. Jansen (Cambridge: Cambridge University Press, 1989), Volume 5.

9. Anthony Giddens, *Social Theory and Modern Sociology* (Stanford: Stanford University Press, 1987), p. 39.

10. Dirkheim, *op. cit.,* p. 5.

11. Mark Borthwick, *Pacific Century: The Emergence of Modern Pacific Asia* (Boulder: Westview Press, 1992), p. 49.

12. The vulnerability of the system in the years preceding the opening of Japan by Perry skips over the achievements of the unifiers, the ambitious and resourceful men who founded modern Japan. On the contribution of Hideyoshi Toyotomi, Ieyasu Tokugawa, and Nobunaga Oda, see Mary Elizabeth Berry, "Public Peace and Private Attachment: The Goals and Conduct of Power in Early Modern Japan." *Journal of Japanese Studies* (Summer 1986).

13. The importance of nation-building efforts do not of course start in these years. See eds. John Whitney Hall, Keiji Nagahara and Kozo Yamamura, *Japan Before Tokugawa: Political Consolidation and Economic Growth, 1500 to 1650* (Princeton: Princeton University Press, 1981).

14. Thomas P. Rohlen, "Learning: The Modernization of Knowledge in the Japanese Political Economy," *The Political Economy of Japan, Volume 3: Culture and Social Dynamics.* eds. S. Kumon and H. Rosovsky (Stanford: Stanford University Press, 1992), p. 325.

15. The economic context in which Perry's mission was undertaken was well articulated in the instructions he was given. They read in part:

> Recent events—the navigation of the ocean by steam, the acquisition and settlement by this country of vast territory on the Pacific, the discovery of gold in that region, the rapid communication across the isthmus which separates the two oceans—have practically brought the countries of the East in closer proximity to our own; although the consequences of these events have scarcely begun to be felt, the intercourse between them has already greatly increased and no limit can be assigned to its future extension.

16. Jon Halliday, *A Political History of Japanese Capitalism* (New York: Monthly Review Press, 1975), p. 34.

17. John W. Dower, "E. H. Norman, Japan and the Uses of History," in *Origins of the Modern Japanese State: Selected Writings of E. H. Norman* (New York: Pantheon, 1975), p. 8; William W. Lockwood, *op. cit.,* p. 12. John Whitney Hall, "Changing Conceptions of the Modernization of Japan." *Japanese Attitudes Toward Modernization,* ed. Marius B. Jansen (Tokyo: Charles E. Tuttle Co., 1982), p. 7.

18. Tessa Morris-Suzuki. *A History of Japanese Economic Thought* (London: Routledge, 1989), p. 35.

19. Marius B. Jansen, "Wisdom Sought Throughout the World," in M. B. Jansen, *Japan and Its World: Two Centuries of Change* (Princeton: Princeton University Press, 1980).

20. On the sense of shared obligation that pervades these relationships and the sense of responsibility to maintain and build social institutions on which everyone in the society depends, see Robert N. Bellah, *Tokugawa Religion: The Values of Pre-Industrial Japan* (Boston: Beacon Press, 1970).

21. See Eugene Soviak, "On the Nature of Western Progress: The Journal of

the Iwakura Embassy,'' *Tradition and Modernization in Japanese Culture*, ed. Donald H. Shively (Princeton: Princeton University Press, 1971).

22. Tessa Morris-Suzuki. *op. cit.*, p. 47. See also *Foreign Employees in Nineteenth-Century Japan*, eds. E. R. Beauchamp and A. Iriye (Boulder: Westview, 1990).

23. As quoted by Lockwood, *op. cit.*, p. 582.

24. G. C. Allen, *A Short Economic History of Japan, 1867–1937* (London: Macmillan, 1946), p. 30.

25. Robert N. Bellah, *Tokugawa Religion* (Boston: Beacon Press, 1957), in which the Isasaki code is cited on p. 187.

26. Gavan McCormack and Yoshio Sugimoto, "Introduction: Democracy and Japan" *Democracy in Contemporary Japan*, eds. G. McCormack and Y. Sugimoto (Armonk: M. E. Sharpe, 1986), p. 10.

27. There were challenges from the old order. The most famous of these is the Satsuma Rebellion of 1977. The disgruntled samurai were put down by a conscript army transported on Mitsubishi ships and supplied with materials by Mitsui Bussan. The police action was financed by the Mitsui Bank. By this time Mitsui was active in mining and processing zinc and gold, salt and sulphur, spinning and weaving cotton and silk (later rayon), and then on into machine tools and beer among its hundreds of subsidiaries. At the time it underwrote the suppression of the Satsuma Rebellion it was already a well-established business empire.

28. On Japan's particular form of nationalism from earlier in this period, see Carol Gluck, *Japan's Modern Myths: Ideology in the Late Meiji Period* (Princeton: Princeton University Press, 1985).

29. Cited by Borthwick. *op. cit.*, p. 135.

30. The activities of the Meiji state is subject to some controversy. Neoclassically oriented economists (e.g., Yutaka Kosai and Yoshitaro Ogino challenge the view attributing economic success in the Meiji Era to the government; see the current debate over industrial policy as an extension of nineteenth-century claims (false in their minds) that government can claim credit for more than improvements in education, the legal system, and building up the infrastructure of the country. I am clearly suggesting the evidence is sufficient to contradict this view for the Meiji Era. I will argue it is equally false for later periods up to and including the post–World War II era.

Yutaka Kosei and Yoshitara Ogino, *The Contemporary Japanese Economy* (Armonk: M. E. Sharpe, 1984), p. 59.

31. Rob Stevens, "Structural origins of Japan's direct foreign investment," *Japan and the Global Economy: Issues and Trends in the 1990s*, ed. J. Morris (London: Routledge, 1991), p. 46. See also E. Patricia Tsurumi, *Factory Girls: Women in the Thread Mills of Meiji Japan* (Princeton: Princeton University Press, 1990).

32. Lockwood, *op. cit.*, p. 303.

33. Robert Evans, Jr., *The Labor Economies of Japan and the United States* (New York: Praeger, 1971), p. 43.

34. Lockwood, *op. cit.*, p. 323.

35. *Ibid.*, p. 200.

36. David Felix has made the divergent evolution of the craft industry sectors the focus of an effort to understand successful later modernizers making the role of traditional producers key to an understanding of path dependent comparative advantage study.

David Felix, "Import Substitution and Late Industrialization: Latin America and Asia Compared," *World Development* 17:9 (1989).

37. Lockwood, *op. cit.*, p. 212.

38. William G. Beasley, *Japanese Imperialism, 1894–1945* (Oxford: Clarendon Press, 1987), p. 258.

39. I say two schools, but if we widen our lens to include the views of other Asian nationals, scholars, and the general public, then we see that East Asian international relations in the 1920s and 1930s "are hostage to mutually insulated historiographies."

John J. Stephan, "Review of Akira Iriye's *The Origin of the Second World War in Asia and the Pacific,*" *Journal of Japanese Studies* (Summer 1988), p. 454.

40. Lockwood, *op. cit.*, p. 537.

41. Lecturing at Keio University Daniel Bell said that

"the big problem for sociology at the beginning of the twentieth century was why capitalism had been so successful in the West, and not in the Orient. Max Weber of course gave the answer. You need something strong enough to break the bonds of traditionalism, mobility, and so on. The question at the end of the Twentieth Century is a different one. It is: Why is capitalism so successful in Japan? Japan is traditionalist; there is little mobility, and the culture is not individualistic."

"How do we explain Japan's impressive growth? The question haunts Western economists."

See interview with Daniel Bell in Richard Swedberg, *Economics and Sociology; Redefining Their Boundaries: Conversations with Economists and Sociologists* (Princeton: Princeton University Press, 1990), p. 228.

42. Halliday, *op. cit.*, p. 56.

43. T. J. Pempel and Keiichi Tsunekawa, "Corporatism without Labour? The Japanese Anomaly," *Trends Toward Corporatist Intermediation*, eds. G. Lembruch and P. Schmitter (London: Sage, 1979).

44. Bernard Eccleston, *State and Society in Post-War Japan* (Cambridge: Polity Press, 1989), p. 73.

45. Masaki Saruta, "Technical Change, Rationalization and Industrial Relations: The Case of Toyota." typescript, February 1990.

46. Taishiro Shirai, *Contemporary Industrial Relations in Japan* (Madison: University of Wisconsin Press, 1983).

47. Andrew Gordon, *The Evolution of Labor Relations in Japan, 1853–1955* (Cambridge: Harvard University Press, 1985).

48. Ichiyo Muto, "Class Struggle in Postwar Japan," G. McCormack and Y. Sugimoto, *op. cit.*, p. 130.

49. *Ibid.*, p. 134.

50. Takafusa Nakamura, *The Postwar Japanese Economy* (Tokyo: University of Tokyo Press, 1981), p. 252.

51. *Ibid.*, p. 254.

52. James P. Womack, Daniel T. Jones, and Daniel Roos, "How Lean Production Can Change the World." *New York Times Sunday Magazine.* September 23, 1990, and James P. Womack, Daniel T. Jones, Daniel Roos, and Donna Sammons Carpenter, *The Machine That Changed the World* (New York: Rawson Associates, published by Macmillan, 1990).

53. Chalmers Johnson, *op. cit.*, p. 197.

54. Robert E. Cole, "Japanese Workers, Unions and the Marxist Appeal," *The Japanese Interpreter* (Summer 1970), as cited by Pempel; see next footnote.

55. Pempel in Katzenstein *op. cit.*, p. 170.

56. Juliet B. Schor, *The Overworked American: The Unexpected Decline of Leisure* (New York: Basic Books, 1992).

Chapter 4

1. Joseph A. Schumpeter, '"The Study of Entrepreneurship," *Joseph A. Schumpeter: The Economics and Sociology of Capitalism.* ed. R. Swedberg (Princeton: Princeton University Press, 1991), p. 411.

2. Sol Sanders, *Honda: The Man and His Machine* (Boston: Little, Brown, 1975), pp. 139–40.

3. Particular measures include the Oil Industry Act of 1934, the Auto Manufacturing and Steel Industry Act of 1936. After the war and increasingly in the 1960s and 1970s as foreign pressure increased and companies were strong enough not to need the same type of control or to want many restrictive policies MITI came to rely on administrative guidance that was not narrowly based on legislation or not specified in legislation at all.

4. Yutaka Kosei, *The Era of High-Speed Growth: Notes on the Postwar Japanese Economy* (Tokyo: Tokyo University Press, 1986), p. 27.

5. *Ibid.*, p. 48.

6. Lockwood, *op. cit.*, p. 61. On the right-wing resurgence and continuities from the prewar regime, see John W. Dower, *Empire and Aftermath: Yoshida Shigero and the Japanese Experience* (Cambridge: Council on East Asian Studies, Harvard University, 1979). My concerns are with the economic side of this period, and so the discussion of the extent of continuity in one of economic institutions and policies is not irrelevant. It is the uses of nationalism in its combined modern izing and authoritarian meanings that is so interesting even if not central to our themes here. See, for example, Herbert P. Bix, "The Showa Emperor's 'Monologue' and the Problem of War Responsibility," *Journal of Japanese Studies* (Summer 1992).

7. David Friedman, *The Misunderstood Miracle: Industrial Development and Political Change in Japan* (Ithaca: Cornell University Press, 1988), p. 2.

8. This also remains the case so that while it is true that most small and medium-sized enterprises do subcontract work for large firms, they also develop their own technologies, which their parent companies draw on. This increases their bargaining power and should be taken into account when one considers what is meant by subcontracting in the Japanese context. See Small and Medium Enterprise Agency, MITI, *White Paper on Small and Medium Enterprises*, 1991, especially Figure 2-29, p. 57.

9. Pempel, *op. cit.*, p. 162.

10. Stephen J. Anderson, "The Political Economy of Japanese Saving: How Postal Savings and Public Pensions Support High Rates of Household Saving in Japan." *Journal of Japanese Studies* (Winter 1990).

11. Things are more complicated, of course. The local postmasters have been a political force in Japan since the end of the last century. They in turn are tied financially and politically by having the ministry rent space in their homes for postal purposes and highly lucrative (and periodically renegotiated) rates. Tanaka kept control of the minister appointment of those responsible for the Ministry of

Post and Telecommunications through twelve cabinets (1957–1982), after which Nakasone took over. See Kent E. Calder, "Linking Welfare and the Developmental State: Postal Savings in Japan," *Journal of Japanese Studies* (Winter 1990).

12. The private banks and indeed even the Ministry of Agriculture, Forestry, and Fishing, with its competitor agricultural savings network, both oppose the postal savings system but to little avail.

13. While there are thousands of trading firms in Japan, nine of them are known as *sogo shosha*. These globe-spanning information and transacting networks trade in everything from instant noodles to jet planes. They build nuclear reactors and oil refineries covering every step from planning and financing to construction and supplying materials. In terms of annual sales they dwarf the gross national products of most nations and function in almost every country in the world. They currently handle about half of Japan's total imports and about 60 percent of its exports. Mitsui and Mitsubishi, the largest, have annual sales of over $100 billion each. Much of this is on trade and sales that does not directly involve Japan. In toto the *sogo shosha* handle 10 percent of world trade among them.

14. See Thomas Alan Schwarz, *America's Germany: John J. McCloy and the Federal Republic of Germany* (Cambridge: Harvard University Press, 1991), especially Chapter 7.

15. On Deming, see Andrea Gabor, *The Man Who Discovered Quality* (New York: Penguin, 1992).

16. Robert C. Angel, *Explaining Economic Policy Failure, Japan in the 1969–1971 International Monetary Crisis* (New York: Columbia University Press, 1991), pp. 9–40. I am obliged to Harry Magdoff for this citation.

17. *Ibid.*, p. 45.

18. As I noted earlier literally meaning, "descent from heaven." The term conveys the relationship between the status of the Japanese elite bureaucrats and the mundane money grubbers of the corporate world and the self-seeking politicians. When the high-ranking bureaucrats retire at about the age of fifty they move on to a career in politics, where they supply most of the prime ministers of the postwar period or are golden parachuted into the private sector at the companies they have regulated as government employees. They of course maintain close ties to their former subordinates and act as a conduit for what has been called Japan, Inc., the close collaborative Japanese governance system. Semiofficial organizations, the government-affiliated special companies such as the Japan External Trade Organization (JETRO), the Export–Import Bank of Japan, and the Employment Promotion Corporation are other bureaucratic safety nets. After working at such positions the former bureaucrats may retire again to yet a new job and an additional generous pension. They end their lives as directors of large companies and advisers with generous compensation packages.

19. See T. J. Pempel, *Policy and Politics in Japan: Creative Conservativism* (Philadelphia: Temple University Press, 1982), pp. 61–62.

20. Beverley Smith, "Democracy Derailed: Citizens' Movements in Historical Perspective," In G. McCormack and Y. Sugimoto, *op. cit.*, p. 164.

21. Chalmers Johnson, "The Industrial Policy Debate Re-examined," *California Management Review* (Fall 1984), p. 74.

22. Morris-Suzuki, *op. cit.*, p. 138.

23. *Ibid.*, p. 140.

24. See Ryoshin Minami, *The Economic Development of Japan: A Quantitative Study* (London, Macmillan, 1986).

25. The investment in modernization and the drive to export, starting in the mid-1950s "represented a life or death gamble," in the eyes of many Japanese economists. There was no guarantee of success, that the products would be good enough for the export market. David Halberstam, in *The Reckoning* (New York: William Morrow and Company, 1986), tells the story of the men sent to America to sell the first Datsuns exported. These were simply terrible, crude, and underpowered. Salesmen privately called them "mobile coffins," partly because of the unbearable heat inside the cars (there was no real heater, the car was heated involuntarily by the engine, and anyone who drove one on a hot day baked). The engine was too small, so the car was way underpowered. It was difficult to start in the winter because the battery was too small. The brakes were weak, and the acceleration poor. To drive one on a U.S. freeway was a dangerous proposition. In hindsight it all seems like it must have been easy.

26. Ken-ichi Miyamoto, "Urban Problems in Japan With Emphasis upon the Period of Rapid Economic Growth," *Japan Institute of International Affairs, Annual Review* (1970), p. 32.

27. Gershenkron reminds us that this tendency to criticize upstarts for lack of originality is long present: "German mining engineers of the sixteenth century accused the English of being but slavish imitators of German methods, and the English fully reciprocated these charges in the fifties and sixties of the last century." *Op. cit.*, p. 8.

28. The term information society seems to have originated in the writings of Yujiro Hayashi, a University of Tokyo professor. By 1969 it had found its way into an Economic Advisory Council report *Japan's Information Society: Vision and Tasks*. See Tessa Morris-Suzuki. "Sources of conflict in the information society. Some social consequences of technological change in Japan since 1973." in G. McCormack and Y. Sugimoto, *op. cit.*

29. Economic Planning Agency, *Economic White Paper for 1987*.

30. Rob Stevens, "Structural origins of Japan's direct foreign investment," in J. Morris, *op. cit.*, p. 51.

31. Richard C. Marston, "Price Behavior in Japanese and U.S. Manufacturing," *Trade with Japan: Has the Door Opened Wider?* ed. P. Krugman (Chicago: University of Chicago Press, 1991), p. 122.

32. For views at variance to mine see: Philip H. Trezise, "Industrial Policy in Japan." *Industrial Vitalization: Toward a National Industrial Policy*, ed. M. E. Dewar. (New York: Pergamon Press, 1982), and R. Gerard Adams and Shinichi Ichimura, "Industrial Policy in Japan," in *Industrial Policies for Growth and Competitiveness: An Economic Perspective*, eds. F. G. Adams and L. R. Klein (Lexington, Massachusetts: D. C. Heath, 1983).

33. Hikari Nohara, "Is Japanese Industrial Relations a Breakthrough: A Hypothesis Relating Japanese Industrial Relations to Those in the U.S. and Europe," unpublished paper, April 1990.

34. The phenomenon has not gone unnoticed in Japan of course. To choose one formulation of the phenomenon from a Japanese perspective:

Japan appears to be rising swiftly from the status of a mere major economic power to that of an economic superpower just as America slides from its position as an economic superpower to that of a mere major economic power. This may sound like monstrous conceit, and of course it does not become us to be arrogant, but neither is there anything to be gained from false humility or servility. When two nations are *trading places* [emphasis added] in this way, frequent and severe outbursts of trade friction are only to be expected, and a comprehensive solution to the problem is in all likelihood an impossibility.

The quote is from Tsuneo Iida, "Decline of a Superpower," *Japan Echo* (Autumn, 1987), p. 22. The popular source is Clyde Prestowitz, Jr., *Trading Places: How We Are Giving Our Future to Japan and How to Reclaim It* (New York: Basic Books, 1988).

35. Bela Belassa and Marcus Noland, *Japan in the World Economy* (Washington, D.C.: Institute for International Economics, 1988), p. 4.

36. Osamu Shimomura. "The 'Japan Problem' Is of America's Making." *Japan Echo* (Autumn 1987), p. 24.

37. Of course, efforts at explaining the Japanese system and the relation of bureaucrat and *keiretsu* to market is at the heart of the dispute over the nature of the Japanese system and the universal applicability of Anglo-American economics. All of these debates are related. The most interesting discussions are for the most part ignored by mainstream economists who are directed to: John O. Hadley, "Governance by Negotiation: A Reappraisal of Bureaucratic Power in Japan," *Journal of Japanese Studies* (Summer 1987); T. J. Pempel, "The Unbundling of 'Japan, Inc.': The Changing Dynamics of Japanese Policy Formation," *Journal of Japanese Studies* (Summer 1987); and Michael L. Gerlach, "Twilight of the *Keiretsu*? A Critical Assessment," *Journal of Japanese Studies* (Winter 1992).

38. Minohei Shinohara, *op. cit.*, p. 82.

39. Steven K. Vogel, "Japanese High Technology, Politics and Power." BRIE Research Paper No. 2, Berkeley Roundtable on the International Economy, University of California (Berkeley, March 1989).

40. The feedback of the Japanese case on economic theory deserves special mention. Thanks in significant measure to the concerns raised by the Japanese example, "No longer can theorists prescribe to policymakers on the assumptions that all firms are in possession of, or have equal access to, all technologies, that technological knowledge is costlessly transferred and absorbed, or that the macroeconomic environment of inflation, risk, and capital costs is unimportant."

Nathan Rosenberg, Ralph Landau, and David C. Mowery, "Introduction," *Technology and the Wealth of Nations*. eds. N. Rosenberg, R. Landau, and D. C. Mowery (Stanford: Stanford University Press, 1992), p. 2.

41. The phrase is from Yasusuke Murakami, "The Japanese Model of Political Economy," in K. Yamamura and Y. Yasuba, *op. cit.*, p. 46.

42. While economists are not in agreement on the matter, the evidence seems to suggest that it is a misconception to believe that these institutions are to be found in Japan's historical practice going back centuries. Whatever the enabling features of the receiving cultural environment,

The separation of ownership from management, management committees, quasi-vertical integration, long-range planning systems, lifetime employment, ambiguously defined jobs, promotions and wage increases by length of service and merit, respect for workers—all these characteristics were formed after 1945 as a result of rational decision, though some of the systems were practiced to some extent by some companies before the war.

Toyohiro Kono, *Strategy and Structure of Japanese Enterprise* (Armonk: M. E. Sharpe, 1984), p. xiii.

43. While the concern in the present study is with Japan, the wider group of late industrializers and especially the Asian newly industrialized countries have followed Japan in its institutional innovations, elite cohesion, and progrowth coalition, as well as in its linkage sequencing. See ed. Frederic C. Deyo, *The Political Economy of the New Asian Industrialization* (Ithaca: Cornell University Press, 1987); Robert Wade, *Governing the Market: Economic Theory and the Role of Government in East Asian Industrialization* (Princeton: Princeton University Press, 1990); and Alice Amsden, *Asia's Next Giant: South Korea and Late Industrialization* (New York: Oxford University Press, 1989). See also Robert Wade, "East Asia's Economic Success: Conflicting Perspectives, Partial Insights, Shaky Evidence," *World Politics* (January 1992), on the general applicability of Rashomon Mirror perceptions.

It is also possible to reread much of the development literature with such cases in mind and appreciate how much the "flaky" subfield in economics has understood about the process of economic growth on the peripheries of the world system. See Pranab Bardhan, "Alternative Approaches to Development Economics," *Handbook of Development Economics*. eds. H. Chenery and T. N. Srinivasan, Volume I (Amsterdam: Elsevier Science Publishers, 1988).

44. Oliver Hart, "Theories of Optimal Capital Structure: A Management Discretion Perspective," *The Deal Decade: What Takeovers and Leveraged Buyouts Mean for Corporate Governance*, ed. M. M. Blair (Washington, D.C.: Brookings Institution, 1993).

45. Efforts to empirically discuss the *keiretsu* form are plagued with definitional problems. There are serious differences in which businesses actually should be classified as *keiretsu*. Different data series define the category differently and in ways that have led to lists overlapping very little. Indeed, the same standard source has made dramatically different counts in different years. In addition to Gerlach, see Gary Saxenhouse, "Comments and Discussion" of Robert Z. Lawrence, "Efficient or Exclusionist? The Import Behavior of Japanese Corporate Groups," *Brookings Papers on Economic Activity* 1 (1991).

46. Albert Ando and Alan Auerbach, "The corporate cost of capital in Japan and the United States: a comparison," and John B. Shoven and Toshiaki Tachibanaki, "The taxation of income from capital in Japan," both in *Government Policy Toward Industry in the United States and Japan*, ed. J. B. Shoven (Cambridge: Cambridge University Press, 1988). See also W. Carl Kester and Timothy A. Luehrman. "The Myth of Japan's Low-Cost Capital," *Harvard Business Review* (May–June 1992).

47. David M. Meerschwan, "The Japanese Financial System and the Cost of Capital," in Krugman, *op. cit.*, p. 193.

48. Michael C. Jensen and William H. Meckling, "Theory of the Firm: Managerial Behavior, Agency Costs, and Ownership Structure," *Journal of Financial Economics* 3 (1976).

49. Meerschwam in Krugman, *op. cit.*, p. 193.

50. Johnson, *op. cit., p. 203.*

51. Yasuke Murakami. "The Japanese Model of Political Economy," in Yamamura and Yasuba, pp. 444–500. See also Merton J. Peck, Richard C. Levin, and Akira Goto, "Picking Losers: Public Policy Toward Declining Industries in Japan," Journal of Japanese Studies (Winter 1987).

52. Quoted by Lockwood, *op. cit.*, p. 331, fn. 14.

53. Lockwood, *op. cit.*, p. 331.

54. The term is used by Robert Reich, *op. cit.*, pp. 178–79.

55. Paul Blustein, "In Japan, the Good Old Days of the '70s and '80s Are Gone Forever," *Washington Post National Weekly Edition*, June 29–July 5, 1992, p. 20.

Chapter 5

1. "How much can Bush bring home?" *Business Week*, January 13, 1992.

2. Steven R. Weissman, "Japan and U.S. Struggle With Resentment," *New York Times*, December 3, 1991, p. A16.

3. James P. Womack, Daniel T. Jones, and Daniel Roos, *The Machine that Changed the World; The Story of Lean Production* (New York: Harper Perennial, 1991).

4. M. Wilkins and F. Hill, *American Business Abroad* (Detroit: Wayne State University, 1964), as quoted in Auerbach, *op. cit.*, p. 223.

5. *The Wheel: A Japanese History* (Tokyo: Cosmo Public Relations Corporation, 1981), p. 29.

6. This is the judgment of Michael Cusmano, whose monograph study is, *The Japanese Automobile Industry: Technology and Management at Nissan and Toyota* (Cambridge: Harvard University Press, Cambridge 1989).

7. James P. Womack et al., *op. cit.*, pp. 77–78.

8. "When GM's Robots Ran Amok," *Economist*, August 10, 1991, p. 65.

9. Harley Shaiken and Stephen Herzenberg, *Automation and Global Production: Automobile Engine Production in Mexico, the United States, and Canada* (San Diego: Center for U.S.–Mexican Studies, University of California, 1987).

10. The Pontiac Le Mans model was made in Korea, as was the Ford Festiva. The Mercury Tracer came from Mexico (although if you bought your Tracer in Canada it came from Taiwan). With 600 car models available in the U.S. market, a customer wishing to be sure to "Buy American," would have been advised to play it safe and purchase a Honda Accord made in Ohio. Many did. It was America's best-selling car. In a kind of perverse tribute we did "Buy American." Even one of the former symbols of American automotive greatness, the Ford muscle car, the Mustang, was manufactured in Mazda's Flat Rock Michigan plant (based on Mazda's 626 model, which was also built there for sale to the U.S. market).

11. Sanders, *op. cit.*, pp. 138–39.

12. The report of the MIT International Vehicles Program's five-year study details much of what had happened. See James P. Womack, Daniel T. Jones and Daniel Roos, *op. cit.*, p. 13.

13. Cusmano, *op. cit.*, p. 381.

14. Cited *ibid.*, p. 307.

15. *Ibid.*, p. 182.

16. Hikari Nohara, "The Average Workers of a Large Japanese Company," Nihon Fukushi University Working Paper, 1990.

17. Especially influential in pulling Americans out of a false sense that the Japanese advantage was simply labor costs was the definitive study of the auto industry by James Harbour and his associates in 1982 showing that the Japanese produced subcompact cars with 42 percent fewer hours of labor and that it was their managerial efficiency that accounted for most of the ($1,643 per car) manufacturing cost advantage they enjoyed. Wage differentials were $550 and was almost totally offset by shipping, port, and duty costs of $485 per car. The net cost advantage amounted to $1,718 in favor of the Japanese subcompact car maker. Quality considerations probably added to the competitive gap. Harbour and Associates,

Inc., "Comparison of Japanese Assembly Plant Located in Japan and U.S. Car Assembly Plant Located in the U.S." (Berkeley, Michigan, 1983). The Harbour and Associates studies were prominently reported in the quality press. See *New York Times*, February 16, 1983.

18. Christopher Scherrer, "Governance of the Automobile Industry: The Transformation of Labor and Supply Relations," *Governance of the American Economy*. eds. J. R. Hollingsworth and L. N. Lindberg (Cambridge: Cambridge University Press, 1991), p. 227, fn. 23.

19. Koichi Shimokawa, "Production and Labour Strategies in Japan," *The Automobile Industry and Its Workers*, eds. S. Tolliday and J. Zeitlin (Cambridge: Polity Press, 1986).

20. For more extensive discussions, see Michael J. Smitka, *Competitive Ties: Subcontracting in the Japanese Automobile Industry* (New York: Columbia University Press, 1991), and also Banri Asanuma, "Manufacturer-Supplier Relationships in Japan and the Concept of Relation-Specific Skill," *Journal of the Japanese and International Economies* 3 (1989).

21. Michael J. Smitka, *op. cit.*, Table 3.7, p. 78.

22. The identification of affiliates and production groups is not a cut and dry procedure, and because of the fluidity in supplier relationships efforts to quantify what is going on can often produce conflicting results. See Eleanor Hadley, "Counterpoint on Business Groupings and Government-Industry Relations in Automobiles," *The Economic Analysis of the Japanese Firm*, ed. Masahiko Aoki (Amsterdam: North-Holland, 1984).

23. Womack et al., *op. cit.*, p. 57.

24. *Ibid.*, p. 80.

25. Kuniko Fujita, "Labor Process," presented University of Milan, April 1988 International Symposium on the Micro Electronics Revolution and Regional Development, Labour Organization and the Future of Post Industrial Societies.

26. Womack et al., *op. cit.*, p. 13.

27. David Friedman, "Beyond the Age of Ford: The Strategic Basis of the Japanese Success in Automobiles," *American Industry in International Competition: Government Policies and Corporate Strategies*. eds. J. Zysman and L. D. Tyson (Ithaca: Cornell University Press, 1983), p. 380.

28. Michael Simka, "The Decline of the Japanese Auto Industry: Domestic and International Implications." Paper presented to the Japan Economic Seminar East Asian Institute, Columbia University (February 20, 1993).

29. *Solidarity*, September 1-15, 1987, p. 13.

30. Constance Holden, "New Toyota-GM Plant's U.S. Model of Japanese Management," *Science*, July 1986, p. 274.

31. Holden, pp. 275-76.

32. Clair Brown and Michael Reich, "When Does Cooperation Work? A Look at NUMMI and GM-Van Nuys," *California Management Review* (Summer 1989); Mike Parker and Jane Slaughter, "Management by Stress," *Technology Review* (October 1988); Harry Katz, *Shifting Gears: Changing Labor Relations in the U.S. Automobile Industry* (Cambridge: MIT Press, 1985); K. Dohse, U. Jurgens, and T. Malsch, "From Fordism to Toyotaism? The Social Organization of the Labor Process in the Japanese Automobile Industry," *Politics and Society* 14:2 (1985); Robert E. Cole and Donald R. Deskins, Jr., "Racial Factors in Site Selection and Employment Patterns of Japanese Auto Firms in America," *California Management Review* (Fall 1988); Chalmers Johnson, "Japanese-Style Management in America," *California Management Review* (Summer 1988).

33. Harley Shaiken, *op. cit.*, p. 80.

34. Richard Florida and Martin Kenny, "Organizational Transplants: The Transfer of Japanese Industrial Organization to the U.S.," *American Sociological Review* (June 1991).

35. *Ibid.*, p. 275.

36. The impression of labor–company antagonism at their American plants is confirmed in Joseph J. Fucini and Suzy Fucini, *Working for the Japanese: Inside Mazda's American Auto Plants*, 1990.

37. "At Saturn, What Workers Want is . . . Fewer Defects," *Business Week*, December 2, 1991, pp. 117–18.

38. "Remove the barriers that hinder the hourly worker" is the twelfth of Deming's famous fourteen points to improve quality. "The hourly worker," he wrote, "is deeply aware of the need for quality. To him, quality means his job. He cannot understand why the management talks about quality and does nothing about it—in fact impedes it."
See W. Edward Deming, *Quality, Productivity and Competitive Position* (Cambridge: MIT Center for Advanced Engineering Study, 1982).

39. Candace Howes, "The Benefits of Youth: The Role of Japanese Fringe Benefits in the Restructuring of the U.S. Motor Vehicle Industry," *International Contributions to Labour Studies* 1 (1991), p. 123.

40. Kuniko Fujita and Richard Child Hill, "Global Production and Regional 'Hollowing Out' in Japan," *Pacific Rim Cities in the World Economy*, ed. M. P. Smith (New Brunswick: Transaction Books, 1989), p. 216; see also Toshihisa Komaki, "Japan Shifts Production to ASEAN States," *Japan Economic Journal*, January 2 and 9, 1988.

41. Doran P. Levin, "Back to School for Honda Workers," *New York Times*, March 29, 1993.

42. "How a Team of Buckeyes Helped Honda Save a Bundle," *Business Week*, September 13, 1993.

43. "Honda; Is It an American Car?" *Business Week*, November 18, 1991, p. 105.

44. Candace Howes, "Japanese Direct Foreign Investment in the U.S. Auto Industry" (Washington, D.C.: Economic Policy Institute, 1993).

45. Harley Shaiken, *op. cit.*, p. 80.

46. David E. Sanger, "Trade Mission Ends in Tension As the 'Big Eight' Meet," *New York Times*, January 10, 1992, p. A11.

47. James Sterngold, "Europeans Ready to Protest if Trade Accord Leaves Them Out," *New York Times*, January 10, 1992, p. A11.

48. "Japan's sudden deceleration: is Detroit winning back share—or is Tokyo giving it up?" *Business Week*, June 8, 1992, p. 26.

49. *Ibid.*

50. Clyde V. Prestowitz, Paul S. Willen, and Larry Chimerine, "The Future of the Auto Industry: It Can Compete, Can It Survive?" (Washington, D.C.: Economic Strategy Institute, 1992). The study also revealed some interesting contrasts between cost structures in the two countries. Higher health care and pension costs in the United States, nearly half of which went to retirees and laid-off workers, added $600 more to the cost of each American car. The auto industry had a clear stake in a quality national health care system and strengthened Social Security.

51. Hiromi Enshu, "Mutual Impacts of U.S.–Japanese Socioeconomic Exchange on Regional Restructuring," Institute for Urban and Regional Development Working Paper 539 (Berkeley: University of California, June 1991), p. 20.

Chapter 6

1. Alan S. Blinder, "Can Japan's Cozy System Come to Terms With Change?" *Business Week*, August 19, 1991, p. 14.

2. Kazuo Koike, "Human Resource Development and Labor–Management Relations," in *The Political Economy of Japan; Volume I: The Domestic Transformation*, eds. K. Yamamura and Y. Yasuba (Stanford: Stanford University Press, 1987), p. 308.

3. National Defense Counsel for Victims of *Karoshi*. *Karoshi: When the Corporate Warrior Dies* (Tokyo: Mado-Sha, 1990), p. 4.

4. David E. Sanger, "Japan Premier Joins Critics of Americans' Work Habits," *New York Times*, February 4, 1992, p. A6.

5. Gavan McCormack, "The Emptiness of Affluence: Vitality, Embolisms and Symbiosis in the Japanese Body Politic" (Luxembourg: Institute for European and International Affairs, 1992), p. 6.

6. Karel van Wolferen, "Rise of an Anti-Social Force," *Times Literary Supplement*, August 31–September 1, 1990, p. 926.

7. The Japan *Karoshi* Foundation, Bunkyo Sogo Law Office, 3-18-11 Hongo, Bunkyo-ku, Tokyo 113, Japan for text. This particular ad appeared in the *New York Times* of September 9, 1991.

8. Details of the manual, confirmed by the Ministry, appeared in the May 19, 1990 *Asahi Shimbun* and other places.

9. National Defense Counsel for Victims of *Karoshi*, *op. cit.*, p. 70.

10. Rob Steven, *Japan's New Imperialism*. (Armonk, New York: M. E. Sharpe, 1990), pp. 49–50.

11. Rob Steven, *Classes in Contemporary Japan* (Cambridge: Cambridge University Press, 1983), p. 193.

12. M. Anne Hill, "Women in the Japanese Economy." Paper presented to World Bank Conference, "Women's Changing Economic Role in Asia," University of Toronto (June 4–5, 1992), p. 1.

13. M. Anne Hill, "Women's Relative Wages in Post-War Japan," *International Review of Comparative Public Policy* (1991). See also Haruo Shimada and Yoshio Higuchi, "An Analysis of Trends in Female Labor Force Participation in Japan," *Journal of Labor Economics* (January 1985).

14. Susan N. Houseman, and Katherine G. Abraham, "Female Workers as a Buffer in the Japanese Economy," *American Economic Association, Papers and Proceedings*, May 1993, p. 45. Also see M. Anne Hill, "Female Labor Force Participation in Developing and Developed Countries—Consideration of the Informal Sector," *Review of Economics and Statistics* (August 1983).

15. David W. Plath, *Work and Life Course in Japan*, cited by Bernard Eccleston, *op. cit.*, p. 67.

16. About one third of men with families leave them behind when faced with transfers requiring a household move. See Takao Minami, "Transfers of Workers and the Separation of Families," *Economic Eye* (Spring 1992).

17. See Alice H. Cook and Hiroko Hayashi, *Working Women in Japan: Discrimination, Resistance, and Reform* (Ithaca: New York State School of Industrial and Labor Relations, Cornell University, 1980), and Takie Sugiyama Lebra, *Japanese Women: Constraint and Fulfillment* (Honolulu: University of Hawaii Press, 1984).

18. Machiko Osawa, "Changing Role of Education and Women Workers in Japan," *Keio Business Review* 24 (1987).

19. Linda N. Edwards, "Equal Employment Opportunity in Japan: A View for the West," *Industrial and Labor Relations Review* (January 1988).

20. Robert J. Smith, "Gender Inequality in Contemporary Japan," *Journal of Japanese Studies* (Winter 1987).

21. Takie Sugiyama Lebra, "Gender and Culture in the Japanese Political Economy: Self-Portrayals of Prominent Business Women," in Kumon and Rosovsky, *op. cit.*, p. 367.

Ian Buruma has characterized the role of women in the following terms, which still reflects a dominant tendency in Japanese society:

[F]rom the lowliest masseuse to the top-flight geisha, they serve to put the Japanese male at ease, to make him forget the tensions of collective company life, to soothe his masculine anxieties, to indulge his whims and flatter his social pride. They are, perhaps increasingly, highly trained mothers.

Ian Buruma, *Behind the Mask: On Sexual Demons, Sacred Mothers, Transvestites, Gangsters and Other Japanese Cultural Heroes* (New York: Penguin Books, 1984), p. 101.

22. Kuniko Fujita, "A World City: The Tokyo Metropolis," International Sociological Association, Research Committee on the Sociology of Urban and Regional Studies, Rio de Janeiro, September 1988.

23. The weekly *Gendai*, which ran an article by the woman who won the sexual harassment suit, preceded it with a six-page spread of glossy photos of a nude woman.

24. Kazuo Sugeno, "The Supreme Court's Hitachi Decision on the Duty to Work Overtime," *Japan Labor Bulletin*, May 1991.

In citing the importance of this case and its larger significance I am not singling out Hitachi for special criticism. It has diverse practices in many of its 800 subsidiaries. (Hitachi is huge—it alone produces nearly 2 percent of Japan's GNP.) It does brilliant work in robotics and supercomputing. Its creative work teams on the frontiers of science demonstrate hierarchical differentiation by gender and abusive expectations of its less-privileged workers. In this it is not unique.

25. *Asahi Shimbun Japan Access*, December 9, 1991, p. 3.

26. *Asahi Shimbun Japan Access*, February 10, 1992, p. 2.

27. Kanemichi Kumagai, "Japanese Style Industrial Relations and Trade Union Rights," statement November 1991.

28. Ryuzo's Saki *Cold Lump of Steel*, based on his experience as a blue-collar worker and the effect of hierarchical differences in fringe benefits and working conditions, won him the New Japanese Literature Prize. Kazuo Watanabe's 1979 novel, *Feeding on the Company*, describes greedy top management, a left-wing union critical of their devious activities, and the chairman of the company union whose job it is to get rid of that union. This book, too, is based on the author's experiences. He was the right-wing union chairman and the book was written to expiate his own guilt. A second novel, which traces the punishment he received from the company after *Feeding the Company* appeared, is a minor best seller, *A Letter of Resignation* (1980).

29. William G. Ouchi, *Theory Z: How American Business Can Meet the Japanese Challenge* (Boston: Addison-Wesley, 1981).

30. Toyota Motor Company, *Labor/Management Relations*. Printed in Japan (1984).

31. Hidesuke Nagashima, "Old Seniority System Being Overhauled," *Mainichi Daily News*, November 21, 1990, p. 6.

32. Novelist Yasuda's Jiro Yasuda has laid out the ways brokerage houses buy

and sell to launder money for clients wishing to evade taxes and buy political fund raisers; see his popular *The Black Wolf of Kabutocho* and *The Collapse of Kabutocho* . Albert J. Alletzhauser's *The House of Nomura: The Inside Story of the Legendary Japanese Financial Dynasty* is also a best seller that serves as a nonfiction preparation to read Yasuda's first book, the 1980 *Money Hunter*, which is about a scheme by MOF officials to turn *Kabutocho*, Tokyo's Wall Street, into a state-operated casino by methodically manipulating prices. We shall discuss these themes less colorfully in Chapter 10.

33. Teruyuki Murakami, from a presentation to the International Trade Union Symposium, "Japanese Style Industrial Relations and Trade Union Rights," Tokyo, November 1991. The conference was sponsored by *Zenroren*, the leftist opposition National Confederation of Trade Unions.

34. Even though the Confederation of Japanese Automobile Workers' Unions, the largest industrywide organization in Japan's private sector, is dedicated to labor solidarity above and beyond the framework of individual enterprises, its official handbook also notes that "a car manufacturer, parts makers, sales dealers, and transportation companies enjoy an extremely close relationship, one which can be likened to a communal relationship where members are bound together by a common fate." JAW, *Organization and Activities*, n.d., p. 5.

35. William Ouchi, *op. cit.*, p. 39.

36. Hikari Nohara, "Reconsidering the Japanese Production System Model," (Melbourne: February 1991), Nihon Fukushi University and Institute of East Asian Studies, University of California Research Paper, p. 10.

37. *Ibid.*, p. 11.

38. *Business Week*, May 12, 1986, p. 52.

39. Hikari Nohara, "Is the Japanese Industrial Relations a Breakthrough: A Hypothesis Relating Japanese Industrial Relations to Those in the United States and Europe," unpublished paper, April 1990, p. 4.

40. Eishi Fujita, "Labor Process and Labor Management: The Case of Toyota" (1990), Typescript.

41. Akio Morita, *Made in Japan* (Baltimore: Penguin, 1988).

42. Koike, *op. cit.*, p. 306.

43. Masanori E. Hashimoto and John Raisian, "Employment Tenure and Earnings Profiles in Japan and the United States," *American Economics Review*, 1985; and Robert L. Clark and Naohiro Ogawa, "The Effect of Mandatory Retirement on Earnings Profiles in Japan," *Industrial and Labor Relations Review* (January 1992).

44. Jane Slaughter, "Management by Stress," *Multinational Monitor* (January–February 1990).

45. Many other companies also refused to seriously reinvest in the low profit steel business. See Abegglen and Salk, *op. cit.*, p. 76.

46. Yoshi Tsurumi, "Labor Relations and Industrial Adjustment in Japan and the U.S.: A Comparative Analysis," *Yale Law & Policy Review* (Spring 1984), p. 219.

47. Yasuo Shingu is quoted in "Structural Changes in Manufacturing," *Japan Close-Up* (July 1990), p. 41.

48. Quoted by Ichiyo Muto, *op. cit.*, p. 129.

49. *Business Week*, May 12, 1986, p. 49.

50. From company material given to the author.

51. The quote from Matsushita is from Hayward and Bessant, *op. cit.*, 1987. The two experts cited are Freeman and Perez, *op. cit.*, p. 37.

52. The survey was by the Dai-Tokyo Marine and Fire Insurance Company and was reported in "Labor Letter," *Wall Street Journal*, April 23, 1991, p. A1.

Chapter 7

1. Masahiko Aoki, "Decentralization–Centralization in Japanese Organization: A Duality Principle," in eds. Shumpei Kumon and Henry Rosovsky, *The Political Economy of Japan, Volume 3, Cultural and Social Dynamics* (Stanford: Stanford University Press, 1992), p. 164.

2. Ronald P. Dore, *Shinohata: A Portrait of a Japanese Village* (New York: Pantheon Books, 1978), p. 97.

3. "FTC Lets Construction Clique Off the Hook; Failure to Pursue Saitama Bid-Rigging Fuels Other Suspicions," *Asahi Shimbun Japan Access*, May 25, 1992, p. 3.

In 1993 construction company documents disclosing the ranking of virtually every major politician in the country (each given a letter grade that determined exactly how large a contribution they would receive twice a year) were made public. Japanese press reports suggested that most construction companies used such a system. The legality of the unethical practice was in dispute since the subterfuges used to circumvent the laws barring excessive contributions seemed to be capable of being interpreted as lawful behavior.

4. Chalmers Johnson, "Tanaka Kakuei, Structural Corruption, and the Advent of Machine Politics in Japan," *Journal of Japanese Studies* (Winter 1986).

5. In the fall of 1992 Hiroyasu Watanabe told investigators that he had illegally given Kanemaru $4 million (paid in the form of 50,000 ten thousand yen notes in a number of shopping bags when they had met for this purpose in a dimly lit parking garage). Watanabe's mob-related company, *Tokyo Sagawa Kyubin*, a parcel delivery firm, had paid out over $17 million, among others, to three former prime ministers, at least two current cabinet ministers, and some other persons of prominence, an amount that set a new record in political corruption in Japan.

6. Steven R. Wiseman, "Japanese Leaders Taken to Task By Political Boss for Bashing U.S.," *New York Times*, February 12, 1992, p. 12.

7. Kent E. Calder, *Crisis and Compensation: Public Policy and Political Stability in Japan* (Princeton: Princeton University Press, 1988), p. 297.

8. Nakamura, *op. cit.*, Chapter 2.

9. See Kosai, *op. cit.*, for a rationale and discussion of a slightly different classification.

10. Yukio Noguchi, "The Development and Present State of Public Finance," *Public Finance in Japan*, ed. T. Shibata (Tokyo: University of Tokyo Press, 1986).

11. *Hekichi* is the designation of a backward and remote region that qualifies for special assistance.

12. Jackson H. Bailey, "The Desperate Search for Jobs," in his *Ordinary People, Extraordinary Lives: Political and Economic Change in a Tohoku Village* (Honolulu: University of Hawaii Press, 1991), p. 149.

13. A significant ethnographic literature exists among which the following are notable instances:

John Embree, *Suye Mura: A Japanese Village* (Chicago: University of Chicago Press, 1939); John F. Embree and Ella Lury Wiswell, *The Women of Suye Mura* (Chicago: University of Chicago Press, 1982); Edward Norbeck, *Takashima: A Japanese Fishing Community* (Salt Lake City: University of Utah Press, 1954); Robert J. Smith, *Kurusu: The Price of Progress in a Japanese Village, 1951–1975* (Stanford: Stanford University Press, 1978), as well as the works by Bailey and Dore cited earlier.

14. Kenichi Miyamoto, *op. cit.*, "Urban Problems . . . ," p. 37.

15. Haruhiro Fukui, "Studies in Policy Making: A Review of the Literature,"

Policy Making in Contemporary Japan, ed. T. J. Pempel (Ithaca: Cornell University Press, 1977).

16. As Miyamoto reports:

> Within major urban areas the population in suburban areas increased most, and the majority of the increased population are households with young couples and children with low income. In other words, they are propertyless workers who have to be provided with housing facilities for livelihood, environment and means of transportation to the center of the cities. Furthermore, they are the households with children of school age that cannot do without educational facilities, clinics, and hospitals. However, due to the fact that suburban areas where they came to live were originally agricultural villages whereby the accumulation of the means of social consumption such as housing, educational facilities, environmental facilities, and means of transportation were not developed, the demand for housing and the means of social consumption occurred explosively.

op. cit., "Urban Problems . . . ," p. 38.

17. It was not only the left candidates who were members of the educated elite. Almost all large-city mayors and governors in these areas had college degrees and about half had attended either Tokyo or Kyoto universities, the two most prestigious in the country, and there was no real difference between progressives and conservatives in this regard.

18. Kyoto has always been a bastion of progressive politics. It has been called the Japanese Bologna after the Italian city with a strong leftist political culture and strong grass-roots support for historical preservation and democratic locally controlled economic policies. Both cities have been extensively studied by scholars for the way local small business people vote for communists and support other insurgent groups and are rewarded by policies favoring local industry prosperity over encouragement of outsiders and large corporate domination. Both Kyoto and Bologna, while large critics, preserve a community structure and spirit. For a study of Bologna, see Robert H. Evans, *Coexistence: Communism and Its Practice in Bologna, 1945-65* (South Bend: University of Notre Dame Press, 1967).

19. Terry MacDougall, "Japanese Urban Local Politics: Towards a Viable Progressive Political Opposition," in *Japan: The Paradox of Progress*, ed. L. Austin (New Haven: Yale University Press, 1976).

20. Ellis S. Krauss, "Opposition in Power: The Development and Maintenance of Leftist Government in Kyoto Prefecture," in *Political Opposition and Local Politics in Japan*, eds. K. Steiner, E. S. Krause and S. C. Flanagan (Princeton: Princeton University Press, 1980).

21. Kazuhiro Ueta, "Environmental Planning in Japan," paper presented to the International Conference on Public Policy Planning, Taipei, Taiwan, June 12–14, 1989.

22. For detailed discussion, see Margaret A. McKean, "The Legal Impact of the Big Four Verdicts," *Environmental Protest and Citizen Politics in Japan* (Berkeley: University of California Press, 1981), p. 61 ff.

23. Compensation of victims is financed by polluters. It took until 1992 for the Tokyo District Court to rule in a Minamata Disease (mercury poisoning) case absolving the prefecture and national governments from legal responsibilities relating to the spread of the disease. The court did award victims $32,000 from the Chisso Corporation, which released the poisonous chemicals into Minamata Bay in the late 1950s, a pitifully small sum after more than three decades of struggle.

The young of the community have left. They cannot fish the waters despite dredging of tons of mercury from what was once one of Japan's richest fishing grounds. They cannot get jobs elsewhere if potential employers learn they are from Minamata. For young people it is almost impossible to find a marriage partner. Yet, even today the town is divided. The victims association wants a memorial and commemorative museum. Other residents, recalling Ibsen's *An Enemy of the People*, want all reminders swept away and the incident eradicated from history so that Chisso, whose factory still dominates the town, will invest further. The government, backed by the courts, refused compensation and waits for the victims to die.

24. Michio Muramatsu and Ronald Aqua, "Japan Confronts Its Cities: Central–Local Relations in a Changing Political Context," in ed. Douglas Ashford, *National Resources and Urban Policy*. (London: Methuen, 1980).

25. Noguchi, *op. cit.*, p. 42.

26. T. J. Pempel, *op. cit.*, p. 57.

27. Kenichi Miyamoto, "Cities Under Contemporary Japanese Capitalism," *Japanese Economic Studies* (Fall 1987), p. 22.

28. *Ibid.*, p. 16.

29. Kenichi Miyamoto, "Urban Policies in the Metropolitan Areas of Japan: Post–World War II to the Present," *Keizei Kenkyu* (*Business Review*), Osaka City University, (May 1985), pp. 91–92.

30. The description of the Tokyo region in the final report stressed this.

"Tokyo, not only as the Japanese capital, but as the worldwide metropolitan center of the international financial market should have higher level function to supply worldwide information to the whole nation and to become useful for the development of international society as well as our country. For this purpose, the Tokyo region should be promoted to pursue the function of a world city."

The report called for even more intensive land use of the Tokyo bay area.

31. Cited by Shujiro Yazawa. "The Technopolis Program in Japan." *Hitotsubashi Journal of Social Studies* 22 (1990), p. 9.

32. Jeffrey Broadbent interviewed an official of the National Land Agency in 1979. That interview conveys a sense of how the national government has not in fact fought concentration in the already crowded Pacific industrial belt despite its rhetoric.

"The Ikeda Cabinet pushed growth in the Pacific Coast Belt area. But we [bureaucrats at the National Land Agency] . . . pushed for the New Industrial Cities (NIC) law to reduce regional differences in income and stop the overconcentration of population. There were two opposing [forces], economic efficiency and regional growth. Two different opinions. All the regional Diet representatives were totally opposed [to further concentration in the Pacific Belt]. The big business leaders [*zaikai*] need the [political] support of all the [LDP] Diet representatives, so they let them ask for [the NIC law. The *zaikai*] asked the bureaucrats to put on a good act [that investment was going to the outlying regions], but to put all the real investment into the Pacific Coast Belt area. . . . In actuality, most of the growth did take place in that [Pacific Coast Belt] area . . . MITI had guidance power, but did not use it.

Jeffrey Broadbent, " 'The Technopolis Strategy' vs. Deindustrialization: High Tech Development Sites in Japan," in Smith, *op. cit.*, pp. 236–37.

33. For more positive assessments in terms of the technological imperative, see Sheridan Tatsuno, *The Technopolis Strategy: Japan, High Technology, and Control of the Twenty-First Century* (Englewood Cliffs: Prentice-Hall, 1986); and eds. Raymond W. Smilor, George Zozmetsky, and David Gison, *Creating the Technopolis: Linking Technology, Commercialization and Economic Development* (Cambridge: Ballinger, 1988).

34. Thus, for example, the Oita Prefecture Technopolis orientation document makes clear that:

> The Technopolis is then built on three basic principles: the integration of agriculture, forestry and fisheries; the fostering of human resources to produce highly skilled and motivated work forces; and decentralization to allow technopolis to develop in harmony with the natural environment and with special local characteristics and traditions and to anticipate the ripple effects of the project.

Tadao Kigazawa cited in Yazawa, *Ibid.*, p. 16.

35. Masayuki Sasaki, "Endogenous Development of Urban Economy in Kanazawa City," a paper presented to the conference "Regional Policies in Asian Areas," 1989, p. 2.

36. Gavan McCormack, "The Price of Affluence: The Political Economy of Japanese Leisure," *New Left Review*, p. 134.

37. Kunihori Yamada, "The Triple Evils of Golf Courses," *Japan Quarterly* (July–September 1990).

38. *Ibid.*, p. 133.

39. The quotation is from a work in progress by Toshio Kamo of the Law Faculty of Osaka City University.

40. Richard Child Hill and Kuniko Fujita, "Japanese Cities in the World Economy," *Japanese Cities in the World Economy: Global Restructuring and Urban–Industrial Change*, eds. K. Fujita and R. C. Hill, (Philadelphia: Temple University Press, 1993).

41. The usual picture of Japanese industry of Hitachi, Toyota, and so on with their satellite suppliers omits the *jiba sangyo*, local industry composed of small and medium-size enterprises concentrated spatially in particular industrial neighborhoods that form into groups engaged in production of products in the same industrial category—fabrics, castings, ceramics, and so on. Osaka alone has sixty *jiba sangyo*. A chamber of commerce survey of August 1989 lists 615 bicycle and parts manufacturers, 58 umbrella companies (with 62 rib and partsmakers) and a host of other *jiba sangyo* groups.

42. Theodore Bestor, *Neighborhood Tokyo* (Stanford: Stanford University Press, 1988).

43. MITI, *op. cit.*, p. 89.

44. Shunichi Teranishi, "New Urban Growth of Tokyo Metropolitan Region and Some Aspects of Environmental Problems in Japan," presented to joint meeting of European Environmental Bureau and Japan Environmental Conference, July 9–11, 1990, Brussels, Belgium.

45. *Asahi Shimbun*, June 3, 1991.

46. I am indebted to a very large number of people for conversations on this subject. Let me mention Takamichi Masai of the editorial board of the *Asahi Shimbun*, Hiroshi Takatsuki, senior editor of the *Mainachi* newspapers, Yoshiaki Takagi, director general of the Bureau of Taxation of the Tokyo Metropolitan government, Yoshitaka Misu, chairman of the Tokyo Metropolitan Government Workers Union, Yukio Tanaka, of the Department of Commerce and Industry of the Osaka Prefecture government, and Michio Sugimoto, director of the Osaka Chamber of Com-

merce. On the relevant statistics see *The White Paper* of the Ministry of Construction, July 1991.

47. Kenichi Miyamoto, "The Decline and Restructuring of the Osaka Metropolitan Area: An Analytical Comparison with the Tokyo Metropolitan Area," in K. Fujita and R. C. Hill, *op. cit.*

48. Kojiro Nakamura. "Endogenous Development in a Local City—An Economic Case Study of Kanazawa as a Model City," *Image of Big Cities in the 21st Century*, ed. T. Shibata (Tokyo: University of Tokyo Press, 1986).

49. *Ibid.*, pp. 8–9.

50. *Ibid.*, p. 7.

51. I may add that one of the community training schools specializes in the traditional crafts of the region so that they are passed on to the young in a formally structured learning environment, thereby keeping alive skills important to the local economy. There is a deep awareness of the importance of urban amenities, historical preservation, the arts and culture of the city, and residents' rights to a quality living environment among the resident decision makers. Such efforts have paid off in other ways as well. Kanazawa has been rated the most comfortable city in Japan in which to live by *Nihon Keizai Shimbun*, the financial daily. Preservation has been a physical, cultural and industrial undertaking. There has been no conflict among these goals of economic development and preservation on the quality of life.

52. T. R. Reid, "Taking Steps to Rein In the High Cost of Land in Japan," *Washington Post*, October 21, 1990.

53. In Kyoto I also visited a Buddhist priest in his rebuilt temple. It was on the roof of a four-story shopping mall in the downtown. He was proud of the solution he had come up with, rather than submit to a forced sale of the property to the *jiageya* (speculators) and *yakuza* (gangsters), after a fire had destroyed the old temple, who demanded that he sell and build his new temple outside central Kyoto. He had entered an arrangement to build the present structure that supported the temple at its traditional location. It seemed an odd and not altogether satisfactory compromise.

54. Haruo Shimada has noted that while there are many measures that would help correct the inefficiencies in land use, such as increasing property taxes and making it easier to sell land by decreasing the income tax on land sales,

> An equally important need is for a comprehensive regional development policy. The greatest obstacle is the national government's strong control of local governments. The need to foster local initiatives is stressed repeatedly, but the concentration of power and authority in the national government makes it almost impossible to prepare an environment conducive to regional development.

Haruo Shimada, "Structural Policies in Japan," in Kernell, *op. cit.*, p. 313.

55. MITI is establishing an Institute of Earth Environment Industrial Technology, which, among other projects, will try to solidify the carbon dioxide gas in the atmosphere with the use of algae, bacteria, and catalytic reactions to produce methanol and organic acids that can be productively recycled and other impressive projects.

Chapter 8

1. Albert J. Alletzhauser, *The House of Nomura: The Inside Story of the Legendary Japanese Financial Dynasty* (New York: HarperPerennial, 1990), p. 294.

2. Borthwick, *op. cit.*, p. 263.

3. Examples from the press abound critical of such arrangements and abuses. An editorial in the *Asahi Shimbun* of January 27, 1992, is not untypical: "Collusion between the LDP and the bureaucracy has assumed such grave proportions that it threatens the very foundations of democracy in Japan."

4. A certain amount of breastbeating boiler plate is employed each time the LDP's "ethical failings" are unmasked and new sets of controls and reforms are proposed. The same document is basically recycled each time. For example, see Political Reform Committee, Liberal Democratic Party, "A Proposal for Political Reform," *Journal of Japanese Studies* 4.22 (Autumn 1989).

5. The faction has traditionally been called an "army corps" because of the exceptional loyalty of its lieutenants and the strong solidarity of its ranks. Any dissent is severely punished. An offender finds a well-financed rival running against him supported vigorously by the rest of the faction. Those who dare cross the faction's decisions "are as good as dead politically." Thus, the contrived solidarity of the faction is enforced by strict discipline. The decomposition of the LDP in the early 1990s made for a new, more fluid situation.

When the skillful kingmaker allows a leader of another faction to become prime minister, he also works to assure that his power is limited and that key cabinet posts go to members of his own faction, not to those whom the prime minister would appoint from his own *ha*. These exceptions are negotiated and then publicly voiced. As the *Asahi Shinbum* reports, "Although the LDP presidential election determines the nation's leadership, the Japanese public has little influence and no choice in the matter."

6. Although Tanaka was arrested in June 1976 for taking $3.8 million in bribes from executives of Marubeni to approve purchase of Lockheed's Tristar, at this writing sixteen years have gone by since he was indicted, but no final judgment on his guilt was rendered. Seven years after his arrest he was sentenced to four years of hard labor in prison, but prolonged appeals left him at liberty.

The Recruit stock-for-favors scandal was front-page news in 1988 and 1989. It involved almost all leaders of the Japanese political Establishment at the time.

7. "Japan Survey," *The Economist*, December 5, 1987, p. 22.

8. "Hidden Japan," *Business Week*, August 26, 1991, p. 35.

9. Michio Muramatsu and Masaru Mabuchi, "Introducing a New Tax in Japan," Kernell, *op. cit.*, p. 197.

10. Eisuke Sakakibara, "The Japanese Politico-Economic System and the Public Sector," Kernell, *ibid.*, p. 53.

11. For those interested in formal modeling of this relation from a political science perspective see Michio Muramatsu. "Center–Local Political Relations in Japan: A Lateral Competition Model," *Journal of Japanese Studies* (Summer 1986).

12. On the system and its expenses, see Gerald L. Curtis, *Election Campaigning Japanese Style* (Tokyo: Kodansha International, 1983).

13. "Japan's Revolution Could End Up as Paralysis," *Business Week*, August 16, 1993, p. 47.

14. James Sterngold, "Conservatives Dominate Japan's New Cabinet," *New York Times*, August 9, 1993, p. A7.

15. Andrew W. Pollack, "Japan Businesses See Little Threat in Vote Results," *New York Times*, July 26, 1993, p. A3.

16. Andrew Glyn, Alan Hughes, Alain Lipietz, and Ajit Singh, "The Rise and Fall of the Golden Age," *The Golden Age of Capitalism: Reinterpreting the Postwar Experience*, eds. S. A. Marglin and J. B. Schor (Oxford: Clarendon Press, 1991), Table 2.13, p. 84.

17. *Ibid.*, p. 42.

18. "America's Hidden Problem," *Business Week*, August 29, 1983, p. 83.

19. Margaret M. Blair, *The Deal Decade: What Takeovers and Leveraged Buyouts Mean for Corporate Governance* (Washington, D.C.: Brookings Institution, 1993).

20. Pempel in Katzenstein, *op. cit.*, p. 152.

21. The *kokyu-kanryo* high-echelon bureaucrats move on, usually in their mid-forties, to soft but well-paid, high-status jobs in both the private sector and in nonprofit organizations controlled by government ministries. There were 6,841 of these organizations in October 1990, according to the Management and Coordination Agency. MITI's Industrial Policy Bureau has approved the establishment of more than 160 nonprofit corporations. *Keidanren*, which has contributed over $1 billion to fund such research institutes, has urged the ministries and agencies to exercise restraint in establishing new ones, but to little effect. The structural corruption here is less commented upon, but it is worth noting.

The *amakudari* phenomenon became a critical issue only in 1991 as part of the securities house scandals and the way the Finance Ministry was perceived as having looked the other way, the result it was commonly said of the former MOF bureaucrats in senior positions at the securities houses being able to obtain favorable treatment from former subordinates anxious to land cushy berths when they themselves "ascended from heaven."

The National Personnel Authority lists hundreds of high-ranking officials who join private companies with close ties to the ministries or agencies they have left that, while it is illegal under the law (retired bureaucrats are prohibited by Article 103 of the Government Official Law from taking positions with ties to ministries or agencies for two years after they leave government service), are routinely granted exemptions. Indeed, the National Personnel Authority list is an enumeration of the exemptions officially granted. Former officials of the MOF numerically head the list.

22. These figures are from Shimada, *op. cit.*, p. 286.

23. *Asahi Shimbun Japan Access*, April 13, 1992, p. 5.

24. The comparisons and contrast between the United States and Japan in the early 1990s is informative. In Japan corporate profits plunged and the stock market was a disaster. Both held up far better in the United States despite a deeper recession. In Japan consumer spending levels were maintained and income distribution became somewhat more equal as land and stock prices fell. As other businesses felt the effect of the downturn hundreds of company presidents resigned to take blame for poor performance. Employment remained high because companies did not lay off workers and the social contract between corporate Japan and its full-time employees for the most part held. Wage rate growth slowed but stayed comfortably at more than twice the rate of price increases. The expense account crowd suffered as did business at fancier restaurants, but businesses where people spent their own money continued to hold their own.

25. Another player was the Japanese life insurance industry, which passed the United States in the value of their policies in 1987. The *seiho* (life insurance companies) are a major force in international finance. In the second half of the 1980s their assets more than doubled as Japanese grew wealthier and spent more on life insurance, thanks in part to the 400,000 door-to-door salespeople, the ubiquitous and seemingly indefatigable life insurance ladies with their detailed knowledge and neighborhood ties. Much of the *seiho* money found its way into U.S. Treasuries.

The insurance companies, securities firms, and banks all lobbied the government to allow them to enter businesses that were the preserve of other sectors of the finance industry. There was fear among regulators that imprudent investments and overextensions would follow a freeing of the reins. As in the United States, and partially with an eye on developments in America, regulators in Japan expressed the same concerns over option trading, brokering bond futures and the use of stock index futures trading instruments would create wider instabilities. The regulators were caught between pressure to accept these new instruments because if they did not the Japanese financial firms would be at an international disadvantage and the knowledge that if they did accept such innovations, then their ability to control Japan's financial markets would seriously be diminished.

26. Kenichi Ohmae, *The Borderless World* (New York: Harper and Row, 1990).

27. Kenichi Ohmae, "The Scandal Behind Japan's Financial Scandals," *Wall Street Journal*, August 6, 1991.

28. What Ohmae and others who question the bad deal the Japanese were getting by financing, with their continued purchases of enormous quantities of Treasury bonds, was the prolonged spending binge that paid for imports from Japan and had an important impact as well on U.S. politics. In acting as they did the Japanese could be seen as "a de facto Republican political action committee," as David Hale has written.

Ohmae has also written that "It is better that the yen remain high until Japan can buy up more American resources and it is better that the U.S. budget deficit continue a bit longer. . . . Japan's prosperity is built on the U.S. budget deficit." Of course, he said that in Japanese for a Japanese audience only. As Japanese investors cooled on the prospects of the U.S. economy Japanese purchases of Treasury bonds did in fact drop from as much as 40 percent in the late 1980s to less than 10 percent in the early 1990s.

The impact of Japanese financial practices is a matter of some controversy. Nomura Research Institute, the largest commercially owned think-tank in the world, warned its clients that Wall Street was ready to tumble just before the 23 percent drop in the Dow on Black Monday October 19, 1987. Some American commentators blame Japanese sell orders with triggering the fall.

David Hale, "Picking Up Reagan's Tab," *Foreign Policy* (Spring 1989), p. 152.

Kenichi Ohmae, as quoted in Chalmers Johnson, "Trade Revisionism and the Future of Japanese–American Relations," *Japan's Economic Structure: Should It Change?* ed. K. Yamamura (Seattle: Society for Japan Studies), 1990, p. 130.

29. Even Mitsui Trust and Banking Company, a core element of the great Mitsui *keiretsu*, found its share prices selling for 80 percent less in 1992 than they did in 1987 because of collapsing property prices. Mitsui, like the other blue-chip banks, had lent to financial companies that had in turn extended hundreds of billions of dollars in loans in the 1980s that had turned sour.

30. The Bank for International Settlement rules allow banks to include 45 percent of the unrealized capital gains on their stock holdings toward the 8 percent (of their risk weighted assets). The Japanese had insisted on including unrealized stock profits in the capital asset ratio calculation in the negotiations leading up to acceptance of the capital adequacy rule in December 1987. The requirement itself is a good thing as a security measure for the international finance system. It was pushed by Western bankers, however, as part of a competitiveness offensive, as they saw it, to level the playing field since Japanese banks were using the rising paper value of their assets to dramatically expand loans. The Japanese without strict capital adequacy requirements at home could lend aggressively at very low rates and in effect earn no profit, but successfully "stealing" markets from U.S.

and European bankers who faced both more substantial constraints and higher profit targets on their lending.

31. Tony Shale, "The Plot that Triggered Tokyo's Plunge," *Europemoney*, May 1990.

32. James Sterngold, "Treasury Official Rebukes Japan," *New York Times*, October 18, 1991, p. D1.

33. As Will Hutton wrote: "It is a 1990s version of Gresham's Law. Deregulated banking drives out regulated banking and all of us pay the price." in "Finance and Economics," *Guardian*, September 10, 1990, p. 10.

34. Alan M. Webber, Interviewer, "Yasuhiro Nakasone: The Statesman as CEO," *Harvard Business Review* (March/April 1989), p. 89.

35. Alletzhauser, *op. cit.*, pp. 10–11.

36. They were more successful in their ruling about the same time against a secret cartel of Japanese plastic wrap manufacturers that industry executives claimed was unfair appeasement of the Americans. They suggested that since such rigged bidding had been going on in their industry for seventeen years and was far from uncommon elsewhere, the government had simply served them up to the Americans to show resolve. This may have been an accurate assessment, but it also showed which way the wind was blowing. The powerful Nomura itself was soon to be brought low by the regulators.

37. James Sterngold, "Japan Takes On the Mob, and the Mob Fights Back," *New York Times*, June 15, 1992, p. A7.

38. James Sterngold, "Testimony On Brokers In Tokyo," *New York Times*, August 30, 1991, p. D6.

39. *Ibid.*

40. It also became known about the same time that Prescott Bush, President George Bush's brother, had been a consultant and received hundreds of thousands of dollars from Mr. Ishii through a series of front companies. Indeed, in a plot twist worthy of Mr. Itami, a Japanese company with reputed *yakuza* ties, sued Prescott Bush in U.S. Federal District Court for swindling them. In pretrial discussions Mr. Bush's lawyers explained the American legal system to the Japanese. If there was any liability, it was to an entity called Prescott Bush & Co. (a shell that had its phone disconnected) and not to the individual they were suing. The Japanese, however, knew enough about American law to point out that if Mr. Bush had purposely undercapitalized his own company with the intent of rendering it incapable of meeting its financial obligations, then they would have his lunch. Thus, international understanding and good will is spread and the process of bringing harmony proceeds.

Ronald Sullivan, "Tokyo Company Sues Bush's Brother for Millions," *New York Times*, June 16, 1992.

41. Karl Marx, *Grundrisse: Foundation of the Critique of Political Economy*, translated by Martin Nicolaus (Baltimore: Penguin Books, 1973), p. 87.

42. Christopher Wood, "Japanese Finance," *The Economist*, December 8, 1990, p. 3.

43. R. Taggart Murphy, "Power Without Purpose: The Crisis of Japan's Global Financial Dominance," *Harvard Business Review* (March–April 1989), p. 72.

44. Akio Kuroda of the Bank's Institute for Monetary and Economic Studies summed up the experience with deregulation writing, "The controllability of the open market rates has not always been satisfactory from the viewpoint of the BOJ." Japanese monetary authorities speak of the need to develop new techniques if they

are to control interest rates in an era of financial globalization. Akio Kuroda, "Book Review," *Journal of Japanese and International Economics* 4 (1990), p. 98.

45. Tohru Machida, "Securities Industry; Growing Competition and the Whiff of Scandal: Troubled Times for a Super-Rich Industry," *Japan Economic Almanac* (1990), p. 73.

46. "Hidden Japan," *Business Week*, August 26, 1991, p. 36.

47. "Guidance: Not All Executives Think Collusion is Bad," *Asahi Shimbun/ Japan Access*, June 15, 1992, p. 2.

48. James Sterngold, "Japan's New Financial Official Plots an Independent Course," *New York Times*, August 5, 1991, p. D8.

Chapter 9

1. Theodore White, "The Danger From Japan," *New York Times Magazine*, July 28, 1985.

2. The British were warned, of course, in alarmist best sellers with such titles as *Made in Germany* and *American Invaders*, but ideology dies hard and the more internationalized wing of British capital continues to thrive to this day. It is that part of the country where most Britons live and work that has known hard times over the long period of the nation's decline. Britain remains competitive in an economist's sense of course, but at a lower and lower relative standard of living.

3. Yung Chul Park and Won-Am Park, "Changing Japanese Trade Patterns and the East Asian NICs." Krugman, *op. cit.*

4. Arthur MacEwan and William K. Tabb, "Instability and Change in the World Economy," *Instability and Change in the World Economy*, eds. Arthur MacEwan and William K. Tabb (New York: Monthly Review Press, 1989).

5. Dominick Salvatore, "How to Solve the U.S.–Japan Trade Problem," *Challenge* (January–February 1991), p. 41.

6. Robert Z. Lawrence, "Imports in Japan: Closed Markets or Minds?" *Brooking Papers on Economic Activity*, 1987.

7. Gary R. Saxonhouse, "Comment," Krugman, *op. cit.*, p. 42. See also Gary R. Saxonhouse, "Differentiated Products, Economies of Scale, and Access to the Japanese Market," Funstra, *op. cit.*

8. Robert Z. Lawrence, "Japan's Different Trade Regime: An Analysis with Particular Reference to *Keiretsu*," and Gary R. Saxonhouse, "What Does Japanese Trade Structure Tell Us About Japanese Trade Policy," both in *Journal of Economic Perspectives* 7:3 (Summer 1993).

9. Osamu, *op. cit.*, p. 26.

10. As quoted in *Asahi Shimbun Japan Access*, June 15, 1992, p. 5.

11. Hideo Sato, "Aiding the Wounded Eagle," *Japan Echo* (Autumn 1987), p. 29.

12. *Ibid.*, p. 30.

13. Kenneth S. Courtis. "The Third Economic Miracle," *Business Tokyo* (November 1989), p. 47.

15. See Marie Anchordoguy, *Computers Inc.: Japan's Challenge to IBM* (Cambridge: Council on East Asian Studies Harvard University, 1987); and Ken-ichi Imai, "Japan's Industrial Policy for High Technology Industry," *Japan's High Technology Industries*, ed. H. Patrick (Seattle: University of Washington Press, 1986).

16. "Hewlett-Packard Digs Deep for a Digital Future," *Business Week*, October 18, 1993, p. 74.

17. "Chipping Away at Japan," *Business Week*, December 7, 1992, p. 120.

18. "Windows on the World of Atoms," *Business Week*, August 30, 1993.

19. Ryutaro Komiya, *op. cit.*, p. 50.

20. "Emboldened Japan Tweaks Trade Partners," *Asahi Shimbun Japan Access*, June 15, 1992, p. 5.

21. The United States still spends over $1 billion per year on agricultural services. Farming produces 2 percent of Gross National Product. The nation as a whole spent only $70 million on manufacturing extension services, so there is a long way to go.

22. William J. Broad, "Clinton Plans to Promote Technology With Pentagon Money," *New York Times*, November 10, 1992, p. C1.

23. "Technology: The Engine of Economic Growth," issued September 21, 1992, by the Clinton–Gore campaign headquarters.

24. David E. Sanger, "US Offers a Trade to Help Build Missile Defense," *New York Times*, September 23, 1993, p. A13.

25. I am here using the criterion for industrial policy suggested by Chalmers Johnson when he wrote that it is "first and all an attitude, and only then a matter of technique." Technique, of course, is involved, and I will get to that aspect shortly.

Chalmers Johnson, "Introduction: The Idea of Industrial Policy," *The Industrial Policy Debate*, ed. C. Johnson (Palo Alto: Institute for Contemporary Studies, 1984), p. 7.

26. John Markoff, "Clinton Proposes Change to Aid Technology," *New York Times*, February 23, 1993, p. 1.

27. See Competitiveness Policy Council, *Building a Competitive Economy* (Washington, D.C.: Competitiveness Policy Council, March 1992).

28. Hiroya Ueno, "Industrial Policy: Its Role and Limits," *Journal of Japanese Trade and Industry* (July/August 1983), p. 34; cited in Chalmers Johnson, "The Industrial Policy Debate Re-examined," *California Management Review* (Fall 1984).

29. Johnson, *ibid.*, p. 74.

30. Robert S. Ozaki, "Japanese Views on Industrial Organization," *Asian Survey* (October 1970), p. 879.

31. Cited by Masahiro Okuno-Fujiwara, "Industrial Policy in Japan: A Political Economy View," Krugman, *op. cit.*, p. 272.

32. Motoshige Itoh, Masahiro Okuno, Kazuharu Kiyono, and Kotaro Suzumura, "Industrial Policy as a Correction to Market Failures," *Industrial Policy of Japan*, eds. R. Komiya, M. Okuno, and K. Suzumura (New York: Academic Press, 1988), p. 233.

33. Paul R. Krugman, "The 'New Theories' of International Trade and the Multinational Enterprise," *The Multinational Corporation in the 1980s*, eds. C. P. Kindleberger and D. B. Audretsch (Cambridge: MIT Press, 1983).

34. Miyohei Shinohara, *Industrial Growth, Trade, and Dynamic Patterns in the Japanese Economy* (Tokyo: University of Tokyo Press, 1982), p. 24.

35. Shimada in Kernell, *op. cit.*, p. 288. See his Figure 1, p. 289, for the numbers.

36. Sakakibara in Kernell, *ibid.*, p. 77.

37. Kernell in Kernell, *ibid.*, p. 372.

38. Daniel I. Okimoto, *Between MITI and the Market: Japanese Industrial Policy for High Technology* (Stanford: Stanford University Press, 1989).

39. I would not want to suggest that the overall balance does not shift over time. There has perhaps been an increases in the importance of the *zoku* in the coordinating and policy formation process in relation to that of the bureaucrats. This allows the

politicians to adjudicate among conflicting interests and to increase their fees for the now more important services they render clients. The corruption of the system may be growing as a result, although such matters are hard to quantify.

As Diet leaders gain ground as compared with bureaucrats, the nature of the accommodation changes, and relative strength shifts in other ways too. Forty percent of the LDP Diet members currently followed their fathers into political careers. Most of these had also had bureaucratic careers. However, under the current allocation of power, in which positions are based on the number of Diet elections won, the value of a bureaucratic career has declined. A Diet member who follows a parent into politics younger will maximize chances of rising to a top party position. There is thus less incentive for retired bureaucrats at the end of a government career to go into politics.

40. Shinohara, *op. cit.*

41. Robert E. Baldwin, "Are Economists' Traditional Trade Policy Views Still Valid?" *Journal of Economic Literature* (June 1992).

42. In this regard Eads and Yamamura offer an important warning:

The crucial point is that the process of industrial policy formulation is not the means of developing the basic consensus about such a vital issue as the relative weights a society must place on growth and equity. That consensus, and the means for maintaining it, are developed elsewhere in the political system. If industrial policy formulation becomes the battleground for deciding these core issues, an effective industrial policy becomes impossible.

George C. Eads and Kozo Yamamura, "The Future of Industrial Policy," K. Yamamura and Y. Yasuba *op. cit.*, p. 429.

43. Komiya, *op. cit.*, pp. 51–52.

44. Eads and Yamamura in Yamamura and Yasuba, *op. cit.*, p. 441.

45. Alfred D. Chandler, Jr., *The Visible Hand . . . op. cit.*, p. 10.

Chapter 10

1. The quote is from an unpublished 1951 Columbia University Master's essay by Charles S. Terry and is cited in Marius B. Jansen, *Changing Attitudes Toward Modernization*, p. 56.

2. C. P. Snow, *The Physicists* (New York: Macmillan, 1981), pp. 159–60; I reencountered this passage in James C. Abegglen and George Stalk, Jr., *Kaisha: The Japanese Corporation: How Marketing, Money, and Manpower Strategy, Not Management Style Make the Japanese World Pace-Setters* (New York: Basic Books, 1985), p. 145.

3. *Australian Financial Review*, April 4, 1989, as cited by Abe David and Ted Wheelwright, *The Third Wave: Australia and Asian Capitalism* (Sydney: Left Book Club Co-operative Ltd., 1989), p. 44.

4. Morris, *op. cit.*, p. 139.

5. For a breakdown of Japanese direct foreign investments in this period, see Neil Reid, "Japanese direct investment in the United States manufacturing sector," Morris, *op. cit.*

6. Shoshichi Sugimoto, "The International Structure of the Contemporary Japanese Economy; The Asian Variant of the Process of World Economic Fusion." Discussion Paper No. 335 Kyoto Institute of Economic Research (September 1991), p. 3.

7. In the mid-1960s total Japanese direct foreign investment was insignificant—$103 million compared, for example, with close to $3 billion for the British—but by the late 1980s Japan's direct foreign investment was over $50 billion, about half of British investment. In the 1990s the gap continued to narrow. Extrapolating the growth trends, Japanese direct foreign investment would eventually challenge America's leading position. The nominal value of foreign assets owned by Japanese nationals rose tenfold between 1980 and 1990, from $150 billion to $1.9 trillion.

8. See JETRO and MITI white papers of the early 1990s for charts linking Japanese firms such as Toshiba, Hitachi, NEC, Sharp, and others by category: Technical cooperation, joint development, joint production, sourcing, sales agreement and so on to major foreign firms. See MITI, *White Paper on International Trade 1991*, JETRO, *White Paper—Investment* (1991), and Shiro Takeda, "International Strategic Coalition among MNC," *Yokohama Keizai Kenkyu* (September 1990).

9. Shinichi Yamoto. "Japan's Trade Lead: Blame Profit Hungry American Firms," *The Brookings Review* (Winter 1989/90).

10. The construction of a regionally articulated division of labor in East Asia has been a major factor in a needed revision in the theory of economic development, which has been the reigning orthodoxy and which takes the individual nation as the unit of analysis. Japan's organization of a regional web of production also suggests the need for a revised calibrating of left core-periphery development modeling. While it is beyond our task to review each of these literatures, as in the case of the theory of the firm, industrial organization, international trade theory, and the economics of development and underdevelopment, the Japanese experience should prompt major rethinking.

11. Cited in Abegglen and Stalk *op. cit.*, p. 260.

12. Kiyoshi Kojima. *Direct Foreign Investment* (Croom Helm, 1978), p. 168.

13. Borthwick, *op. cit.*, p. 517.

14. S. Nakano. "Japanese Direct Investment in Asian Newly Developing Countries and Intra-Firm Division of Labour," *The Developing Economies* 18 (1980); and Tessa Morris-Suzuki, "Japan's Role in the New Industrial Division of Labour—a reassessment," *Journal of Contemporary Asia* 14 (1984).

15. Twu Jaw-Yann, "The Coming Era of the Sea of Japan," *Japan Echo* Special Issue (1992); and Jonathan Standing, "Asian Ambitions," *Tokyo Business* (July 1992).

16. James Sterngold, "Anger at Tokyo Grows in Asia," *New Yotk Times*, April 13, 1993, p. D1.

17. Tessa Morris-Suzuki, "Reshaping the International Division of Labour: Japanese Manufacturing Investment in South-East Asia," in Morris, *op. cit.*, p. 135.

18. Cited in Bernard Wysocki, Jr., "Guiding Hand: In Asia, the Japanese Hope to 'Coordinate' What Nations Produce," *The Wall Street Journal*, August 20, 1990.

19. See Masaru Tamamoto, "Japan's Uncertain Role," *World Policy Journal* (Fall 1991).

20. See Pasuk Phongpaichit, "Japan's Investment and Local Capital in ASEAN since 1985," in Shoichi Yamashita, ed., *Transfer of Japanese Technology and Management to the ASEAN Countries* (Tokyo: University of Tokyo, 1991).

21. Masaharu Hanazaki, "Industrial and Trade Structures of Asian Newly Industrialized Economies," in Shojiro Tokunaga, *Japan's Foreign Investment and Asian Economic Interdependence* (Tokyo: University of Tokyo, 1992).

22. Eighty percent of Japan's bilateral loan assistance is to its economically more advanced neighbors in which Japanese businesses have the greatest interest. A

lower percentage of Japan's official development assistance is in the form of actual grants than for any of the eighteen countries that make up the Development Assistance Committee of the OECD.

23. Peter Rimmer, "Reshaping Western Pacific Rim Cities: Japanese Planning Ideas in Transit," Fujita and Hill, *op. cit.*

24. Thomas L. Friedman, "Asia Pacific Alignment Is Off to an Upbeat Start," *New York Times*, March 21, 1994, p. A10.

25. Thomas L. Friedman, "Looking to Asia, Bentsen Sees History in Making," *New York Times*, March 19, 1994, p. D1.

26. C. Fred Bergsten, "APEC and World Trade: A Force for Worldwide Liberalization," *Foreign Affairs*, May/June, 1994.

27. Borthwick, *op. cit.*, p. 527.

28. U.S. Department of Defense, Office for International Security Affairs, "A Strategic Framework for the Asian Pacific Rim: Looking Forward Toward the 21st Century," (April 1990).

29. Japan is the largest aid giver in absolute terms, but only the eighth largest giver of foreign aid in relation to economic capacity. In 1990 its foreign aid was equal to only four-tenths of one percent of Gross National Product.

30. Robert M. Orr, Jr., "The Rising Sum: What Makes Japan Give?" *The International Economy* (September/October 1989); and Margaret M. Ensign, *Doing Good or Doing Well? Japan's Foreign Aid Program* (New York: Columbia University Press, 1992).

31. Edward J. Lincoln, "Japan in the 1990s, A New Kind of World Power," *The Brookings Review* (Spring 1992).

32. James Sterngold, "Japan's New Financial Official Plots an Independent Course," *New York Times*, August 5, 1991, p. D8.

33. In the case of Poland the forgiveness had a lot to do with domestic politics and rewarding a country that had gone further than any other former communist nation in imposing austerity and a sudden free market on its citizens. The case of Egypt was widely understood as a payoff for support in the U.S. coalition against Saddam Hussein.

34. Barnaby J. Feder, "Business Chiefs Praise Clinton for Stand on Japan," *New York Times*, February 21, 1994, p. D1.

35. "Help Wanted From the Multinationals," *Business Week*, February 29, 1988, p. 69.

36. Fumio Komoda, "Japanese Studies on Technology Transfer To Developing Countries: A Survey," *The Developing Economies* (December 1986), p. 409.

37. Kravis and Lipsey, *op. cit.*, p. 12.

38. "Japan Takes a Good Hard Look at Itself, Is Its Brand of Capitalism Simply Better?" *Business Week*, February 17, 1992, p. 33.

39. Leonard Silk, "A Japanese Shift Away from U.S.," *New York Times*, September 27, 1991, p. D2.

40. See *Tokyo Business Today* (July 1990) for statistical table on Japanese direct foreign investment in Asia.

41. Takahashi Hoshino, "Japanese Manufacturers Taking Root in Local Communities of the U.S.A.," *Economic Review*, Long Term Credit Bank of Japan 96 (1989); Shinjiro Hagiwara, "Dramatic Increase of Japan's Direct Foreign Investment into the U.S. and Completion among Multinationals," *Shinnihon Shuppansha* 331 (1991); and discussion in Hiromi Enshu, "Regional Development and Transplant Experience," (Kobe: Graduate School of Science and Technology Kobe University, 1991).

42. The Japan Economic Institute in Washington publishes periodic studies, *Japan's Expanding US Manufacturing Presence*, based on survey data. The data is discussed extensively in Neil Reid, "Japanese Direct Investment in the United States Manufacturing Sector," in Morris, *op. cit.* An alarmist account can be found in Martin Tolchin and Susan Tolchin, *Buying Into America: How Foreign Money is Changing the Face of Our Nation* (New York: Times Books, 1988).

43. Marunouchi, the hot growth area for business headquarters in Tokyo, is also known as Mitsubishi Village since the headquarters of many of the twenty-eight core companies that make up the group are to be found there. With sales of over $200 billion at the start of the 1990s, Mitsubishi represented a level of financial power unknown in the United States where trendy drinkers of Kirin beer and owners of some models of U.S.-name-plate cars do not realize they have bought Mitsubishi products. Few realized when a Mitsubishi company bought Rockefeller Center just who had purchased the landmark property of America's greatest capitalist family or that Japan's leading economic power was replicating the formula that had succeeded so well at home in the United States. American resistance to increased Japanese ownership kept direct investment within limits that have little to do with free markets, but the model of a different and perhaps better way of organizing capitalist markets is evident in the Mitsubishi example.

44. *"Last Action Hero*—or First $60 Million Commercial?" *Business Week*, April 12, 1993.

45. Akio Morita, "Toward a Convergence of Corporate Cultures and the Implications for Trilateral Relations," *Trialogue* 44 (1992); and "Nihon-gata Keiei ga Abunai," (A Critical Moment for Japanese Management?) *Bungei Shunju* (February 1992).

46. Cited in "Debate Broadens on Bigger Share for Labor," *Asahi Shimbun Japan Access*, February 10, 1992, p. 2; see also Haruo Shimada, "The Desperate Need for New Values in Japanese Corporate Behavior," *Journal of Japanese Studies* (Winter 1991).

47. Department of Industrial Policy, MITI, *2000 Nen no Sangyo Kozo: Keizai Koritsu Jushi wo Koeta Sangyo Seisaku no Tenbo*, 1990, p. 14. The translation is by Hiromi Enshu.

Chapter 11

1. Nishimura was a government official both before and after the Meiji Restoration. He was a Confucian-oriented modernizer who wrote over 130 books. This passage is by Donald H. Shively in Jensen, *op. cit.*, p. 227.

2. Giddens *op. cit.*, p. 43.

3. There is controversy on the issue of whether labor shortages are to be expected. See Yasuo Kuwahara, "Are Workers Really in Short Supply?" *Japan Labor Bulletin* (March 1990).

4. William Lazonick, *Business Organization and the Myth of the Market Economy* (Cambridge: Cambridge University Press, 1982), p. 95.

5. Ouchi, *op. cit.*

6. There are a number of important and related theoretical contributions on the payments above market wages (by Akerlof), egalitarian pay systems (Lazear), managers who value the interests of stakeholders (Kotter and Heskett), coordination and organizational learning (Marengo), organization and markets (Simon),

and so forth that are also insightful with regard to the issues raised here but are posed in an ahistorical frame. This wider literature cannot be surveyed here, but see references to these authors at the end of the book.

7. Stephen A. Marglin, "Lessons of the Golden Age: An Overview," in Marglin and Schor, *op. cit.*, p. 25.

8. The difference between the organic institutionalism that characterizes my approach here and the property rights version of "the new institutionalism" of the finance literature that privileges the role of the risk bearer and the primacy of the ownership of capital is drawn best by a comparison to such classics of that literature as Eugene Fama, "Agency Problems and the Theory of the Firm," *Journal of Political Economy* 88 (1980); and Jensen and Meckling, (1976). This literature has a very different understanding of "efficient markets" that would be exceedingly misleading as applied both to my understanding of the Japanese economy and, I think, for our own as well. For a critique of their terminology and its theoretical uses, see David Teece, "Toward an Economic Theory of the Multiproduct Firm." *Journal of Economic Behavior and Organization* 3 (1982).

9. Steven Greenhouse, "The Calls for an Industrial Policy Grow Louder," *New York Times*, July 19, 1992, p. F5.

10. Axelrod, *op. cit.*

11. Robert Alan Feldman in Krugman, *op. cit.*, p. 224.

12. Merry White *op. cit.*, p. 79.

13. Commission on the Skills of the American Workforce, *America's Choice: High Skills or Low Wages!* (Rochester, New York: National Center on Education and the Economy, 1990).

14. There is a tendency both on the free-market Right and on the Marxist Left to underestimate the ways Japan is different by presuming capitalism is capitalism. The specifics of a social formation matter a great deal and understanding them is essential to do good theoretical work. This is because "the same economic base . . . can exhibit endless variations and deviations in its appearance as a result of countless empirical circumstances—natural conditions, race relations, outside historic influences, etc.—and these must be carefully analyzed in terms of the empirically given circumstances."
Karl Marx. *Capital* Volume III, Chapter 47, part 2, pp. 798–99, of the International Publishers edition.

15. Karl Marx, however, was a unique thinker in that the seemingly smallest construct or social category, the commodity, was his starting point in presenting his theory of *Capital*. In the single product sold on the market to realize surplus value, to turn a profit, is embedded and integrally encompasses his vast system. Exchange is a moment in a totality to which it is dialectically a part and whose other relations it includes in its definition. Thus, the manner in which a commodity is embedded in the wider system set different terms for understanding capitalism than in neoclassical theorizing. The differences, which need not detain us, are embodied in commodity exchange and are connected intimately to the totality. Nothing remains constant when a change takes place in one part of the totality. The possibility of unconnectedness in the social world, the assumption of *ceteris paribus*, is a fetishism.

16. Karl Polanyi, *The Great Transformation: The Politics and Economic Origins of Our Times* (Boston: Beacon Press, 1944), p. 68.

17. Given the intellectual division of labor in the academy many of the concepts important to understanding the cultural economy and the distinguishing character-

istics of economic institutions embedded in them are being developed within sociology departments. Max Weber, arguably the Adam Smith of the discipline, perhaps more than any other figure, surely makes us aware of the network of contractual relationships and the ways control can be exercised based on sanctions and expectations and customs that structure, constrain, and guide self-interest, modes of regulating markets, and the relation of formal and substantive rationality in economic action. Weber was an economist, although he is disowned by economists. Indeed, he was a key figure in trying to hold together the social sciences resulting from the schism of the *Methodenstreit* debate at the turn of the century.

18. As Murakami and Rohlen make clear, what makes sense in a particular societal context "does not easily survive reduction to universal constructions of rationality."

Yasusuke Murakami and Thomas P. Rohlen, "Socio-Exchange Aspects of the Japanese Political Economy." Kumon and Rosovsky, *op. cit.*, p. 70.

Shared meanings are accompanied by personal attributes that are part of social exchange—sensitivity, patience, politeness, and generosity, which are absent or at least irrelevant in perfectly competitive markets that are by definition depersonalized. Mutual flexibility, trust, and friendship are of no account in such market exchange. Capacity to cooperate for mutual benefit are proven over time and longer time horizons come to be assumed as relationships succeed. There is more to gain from continuation of trust, so once a history is built it is difficult for outsiders to offer "a better deal." Cultural specificity is essential to modeling such possibilities. For more orthodox presentations of relational contracting, see Oliver D. Hart, "Incomplete Contracts and the Theory of the Firm," *The Nature of the Firm: Origins, Evolution, and Development*, eds. O. E. Williamson and S. G. Winter (New York: Oxford University Press, 1991). The ethnocentricity of economists extends to neo-Marxists, who, while placing attention on contested exchange, are hardly less guilty of abstraction based on limited cultural expectations. See Samuel Bowles and Herbert Gintis, "The Revenge of Homo Economicus: Contested Exchange and the Revival of Political Economy," *Journal of Economic Perspectives* (Winter 1993).

19. Armen Alchian and Harold Demetz, "Production, Information Costs and Economic Organization," *American Economic Review* 62 (1972), p. 777.

20. R. H. Coase, "The Nature of the Firm," *Economica* New Series (1937) in *Readings in Price Theory*, eds. G. Stigler and K. E. Boulding (Chicago: Richard D. Irwin, 1952), p. 341.

21. Clapham, *op. cit.*

22. Giddens, *op. cit.*, p. 48.

23. Douglass North, an important influence among economists working from the sort of perspective offered here, writes:

> Institutions are the rules of the game in a society or, more formally, are the humanly derived constraints that shape human interaction. In consequence they structure incentives in human exchange, whether political, social, or economic. Institutional change shapes the way societies evolve through time and hence in the key to understanding historical change. . . . Institutions reduce uncertainty by providing a structure to everyday life. They are a guide to human interaction. . . . Institutions include any form of constraint that human beings devise to shape human interaction. . . . Institutions affect the performance of the economy by their effect on the cost of exchange and production.

Douglass C. North, *Institutions, Institutional Change and Economic Performance* (Cambridge: Cambridge University Press, 1990), pp. 3–5.

24. Richard Boyd, "Government–Industry Relations in Japan. Access, Communications, and Competitive Collaborations," *Comparative Government–Industry Relations: Western Europe, the United States, and Japan*, eds. S. Wilks and M. Wright (Oxford: Clarendon Press, 1987).

25. John J. Wallis and Douglass C. North, "Measuring the Transaction Sector in the American Economy, 1870–1970," *Long-Term Factors in American Economic Growth*, eds. S. L. Engerman and R. E. Gallman (Chicago: University of Chicago Press, 1986).

26. Steven R. Weisman, "How Do Japan's Students Do It? They Cram," *New York Times*, April 27, 1992, p. A8.

27. Merry White, *op. cit.*, pp. 4–5.

28. See Teruhisa Horio, *Educational Thought and Ideology in Modern Japan* (Tokyo: University of Tokyo Press 1988). Dr. Horio is dean of the faculty of education at the University of Tokyo and philosophically committed to individual rights and from such a stance is critical of state domination of education serving national and economic elite goals.

29. "Leona Esaki: Nobel Laureate Has Chance to Rescue Tsukuba," *Asahi Shimbun Japan Access*, April 20, 1992, p. 7.

30. It should be pointed out that the Japanese do far worse at the college level, where "graduation is automatic, transfer of knowledge incidental, and accountability nonexistent" (in John Zeugner's flavorful summary, Rohlen, *op. cit.*, p. 346). Corporations seem to prefer things this way. They want to shape their young recruits and impart their own corporate culture as part of skill training on the job.

31. "Work Need Not Be a Grind, Say Recruits," *Asahi Shimbun Japan Access*, December 9, 1991, p. 6.

32. The estimate is by the Asahi Mutual Life Insurance Company research staff.

33. Michael Dertouzos, Richard K. Lester, Robert M. Solow and the MIT Commission on Industrial Productivity, *Made in America: Regaining the Competitive Edge* (Cambridge: The MIT Press, 1989), p. 91.

34. *Ibid.*

35. Steven Greenhouse, "The Coming Crisis of the American Workforce," *The New York Times*, June 7, 1992, p. 14.

36. Ryunosuke Akutagawa, *op. cit.*, p. 17.

Chapter 12

1. The most direct statement of the views of the Japanese Establishment to date is perhaps the report by the Japan Economic Research Institute (JERI), "Thoughts on Global Grand Designs—In Search of a Better Life," from which the preceding quotes are taken. The JERI was formed in 1962 by the nation's four most influential business organizations: Keidanren, Keizai Doyukai, the Japanese Chamber of Commerce and Industry, and Nihon Boeki Kai, the Japan Foreign Trade Council. Among the thirty influentials responsible for the report were former top bureaucrats at the MOF, MITI, and the Defense Agency.

2. John Markoff, "Rethinking the National Chip Policy," *New York Times*, July 14, 1992, p. D1.

3. On issues involved in international strategic alliances or collaborative ventures see David C. Mowery, "International Collaborative Ventures and the Commercialization of New Technologies," in eds. Nathan Rosenberg, Ralph Landau

and David C. Mowery, *Technology and the Wealth of Nations* (Palo Alto: Stanford University Press, 1992).

4. *Ibid.*

5. See interview in *Japan Times Weekly International Edition*, January 14–20, 1991, p. 7.

6. Paul Kennedy, *The Rise and Fall of the Great Powers: Economic Change and Military Conflict from 1500 to 2000* (New York: Random House, 1987).

7. The Economic Planning Agency devoted an entire chapter in a 1990 economic White Paper to the issue of labor's share of national income, which the report noted was "relatively low" in Japan. It should be noted that such international comparisons are not exact because of different composition of small entrepreneurial activities versus wage labor.

8. Takeshi Nagano, president of *Nikkeiren* (the Japan Federation of Employers' Associations discussed in Chapter 8), criticized Morita and others who held such views, claiming that Japan needed funds for investment, but it seemed that a new thinking was in the air. Many companies thought it better if Japan slowed its productionist pace and worked on increasing consumption. As this is written each passing day carries stories about yet another major company insisting its workers and managers take longer holidays. Foreign aid, mostly to the United States in various guises, but to developing nations as well, grows by leaps and bounds. Japan is depending less on exports and is importing more. Even land prices are coming down and the distribution system is beginning to change as more department stores and others purchase directly from foreign producers, bypassing the middle layers of the system. In a 1990 report MITI declared we cannot be a "companyist nation," suggesting a willingness to open the cozy semipermanent relations that outsiders complain characterize the Japanese economy.

"Japan just may be ready to change its ways," *Business Week*, January 27, 1992, p. 30; and Akio Morita, "Japanese Way of Business in Crisis," *Bungei Shunju*, February 1992.

9. James Weinstein, *The Liberal Ideal in the Corporate State* (Boston: Beacon Press, 1968).

10. Lester Thurow, *op. cit.*

11. Hall, *op. cit.*, p. 17.

12. Stephen Gill, "The Emerging World Order and European Change," *Socialist Register 1992*, eds. R. Miliband and L. Panitch (London: Merlin Press, 1992), p. 165; see also Stephen Gill and David Law, "Global Hegemony and the Structural Power of Capital," *International Studies Quarterly* 33:4 (1989).

13. Stephen A. Marglin, "What Do Bosses Do? The Origin and Functions of Hierarchy in Capitalist Production," *Review of Radical Political Economics* 6:2 (Summer 1974), p. 34.

14. John E. Chubb and Paul E. Peterson, "Political Institutions and the American Economy," *Parallel Politics: Economic Policymaking in the United States and Japan*, ed. S. Kernell (Washington, D.C.: Brookings Institution, 1991), p. 19.

15. William N. Cooke, "Improving Productivity and Quality Through Collaboration," *Industrial Relations* 28 (1989).

16. Kelly and Harrison, *op. cit.*

17. Barry Bluestone and Irving Bluestone, *Negotiating the Future: A Labor Perspective on American Business* (New York: Basic Books, 1993).

18. Albert O. Hirschman, *Exit, Voice, and Loyalty: Responses to Decline in Firms, Organizations and States* (Cambridge: Harvard University Press, 1970).

19. An expanding literature now exists that supports such views. See eds. Lawrence Mishel and Paula B. Voos, *Unions and Economic Competitiveness* (Armonk, New York: M. E. Sharpe, 1992); Richard Freeman, "Individual Mobility and Union Voice in the Labor Market," *American Economic Review, Papers and Proceedings* (May 1976); Charles Brown and James Medoff, "Trade Unions in the Productivity Process," *Journal of Political Economy* (June 1978); and Guillermo J. Grenier, *Inhman Relations: Quality Circles and Anti-Unionism in American Industry* (Philadelphia: Temple University Press, 1988).

20. There is recognition in some sectors of the labor movement that this is a necessary direction. See eds. Andy Banks and John Metzgar, "Participation in Management: Union Organizing on a New Terrain," *Labor Research Review*, Special Issue (Fall 1990).

21. Bennett Harrison and Barry Bluestone, "Wage Polarization in the U.S. and the 'Flexibility' Debate," *Cambridge Journal of Economics* 14 (September 1990); and David I. Levine and Laura D'Andrea Tyson, "Participatory Productivity and the Firm's Environment." *Paying for Productivity*, ed. A. S. Blinder (Washington, D.C.: Brookings Institution, 1990).

22. I have featured Ishihara, as well as Morita for that matter, because they are articulate representatives of important aspects of Japanese public life and policy debate. They are not unique in their ways of thinking. On the matter here at hand, in May 1994 the newly appointed Justice Minister, Shigeto Nagano, the former chief of staff of the army, told the *Mainichi Shimbun* that Japan's war in Asia was to liberate the colonies and criticized the man who appointed him, then prime minister Hosokawa, for labeling Japan's invasion of Asia "a war of aggression." He also denied the Rape of Nanking happened. Nagano was forced to resign because of the impact his statement had on trade prospects with Korea and China, among other neighbors.

A different story of Japanese soldiers beheading captives and engaging in unmentionable acts as required not to lose face before their officers and fellow soldiers is told by the participants of wholesale massacres of civilians in Haruko Taya Cook and Theodore F. Cook, *Japan at War: An Oral History* (New York: The Free Press, 1992); and John H. Dower, *War Without Mercy* (New York: Pantheon, 1986). The city was burned, 20,000 women raped, and 150,000-plus civilians estimated murdered.

23. Shintaro Ishihara, "Forget Pearl Harbour," *The Economist*, November 30, 1991, p. 21.

24. John Stephan has commented, "East Asian international relations in the 1920s and 1930s are hostage to mutually insulated historiographies." Koreans, Philippinos, Chinese, and others have their own views on these events.

John J. Stephan, "Review of Akira Iriye's *The Origin of the Second World War in Asia and the Pacific*," *Journal of Japanese Studies* (Summer 1988), p. 454.

25. The phrase was used in this context by Masamichi Inoki, a former head of the Defense Academy.

26. The overseas deployment of the SDF was at first limited to a special 2,000-member unit that could be deployed only in such peacekeeping tasks as providing food and rebuilding hospitals. Leftist opposition parties argued that the move was nothing short of "a rejection of the most critical element of Japan's postwar national identity and could lead to disaster. Even with the amendments attached, we consider this a quantum leap from what public opinion used to be," a senior Foreign official responsible for getting the bill passed said. "The concept is in place."

David E. Sanger, "Japan's Parliament Votes to End Ban on Sending Troops Abroad," *New York Times*, June 16, 1992, p. A1.

27. Yasushi Akashi, "The United Nations Transitional Authority in Cambodia," *Trialogue* 44 (1992), p. 11.

28. In this regard, see discussion of the 1992 Gulf crisis in Takashi Inoguchi, "Japan's Response to the Gulf Crisis: An Analytic Overview," *Journal of Japanese Studies* (Summer 1991) and Jiro Yamaguchi, "The Gulf War and the Transformation of Japanese Constitutional Politics," *Journal of Japanese Studies* (Winter 1992).

29. *Asahi Shimbun Japan Access*, December 30, 1991, p. 15.

30. "Environment: Global Issue is Ideal Diversion," *Asahi Shimbun Japan Access*, March 30, 1992, p. 3.

31. Ishihara, *op. cit.*

32. Ivan P. Hall, "Samurai Legacies, American Illusions," *The National Interest* (Summer 1992), p. 25.

33. As quoted by Morris-Suzuki, *op. cit.*, p. 192.

Bibliography of Works Cited

Abegglen, J. C., and Stalk, Jr., G. (1985) *Kaisha: The Japanese Corporation: How Marketing, Money, and Manpower Strategy, Not Management Style Make the Japanese World Pace-Setters*. Basic Books, New York.

Adams, F. G., and Klein, L. R., eds. (1983) *Industrial Policies for Growth and Competitiveness: An Economic Perspective*. D. C. Heath, Boston.

Adams, R. G., and Ichimura, S. (1983) "Industrial Policy in Japan." *Industrial Policies for Growth and Competitiveness: An Economic Perspective*. eds. F. G. Adams and L. R. Klein. D. C. Heath, Boston.

Akerlof, G. (1982) "Labor Contracts as Partial Gift Exchange." *Quarterly Journal of Economics* (97).

Alchian, A. A. (1950) "Uncertainty, Evolution and Economic Theory." *Journal of Political Economy* (58).

Alchian, A., and Demetz, H. (1972) "Production, Information Costs and Economic Organization." *American Economic Review* (62).

Allen, G. C. (1946) *A Short Economic History of Japan, 1867–1937*. Macmillan, London.

Alletzhauser, A. J. (1990) *The House of Nomura: The Inside Story of the Legendary Japanese Financial Dynasty*. HarperPerennial, New York.

Almond, G., and Coleman, J. S. (1960) *The Politics of Developing Areas*. Princeton University Press, Princeton.

Alt, J. (1979) *The Politics of Economic Decline*. Cambridge University Press, New York.

Amin, A. (1991) "Flexible Specialization and Small Firms in Italy: Myths and Realities." *Farewell to Flexibility*. ed. A. Pollert. Basil Blackwell, Cambridge.

Amsden, A. H. (1989) *Asia's Next Giant: South Korea and Late Industrialization*. Oxford University Press, New York.

Anderson, S. J. (1990) "The Political Economy of Japanese Saving: How Postal Savings and Public Pensions Support High Rates of Household Saving in Japan." *Journal of Japanese Studies* (Winter).

Ando, A., and Auerbach, A. (1988) "The Corporate Cost of Capital in Japan and the United States: A Comparison." *Government Policy Toward Industry in the United States and Japan*. ed. J. B. Shoven. Cambridge University Press, Cambridge.

Angel, R. C. (1991) *Explaining Economic Policy Failure, Japan in the 1969–1971 International Monetary Crisis*. Columbia University Press, New York.

Aoki, M. (1988) *Information, Incentives and Bargaining in the Japanese Economy*. Cambridge University Press, New York.

Asanuma, B. (1985) "Japan's *Keiretsu* System: The Case of the Automobile Industry." *Japanese Economic Studies* (13:4).

Asanuma, B. (1989) "Manufacturer–Supplier Relationships in Japan and the Concept of Relation-Specific Skill." *Journal of the Japanese and International Economies* (3).

Auerbach, P. (1988) *Competition: The Economics of Industrial Change.* Basil Blackwell, Cambridge.

Austin, L., ed. (1976) *Japan: The Paradox of Progress.* Yale University Press, New Haven.

Axelrod, R. (1984) *The Evolution of Cooperation.* Basic Books, New York.

Bagguley, P. (1991) "Post-Fordism and Enterprise Culture." *Enterprise Culture.* eds. R. Keats and N. Abercrombie. Routledge, London.

Bailey, J. H. (1991) *Ordinary People, Extraordinary Lives: Political and Economic Change in a Tohoku Village.* University of Hawaii Press, Honolulu.

Baldwin, R. E. (1992) "Are Economists' Traditional Trade Policy Views Still Valid?" *Journal of Economic Literature* (June).

Bander, J. A. (1986) "Rationales for Strategic Trade and Industrial Policy." *Strategic Trade Policy and the New International Economics.* ed. P. Krugman. MIT Press, Cambridge.

Banks, A., and Metzgar, J., eds. (1990) "Participation in Management: Union Organizing on a New Terrain." *Labor Research Review* (Fall).

Barthes, R. (1982) *Empire of Signs.* Jonathan Cape, London.

Beasley, W. G. (1987) *Japanese Imperialism, 1894–1945.* Clarendon Press, Oxford.

Beasley, W. G. (1972) *The Meiji Restoration.* Stanford University Press, Stanford.

Beauchamp, E. R., and Iriye, A., eds. (1990) *Foreign Employees in Nineteenth-Century Japan.* Westview, Boulder.

Belassa, B., and Noland, M. (1988) *Japan in the World Economy.* Institute for International Economics, Washington, D.C.

Bellah, R. N. (1970) *Tokugawa Religion: The Values of Pre-Industrial Japan.* Beacon Press, Boston.

Benedict, R. (1946) *The Chrysanthemum and the Sword: Patterns of Japanese Culture.* Houghton, Mifflin Company, Boston.

Best, M. H. (1990) *The New Competition: Institutions of Industrial Restructuring.* Polity Press, Cambridge.

Bestor, T. (1988) *Neighborhood Tokyo.* Stanford University Press, Stanford.

Bix, H. P. (1992) "The Showa Emperor's 'Monologue' and the Problem of War Responsibility." *Journal of Japanese Studies* (Summer).

Blair, M. M. (1993) *The Deal Decade: What Takeovers and Leveraged Buyouts Mean for Corporate Governance.* Brookings Institution, Washington, D.C.

Bluestone, B., and Bluestone, I. (1993) *Negotiating the Future: A Labor Perspective on American Business.* Basic Books, New York.

Boff, L. (1991) *New Evangelization.* Orbis Books, Maryknoll.

Borthwick, M. (1992) *Pacific Century: The Emergence of Modern Pacific Asia.* Westview Press, Boulder.

Bowles, S., and Gintis, H. (1993) "The Revenge of Homo Economicus: Contested Exchange and the Revival of Political Economy." *Journal of Economic Perspectives* (Winter).

Bowles, S., Gordon, D. M., and Weiskopf, T. E. (1990) *After the Wasteland: A Democratic Economics for the Year 2000.* M. E. Sharpe, Armonk.

Branscomb, L. M. (1992) "Does America Need a Technology Policy?" *Harvard Business Review* (March–April).

Braverman, H. (1974) *Labor and Monopoly Capital*. Monthly Review Press, New York.

Bresnan, J. (1994) *From Dominoes to Dynamos: The Transformation of Southeast Asia*. Council of Foreign Relations Press, New York.

Brown, C., and Medoff, J. (1978) "Trade Unions in the Productivity Process." *Journal of Political Economy* (June).

Brown, C., and Reich, M. (1989) "When Does Cooperation Work? A Look at NUMMI and GM-Van Nuys." *California Management Review* (Summer).

Bulow, J., Summers, L. H., and Summers, V. P. (1990) "Distinguishing Debt from Equity in the Junk Bond Era." *Debt, Taxes and Corporate Restructuring*. eds. J. B. Shoven and J. Waldfogel. Brookings Institution, Washington, D.C.

Buruma, I. (1984) *Behind the Mask: On Sexual Demons, Sacred Mothers, Transvestites, Gangsters and Other Japanese Cultural Heroes*. Penguin Books, Baltimore.

Buruma, I. (1991) "The Peace Axis." *New York Review of Books* (April 25).

Boyd, R. (1987) "Government–Industry Relations in Japan. Access, Communications and Competitive Collaborations." *Comparative Government–Industry Relations: Western Europe, the United States, and Japan*. eds. S. Wilks and M. Wright. Clarendon Press, Oxford.

Breziz, E. S., Krugman, P., and Tsiddon, D. (1993) "Leapfrogging in International Competition: A Theory of Cycles in National Technological Leadership." *American Economic Review* (December).

Brinton, M. C. (1988) "The Social-Institutional Bases of Gender Stratification: Japan as an Illustrative Case." *American Journal of Sociology*. September (94:2).

Calder, K. E. (1988) *Crisis and Compensation: Public Policy and Political Stability in Japan*. Princeton University Press, Princeton.

Calder, K. E. (1990) "Linking Welfare and the Developmental State: Postal Savings in Japan." *Journal of Japanese Studies* (Winter).

Chandler, Jr., A. D. (1966) *Strategy and Structure: Chapters in the History of the Industrial Enterprise*. Anchor Books, Garden City.

Chandler, Jr., A. D. (1977) *The Visible hand: The Management Revolution in America*. Harvard University Press, Cambridge.

Chiba, K. (1992) "A 'Worm's Eye' View of GATT." *Trialogue* (43).

Choate, P. (1990) *Agents of Influence: How Japan's Lobbyists in the United States Manipulate America's Political and Economic System*. Knopf, New York.

Chubb, J. E., and Peterson, P. E. (1991) "Political Institutions and the American Economy." *Parallel Politics: Economic Policymaking in the United States and Japan*. ed. S. Kernell. Brookings Institution, Washington, D.C.

Clapham, J. H. (1922) "Of Empty Boxes." *The Economic Journal* (XXXXII).

Clark, R. L., and Ogawa, N. (1992) "The Effect of Mandatory Retirement on Earnings Profiles in Japan." *Industrial and Labor Relations Review* (January).

Clauson, D. (1980) *Bureaucracy and the Labor Process: The Transformation of U.S. Industry, 1860–1920*. Monthly Review Press, New York.

Coase, R. H. (1937) "The Nature of the Firm." *Economica* (New Series, IV).

Cohen, L., and Noll, R. (1991) *The Technology Pork Barrel*. Brookings Institution, Washington, D.C.

Cole, R. E., and Deskins, Jr., D. R. (1988) "Racial Factors in Site Selection and Employment Patterns of Japanese Auto Firms in America." *California Management Review* (Fall).

Commission on the Skills of the American Workforce. (1990) *America's Choice:*

High Skills or Low Wages! National Center on Education and the Economy, Rochester, New York.

Competitiveness Policy Council. (1992) *Building a Competitive Economy* (March).

Cook, A. H., and Hayashi, H. (1980) *Working Women in Japan: Discrimination, Resistance, and Reform.* New York State School of Industrial and Labor Relations, Cornell University, Ithaca.

Cook, H. T., and Cook, T. F. (1992) *Japan at War: An Oral History.* The Free Press, New York.

Cooke, W. (1989) "Improving Productivity and Quality Through Collaboration." *Industrial Relations* (28).

Cooke, W. N. (1989) "Improving Productivity and Quality Through Collaboration." *Industrial Relations* (28).

Courtis, K. S. (1989) "The Third Economic Miracle." *Business Tokyo* (November).

Crichton, M. (1992) *Rising Sun.* Alfred A. Knopf, New York.

Curtis, G. L. (1983) *Election Campaigning Japanese Style.* Kodansha International, Tokyo.

Cusmano, M. (1989) *The Japanese Automobile Industry: Technology and Management at Nissan and Toyota.* Harvard University Press, Cambridge.

David, A., and Wheelwright, T. (1989) *The Third Wave: Australia and Asian Capitalism.* Left Book Club Co-operative Ltd., Sydney.

Deming, W. E. (1982) *Quality, Productivity and Competitive Position.* MIT Center for Advanced Engineering Study, Cambridge.

Dertouzos, M., Lester, R. K., Solow, R. N., and the MIT Commission on Industrial Productivity (1989) *Made in America: Regaining the Competitive Edge.* The MIT Press, Cambridge.

Dewar, M. E., ed. (1982) *Industrial Vitalization: Toward a National Industrial Policy.* Pergamon Press, New York.

Dohse, K., Jurgens, U., and Malsch, T. (1985) "From Fordism to Toyotaism? The Social Organization of the Labor Process in the Japanese Automobile Industry." *Politics and Society* (14).

Dore, R. P. (1983) "Goodwill and the Spirit of Market Capitalism." *British Journal of Sociology* (34).

Dore, R. P. (1978) *A Portrait of a Japanese Village.* Pantheon Books, New York.

Dore, R. P. (1987) *Taking Japan Seriously: A Confucian Perspective on Leading Economic Issues.* Stanford University Press, Stanford.

Dower, J. W. (1979) *Empire and Aftermath: Yoshida Higeru and the Japanese Experience.* Council on East Asian Studies, Harvard University, Cambridge.

Dower, J. W. (1975) *Origins of the Modern Japanese State: Selected Writings of E. H. Norman.* Pantheon, New York.

Dower, J. W. (1986) *War Without Mercy.* Pantheon, New York.

Durkheim, E. (1964) *The Rules of Sociological Method.* The Free Press, New York.

Eatwell, J., Milgate, M., and Newman, P., eds. (1989) *The New Palgrave: Economic Development.* W. W. Norton & Company, New York.

Eccleston, B. (1989) *State and Society in Post-War Japan.* Polity Press, Cambridge.

Edwards, L. N. (1988) "Equal Employment Opportunity in Japan: A View for the West." *Industrial and Labor Relations Review* (January).

Enshu, H. (1991) "Mutual Impacts of U.S.–Japanese Socioeconomic Exchange on Regional Restructuring." Institute for Urban and Regional Development, University of California, Berkeley (June).

Ensign, M. M. (1992) *Doing Good or Doing Well? Japan's Foreign Aid Program*. Columbia University Press, New York.

Evans, Jr., R. (1971) *The Labor Economics of Japan and the United States*. Praeger, New York.

Evans, R. H. (1967) *Coexistence: Communism and Its Practice in Bologna, 1945-65*. University of Notre Dame, South Bend.

Fabricant, S. (1954) *Economic Progress and Economic Growth*. National Bureau of Economic Research, New York.

Fallows, J. (1989) "Containing Japan." *The Atlantic* (May).

Fama, E. (1980) "Agency Problems and the Theory of the Firm." *Journal of Political Economy* (88).

Felix, D. (1989) "Import Substitution and Late Industrialization: Latin America and Asia Compared." *World Development* (17).

First Domestic Research Division, Research Bureau (1992) *Economic Survey of Japan (1991-1992): Seeking for a New Perspective beyond the Adjustment Process*. Economic Planning Agency, Japanese Government, Tokyo.

Flamm, K. (1991) "Making New Rules: High-Tech Trade Friction and the Semi-Conductor Industry." *The Brookings Review* (Spring).

Flamm, K. (1993) "Semiconductor Dependency and Strategic Trade Policy." *Brookings Papers on Economic Activity* (1).

Florida, R., and Kenny, M. (1991) "Organizational Transplants: The Transfer of Japanese Industrial Organization to the U.S." *American Sociological Review* (June).

Foster, J. B. (1988) "The Fetish of Fordism." *Monthly Review* (March).

Freeman, C., and Perez, C. (1988) "Structural Crisis of Adjustment: Business Cycles and Investment Behavior." *Technical Change and Economic Theory*. eds. G. Dosi et al., Pinter, London.

Freeman, R. (1976) "Individual Mobility and Union Voice in the Labor Market." *American Economic Review, Papers and Proceedings* (May).

Friedman, D. (1983) "Beyond the Age of Ford: The Strategic Basis of the Japanese Success in Automobiles." *American Industry in International Competition: Government Policies and Corporate Strategies*. eds. J. Zysman and L. D. Tyson. Cornell University Press, Ithaca.

Friedman, D. (1988) *The Misunderstood Miracle: Industrial Development and Political Change in Japan*. Cornell University Press, Ithaca.

Friedman, G., and LeBard, M. (1991) *The Coming War with Japan*. St. Martin's Press, New York.

Friedman, R. A. (1991) "Comment." *Trade with Japan: Has the Door Opened Wider?* ed. P. Krugman. University of Chicago Press, Chicago.

Fucini, J. J., and Fucini, S. (1990) *Working for the Japanese: Inside Mazda's American Auto Plants*.

Fujita, K. (1988) "Labor Process." International Symposium on the Micro Electronics Revolution and Regional Development, Labour Organization and the Future of Post Industrial Societies, Milan.

Fujita, K., and Hill, R. C. (1989) "Global Production and Regional 'Hollowing Out' in Japan." *Pacific Rim Cities in the World Economy*. ed. M. P. Smith. Transaction Books, New Brunswick.

Fujita, K., and Hill, R. C., eds. (1993) *Japanese Cities in the World Economy*. Temple University Press, Philadelphia.

Fukui, H. (1977) "Studies in Policy Making: A Review of the Literature." *Policy Making in Contemporary Japan.* ed. T. J. Pempel. Cornell University Press, Ithaca.

Gabor, A. (1992) *The Man Who Discovered Quality.* Penguin, Baltimore.

Geertz, C. (1973) *The Interpretation of Culture.* Basic Books, New York.

Genther, P., and Dalton, D. H. (1990) *Japanese Direct Investment in U.S. Manufacturing.* U.S. Department of Commerce.

Gerlach, M. L. (1992) *Alliance Capitalism: The Social Organization of Japanese Business.* University of California Press, Berkeley.

Gershenkron, A. (1962) *Economic Backwardness in Historical Perspective.* Harvard University Press, Cambridge.

Giddens, A. (1987) *Social Theory and Modern Sociology.* Stanford University Press, Stanford.

Gill, S., and Law, D. (1989) "Global hegemony and the structural power of capital." *International Studies Quarterly* (33).

Gold, B. (1979) *Productivity, Technology, and Capital.* Lexington Books, Lexington, Mass.

Gluck, C. (1985) *Japan's Modern Myths: Ideology in the Late Meiji Period.* Princeton University Press, Princeton.

Glyn, A., Hughes, A., Lipietz, A., and Singh, A. (1991) "The Rise and Fall of the Golden Age." *The Golden Age of Capitalism: Reinterpreting the Postwar Experience.* eds. S. A. Marglin and J. B. Schor. Clarendon Press, Oxford.

Gordon, A. (1985) *The Evolution of Labor Relations in Japan, 1853–1955.* Harvard University Press, Cambridge.

Grenier, G. J. (1988) *Inhuman Relations: Quality Circles and Anti-Unionism in American Industry.* Temple University Press, Philadelphia.

Griliches, Z. (1994) "Productivity, R & D, and the Data Constraint." *American Economic Review* (March).

Hadley, J. O. (1987) "Governance by Negotiation: A Reappraisal of Bureaucratic Power in Japan." *Journal of Japanese Studies* (Summer).

Halberstam, D. (1986) *The Reckoning.* William Morrow and Company, New York.

Hale, D. "Picking Up Reagan's Tab." *Foreign Policy* (Spring).

Haley, J. (1978) "The Myth of the Reluctant Litigant." *Journal of Japanese Studies* (Summer).

Hall, I. P. (1992) "Samurai Legacies, American Illusions." *The National Interest* (Summer).

Halliday, J. (1975) *A Political History of Japanese Capitalism.* Monthly Review Press, New York.

Hanazaki, M. (1992) "Industrial and Trade Structures of Asian Newly Industrialized Economies," in Tokunaga, S., ed. *Japan's Foreign Investment and Asian Economic Interdependence.* University of Tokyo, Tokyo.

Harris, M. (1979) *Cultural Materialism.* Random House, New York.

Harrison, B., and Bluestone, B. (1990) "Wage Polarization in the U.S. and the 'Flexibility' Debate." *Cambridge Journal of Economics* (14).

Hart, J. A. (1993) *Rival Capitalists: International Competitiveness in the United States, Japan and Western Europe.* Cornell University Press, Ithaca.

Hart, O. (1992) "Theories of Optimal Capital Structure: A Management Discretion Perspective." *The Deal Decade: What Takeovers and Leveraged Buyouts Mean for Corporate Governance.* ed. M. M. Blair. Brookings Institution, Washington, D.C.

Hart, O. D. (1991) "Incomplete Contracts and the Theory of the Firm." *The Nature of the Firm; Origins, Evolution, and Development*. eds. O. E. Williamson and S. G. Winter. Oxford University Press, New York.

Hashimoto, M. E., and Raisian, J. (1985) "Employment Tenure and Earnings Profiles in Japan and the United States." *American Economics Review*, September (75:4).

Hayes, R. H., and Abernathy, W. (1980) "Managing Our Way to Economic Decline." *Harvard Business Review* (September–October).

Hibbett, H. (1952) "Introduction" to Ryunosake Akuntagawa. *Rashomon and Other Stories*. Charles E. Tuttle, Tokyo.

Hill, M. A. (1983) "Female Labor Force Participation in Developing and Developed Countries—Consideration of the Informal Sector." *Review of Economics and Statistics* (August).

Hill, M. A. (1992) "Women in the Japanese Economy." World Bank Conference "Women's Changing Economic Role in Asia" University of Toronto (June 4–5).

Hill, R. C. (1991) "Foundation Firms and Industrial Districts; Organizational and Territorial Restructuring in the U.S. and Japanese Automobile Industries." Conference on Globalization and the City. Ritsumeikan University, Kyoto, Japan (December 21).

Hill, R. C., and Fujita, K. (1992) "Japanese Cities in the World Economy." *Japanese Cities in the World Economy: Global Restructuring and Urban-Industrial Change*. eds. K. Fujita and R. C. Hill. Temple University Press, Philadelphia.

Hirschman, A. O. (1970) *Exit, Voice, and Loyalty: Responses to Decline in Firms, Organizations and States*. Harvard University Press, Cambridge.

Hirsh, B. T., and Link, A. N. (1987) "Labor Union Effects on Innovation Activity." *Journal of Labor Research* (Fall).

Holden, C. (1986) "New Toyota-GM Plant's U.S. Model of Japanese Management." *Science* (July).

Hollingsworth, J. R., and Lindberg, L. N., eds. (1991) *Governance of the American Economy*. Cambridge University Press, Cambridge.

Hollingsworth, J. R., Schmitter, P. C., and Streeck, W., eds. (1994) *Governing Capitalist Economies: Performance and Control of Economic Sectors*. Oxford University Press, New York.

Horio, T. (1988) *Educational Thought and Ideology in Modern Japan*. University of Tokyo Press, Tokyo.

Houseman, S. N., and Abraham, K. G. (1993) "Female Workers as a Buffer in the Japanese Economy." *American Economics Association, Papers and Proceedings* (May).

Howes, C. (1991) "The Benefits of Youth: The Role of Japanese Fringe Benefits in the Restructuring of the U.S. Motor Vehicle Industry." *International Contributions to Labour Studies* (1).

Howes, C. (1993) "Japanese Direct Foreign Investment in the U.S. Auto Industry." Economic Policy Institute, Washington, D.C.

Hwang, D. H. (1988) *M. Butterfly*. Dramatists Play Service, New York.

Imai, K. (1992) "Japan's Corporate Networks." *The Political Economy of Japan; Volume 3, Cultural and Social Dynamics*. eds. S. Kumon and H. Rosovsky. Stanford University Press, Stanford.

Imai, K., and Itami, H. (1984) "Interpenetration of Organization and Market. Japan's Firm and Market in Comparison with the U.S." *International Journal of Industrial Organization* (December).

Inagami, T. (1991) "A New Employment Vision for Long-Life Society." *Japan Labor Bulletin* (April).

Ishihara, S. "Forget Pearl Harbour." *The Economist* (November 30).

Ishihara, S. (1991) *The Japan That Can Say No: Why Japan Will Be First Among Equals.* Simon and Schuster, New York.

Ivy, M. (1989) "Critical Texts, Mass Artifacts: The Consumption of Knowledge in Postmodern Japan." M. Miyoshi and D. H. Harootunian, eds., *Postmodernism and Japan.* Duke University Press, Durham.

Jansen, M. B. ed. (1989) *The Cambridge History of Japan, Volume 5: The Nineteenth Century.* Cambridge University Press, Cambridge.

Jansen, M. B. (1969) *Changing Japanese Attitudes Toward Modernization.* Charles E. Tuttle, Tokyo.

Jansen, M. B. (1980) "Wisdom Sought Throughout the World." *Japan and Its World: Two Centuries of Change.* Princeton University Press.

Jensen, M. C. (1986) "Agency Costs of Free Cash Flow, Corporate Finance, and Takeovers." *American Economic Review, Papers and Proceedings* (May).

Jensen, M. C., and Meckling, W. H. (1976) "Theory of the Firm: Managerial Behavior, Agency Costs and Ownership Structure." *Journal of Financial Economics* (3).

Johnson, C. (1987) "How to Think About Economic Competition From Japan." *Journal of Japanese Studies* (13:2).

Johnson, C. (1984) "Industrial Policy Debate Re-examined." *California Management Review* (Fall).

Johnson, C. (1988) "Japanese-Style Management in America." *California Management Review* (Summer).

Johnson, C. (1982) *MITI and the Japanese Miracle: The Growth of Industrial Policy, 1925-1975.* Stanford University Press, Stanford.

Johnson, C. (1986) "Tanaka Kakuei, Structural Corruption, and the Advent of Machine Politics in Japan." *Japanese Studies* (Winter).

Johnson, S. (1991) *The Japanese Through American Eyes.* Stanford University Press, Stanford.

Katz, H. (1985) *Shifting Gears: Changing Labor Relations in the U.S. Automobile Industry.* MIT Press, Cambridge.

Katzenstein, P. (1987) *Power and Politics in West Germany: The Growth of the Semisovereign State.* Temple University Press, Philadelphia.

Junkerman, J. (1983) "The Japanese Model." *The Progressive* (May).

Kearns, R. (1992) *Zaibatsu America.* Free Press, New York.

Keat, R., and Abercrombie, N. (1991) *Enterprise Culture.* Routledge, London.

Keene, D. (1969) *The Japanese Discover Europe, 1720-1830.* Stanford University Press, Stanford.

Kelman, S. (1990) "The 'Japanization' of the United States?" *The Public Interest* (Winter).

Kelley, M. R., and Harrison, B. (1992) "Unions, Technology, and Labor-Management Cooperation." *Unions and Economic Competitiveness.* eds. L. Mishel and P. Voos. M. E. Sharpe, Armonk.

Kernell, S. (1991) "The Need for Comparative Analysis." *Parallel Politics: Economic Policymaking in Japan and the United States.* ed. S. Kernell. The Brookings Institution, Washington, D.C.

Kester, W. C. (1991) *Japanese Takeovers: The Global Contest for Corporate Control.* Harvard Business School Press, Boston.

Kester, W. C., and Luehrman, T. A. (1992) "The Myth of Japan's Low-Cost Capital." *Harvard Business Review* (May–June).

Kinzley, W. D. (1990) *Industrial Harmony in Modern Japan: The Invention of a Tradition*. Routledge, London.

Koike, K. (1987) "Human Resource Development and Labor–Management Relations." *The Political Economy of Japan; Volume I: The Domestic Transformation*. eds. K. Yamamura and Y. Yasuba. Stanford University Press, Stanford.

Koike, K. (1988) *Understanding Industrial Relations in Modern Japan*. St. Martin's Press, New York.

Kojima, K. (1978) *Direct Foreign Investment*. Croom Helm, London.

Komiya, R. (1990) *The Japanese Economy: Trade, Industry, and Government*. University of Tokyo, Tokyo.

Komiya, R., Okuno, M., and Suzumura, K. (1988) *Industrial Policy of Japan*. Academic Press, New York.

Komoda, F. (1986) "Japanese Studies on Technology Transfer To Developing Countries: A Survey." *The Developing Economies* (December).

Kono, T. (1984) *Strategy and Structure of Japanese Enterprise*. M. E. Sharpe, Armonk.

Kosei, Y. (1986) *The Era of High-Speed Growth: Notes on the Postwar Japanese Economy*. Tokyo University Press, Tokyo.

Kosei, Y., and Ogino, Y. (1984) *The Contemporary Japanese Economy*. M. E. Sharpe, Armonk.

Kotter, J., and Heskett, J. (1992) *Corporate Culture and Performance*. The Free Press, New York.

Krauss, E. S. (1980) "Opposition in Power: The Development and Maintenance of Leftist Government in Kyoto Prefecture." *Political Opposition and Local Politics in Japan*. eds. K. Steiner, E. S. Krauss, and S. C. Flanagan. Princeton University Press, Princeton.

Kravis, I. B., and Lipsey, R. E. (1992) "Parent Firms and Their Foreign Subsidiaries in Goods and Service Industries." *International Trade and Finance Association*, 1992 Proceedings, edited by K. Fatemi.

Kravis, I. B., and Lipsey, R. E. (1992) "Sources of Competitiveness of the United States and Its Multinational Firms." *Review of Economics and Statistics* 74:2 (May).

Krugman, P. R. (1983) "The 'New Theories' of International Trade and the Multinational Enterprise." *The Multinational Corporation in the 1980s*. eds. C. P. Kindleberger and D. B. Audretsch. MIT Press, Cambridge.

Krugman, P. R., ed. (1991) *Trade with Japan: Has the Door Opened Wider?* University of Chicago Press, Chicago.

Kuroda, A. (1990) "Book Review." *Journal of Japanese and International Economics* (4).

Kuroda, M. (1992) "Hardly Anyone Wants to Deal With Us." in *Bungei Shunju*. *World Press Review* (April).

Kuwahara, Y. (1990) "Are Workers Really in Short Supply?" *Japan Labor Bulletin* (March).

Lawrence, R. Z. (1987) "Imports in Japan: Closed Markets or Minds?" *Brookings Papers on Economic Activity*.

Lawrence, R. Z. (1993) "Japan's Different Trade Regime: An Analysis with Particular Reference to *Keiretsu*." *Journal of Economic Perspectives* (7:3) (Summer).

Lazonick, W. (1992) *Business Organization and the Myth of the Market Economy*. Cambridge University Press, Cambridge.

Lebra, T. S. (1992) "Gender and Culture in the Japanese Political Economy: Self-

Portrayals of Prominent Business Women." *The Political Economy of Japan,
Volume 3, Cultural and Social.* eds. S. Kumon and H. Rosovsky. Stanford
University Press, Stanford.

Lebra, T. S. (1984) *Japanese Women: Constraint and Fulfillment.* University of Hawaii
Press, Honolulu.

Leibenstein, H. (1982) "The Prisoners' Dilemma in the Invisible Hand: An Analysis of Intrafirm Productivity." *American Economic Review, Papers and Proceedings* (72).

Levine, D. I., and Tyson, L. D. (1990) "Participatory Productivity and the Firm's
Environment." *Paying for Productivity.* ed. A. S. Blinder. Brookings Institution, Washington, D.C.

Levine, S. B., and Kawada, H. (1980) *Human Resources in Japanese Industrial Development.* Princeton University Press, Princeton.

Lincoln, E. J. (1992) "Japan in the 1990s, A New Kind of World Power." *The
Brookings Review* (Spring).

Lipietz, A. (1987) *Mirages and Miracles: The Crisis of Global Fordism.* Verso, London.

Lippmann, W. (1922) "The World Outside and the Pictures in Our Heads." *Public
Opinion. Images of Man.* (1960) ed. C. W. Mills. George Braziller, New York.

Lockwood, W. (1954) *The Economic Development of Japan: Growth and Structural
Change 1868–1938.* Princeton University Press, Princeton.

MacEwan, A., and Tabb, W. K., eds. (1989) *Instability and Change in the World
Economy.* Monthly Review Press, New York.

Magdoff, H. (1992) "Globalization—To What End? Part I." *Monthly Review* (February).

Mansfield, E. (1988) "Innovation in Japan and the United States." *Science*, September 30.

Marengo, L. (1992) "Coordination and Organizational Learning in the Firm."
Journal of Evolutionary Economics (2).

Marglin, S. A. (1974) "What Do Bosses Do? The Origin and Functions of Hierarchy
in Capitalist Production." *Review of Radical Political Economics* (6).

Marglin, S. A., and Schor, J. B., eds. (1991) *The Golden Age of Capitalism: Reinterpreting the Postwar Experience.* Clarendon Press, Oxford.

Marshall, A. (1970) *Industry and Trade.* Augustus M. Kelley, Chicago.

Marston, R. C. (1991) "Price Behavior in Japanese and U.S. Manufacturing." *Trade
with Japan: Has the Door Opened Wider?.* ed. P. Krugman. University of Chicago Press, Chicago.

Marx, K. (1973) *Grundrisse: Foundation of the Critique of Political Economy.* Penguin
Books, Baltimore.

Marx, K. (1971) *Capital*, Volume III. International Publishers, New York.

Mathews, R. C. O., Feinstein, C., and Odling-Smee, J. (1983) *British Economic
Growth, 1856–1973.* Stanford University Press, Stanford.

Maull, H. W. (1990–91) "Germany and Japan: The New Civilian Powers." *Foreign
Affairs* (Winter).

McCormack, G. (1986) "Crime, Confession, and Control in Contemporary Japan."
Democracy in Contemporary Japan. eds. G. McCormack and Y. Sugimoto.
M. E. Sharpe, Armonk.

McCormack, G. (1992) "The Emptiness of Affluence: Vitality, Embolisms and
Symbiosis in the Japanese Body Politic." Institute for European and International Affairs, Luxembourg.

McCormack, G. "The Price of Affluence: The Political Economy of Japanese Leisure." *New Left Review*. July–August (188).

McKean, M. A. (1981) "The Legal Impact of the Big Four Verdicts." *Environmental Protest and Citizen Politics in Japan*. University of California Press, Berkeley.

Minami, R. (1986) *The Economic Development of Japan: A Quantitative Study*. London, Macmillan.

Miyamoto, K. (1970) "Urban Problems in Japan With Emphasis upon the Period of Rapid Economic Growth." *Japan Institute of International Affairs, Annual Review*.

Miyamoto, K. (1975) "The Fiscal Crisis of Local Government." *Japan Echo* (II).

Miyamoto, K. (1985) "Urban Policies in the Metropolitan Areas of Japan: Post-World War II to the Present." *Keizei Kenkyu (Business Review)*. Osaka City University (May).

Miyamoto, K. (1987) "Under Contemporary Japanese Capitalism." *Japanese Economic Studies* (Fall).

Morita, A. with Reingold, E. M., and Shimomura, M. (1986) *Made in Japan: Akio Morita and Sony*. Dutton, New York.

Morita, A. (1992) "Nihon-gata Keiei ga Abunai" (A Critical Moment for Japanese Management?). *Bungei Shunju* (February).

Morita, A. (1992) "Toward a Convergence of Corporate Cultures and the Implications for Trilateral Relations." *Trialogue* (44).

Morris, J. ed. (1991) *Japan and the Global Economy: Issues and Trends in the 1990s*. Routledge, London.

Morris-Suzuki, T. (1989) *A History of Japanese Economic Thought*. Routledge, London.

Morris-Suzuki, T. (1984) "Japan's Role in the New Industrial Division of Labour—A Reassessment." *Journal of Contemporary Asia* (14).

Mowery, D. C. (1992) "International Collaborative Ventures and the Commercialization of New Technologies." *Technology and the Wealth of Nations*. eds. N. Rosenberg, R. Landau, and D. C. Mowery. Stanford University Press, Stanford.

Muramatsu, M. (1986) "Center–Local Political Relations in Japan: A Lateral Competition Model." *Journal of Japanese Studies* (Summer).

Muramatsu, M. (1987) "In Search of National Identity: The Politics and Policies of the Nakasone Administration." *Journal of Japanese Studies* (Summer).

Muramatsu, M., and Aqua, R. (1980) "Japan Controls Its Cities: Central–Local Relations in a Changing Political Context." *National Resources and Urban Policy*. ed. D. Ashford. Metheun, London.

Murphy, R. T. (1989) "Power Without Purpose: The Crisis of Japan's Global Financial Dominance. *Harvard Business Review* (March–April).

Nakamura, T. (1981) *The Postwar Japanese Economy*. University of Tokyo Press, Tokyo.

Nakano, S. (1980) "Japanese Direct Investment in Asian Newly Developing Countries and Intra-Firm Division of Labour." *The Developing Economies* (18).

Nakazawa, K. (1989) "Flaws in the 'Containing Japan' Thesis." *Japan Echo* (Winter).

National Defense Council for Victims of *Karoshi*. (1990) *Karoshi: When the Corporate Warrior Dies*. Mado-Sha, Tokyo.

Nelson, R. R., and Wright, G. (1992) "The Rise and Fall of American Technological Leadership." *Journal of Economic Literature* (December).

Nivola, P. S. (1991) "More Like Them? The Political Feasibility of Strategic Trade Policy." *The Brookings Review* (Spring).

Nohara, H. (1990) "The Average Workers of a Large Japanese Company." Nihon Fukushi University Working Paper.

Nohara, H. (1990) "Is the Japanese Industrial Relations a Breakthrough: A Hypothesis Relating Japanese Industrial Relations to Those in the U.S. and Europe." Nihon Fukushi University Working Paper.

Noponen, H., Graham, J., and Markusen, A. R. eds. (1993) *Trading Industries, Trading Regions: International Trade, American Industry, and Regional Economic Development.* Guilford Press, New York.

North, D. C. (1990) *Institutions, Institutional Change and Economic Performance.* Cambridge University Press, Cambridge.

Ohmae, K. (1990) *The Borderless World.* New York: Harper and Row, New York.

Okimoto, D. I. (1989) *Between MITI and the Market: Japanese Industrial Policy for High Technology.* Stanford University Press, Stanford.

Okuno-Fujiwara, M. (1988) "Interdependence of Industries, Coordination Failure and Strategic Promotion of Industry." *Journal of International Economics* (25).

Orr, Jr., R. M. (1989) "The Rising Sum: What Makes Japan Give?" *The International Economy* (September/October).

Osamu, S. (1987) "The 'Japan Problem' Is of America's Making." *Japan Echo* (Autumn).

Osawa, M. (1987) "Changing Role of Education and Women Workers in Japan." *Keio Business Review* (24).

Ouchi, W. G. (1981) *Theory Z: How American Business Can Meet the Japanese Challenge.* Addison-Wesley, Reading, Mass.

Ozaki, R. S. (1970) "Japanese Views on Industrial Organization." *Asian Survey* (October).

Pack, H. (1994) "Endogenous Growth Theory: Intellectual Appeal and Empirical Shortcomings." *Journal of Economic Perspectives* (Winter).

Parker, M., and Slaughter, J. (1988) "Management by Stress." *Technology Review* (October).

Pascale, R., and Rohlen, T. P. (1983) "The Mazda Turnaround." *Journal of Japanese Studies* (9).

Peck, M. J., Levin, R. C., and Goto, A. (1987) "Picking Losers: Public Policy Toward Declining Industries in Japan." *Journal of Japanese Studies* (Winter).

Pelikan, P. (1987) "The Formation of Incentive Mechanisms in Different Economic Systems." *Incentives and Economic Systems.* ed. S. Hedlund. New York University Press, New York.

Pempel, T. J. (1982) *Policy and Politics in Japan: Creative Conservativism.* Temple University Press, Philadelphia.

Pempel, T. J. (1987) "The Unbundling of 'Japan, Inc.': The Changing Dynamics of Japanese Policy Formation." *Journal of Japanese Studies* (Summer).

Pempel, T. J., and Tsunekawa, K. (1979) "Corporatism without Labour? The Japanese Anomaly." *Trends Toward Corporatist Intermediation.* eds. G. Lembruch and P. Sage, London.

Phillips, K. P. (1992) "U.S. Industrial Policy: Inevitable and Ineffective." *Harvard Business Review* (July–August).

Phongpaichit, P. (1991) "Japan's Investment and Local Capital in ASEAN since

1985." in Yamashita, S., ed., *Transfer of Japanese Technology and Management to the ASEAN Countries*. University of Tokyo, Tokyo.

Plath, D. W. (1983) *Work and Life Course in Japan*. State University of New York Press, Albany.

Polanyi, K. (1944) *The Great Transformation: The Politics and Economic Origins of Our Times*. Beacon Press, Boston.

Political Reform Committee, Liberal Democratic Party (1989) "A Proposal for Political Reform." *Journal of Japanese Studies* (Autumn).

Pollert, A. (1991) *Farewell to Flexibility?* Basil Blackwell, Oxford.

Porter, M. E. (1990) "The Competitiveness of Nations." *Harvard Business Review* (March–April).

Prestowitz, Jr., C. V. (1988) *Trading Places: How We Are Giving Our Future to Japan and How to Reclaim It*. Basic Books, New York.

Prestowitz, Jr., C. V., Willen, P. S., and Chimerine, L. (1992) "The Future of the Auto Industry: It Can Compete, Can It Survive?" Economic Strategy Institute, Washington, D.C.

Prowse, M. (1992) "Is America in Decline?" *Harvard Business Review* (July–August).

Putterman, L., ed. (1986) *The Economic Nature of the Firm, A Reader*. Cambridge University Press, Cambridge.

Pyle, K. B. (1987) "In Pursuit of a Grand Design: Nakasone Betwixt the Past and the Future." *Journal of Japanese Studies* (Summer).

Ramseyer, J. M. (1988) "Reluctant Litigant Revisited: Rationality and Disputes in Japan." *Journal of Japanese Studies* (Winter).

Reich, R. B. (1992) *The Work of Nations: Preparing Ourselves for 21st Century Capitalism*. Vintage Books, New York.

Rohlen, T. P. (1983) *Japan's High Schools*. University of California Press, Berkeley.

Rohlen, T. P. (1992) "Learning: The Modernization of Knowledge in the Japanese Political Economy." *The Political Economy of Japan, Volume 3: Cultural and Social Dynamics*. eds. S. Kumon and H. Rosovsky. Stanford University Press, Stanford.

Rosenberg, N. (1976) *Perspectives on Technology*. Cambridge University Press, Cambridge.

Rosenberg, N., Landau, R., and Mowery, D. C. (1992) *Technology and the Wealth of Nations*. Stanford University Press, Stanford.

Rosenberg, N., and Steinmueller, W. E. (1988) "Why Are Americans Such Poor Imitators?" *American Economic Review* (May).

Rostow, W. W. (1960) *The Stages of Economic Growth*. Cambridge University Press, Cambridge.

Said, E. W. (1993) *Culture and Imperialism*. Alfred A. Knopf, New York.

Said, E. W. (1978) *Orientalism*. Random House, New York.

Salvatore, D. (1991) "How to Solve the U.S.-Japan Trade Problem." *Challenge* (January–February).

Samuels, R. J. (1987) *The Business of the Japanese State: Energy Markets in Comparative Historical Perspective*. Cornell University Press, Ithaca.

Sanders, S. (1975) *Honda: The Man and His Machine*. Little, Brown, Boston.

Saruta, M. (1990) "Technical Change, Rationalization and Industrial Relations: The Case of Toyota." Typescript.

Sato, H. (1987) "Aiding the Wounded Eagle." *Japan Echo* (Autumn).

Saxenhouse, G. R. (1991) "Comments and Discussion" of Robert Z. Lawrence,

"Efficient or Exclusionist? The Import Behavior of Japanese Corporate Groups." *Brookings Papers on Economic Activity* (1).

Saxonhouse, G. R. (1993) "What Does Japanese Trade Structure Tell Us About Japanese Trade Policy?" *Journal of Economic Perspectives* (7:3) (Summer).

Scherrer, C. (1991) "Governance of the Automobile Industry: The Transformation of Labor and Supply Relations." *Governance of the American Economy*. eds. J. R. Hollingsworth and L. N. Lindberg, Cambridge University Press, Cambridge.

Schor, J. B. (1992) *The Overworked American: The Unexpected Decline of Leisure*. Basic Books, New York.

Seidensticker, E. (1983) *Low City, High City: Tokyo From Edo to the Earthquake: How the Shogun's Ancient Capital Became a Great Modern City, 1867–1923*. Charles E. Tuttle, Tokyo.

Servan-Schreiber, J. J. (1969) *The American Challenge*. Avon Books, New York.

Shaiken, H., and Herzenberg, S. (1987) *Automation and Global Production: Automobile Engine Production in Mexico, the United States, and Canada*. Center for U.S.-Mexican Studies, University of California, San Diego.

Shale, S. (1990) "The Plot that Triggered Tokyo's Plunge." *Europemoney* (May).

Shibata, T. ed. (1986) *Public Finance in Japan*. University of Tokyo Press, Tokyo.

Shimada, H. (1991) "The Desperate Need for New Values in Japanese Corporate Behavior." *Journal of Japanese Studies* (Winter).

Shimada, H. (1985) "The Labor Crisis: A Strategic Response to Structural Changes." *Japan Labor Bulletin* (November).

Shimada, H., and Higuchi, Y. (1985) "An Analysis of Trends in Female Labor Force Participation in Japan." *Journal of Labor Economics* (January).

Shimokawa, K. (1986) "Production and Labour Strategies in Japan." *The Automobile Industry and Its Workers*. eds. S. Tolliday and J. Zeitlin. Polity Press, Cambridge.

Shinohara, M. (1982) *Industrial Growth, Trade, and Dynamic Patterns in the Japanese Economy*. University of Tokyo Press, Tokyo.

Shinya, A. (1991) *Shoshaman: A Tale of Corporate Japan*. University of California Press, Berkeley.

Shirai, T. (1983) *Contemporary Industrial Relations in Japan*. University of Wisconsin Press, Madison.

Shishido, Z. (1989) "A Texan Raid on a Japanese Company." *Japan Echo* (Winter).

Simka, M. (1993) "The Decline of the Japanese Auto Industry: Domestic and International Implications." Japan Economic Seminar East Asian Institute, Columbia University (February 20).

Simon, H. (1991) "Organizations and Markets." *Journal of Economic Perspectives* (2).

Shoven, J. B., and Tachibanaki, T. (1988) "The Taxation of Income from Capital in Japan." *Government Policy Toward Industry in the United States and Japan*. ed. J. B. Shoven. Cambridge University Press, Cambridge.

Shoven, J. B., and Waldfogel, J. eds. (1990) *Debt, Taxes and Corporate Restructuring*. Brookings Institution, Washington, D.C.

Schumpeter, J. A. (1991) "The Study of Entrepreneurship." *Joseph A. Schumpeter: The Economics and Sociology of Capitalism*. ed. R. Swedberg, Princeton University Press, Princeton.

Slaughter, J. (1990) "Management by Stress." *Multinational Monitor* (January–February).

Small and Medium Enterprise Agency, MITI. (1991) *White Paper on Small and Medium Enterprises*. Ministry of International Trade and Industry, Tokyo.

Smilor, R. W., Zozmetsky, G., and Gison, D., eds. (1988) *Creating the Technopolis: Linking Technology, Commercialization and Economic Development*. Ballinger, Cambridge.

Smith, M. P. ed. (1989) *Pacific Rim Cities in the World Economy*. Transaction Books, New Brunswick.

Smith, R. J. (1987) "Gender Inequality in Contemporary Japan." *Journal of Japanese Studies* (Winter).

Smitka, M. J. (1991) *Competitive Ties: Subcontracting in the Japanese Automobile Industry*. Columbia University Press, New York.

Soviak, E. (1971) "On the Nature of Western Progress: The Journal of the Iwakura Embassy." *Tradition and Modernization in Japanese Culture*. ed. D. H. Shively. Princeton University Press, Princeton.

Standing, J. (1992) "Asian Ambitions." *Tokyo Business* (July).

Steiner, K., Krauss, E. S., and Flanagan, S. C., eds. (1980) *Political Opposition and Local Politics in Japan*. Princeton University Press, Princeton.

Stephan, J. S. (1988) "Review of Akira Iriye's *The Origin of the Second World War in Asia and the Pacific*." *Journal of Japanese Studies* (Summer).

Stevens, R. (1983) *Classes in Contemporary Japan*. Cambridge University Press, Cambridge.

Stevens, R. (1990) *Japan's New Imperialism*. M. E. Sharpe, Armonk.

Sugeno, K. (1991) "The Supreme Court's Hitachi Decision on the Duty to Work Overtime." *Japan Labor Bulletin* (May).

Sugimoto, S. (1991) "The International Structure of the Contemporary Japanese Economy; The Asian Variant of the Process of World Economic Fusion." Discussion Paper No. 335 Kyoto Institute of Economic Research (September).

Swedberg, R. (1990) *Economics and Sociology; Redefining Their Boundaries: Conversations with Economists and Sociologists*. Princeton University Press, Princeton.

Takeda, S. (1990) "International Strategic Coalition among MNC." *Yokohama Keizai Kenkyu* (September).

Takeshita, N. (1988) *The Furusato Concert: Toward a Humanistic and Prosperous Japan*. Simul International, Tokyo.

Tamamoto, M. (1991) "Japan's Uncertain Role." *World Policy Journal* (Fall).

Tasker, P. (1987) *Inside Japan: Wealth, Work and Power in the New Japanese Empire*. Penguin Books, London.

Tatsuno, S. (1986) *The Technopolis Strategy: Japan, High Technology, and Control of the Twenty-First Century*. Prentice-Hall, Englewood Cliffs.

Teece, D. (1982) "Toward an Economic Theory of the Multiproduct Firm." *Journal of Economic Behavior and Organization* (3).

Thurow, L. C. (1992) *Head to Head: Coming Economic Battles Among Japan, Europe, and America*. William Morrow and Company, New York.

Tokunaga, S. (1992) "Japan's FDI-Promoting Systems and Intra-Asia Networks: New Investment and Trade Systems Created by the Borderless Economy," in Tokunaga, S. ed., *Japan's Foreign Investment and Asian Economic Interdependence*. University of Tokyo Press, Tokyo.

Tominomori, K. (1985) "Unemployment in Japan." *Hokudai Economic Papers*(XIV).

Trezise, P. H. (1982) "Industrial Policy in Japan." *Industrial Vitalization: Toward a National Industrial Policy* ed. M. E. Dewar. Pergamon Press, New York.

Tsuneo, I. (1987) "Decline of a Superpower." *Japan Echo* (Autumn).

Tsuru, S. (1993) *Japan's Capitalism: Creative Defeat and Beyond*. Cambridge University Press, Cambridge.

Tsurumi, E. P. (1990) *Factory Girls: Women in the Thread Mills of Meiji Japan*. Princeton University Press, Princeton.

Tsurumi, Y. (1984) "Labor Relations and Industrial Adjustment in Japan and the U.S.: A Comparative Analysis." *Yale Law & Policy Review* (Spring).

Twu, J-Y. (1992) "The Coming Era of the Sea of Japan." *Japan Echo* (Special Issue).

Tyson, L. D. (1992) *Who's Bashing Whom? Trade Conflict in High-Technology Industries*. Institute for International Economics, Washington, D.C.

Ueno, H. (1983) "Industrial Policy: Its Role and Limits." *Journal of Japanese Trade and Industry* (July–August).

Ueta, K. (1989) "Environmental Planning in Japan." International Conference on Public Policy Planning. Taipei, Taiwan (June 12–14).

Unger, D., and Blackburn, P., eds. (1993) *Japan's Emerging Global Role*. Lynne Rienner, Boulder.

Upham, F. (1987) *Law and Social Change in Postwar Japan*. Harvard University Press, Cambridge.

van Wolferen, K. (1990) "Rise of an Anti-Social Force," *Times Literary Supplement* (August 31–September 1).

Vogel, S. K. (1989) "Japanese High Technology, Politics and Power." Berkeley Roundtable on the International Economy, University of California, Berkeley.

Wade, R. (1990) *Governing the Market: Economic Theory and the Role of Government in East Asian Industrialization*. Princeton University Press, Princeton.

Wallis, J. J., and North, D. C. (1986) "Measuring the Transaction Sector in the American Economy, 1870–1970." *Long-Term Factors in American Economic Growth*. eds. S. L. Engerman and R. E. Gallman, University of Chicago Press, Chicago.

Wallerstein, I. (1990) "Culture as the Ideological Battleground of the Modern World-System." *Global Culture: Nationalism, Globalism and Modernity*. ed. M. Featherstone. Sage, Beverly Hills.

Webber, A. H., Interviewer. (1989) "Yasuhiro Nakasone: The Statesman as CEO." *Harvard Business Review* (March/April).

Weber, M. (1947) *The Theory of Social and Economic Organization*. ed. T. Parsons. Oxford University Press, New York.

White, M. (1987) *The Japanese Educational Challenge*. Kodansha International, Tokyo.

Wilks, S., and Wright, M., eds. (1987) *Comparative Government-Industry Relations: Western Europe, the United States, and Japan*. Clarendon Press, Oxford.

Winter, S. G. (1991) "On Coase, Competence, and the Corporation." *The Nature of the Firm: Origins, Evolution, and Development*. eds. O. E. Williamson and S. G. Winter. Oxford University Press, Oxford.

Womack, J. P., Jones, D. T., and Roos, D. (1991) *The Machine that Changed the World; The Story of Lean Production*. Harper Perennial, New York.

Wood, C. (1990) "Japan Survey." *The Economist* (December 8).

Woodiwiss, A. (1992) *Law, Labour and Society in Japan: From repression to reluctant recognition*. Routledge, London.

Yamada, K. (1990) "The Triple Evils of Golf Courses." *Japan Quarterly* (July–September).

Yamamura, K., and Yasuba, Y., eds. (1987) *The Political Economy of Japan, Volume I, The Domestic Transformation*. Stanford University Press, Stanford.

Yamoto, Y. (1989/90) "Japan's Trade Lead: Blame Profit Hungry American Firms." *The Brookings Review* (Winter).

Yazawa, S. (1990) "The Technopolis Program in Japan." *Hitotsubashi Journal of Social Studies* (22).

Young, M. K. (1984) "Judicial Review of Administrative Guidance: Governmentally Encouraged Consensual Dispute Resolution in Japan." *Columbia Law Review* (84).

Yoshitomi, M. (1989) "Treating American Janophobia." *Japan Echo* (Winter).

Zysman, J., and Tyson, L. D. eds. (1983) *American Industry in International Competition: Government Policies and Corporate Strategies*. Cornell University Press, Ithaca.

Index